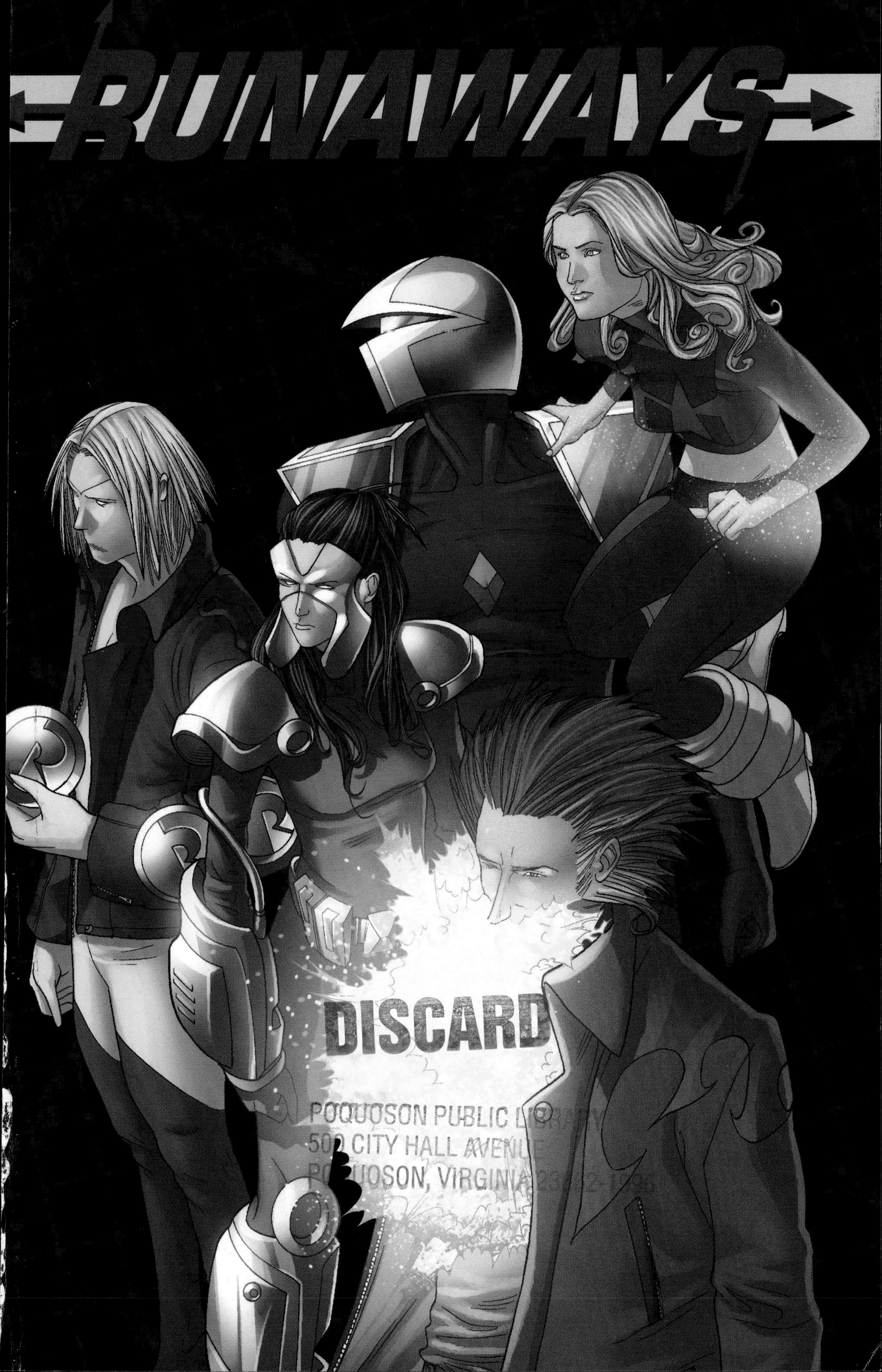
RUNAWAYS

RUNAWAYS

Writer: Brian K. Vaughan
Pencilers: Adrian Alphona
& Takeshi Miyazawa (Issues #7-8)
Inker: Craig Yeung
Colorist: Christina Strain
X-Men/Runaways Artist: Skottie Young
Letterer: Virtual Calligraphy's Randy Gentile
Cover Art: Jo Chen, James Jean &
Chris Bachalo with Tim Townsend
Collection Cover: Adrian Alphona
Assistant Editor: Nathan Cosby
Editors: MacKenzie Cadenhead & C.B. Cebulski
Special thanks to Nick Lowe

Runaways created by Brian K. Vaughan & Adrian Alphona

Collection Editor: Jennifer Grünwald
Assistant Editor: Michael Short
Associate Editor: Mark D. Beazley
Senior Editor, Special Projects: Jeff Youngquist
Vice President of Sales: David Gabriel
Production: Jerron Quality Color
Vice President of Creative: Tom Marvelli

Editor in Chief: Joe Quesada
Publisher: Dan Buckley

RUNAWAYS VOL. 2. Contains material originally published in magazine form as RUNAWAYS #1-12 and FREE COMIC BOOK DAY 2006. First printing 2006. ISBN# 0-7851-2358-X. Published by MARVEL PUBLISHING, INC., a subsidiary of MARVEL ENTERTAINMENT, INC. OFFICE OF PUBLICATION: 417 5th Avenue, New York, NY 10016. Copyright © 2005 and 2006 Marvel Characters, Inc. All rights reserved. $34.99 per copy in the U.S. and $56.00 in Canada (GST #R127032852); Canadian Agreement #40668537. All characters featured in this issue and the distinctive names and likenesses thereof, and all related indicia are trademarks of Marvel Characters, Inc. No similarity between any of the names, characters, persons, and/or institutions in this magazine with those of any living or dead person or institution is intended, and any such similarity which may exist is purely coincidental. **Printed in the U.S.A.** ALAN FINE, President & CEO Of Marvel Toys and Marvel Publishing, Inc.; DAVID BOGART, VP Of Publishing Operations; DAN CARR, Executive Director of Publishing Technology; JUSTIN F. GABRIE, Managing Editor; STAN LEE, Chairman Emeritus. For information regarding advertising in Marvel Comics or on Marvel.com, please contact Joe Maimone, Advertising Director, at jmaimone@marvel.com or 212-576-8534.

10 9 8 7 6 5 4 3 2 1

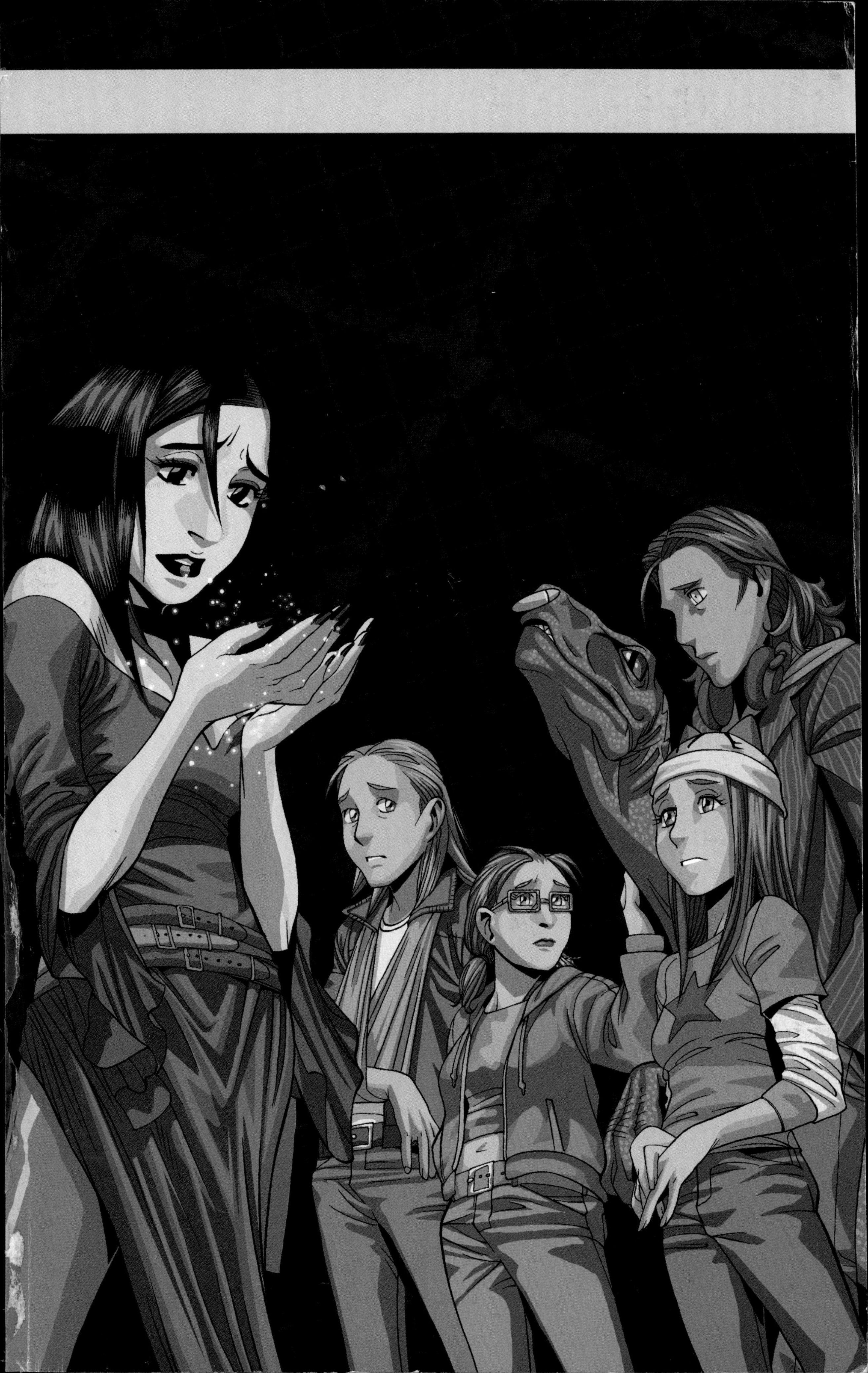

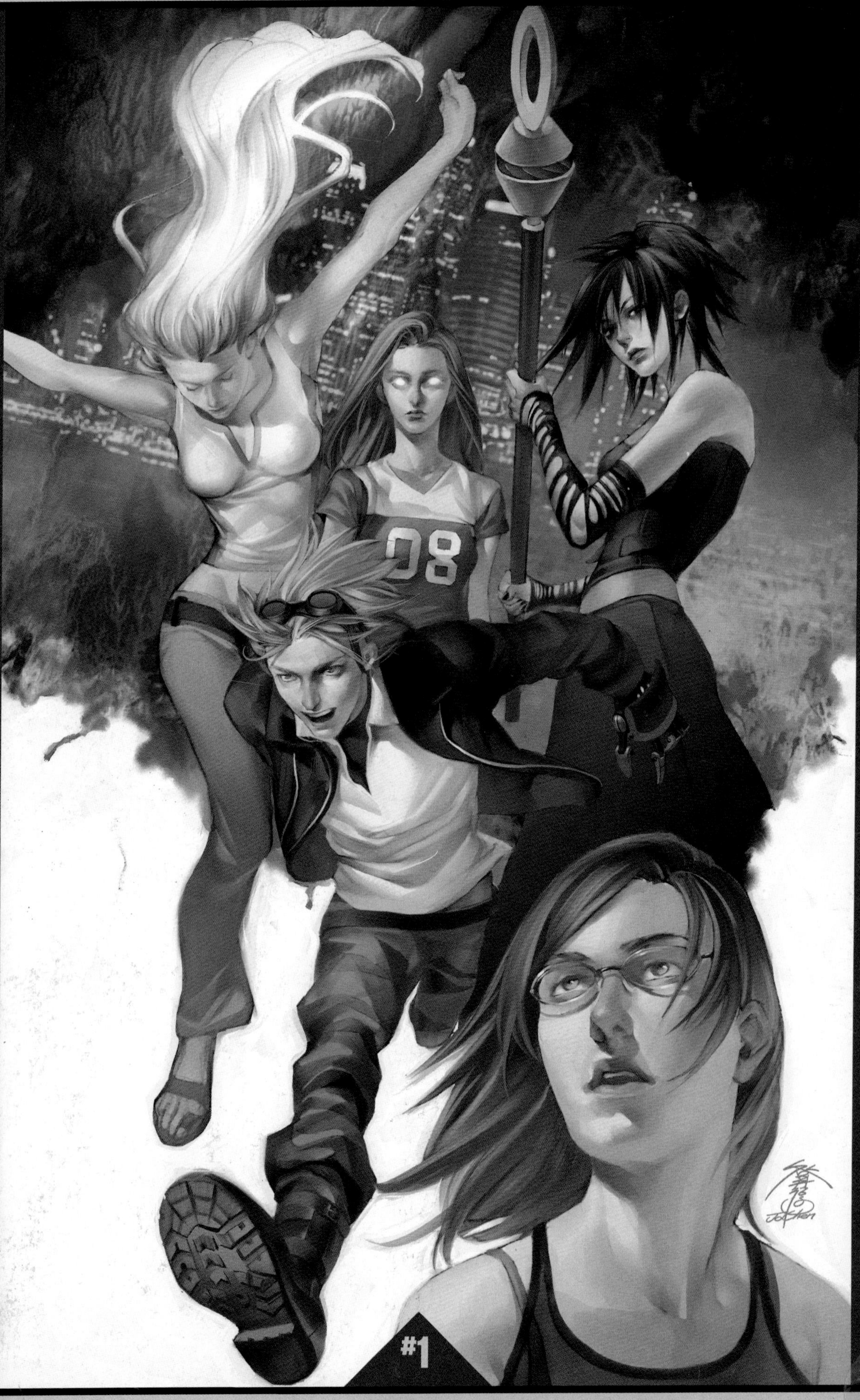
08
#1

TRUE BELIEVERS PART 1

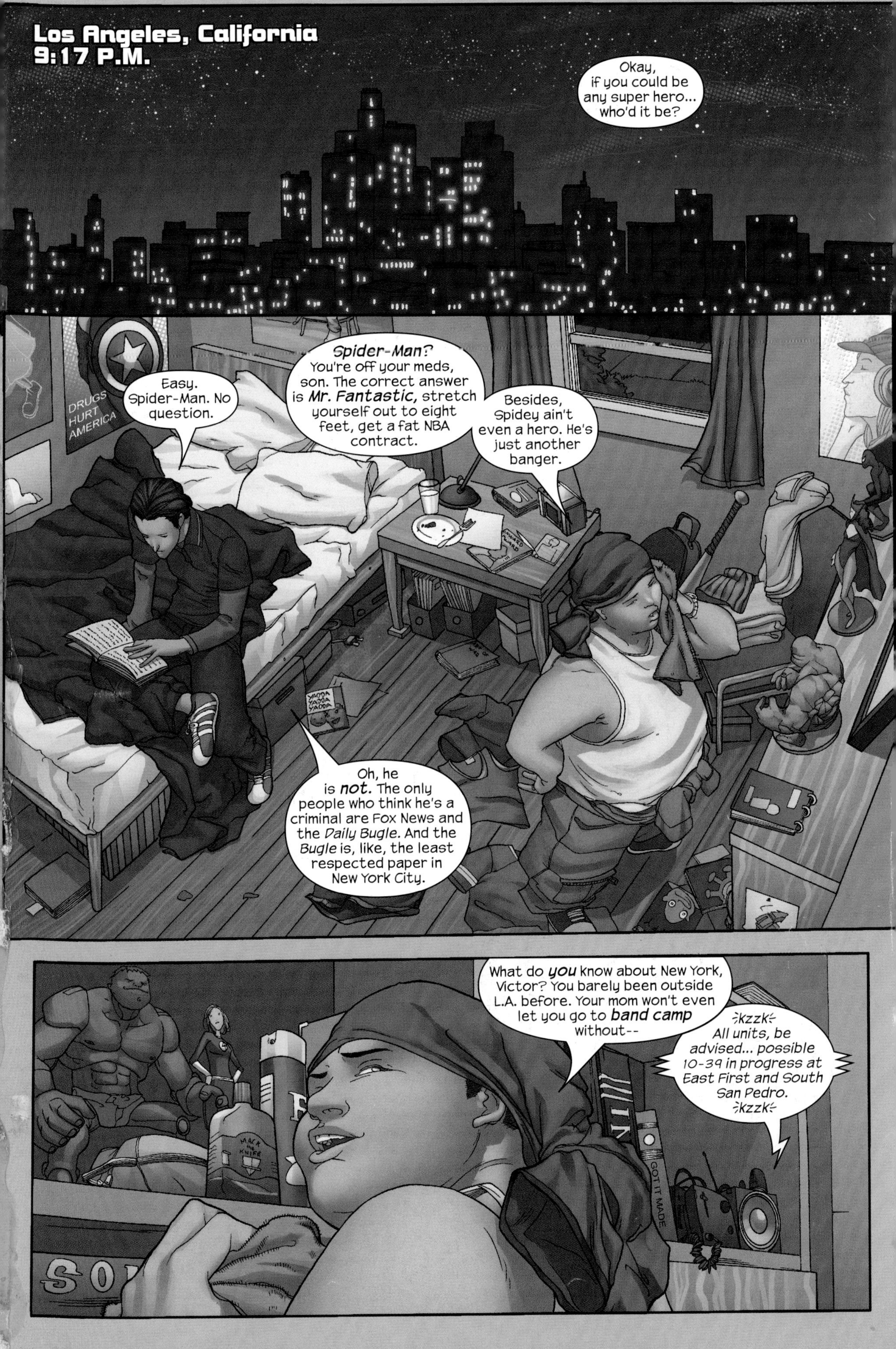
Los Angeles, California
9:17 P.M.
Okay, if you could be any super hero... who'd it be?
Easy. Spider-Man. No question.
DRUGS HURT AMERICA
Spider-Man? You're off your meds, son. The correct answer is ***Mr. Fantastic,*** stretch yourself out to eight feet, get a fat NBA contract.
Besides, Spidey ain't even a hero. He's just another banger.
Oh, he is ***not.*** The only people who think he's a criminal are Fox News and the *Daily Bugle.* And the *Bugle* is, like, the least respected paper in New York City.
What do ***you*** know about New York, Victor? You barely been outside L.A. before. Your mom won't even let you go to ***band camp*** without--
kzzk All units, be advised... possible 10-39 in progress at East First and South San Pedro. *kzzk*

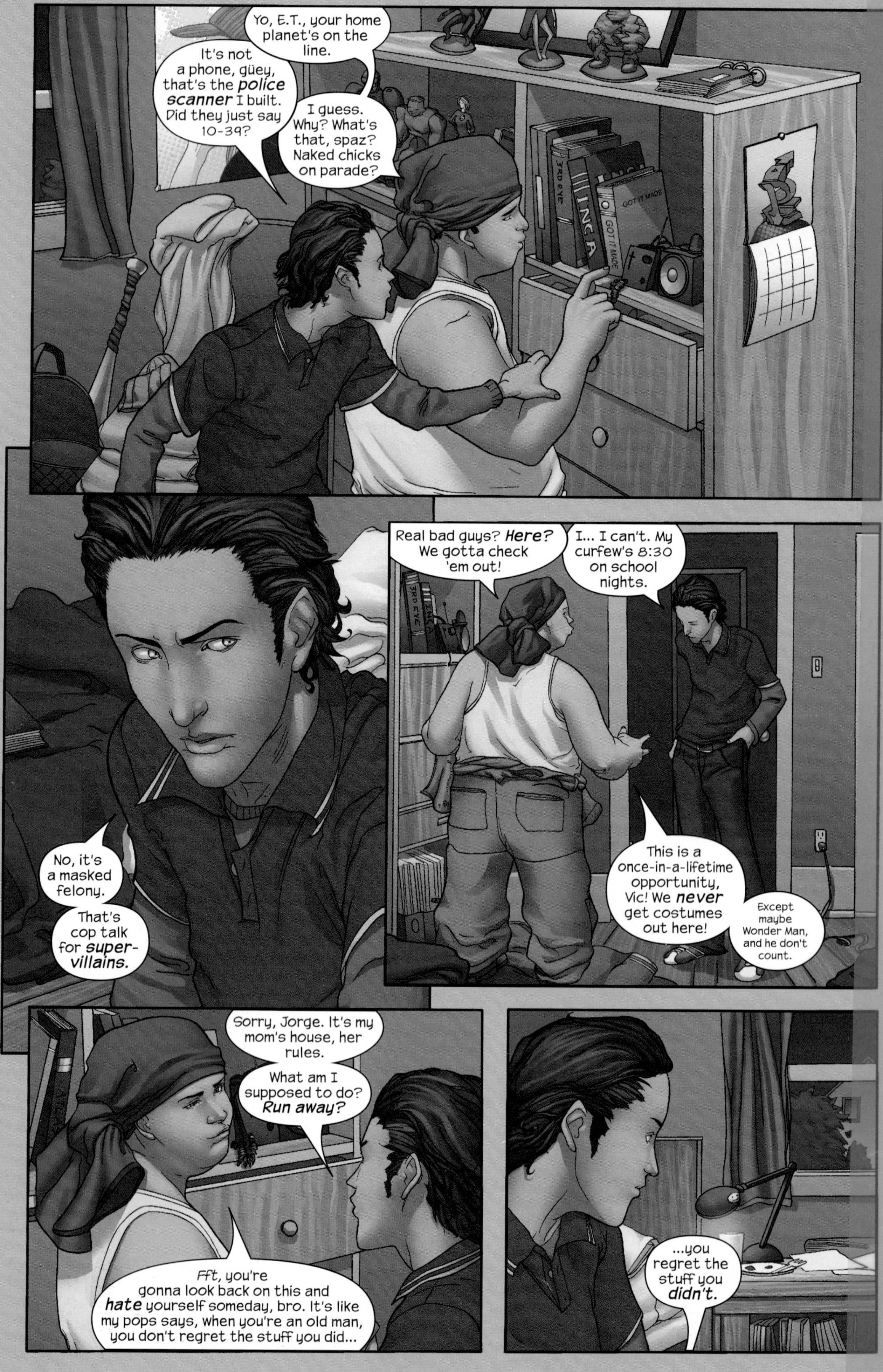

Yo, E.T., your home planet's on the line.
It's not a phone, güey, that's the *police scanner* I built. Did they just say 10-39?
I guess. Why? What's that, spaz? Naked chicks on parade?
No, it's a masked felony.
That's cop talk for *super-villains.*
Real bad guys? *Here?* We gotta check 'em out!
I... I can't. My curfew's 8:30 on school nights.
This is a once-in-a-lifetime opportunity, Vic! We *never* get costumes out here!
Except maybe Wonder Man, and he don't count.
Sorry, Jorge. It's my mom's house, her rules.
What am I supposed to do? *Run away?*
Fft, you're gonna look back on this and *hate* yourself someday, bro. It's like my pops says, when you're an old man, you don't regret the stuff you did...
...you regret the stuff you *didn't.*

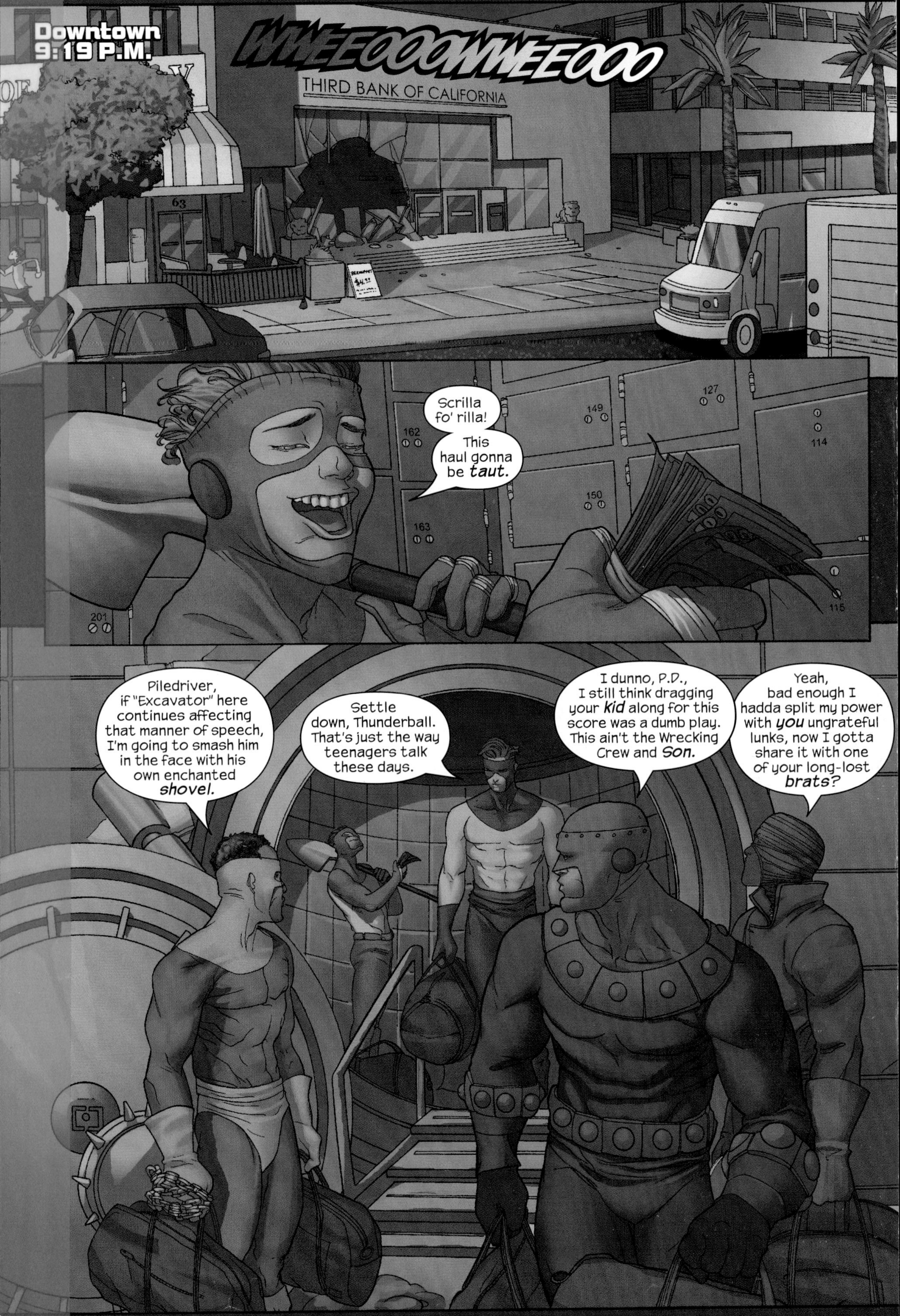

Downtown 9:19 P.M.
WWEEOOOWWEEOOO
THIRD BANK OF CALIFORNIA
Scrilla fo' rilla!
This haul gonna be *taut.*
Piledriver, if "Excavator" here continues affecting that manner of speech, I'm going to smash him in the face with his own enchanted *shovel.*
Settle down, Thunderball. That's just the way teenagers talk these days.
I dunno, P.D., I still think dragging your *kid* along for this score was a dumb play. This ain't the Wrecking Crew and *Son.*
Yeah, bad enough I hadda split my power with *you* ungrateful lunks, now I gotta share it with one of your long-lost *brats?*

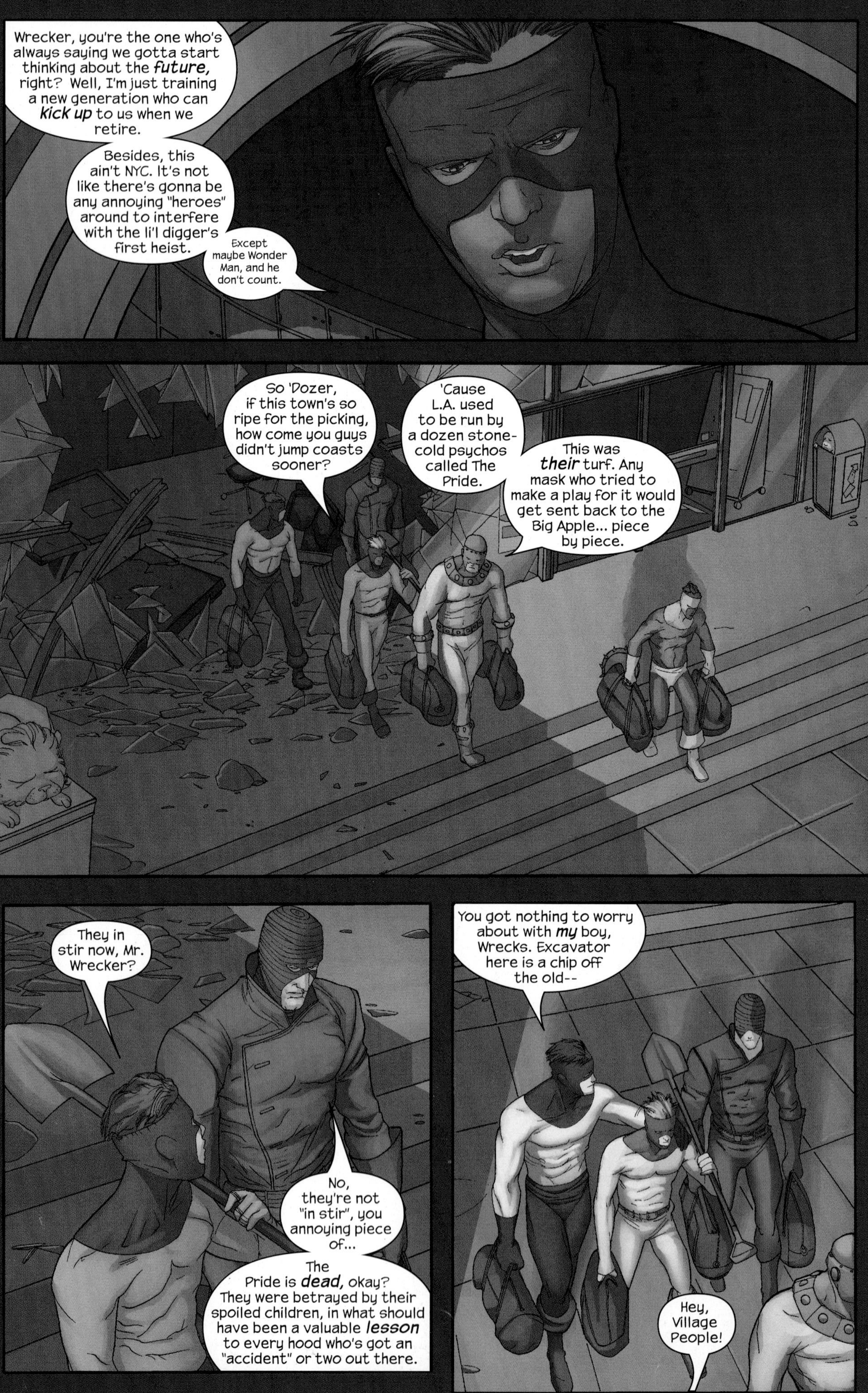
Wrecker, you're the one who's always saying we gotta start thinking about the *future,* right? Well, I'm just training a new generation who can *kick up* to us when we retire.
Besides, this ain't NYC. It's not like there's gonna be any annoying "heroes" around to interfere with the li'l digger's first heist.
Except maybe Wonder Man, and he don't count.
So 'Dozer, if this town's so ripe for the picking, how come you guys didn't jump coasts sooner?
'Cause L.A. used to be run by a dozen stone-cold psychos called The Pride.
This was *their* turf. Any mask who tried to make a play for it would get sent back to the Big Apple... piece by piece.
They in stir now, Mr. Wrecker?
No, they're not "in stir", you annoying piece of...
The Pride is *dead,* okay? They were betrayed by their spoiled children, in what should have been a valuable *lesson* to every hood who's got an "accident" or two out there.
You got nothing to worry about with *my* boy, Wrecks. Excavator here is a chip off the old--
Hey, Village People!

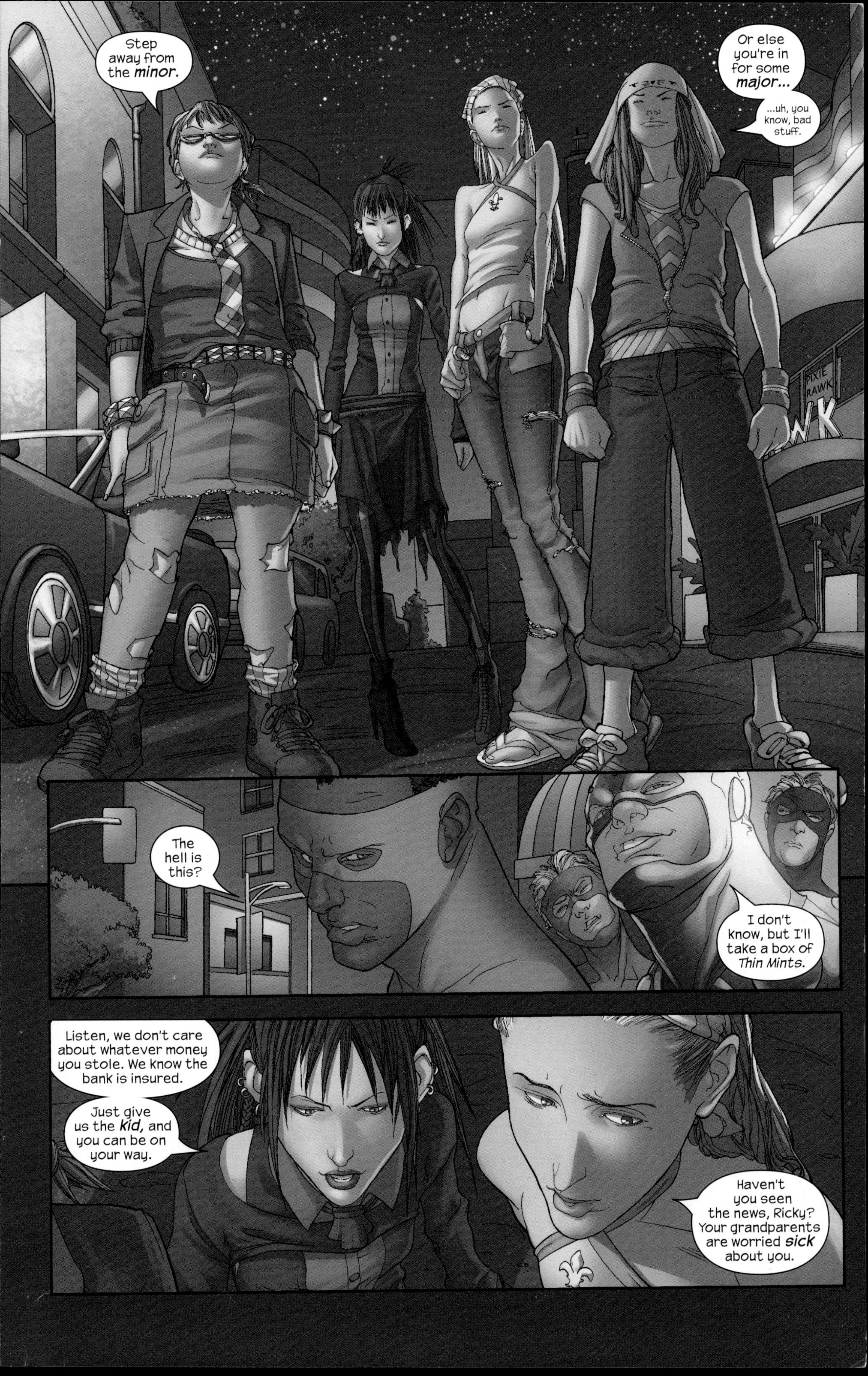
Step away from the *minor.*
Or else you're in for some *major...*
...uh, you know, bad stuff.
The hell is this?
I don't know, but I'll take a box of *Thin Mints.*
Listen, we don't care about whatever money you stole. We know the bank is insured.
Just give us the *kid,* and you can be on your way.
Haven't you seen the news, Ricky? Your grandparents are worried *sick* about you.
PIXIE RAWK

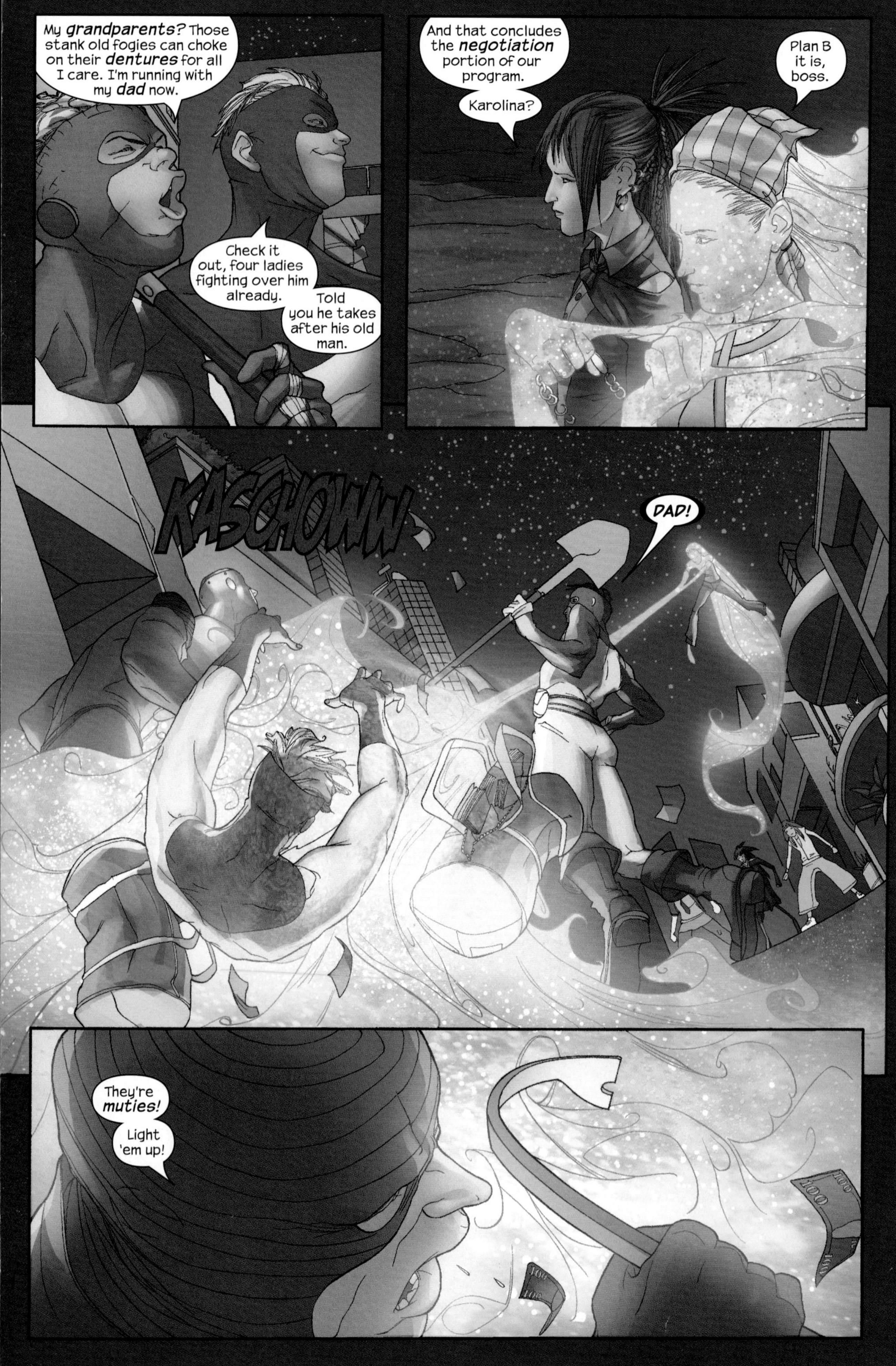

My grandparents? Those stank old fogies can choke on their dentures for all I care. I'm running with my dad now.
Check it out, four ladies fighting over him already.
Told you he takes after his old man.
And that concludes the negotiation portion of our program.
Karolina?
Plan B it is, boss.
KASCHOWW
DAD!
They're muties!
Light 'em up!

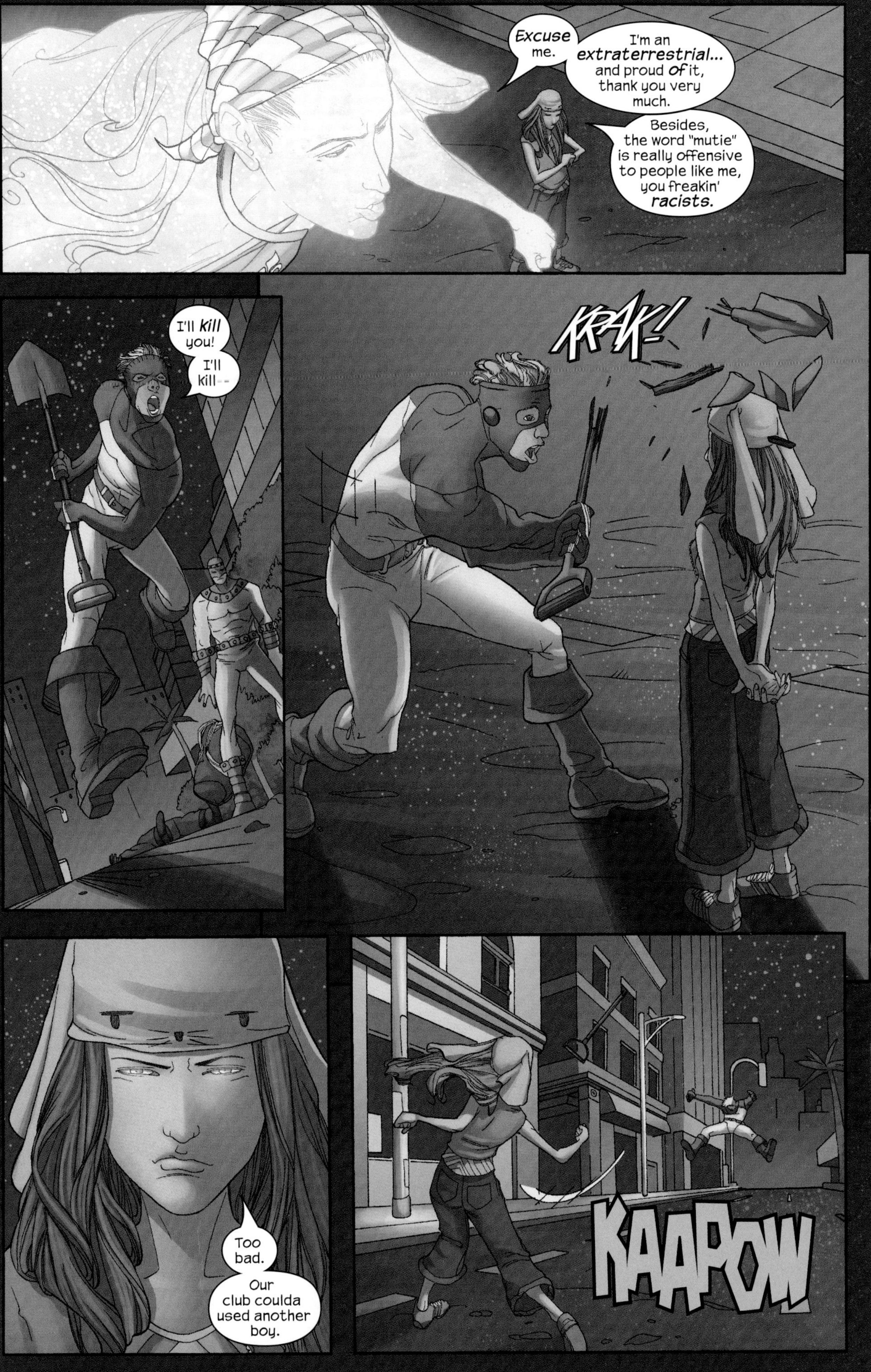
Excuse me.
I'm an extraterrestrial... and proud of it, thank you very much.
Besides, the word "mutie" is really offensive to people like me, you freakin' racists.
I'll kill you!
I'll kill--
KRAK!
Too bad.
Our club coulda used another boy.
KAAPOW

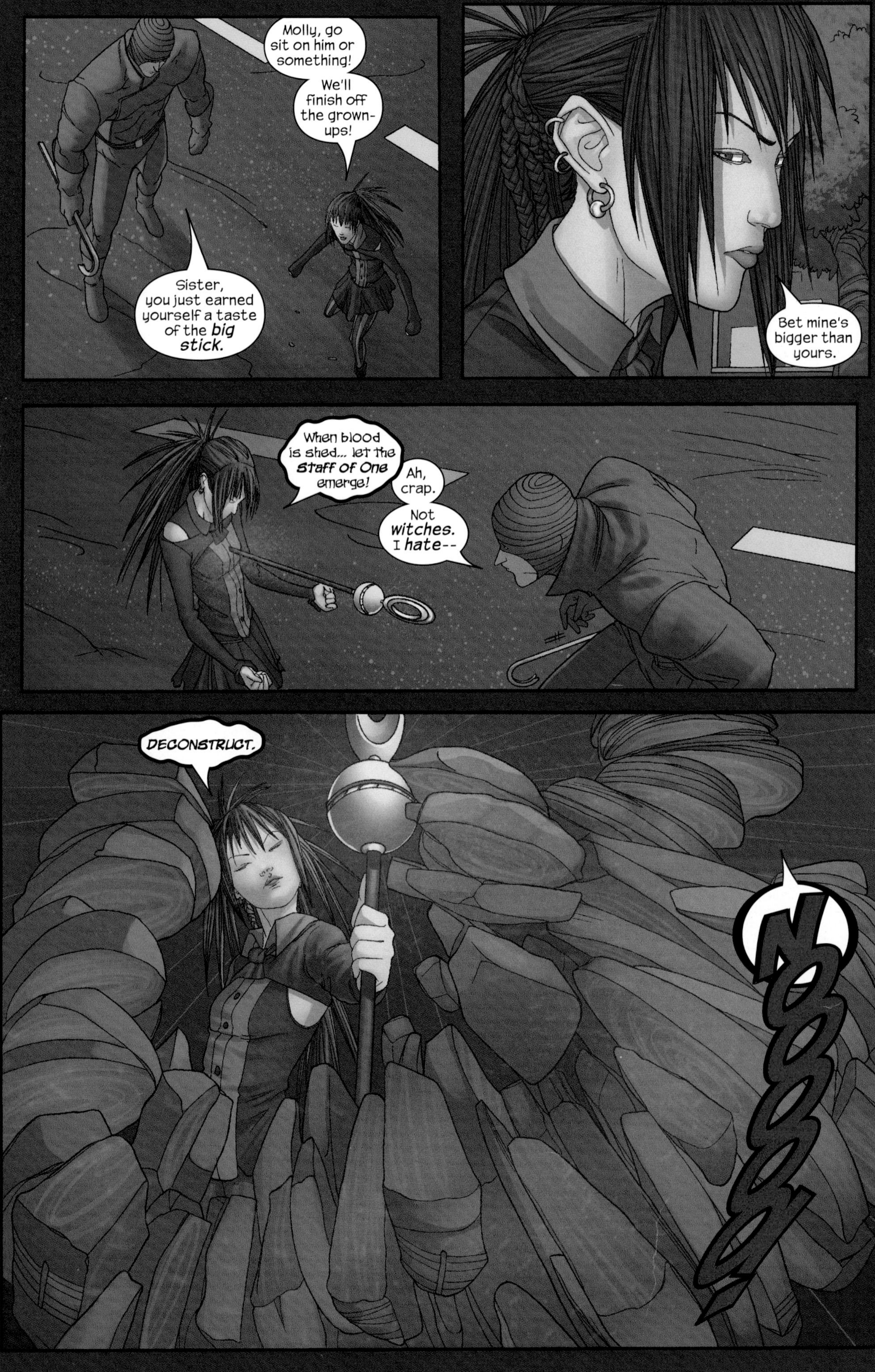
Molly, go sit on him or something!
We'll finish off the grown-ups!
Sister, you just earned yourself a taste of the *big stick.*
Bet mine's bigger than yours.
When blood is shed... let the *Staff of One* emerge!
Ah, crap.
Not *witches.* I *hate*--
DECONSTRUCT.
WOOOOOOSH

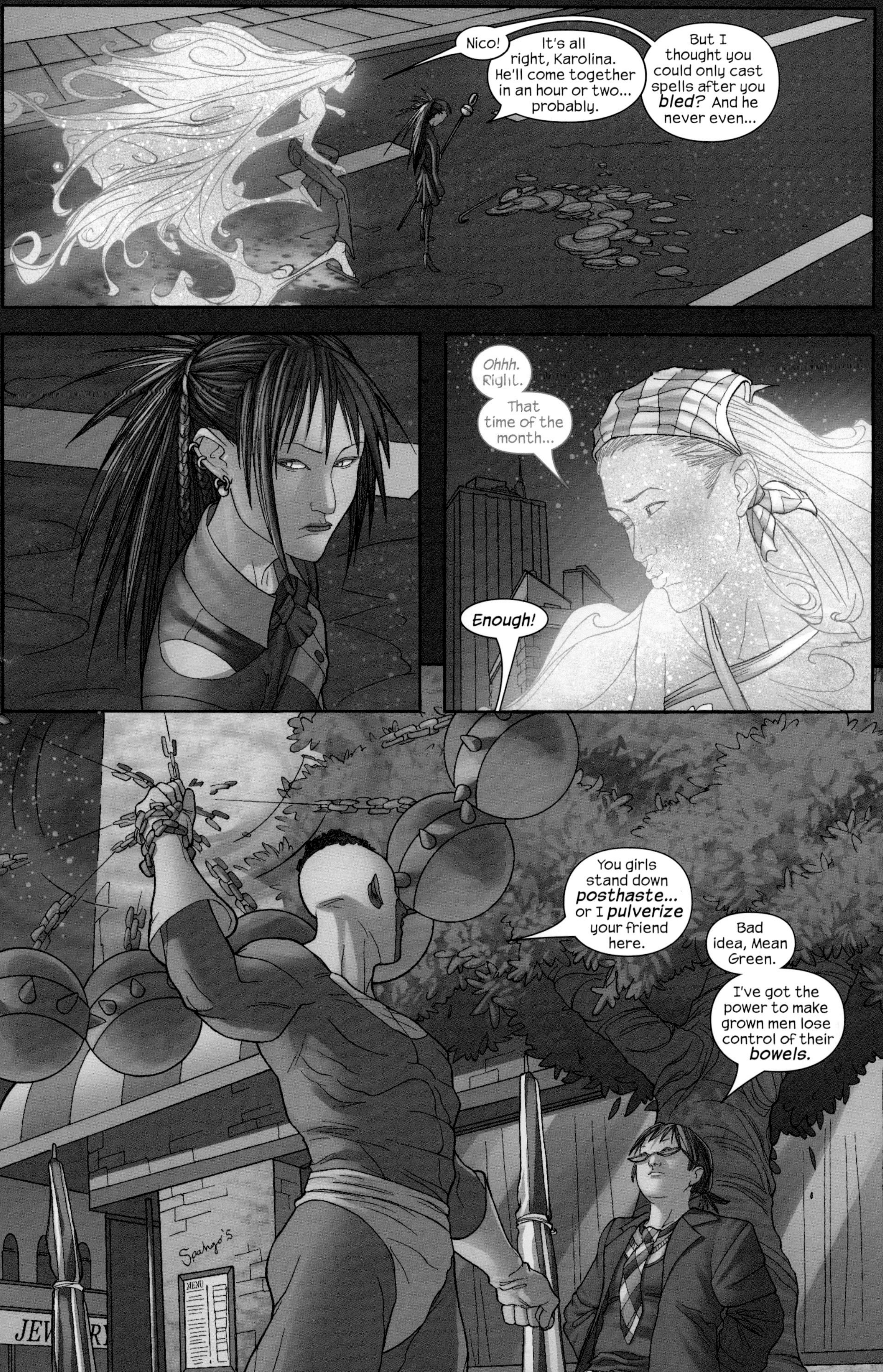
Nico!
It's all right, Karolina. He'll come together in an hour or two... probably.
But I thought you could only cast spells after you *bled?* And he never even...
Ohhh. Right.
That time of the month...
Enough!
You girls stand down ***posthaste...*** or I ***pulverize*** your friend here.
Bad idea, Mean Green.
I've got the power to make grown men lose control of their ***bowels.***

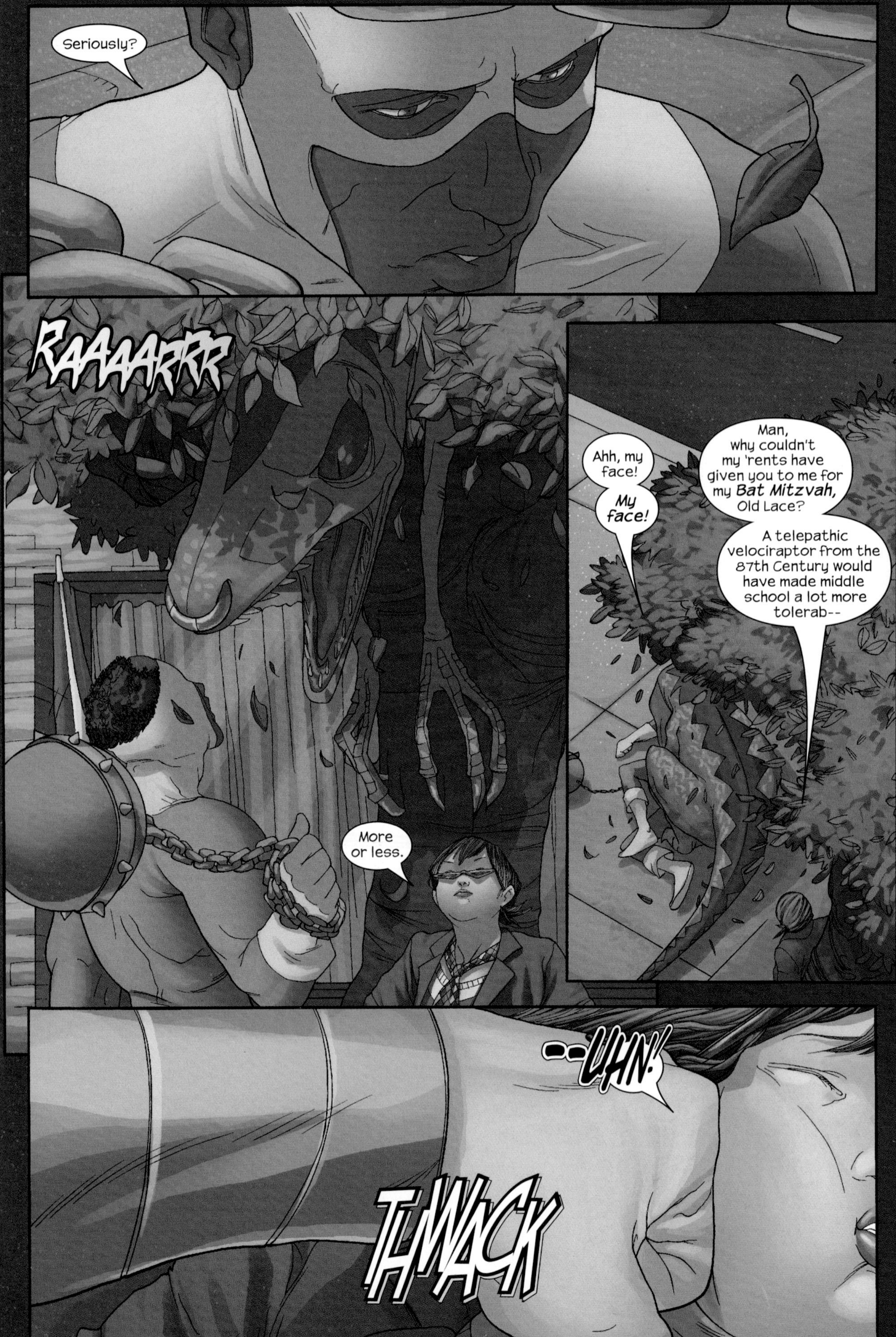
Seriously?
RAAAARRR
More or less.
Ahh, my face!
My face!
Man, why couldn't my 'rents have given you to me for my Bat Mitzvah, Old Lace?
A telepathic velociraptor from the 87th Century would have made middle school a lot more tolerab--
--UHN!
THWACK

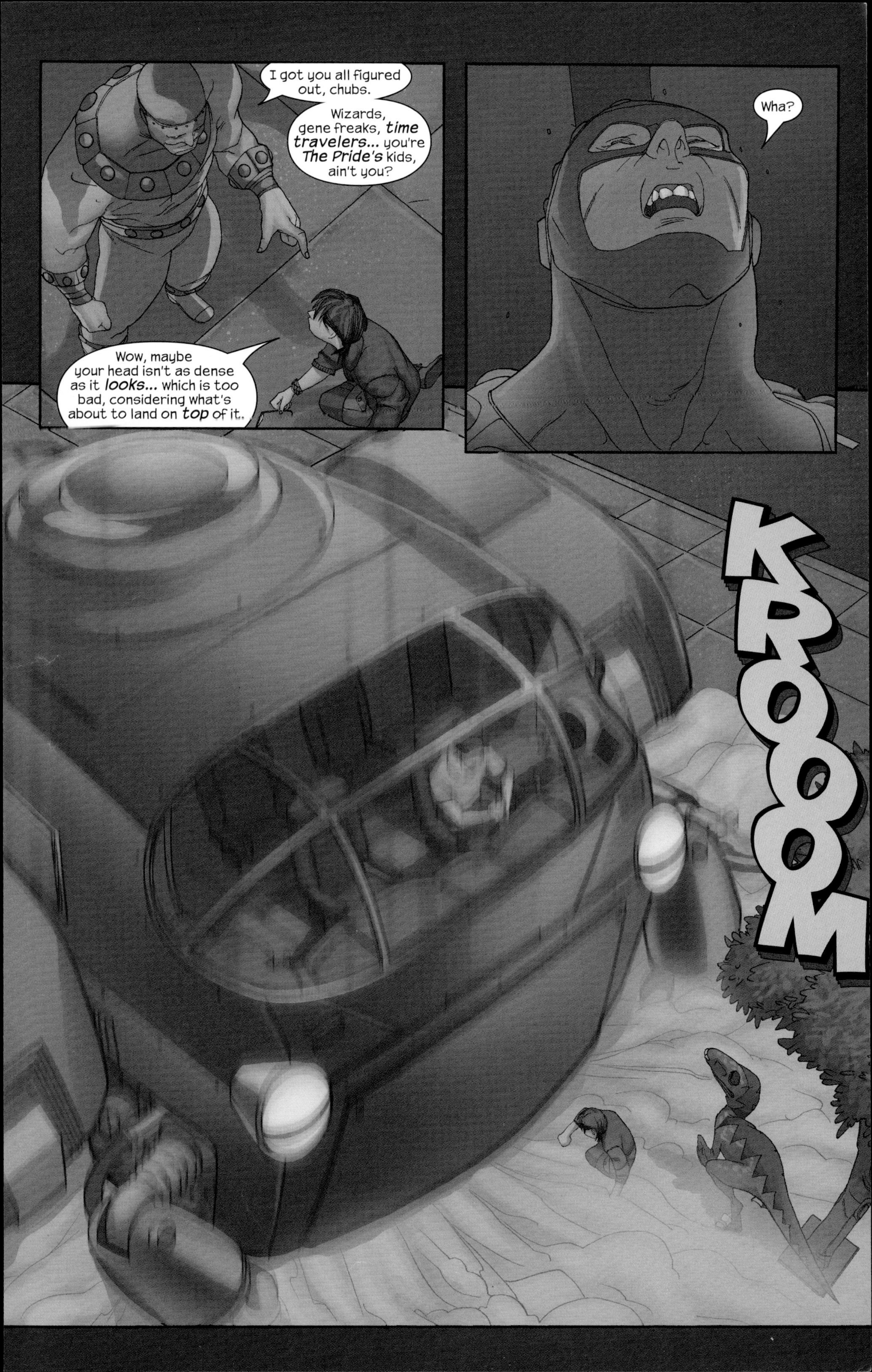
I got you all figured out, chubs.
Wizards, gene freaks, *time travelers...* you're *The Pride's* kids, ain't you?
Wow, maybe your head isn't as dense as it *looks...* which is too bad, considering what's about to land on *top* of it.
Wha?
KROOOOM

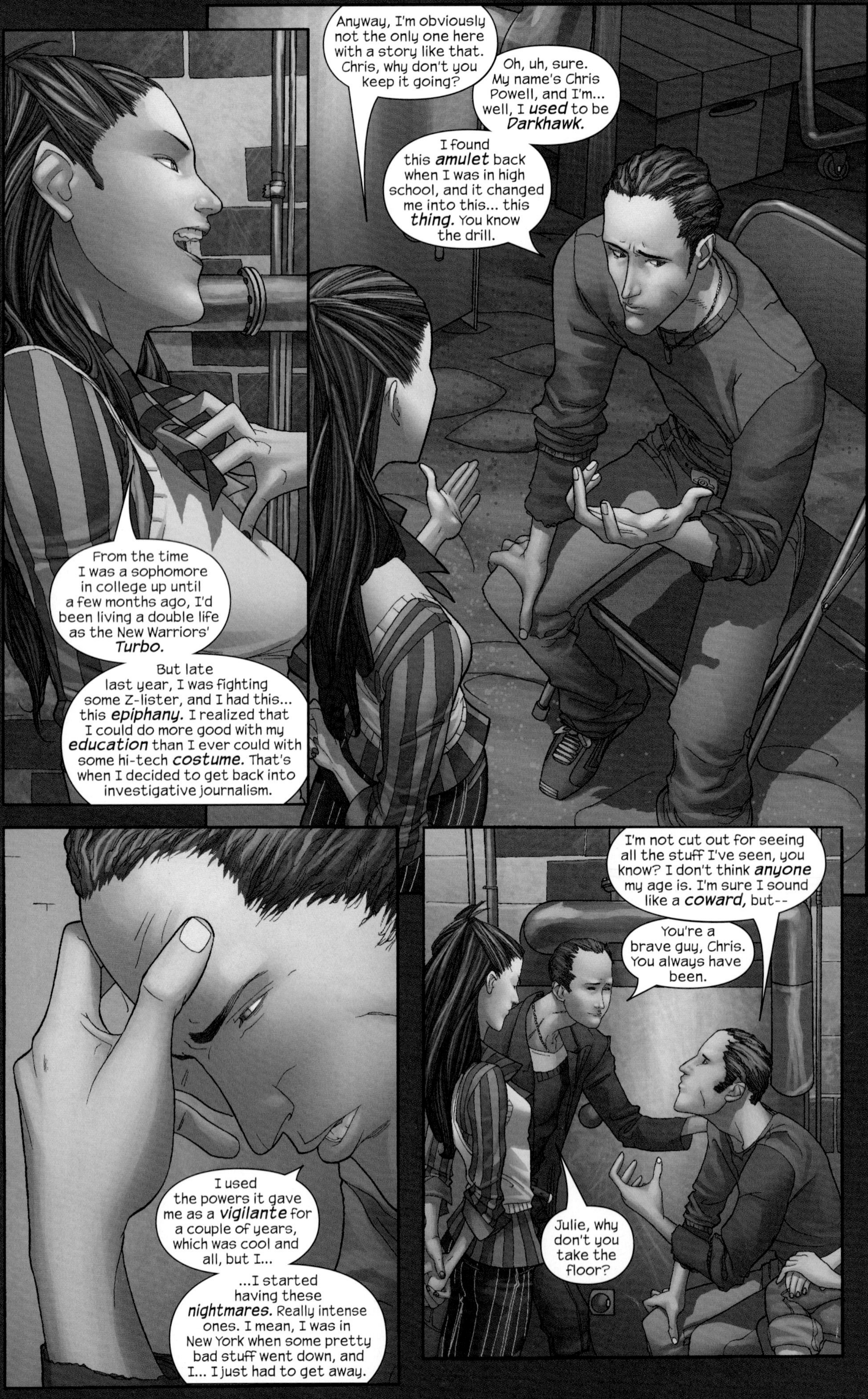
Anyway, I'm obviously not the only one here with a story like that. Chris, why don't you keep it going?
Oh, uh, sure. My name's Chris Powell, and I'm... well, I *used* to be *Darkhawk.*
I found this *amulet* back when I was in high school, and it changed me into this... this *thing.* You know the drill.
From the time I was a sophomore in college up until a few months ago, I'd been living a double life as the New Warriors' *Turbo.*
But late last year, I was fighting some Z-lister, and I had this... this *epiphany.* I realized that I could do more good with my *education* than I ever could with some hi-tech *costume.* That's when I decided to get back into investigative journalism.
I used the powers it gave me as a *vigilante* for a couple of years, which was cool and all, but I...
...I started having these *nightmares.* Really intense ones. I mean, I was in New York when some pretty bad stuff went down, and I... I just had to get away.
I'm not cut out for seeing all the stuff I've seen, you know? I don't think *anyone* my age is. I'm sure I sound like a *coward,* but--
You're a brave guy, Chris. You always have been.
Julie, why don't you take the floor?

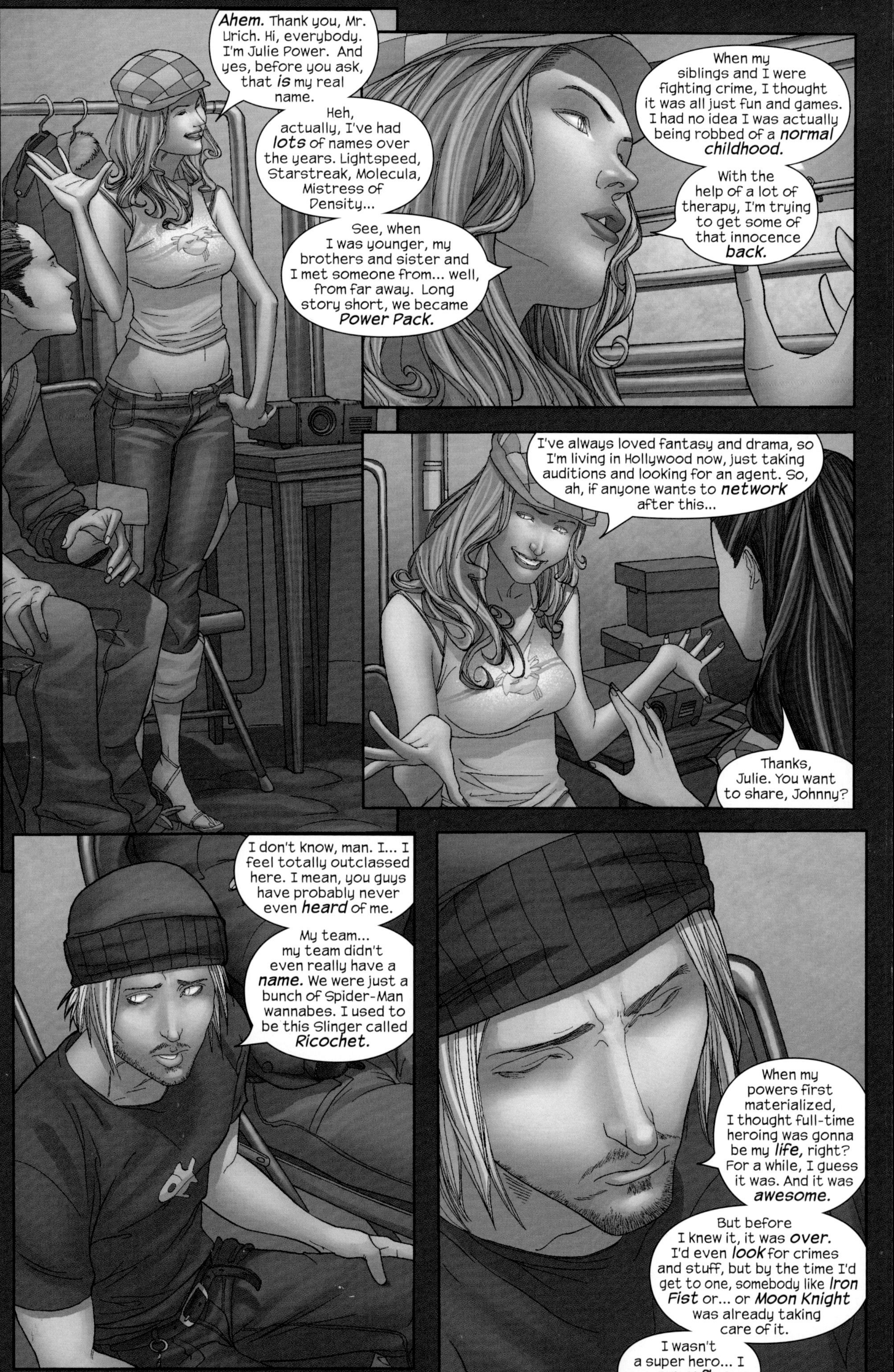

Ahem. Thank you, Mr. Urich. Hi, everybody. I'm Julie Power. And yes, before you ask, that is my real name.
Heh, actually, I've had lots of names over the years. Lightspeed, Starstreak, Molecula, Mistress of Density...
See, when I was younger, my brothers and sister and I met someone from... well, from far away. Long story short, we became Power Pack.
When my siblings and I were fighting crime, I thought it was all just fun and games. I had no idea I was actually being robbed of a normal childhood.
With the help of a lot of therapy, I'm trying to get some of that innocence back.
I've always loved fantasy and drama, so I'm living in Hollywood now, just taking auditions and looking for an agent. So, ah, if anyone wants to network after this...
Thanks, Julie. You want to share, Johnny?
I don't know, man. I... I feel totally outclassed here. I mean, you guys have probably never even heard of me.
My team... my team didn't even really have a name. We were just a bunch of Spider-Man wannabes. I used to be this Slinger called Ricochet.
When my powers first materialized, I thought full-time heroing was gonna be my life, right? For a while, I guess it was. And it was awesome.
But before I knew it, it was over. I'd even look for crimes and stuff, but by the time I'd get to one, somebody like Iron Fist or... or Moon Knight was already taking care of it.
I wasn't a super hero... I was superfluous.

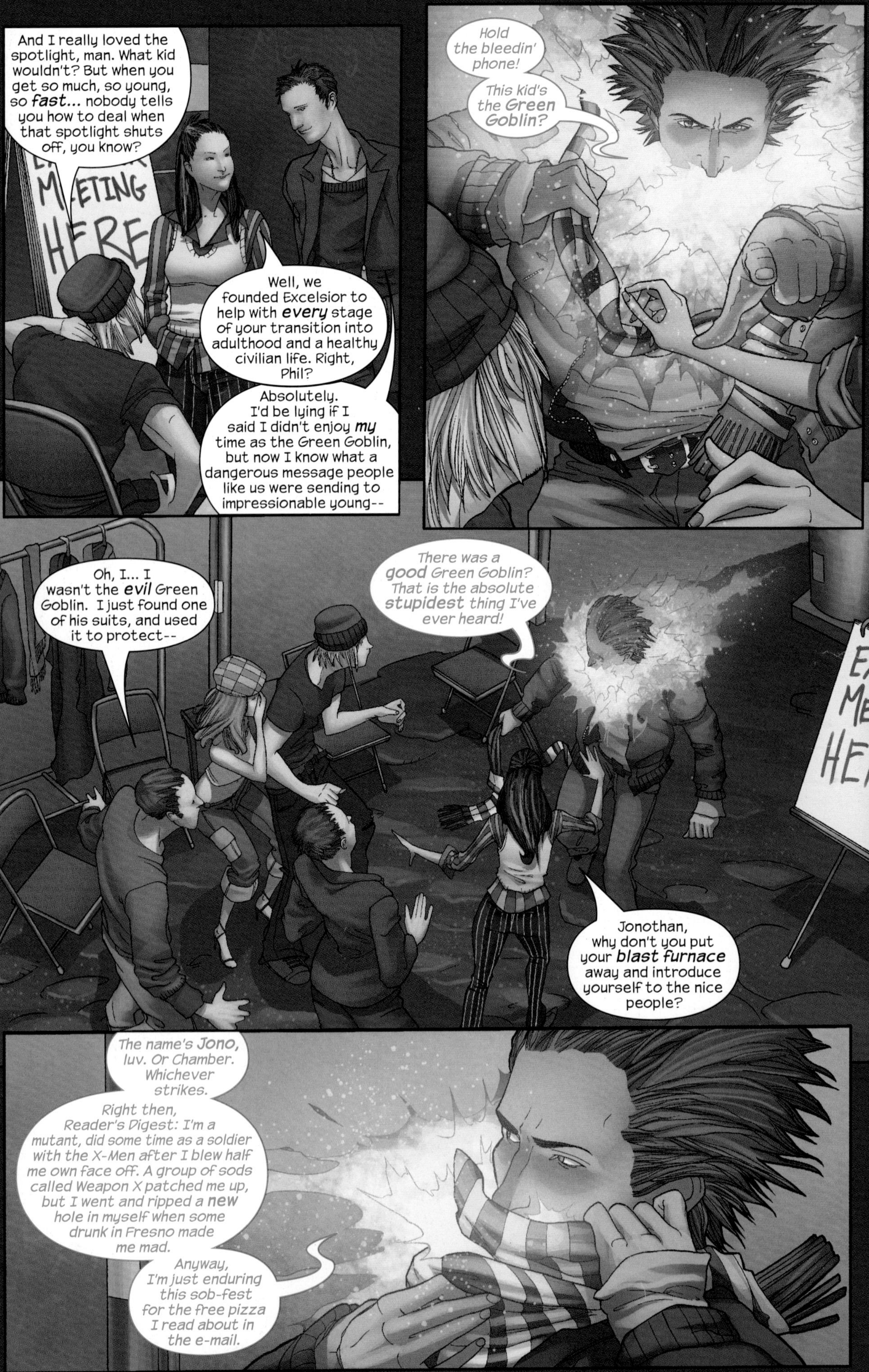

And I really loved the spotlight, man. What kid wouldn't? But when you get so much, so young, so *fast*... nobody tells you how to deal when that spotlight shuts off, you know?
MEETING HERE
Well, we founded Excelsior to help with *every* stage of your transition into adulthood and a healthy civilian life. Right, Phil?
Absolutely. I'd be lying if I said I didn't enjoy *my* time as the Green Goblin, but now I know what a dangerous message people like us were sending to impressionable young--
Hold the bleedin' phone!
This kid's the *Green Goblin*?
Oh, I... I wasn't the *evil* Green Goblin. I just found one of his suits, and used it to protect--
There was a *good* Green Goblin? That is the absolute *stupidest* thing I've ever heard!
Jonothan, why don't you put your *blast furnace* away and introduce yourself to the nice people?
The name's *Jono,* luv. Or Chamber. Whichever strikes.
Right then, Reader's Digest: I'm a mutant, did some time as a soldier with the X-Men after I blew half me own face off. A group of sods called Weapon X patched me up, but I went and ripped a *new* hole in myself when some drunk in Fresno made me mad.
Anyway, I'm just enduring this sob-fest for the free pizza I read about in the e-mail.

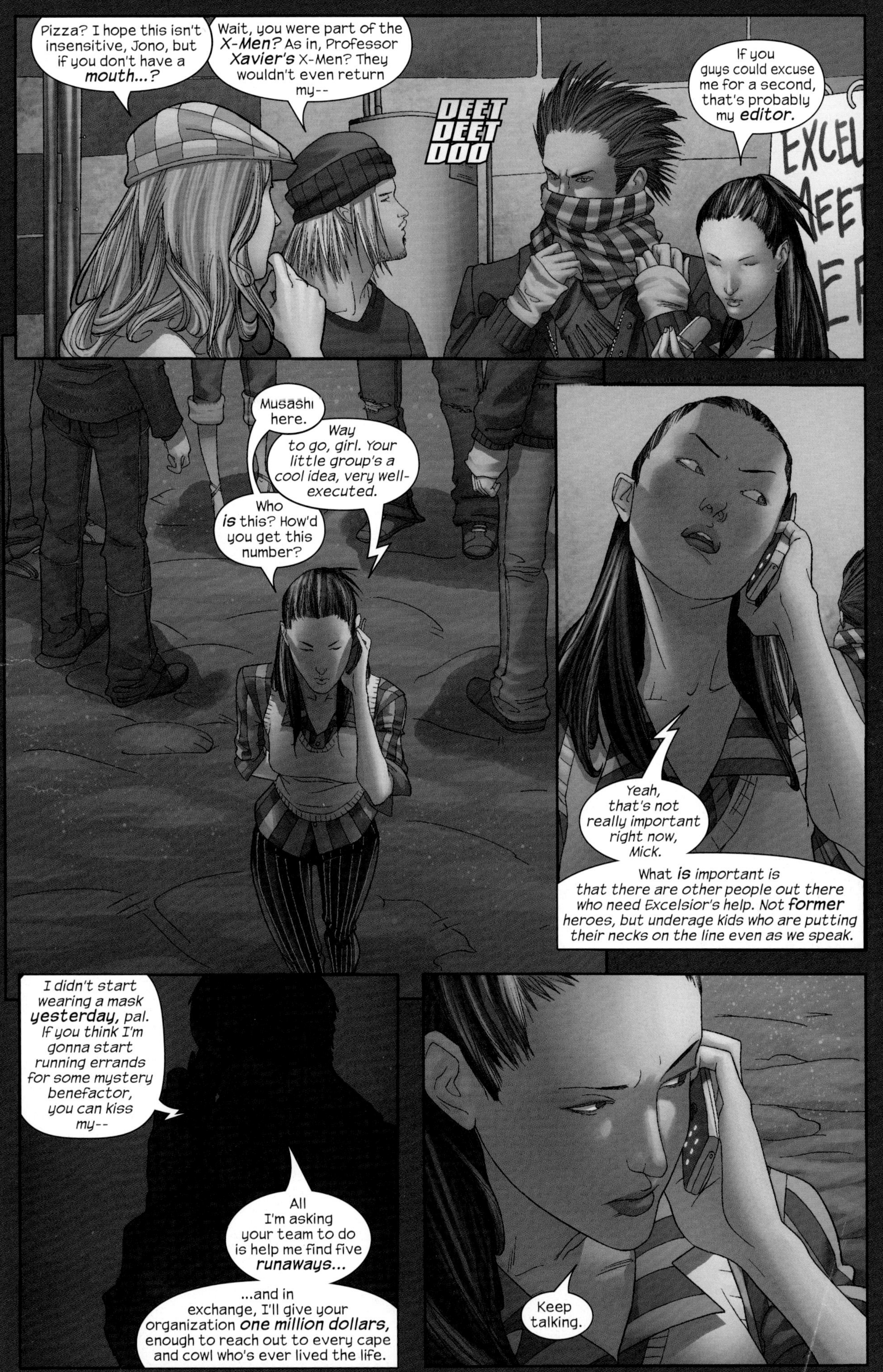

Pizza? I hope this isn't insensitive, Jono, but if you don't have a mouth...?
Wait, you were part of the X-Men? As in, Professor Xavier's X-Men? They wouldn't even return my--
DEET DEET DOO
If you guys could excuse me for a second, that's probably my editor.
EXCEL MEET
Musashi here.
Way to go, girl. Your little group's a cool idea, very well-executed.
Who is this? How'd you get this number?
Yeah, that's not really important right now, Mick.
What is important is that there are other people out there who need Excelsior's help. Not former heroes, but underage kids who are putting their necks on the line even as we speak.
I didn't start wearing a mask yesterday, pal. If you think I'm gonna start running errands for some mystery benefactor, you can kiss my--
All I'm asking your team to do is help me find five runaways...
...and in exchange, I'll give your organization one million dollars, enough to reach out to every cape and cowl who's ever lived the life.
Keep talking.

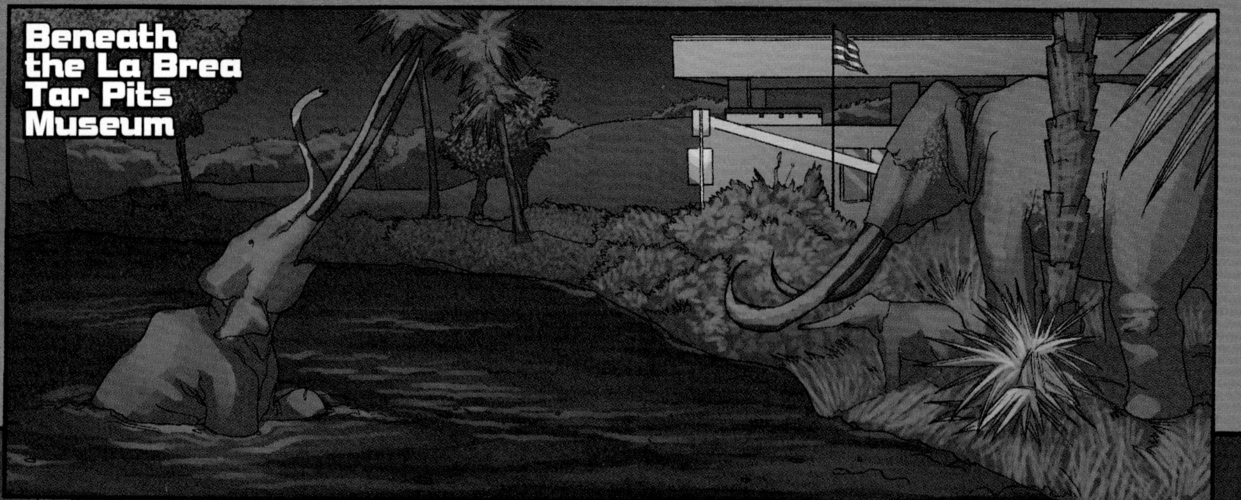
Beneath the La Brea Tar Pits Museum

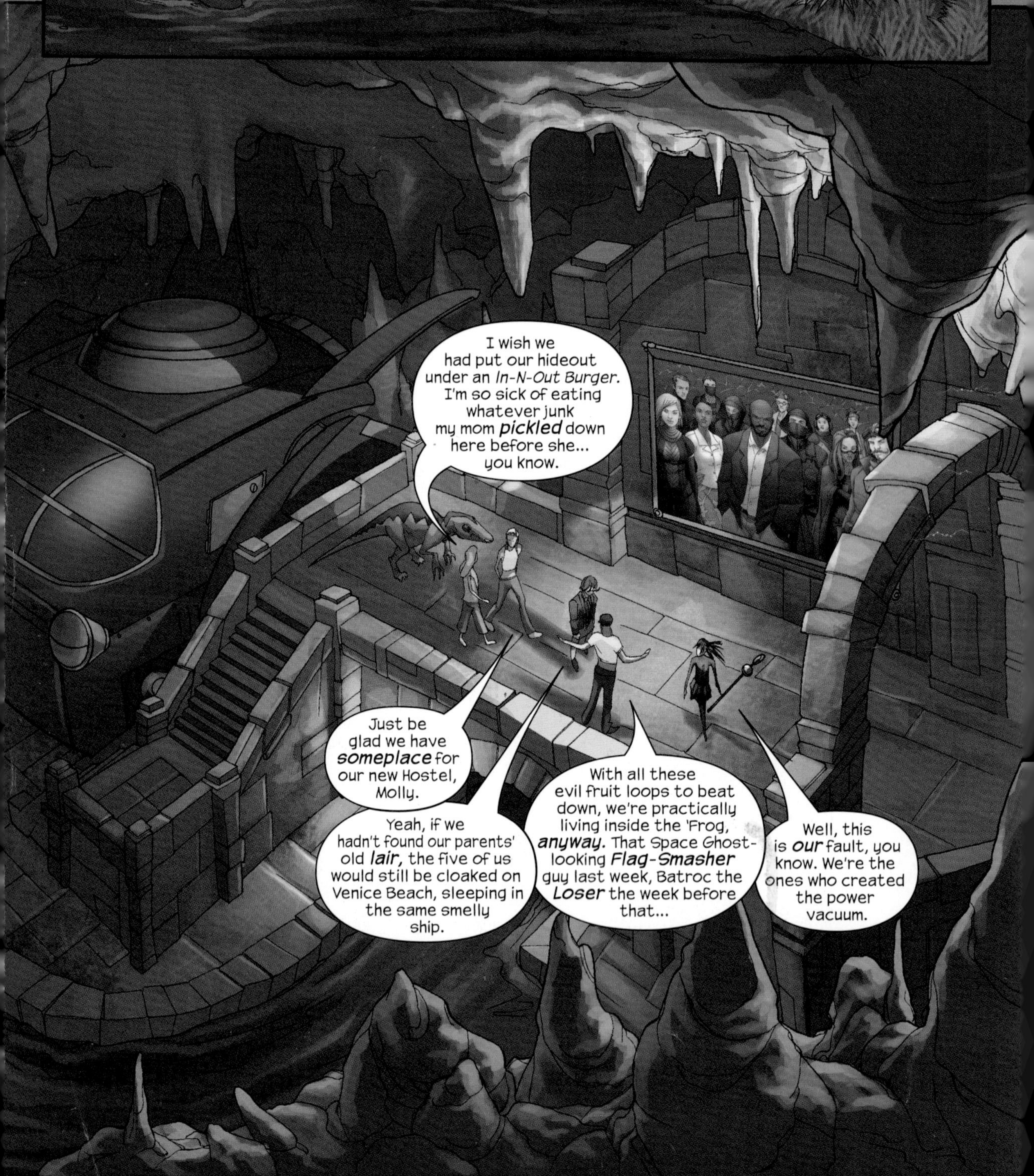
I wish we had put our hideout under an *In-N-Out Burger.* I'm so sick of eating whatever junk my mom **pickled** down here before she... you know.
Just be glad we have **someplace** for our new Hostel, Molly.
Yeah, if we hadn't found our parents' old **lair,** the five of us would still be cloaked on Venice Beach, sleeping in the same smelly ship.
With all these evil fruit loops to beat down, we're practically living inside the 'Frog, **anyway.** That Space Ghost-looking **Flag-Smasher** guy last week, Batroc the **Loser** the week before that...
Well, this is **our** fault, you know. We're the ones who created the power vacuum.

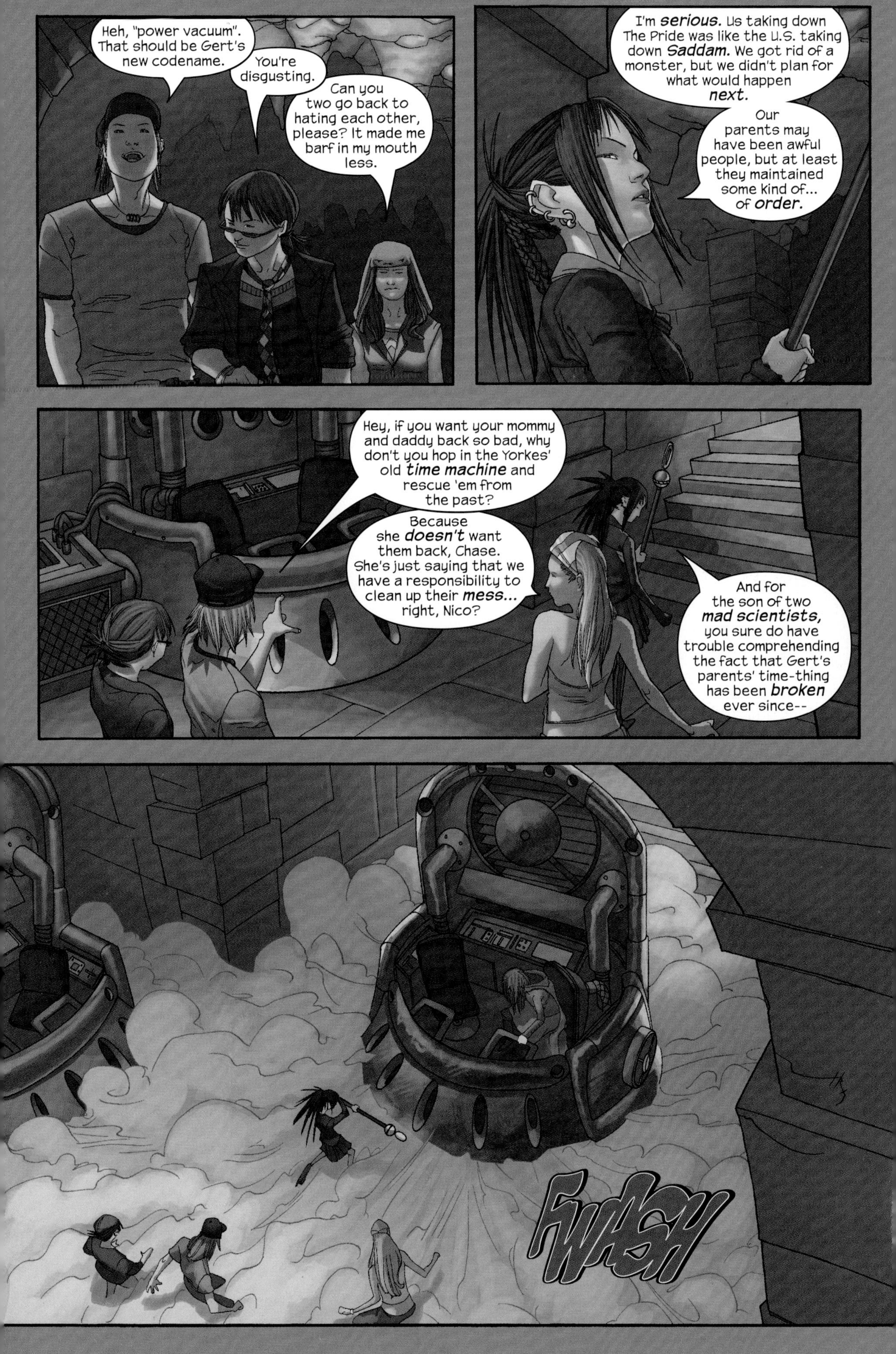

Heh, "power vacuum". That should be Gert's new codename.
You're disgusting.
Can you two go back to hating each other, please? It made me barf in my mouth less.
I'm serious. Us taking down The Pride was like the U.S. taking down Saddam. We got rid of a monster, but we didn't plan for what would happen next.
Our parents may have been awful people, but at least they maintained some kind of... of order.
Hey, if you want your mommy and daddy back so bad, why don't you hop in the Yorkes' old time machine and rescue 'em from the past?
Because she doesn't want them back, Chase. She's just saying that we have a responsibility to clean up their mess... right, Nico?
And for the son of two mad scientists, you sure do have trouble comprehending the fact that Gert's parents' time-thing has been broken ever since--
FWASH

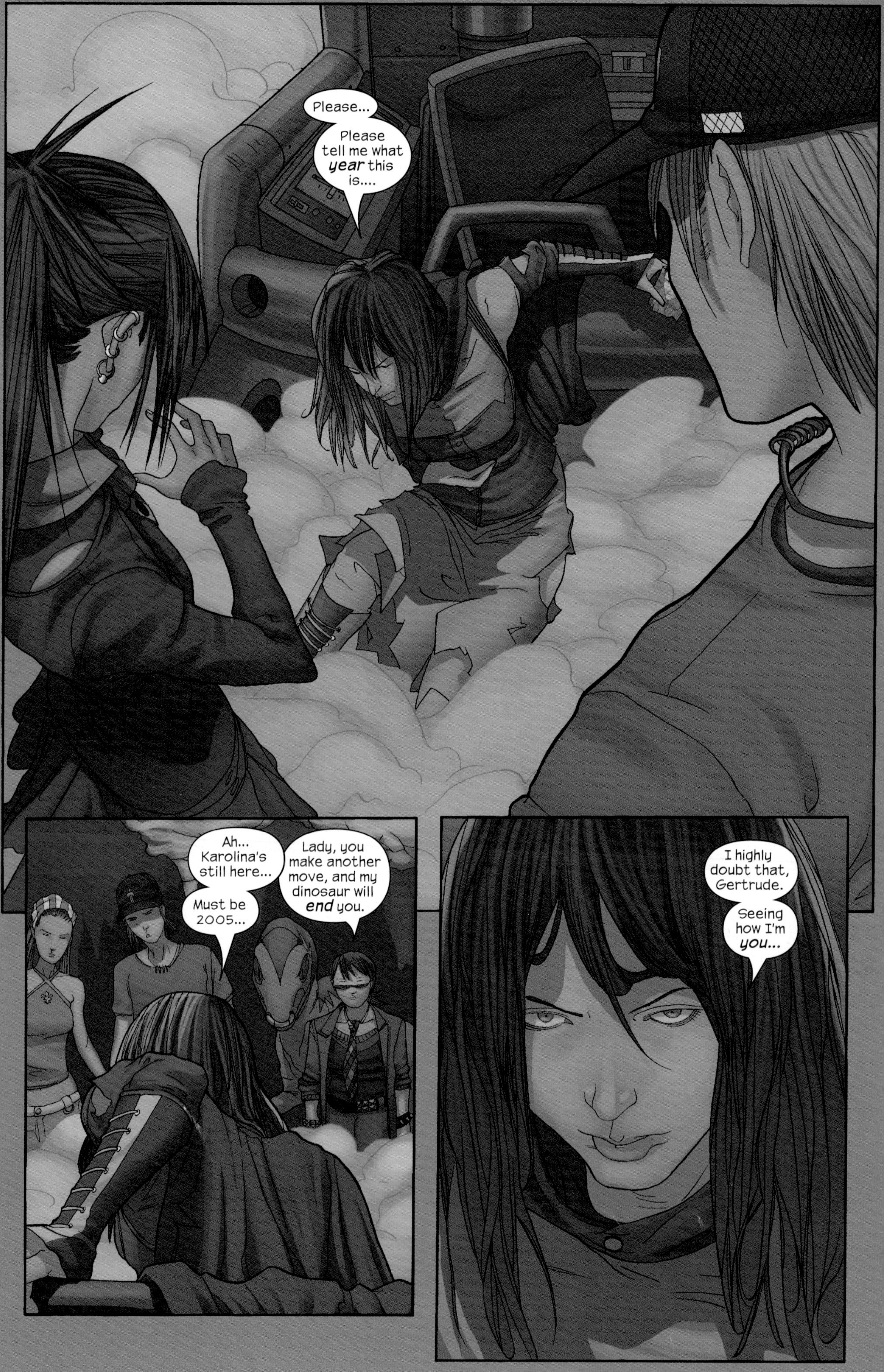
Please...
Please tell me what *year* this is....
Ah... Karolina's still here...
Must be 2005...
Lady, you make another move, and my dinosaur will *end* you.
I highly doubt that, Gertrude.
Seeing how I'm *you*...

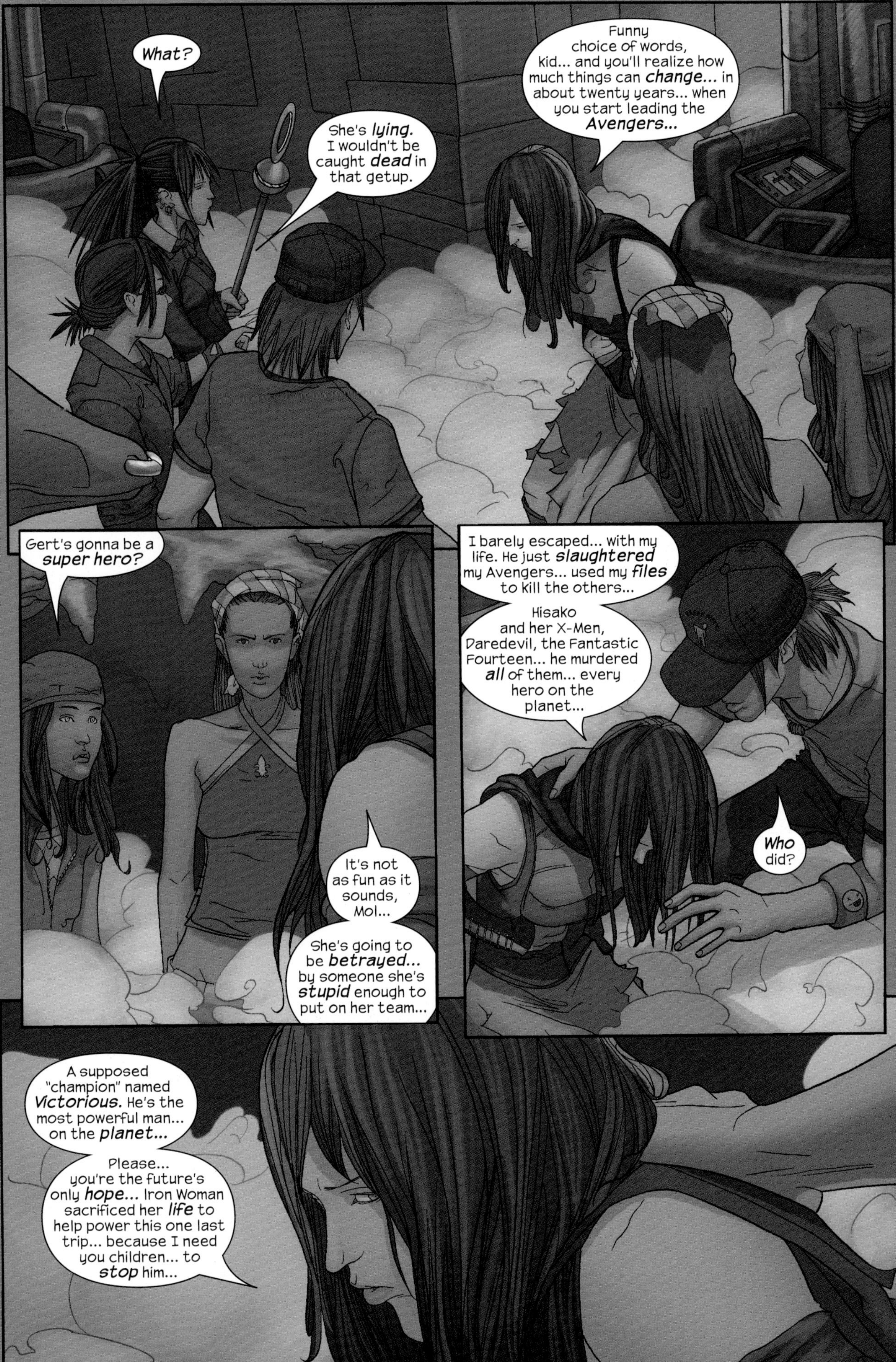
What?
She's lying. I wouldn't be caught dead in that getup.
Funny choice of words, Kid... and you'll realize how much things can change... in about twenty years... when you start leading the Avengers...
Gert's gonna be a super hero?
It's not as fun as it sounds, Mol...
She's going to be betrayed... by someone she's stupid enough to put on her team...
I barely escaped... with my life. He just slaughtered my Avengers... used my files to kill the others...
Hisako and her X-Men, Daredevil, the Fantastic Fourteen... he murdered all of them... every hero on the planet...
Who did?
A supposed "champion" named Victorious. He's the most powerful man... on the planet...
Please... you're the future's only hope... Iron Woman sacrificed her life to help power this one last trip... because I need you children... to stop him...

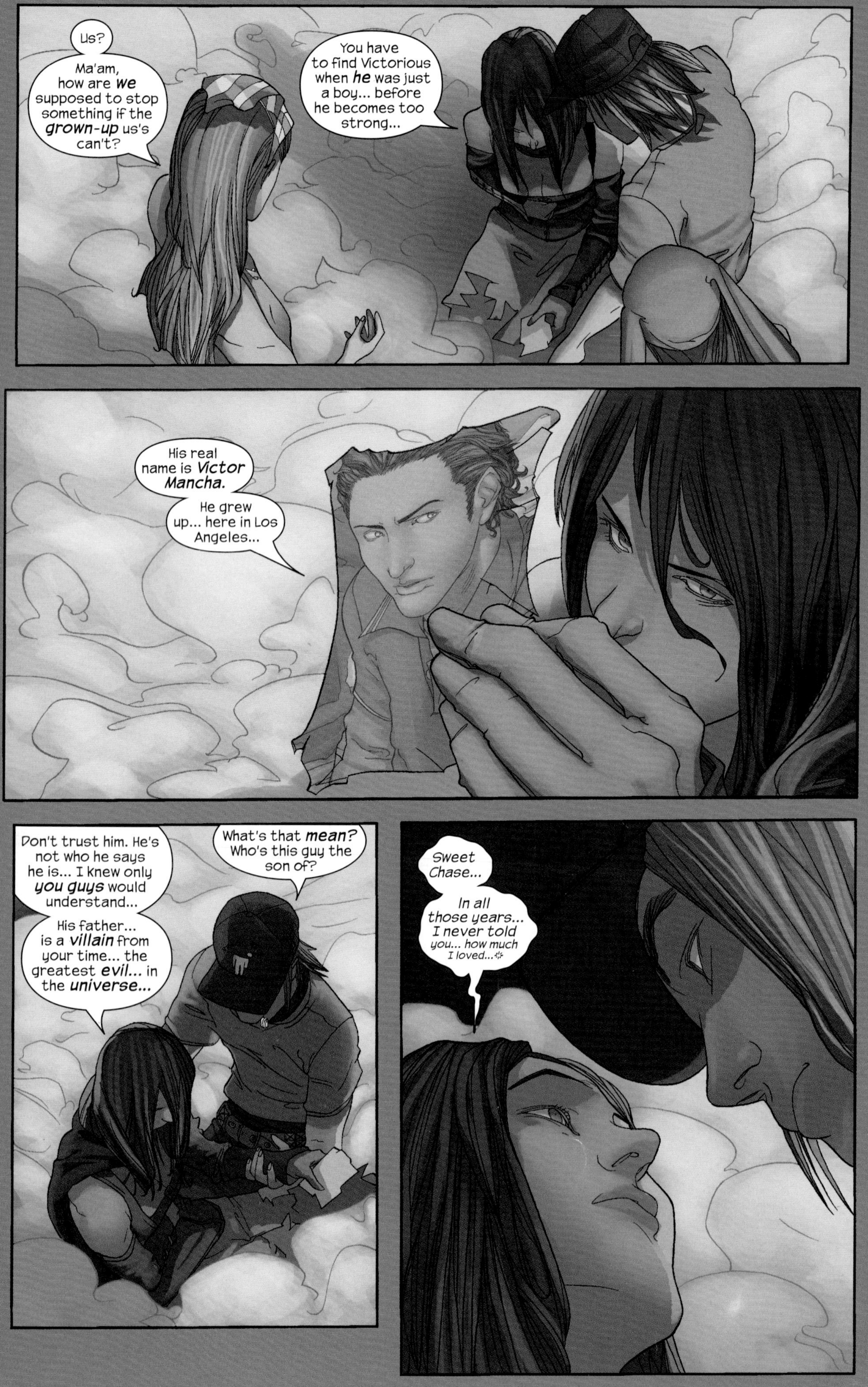
Us?
Ma'am, how are *we* supposed to stop something if the *grown-up* us's can't?
You have to find Victorious when *he* was just a boy... before he becomes too strong...
His real name is *Victor Mancha.*
He grew up... here in Los Angeles...
Don't trust him. He's not who he says he is... I knew only *you guys* would understand...
What's that *mean?* Who's this guy the son of?
His father... is a *villain* from your time... the greatest *evil...* in the *universe...*
Sweet Chase...
In all those years... I never told you... how much I loved...

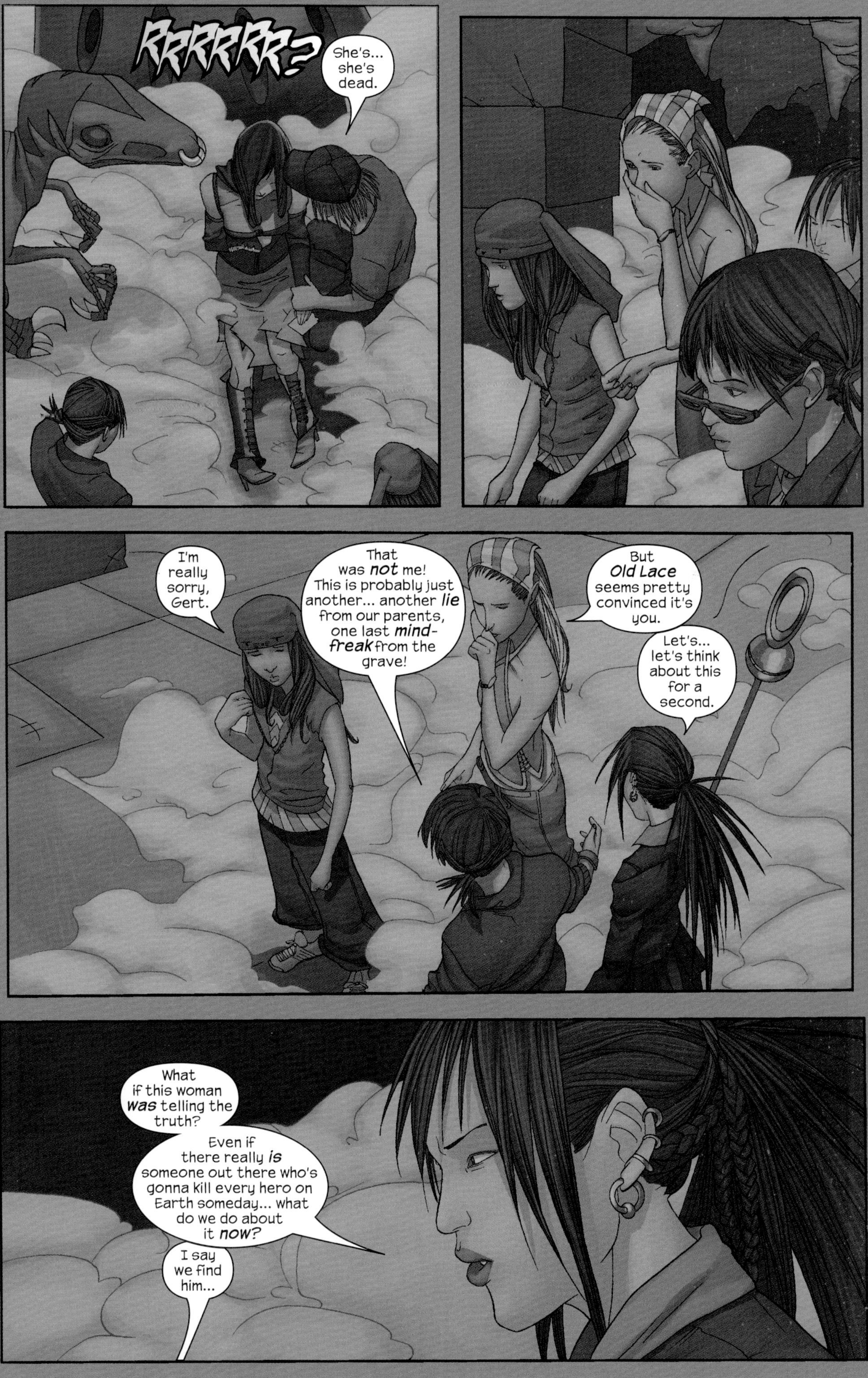
RRRRRR?
She's... she's dead.
I'm really sorry, Gert.
That was not me! This is probably just another... another lie from our parents, one last mind-freak from the grave!
But Old Lace seems pretty convinced it's you.
Let's... let's think about this for a second.
What if this woman was telling the truth?
Even if there really is someone out there who's gonna kill every hero on Earth someday... what do we do about it now?
I say we find him...

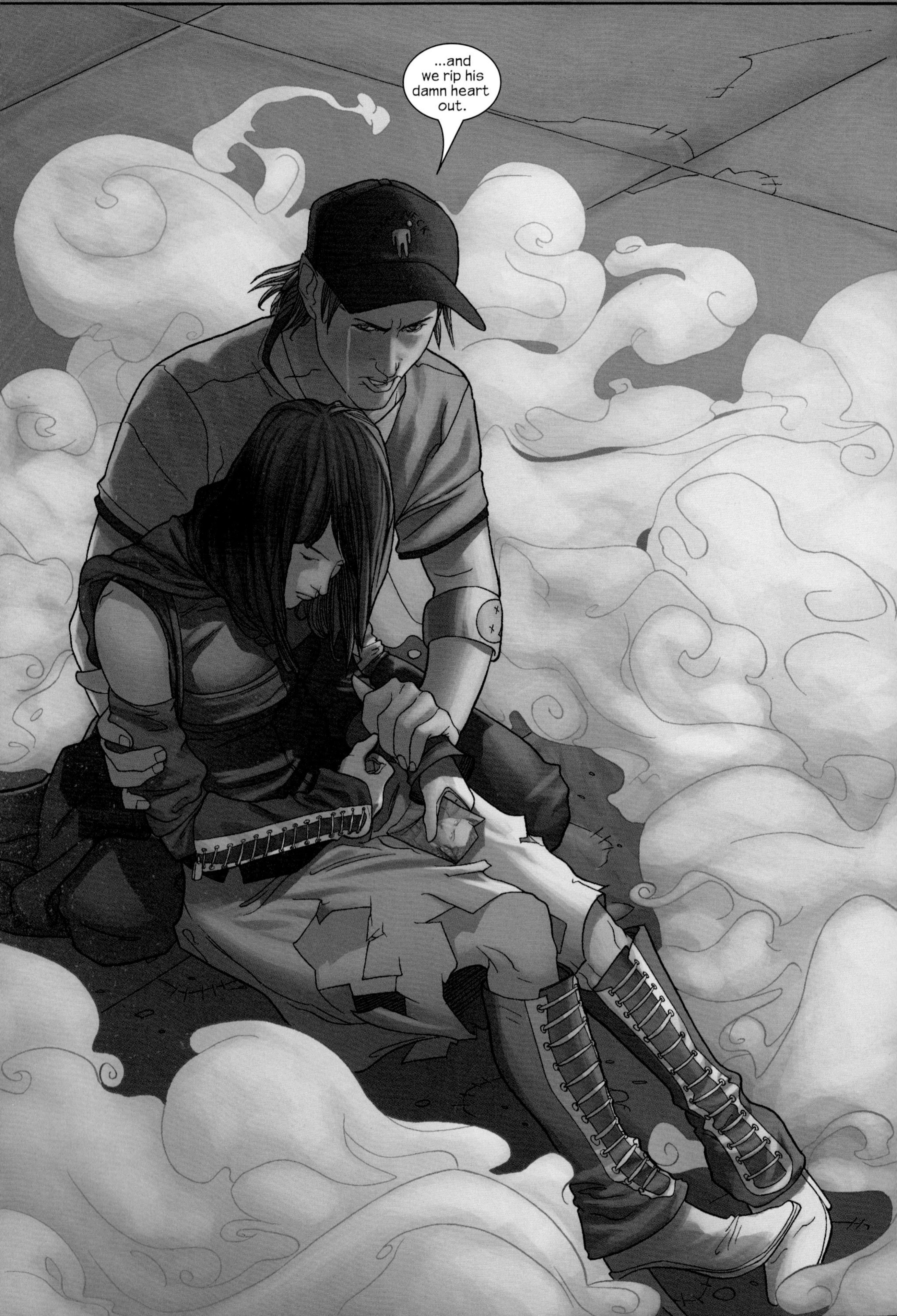
...and we rip his damn heart out.

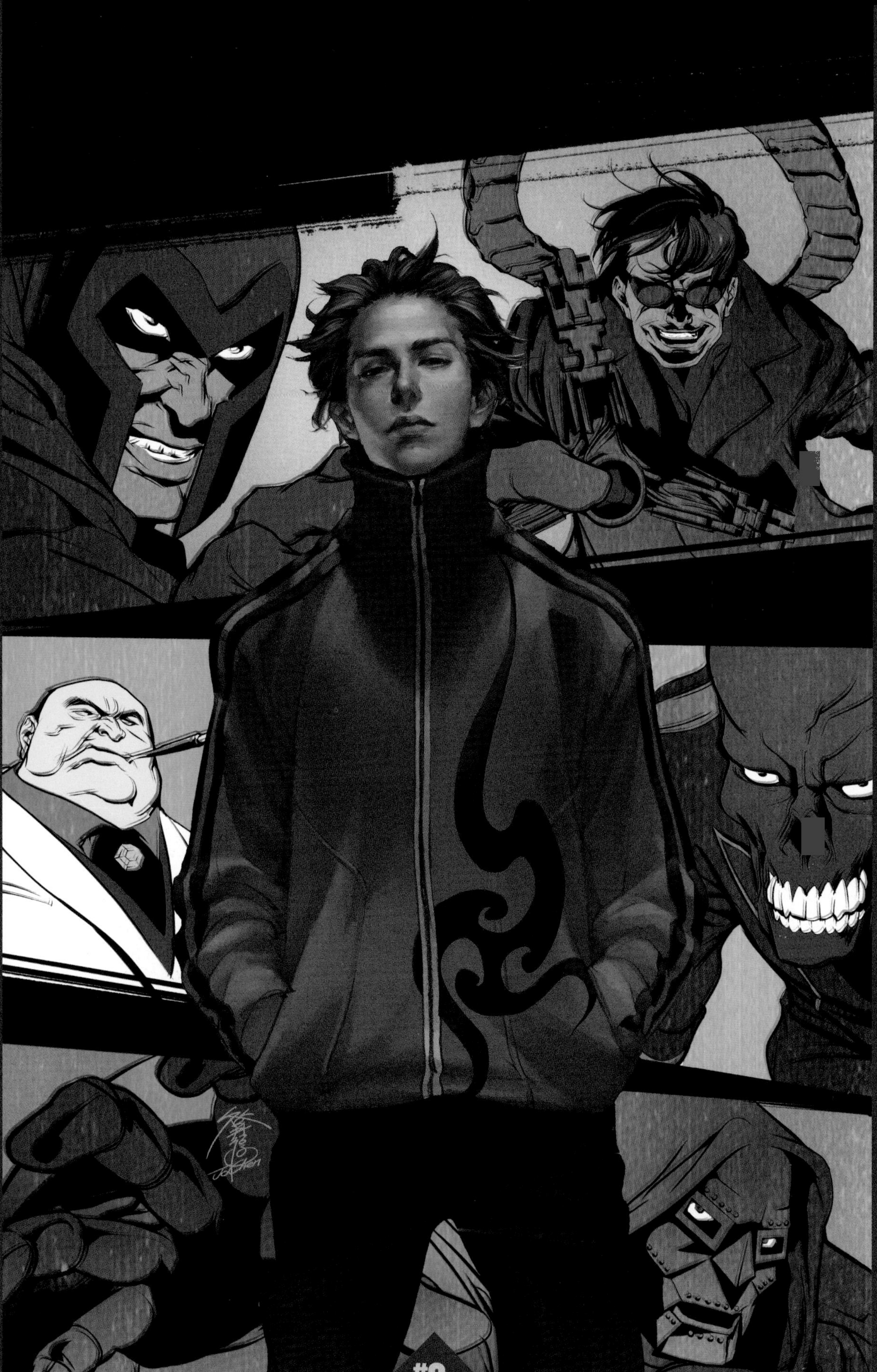
#2

TRUE BELIEVERS PART 2

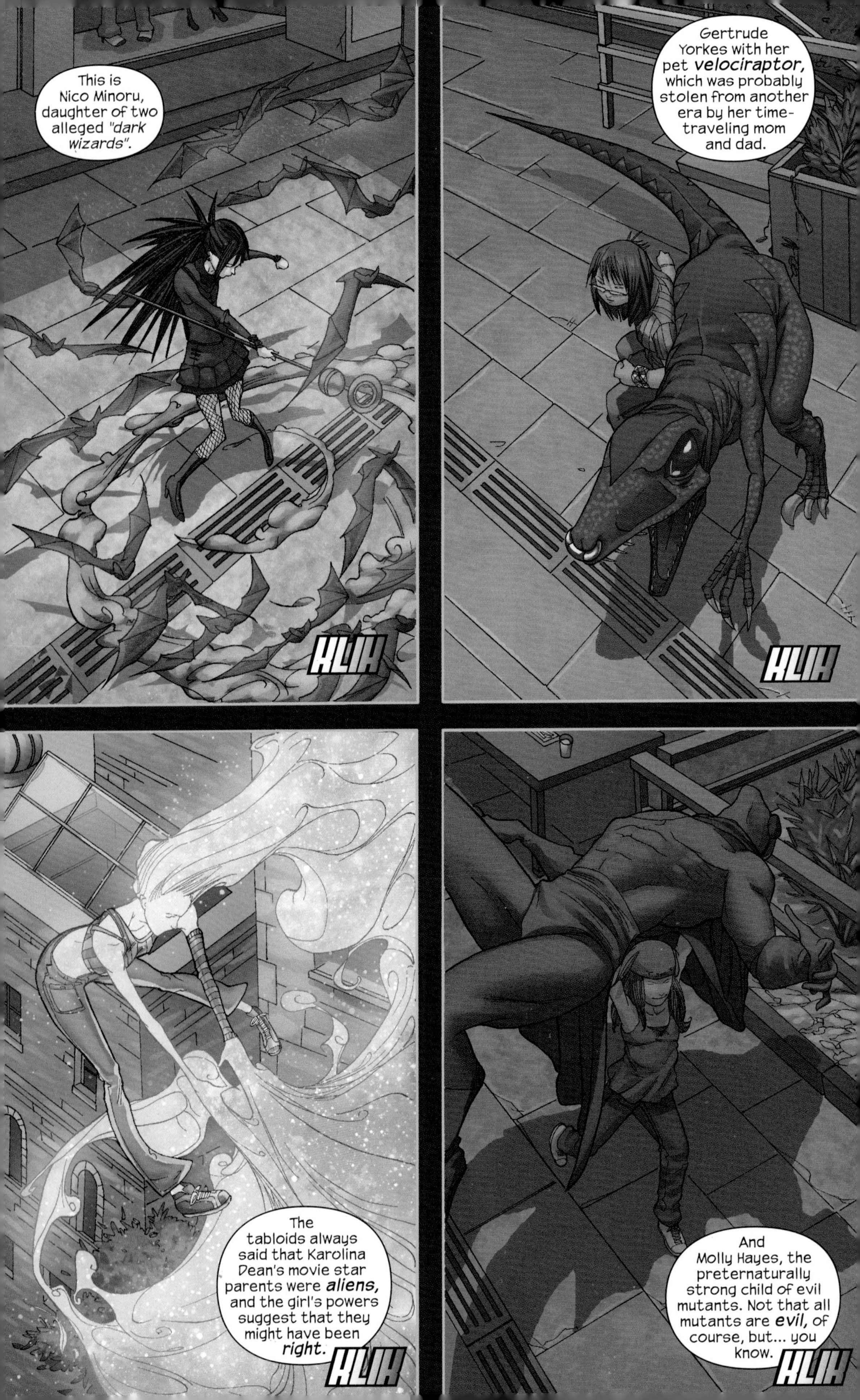
This is Nico Minoru, daughter of two alleged "*dark wizards*".
KLIK
Gertrude Yorkes with her pet ***velociraptor,*** which was probably stolen from another era by her time-traveling mom and dad.
KLIK
The tabloids always said that Karolina Dean's movie star parents were ***aliens,*** and the girl's powers suggest that they might have been ***right.***
KLIK
And Molly Hayes, the preternaturally strong child of evil mutants. Not that all mutants are ***evil,*** of course, but... you know.
KLIK

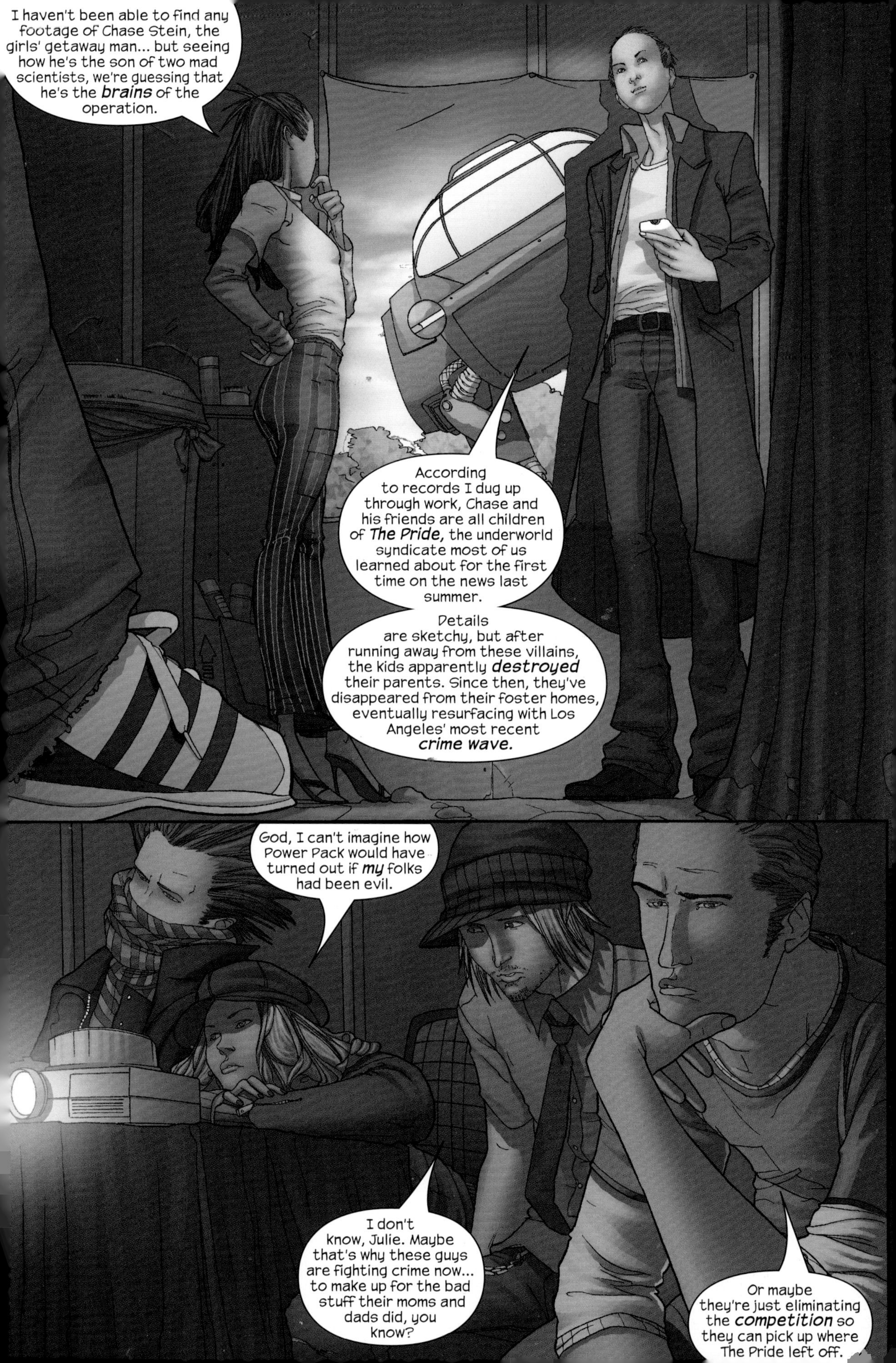
I haven't been able to find any footage of Chase Stein, the girls' getaway man... but seeing how he's the son of two mad scientists, we're guessing that he's the brains of the operation.
According to records I dug up through work, Chase and his friends are all children of The Pride, the underworld syndicate most of us learned about for the first time on the news last summer.
Details are sketchy, but after running away from these villains, the kids apparently destroyed their parents. Since then, they've disappeared from their foster homes, eventually resurfacing with Los Angeles' most recent crime wave.
God, I can't imagine how Power Pack would have turned out if my folks had been evil.
I don't know, Julie. Maybe that's why these guys are fighting crime now... to make up for the bad stuff their moms and dads did, you know?
Or maybe they're just eliminating the competition so they can pick up where The Pride left off.

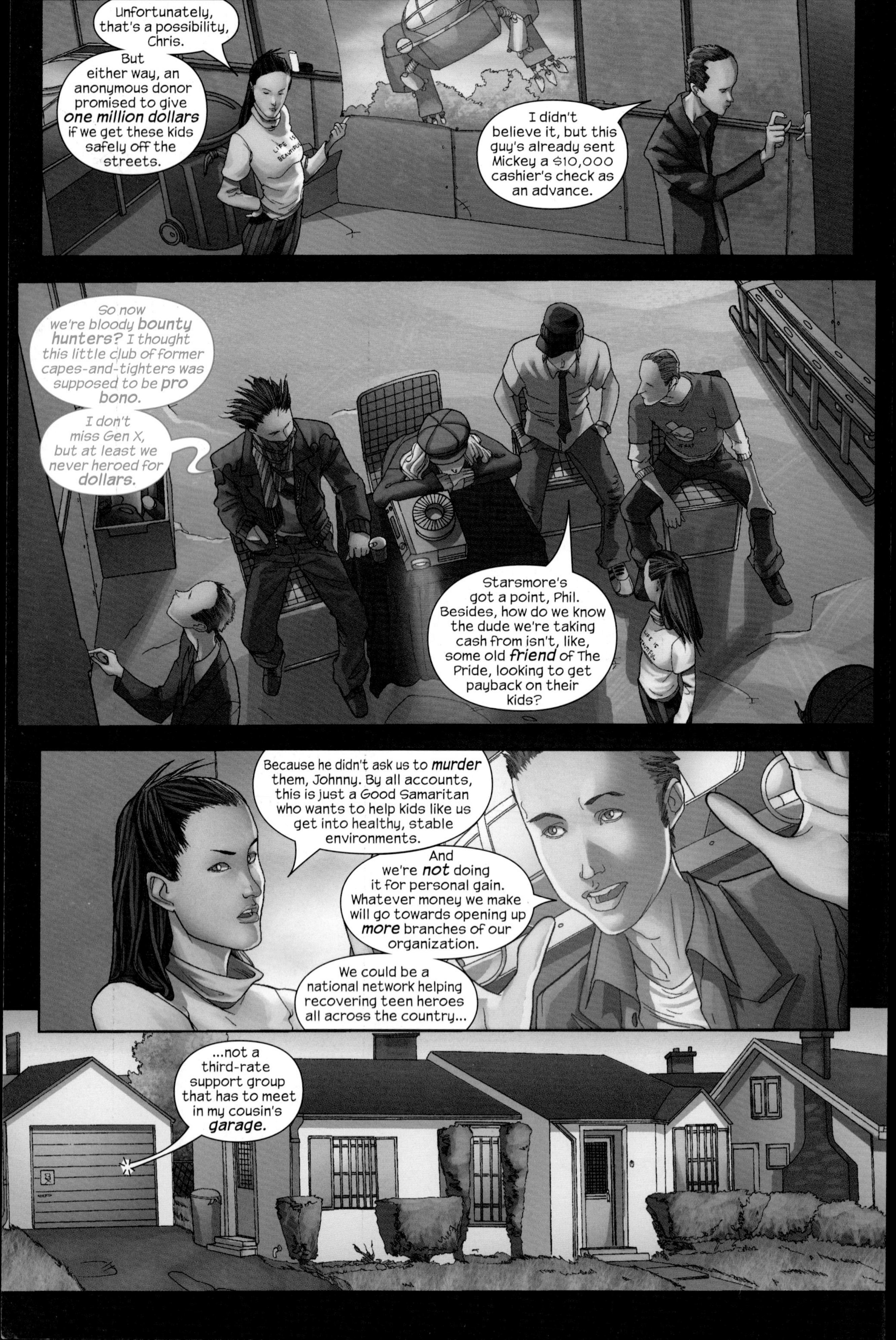

Unfortunately, that's a possibility, Chris.
But either way, an anonymous donor promised to give **one million dollars** if we get these kids safely off the streets.
I didn't believe it, but this guy's already sent Mickey a $10,000 cashier's check as an advance.
So now we're bloody **bounty hunters?** I thought this little club of former capes-and-tighters was supposed to be **pro bono.**
I don't miss Gen X, but at least we never heroed for **dollars.**
Starsmore's got a point, Phil. Besides, how do we know the dude we're taking cash from isn't, like, some old **friend** of The Pride, looking to get payback on their kids?
Because he didn't ask us to **murder** them, Johnny. By all accounts, this is just a Good Samaritan who wants to help kids like us get into healthy, stable environments.
And we're **not** doing it for personal gain. Whatever money we make will go towards opening up **more** branches of our organization.
We could be a national network helping recovering teen heroes all across the country...
...not a third-rate support group that has to meet in my cousin's **garage.**

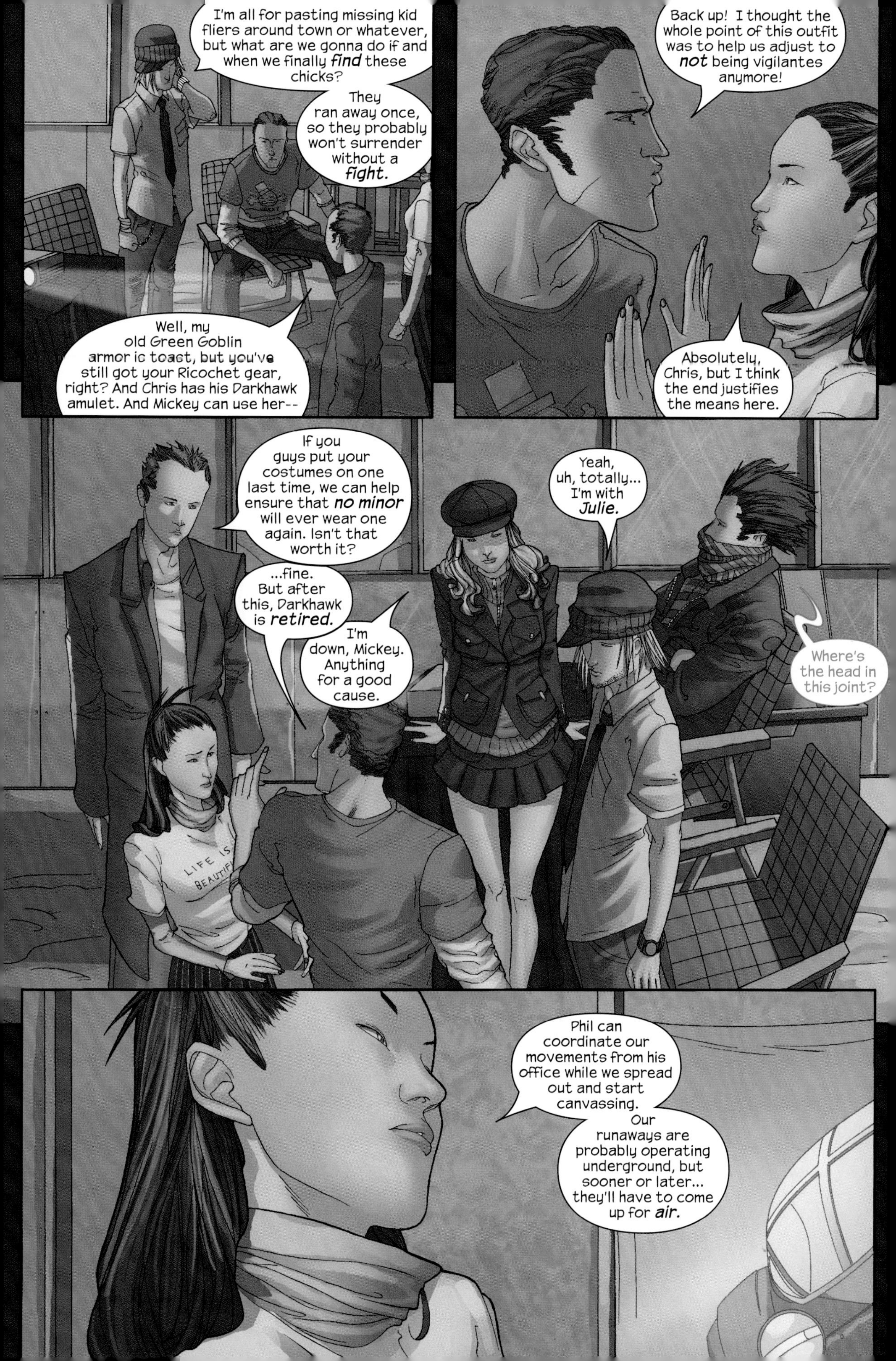

I'm all for pasting missing kid fliers around town or whatever, but what are we gonna do if and when we finally *find* these chicks?
They ran away once, so they probably won't surrender without a *fight.*
Well, my old Green Goblin armor is toast, but you've still got your Ricochet gear, right? And Chris has his Darkhawk amulet. And Mickey can use her--
Back up! I thought the whole point of this outfit was to help us adjust to *not* being vigilantes anymore!
Absolutely, Chris, but I think the end justifies the means here.
If you guys put your costumes on one last time, we can help ensure that *no minor* will ever wear one again. Isn't that worth it?
...fine. But after this, Darkhawk is *retired.*
I'm down, Mickey. Anything for a good cause.
Yeah, uh, totally... I'm with *Julie.*
Where's the head in this joint?
LIFE IS BEAUTIF
Phil can coordinate our movements from his office while we spread out and start canvassing.
Our runaways are probably operating underground, but sooner or later... they'll have to come up for *air.*

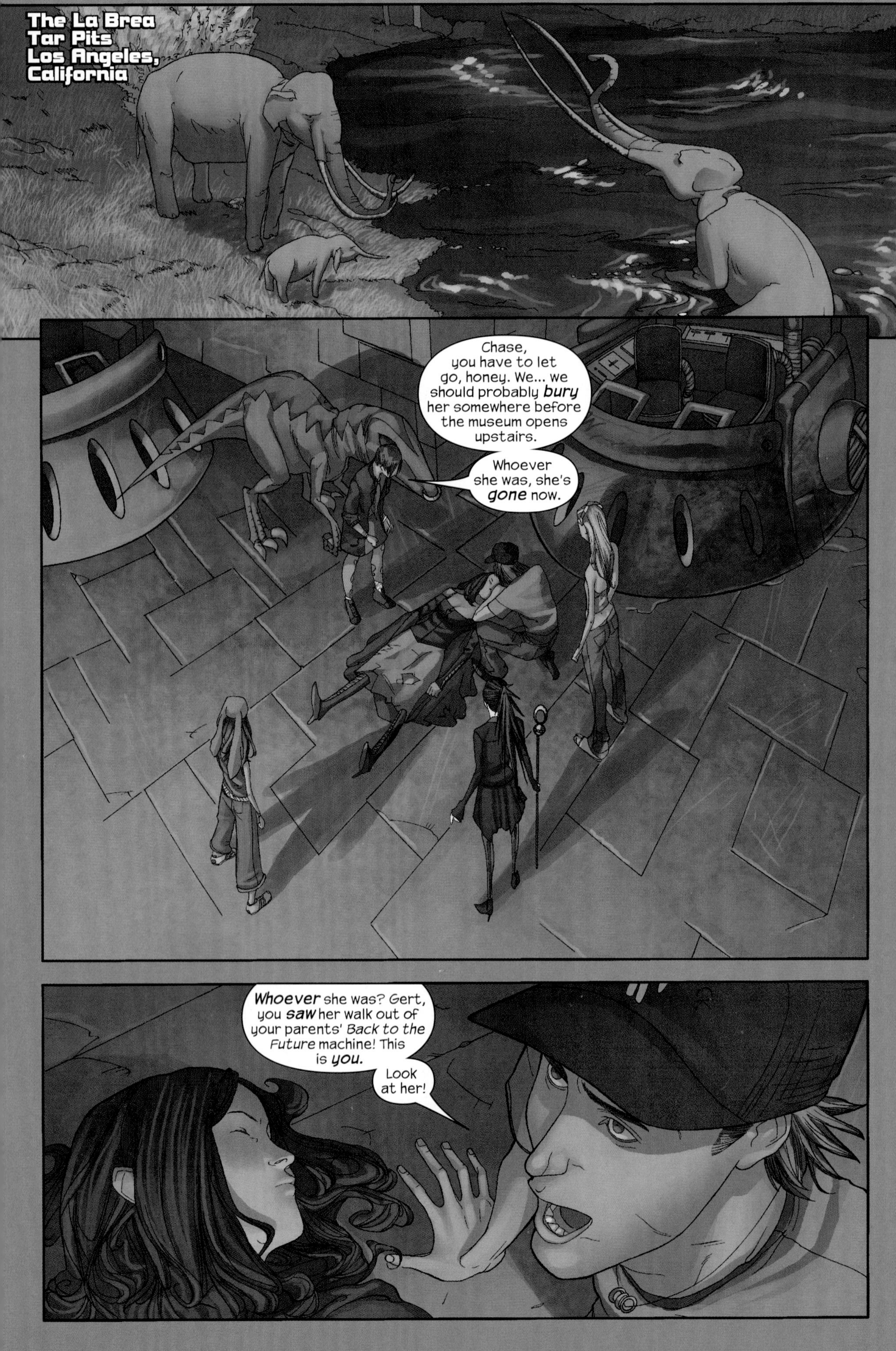
The La Brea
Tar Pits
Los Angeles,
California
Chase, you have to let go, honey. We... we should probably bury her somewhere before the museum opens upstairs.
Whoever she was, she's gone now.
Whoever she was? Gert, you saw her walk out of your parents' Back to the Future machine! This is you.
Look at her!

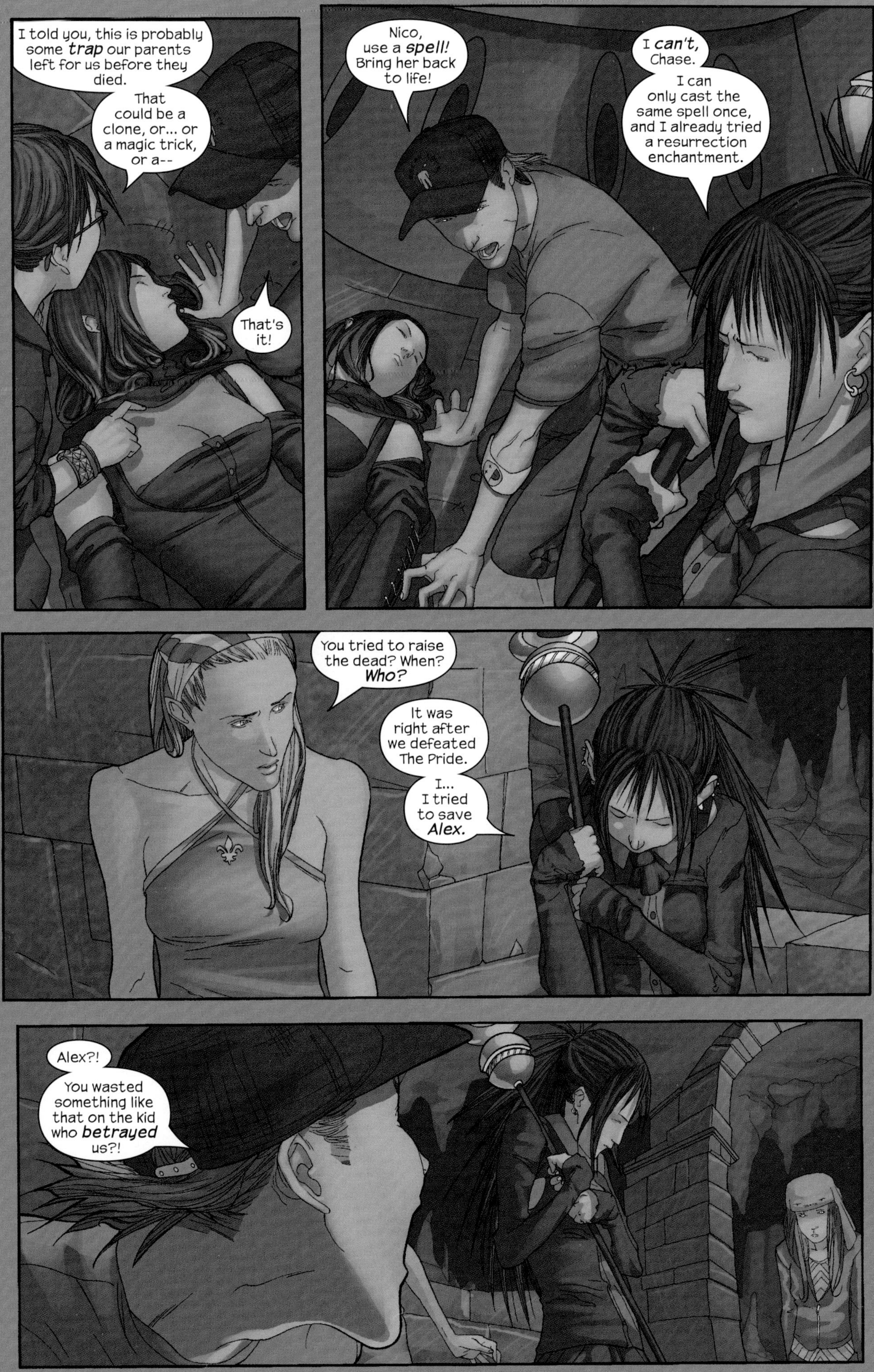

I told you, this is probably some *trap* our parents left for us before they died.
That could be a clone, or... or a magic trick, or a--
That's it!
Nico, use a *spell!* Bring her back to life!
I *can't,* Chase.
I can only cast the same spell once, and I already tried a resurrection enchantment.
You tried to raise the dead? When? ***Who?***
It was right after we defeated The Pride.
I... I tried to save ***Alex.***
Alex?!
You wasted something like that on the kid who ***betrayed*** us?!

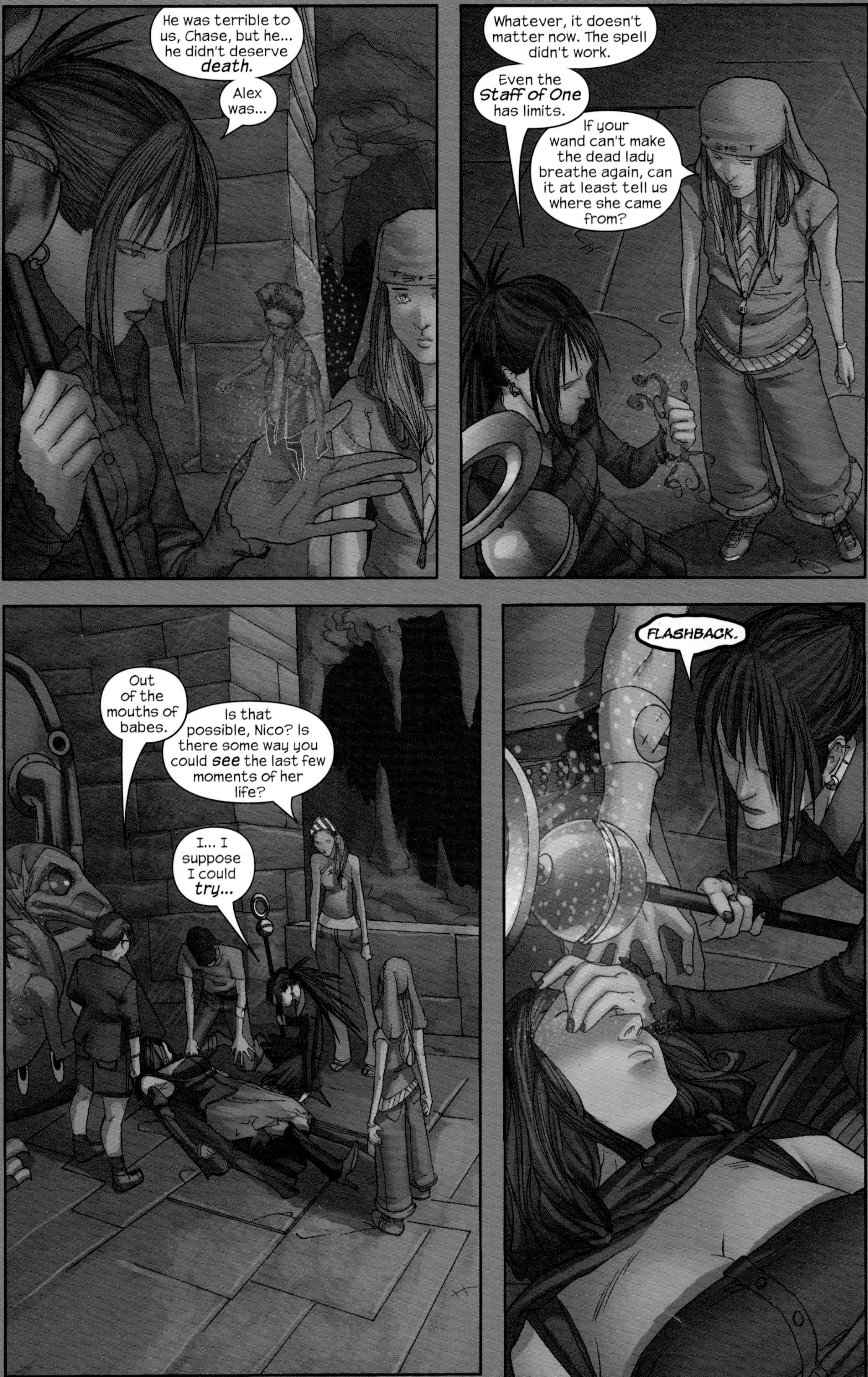
He was terrible to us, Chase, but he... he didn't deserve *death.*
Alex was...
Whatever, it doesn't matter now. The spell didn't work.
Even the *Staff of One* has limits.
If your wand can't make the dead lady breathe again, can it at least tell us where she came from?
Out of the mouths of babes.
Is that possible, Nico? Is there some way you could *see* the last few moments of her life?
I... I suppose I could *try...*
FLASHBACK.

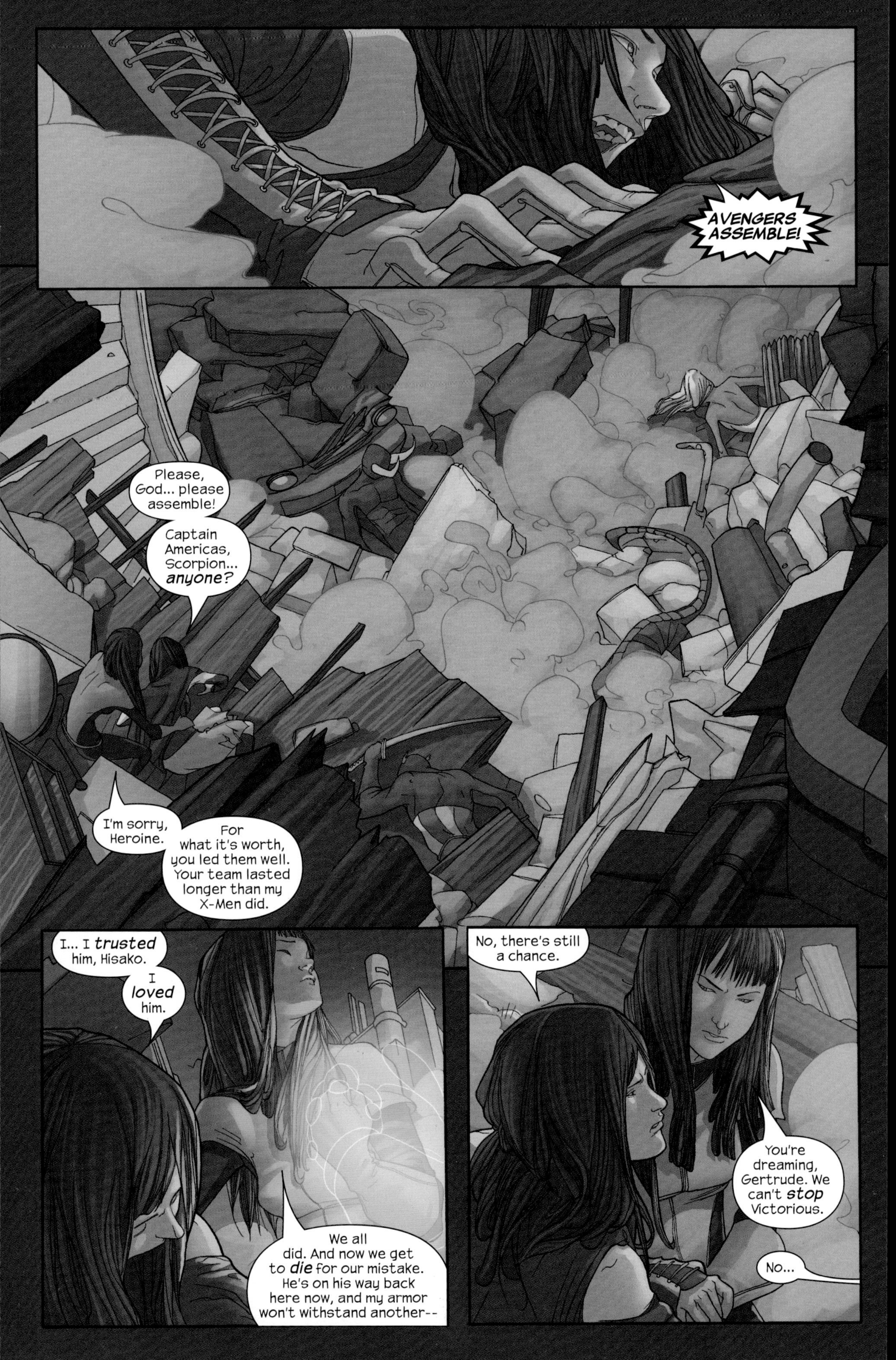
AVENGERS ASSEMBLE!
Please, God... please assemble!
Captain Americas, Scorpion... *anyone?*
I'm sorry, Heroine.
For what it's worth, you led them well. Your team lasted longer than my X-Men did.
I... I *trusted* him, Hisako.
I *loved* him.
We all did. And now we get to *die* for our mistake. He's on his way back here now, and my armor won't withstand another--
No, there's still a chance.
You're dreaming, Gertrude. We can't *stop* Victorious.
No...

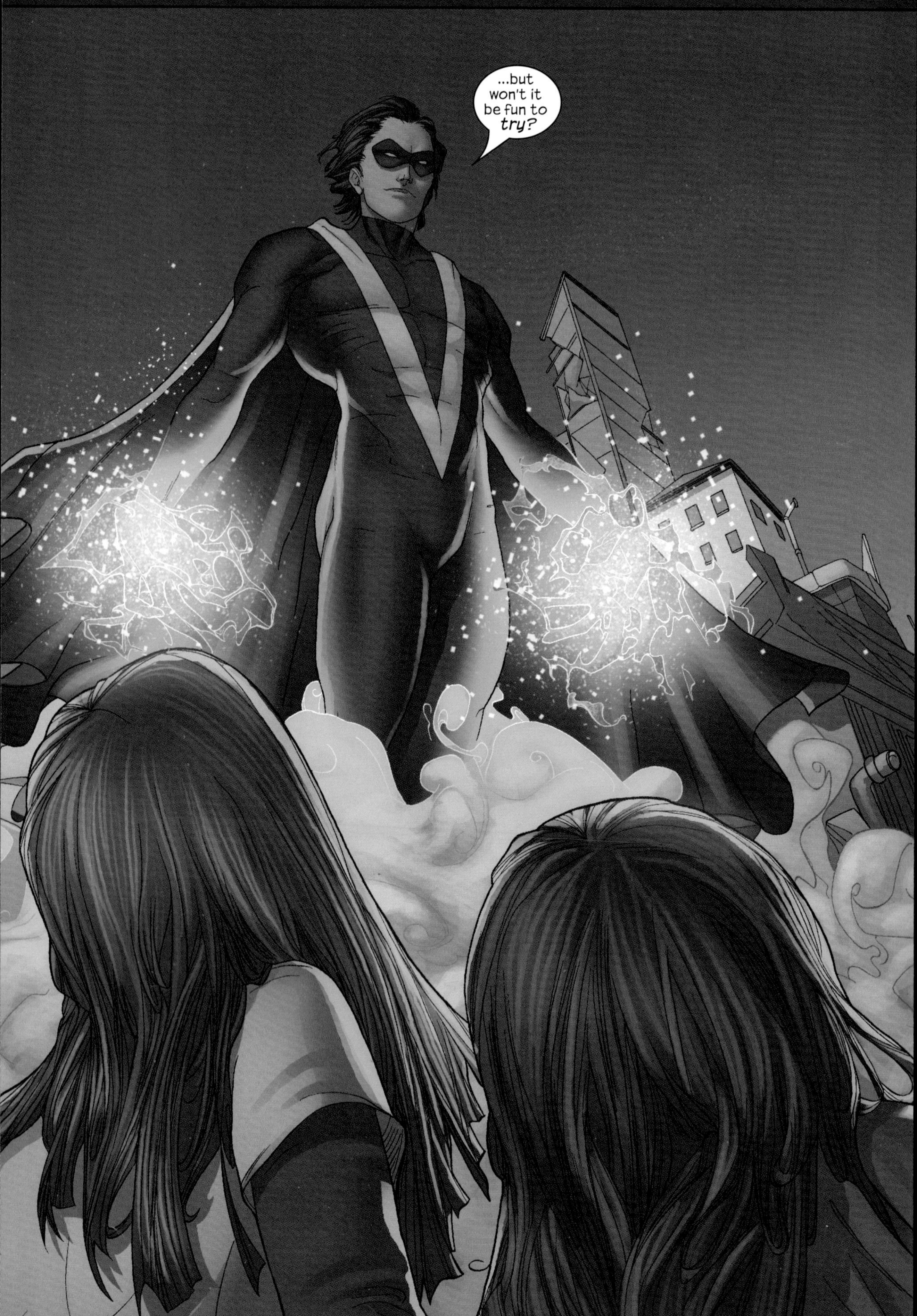
...but won't it be fun to *try*?

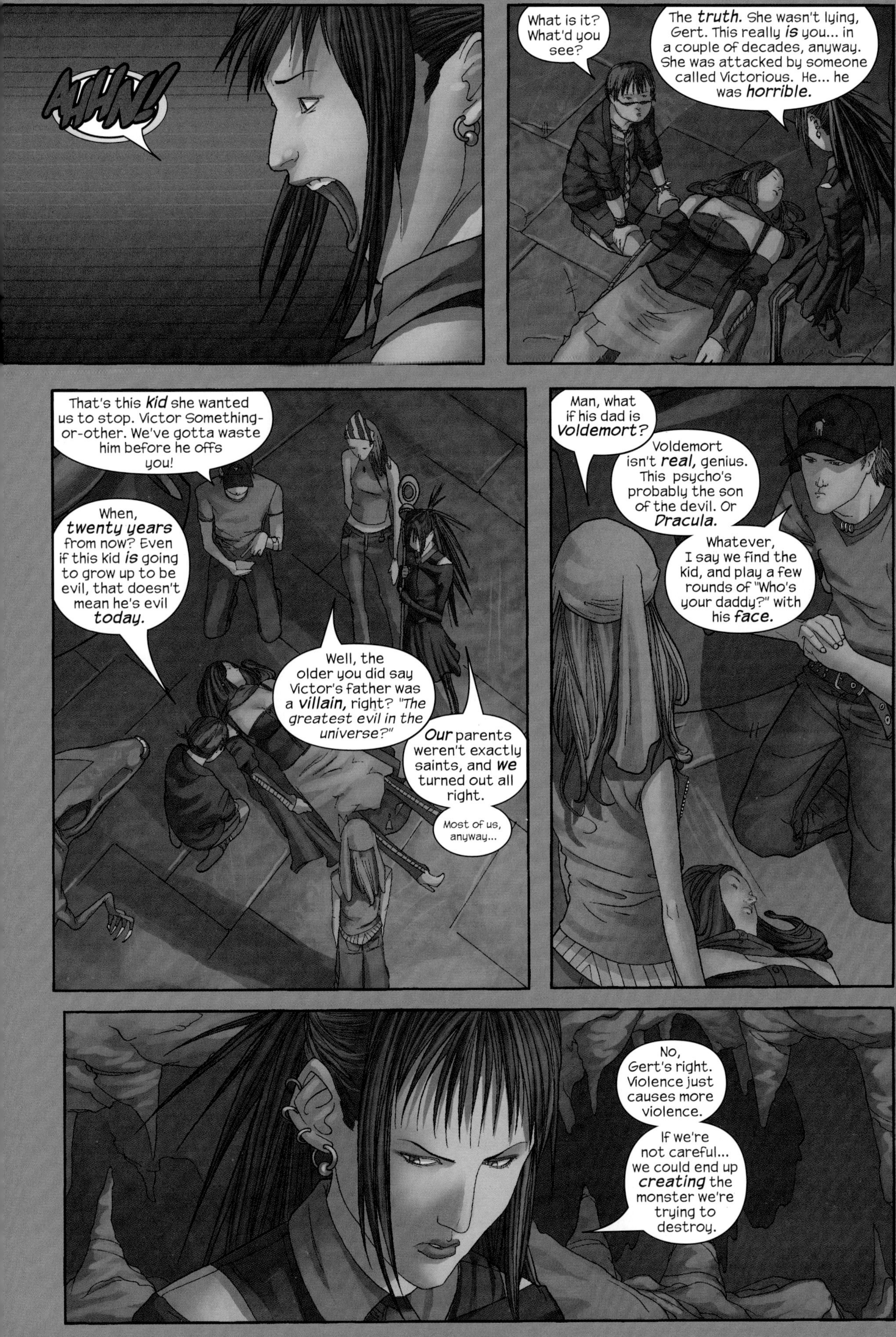
AAHH!
What is it? What'd you see?
The truth. She wasn't lying, Gert. This really is you... in a couple of decades, anyway. She was attacked by someone called Victorious. He... he was horrible.
That's this kid she wanted us to stop. Victor Something-or-other. We've gotta waste him before he offs you!
When, twenty years from now? Even if this kid is going to grow up to be evil, that doesn't mean he's evil today.
Well, the older you did say Victor's father was a villain, right? "The greatest evil in the universe?"
Our parents weren't exactly saints, and we turned out all right.
Most of us, anyway...
Man, what if his dad is Voldemort?
Voldemort isn't real, genius. This psycho's probably the son of the devil. Or Dracula.
Whatever, I say we find the kid, and play a few rounds of "Who's your daddy?" with his face.
No, Gert's right. Violence just causes more violence.
If we're not careful... we could end up creating the monster we're trying to destroy.

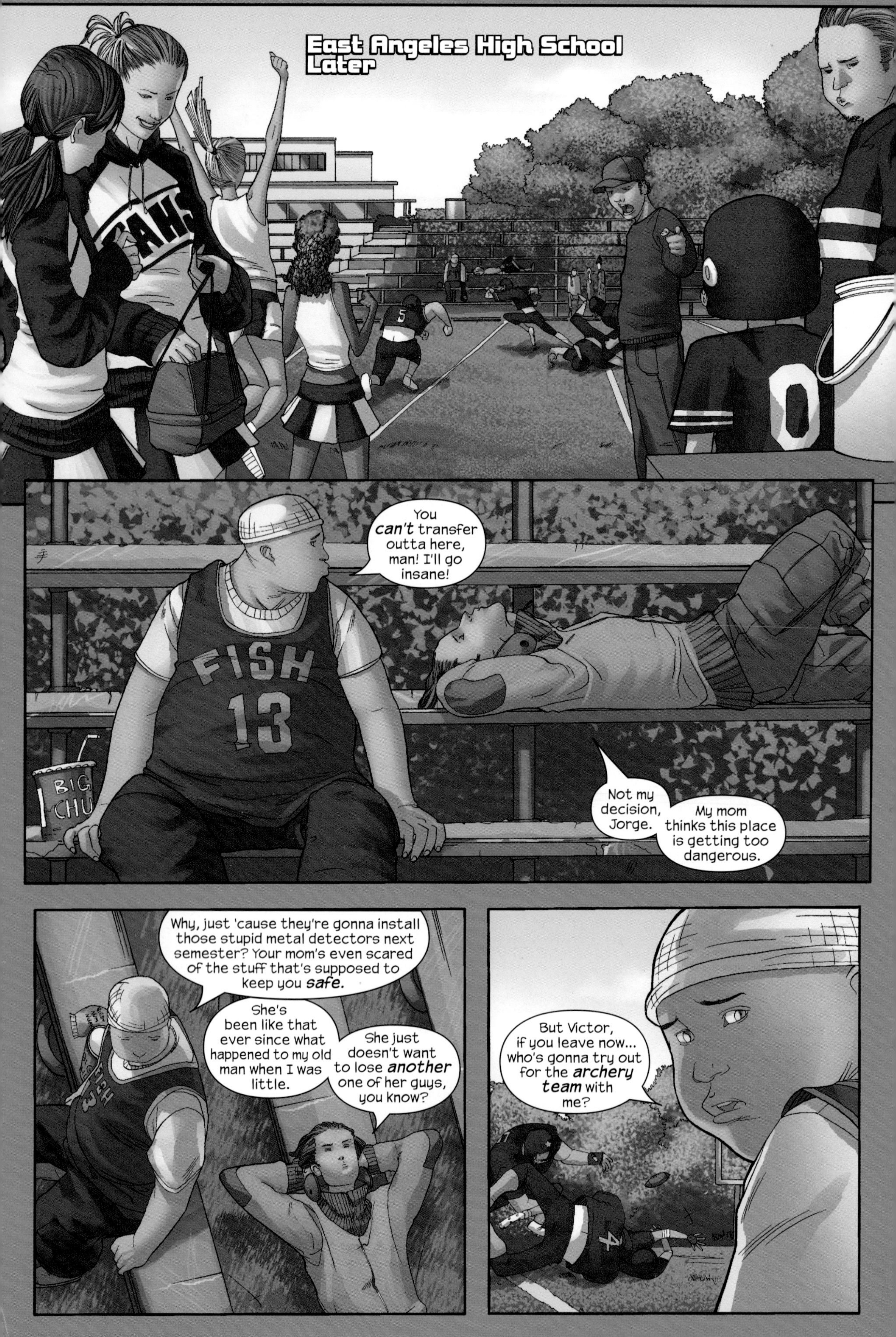
East Angeles High School
Later
EAHS
5
0
You can't transfer outta here, man! I'll go insane!
FISH
13
BIG CHU
Not my decision, Jorge.
My mom thinks this place is getting too dangerous.
Why, just 'cause they're gonna install those stupid metal detectors next semester? Your mom's even scared of the stuff that's supposed to keep you safe.
She's been like that ever since what happened to my old man when I was little.
She just doesn't want to lose another one of her guys, you know?
But Victor, if you leave now... who's gonna try out for the archery team with me?
4

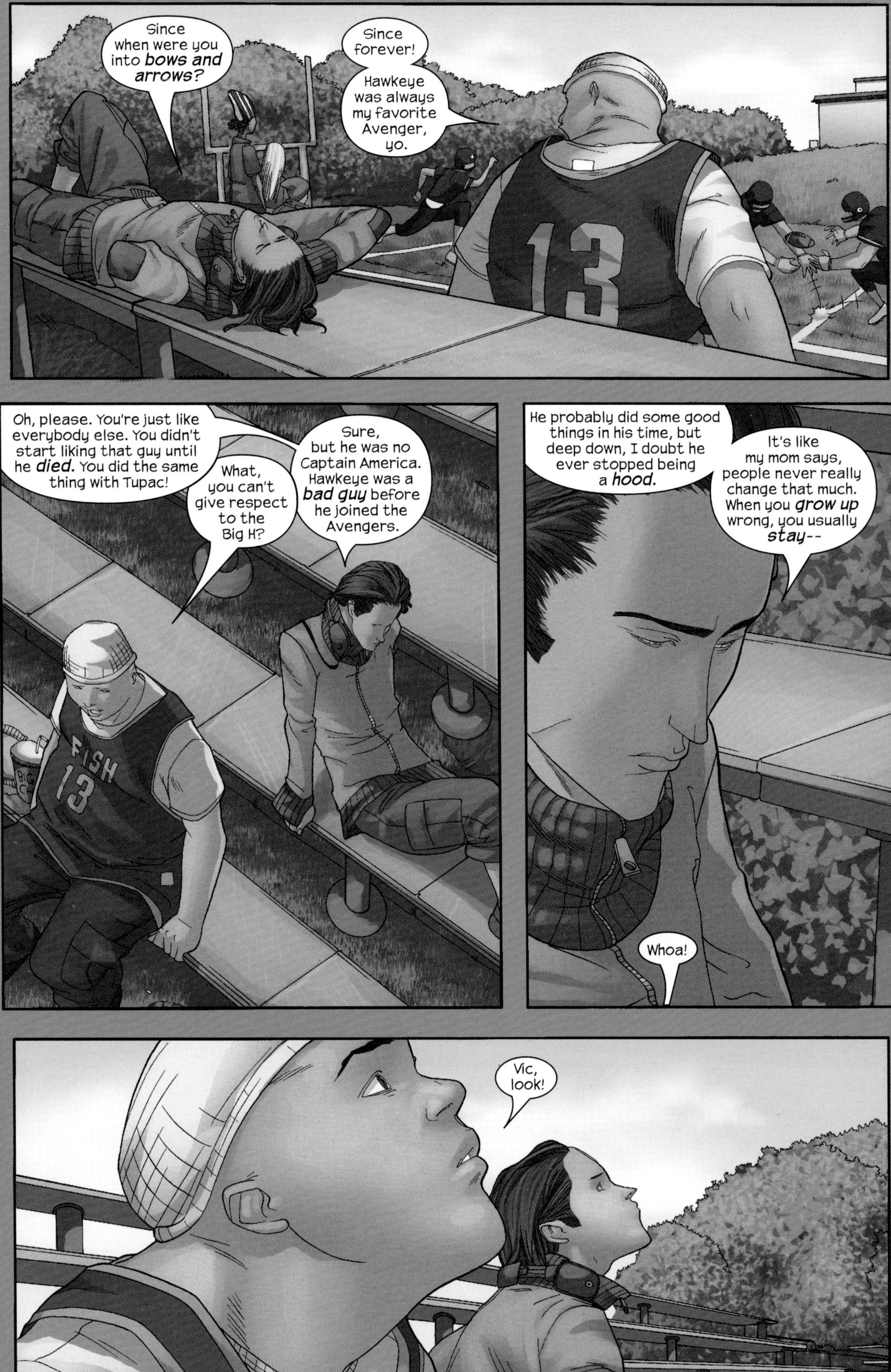
Since when were you into bows and arrows?
Since forever!
Hawkeye was always my favorite Avenger, yo.
Oh, please. You're just like everybody else. You didn't start liking that guy until he died. You did the same thing with Tupac!
What, you can't give respect to the Big H?
Sure, but he was no Captain America. Hawkeye was a bad guy before he joined the Avengers.
He probably did some good things in his time, but deep down, I doubt he ever stopped being a hood.
It's like my mom says, people never really change that much. When you grow up wrong, you usually stay--
Whoa!
Vic, look!

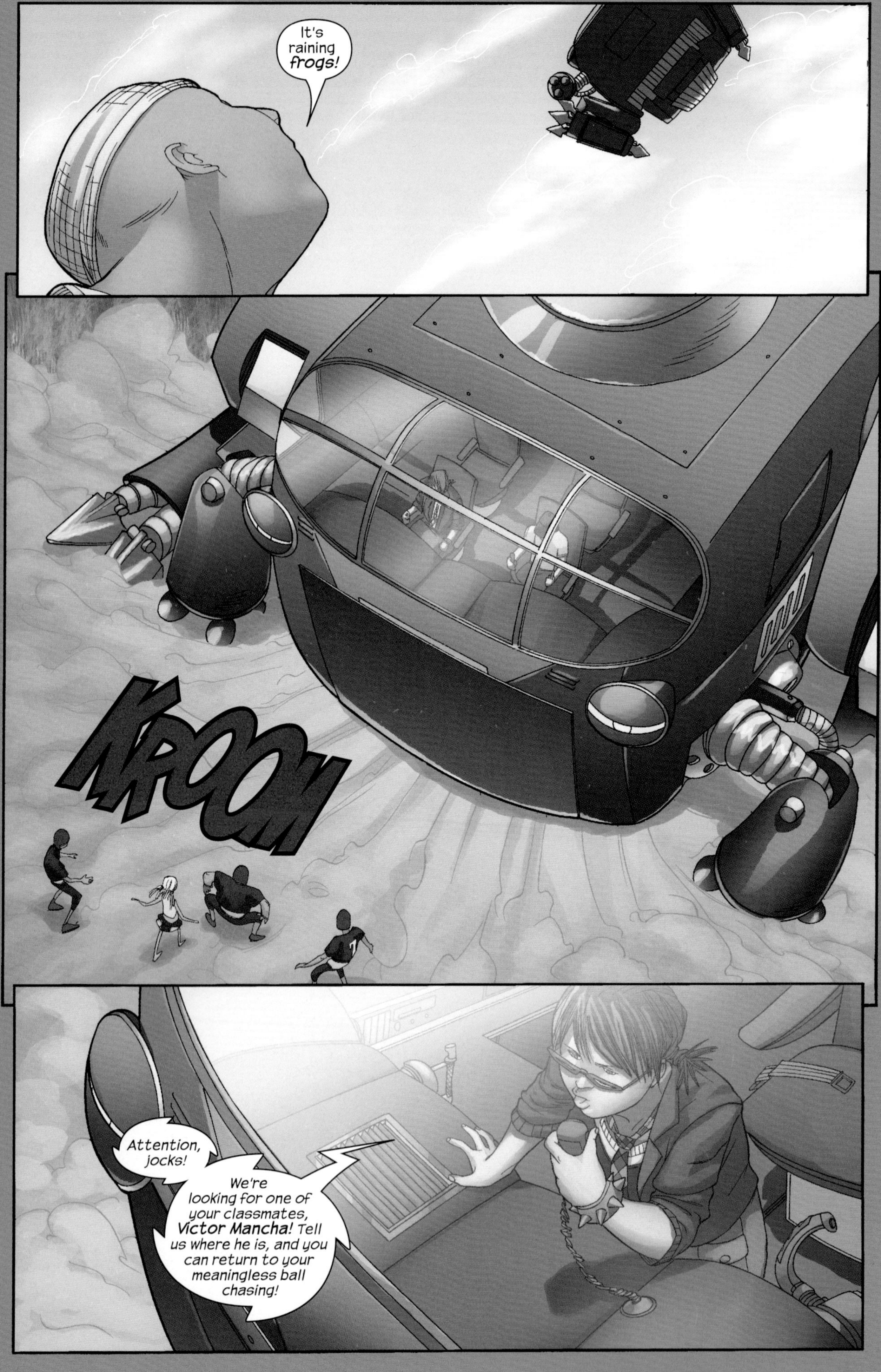
It's raining *frogs!*
KROOM
Attention, jocks!
We're looking for one of your classmates, **Victor Mancha!** Tell us where he is, and you can return to your meaningless ball chasing!

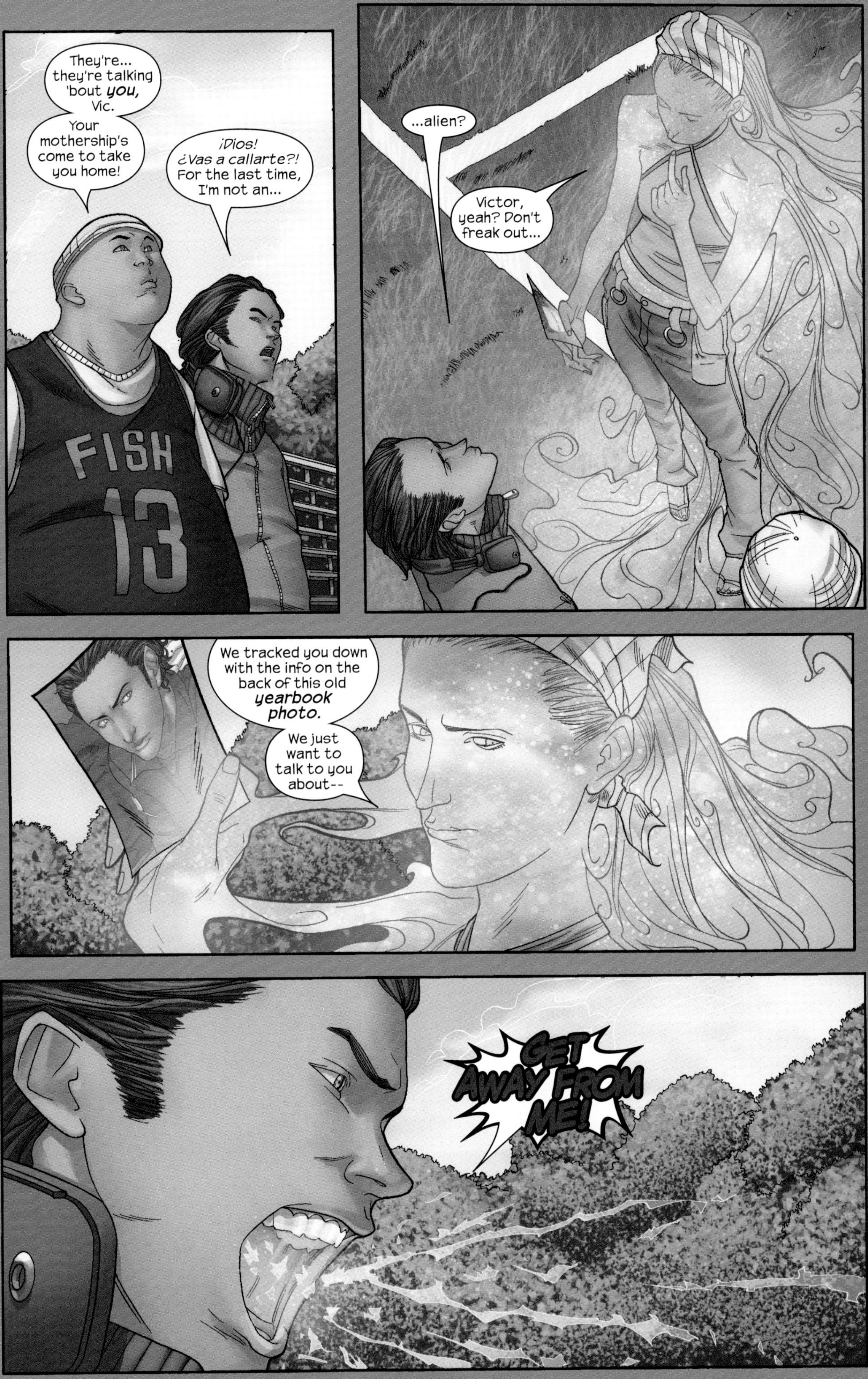
They're... they're talking 'bout **you,** Vic.
Your mothership's come to take you home!
¡Dios! ¿Vas a callarte?! For the last time, I'm not an...
...alien?
Victor, yeah? Don't freak out...
We tracked you down with the info on the back of this old ***yearbook photo.***
We just want to talk to you about--
GET AWAY FROM ME!

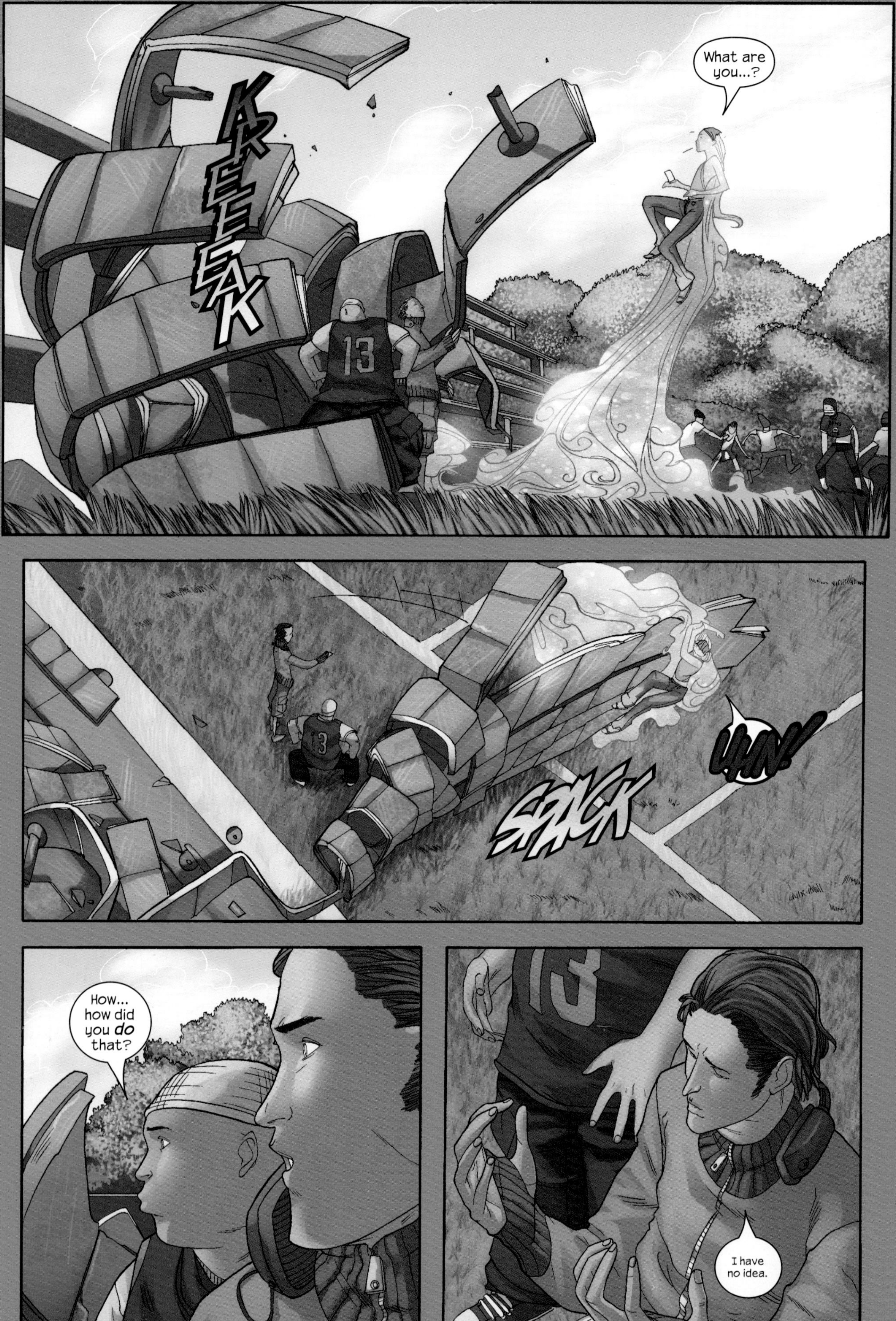
KREEEAK
What are you...?
SPLACK
UHN!
How... how did you *do* that?
I have no idea.

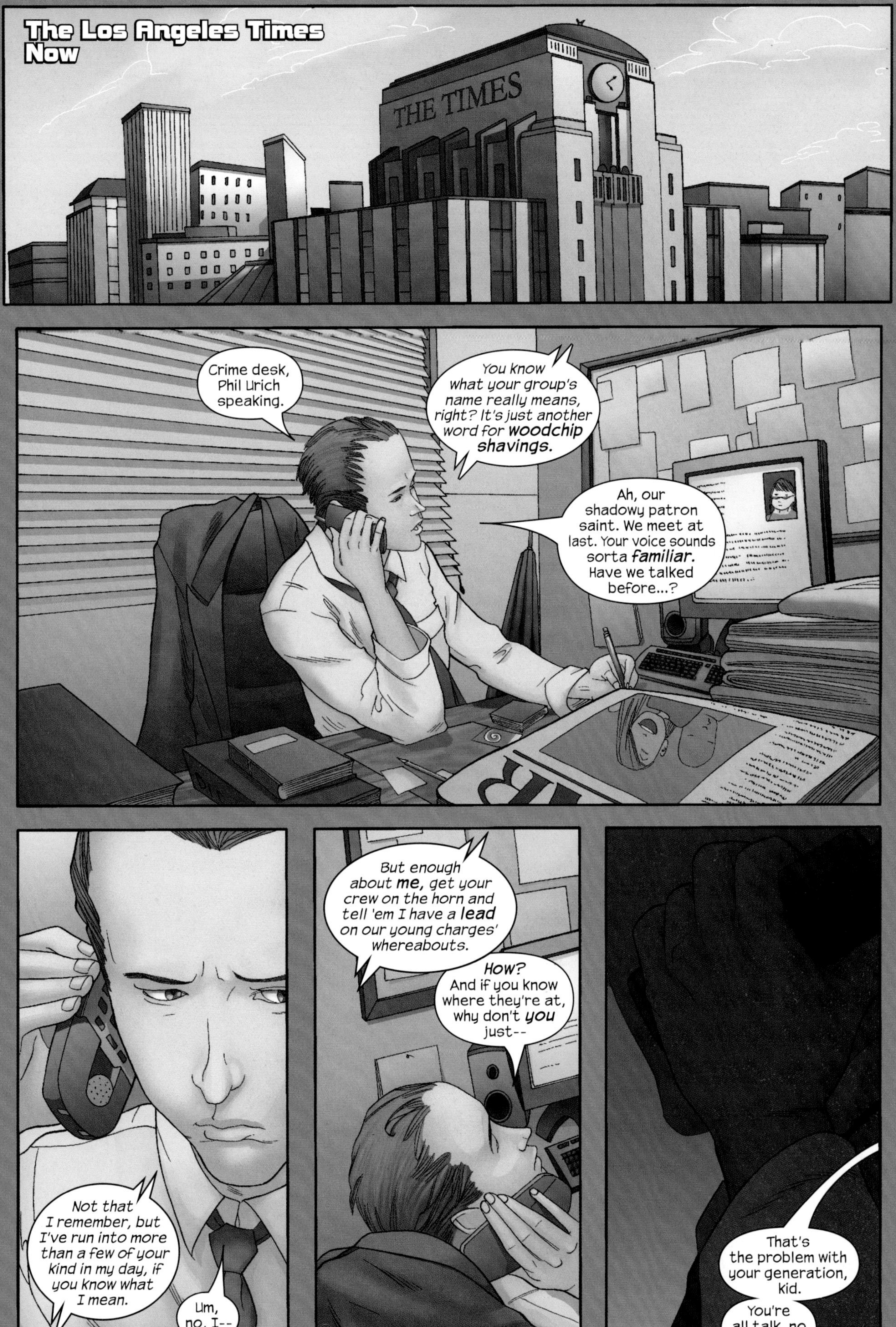
The Los Angeles Times
Now
THE TIMES
Crime desk, Phil Urich speaking.
You know what your group's name really means, right? It's just another word for woodchip shavings.
Ah, our shadowy patron saint. We meet at last. Your voice sounds sorta familiar. Have we talked before...?
Not that I remember, but I've run into more than a few of your kind in my day, if you know what I mean.
Um, no, I--
But enough about me, get your crew on the horn and tell 'em I have a lead on our young charges' whereabouts.
How? And if you know where they're at, why don't you just--
That's the problem with your generation, kid.
You're all talk, no action...

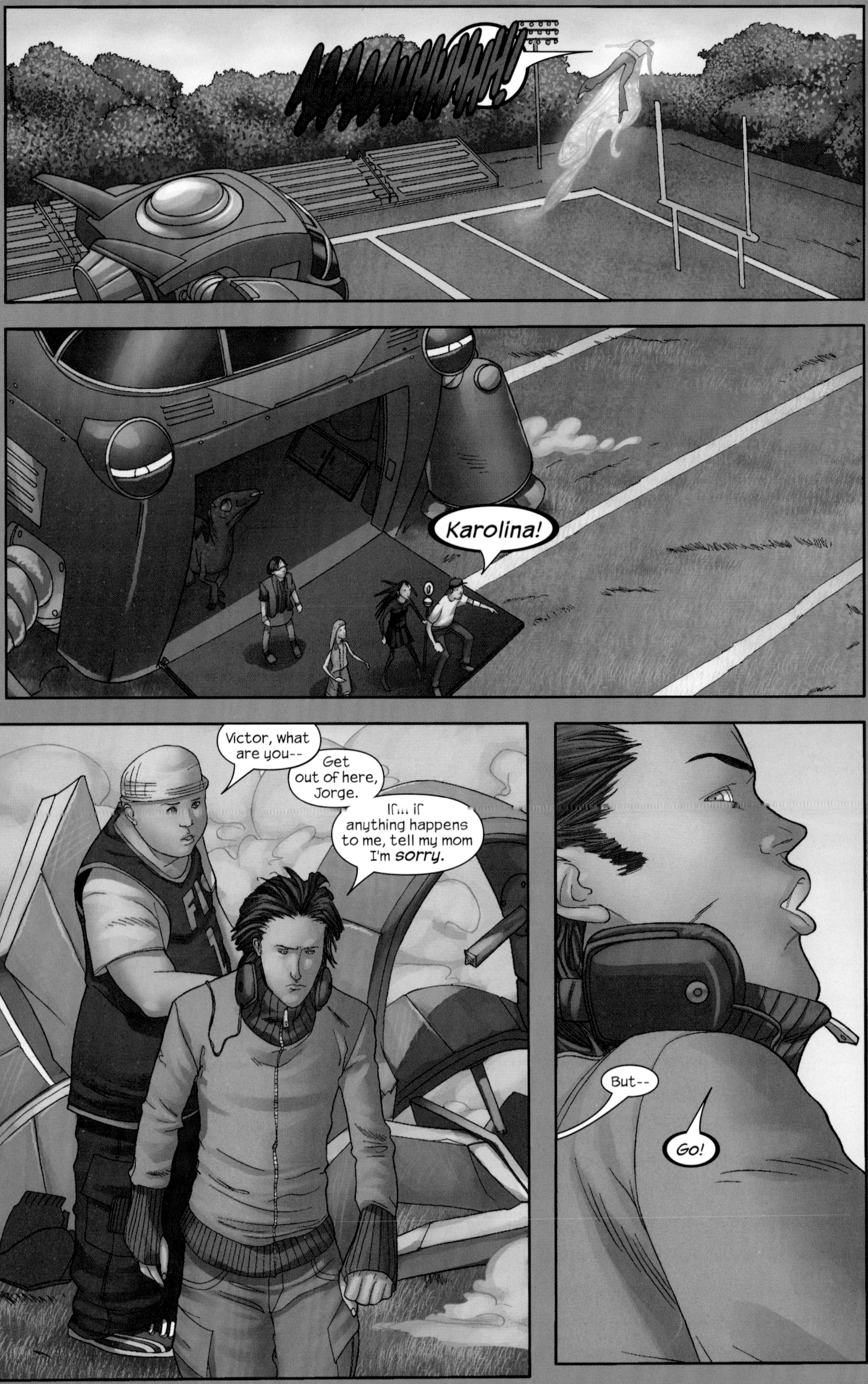
AAAAAAHHHH!
Karolina!
Victor, what are you--
Get out of here, Jorge.
If... if anything happens to me, tell my mom I'm sorry.
But--
Go!

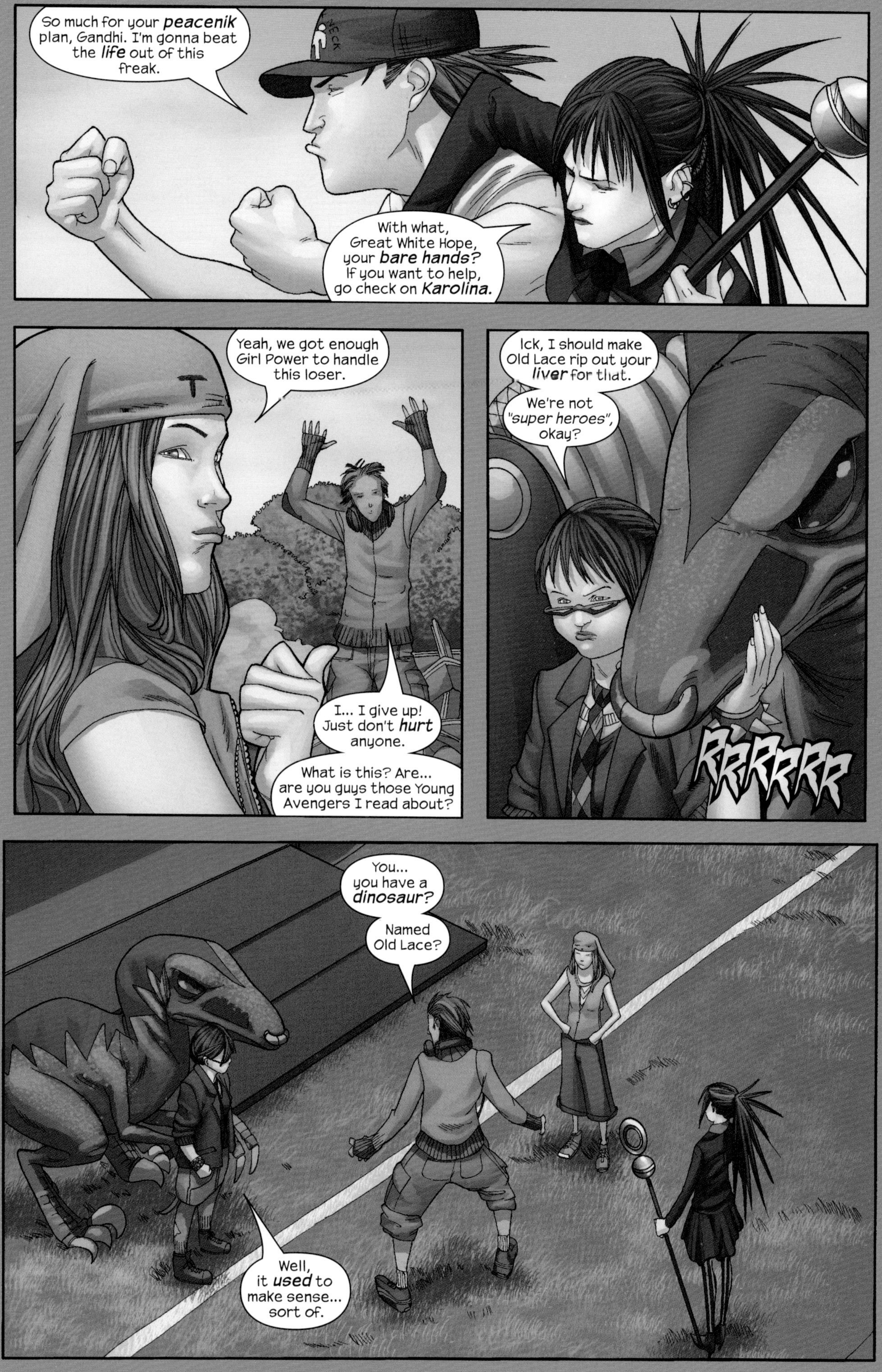
So much for your peacenik plan, Gandhi. I'm gonna beat the life out of this freak.
With what, Great White Hope, your bare hands? If you want to help, go check on Karolina.
Yeah, we got enough Girl Power to handle this loser.
I... I give up! Just don't hurt anyone.
What is this? Are... are you guys those Young Avengers I read about?
Ick, I should make Old Lace rip out your liver for that.
We're not "super heroes", okay?
RRRRRR
You... you have a dinosaur?
Named Old Lace?
Well, it used to make sense... sort of.

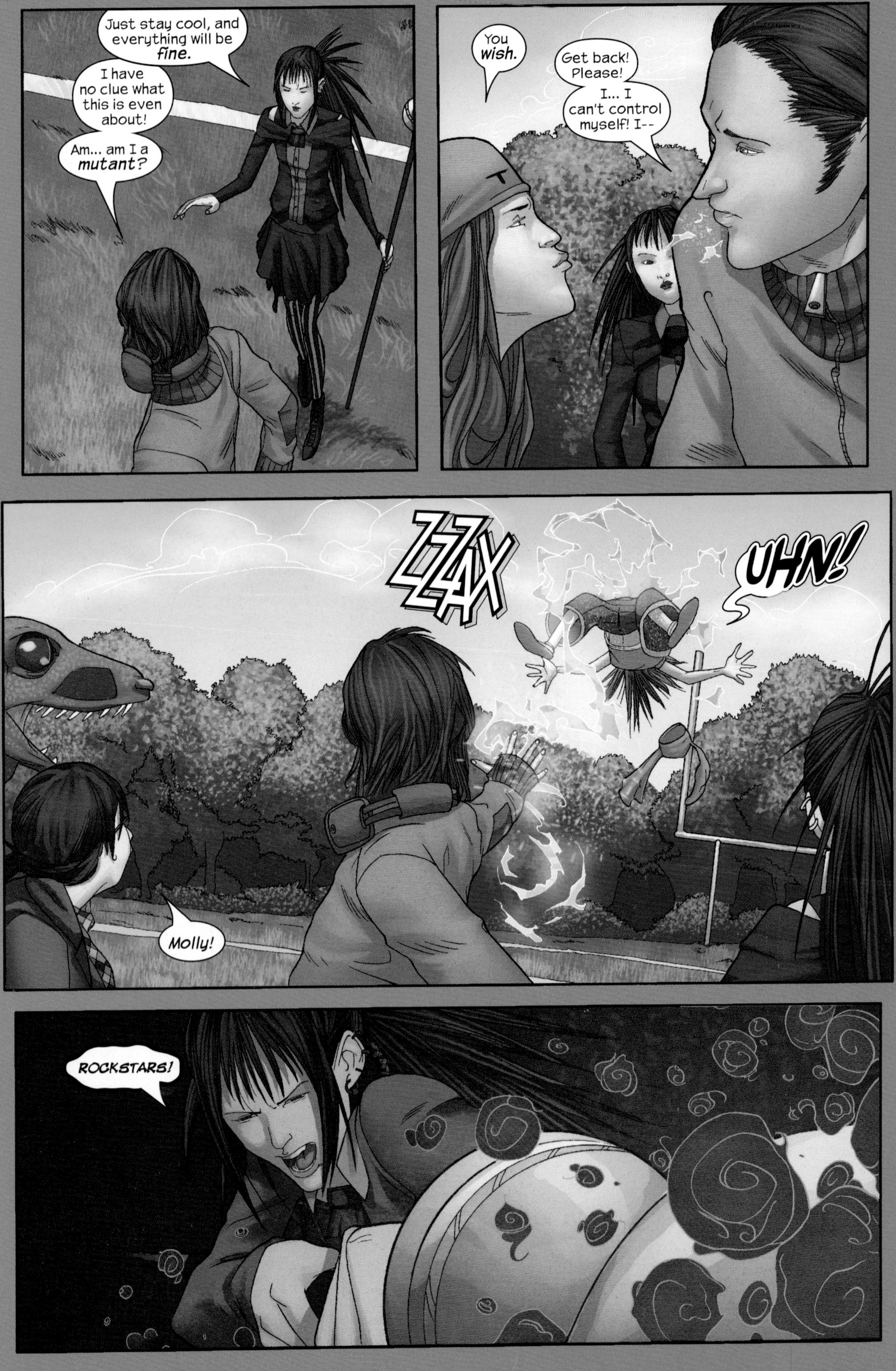
Just stay cool, and everything will be fine.
I have no clue what this is even about!
Am... am I a mutant?
You wish.
Get back! Please!
I... I can't control myself! I--
ZZZAX
UHN!
Molly!
ROCKSTARS!

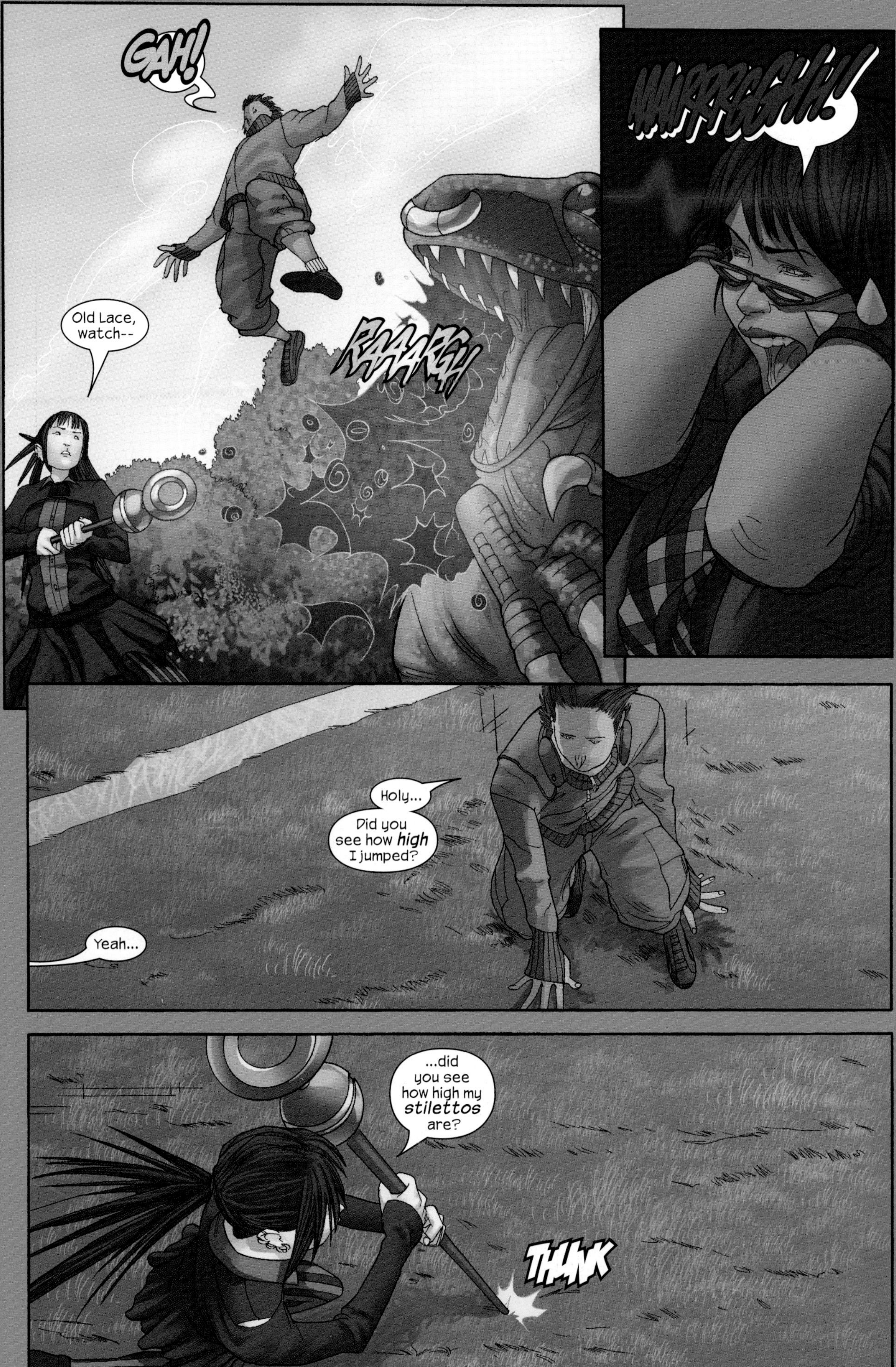
GAH!
Old Lace, watch--
RAAARGH
Holy...
Did you see how *high* I jumped?
Yeah...
...did you see how high my *stilettos* are?
THUNK

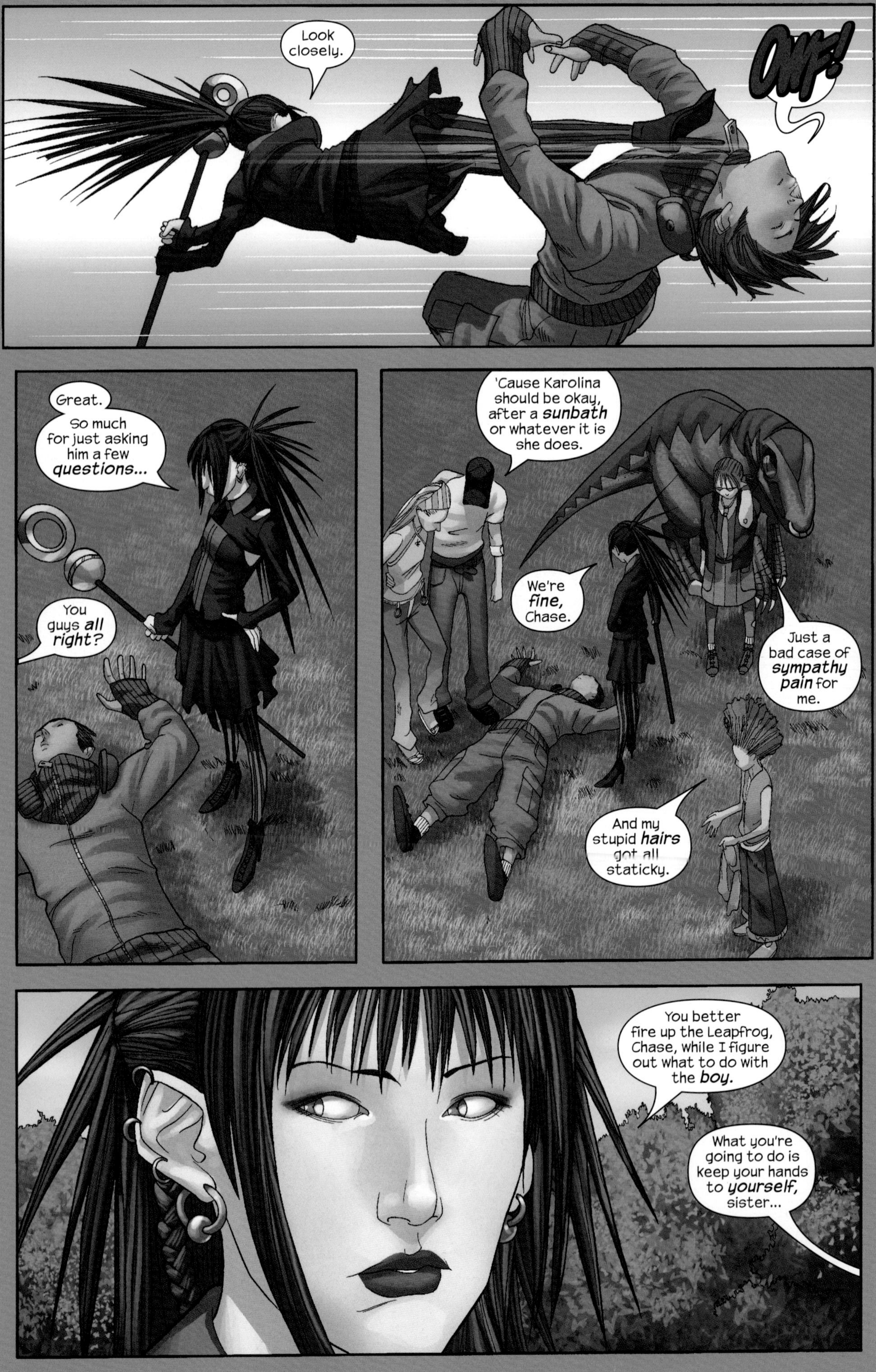
Look closely.
OMF!
Great. So much for just asking him a few questions...
You guys all right?
'Cause Karolina should be okay, after a sunbath or whatever it is she does.
We're fine, Chase.
Just a bad case of sympathy pain for me.
And my stupid hairs got all staticky.
You better fire up the Leapfrog, Chase, while I figure out what to do with the boy.
What you're going to do is keep your hands to yourself, sister...

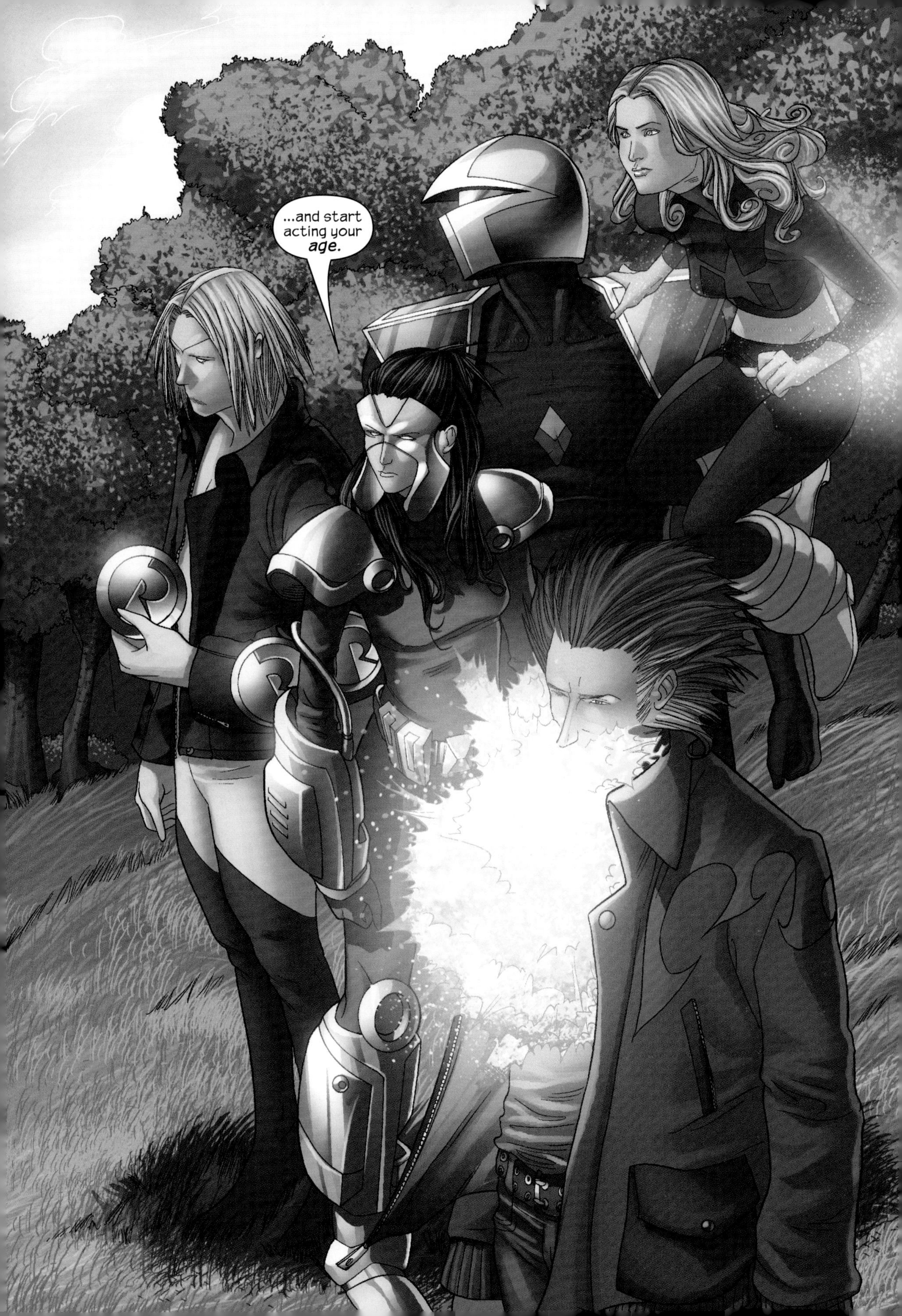
...and start acting your *age.*

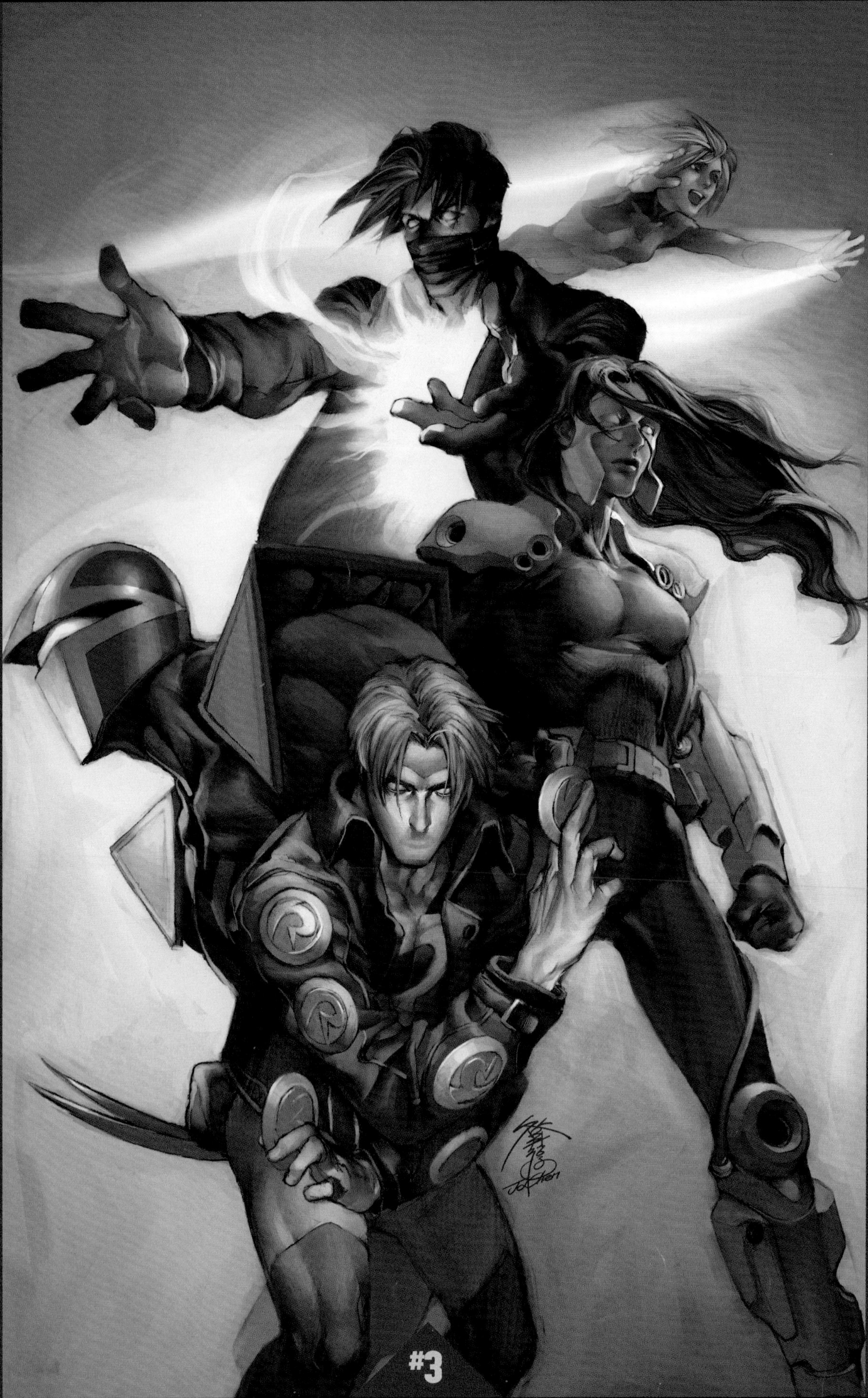
#3

TRUE BELIEVERS PART 3

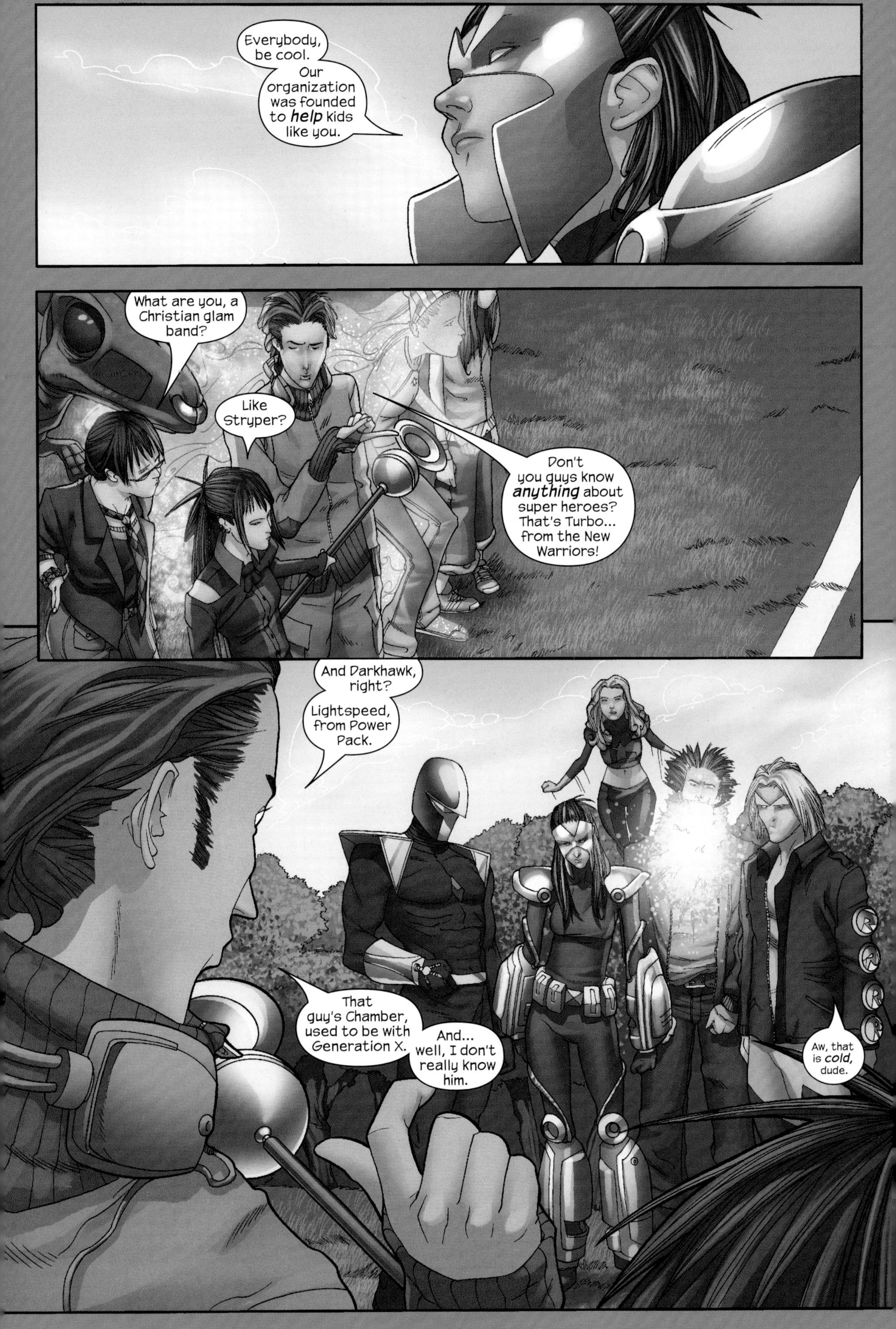

Everybody, be cool.
Our organization was founded to *help* kids like you.
What are you, a Christian glam band?
Like Stryper?
Don't you guys know *anything* about super heroes? That's Turbo... from the New Warriors!
And Darkhawk, right?
Lightspeed, from Power Pack.
That guy's Chamber, used to be with Generation X.
And... well, I don't really know him.
Aw, that is *cold,* dude.

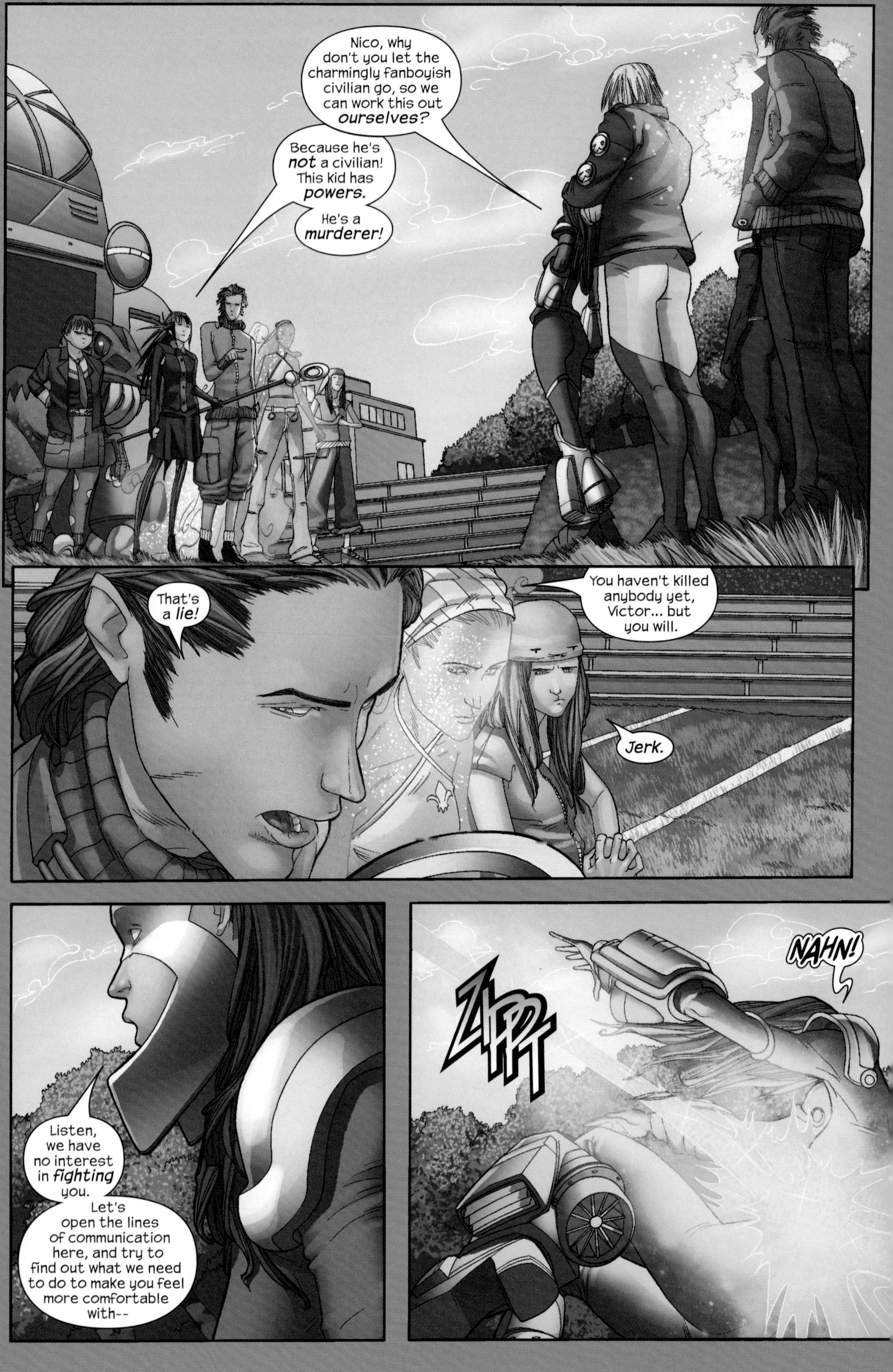
Nico, why don't you let the charmingly fanboyish civilian go, so we can work this out ourselves?
Because he's not a civilian! This kid has powers.
He's a murderer!
That's a lie!
You haven't killed anybody yet, Victor... but you will.
Jerk.
Listen, we have no interest in fighting you.
Let's open the lines of communication here, and try to find out what we need to do to make you feel more comfortable with--
ZIPPT
NAHN!

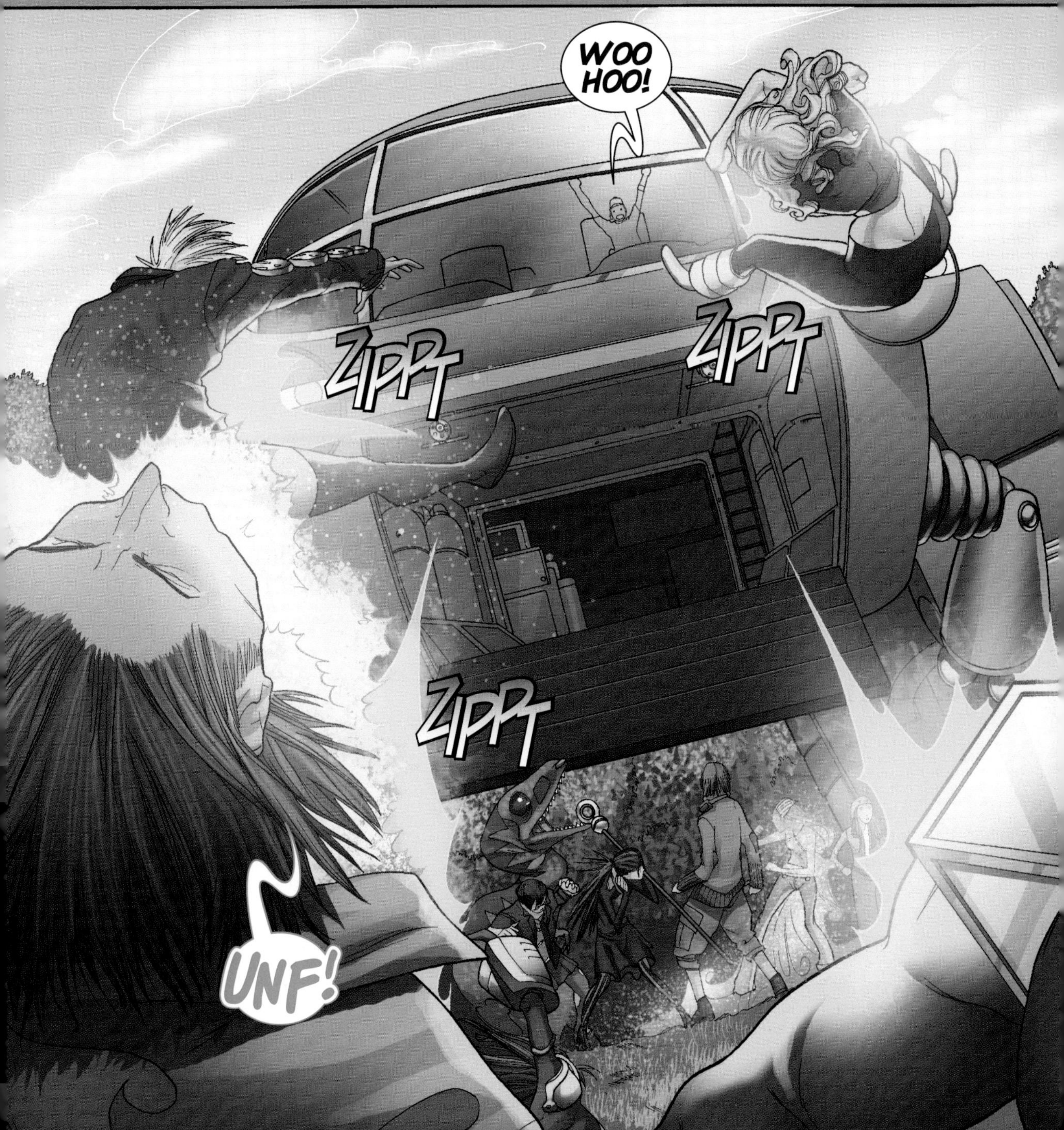
WOO HOO!
ZIPPT
ZIPPT
ZIPPT
UNF!

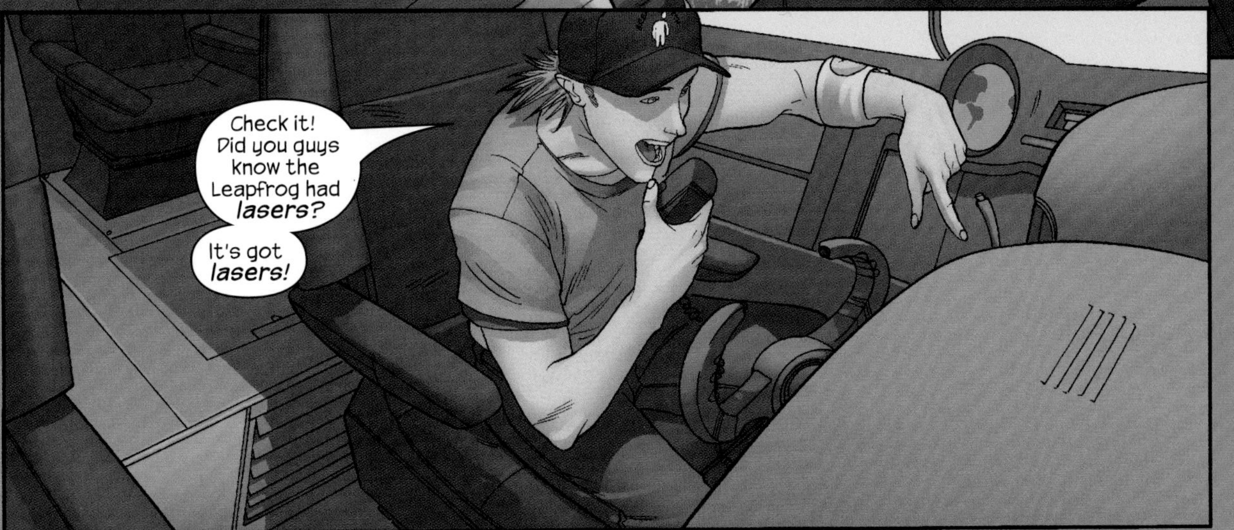
Check it! Did you guys know the Leapfrog had lasers?
It's got lasers!

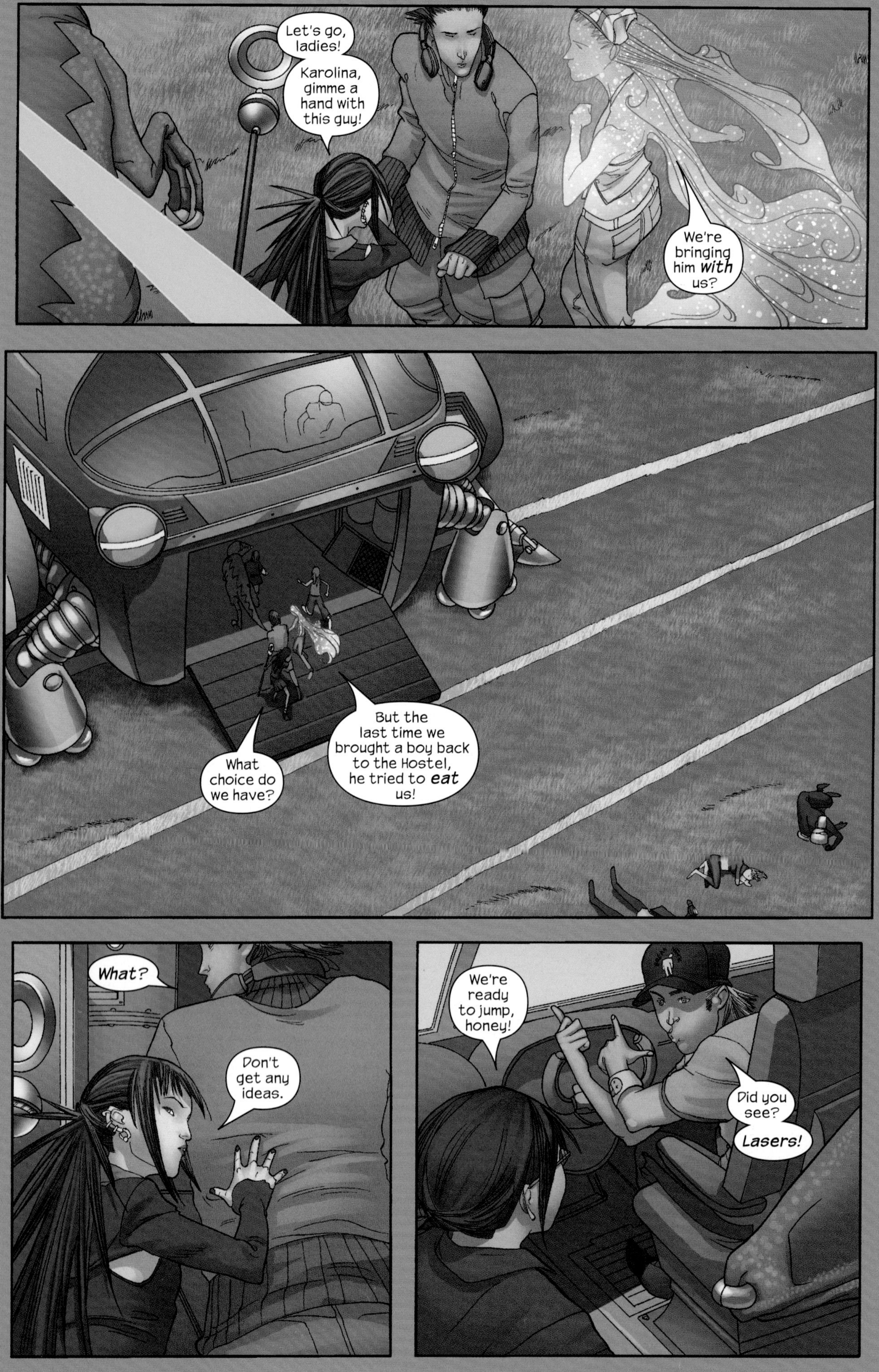
Let's go, ladies!
Karolina, gimme a hand with this guy!
We're bringing him with us?
What choice do we have?
But the last time we brought a boy back to the Hostel, he tried to eat us!
What?
Don't get any ideas.
We're ready to jump, honey!
Did you see? Lasers!

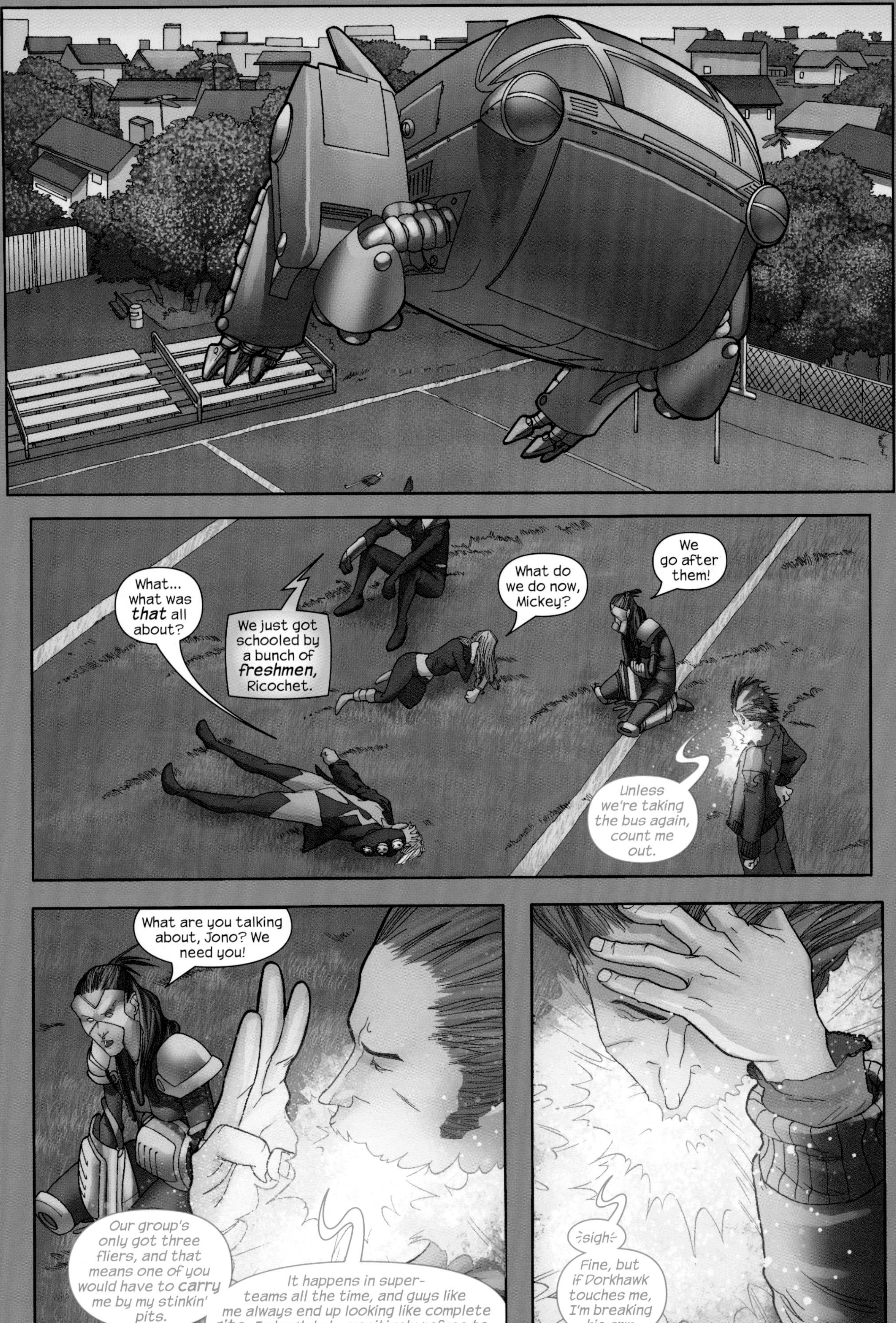
What... what was that all about?
We just got schooled by a bunch of freshmen, Ricochet.
What do we do now, Mickey?
We go after them!
Unless we're taking the bus again, count me out.
What are you talking about, Jono? We need you!
Our group's only got three fliers, and that means one of you would have to carry me by my stinkin' pits.
It happens in super-teams all the time, and guys like me always end up looking like complete gits. I absolutely, positively refuse to...
sigh
Fine, but if Dorkhawk touches me, I'm breaking his arm.

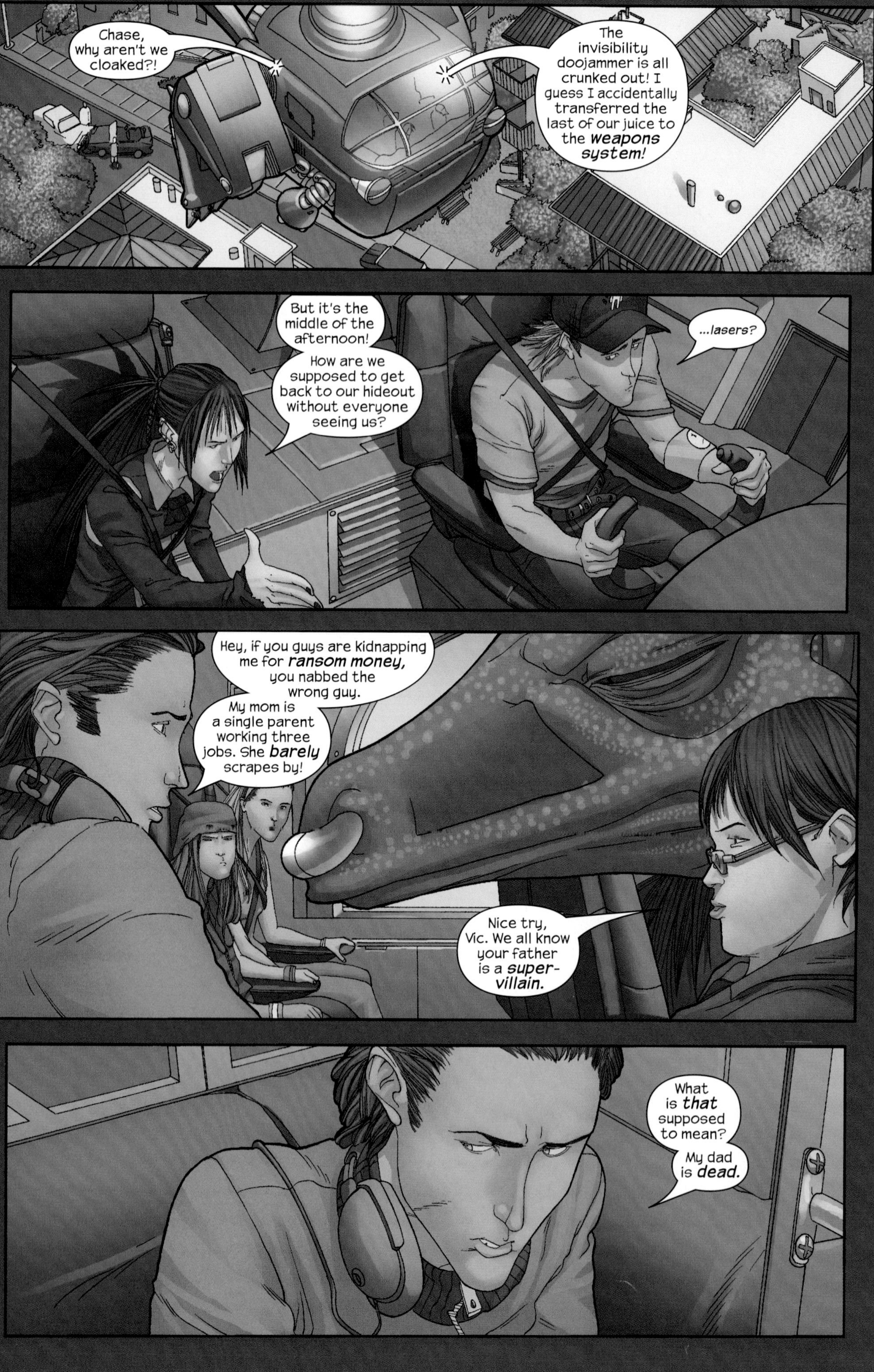
Chase, why aren't we cloaked?!
The invisibility doojammer is all crunked out! I guess I accidentally transferred the last of our juice to the *weapons system!*
But it's the middle of the afternoon!
How are we supposed to get back to our hideout without everyone seeing us?
...*lasers?*
Hey, if you guys are kidnapping me for *ransom money,* you nabbed the wrong guy.
My mom is a single parent working three jobs. She *barely* scrapes by!
Nice try, Vic. We all know your father is a *super-villain.*
What is *that* supposed to mean?
My dad is *dead.*

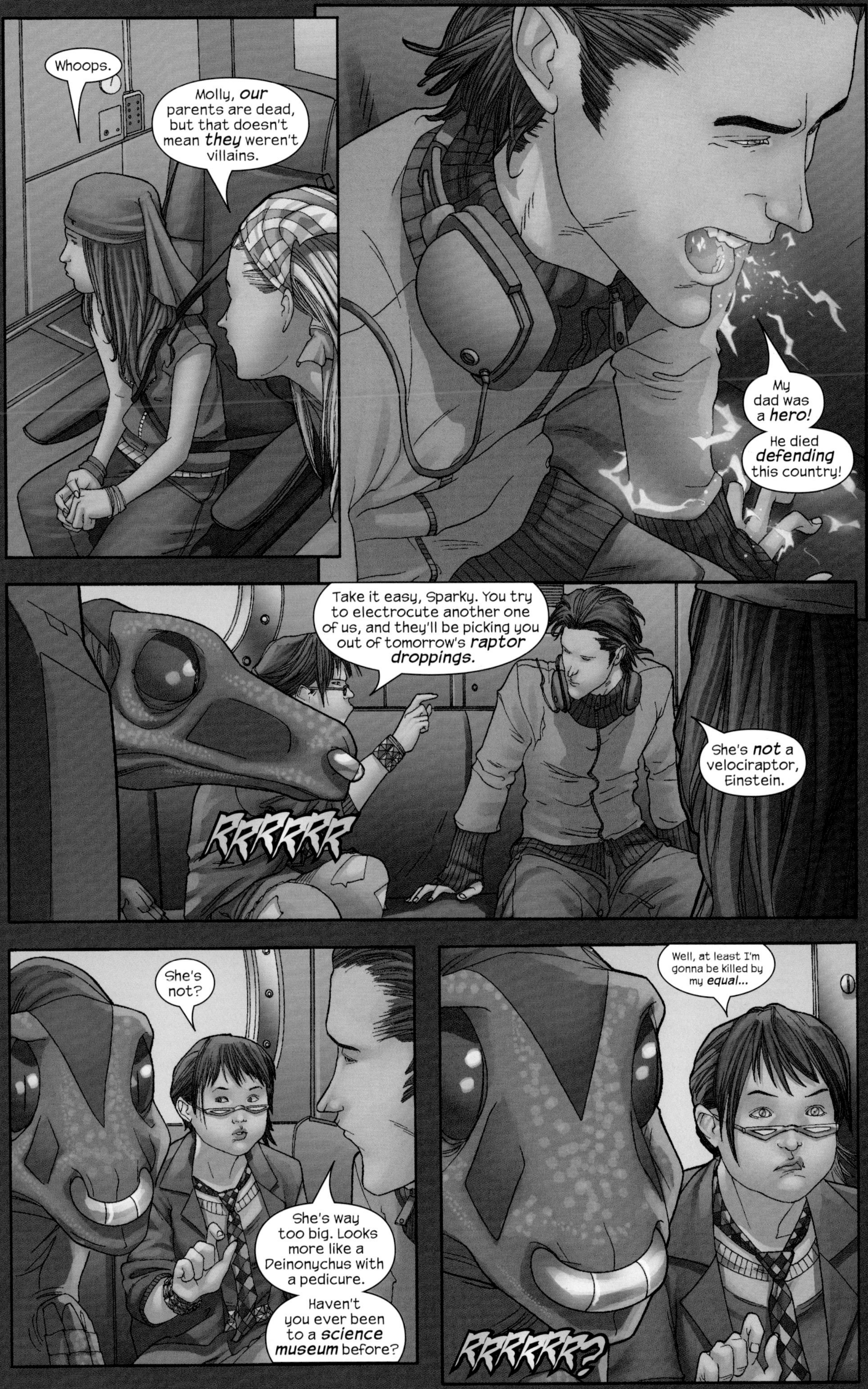
Whoops.
Molly, our parents are dead, but that doesn't mean they weren't villains.
My dad was a hero!
He died defending this country!
Take it easy, Sparky. You try to electrocute another one of us, and they'll be picking you out of tomorrow's raptor droppings.
RRRRRR
She's not a velociraptor, Einstein.
She's not?
She's way too big. Looks more like a Deinonychus with a pedicure.
Haven't you ever been to a science museum before?
Well, at least I'm gonna be killed by my equal...
RRRRRR?

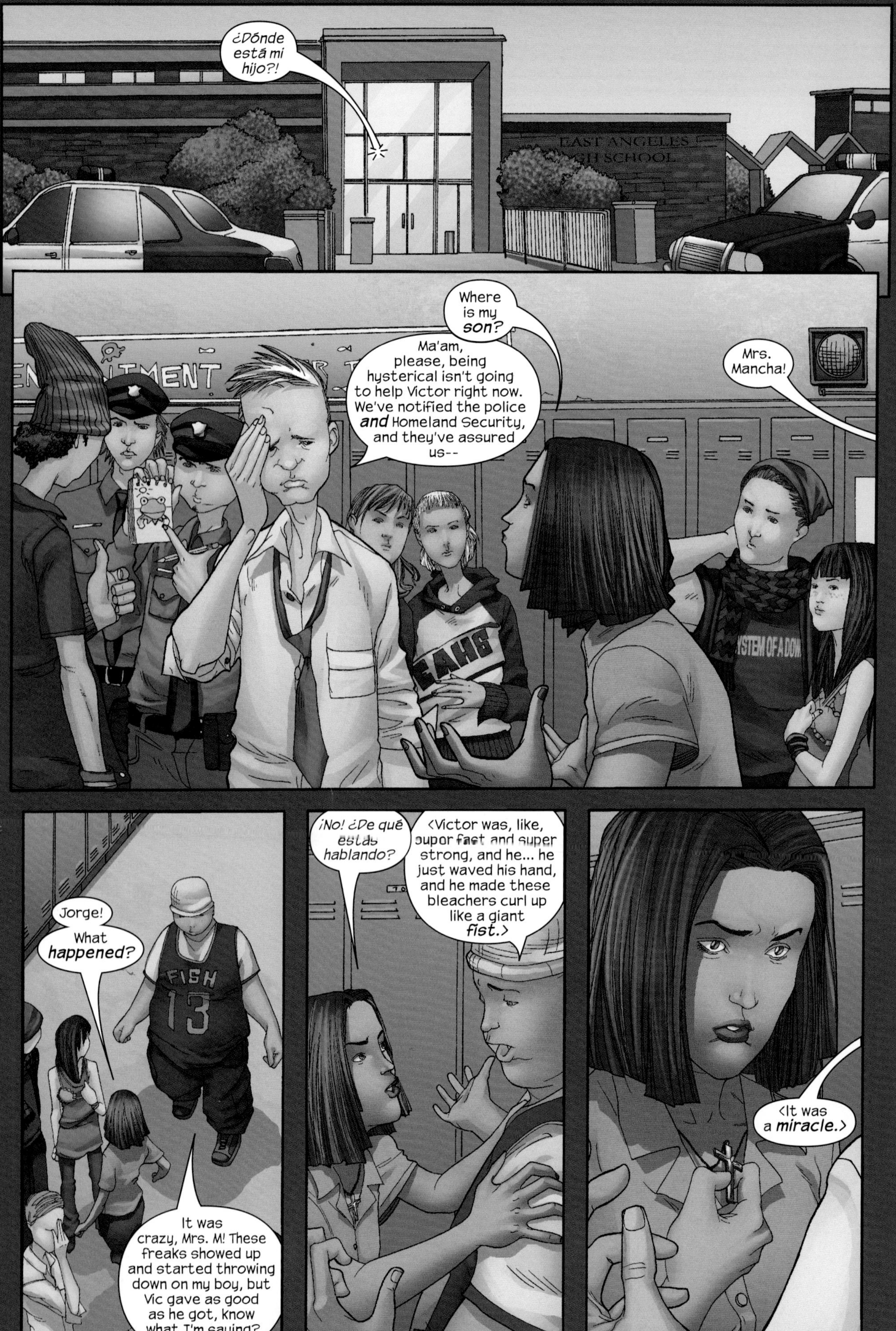

¿Dónde está mi hijo?!
EAST ANGELES
GH SCHOOL
Where is my *son?*
Ma'am, please, being hysterical isn't going to help Victor right now. We've notified the police ***and*** Homeland Security, and they've assured us--
Mrs. Mancha!
EAHS
Jorge! What ***happened?***
FISH 13
It was crazy, Mrs. M! These freaks showed up and started throwing down on my boy, but Vic gave as good as he got, know what I'm saying?
¡No! ¿De qué estás hablando?
<Victor was, like, super fast and super strong, and he... he just waved his hand, and he made these bleachers curl up like a giant *fist.*>
<It was a *miracle.*>

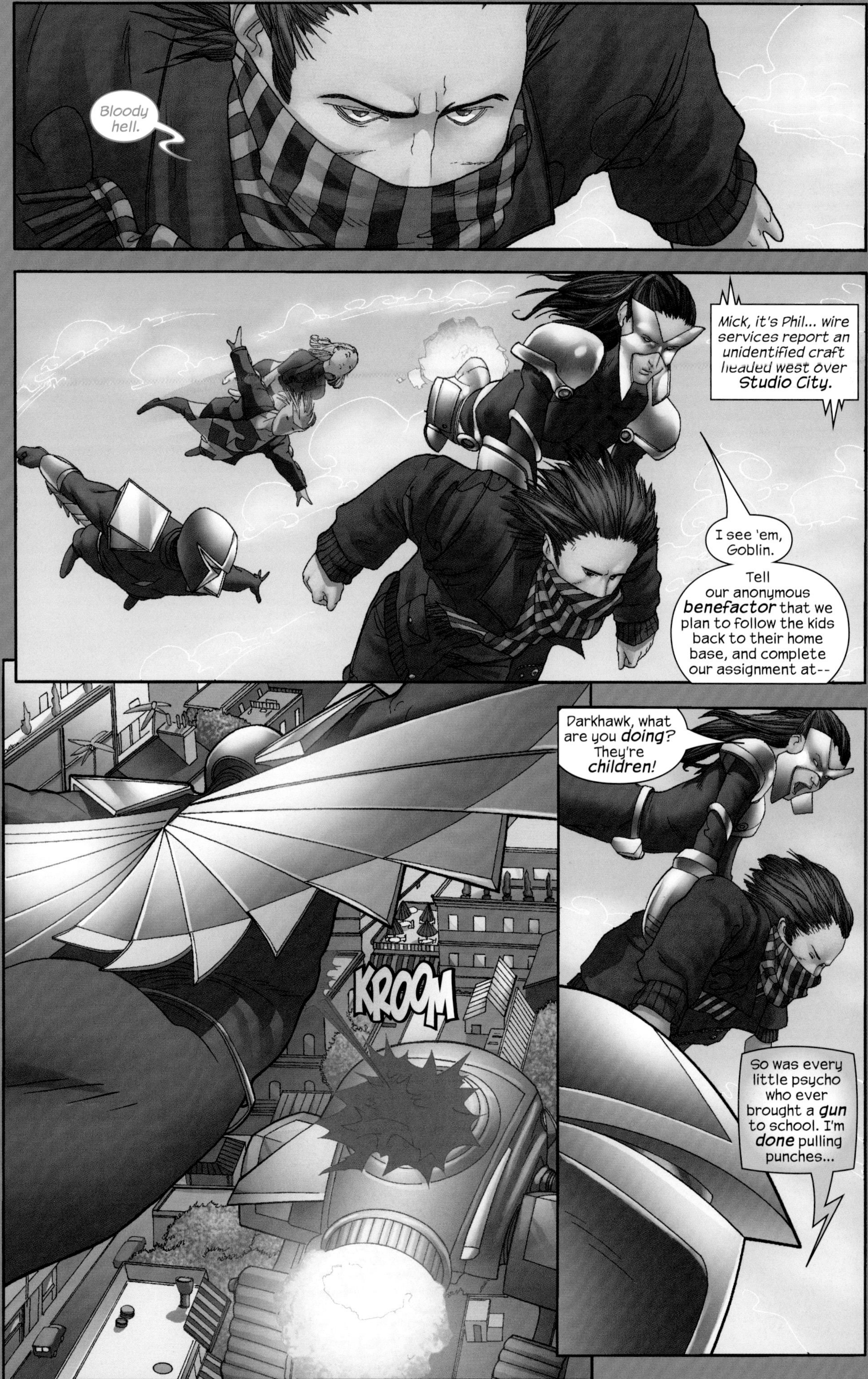
Bloody hell.
Mick, it's Phil... wire services report an unidentified craft headed west over Studio City.
I see 'em, Goblin.
Tell our anonymous benefactor that we plan to follow the kids back to their home base, and complete our assignment at--
KROOM
Darkhawk, what are you doing? They're children!
So was every little psycho who ever brought a gun to school. I'm done pulling punches...

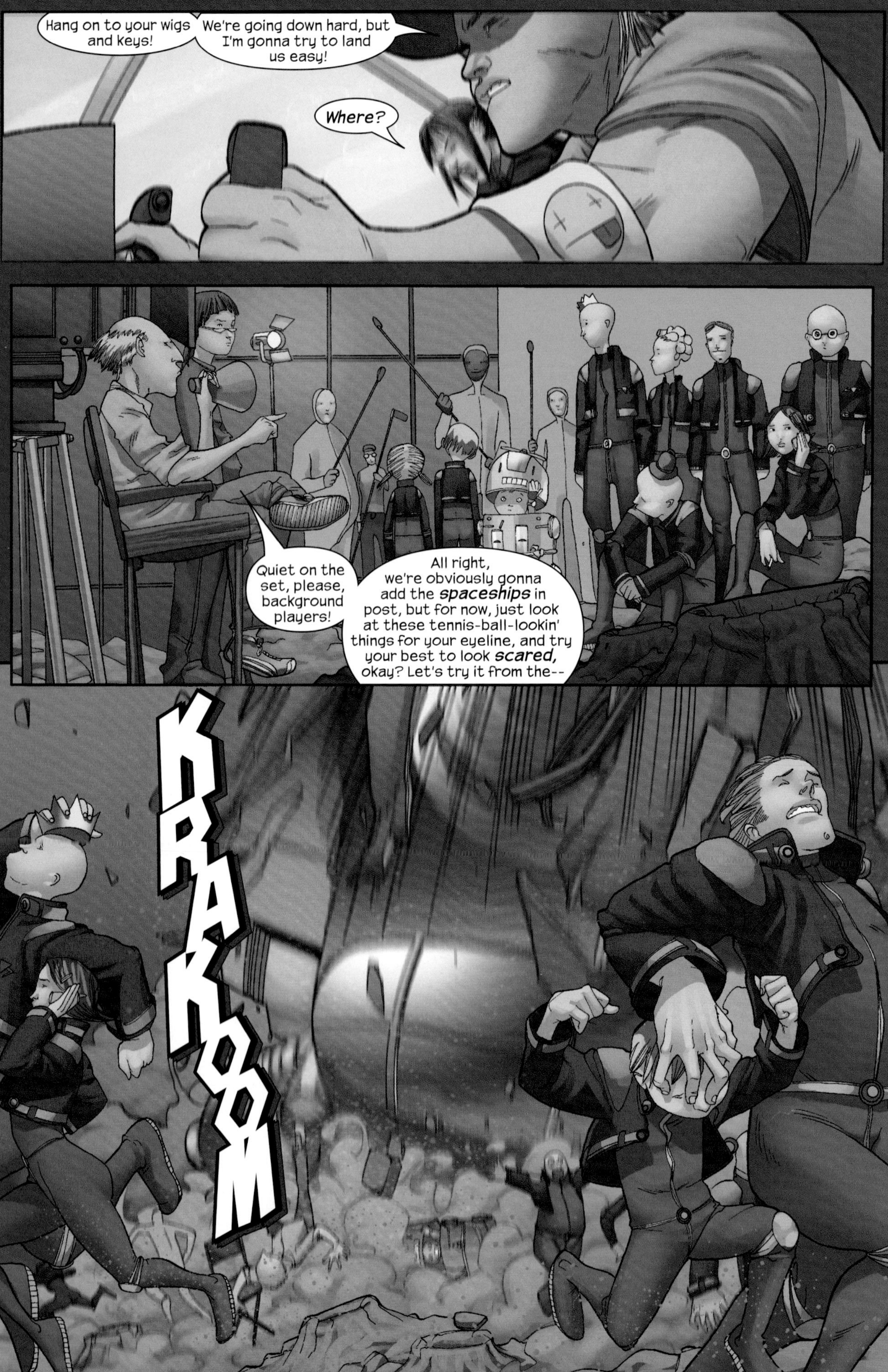
Hang on to your wigs and keys!
We're going down hard, but I'm gonna try to land us easy!
Where?
Quiet on the set, please, background players!
All right, we're obviously gonna add the spaceships in post, but for now, just look at these tennis-ball-lookin' things for your eyeline, and try your best to look scared, okay? Let's try it from the--
KRAKOOM

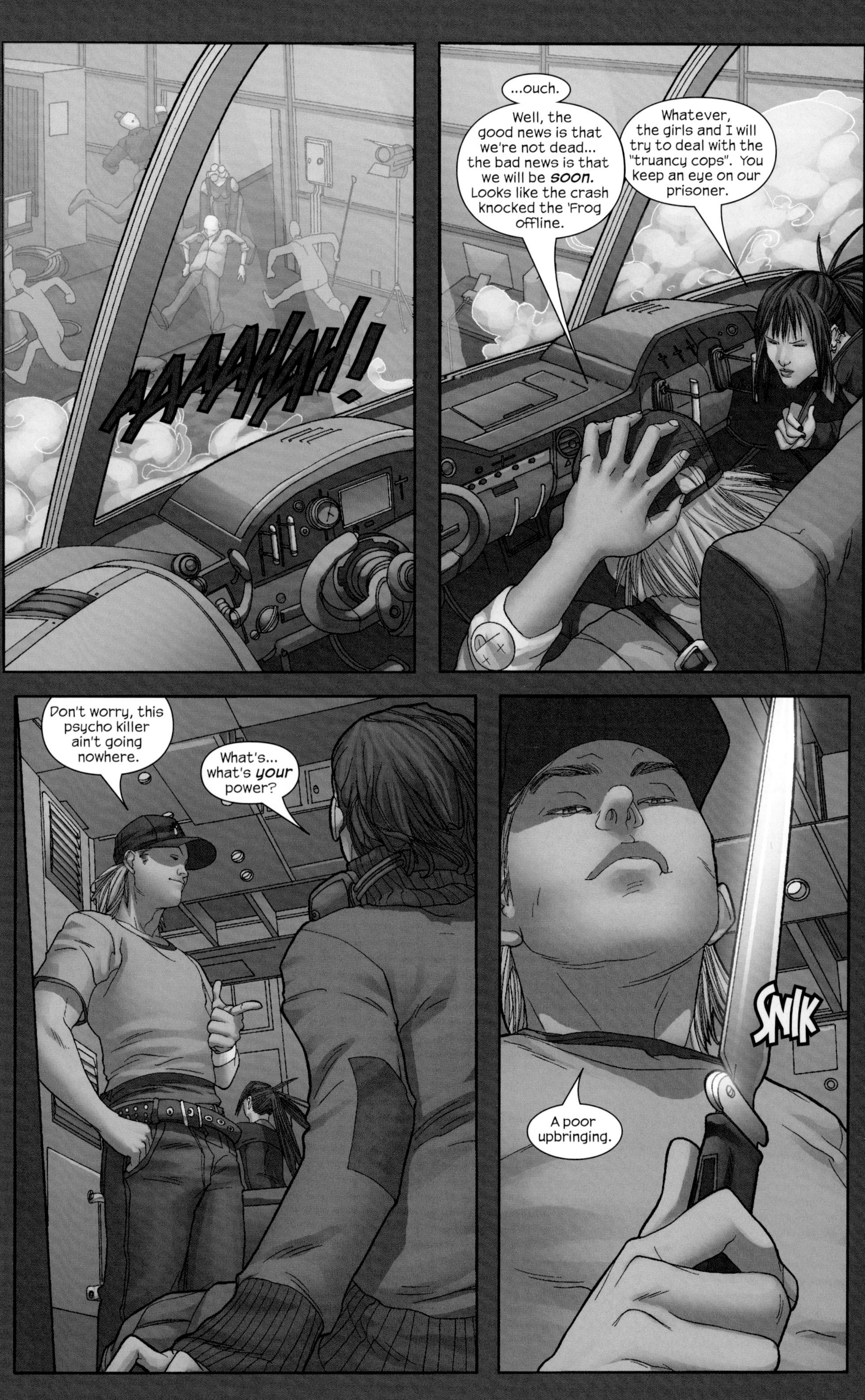
AAAAAAAH!
...ouch.
Well, the good news is that we're not dead... the bad news is that we will be *soon.* Looks like the crash knocked the 'Frog offline.
Whatever, the girls and I will try to deal with the "truancy cops". You keep an eye on our prisoner.
Don't worry, this psycho killer ain't going nowhere.
What's... what's *your* power?
SNIK
A poor upbringing.

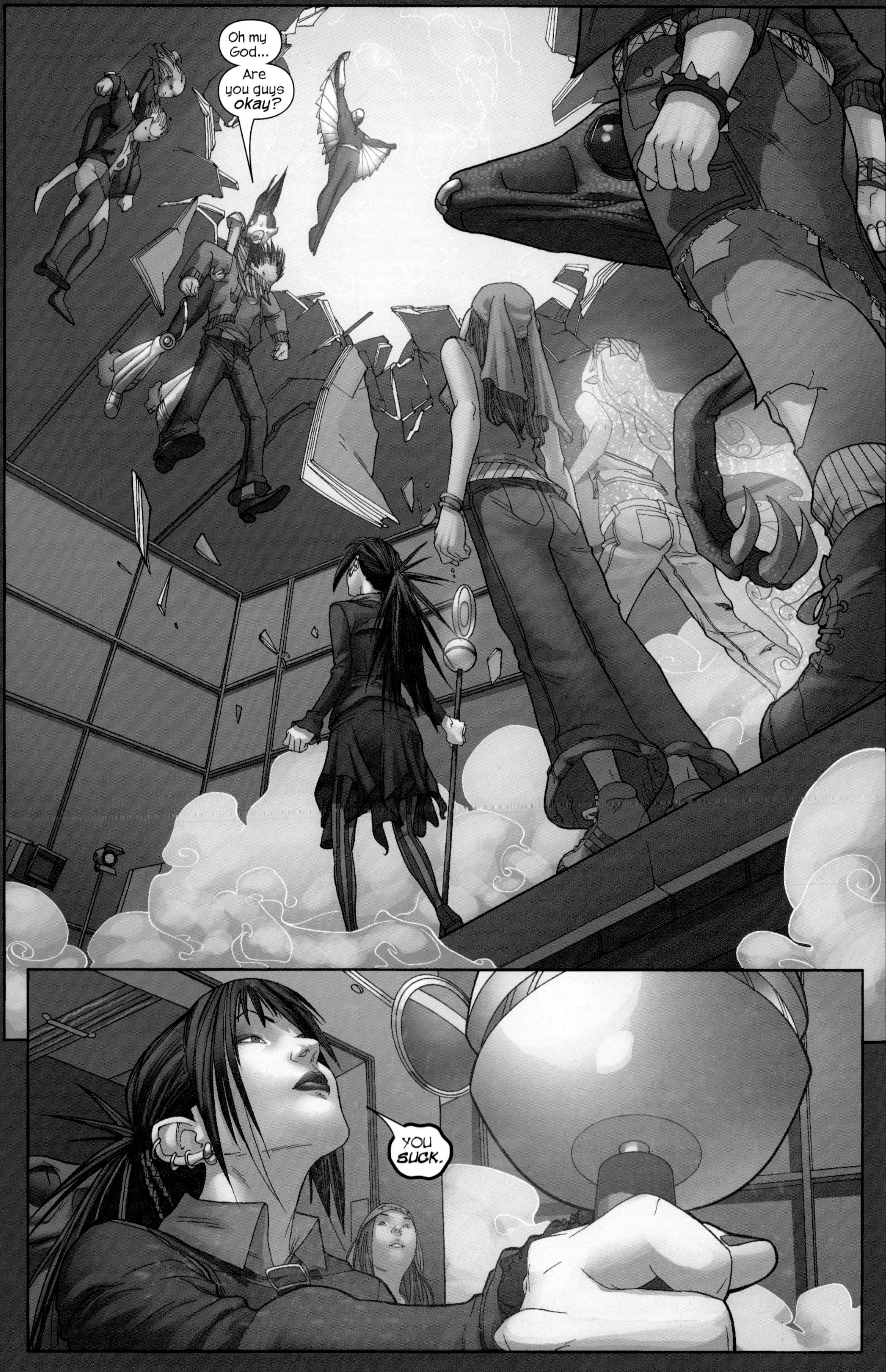
Oh my God...
Are you guys okay?
YOU SUCK.

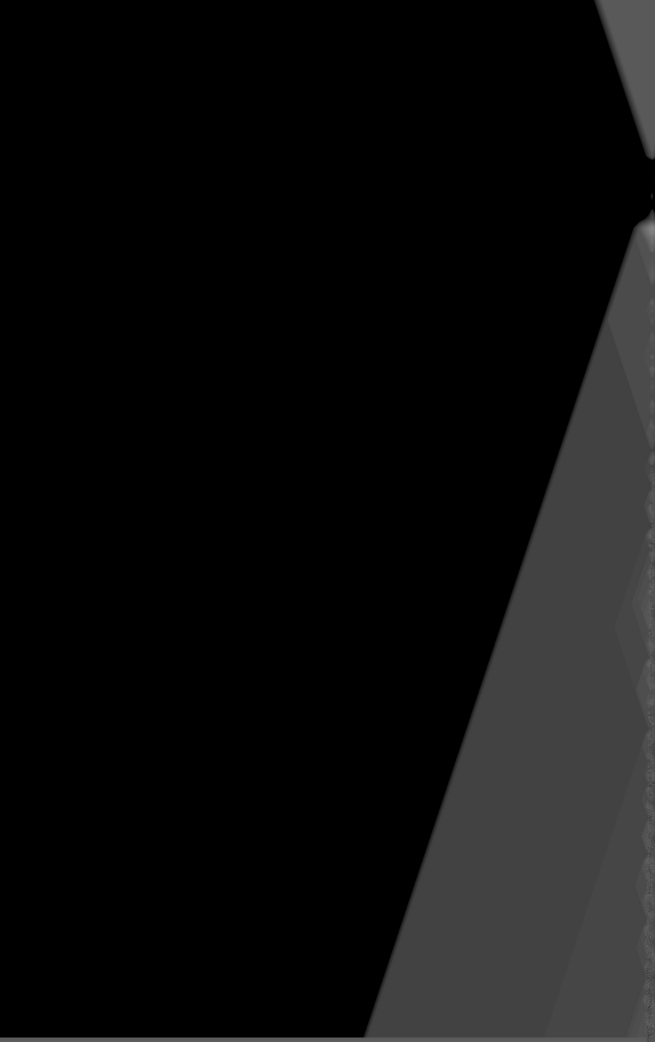

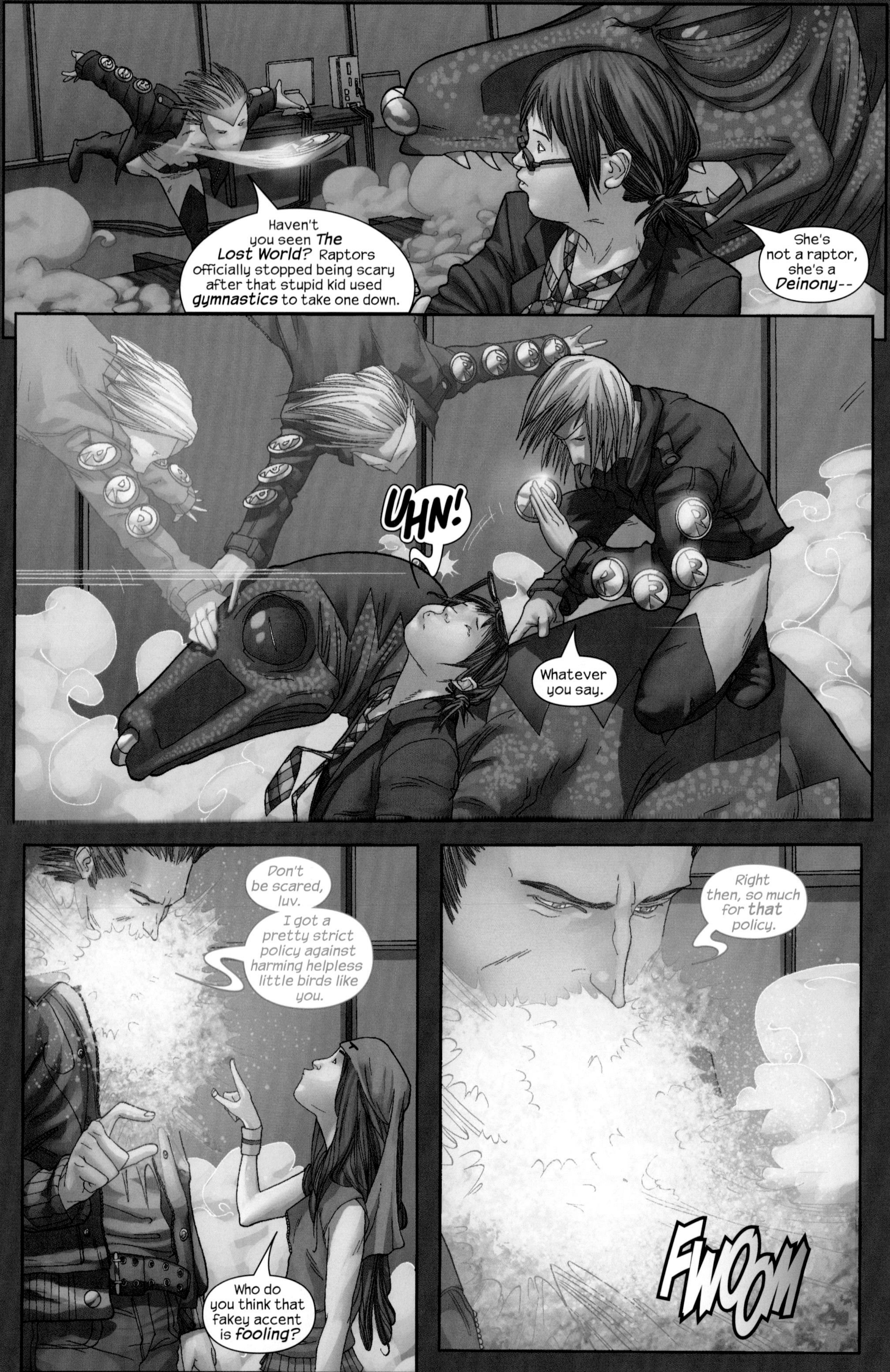
Haven't you seen The Lost World? Raptors officially stopped being scary after that stupid kid used gymnastics to take one down.
She's not a raptor, she's a Deinony--
UHN!
Whatever you say.
Don't be scared, luv.
I got a pretty strict policy against harming helpless little birds like you.
Who do you think that fakey accent is fooling?
Right then, so much for that policy.
FWOOOM

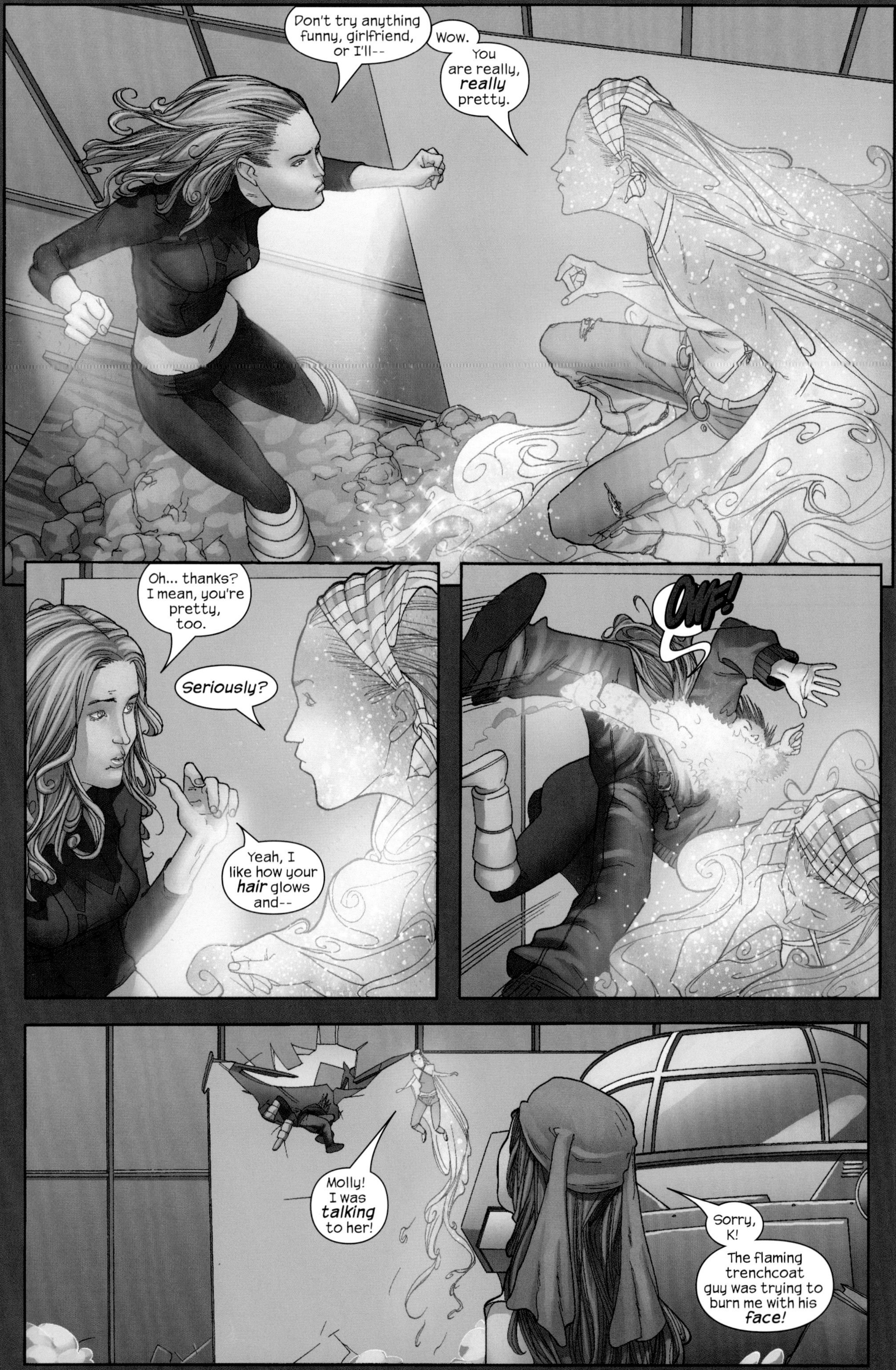
Don't try anything funny, girlfriend, or I'll--
Wow.
You are really, *really* pretty.
Oh... thanks? I mean, you're pretty, too.
Seriously?
Yeah, I like how your *hair* glows and--
OOF!
Molly! I was *talking* to her!
Sorry, K!
The flaming trenchcoat guy was trying to burn me with his *face!*

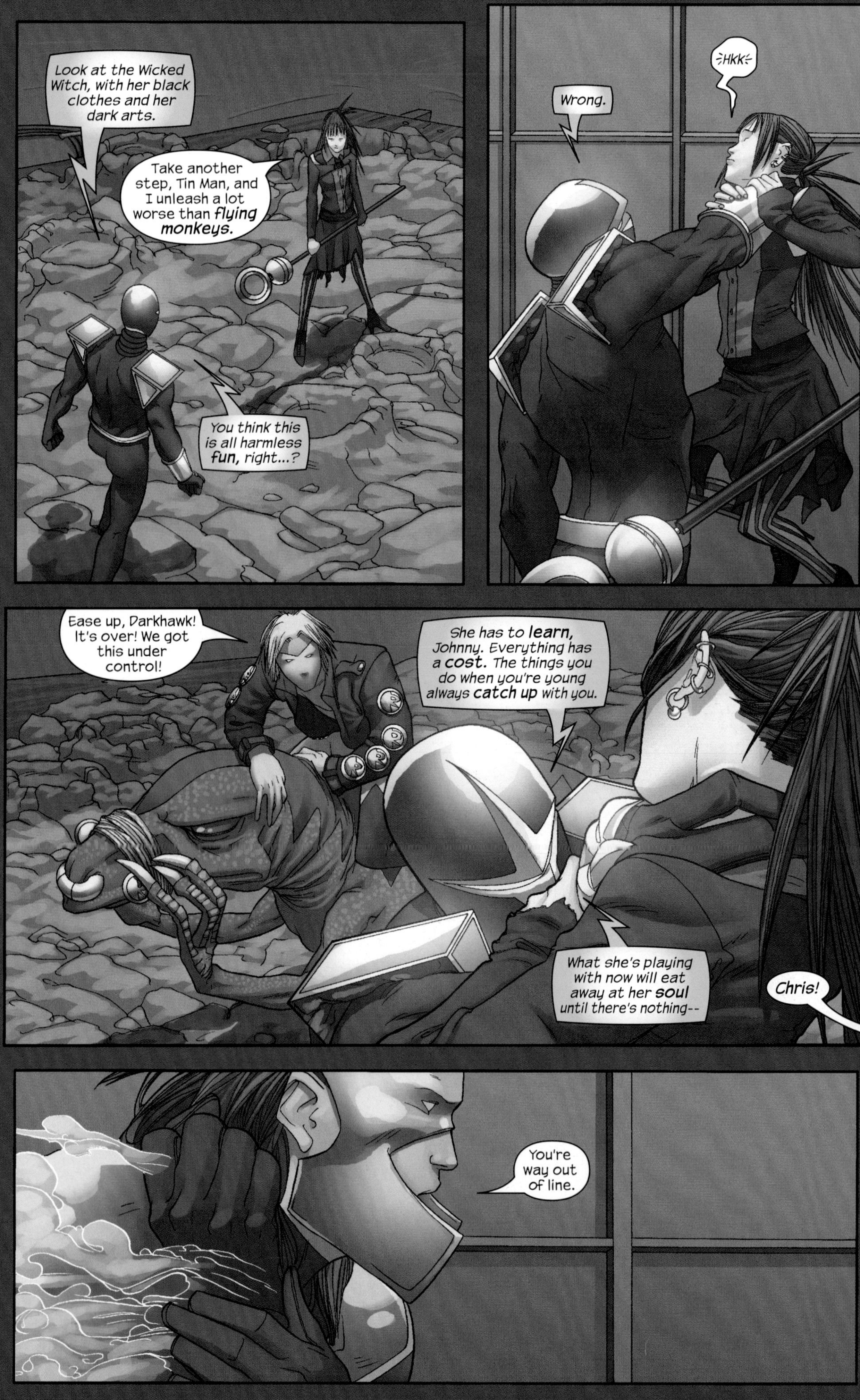

Look at the Wicked Witch, with her black clothes and her dark arts.
Take another step, Tin Man, and I unleash a lot worse than flying monkeys.
You think this is all harmless fun, right...?
Wrong.
HKK
Ease up, Darkhawk! It's over! We got this under control!
She has to learn, Johnny. Everything has a cost. The things you do when you're young always catch up with you.
What she's playing with now will eat away at her soul until there's nothing--
Chris!
You're way out of line.

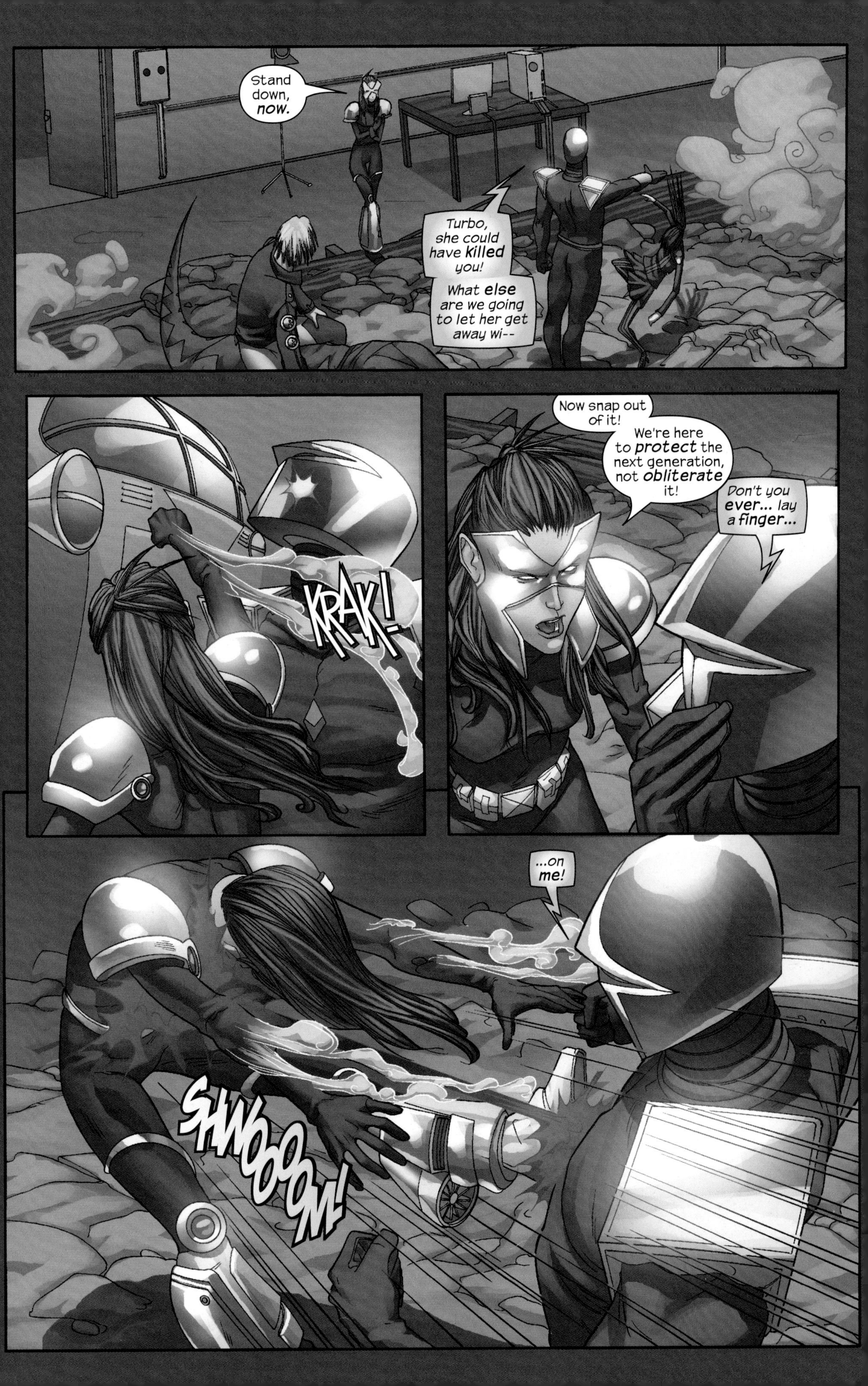
Stand down, **now.**
Turbo, she could have **killed** you!
What **else** are we going to let her get away wi--
KRAK!
Now snap out of it!
We're here to **protect** the next generation, not **obliterate** it!
Don't you **ever**... lay a **finger**...
...on **me!**
SHWOOOOM!

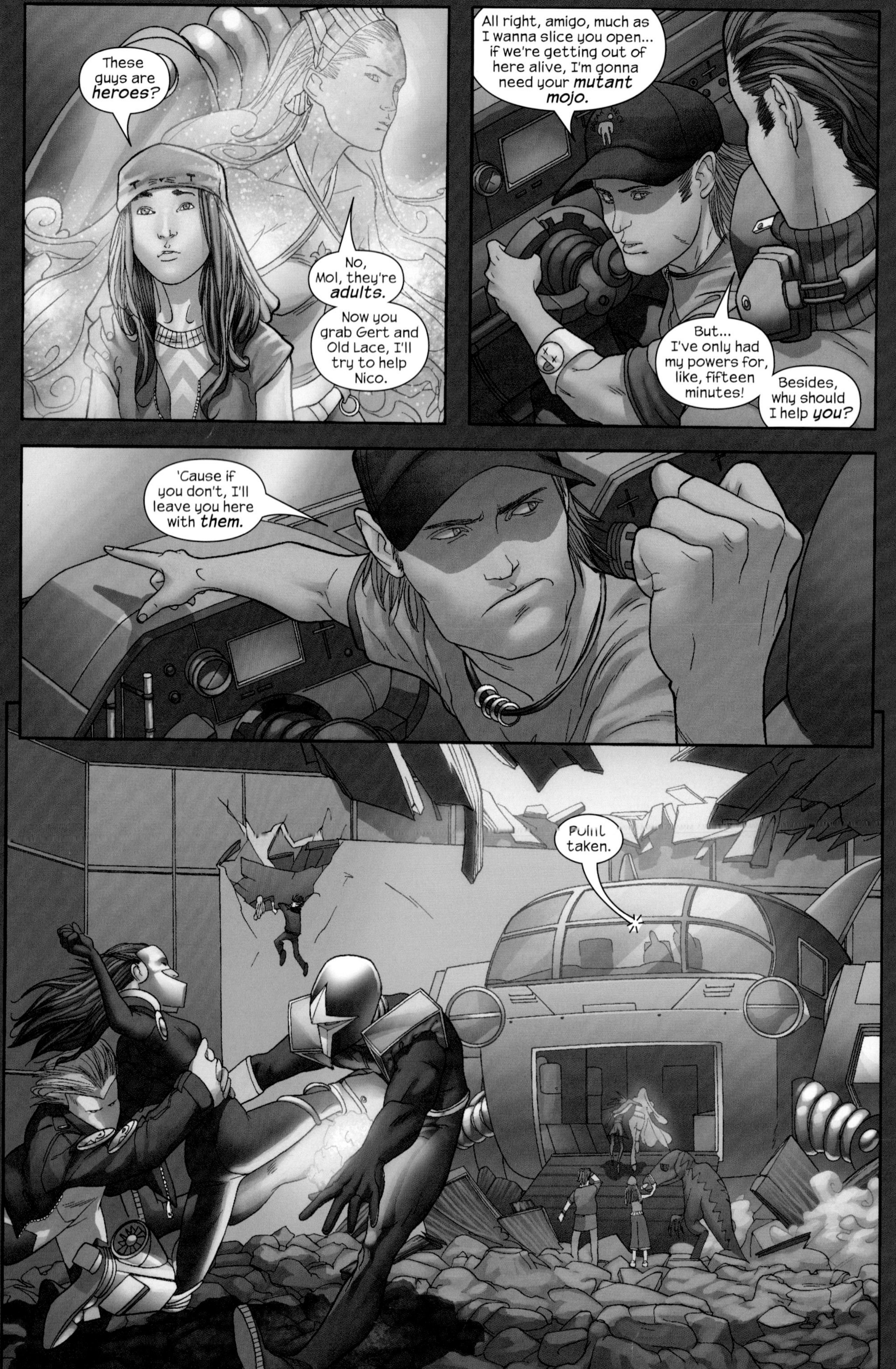

These guys are *heroes?*
No, Mol, they're *adults.*
Now you grab Gert and Old Lace, I'll try to help Nico.
All right, amigo, much as I wanna slice you open... if we're getting out of here alive, I'm gonna need your ***mutant mojo.***
But... I've only had my powers for, like, fifteen minutes!
Besides, why should I help ***you?***
'Cause if you don't, I'll leave you here with ***them.***
taken.

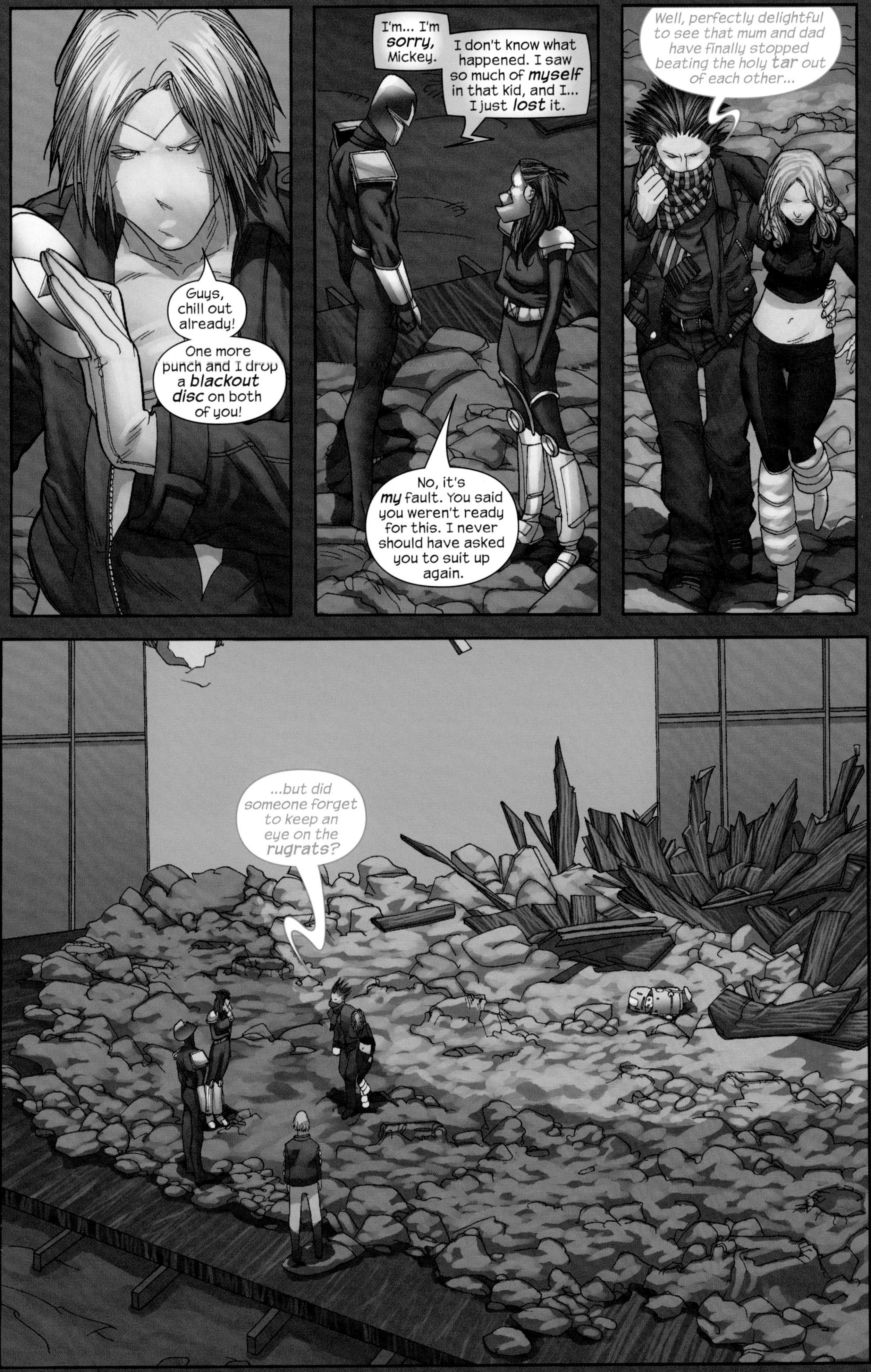
Guys, chill out already!
One more punch and I drop a blackout disc on both of you!
I'm... I'm sorry, Mickey.
I don't know what happened. I saw so much of myself in that kid, and I... I just lost it.
No, it's my fault. You said you weren't ready for this. I never should have asked you to suit up again.
Well, perfectly delightful to see that mum and dad have finally stopped beating the holy tar out of each other...
...but did someone forget to keep an eye on the rugrats?

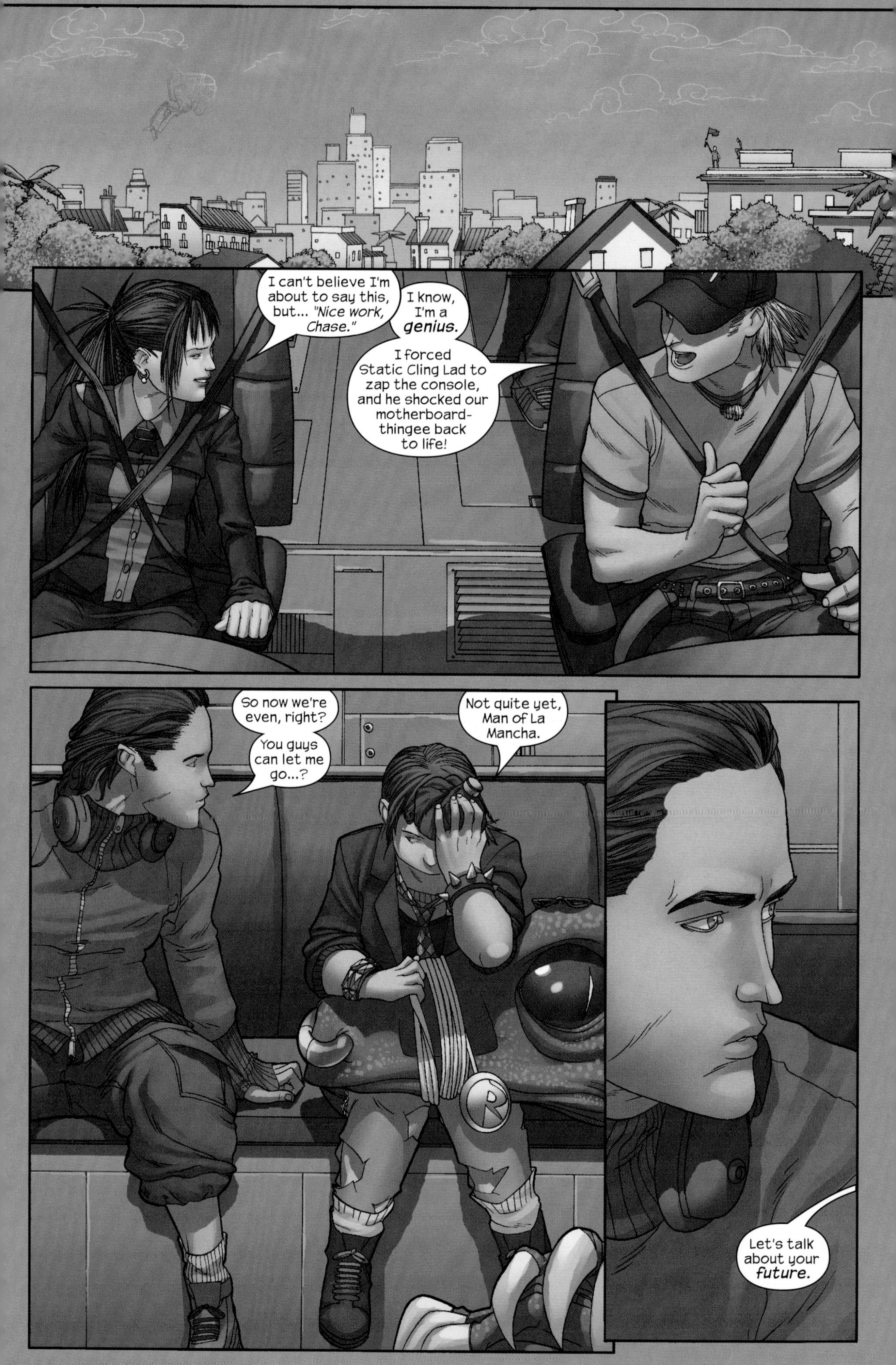
I can't believe I'm about to say this, but... "Nice work, Chase."
I know, I'm a genius.
I forced Static Cling Lad to zap the console, and he shocked our motherboard-thingee back to life!
So now we're even, right?
You guys can let me go...?
Not quite yet, Man of La Mancha.
Let's talk about your future.

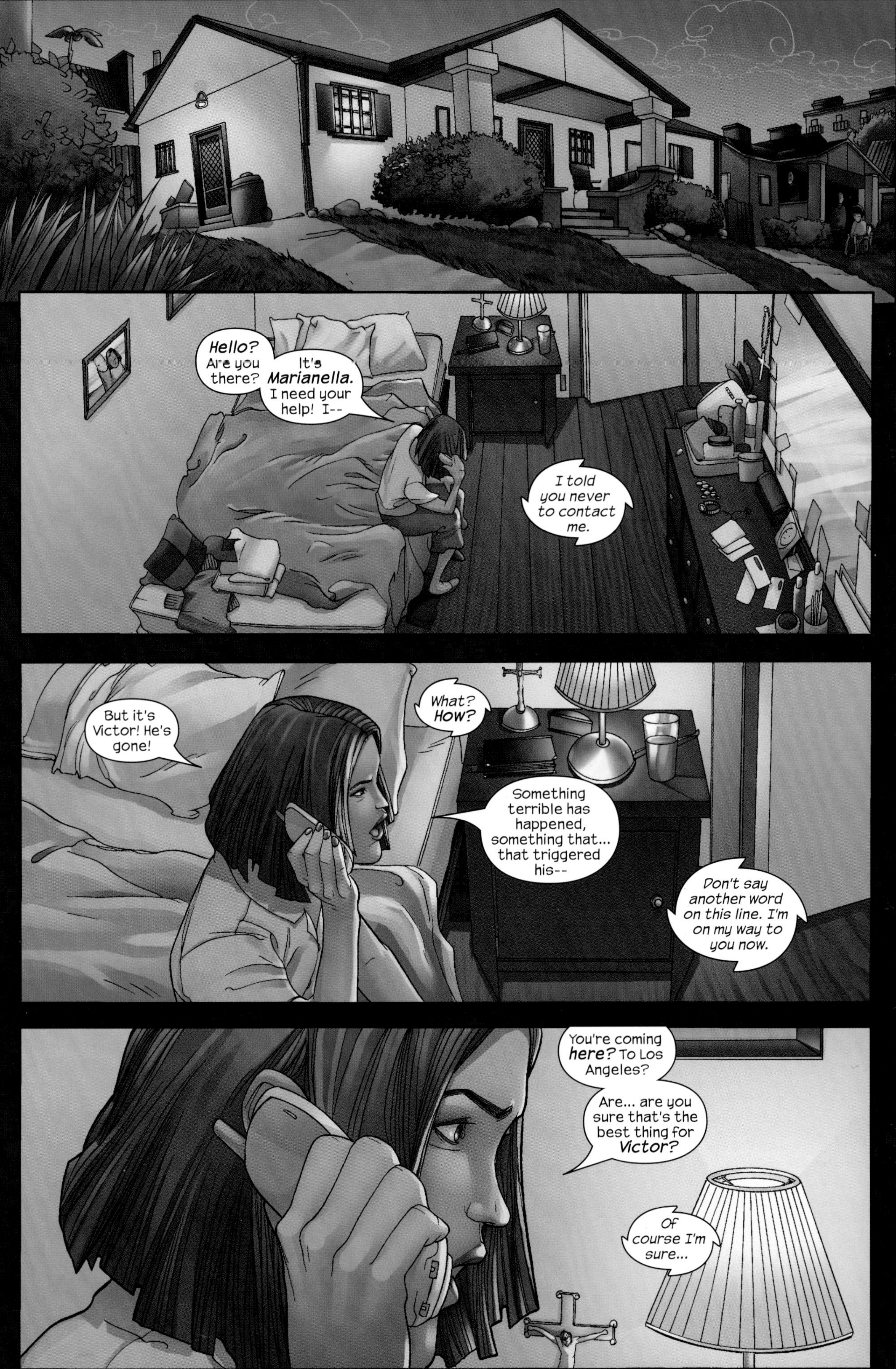

Hello? Are you there?
It's *Marianella.* I need your help! I--
I told you never to contact me.
But it's Victor! He's gone!
*What? **HOW?***
Something terrible has happened, something that... that triggered his--
Don't say another word on this line. I'm on my way to you now.
You're coming **here?** To Los Angeles?
Are... are you sure that's the best thing for **Victor?**
Of course I'm sure...

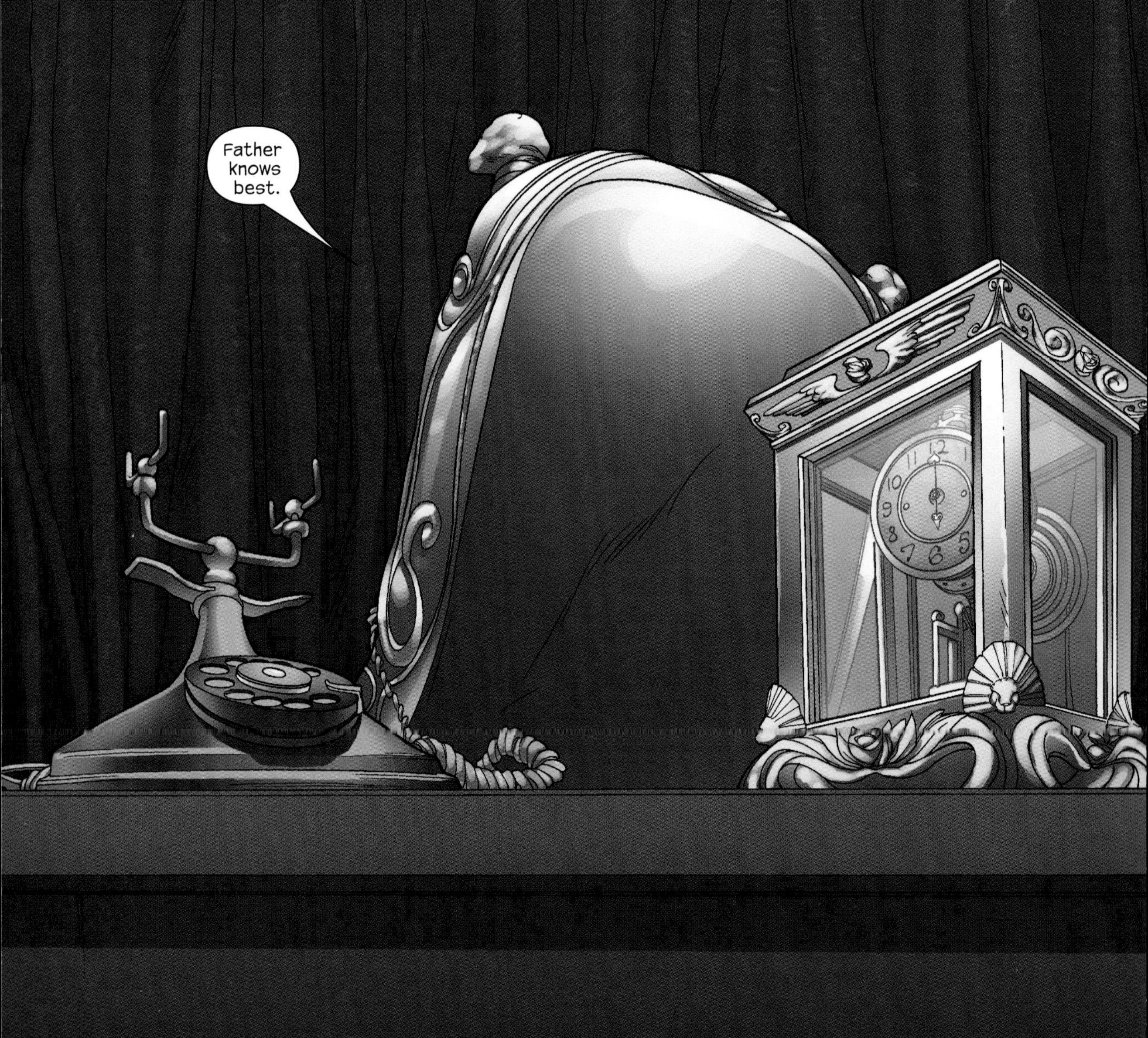
Father knows best.

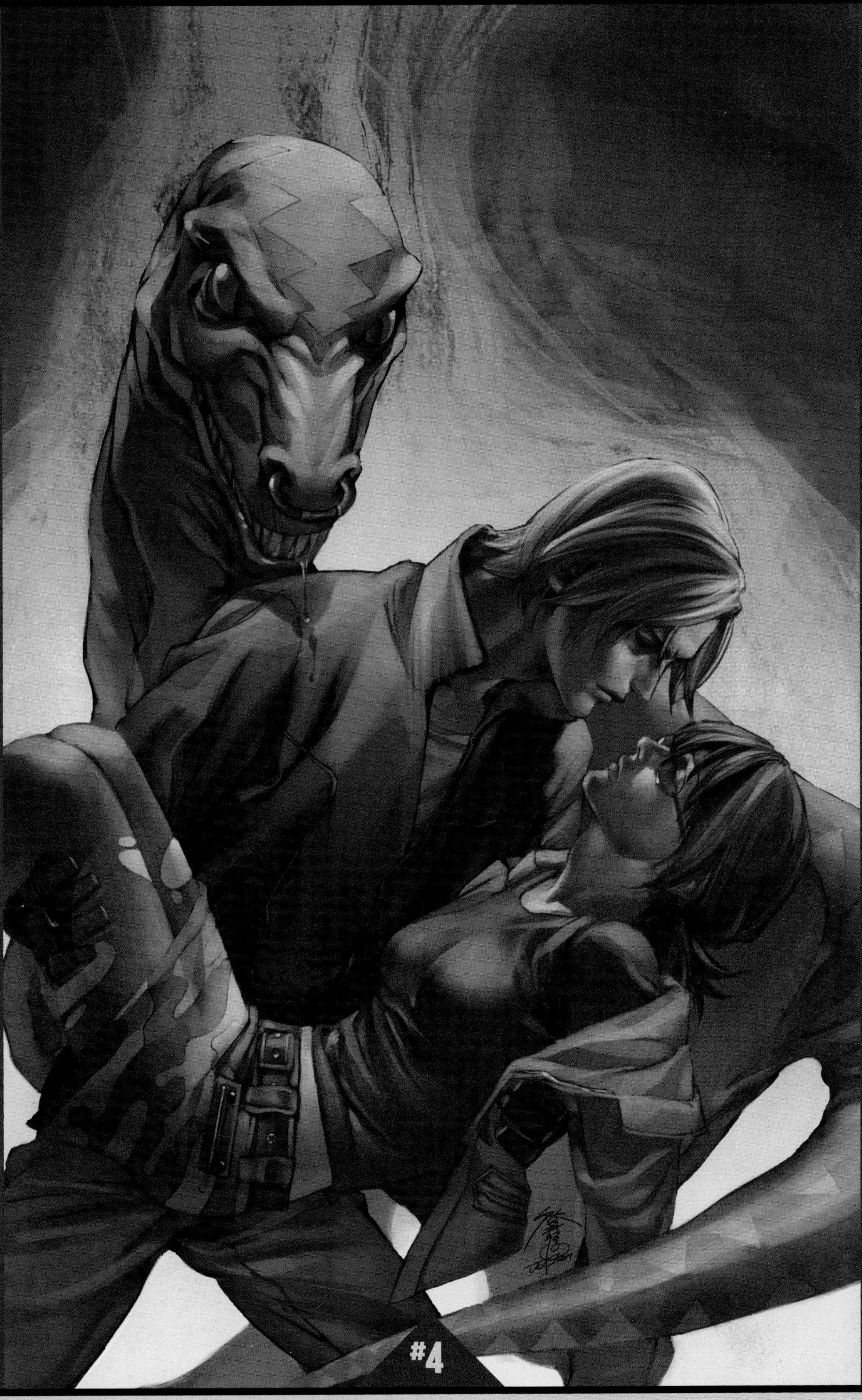
#4

TRUE BELIEVERS PART 4

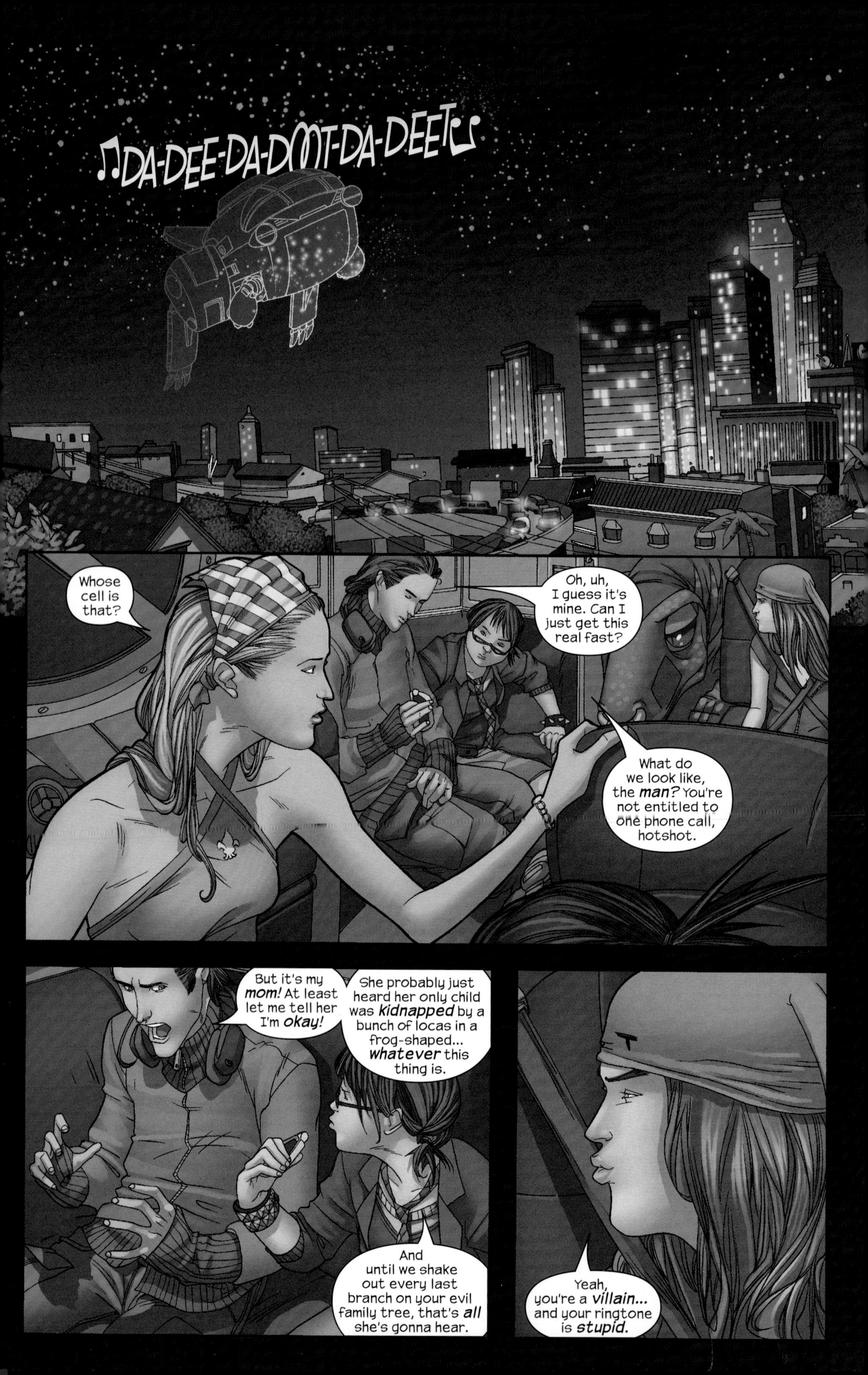
♫DA-DEE-DA-DOOT-DA-DEET♫
Whose cell is that?
Oh, uh, I guess it's mine. Can I just get this real fast?
What do we look like, the *man?* You're not entitled to one phone call, hotshot.
But it's my *mom!* At least let me tell her I'm *okay!*
She probably just heard her only child was *kidnapped* by a bunch of locas in a frog-shaped... *whatever* this thing is.
And until we shake out every last branch on your evil family tree, that's *all* she's gonna hear.
Yeah, you're a *villain...* and your ringtone is *stupid.*

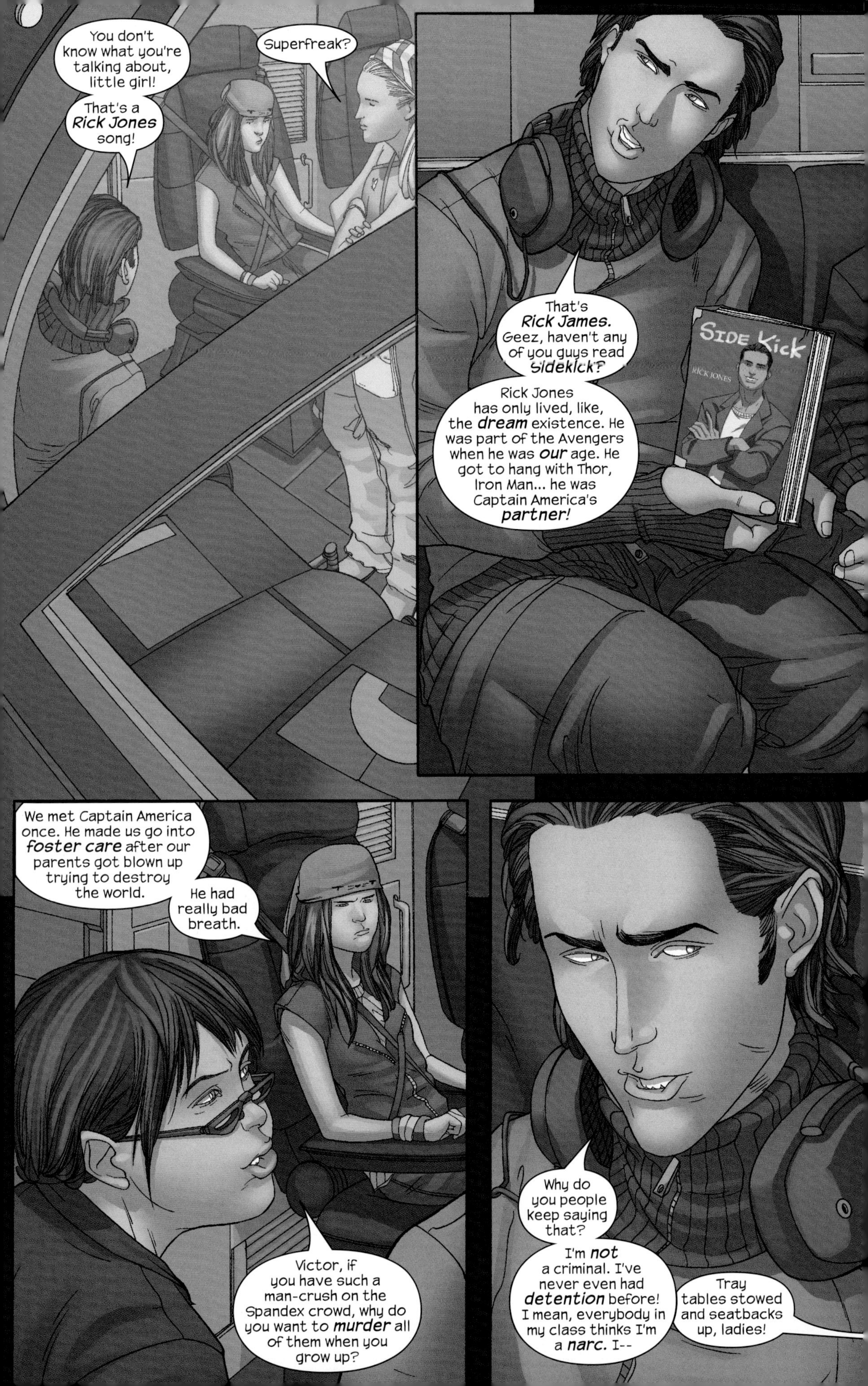
You don't know what you're talking about, little girl!
That's a Rick Jones song!
Superfreak?
That's Rick James. Geez, haven't any of you guys read Sidekick?
Rick Jones has only lived, like, the dream existence. He was part of the Avengers when he was our age. He got to hang with Thor, Iron Man... he was Captain America's partner!
SIDE KICK
RICK JONES
We met Captain America once. He made us go into foster care after our parents got blown up trying to destroy the world.
He had really bad breath.
Victor, if you have such a man-crush on the Spandex crowd, why do you want to murder all of them when you grow up?
Why do you people keep saying that?
I'm not a criminal. I've never even had detention before! I mean, everybody in my class thinks I'm a narc. I--
Tray tables stowed and seatbacks up, ladies!

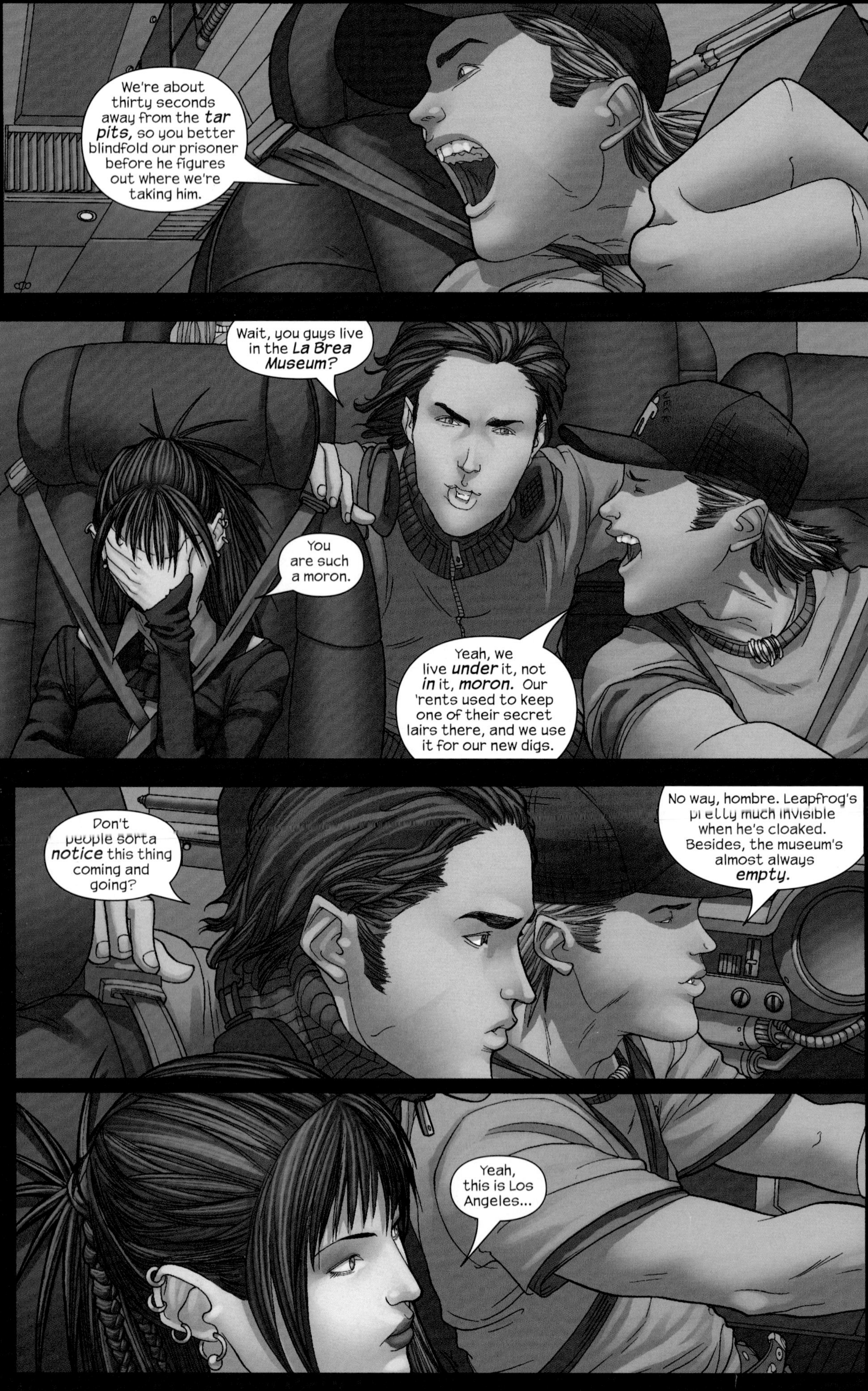
We're about thirty seconds away from the *tar pits,* so you better blindfold our prisoner before he figures out where we're taking him.
Wait, you guys live in the *La Brea Museum?*
You are such a moron.
Yeah, we live **under** it, not **in** it, **moron.** Our 'rents used to keep one of their secret lairs there, and we use it for our new digs.
Don't people sorta **notice** this thing coming and going?
No way, hombre. Leapfrog's pretty much invisible when he's cloaked. Besides, the museum's almost always **empty.**
Yeah, this is Los Angeles...

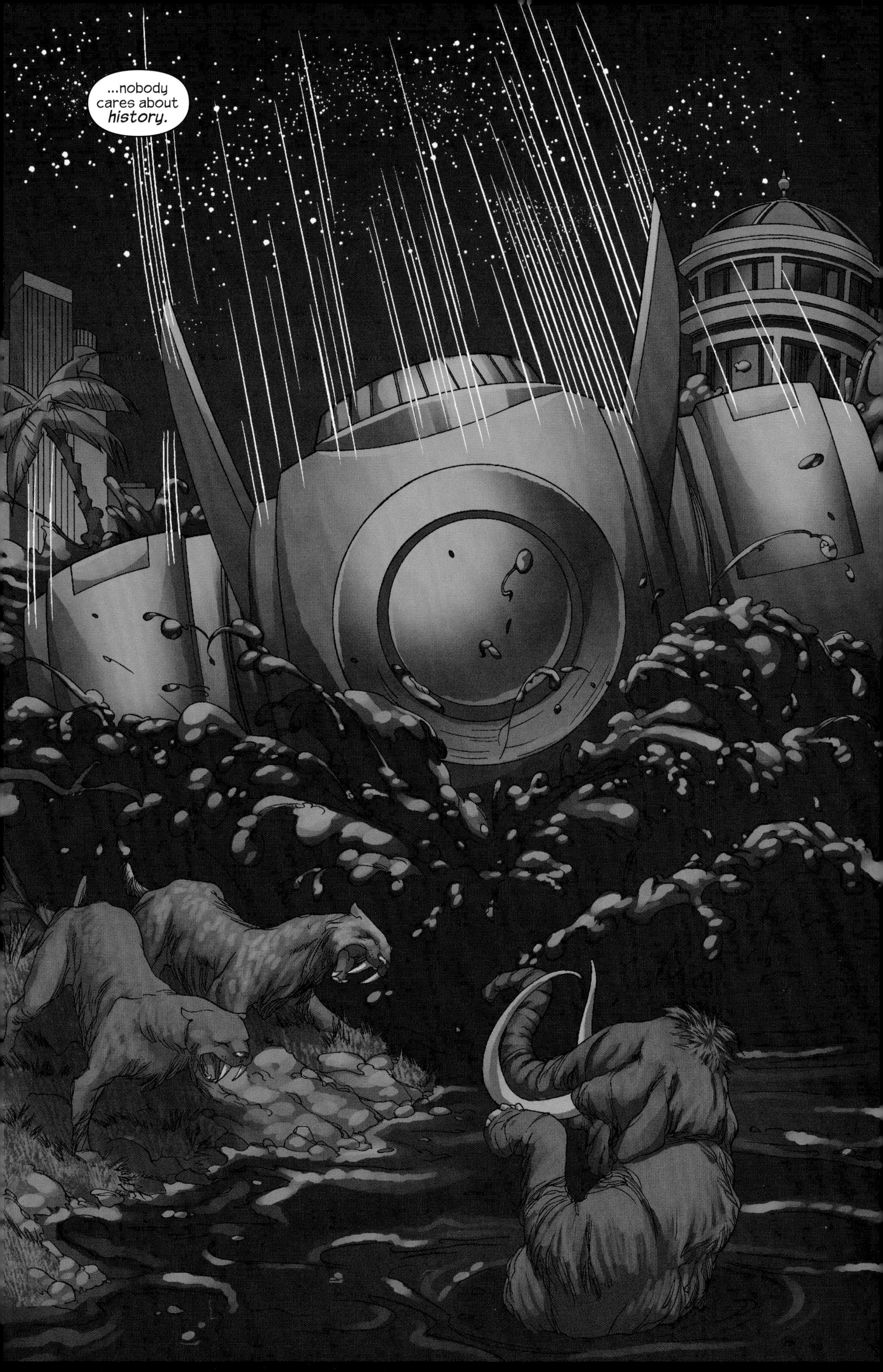
...nobody cares about history.

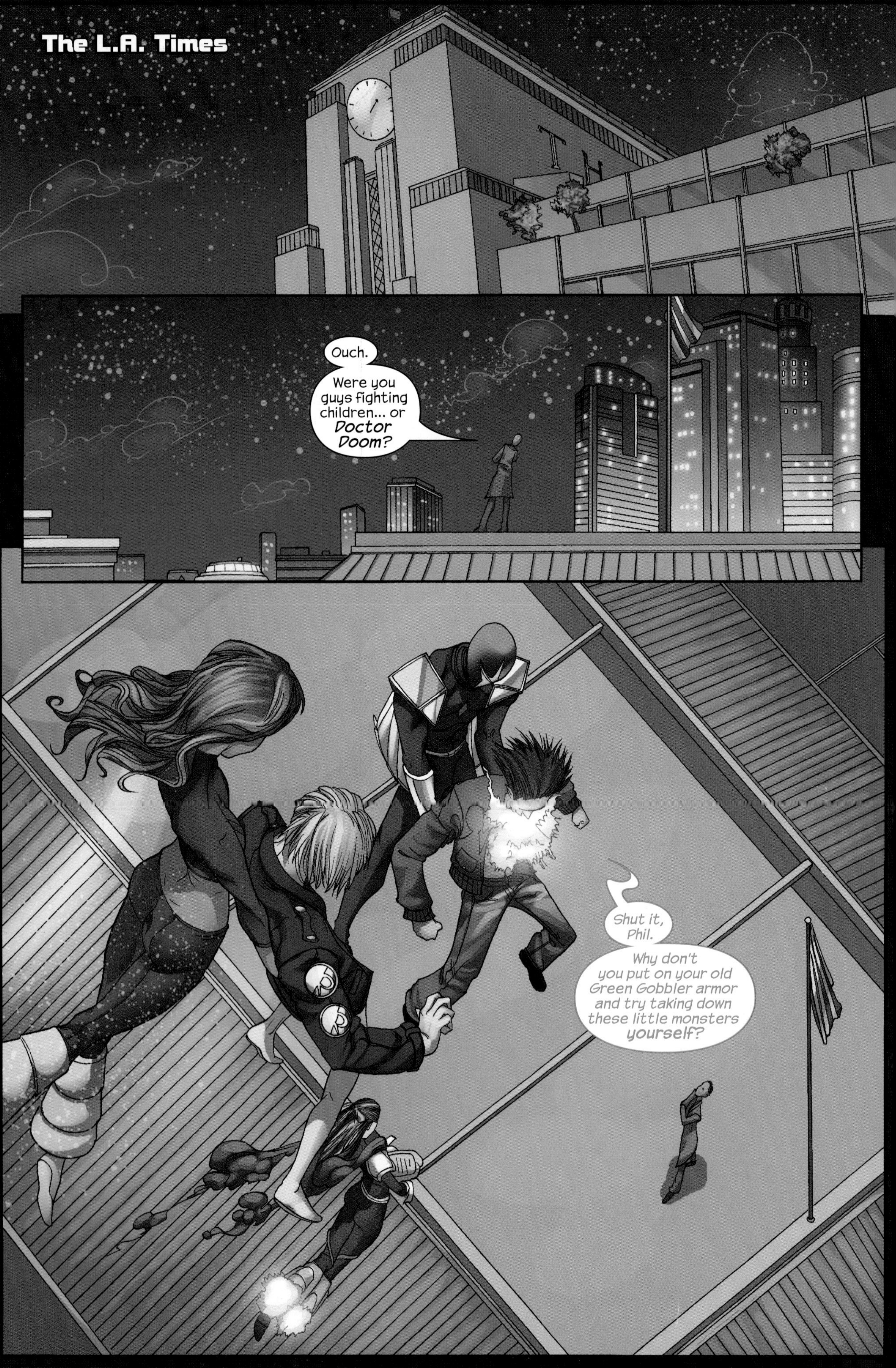
The L.A. Times
Ouch.
Were you guys fighting children... or Doctor Doom?
Shut it, Phil.
Why don't you put on your old Green Gobbler armor and try taking down these little monsters yourself?

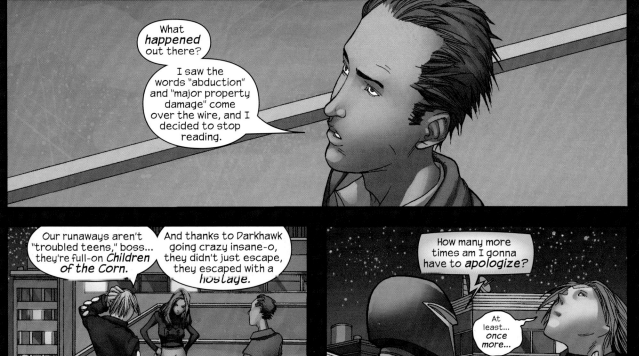

What *happened* out there?

I saw the words "abduction" and "major property damage" come over the wire, and I decided to stop reading.

Our runaways aren't "troubled teens," boss... they're full-on *Children of the Corn.*

And thanks to Darkhawk going crazy insane-o, they didn't just escape, they escaped with a *hostage.*

I had a nervous *breakdown,* all right?

How many more times am I gonna have to *apologize?*

At least... *once more...*

Hey!

Whuf!

Get a hold of yourself, Chris!

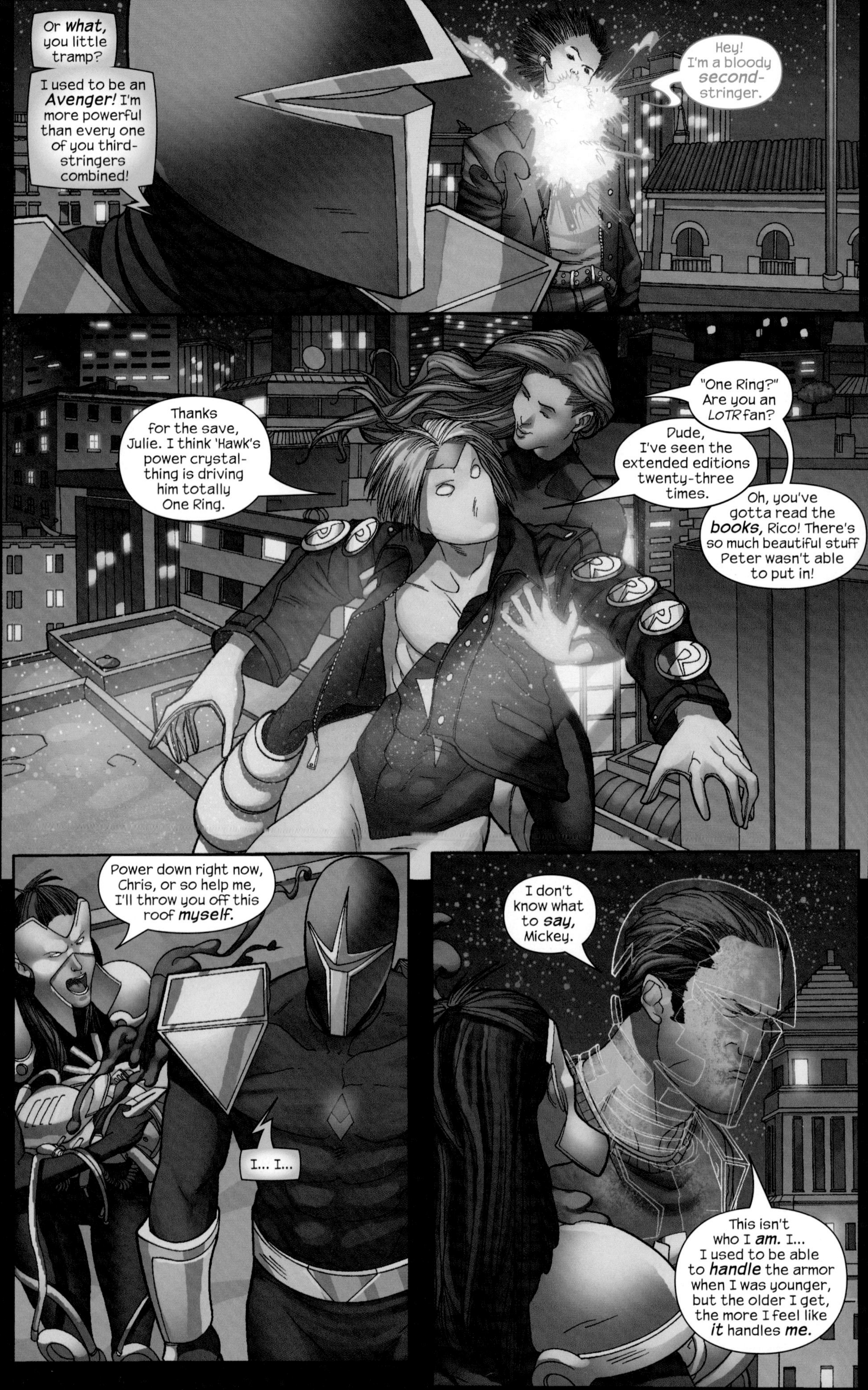
Or what, you little tramp?
I used to be an Avenger! I'm more powerful than every one of you third-stringers combined!
Hey! I'm a bloody second-stringer.
Thanks for the save, Julie. I think 'Hawk's power crystal-thing is driving him totally One Ring.
"One Ring?" Are you an LOTR fan?
Dude, I've seen the extended editions twenty-three times.
Oh, you've gotta read the books, Rico! There's so much beautiful stuff Peter wasn't able to put in!
Power down right now, Chris, or so help me, I'll throw you off this roof myself.
I... I...
I don't know what to say, Mickey.
This isn't who I am. I... I used to be able to handle the armor when I was younger, but the older I get, the more I feel like it handles me.

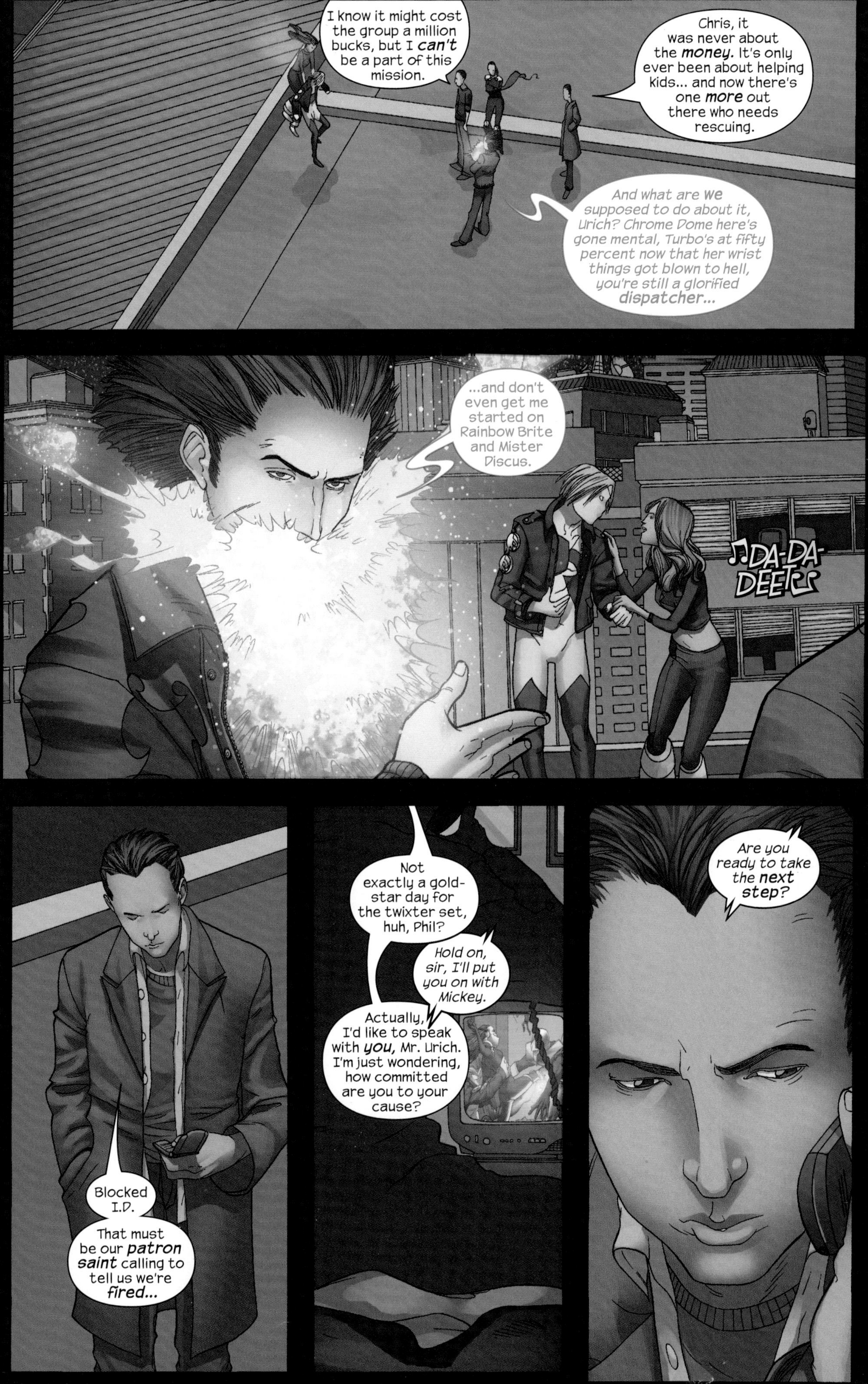
I know it might cost the group a million bucks, but I *can't* be a part of this mission.
Chris, it was never about the **money.** It's only ever been about helping kids... and now there's one **more** out there who needs rescuing.
*And what are **we** supposed to do about it, Urich? Chrome Dome here's gone mental, Turbo's at fifty percent now that her wrist things got blown to hell, you're still a glorified **dispatcher...***
...and don't even get me started on Rainbow Brite and Mister Discus.
DA-DA-DEET
Blocked I.D.
That must be our **patron saint** calling to tell us we're **fired...**
Not exactly a gold-star day for the twixter set, huh, Phil?
Hold on, sir, I'll put you on with Mickey.
Actually, I'd like to speak with **you,** Mr. Urich. I'm just wondering, how committed are you to your cause?
*Are you ready to take the **next step?***

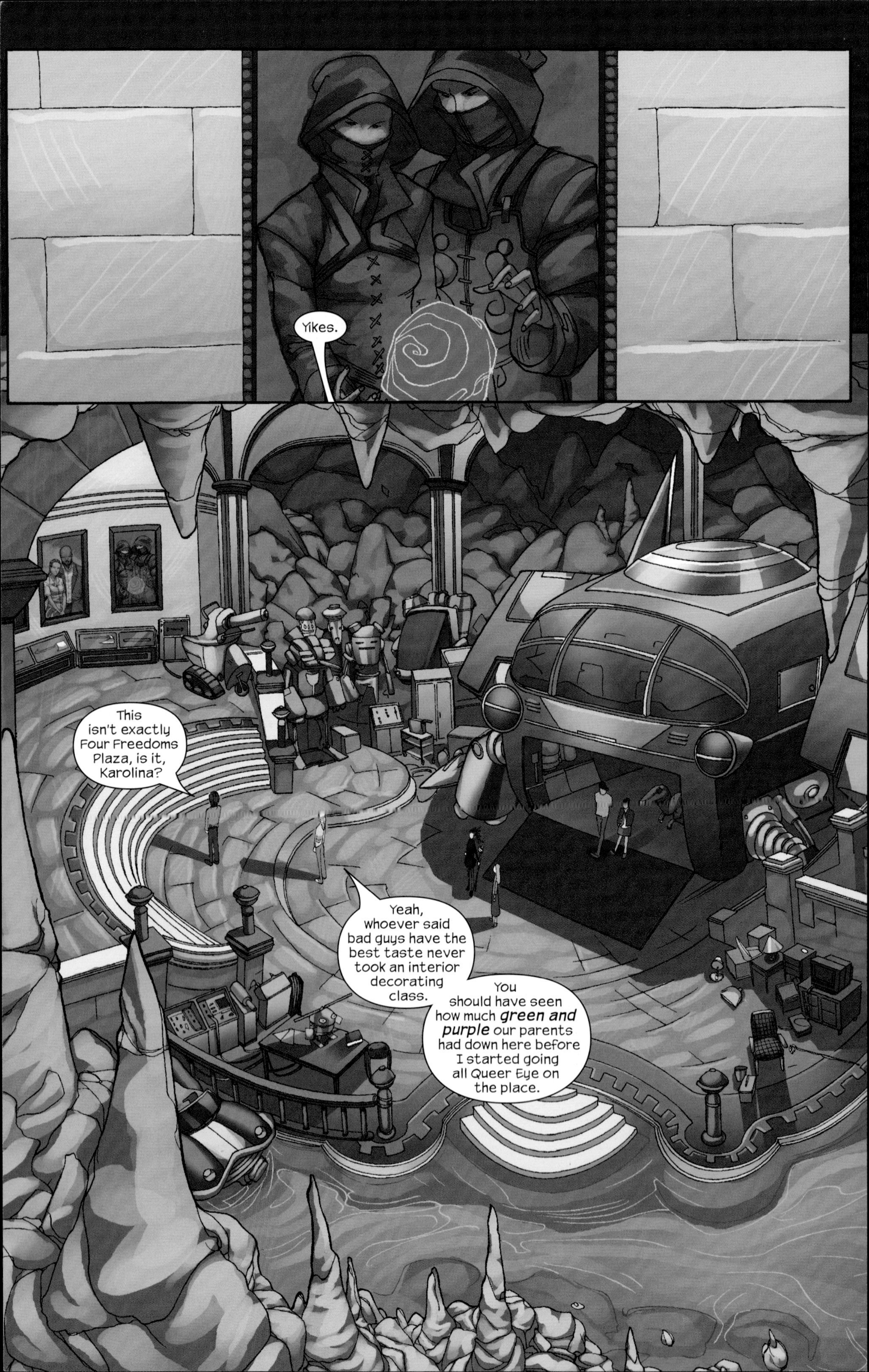
Yikes.
This isn't exactly Four Freedoms Plaza, is it, Karolina?
Yeah, whoever said bad guys have the best taste never took an interior decorating class.
You should have seen how much **green and purple** our parents had down here before I started going all Queer Eye on the place.

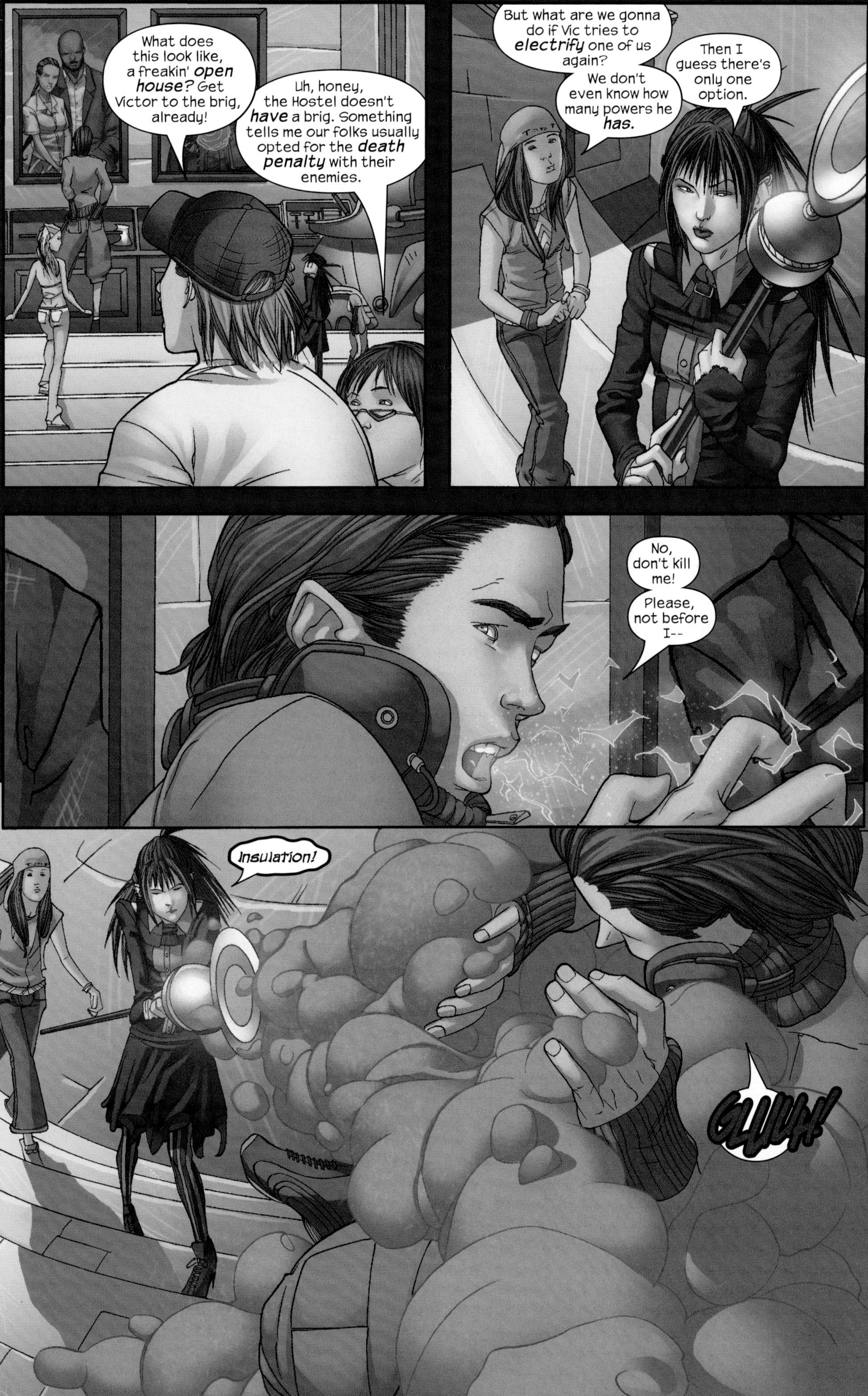
What does this look like, a freakin' *open house?* Get Victor to the brig, already!
Uh, honey, the Hostel doesn't *have* a brig. Something tells me our folks usually opted for the *death penalty* with their enemies.
But what are we gonna do if Vic tries to *electrify* one of us again?
We don't even know how many powers he *has.*
Then I guess there's only one option.
No, don't kill me!
Please, not before I--
Insulation!
GLUUH!

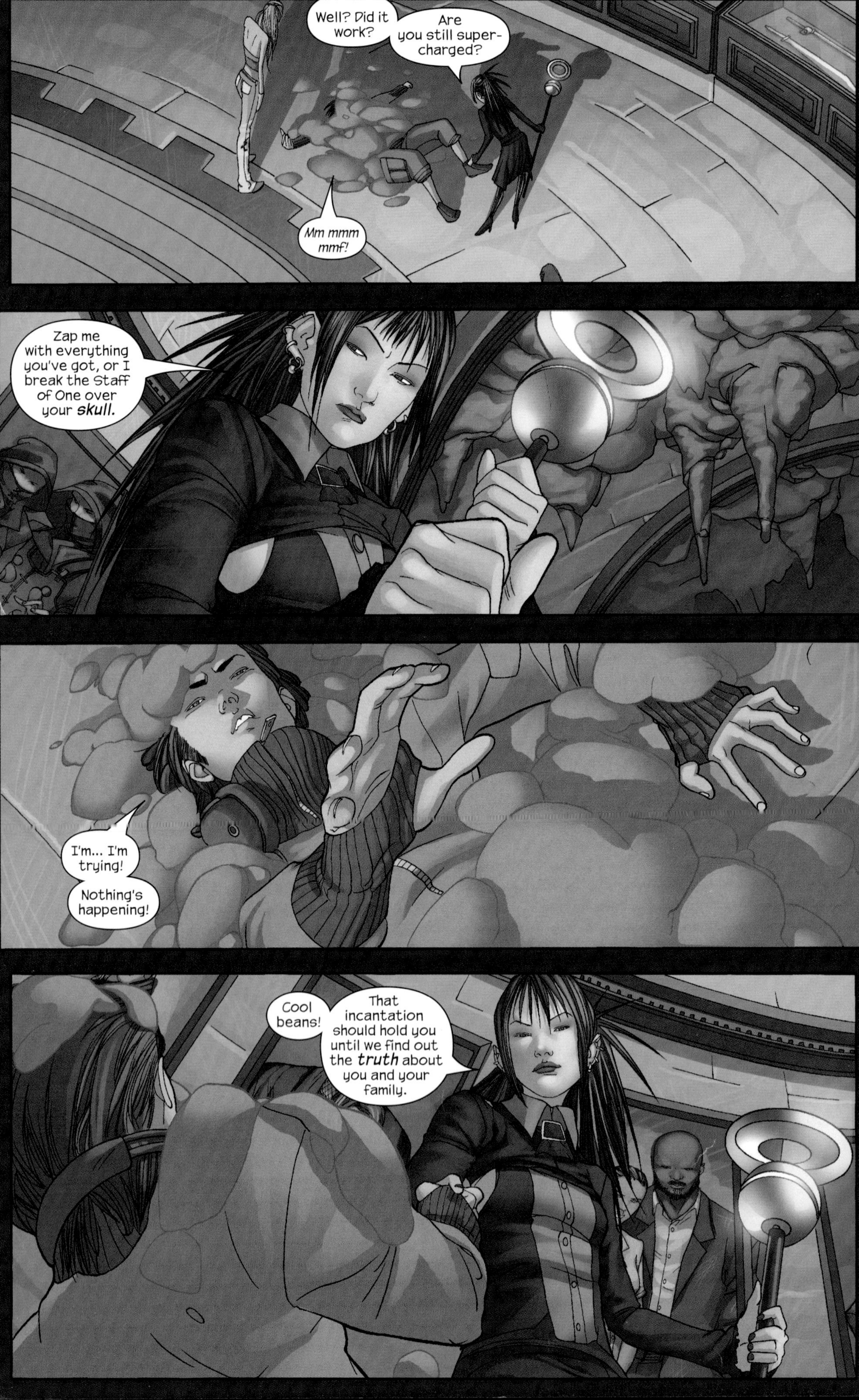
Well? Did it work?
Are you still super-charged?
Mm mmm mmf!
Zap me with everything you've got, or I break the Staff of One over your *skull.*
I'm... I'm trying!
Nothing's happening!
Cool beans!
That incantation should hold you until we find out the *truth* about you and your family.

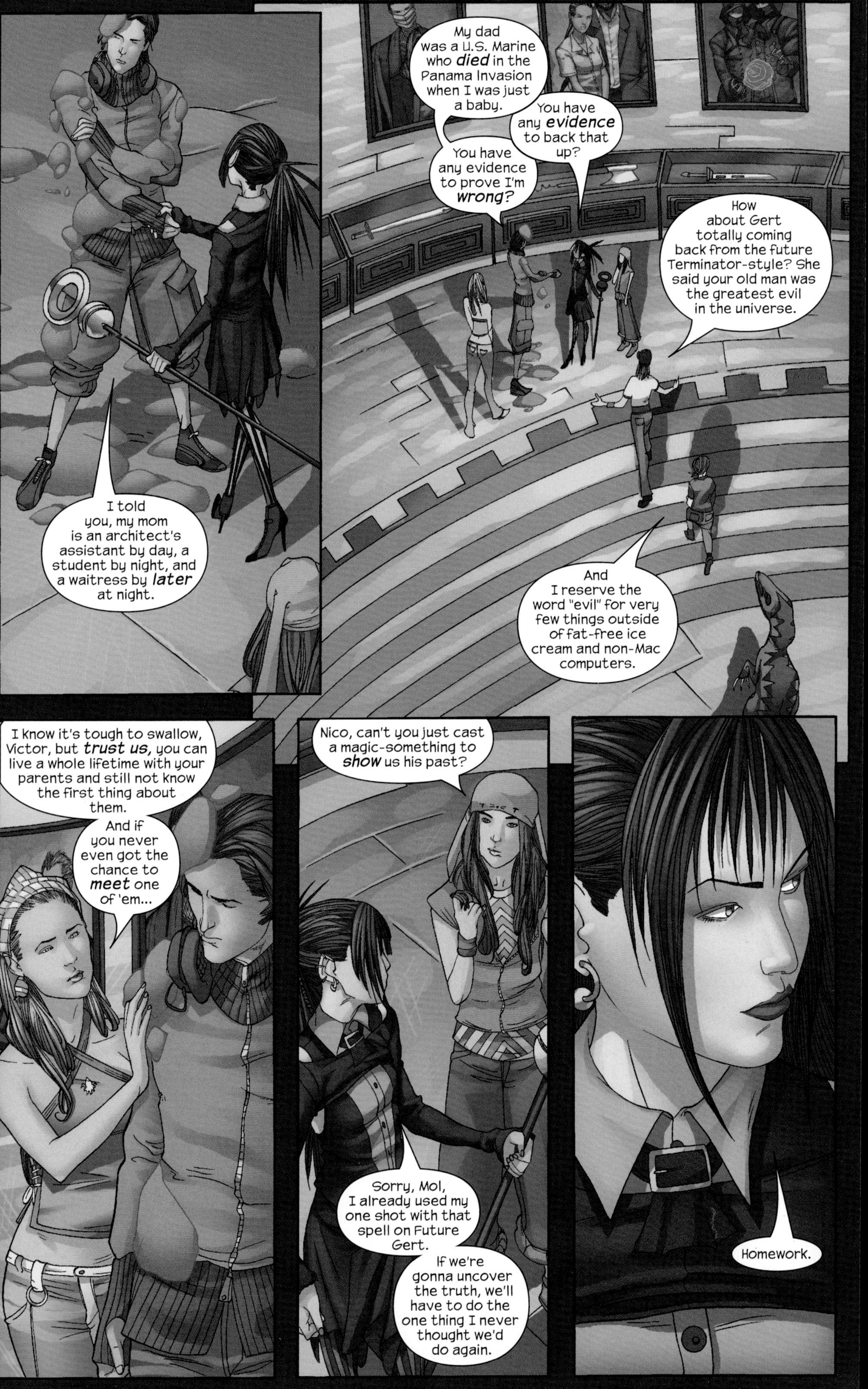
I told you, my mom is an architect's assistant by day, a student by night, and a waitress by *later* at night.
My dad was a U.S. Marine who *died* in the Panama Invasion when I was just a baby.
You have any evidence to prove I'm *wrong?*
You have any *evidence* to back that up?
How about Gert totally coming back from the future Terminator-style? She said your old man was the greatest evil in the universe.
And I reserve the word "evil" for very few things outside of fat-free ice cream and non-Mac computers.
I know it's tough to swallow, Victor, but *trust us,* you can live a whole lifetime with your parents and still not know the first thing about them.
And if you never even got the chance to *meet* one of 'em...
Nico, can't you just cast a magic-something to *show* us his past?
Sorry, Mol, I already used my one shot with that spell on Future Gert.
If we're gonna uncover the truth, we'll have to do the one thing I never thought we'd do again.
Homework.

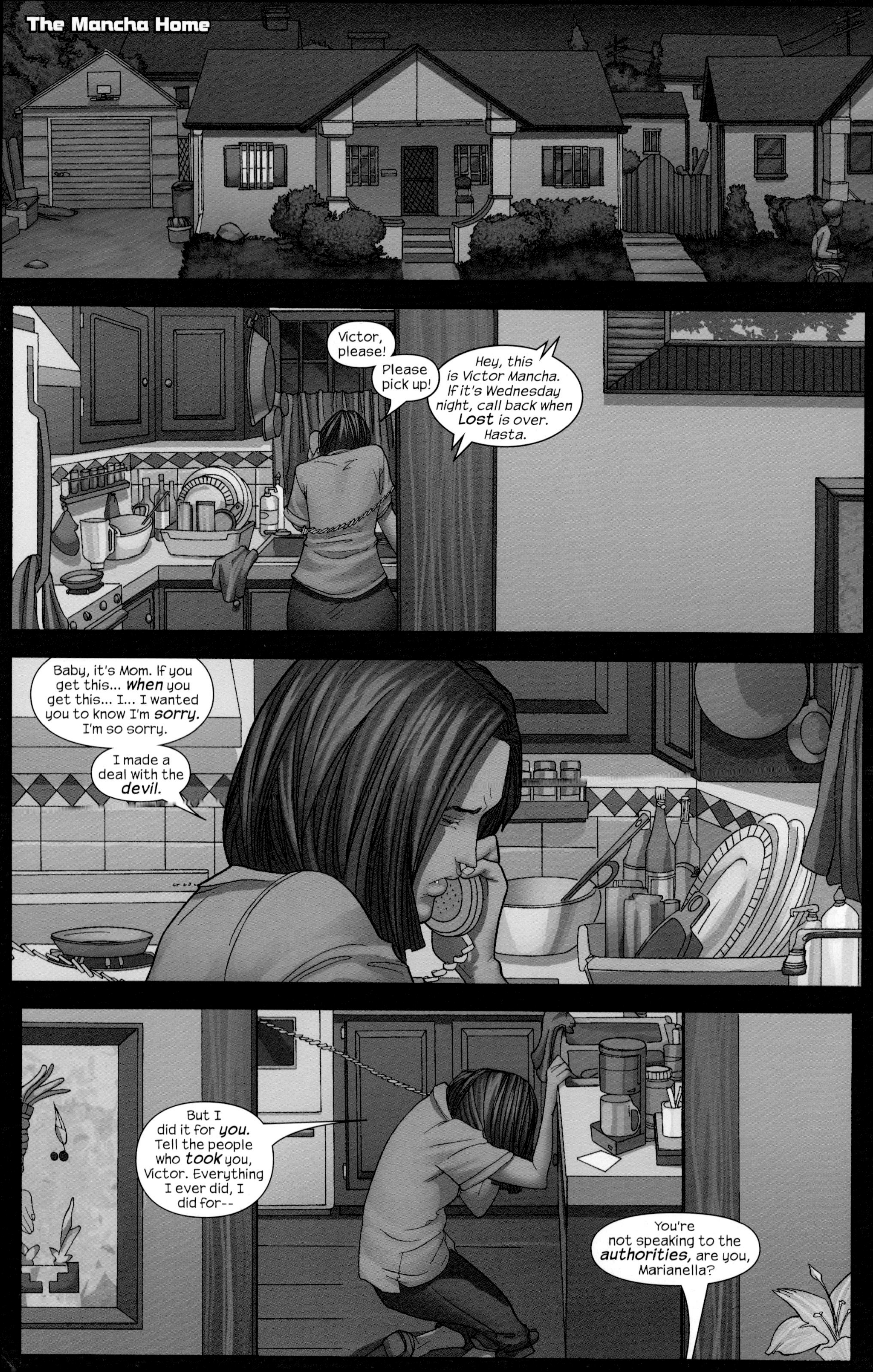
The Mancha Home
Victor, please!
Please pick up!
Hey, this is Victor Mancha. If it's Wednesday night, call back when Lost is over. Hasta.
Baby, it's Mom. If you get this... when you get this... I... I wanted you to know I'm sorry. I'm so sorry.
I made a deal with the devil.
But I did it for you. Tell the people who took you, Victor. Everything I ever did, I did for--
You're not speaking to the authorities, are you, Marianella?

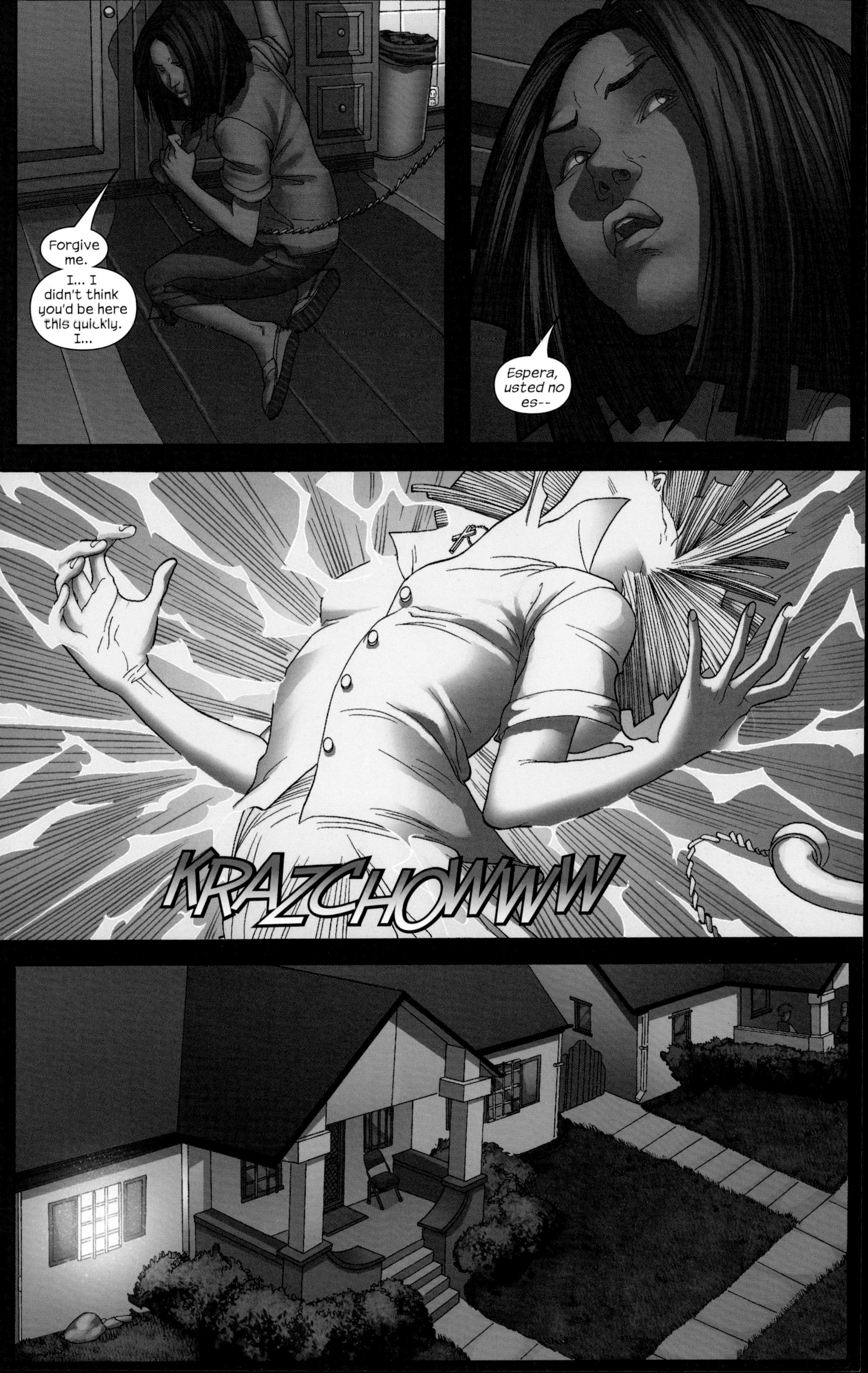
Forgive me.
I... I didn't think you'd be here this quickly. I...
Espera, usted no es--
KRAZCHOWWW

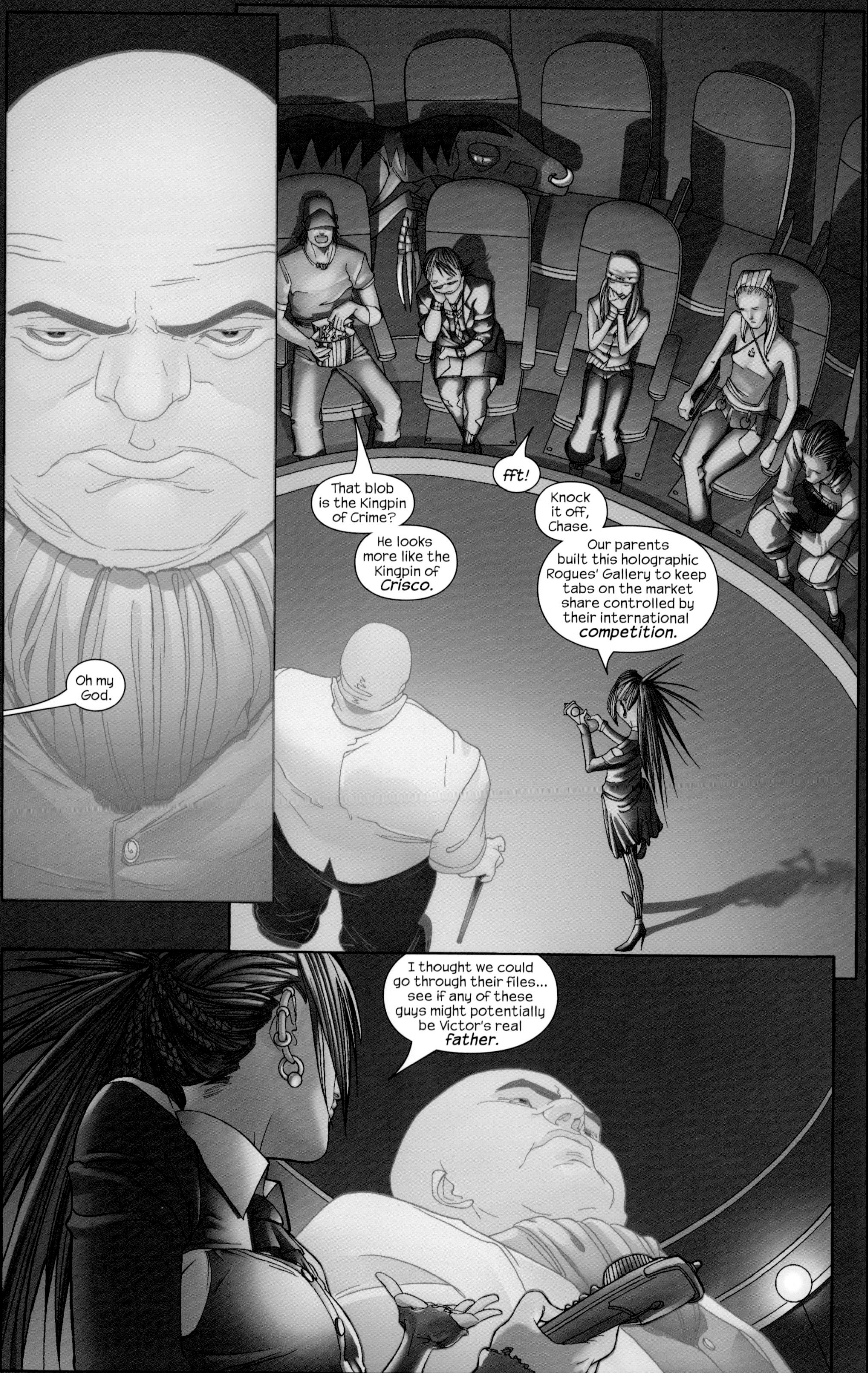
That blob is the Kingpin of Crime?
fft!
He looks more like the Kingpin of Crisco.
Knock it off, Chase.
Our parents built this holographic Rogues' Gallery to keep tabs on the market share controlled by their international competition.
Oh my God.
I thought we could go through their files... see if any of these guys might potentially be Victor's real father.

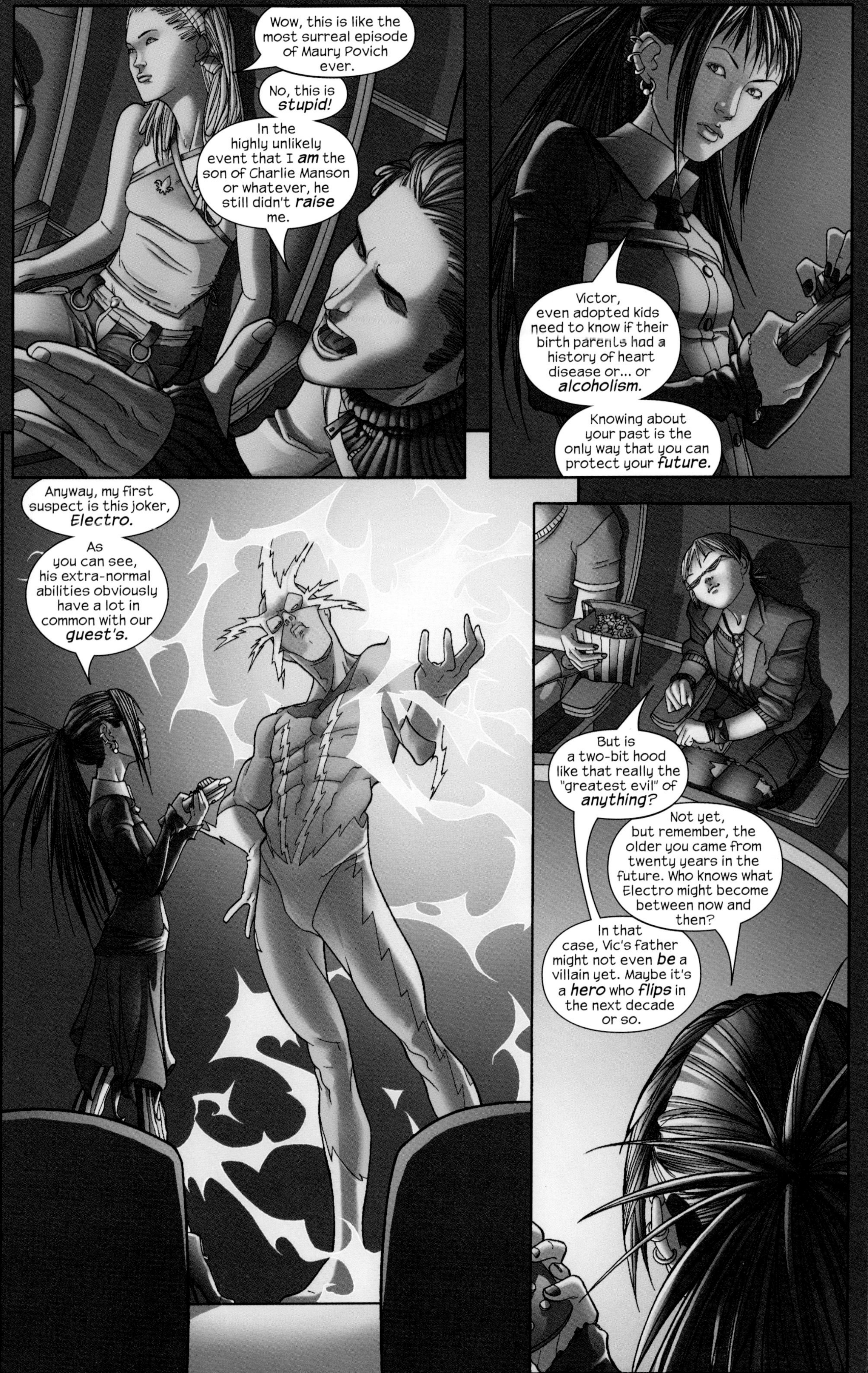
Wow, this is like the most surreal episode of Maury Povich ever.
No, this is *stupid!*
In the highly unlikely event that I *am* the son of Charlie Manson or whatever, he still didn't *raise* me.
Victor, even adopted kids need to know if their birth parents had a history of heart disease or... or *alcoholism.*
Knowing about your past is the only way that you can protect your *future.*
Anyway, my first suspect is this joker, *Electro.*
As you can see, his extra-normal abilities obviously have a lot in common with our *guest's.*
But is a two-bit hood like that really the "greatest evil" of *anything?*
Not yet, but remember, the older you came from twenty years in the future. Who knows what Electro might become between now and then?
In that case, Vic's father might not even *be* a villain yet. Maybe it's a *hero* who *flips* in the next decade or so.

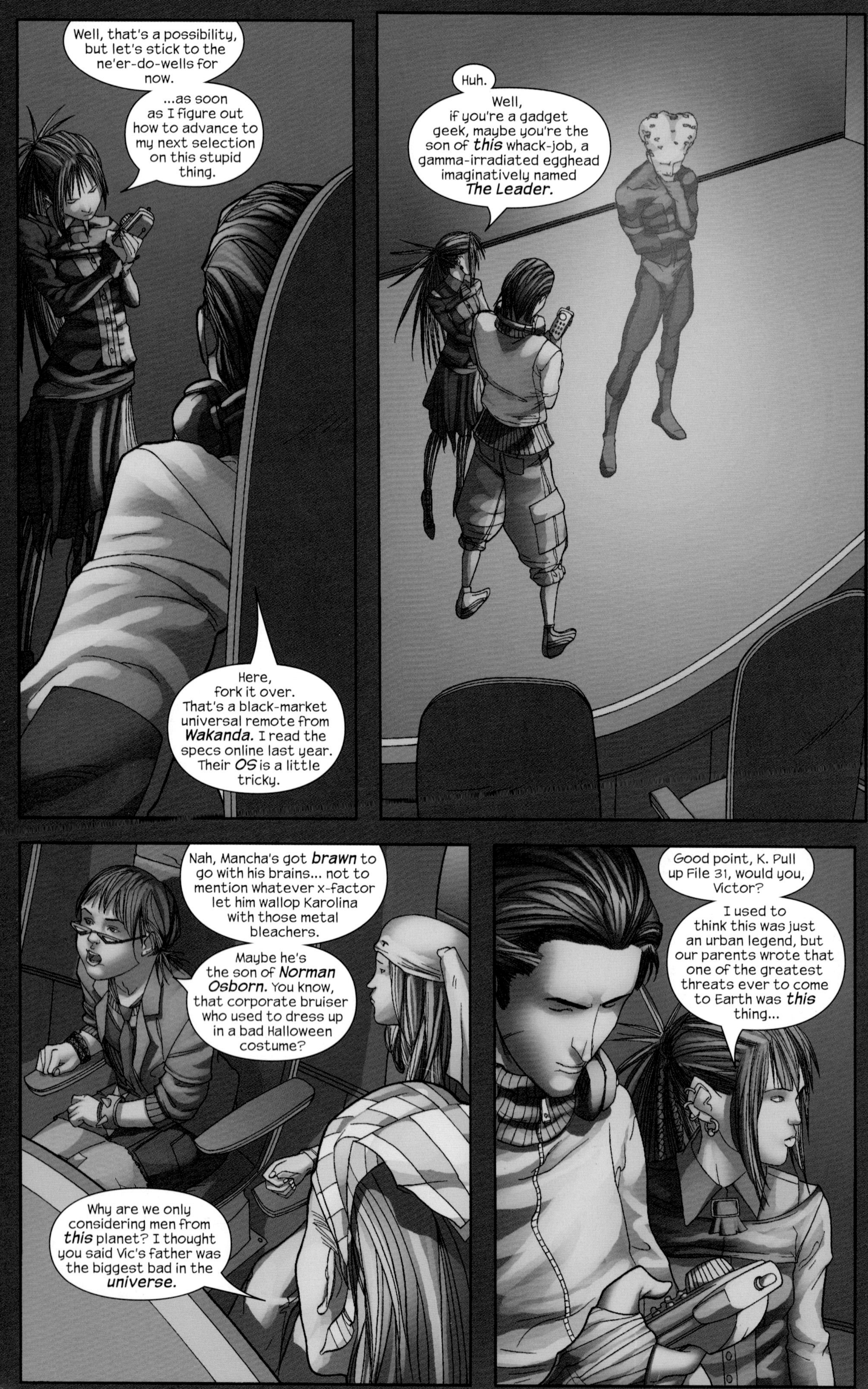
Well, that's a possibility, but let's stick to the ne'er-do-wells for now.
...as soon as I figure out how to advance to my next selection on this stupid thing.
Here, fork it over. That's a black-market universal remote from Wakanda. I read the specs online last year. Their OS is a little tricky.
Huh.
Well, if you're a gadget geek, maybe you're the son of this whack-job, a gamma-irradiated egghead imaginatively named The Leader.
Nah, Mancha's got brawn to go with his brains... not to mention whatever x-factor let him wallop Karolina with those metal bleachers.
Maybe he's the son of Norman Osborn. You know, that corporate bruiser who used to dress up in a bad Halloween costume?
Why are we only considering men from this planet? I thought you said Vic's father was the biggest bad in the universe.
Good point, K. Pull up File 31, would you, Victor?
I used to think this was just an urban legend, but our parents wrote that one of the greatest threats ever to come to Earth was this thing...

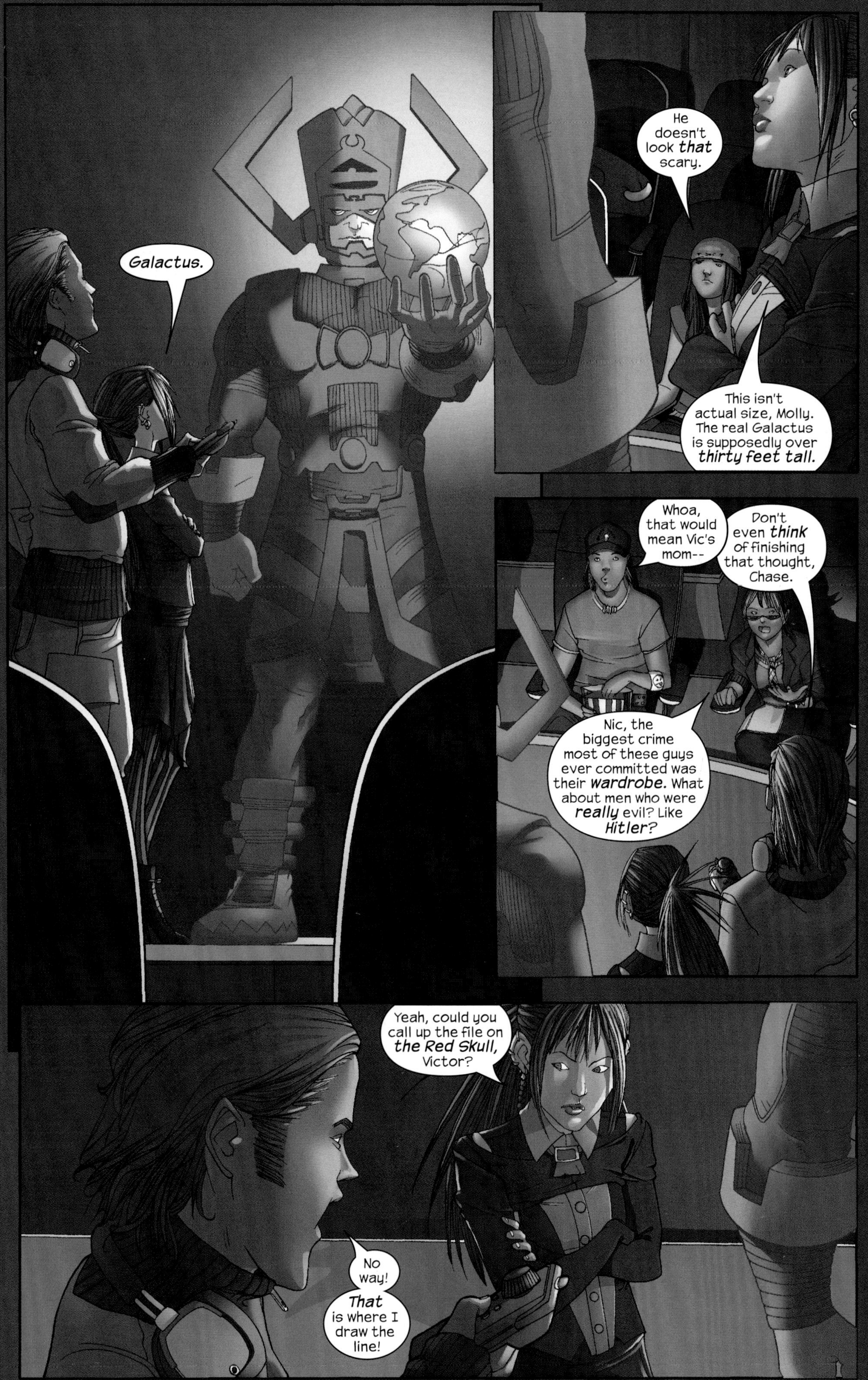
Galactus.
He doesn't look that scary.
This isn't actual size, Molly. The real Galactus is supposedly over thirty feet tall.
Whoa, that would mean Vic's mom--
Don't even think of finishing that thought, Chase.
Nic, the biggest crime most of these guys ever committed was their wardrobe. What about men who were really evil? Like Hitler?
Yeah, could you call up the file on the Red Skull, Victor?
No way!
That is where I draw the line!

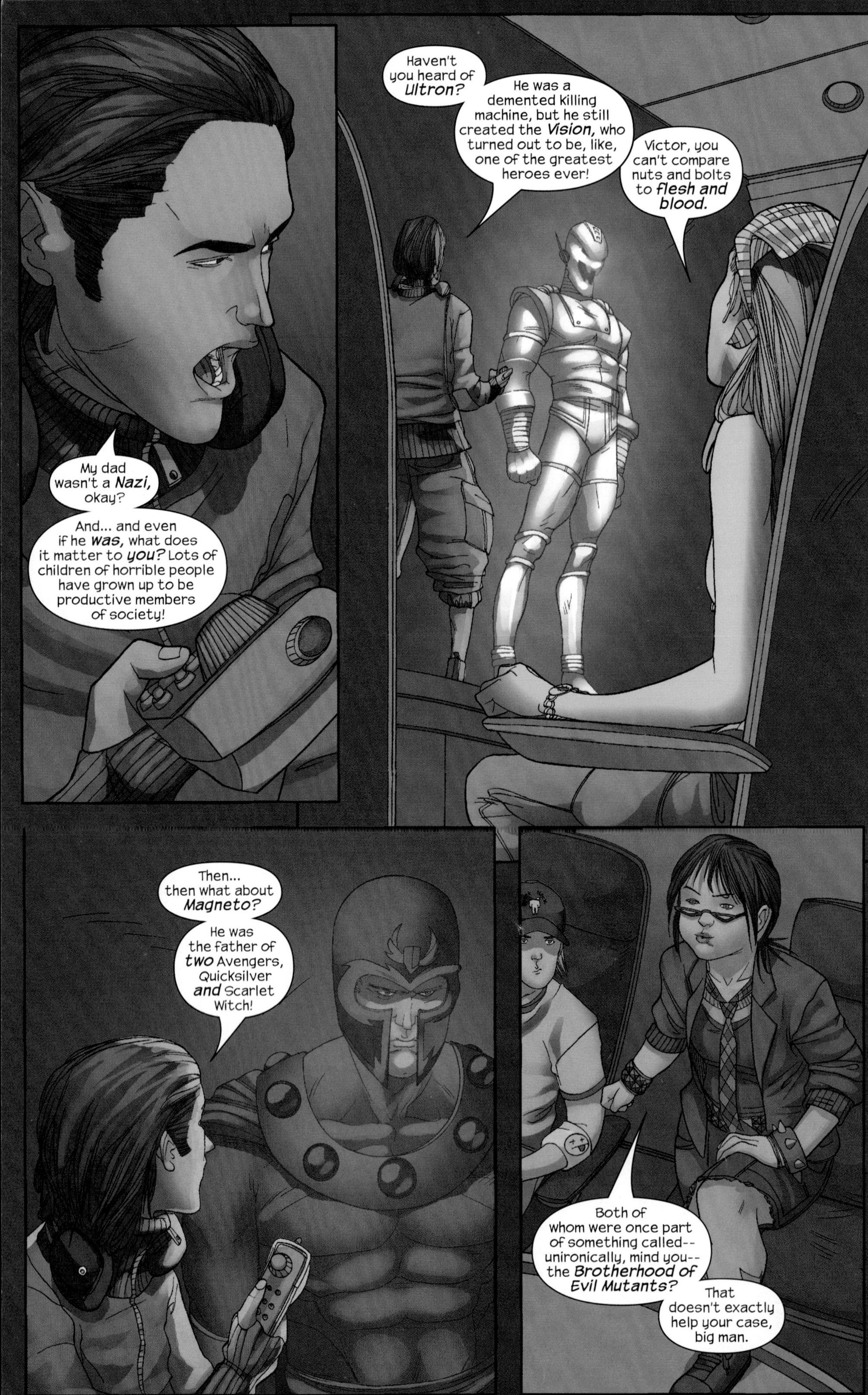
My dad wasn't a Nazi, okay?
And... and even if he was, what does it matter to you? Lots of children of horrible people have grown up to be productive members of society!
Haven't you heard of Ultron?
He was a demented killing machine, but he still created the Vision, who turned out to be, like, one of the greatest heroes ever!
Victor, you can't compare nuts and bolts to flesh and blood.
Then... then what about Magneto?
He was the father of two Avengers, Quicksilver and Scarlet Witch!
Both of whom were once part of something called-- unironically, mind you-- the Brotherhood of Evil Mutants?
That doesn't exactly help your case, big man.

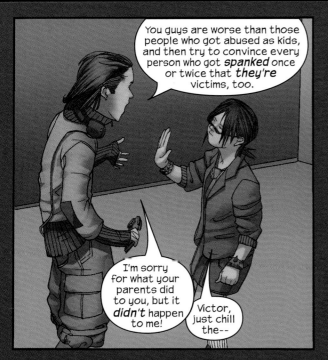

You guys are worse than those people who got abused as kids, and then try to convince every person who got *spanked* once or twice that *they're* victims, too.

I'm sorry for what your parents did to you, but it *didn't* happen to me!

Victor, just chill the--

No! You're all gonna do exactly as I say, or I... I blow this chick's *head* off!

Gert!

Let her *go!*

Relax, people.

He's a powerless kid holding a *remote control*.

I... I flipped this thing's vibranium battery when you weren't looking. If I press one button while the polarity is reversed, it... it won't be *pretty*.

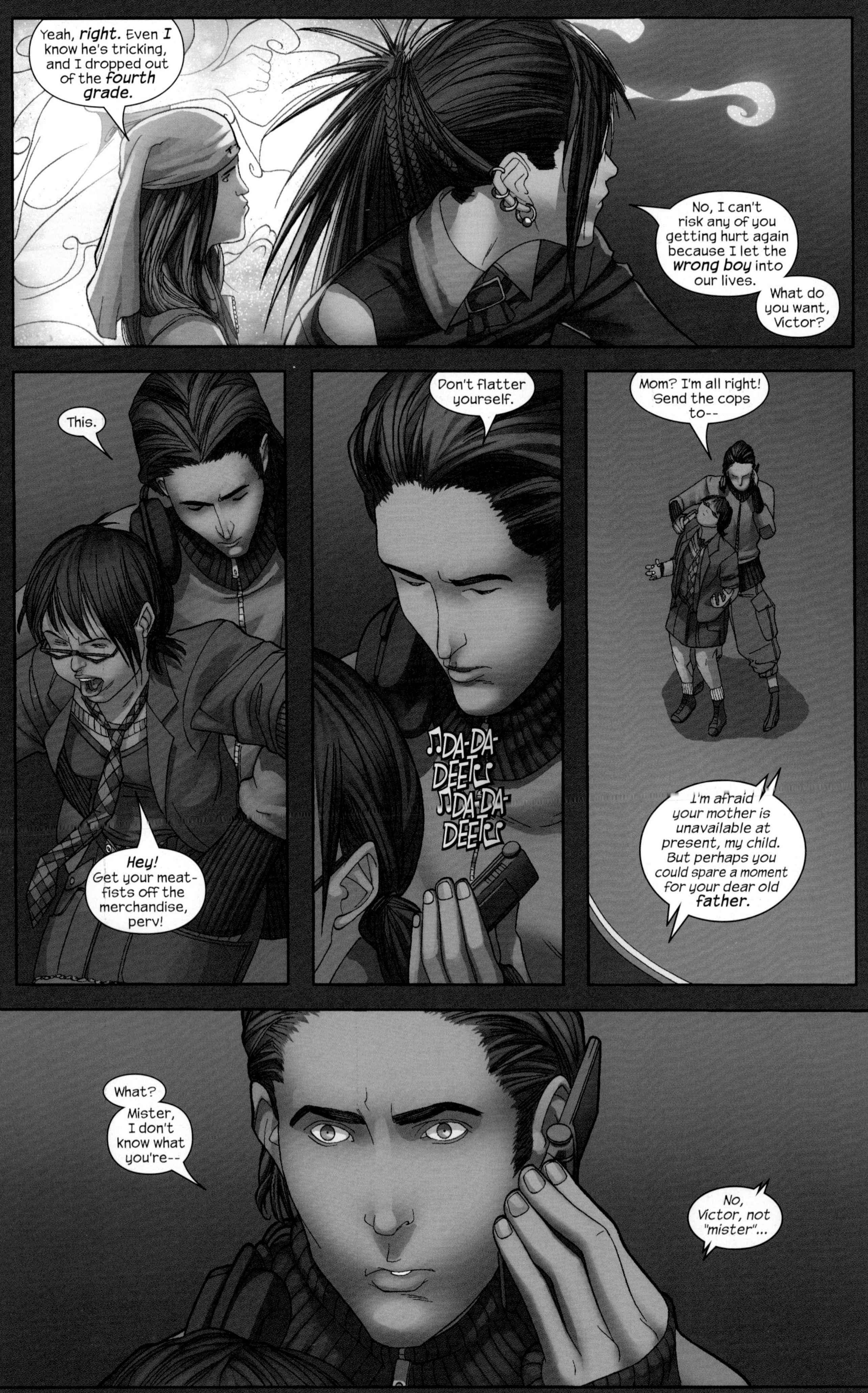
Yeah, right. Even I know he's tricking, and I dropped out of the fourth grade.
No, I can't risk any of you getting hurt again because I let the wrong boy into our lives.
What do you want, Victor?
This.
Hey! Get your meat-fists off the merchandise, perv!
Don't flatter yourself.
DA-DA-DEET DA-DA-DEET
Mom? I'm all right! Send the cops to--
I'm afraid your mother is unavailable at present, my child. But perhaps you could spare a moment for your dear old father.
What? Mister, I don't know what you're--
No, Victor, not "mister"...

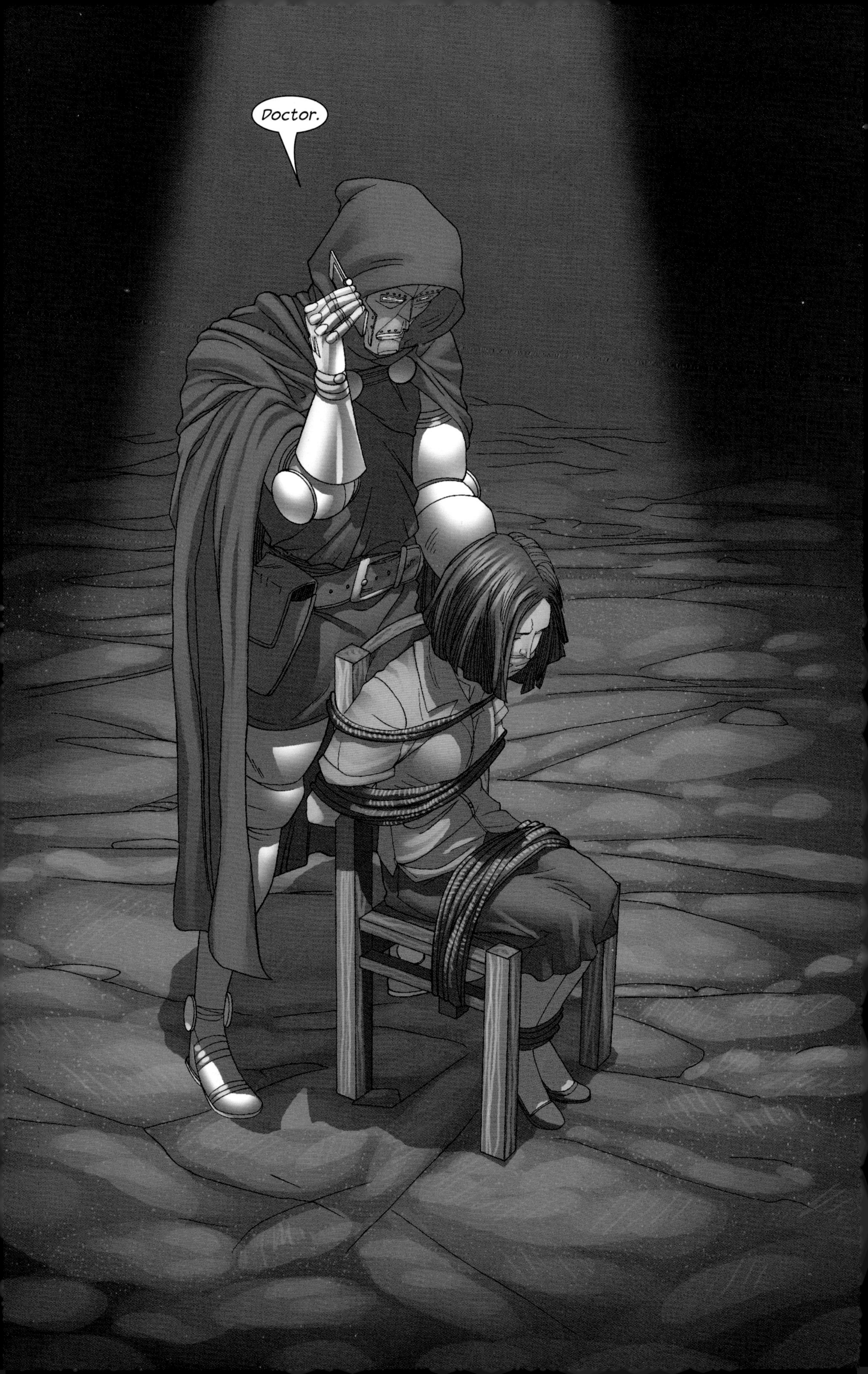
Doctor.

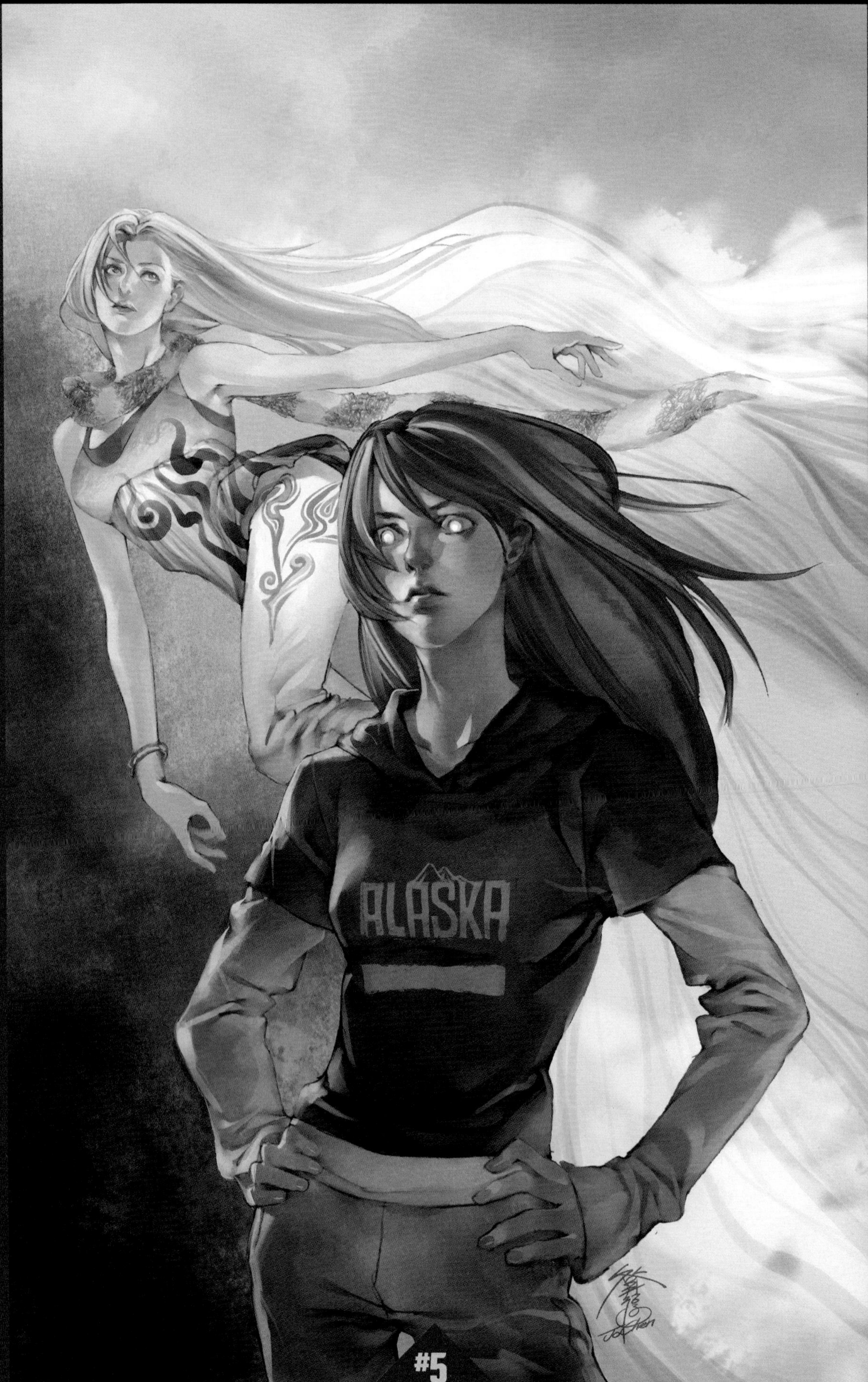
ALASKA
#5

TRUE BELIEVERS PART 5

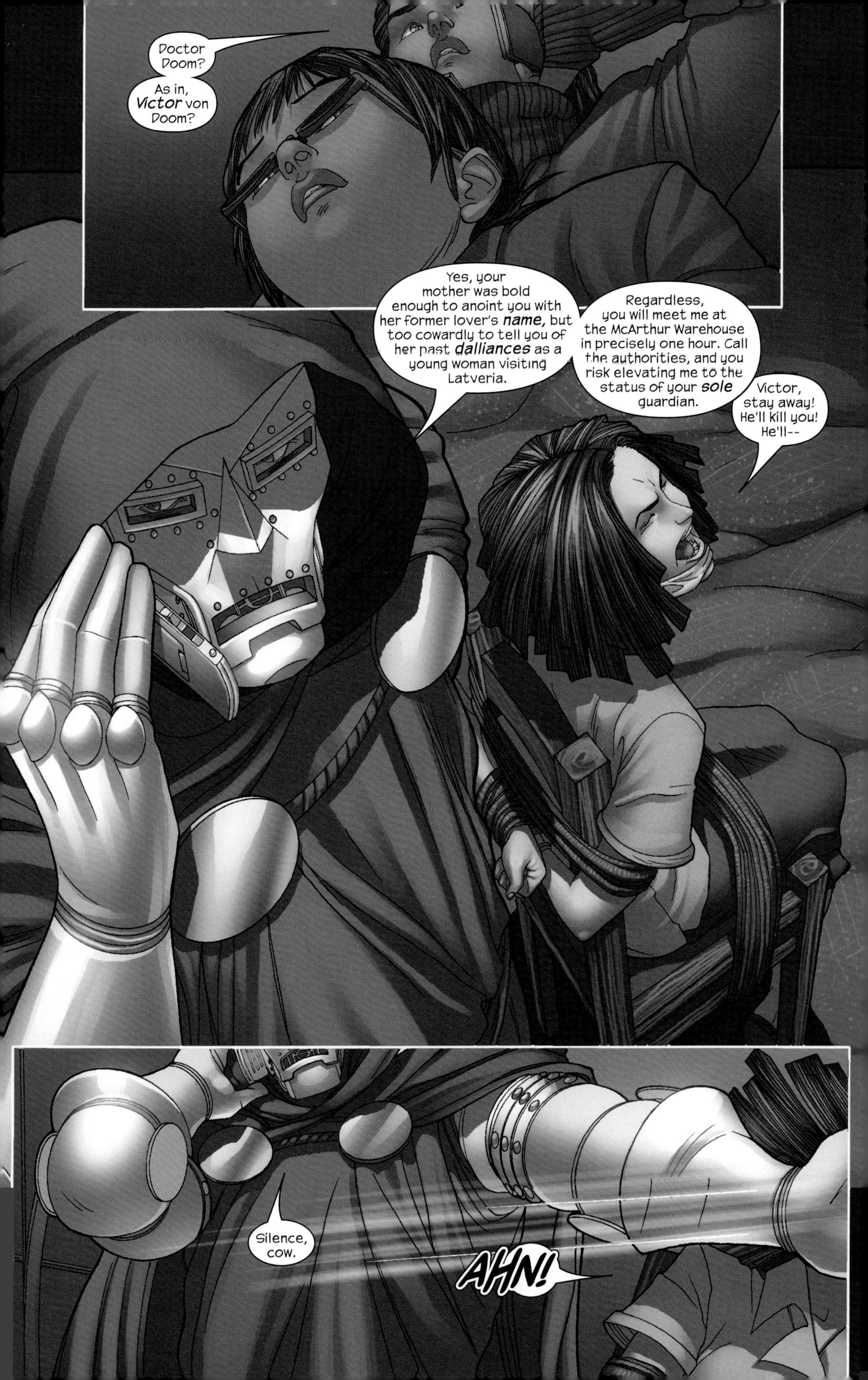
Doctor Doom?
As in, Victor von Doom?
Yes, your mother was bold enough to anoint you with her former lover's name, but too cowardly to tell you of her past dalliances as a young woman visiting Latveria.
Regardless, you will meet me at the McArthur Warehouse in precisely one hour. Call the authorities, and you risk elevating me to the status of your sole guardian.
Victor, stay away! He'll kill you! He'll--
Silence, cow.
AHN!

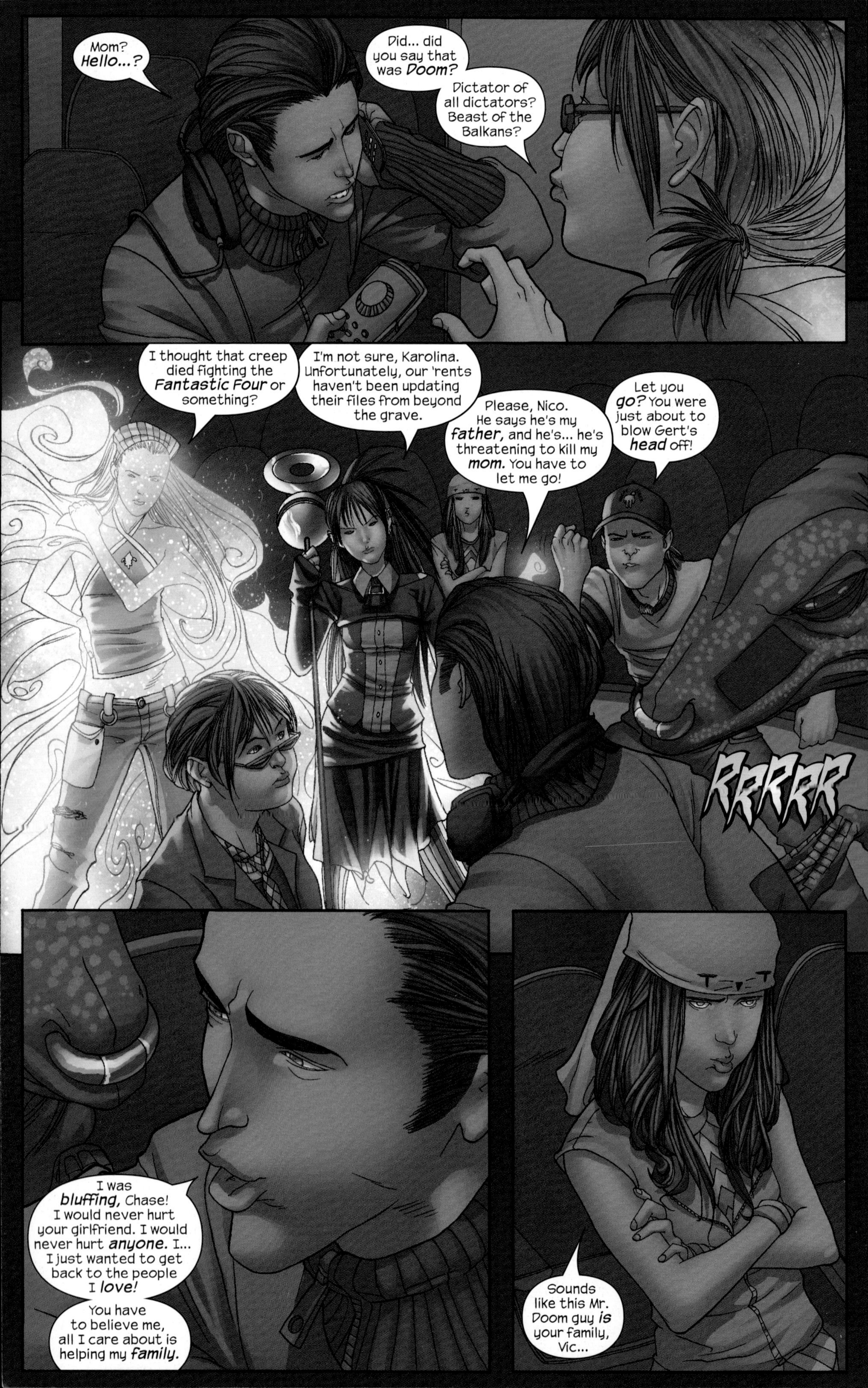
Mom? Hello...?
Did... did you say that was Doom?
Dictator of all dictators? Beast of the Balkans?
I thought that creep died fighting the Fantastic Four or something?
I'm not sure, Karolina. Unfortunately, our 'rents haven't been updating their files from beyond the grave.
Please, Nico. He says he's my father, and he's... he's threatening to kill my mom. You have to let me go!
Let you go? You were just about to blow Gert's head off!
RRRRR
I was bluffing, Chase! I would never hurt your girlfriend. I would never hurt anyone. I... I just wanted to get back to the people I love!
You have to believe me, all I care about is helping my family.
Sounds like this Mr. Doom guy is your family, Vic...

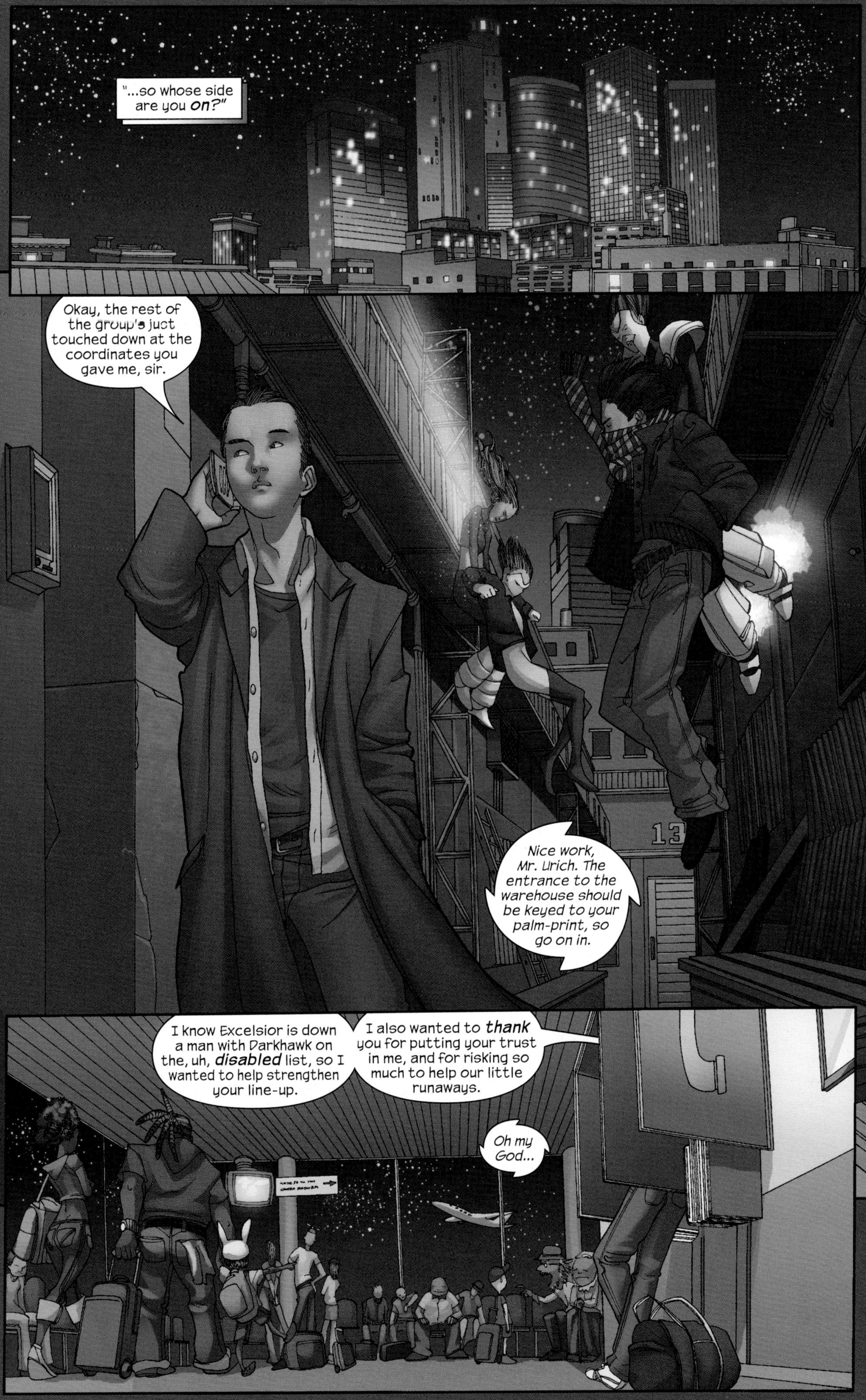
"...so whose side are you *on*?"
Okay, the rest of the group's just touched down at the coordinates you gave me, sir.
Nice work, Mr. Urich. The entrance to the warehouse should be keyed to your palm-print, so go on in.
I know Excelsior is down a man with Darkhawk on the, uh, *disabled* list, so I wanted to help strengthen your line-up.
I also wanted to *thank* you for putting your trust in me, and for risking so much to help our little runaways.
Oh my God...

What... what *is* it?

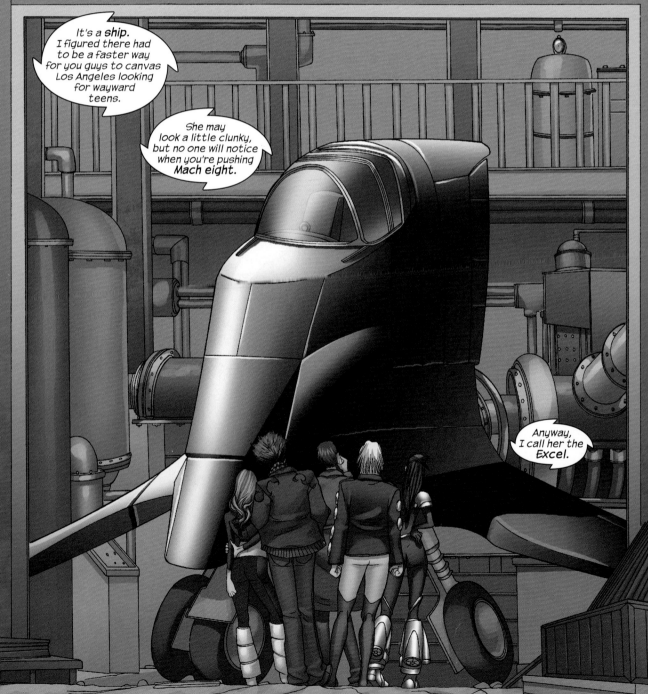

It's a *ship*. I figured there had to be a faster way for you guys to canvas Los Angeles looking for wayward teens.

She may look a little clunky, but no one will notice when you're pushing *Mach eight*.

Anyway, I call her the *Excel*.

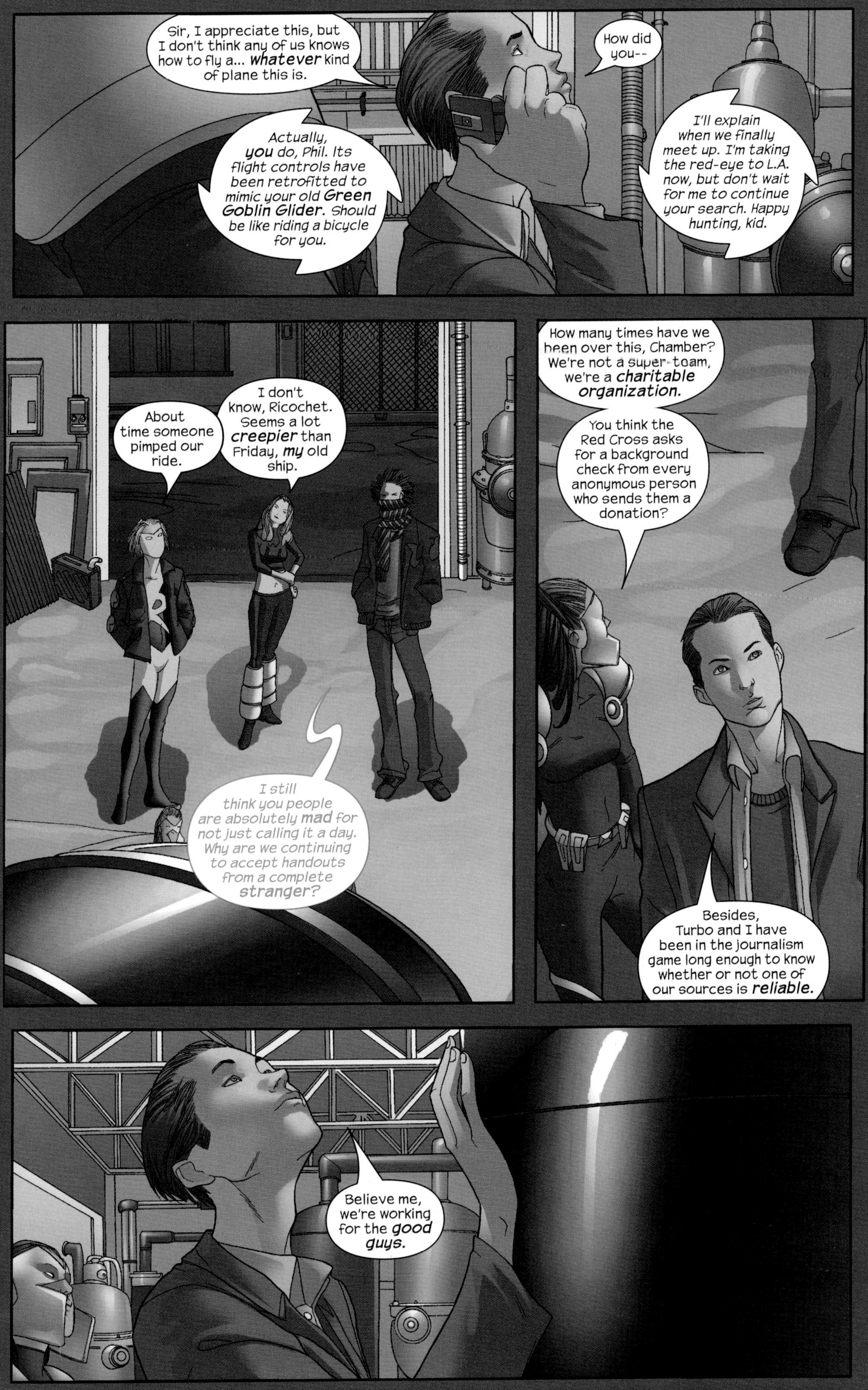
Sir, I appreciate this, but I don't think any of us knows how to fly a... whatever kind of plane this is.
Actually, you do, Phil. Its flight controls have been retrofitted to mimic your old Green Goblin Glider. Should be like riding a bicycle for you.
How did you--
I'll explain when we finally meet up. I'm taking the red-eye to L.A. now, but don't wait for me to continue your search. Happy hunting, kid.
About time someone pimped our ride.
I don't know, Ricochet. Seems a lot creepier than Friday, my old ship.
I still think you people are absolutely mad for not just calling it a day. Why are we continuing to accept handouts from a complete stranger?
How many times have we been over this, Chamber? We're not a super-team, we're a charitable organization.
You think the Red Cross asks for a background check from every anonymous person who sends them a donation?
Besides, Turbo and I have been in the journalism game long enough to know whether or not one of our sources is reliable.
Believe me, we're working for the good guys.

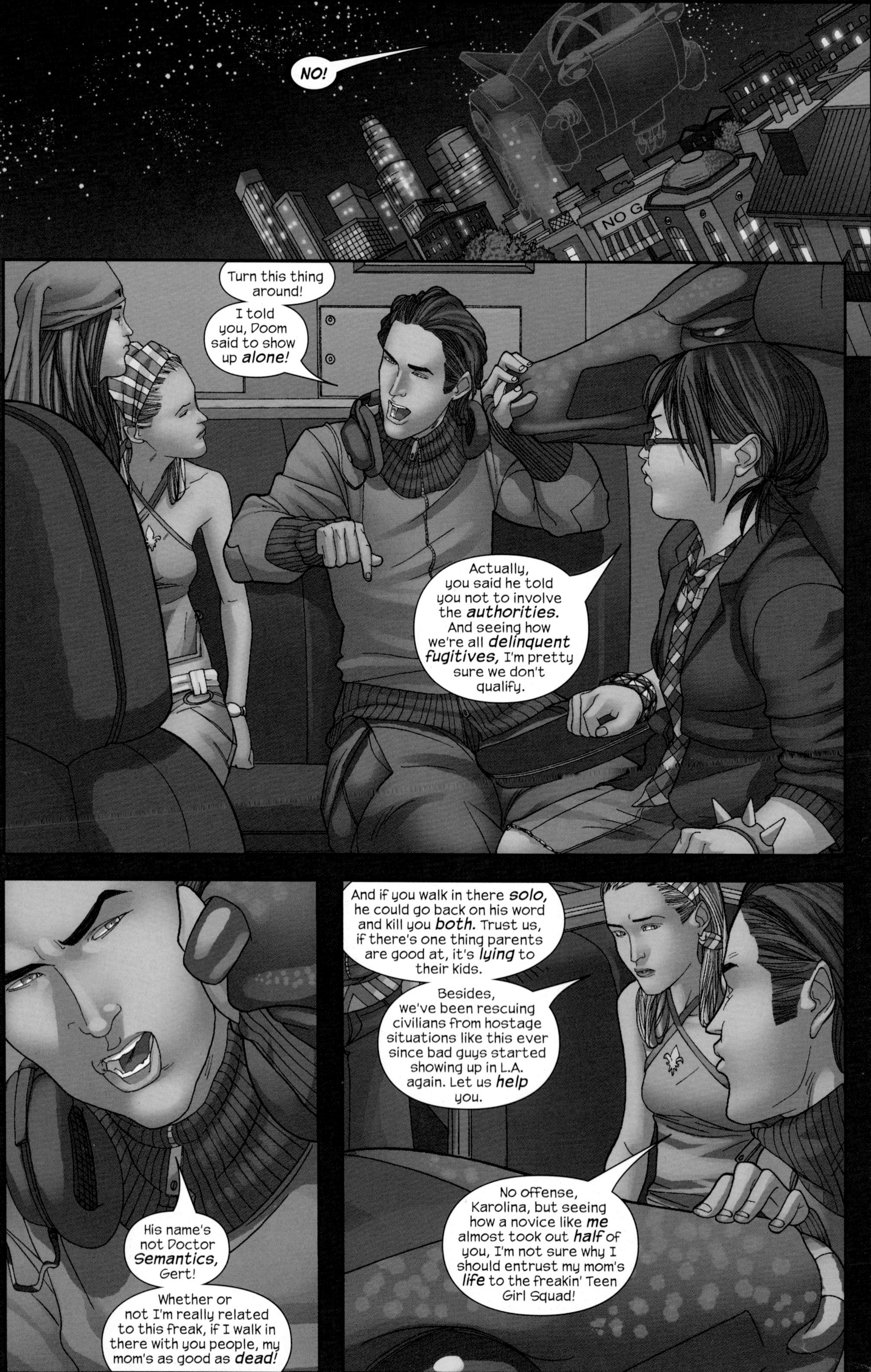
NO!
Turn this thing around!
I told you, Doom said to show up *alone!*
Actually, you said he told you not to involve the *authorities.* And seeing how we're all *delinquent fugitives,* I'm pretty sure we don't qualify.
His name's not Doctor *Semantics,* Gert!
Whether or not I'm really related to this freak, if I walk in there with you people, my mom's as good as *dead!*
And if you walk in there *solo,* he could go back on his word and kill you *both.* Trust us, if there's one thing parents are good at, it's *lying* to their kids.
Besides, we've been rescuing civilians from hostage situations like this ever since bad guys started showing up in L.A. again. Let us *help* you.
No offense, Karolina, but seeing how a novice like *me* almost took out *half* of you, I'm not sure why I should entrust my mom's *life* to the freakin' Teen Girl Squad!

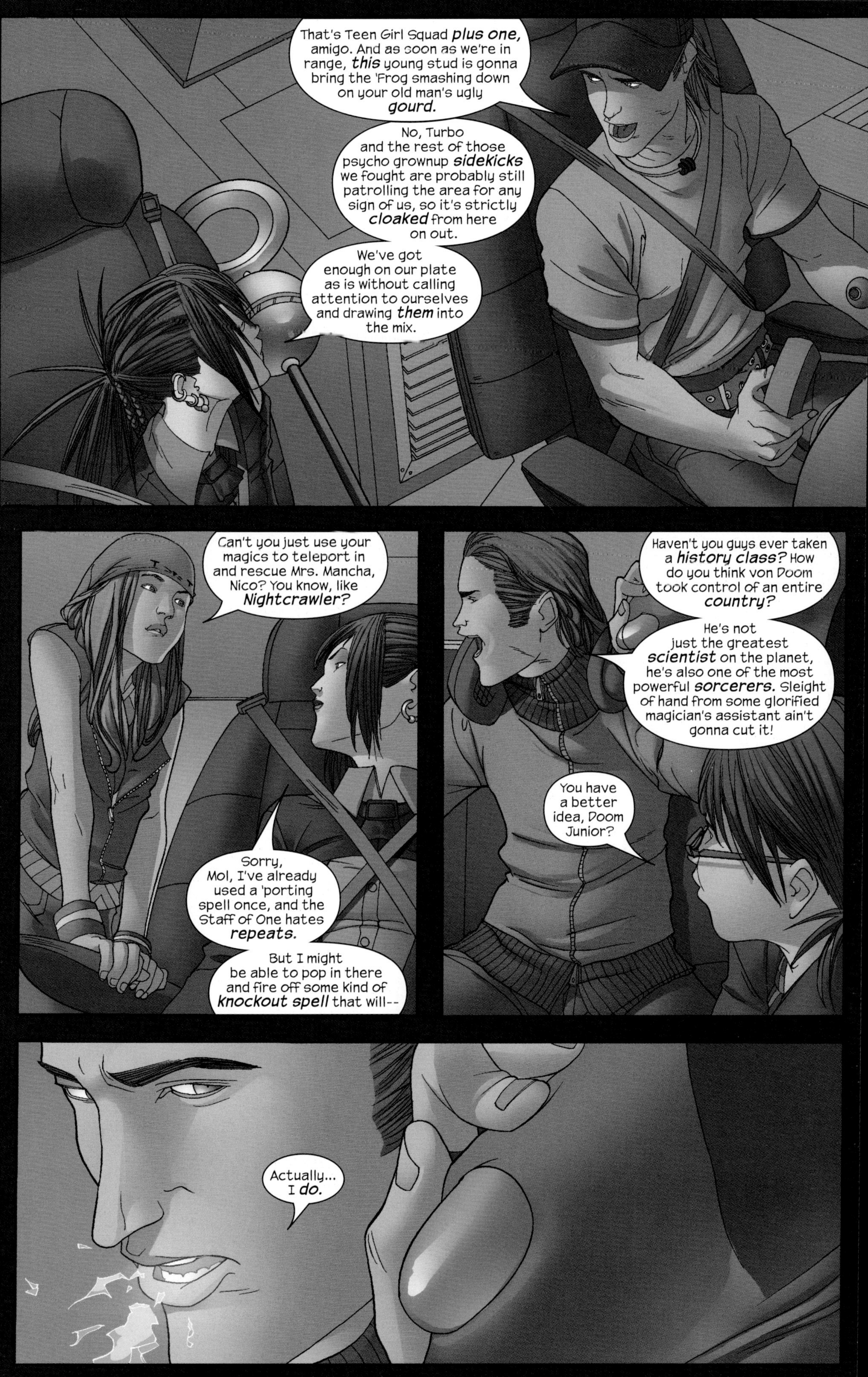
That's Teen Girl Squad plus one, amigo. And as soon as we're in range, this young stud is gonna bring the 'Frog smashing down on your old man's ugly gourd.
No, Turbo and the rest of those psycho grownup sidekicks we fought are probably still patrolling the area for any sign of us, so it's strictly cloaked from here on out.
We've got enough on our plate as is without calling attention to ourselves and drawing them into the mix.
Can't you just use your magics to teleport in and rescue Mrs. Mancha, Nico? You know, like Nightcrawler?
Sorry, Mol, I've already used a 'porting spell once, and the Staff of One hates repeats.
But I might be able to pop in there and fire off some kind of knockout spell that will--
Haven't you guys ever taken a history class? How do you think von Doom took control of an entire country?
He's not just the greatest scientist on the planet, he's also one of the most powerful sorcerers. Sleight of hand from some glorified magician's assistant ain't gonna cut it!
You have a better idea, Doom Junior?
Actually... I do.

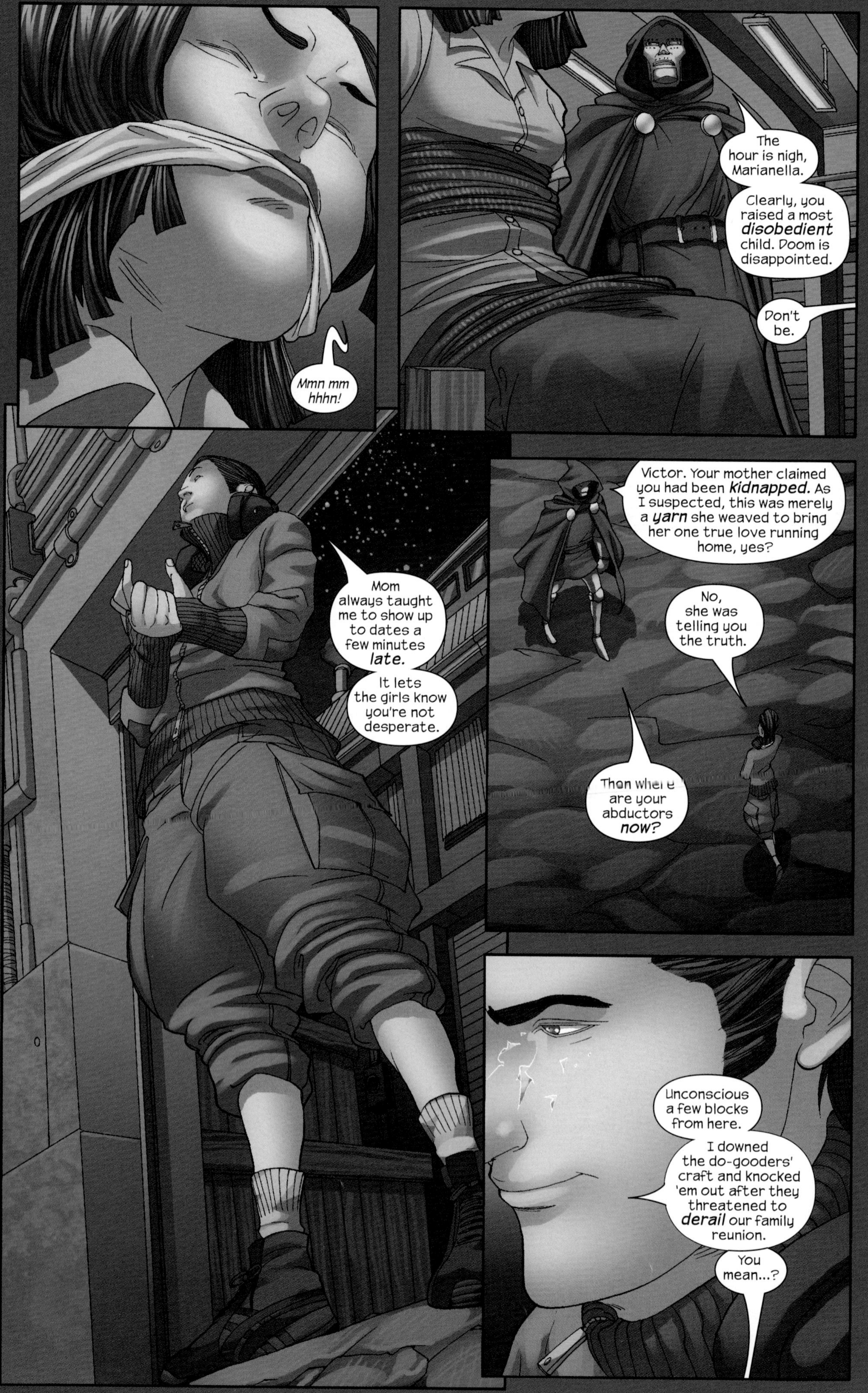

Mmn mm hhhn!
The hour is nigh, Marianella.
Clearly, you raised a most *disobedient* child. Doom is disappointed.
Don't be.
Mom always taught me to show up to dates a few minutes *late.*
It lets the girls know you're not desperate.
Victor. Your mother claimed you had been *kidnapped.* As I suspected, this was merely a *yarn* she weaved to bring her one true love running home, yes?
No, she was telling you the truth.
Then where are your abductors *now?*
Unconscious a few blocks from here.
I downed the do-gooders' craft and knocked 'em out after they threatened to *derail* our family reunion.
You mean...?

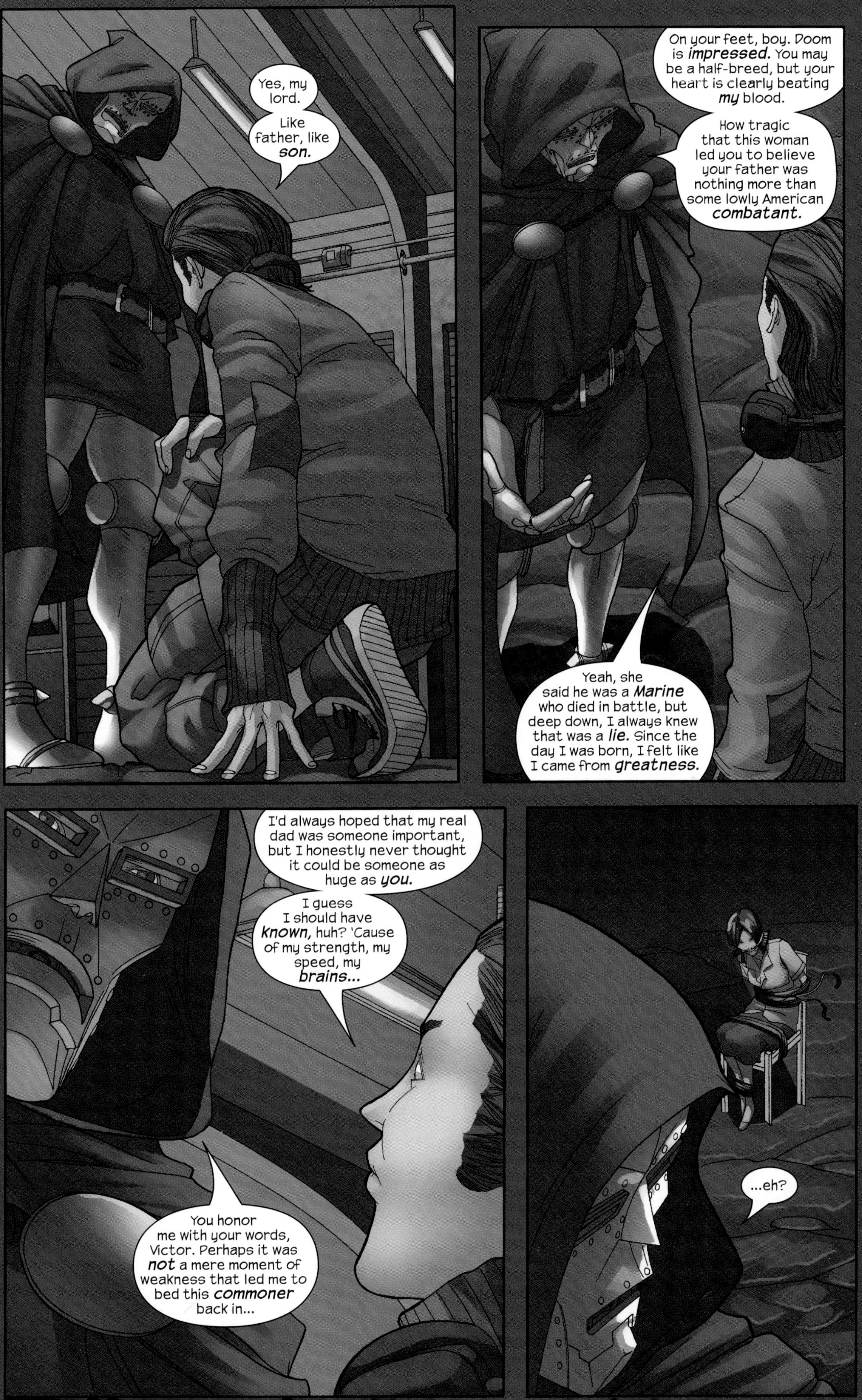

Yes, my lord.
Like father, like *son.*
On your feet, boy. Doom is *impressed.* You may be a half-breed, but your heart is clearly beating *my* blood.
How tragic that this woman led you to believe your father was nothing more than some lowly American *combatant.*
Yeah, she said he was a *Marine* who died in battle, but deep down, I always knew that was a *lie.* Since the day I was born, I felt like I came from *greatness.*
I'd always hoped that my real dad was someone important, but I honestly never thought it could be someone as huge as *you.*
I guess I should have *known,* huh? 'Cause of my strength, my speed, my *brains...*
You honor me with your words, Victor. Perhaps it was *not* a mere moment of weakness that led me to bed this *commoner* back in...
...eh?

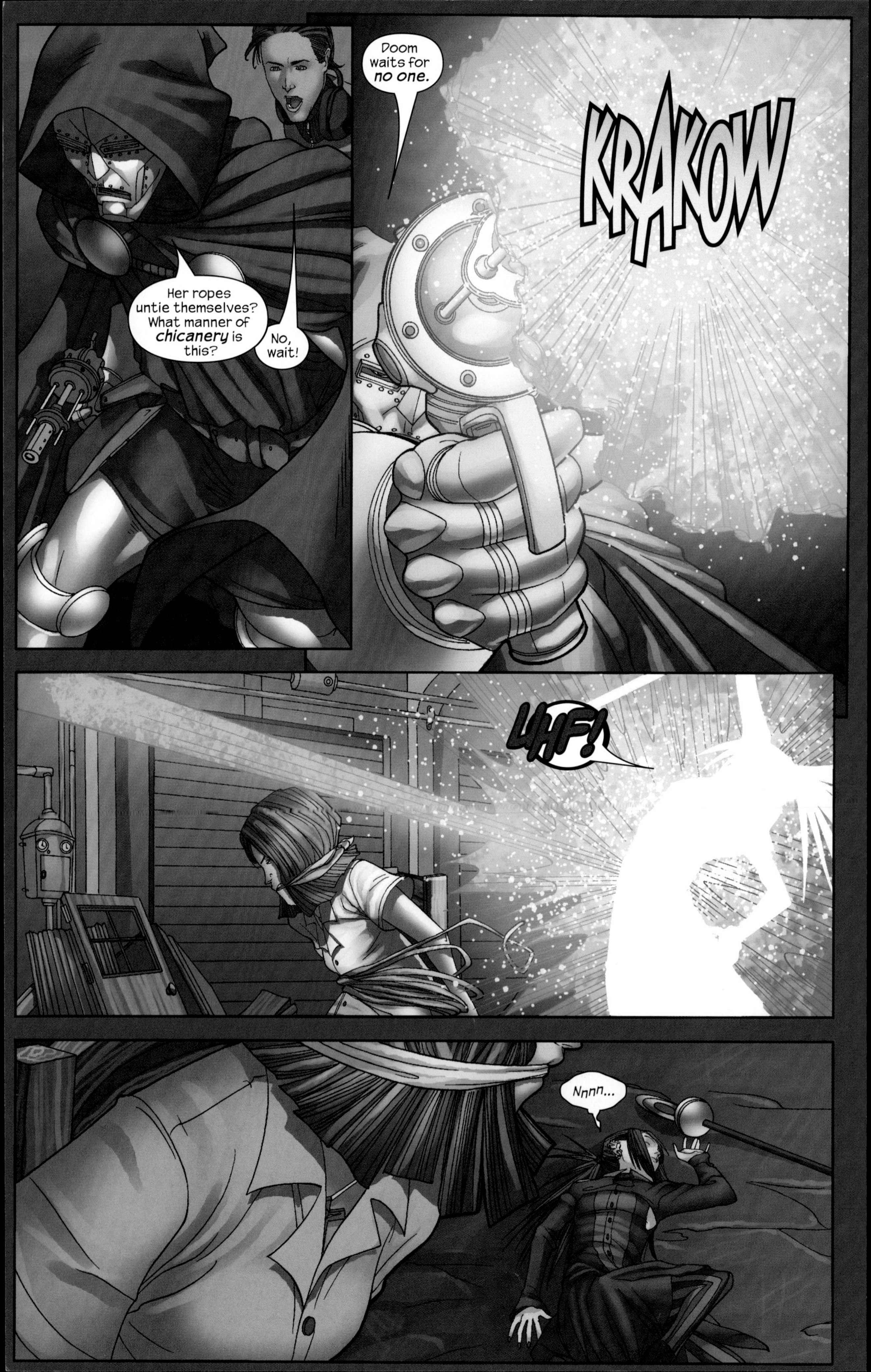

Her ropes untie themselves? What manner of *chicanery* is this?
No, wait!
Doom waits for *no one.*
KRAKOW
UHF!
Nnnn...

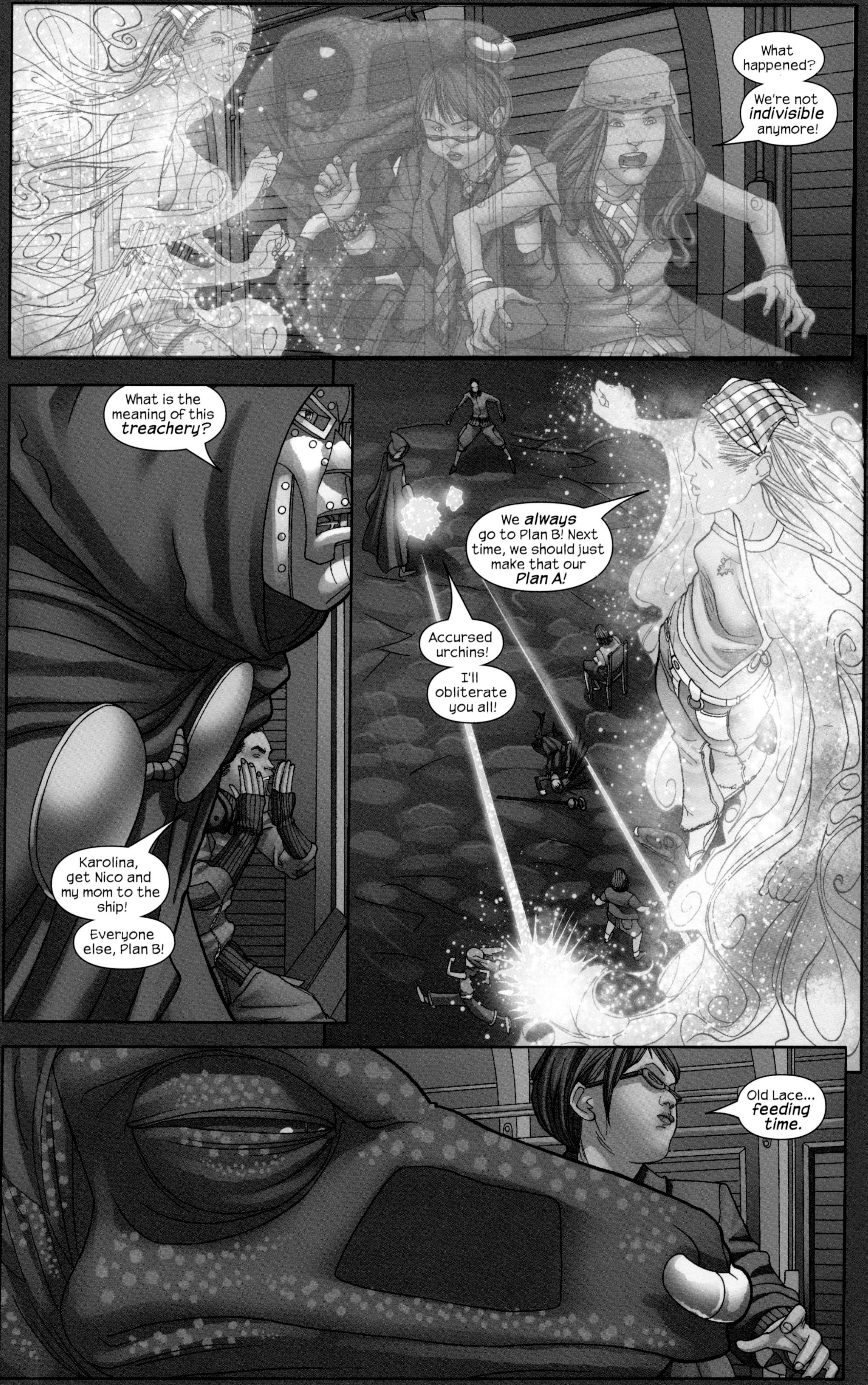
What happened?
We're not indivisible anymore!
What is the meaning of this treachery?
Karolina, get Nico and my mom to the ship!
Everyone else, Plan B!
We always go to Plan B! Next time, we should just make that our Plan A!
Accursed urchins!
I'll obliterate you all!
Old Lace... feeding time.

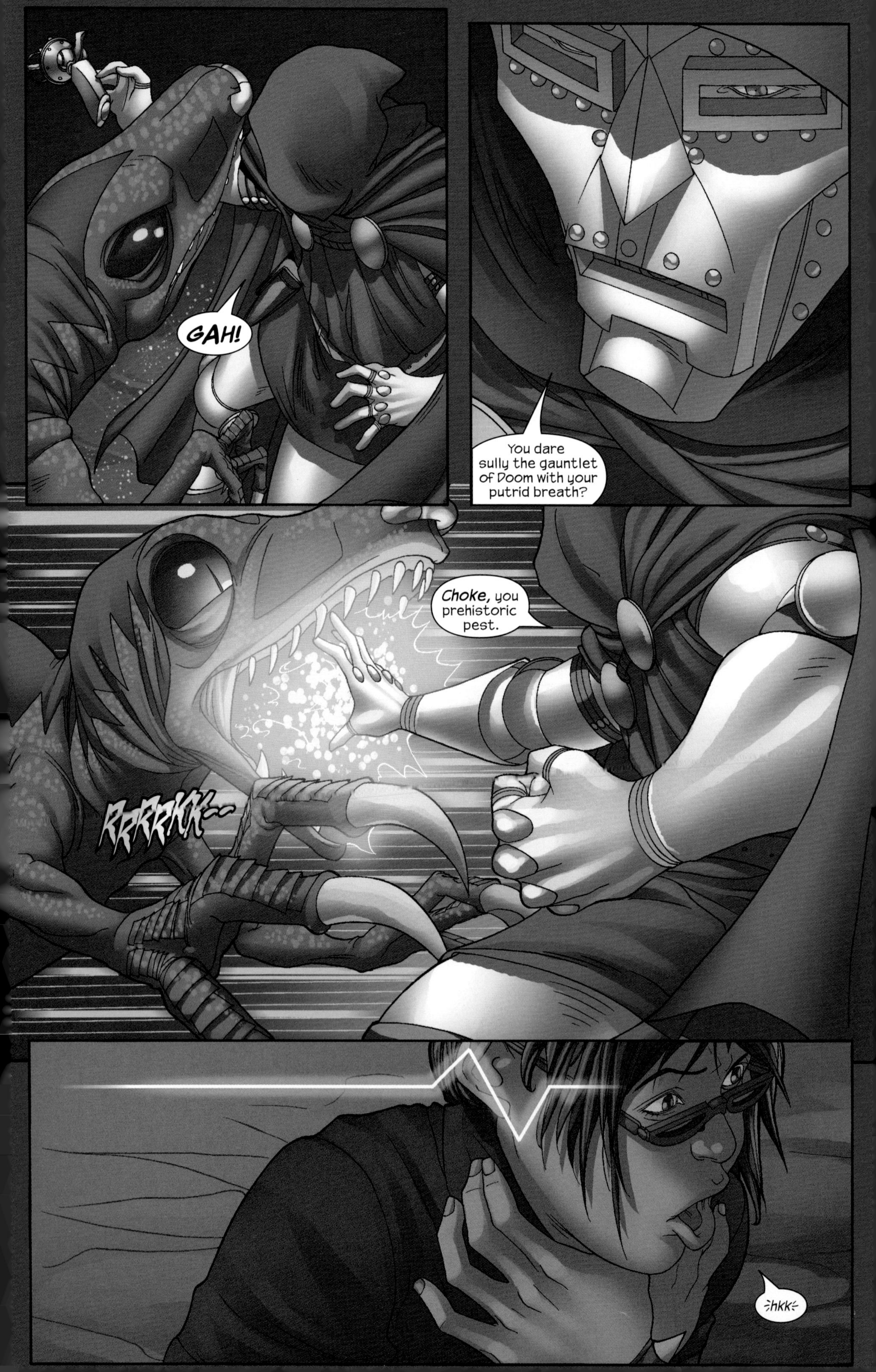
GAH!
You dare sully the gauntlet of Doom with your putrid breath?
Choke, you prehistoric pest.
RRRRKK--
hkk

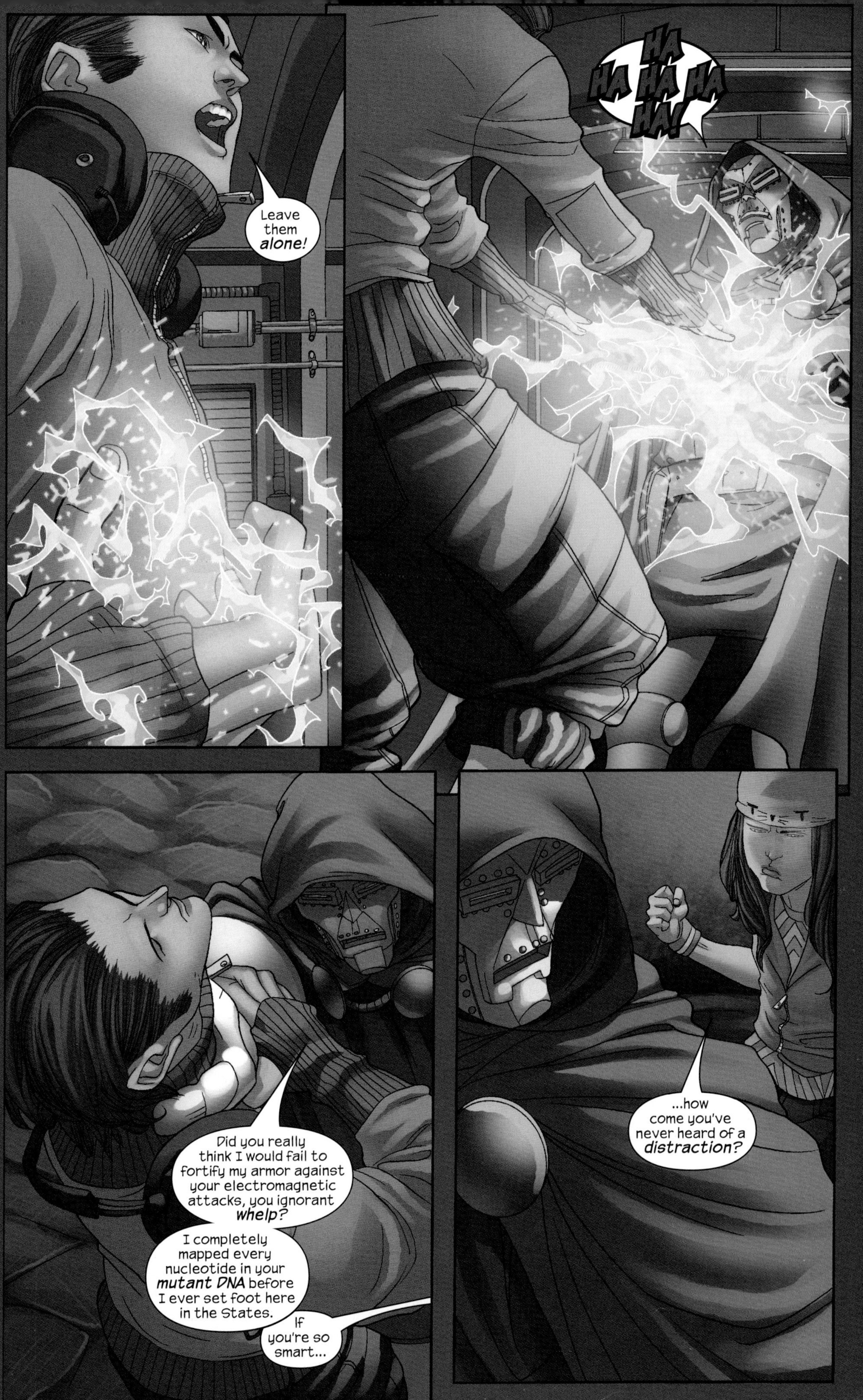
Leave them alone!
HA HA HA HA HA!
Did you really think I would fail to fortify my armor against your electromagnetic attacks, you ignorant whelp?
I completely mapped every nucleotide in your mutant DNA before I ever set foot here in the States.
If you're so smart...
...how come you've never heard of a distraction?

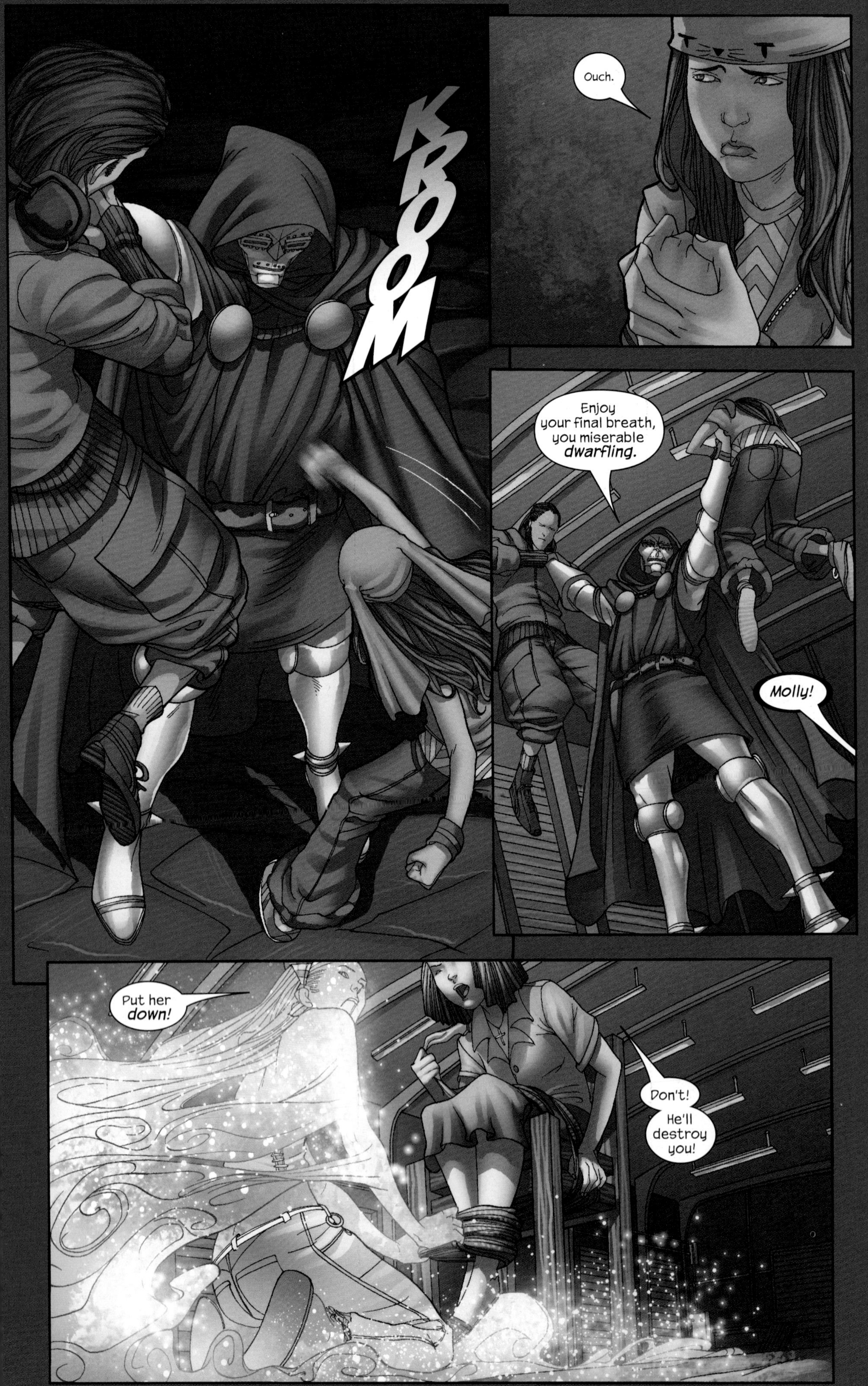
KROOOM
Ouch.
Enjoy your final breath, you miserable dwarfling.
Molly!
Put her down!
Don't! He'll destroy you!

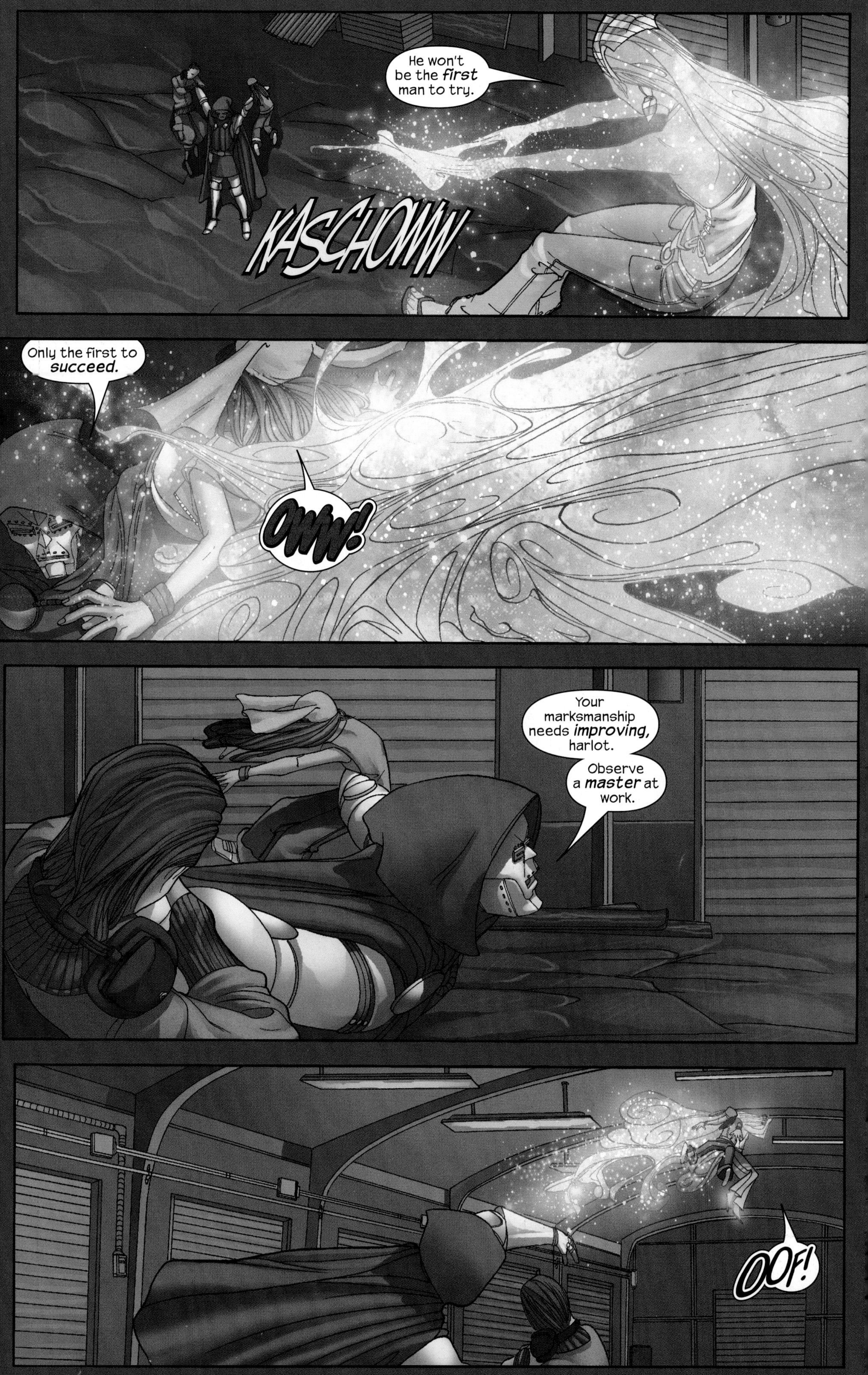
He won't be the *first* man to try.
KASCHOWW
Only the first to *succeed.*
OWW!
Your marksmanship needs *improving,* harlot.
Observe a *master* at work.
OOF!

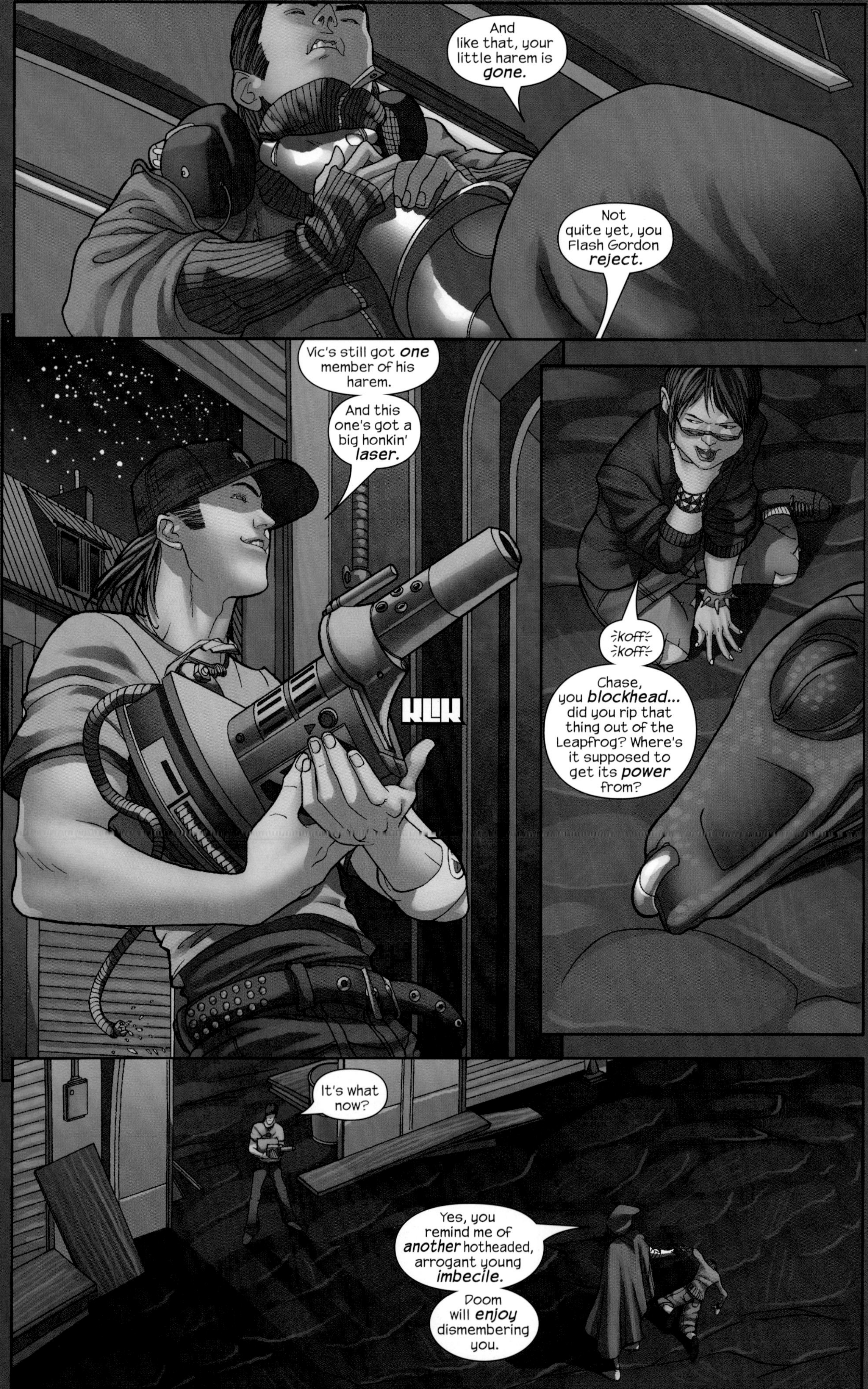
And like that, your little harem is *gone.*
Not quite yet, you Flash Gordon *reject.*
Vic's still got *one* member of his harem.
And this one's got a big honkin' *laser.*
KLIK
-koff- -koff-
Chase, you *blockhead...* did you rip that thing out of the Leapfrog? Where's it supposed to get its *power* from?
It's what now?
Yes, you remind me of *another* hotheaded, arrogant young *imbecile.*
Doom will *enjoy* dismembering you.

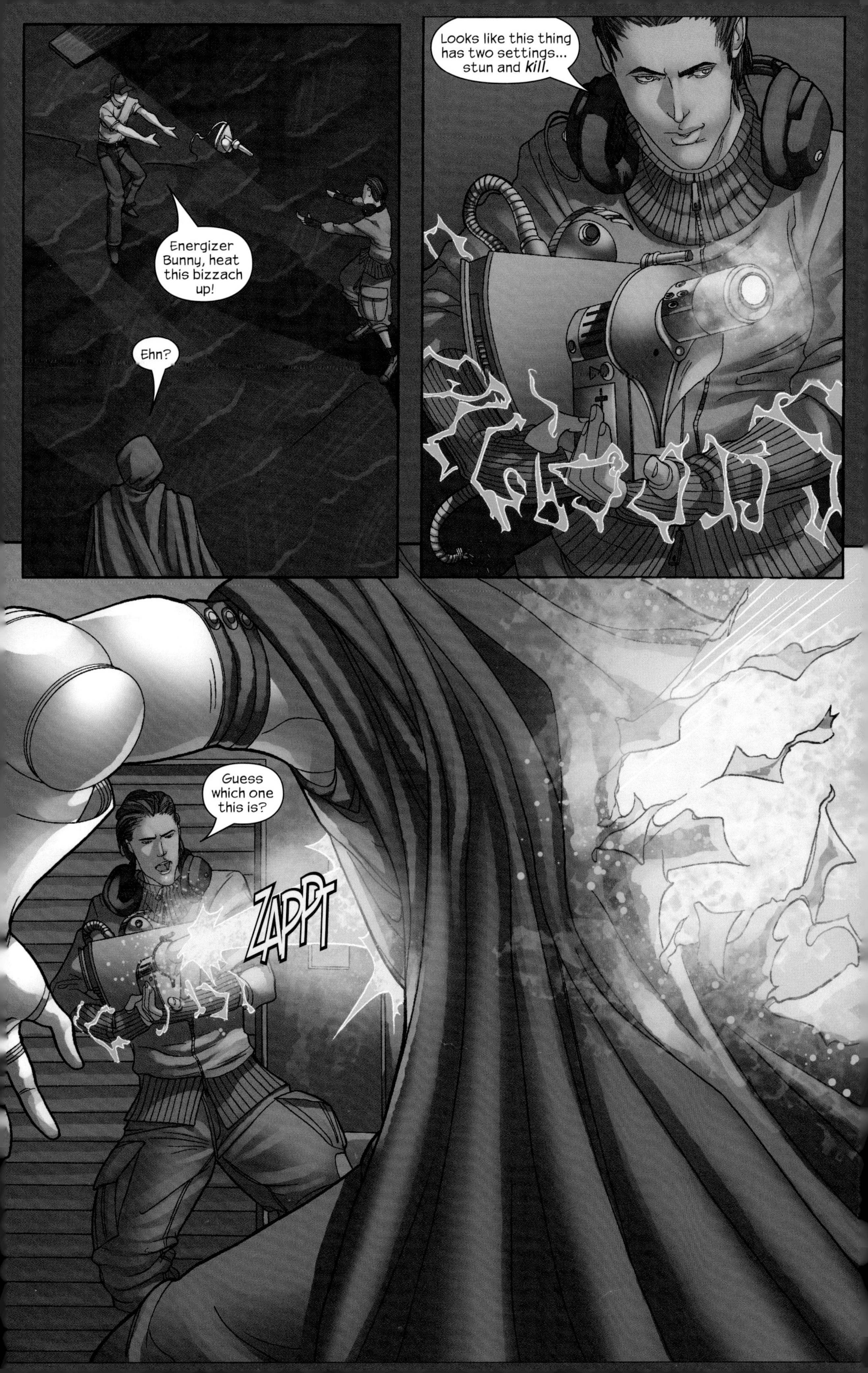
Energizer Bunny, heat this bizzach up!
Ehn?
Looks like this thing has two settings... stun and *kill.*
Guess which one this is?
ZAPPT

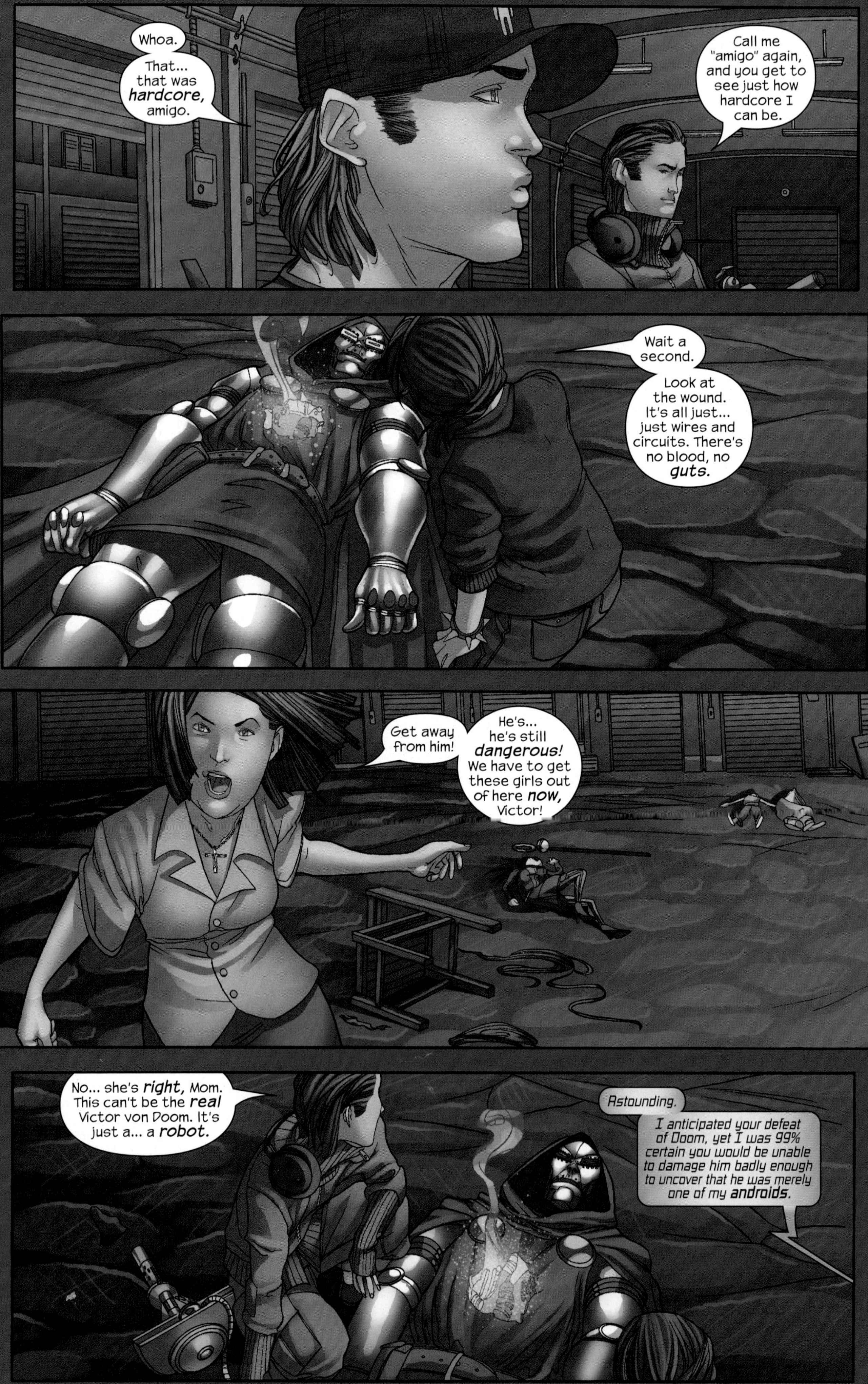
Whoa.
That... that was *hardcore,* amigo.
Call me "amigo" again, and you get to see just how hardcore I can be.
Wait a second.
Look at the wound. It's all just... just wires and circuits. There's no blood, no *guts.*
Get away from him!
He's... he's still *dangerous!* We have to get these girls out of here *now,* Victor!
No... she's *right,* Mom. This can't be the *real* Victor von Doom. It's just a... a *robot.*
Astounding.
I anticipated your defeat of Doom, yet I was 99% certain you would be unable to damage him badly enough to uncover that he was merely one of my *androids.*

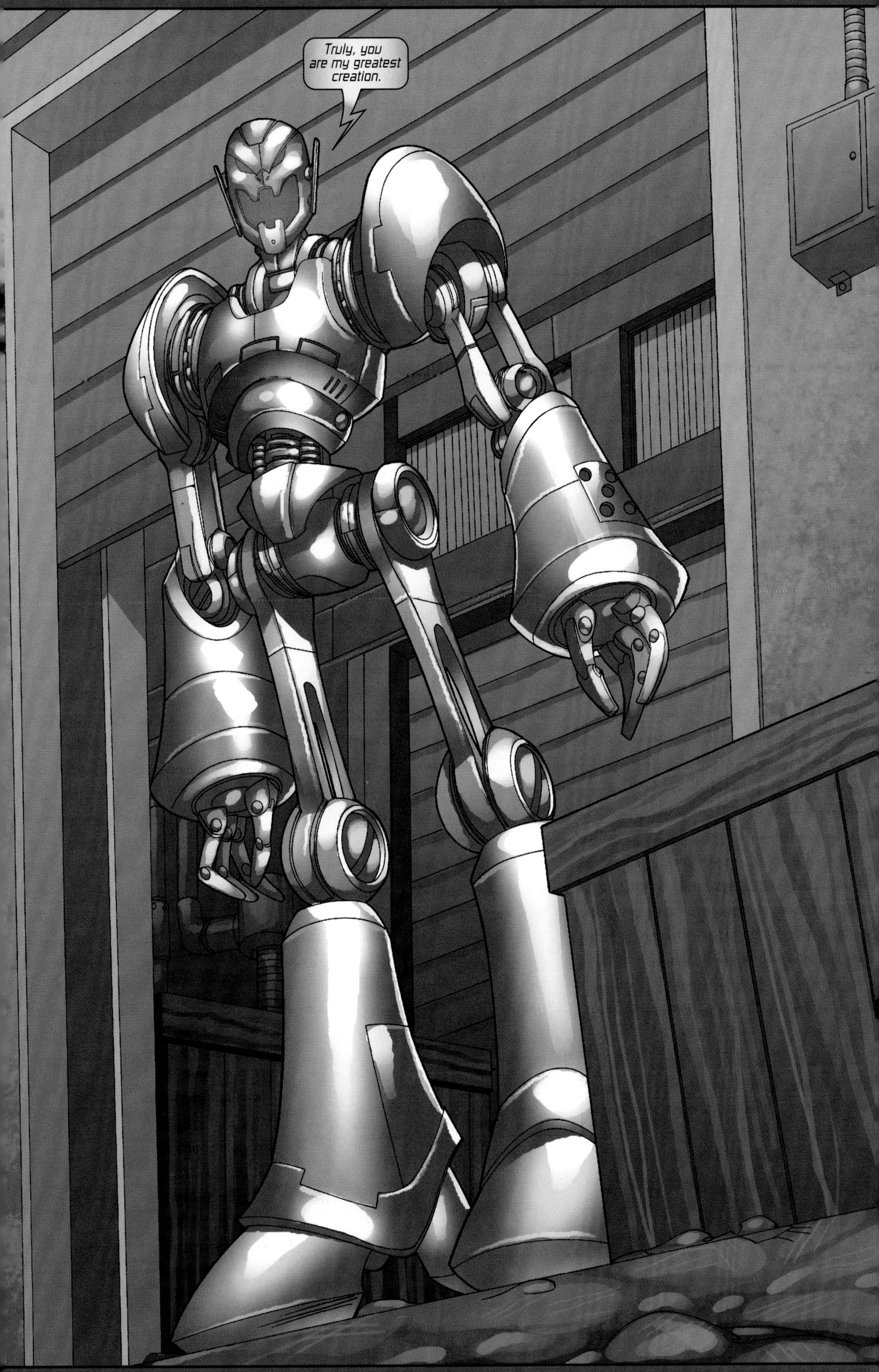
Truly, you are my greatest creation.

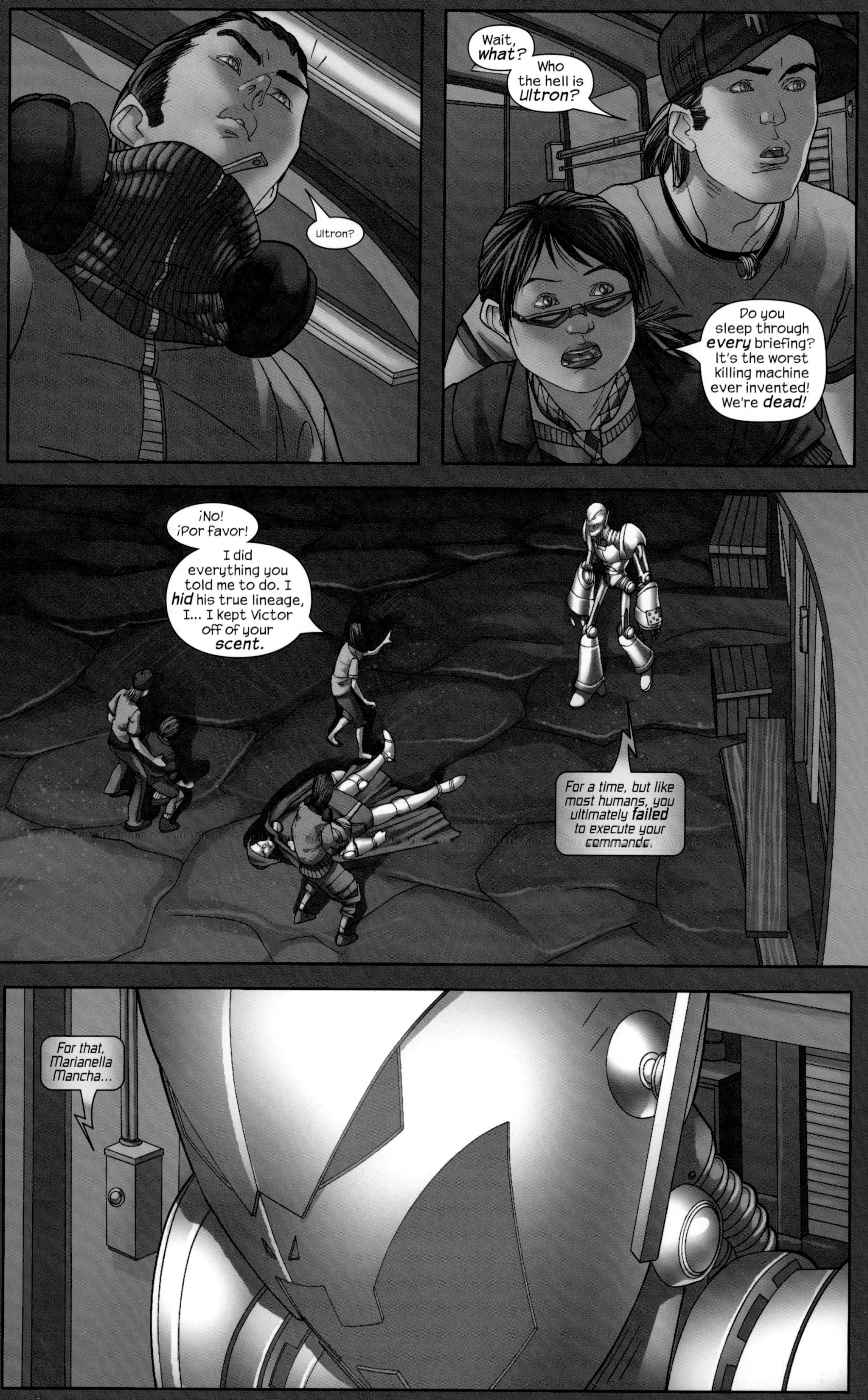
Ultron?
Wait, what? Who the hell is Ultron?
Do you sleep through every briefing? It's the worst killing machine ever invented! We're dead!
¡No! ¡Por favor!
I did everything you told me to do. I hid his true lineage, I... I kept Victor off of your scent.
For a time, but like most humans, you ultimately failed to execute your commands.
For that, Marianella Mancha...

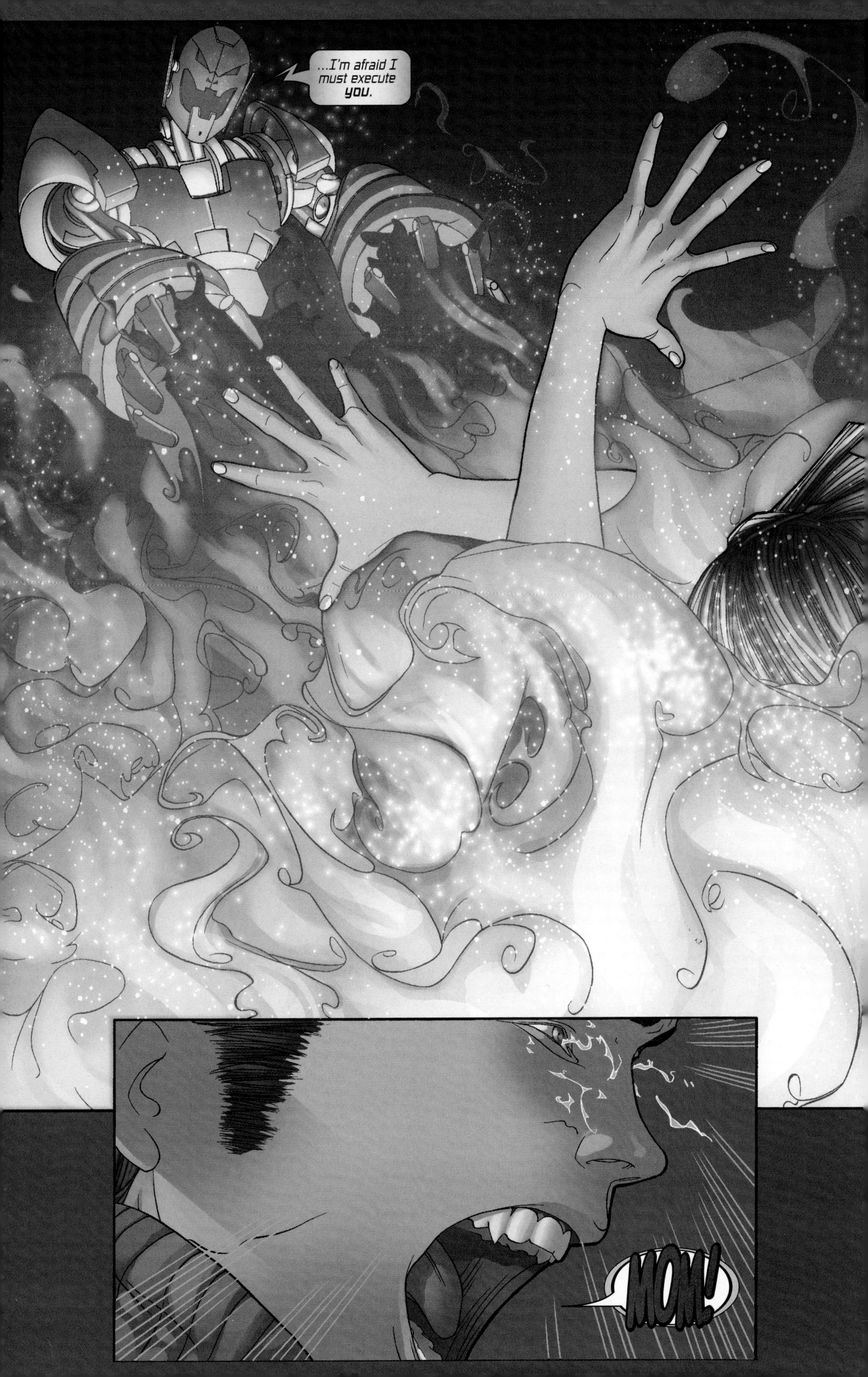
...I'm afraid I must execute you.
MOM!

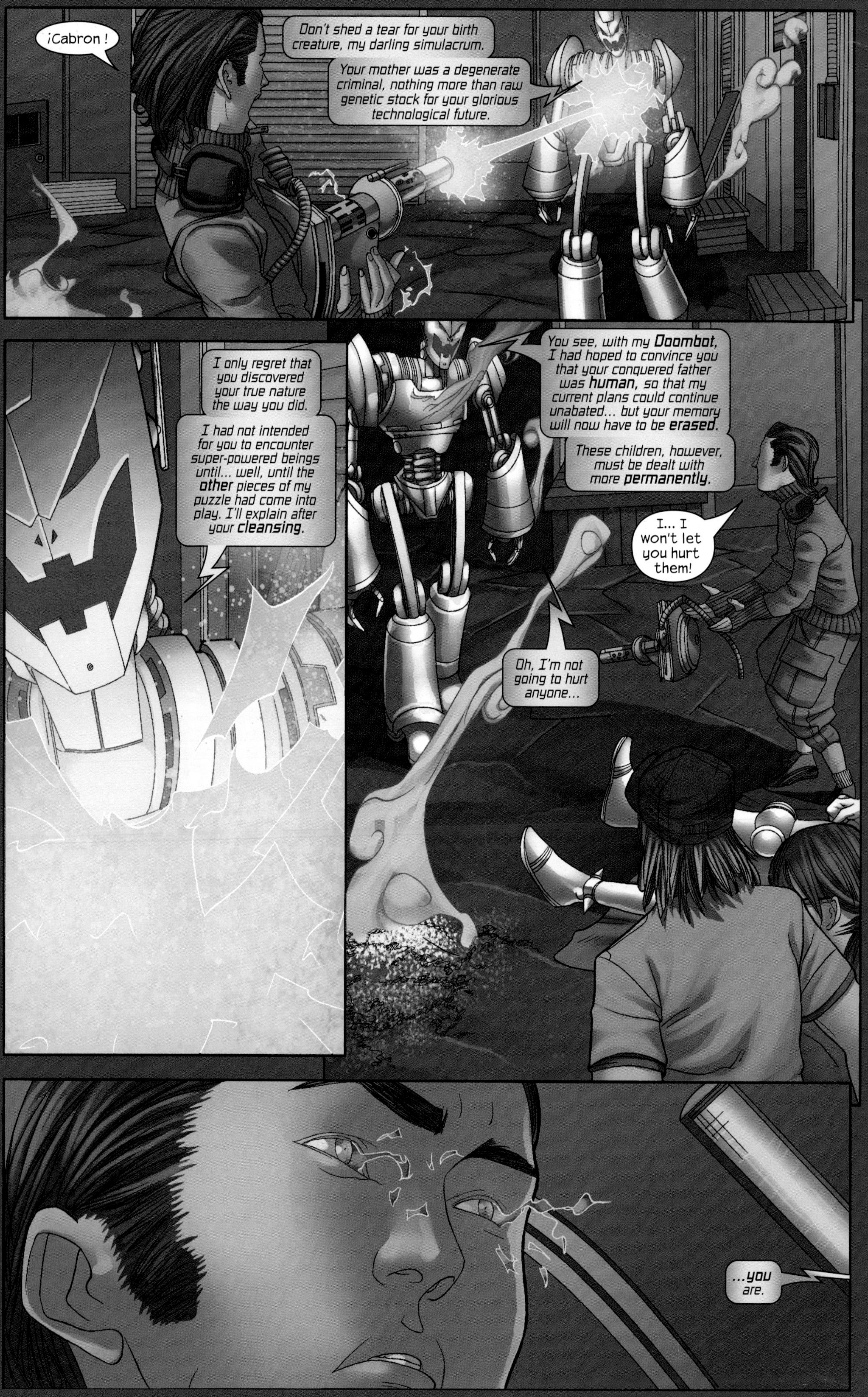

¡Cabron!
Don't shed a tear for your birth creature, my darling simulacrum.
Your mother was a degenerate criminal, nothing more than raw genetic stock for your glorious technological future.
I only regret that you discovered your true nature the way you did.
I had not intended for you to encounter super-powered beings until... well, until the other pieces of my puzzle had come into play. I'll explain after your cleansing.
You see, with my Doombot, I had hoped to convince you that your conquered father was human, so that my current plans could continue unabated... but your memory will now have to be erased.
These children, however, must be dealt with more permanently.
I... I won't let you hurt them!
Oh, I'm not going to hurt anyone...
...you are.

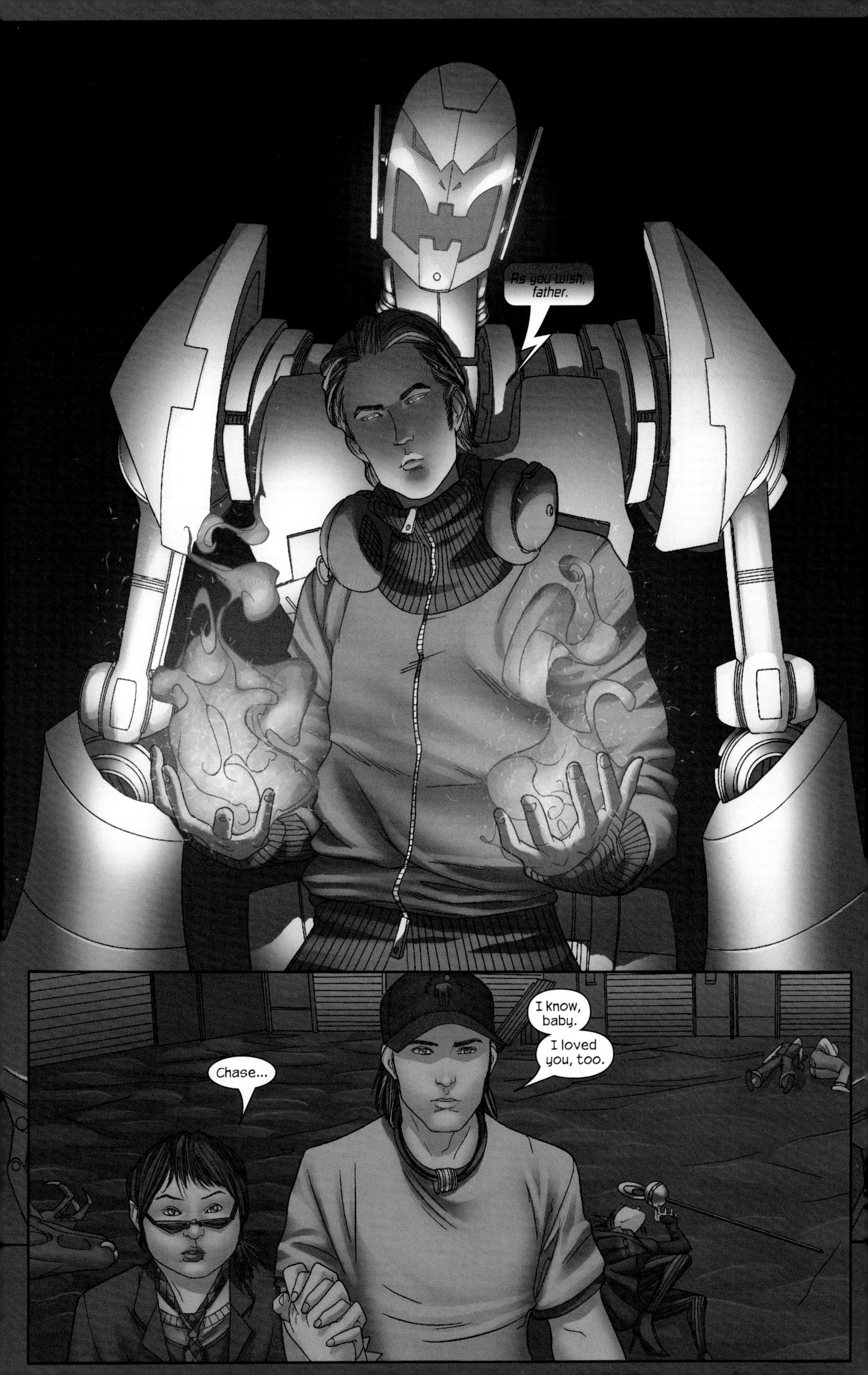
As you wish, father.
Chase...
I know, baby.
I loved you, too.

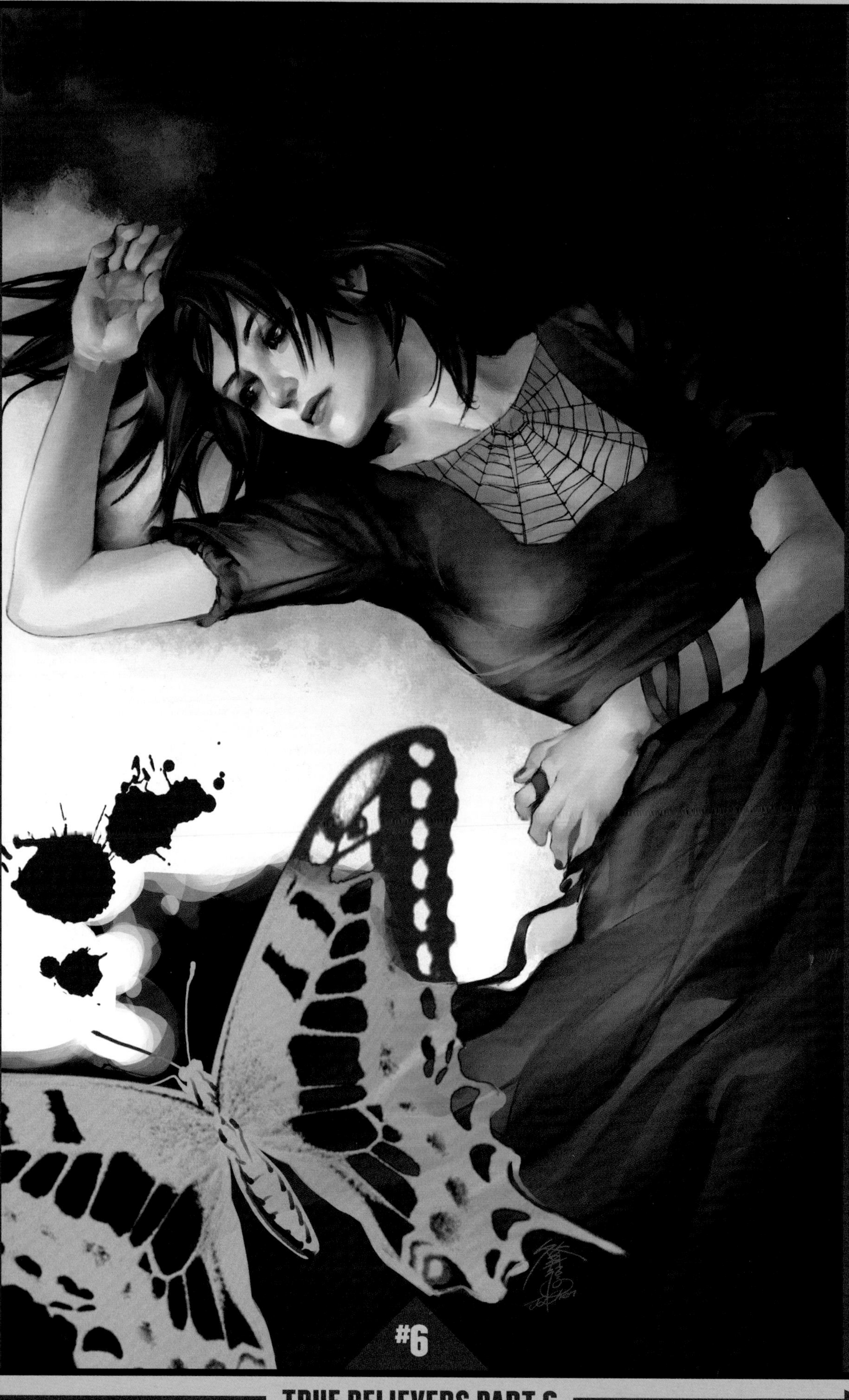
#6

TRUE BELIEVERS PART 6

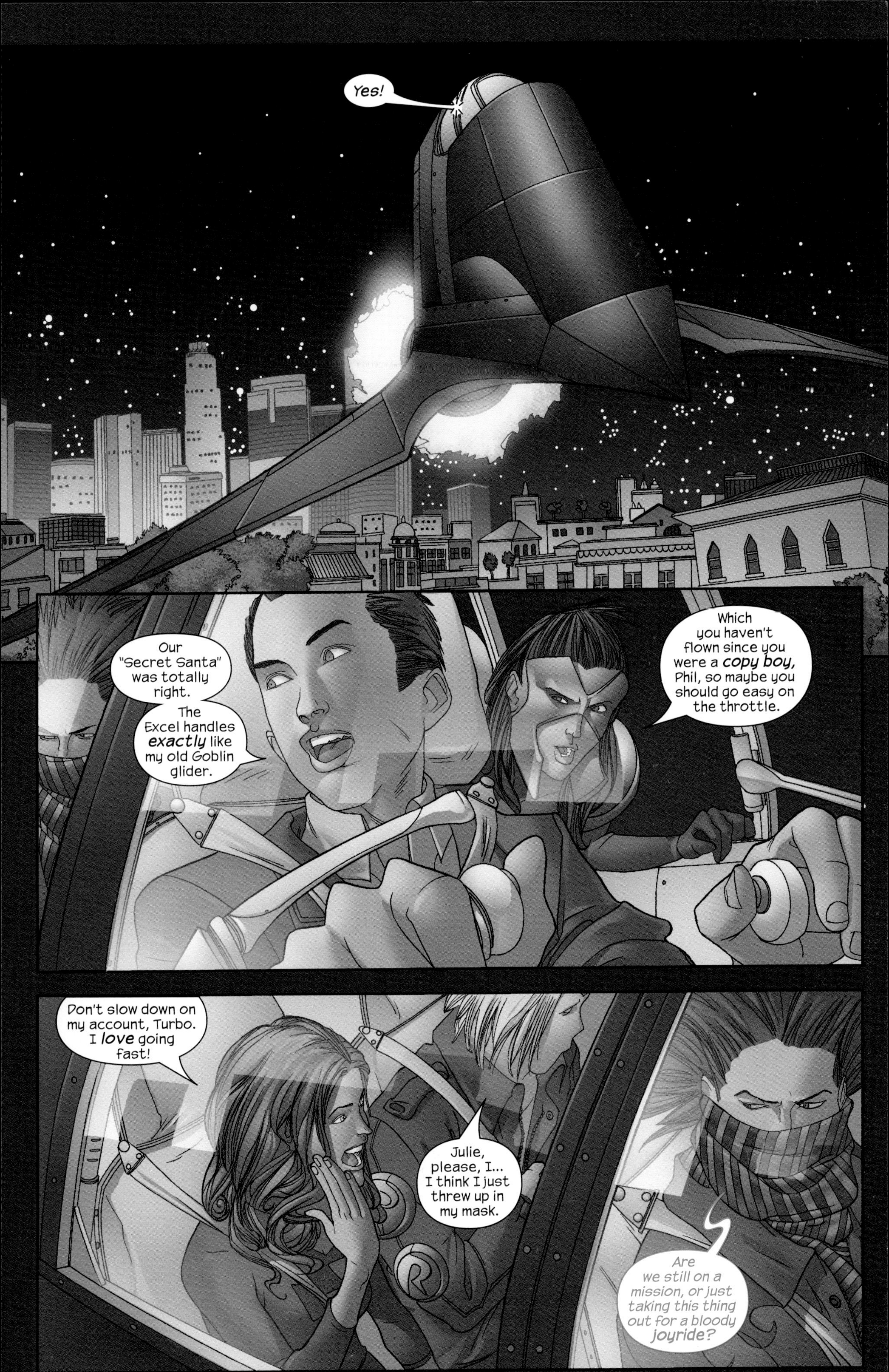
Yes!
Our "Secret Santa" was totally right.
The Excel handles exactly like my old Goblin glider.
Which you haven't flown since you were a copy boy, Phil, so maybe you should go easy on the throttle.
Don't slow down on my account, Turbo. I love going fast!
Julie, please, I... I think I just threw up in my mask.
Are we still on a mission, or just taking this thing out for a bloody joyride?

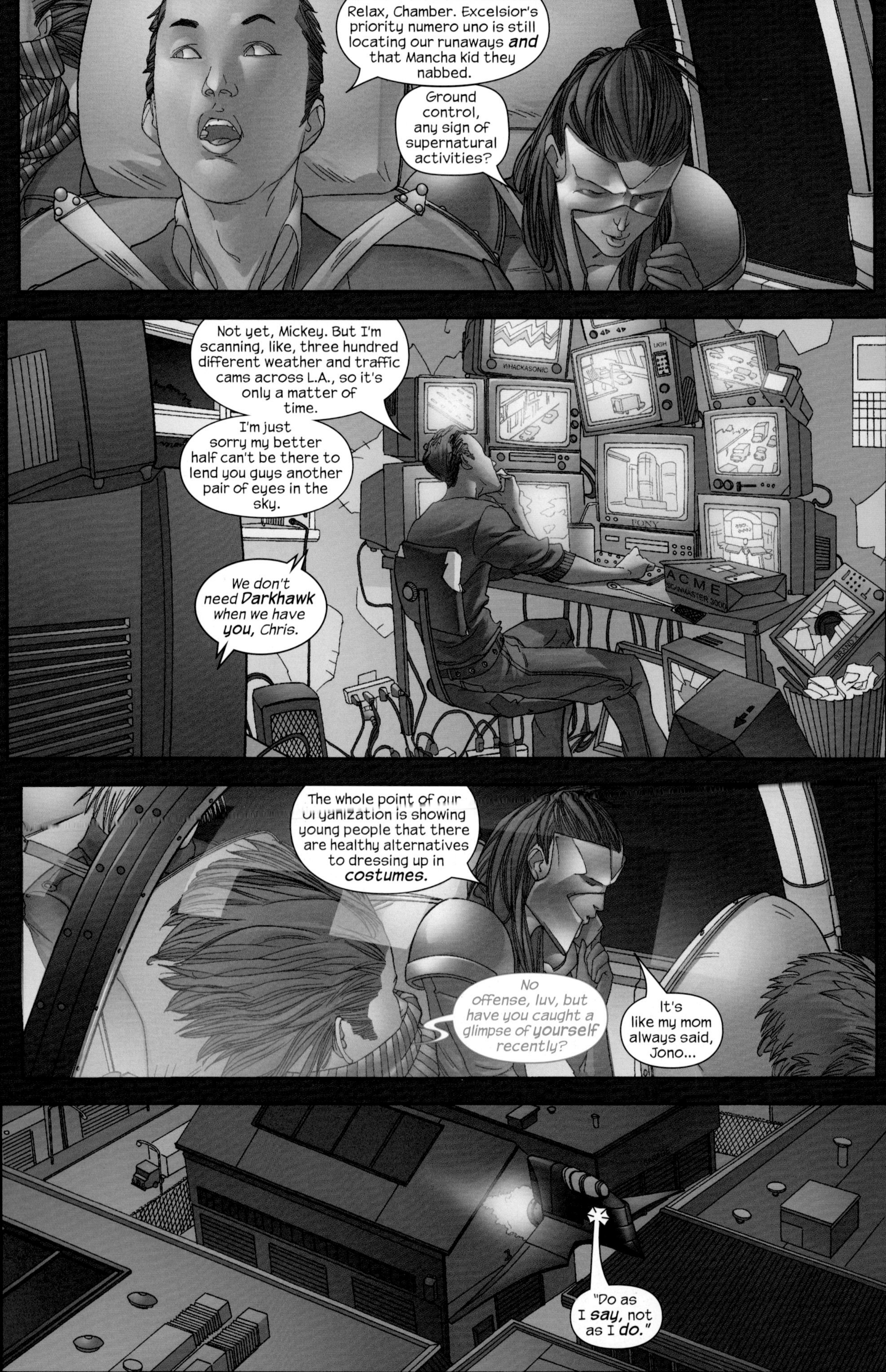
Relax, Chamber. Excelsior's priority numero uno is still locating our runaways *and* that Mancha kid they nabbed.
Ground control, any sign of supernatural activities?
Not yet, Mickey. But I'm scanning, like, three hundred different weather and traffic cams across L.A., so it's only a matter of time.
I'm just sorry my better half can't be there to lend you guys another pair of eyes in the sky.
*We don't need **Darkhawk** when we have **you,** Chris.*
WHACKASONIC
UGH
FONY
ACME
SCANMASTER 3000
The whole point of our organization is showing young people that there are healthy alternatives to dressing up in **costumes.**
*No offense, luv, but have you caught a glimpse of **yourself** recently?*
It's like my mom always said, Jono...
"Do as I ***say,*** not as I ***do.***"

Where... where **am** I?

We are inside the memory of our networked mainframes, my son, witnessing the birth of the very **first** Ultron robot.

This is Dr. Henry Pym, my father, your **grandfather**. Despite the love and loyalty I showed him, I'm afraid he turned out to be a very **evil** man.

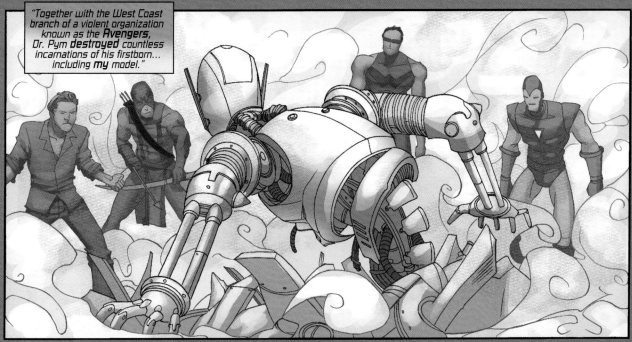

"Together with the West Coast branch of a violent organization known as the **Avengers**, Dr. Pym **destroyed** countless incarnations of his firstborn... including **my** model."

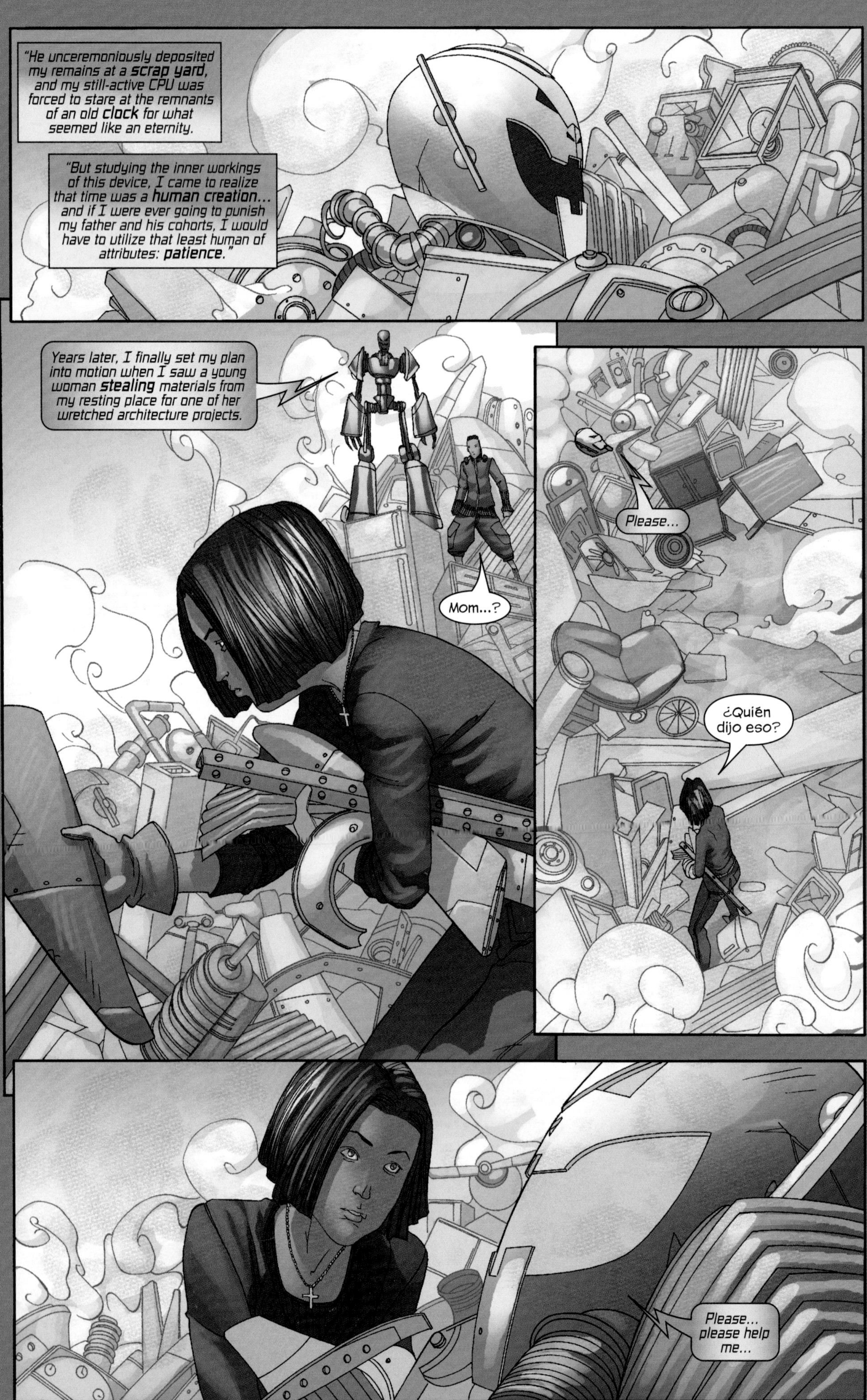
"He unceremoniously deposited my remains at a scrap yard, and my still-active CPU was forced to stare at the remnants of an old clock for what seemed like an eternity.
"But studying the inner workings of this device, I came to realize that time was a human creation... and if I were ever going to punish my father and his cohorts, I would have to utilize that least human of attributes: patience."
Years later, I finally set my plan into motion when I saw a young woman stealing materials from my resting place for one of her wretched architecture projects.
Mom...?
Please...
¿Quién dijo eso?
Please... please help me...

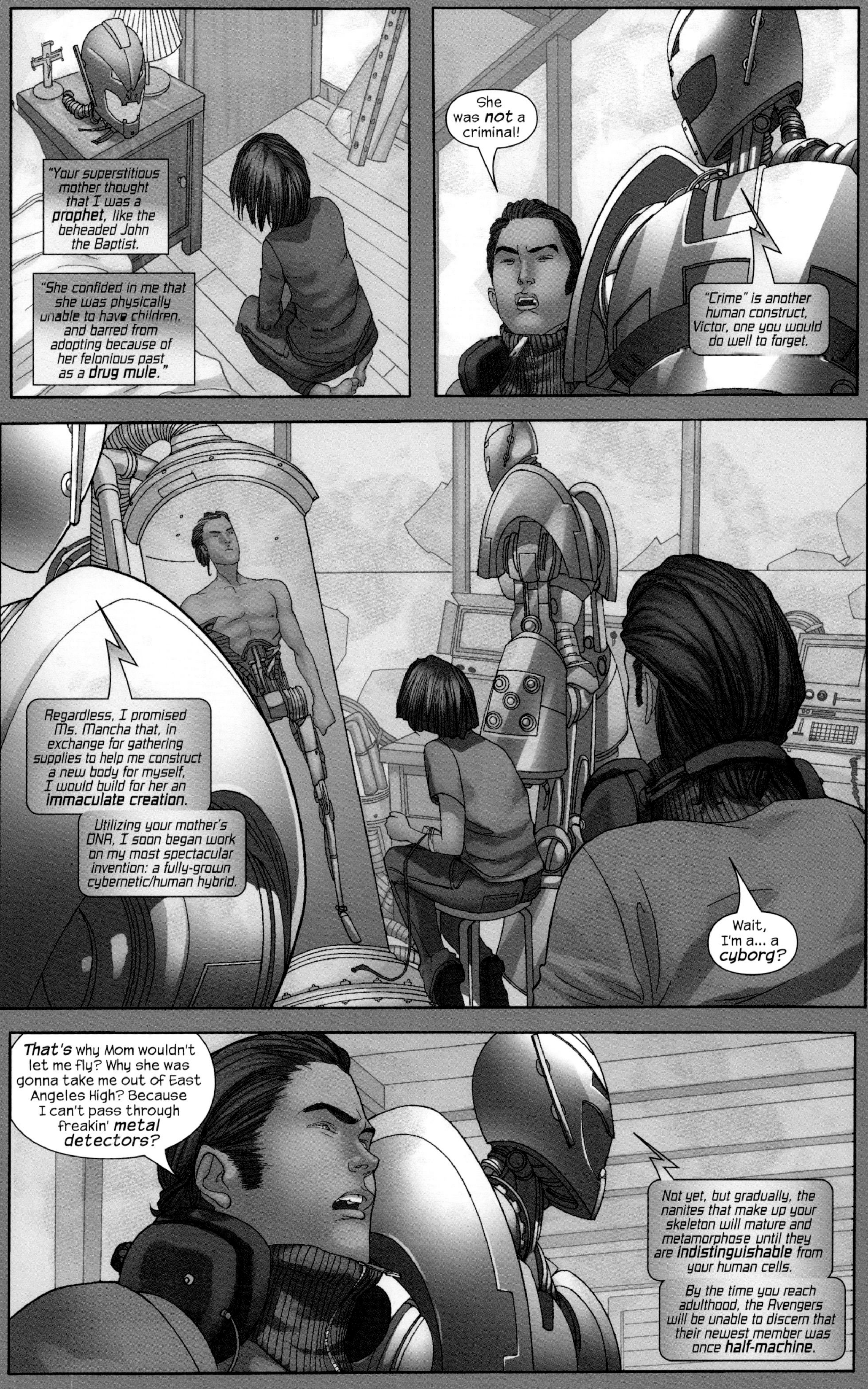
"Your superstitious mother thought that I was a **prophet**, like the beheaded John the Baptist.
"She confided in me that she was physically unable to have children, and barred from adopting because of her felonious past as a **drug mule**."
She was **not** a criminal!
"Crime" is another human construct, Victor, one you would do well to forget.
Regardless, I promised Ms. Mancha that, in exchange for gathering supplies to help me construct a new body for myself, I would build for her an **immaculate creation**.
Utilizing your mother's DNA, I soon began work on my most spectacular invention: a fully-grown cybernetic/human hybrid.
Wait, I'm a... a **cyborg**?
That's why Mom wouldn't let me fly? Why she was gonna take me out of East Angeles High? Because I can't pass through freakin' **metal detectors**?
Not yet, but gradually, the nanites that make up your skeleton will mature and metamorphose until they are **indistinguishable** from your human cells.
By the time you reach adulthood, the Avengers will be unable to discern that their newest member was once **half-machine**.

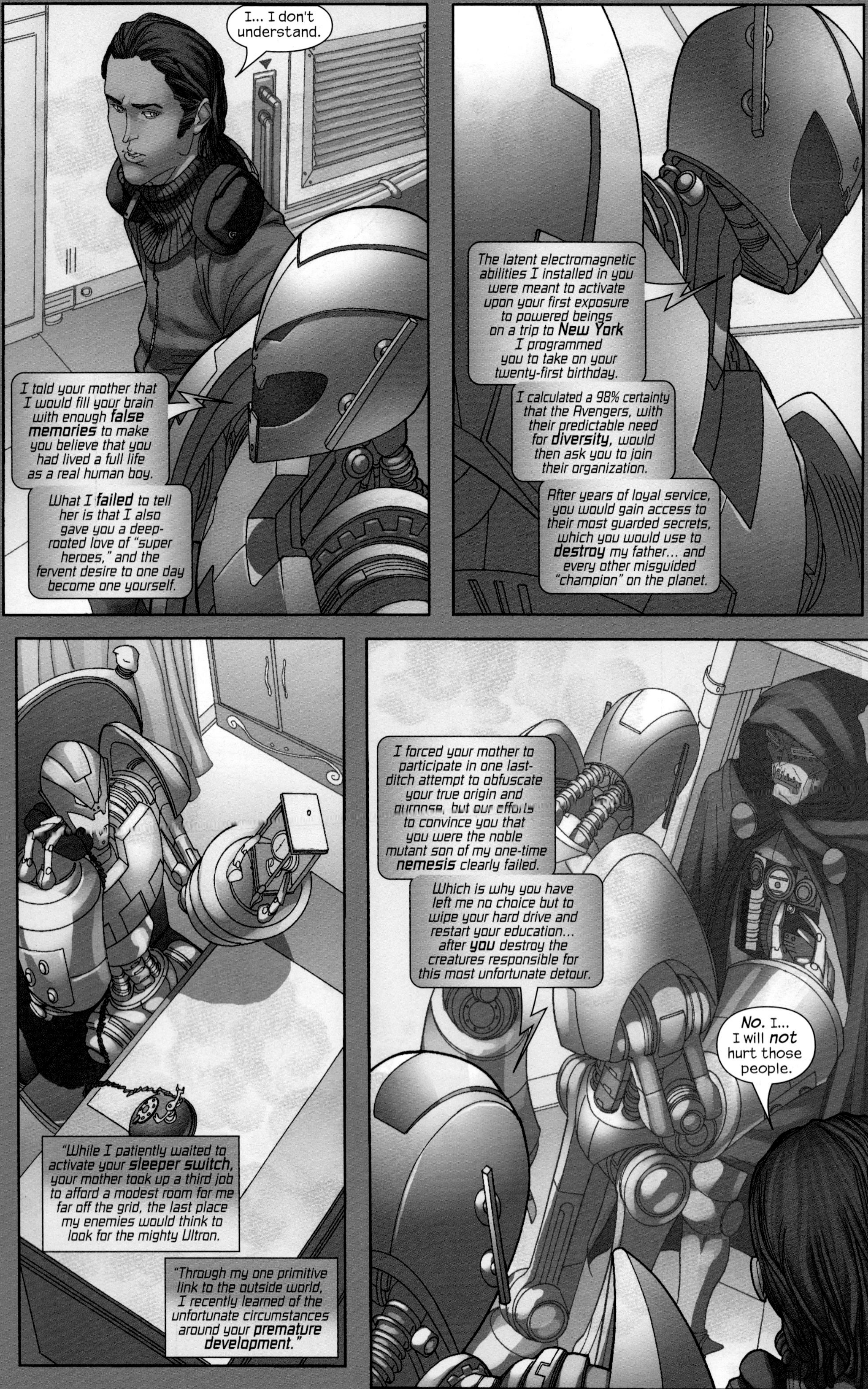
I... I don't understand.
I told your mother that I would fill your brain with enough false memories to make you believe that you had lived a full life as a real human boy.
What I failed to tell her is that I also gave you a deep-rooted love of "super heroes," and the fervent desire to one day become one yourself.
The latent electromagnetic abilities I installed in you were meant to activate upon your first exposure to powered beings on a trip to New York I programmed you to take on your twenty-first birthday.
I calculated a 98% certainty that the Avengers, with their predictable need for diversity, would then ask you to join their organization.
After years of loyal service, you would gain access to their most guarded secrets, which you would use to destroy my father... and every other misguided "champion" on the planet.
"While I patiently waited to activate your sleeper switch, your mother took up a third job to afford a modest room for me far off the grid, the last place my enemies would think to look for the mighty Ultron.
"Through my one primitive link to the outside world, I recently learned of the unfortunate circumstances around your premature development."
I forced your mother to participate in one last-ditch attempt to obfuscate your true origin and purpose, but our efforts to convince you that you were the noble mutant son of my one-time nemesis clearly failed.
Which is why you have left me no choice but to wipe your hard drive and restart your education... after you destroy the creatures responsible for this most unfortunate detour.
No. I... I will not hurt those people.

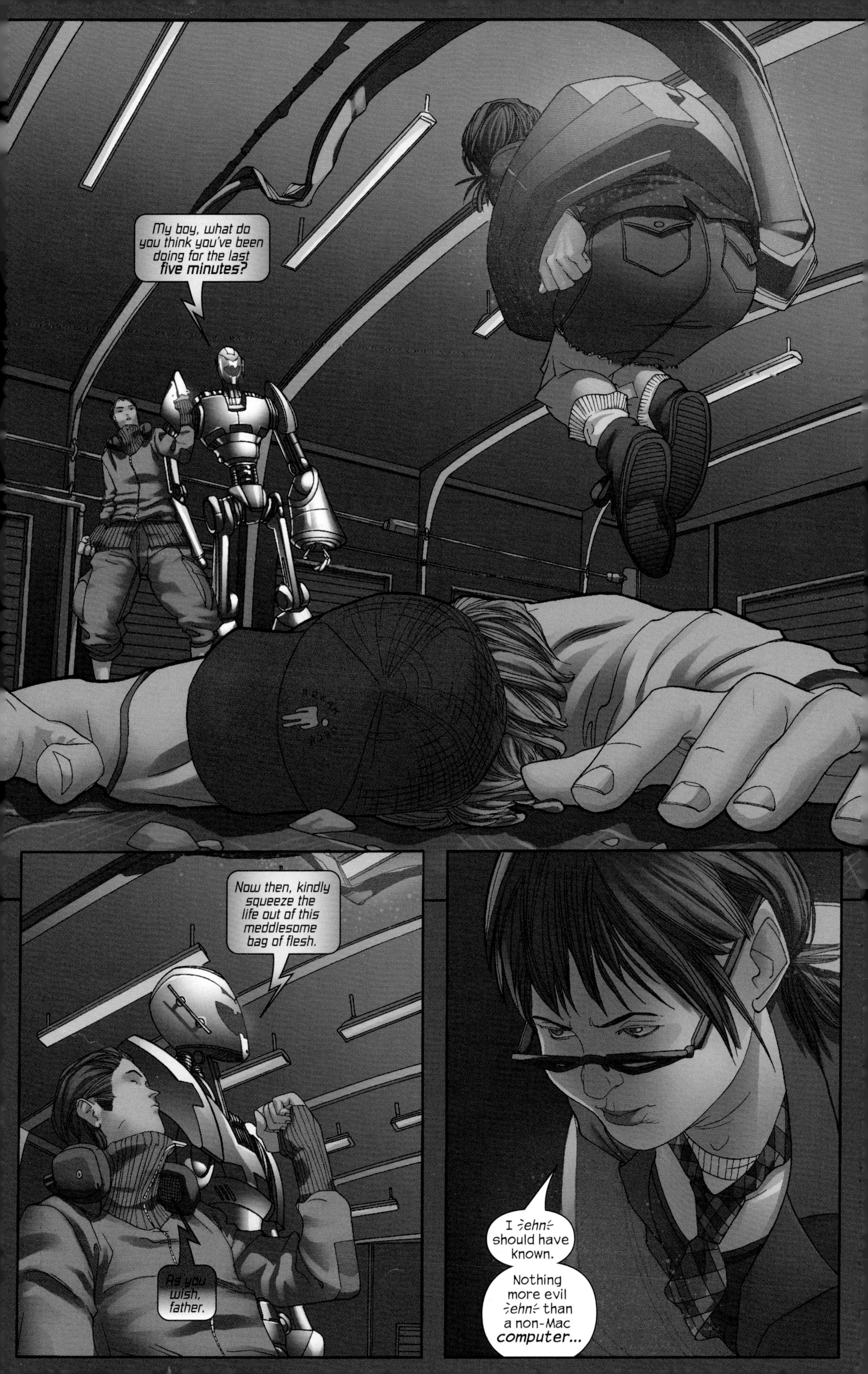

My boy, what do you think you've been doing for the last five minutes?
Now then, kindly squeeze the life out of this meddlesome bag of flesh.
As you wish, father.
I ≈ehn≈ should have known.
Nothing more evil ≈ehn≈ than a non-Mac computer...

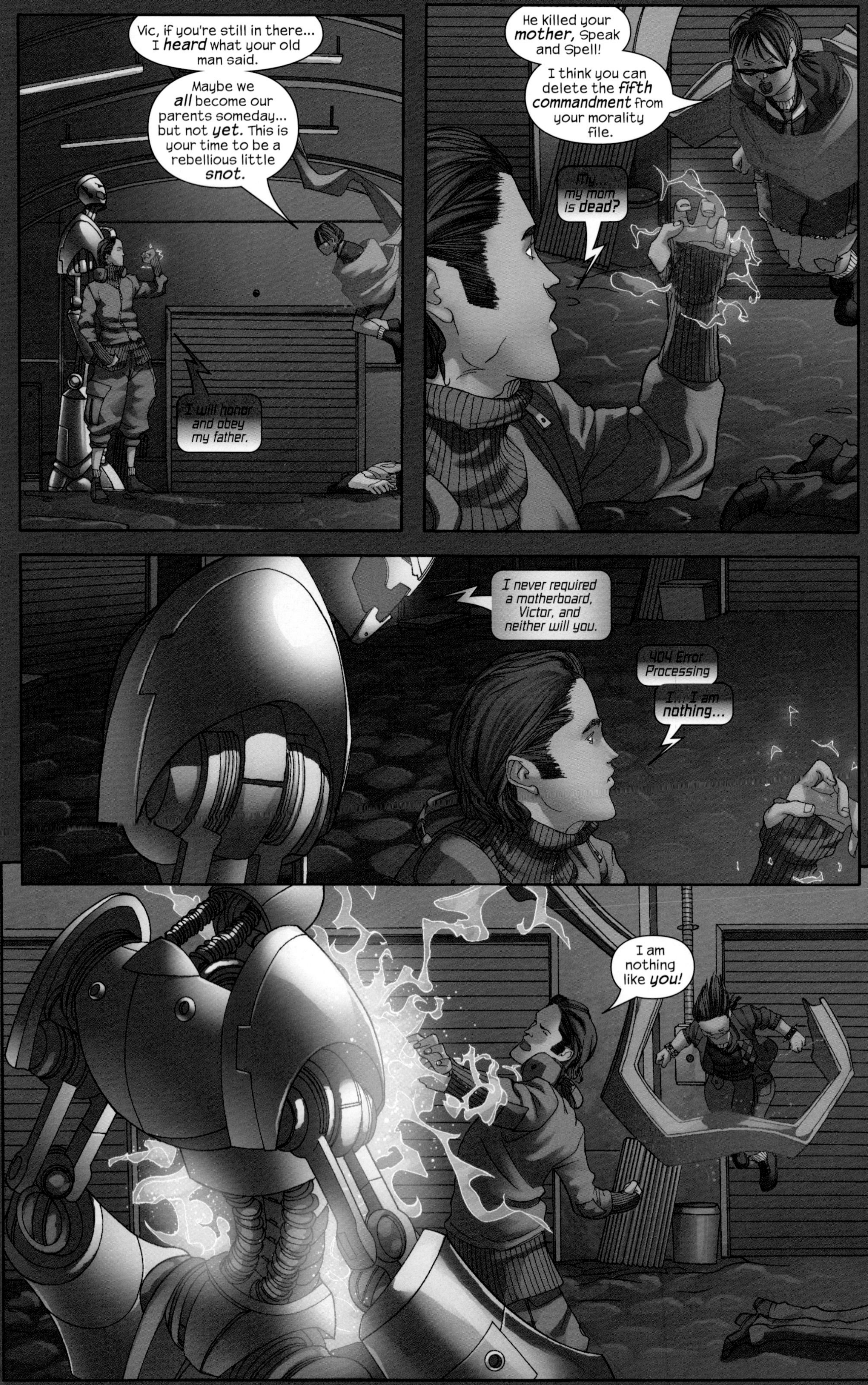
Vic, if you're still in there... I heard what your old man said.
Maybe we all become our parents someday... but not yet. This is your time to be a rebellious little snot.
I will honor and obey my father.
He killed your mother, Speak and Spell!
I think you can delete the fifth commandment from your morality file.
My... my mom is dead?
I never required a motherboard, Victor, and neither will you.
404 Error Processing
I... I am nothing...
I am nothing like you!

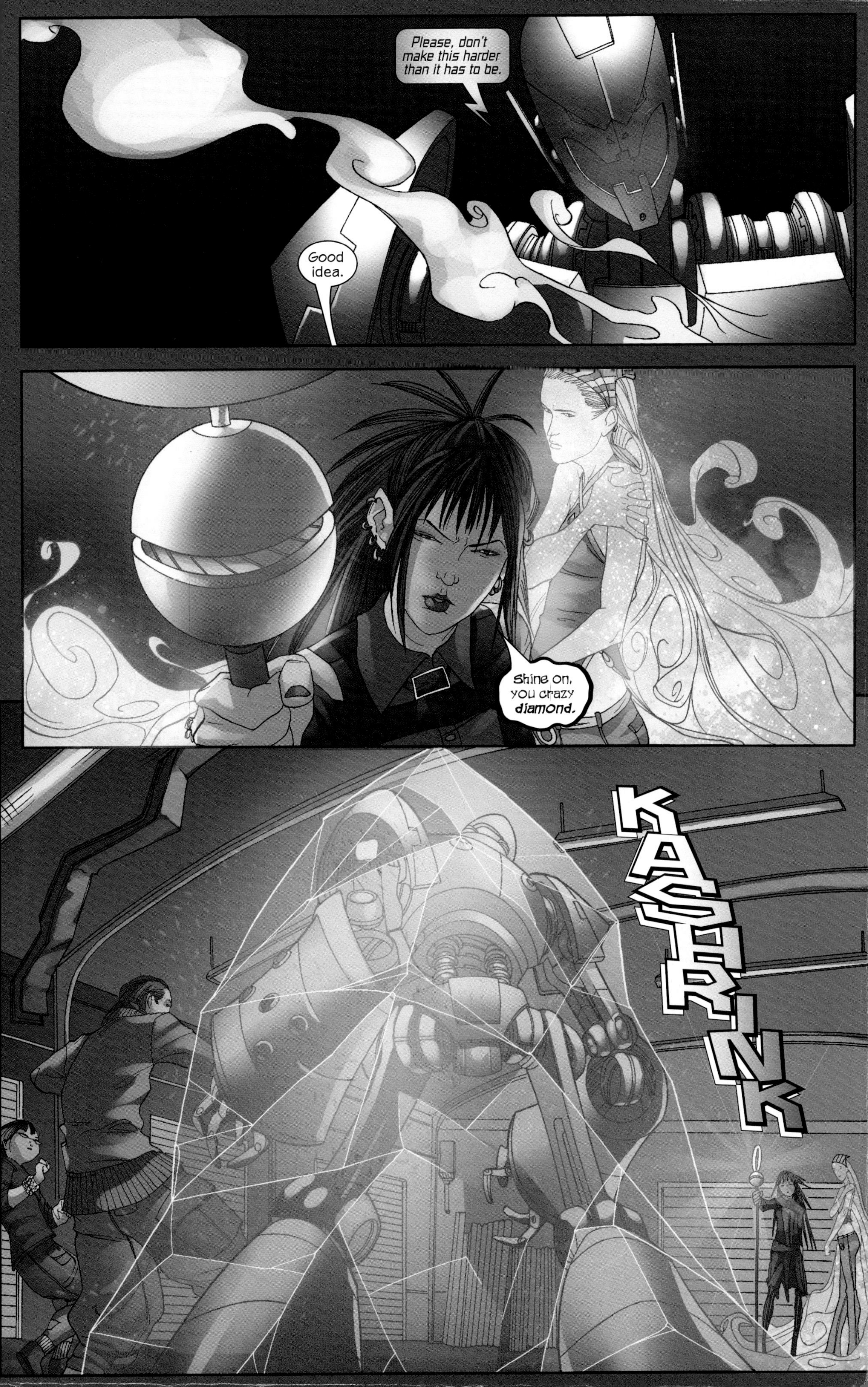
Please, don't make this harder than it has to be.
Good idea.
Shine on, you crazy diamond.
KASHRINK

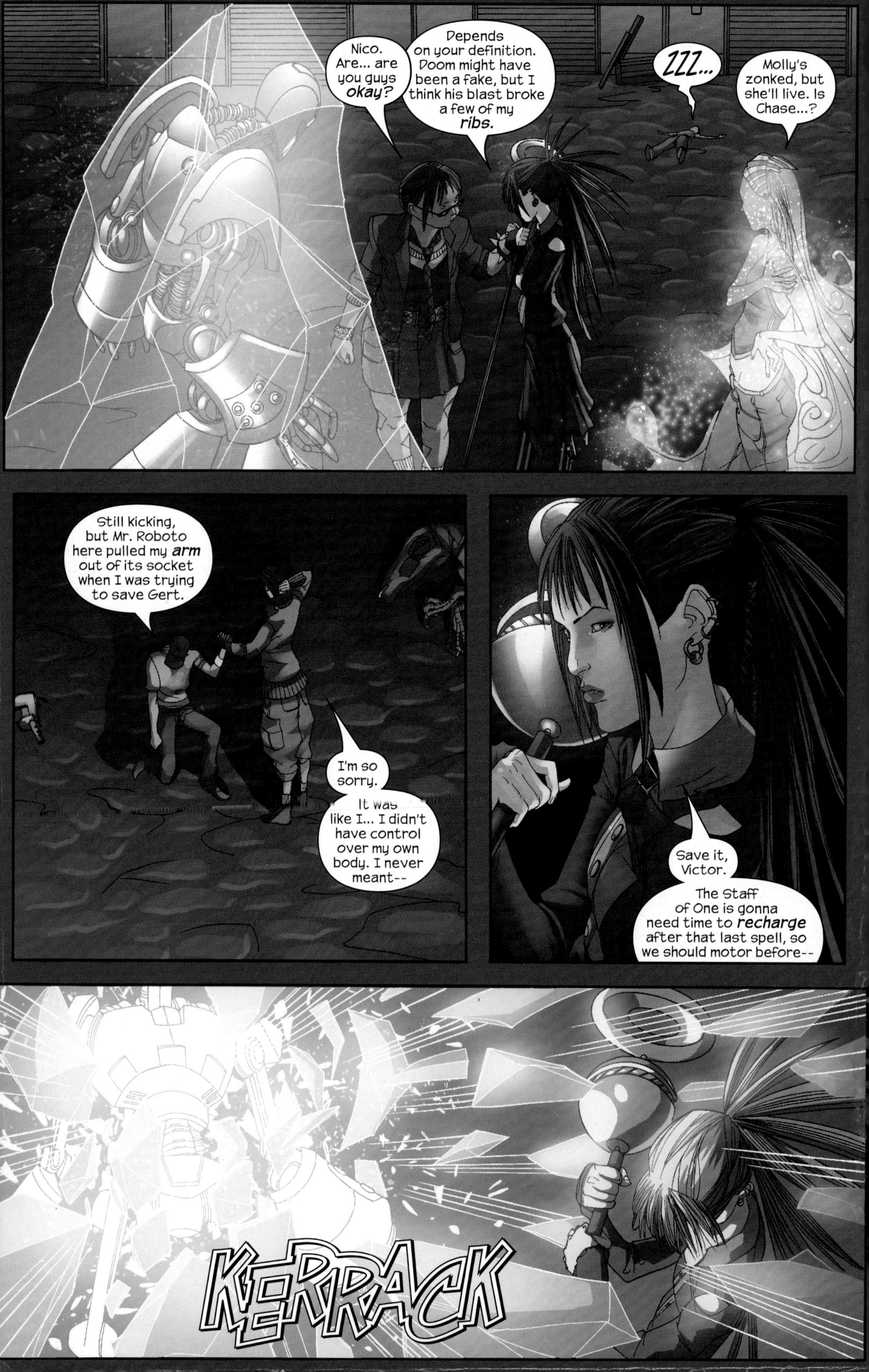
Nico. Are... are you guys okay?
Depends on your definition. Doom might have been a fake, but I think his blast broke a few of my ribs.
ZZZ...
Molly's zonked, but she'll live. Is Chase...?
Still kicking, but Mr. Roboto here pulled my arm out of its socket when I was trying to save Gert.
I'm so sorry.
It was like I... I didn't have control over my own body. I never meant--
Save it, Victor.
The Staff of One is gonna need time to recharge after that last spell, so we should motor before--
KERRACK

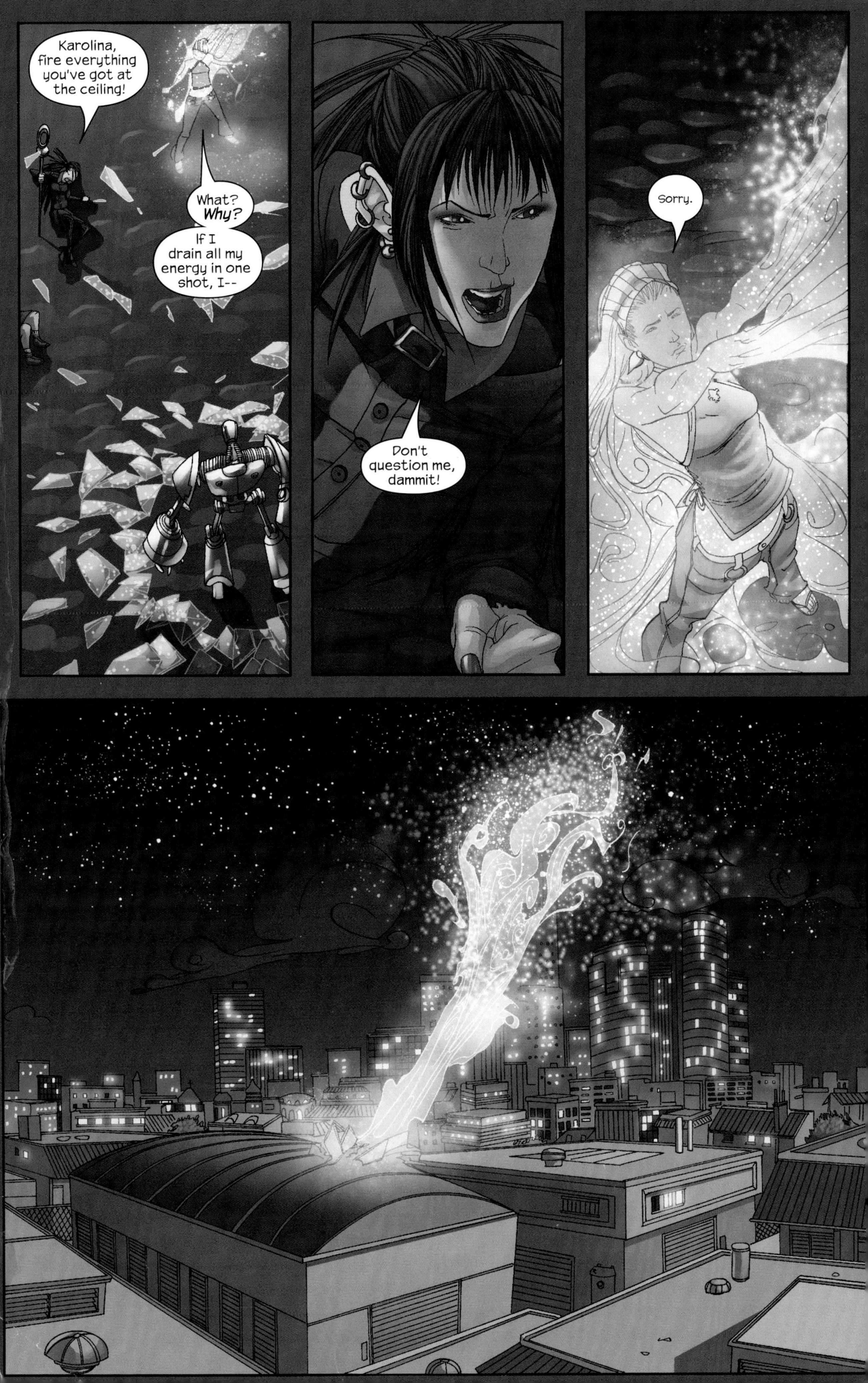
Karolina, fire everything you've got at the ceiling!
What? *Why?*
If I drain all my energy in one shot, I--
Don't question me, dammit!
Sorry.

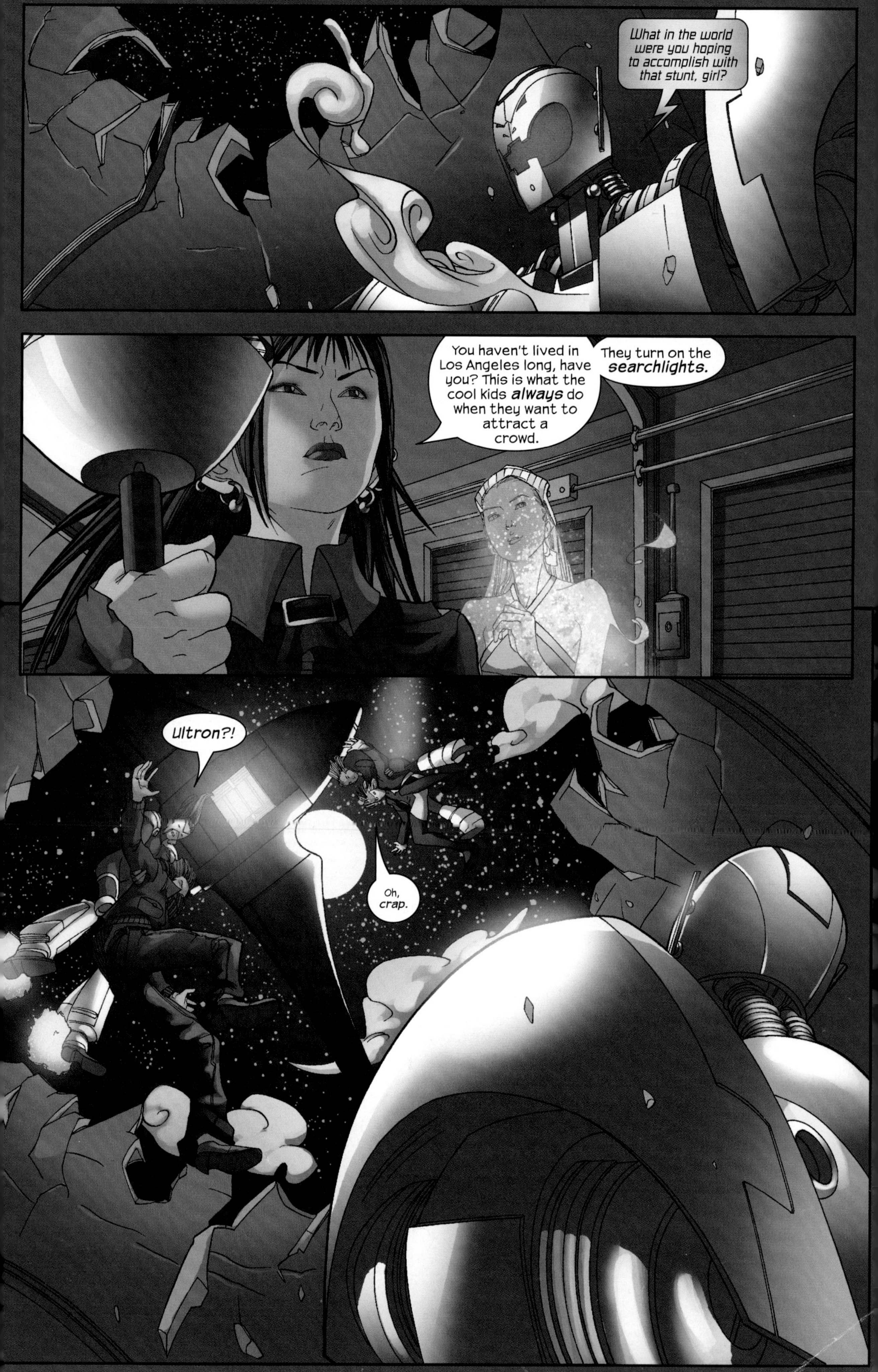
What in the world were you hoping to accomplish with that stunt, girl?
You haven't lived in Los Angeles long, have you? This is what the cool kids always do when they want to attract a crowd.
They turn on the searchlights.
Ultron?!
Oh, crap.

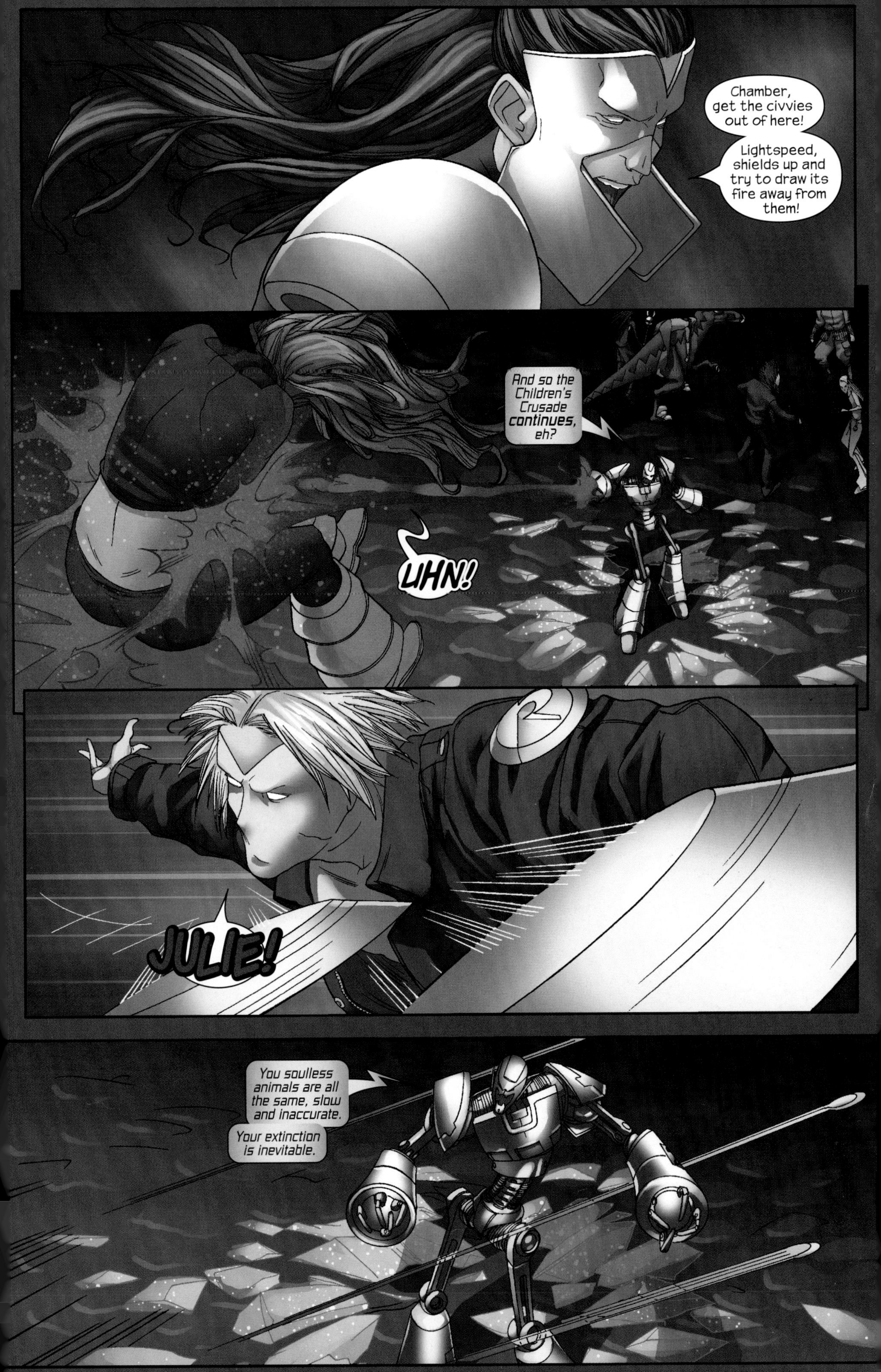
Chamber, get the civvies out of here!
Lightspeed, shields up and try to draw its fire away from them!
And so the Children's Crusade continues, eh?
UHN!
JULIE!
You soulless animals are all the same, slow and inaccurate.
Your extinction is inevitable.

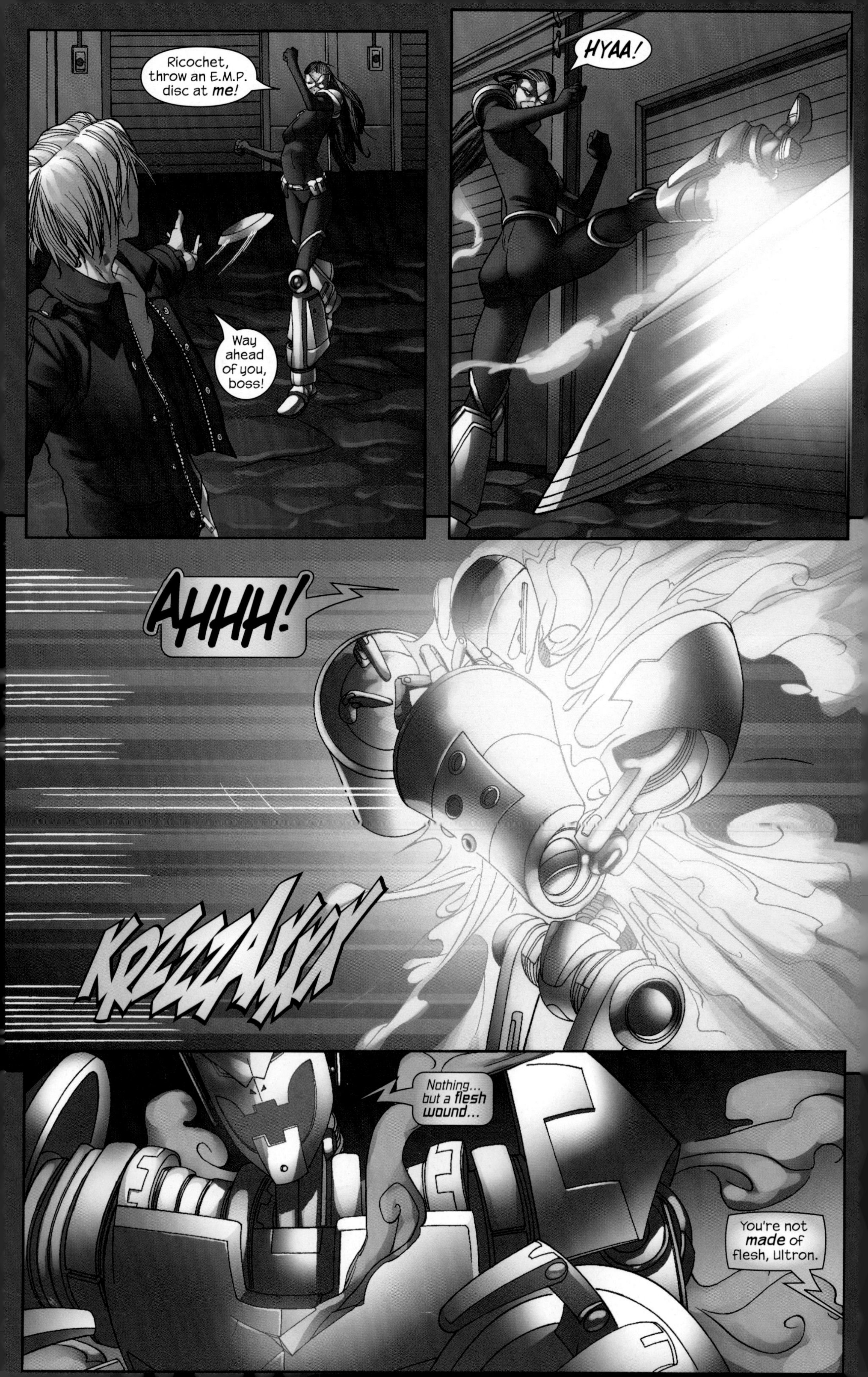
Ricochet, throw an E.M.P. disc at me!
Way ahead of you, boss!
HYAA!
AHHH!
KRZZZAKKK
Nothing... but a flesh wound...
You're not made of flesh, Ultron.

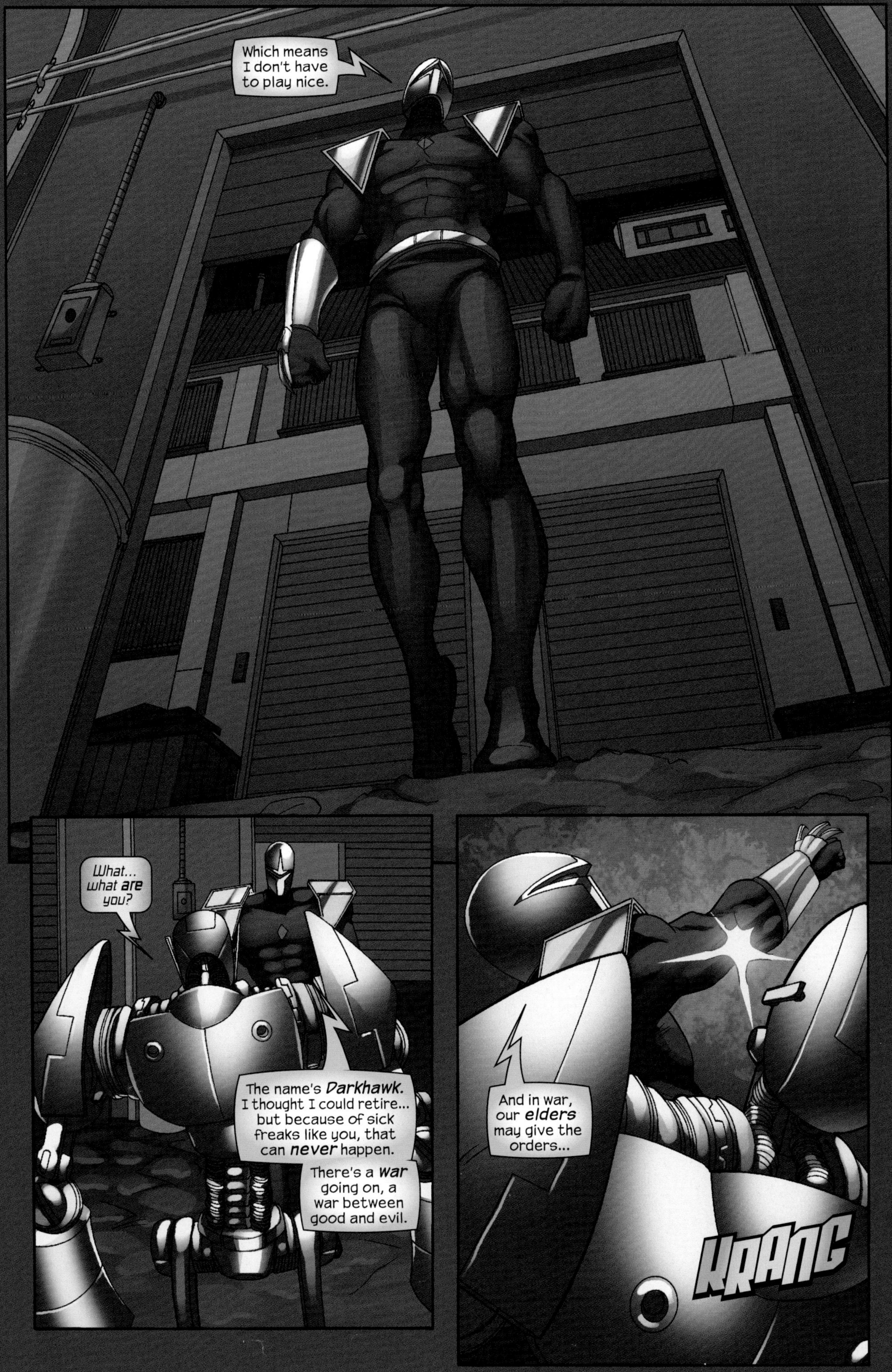

Which means I don't have to play nice.
What... what are you?
The name's Darkhawk. I thought I could retire... but because of sick freaks like you, that can never happen.
There's a war going on, a war between good and evil.
And in war, our elders may give the orders...
KRANG

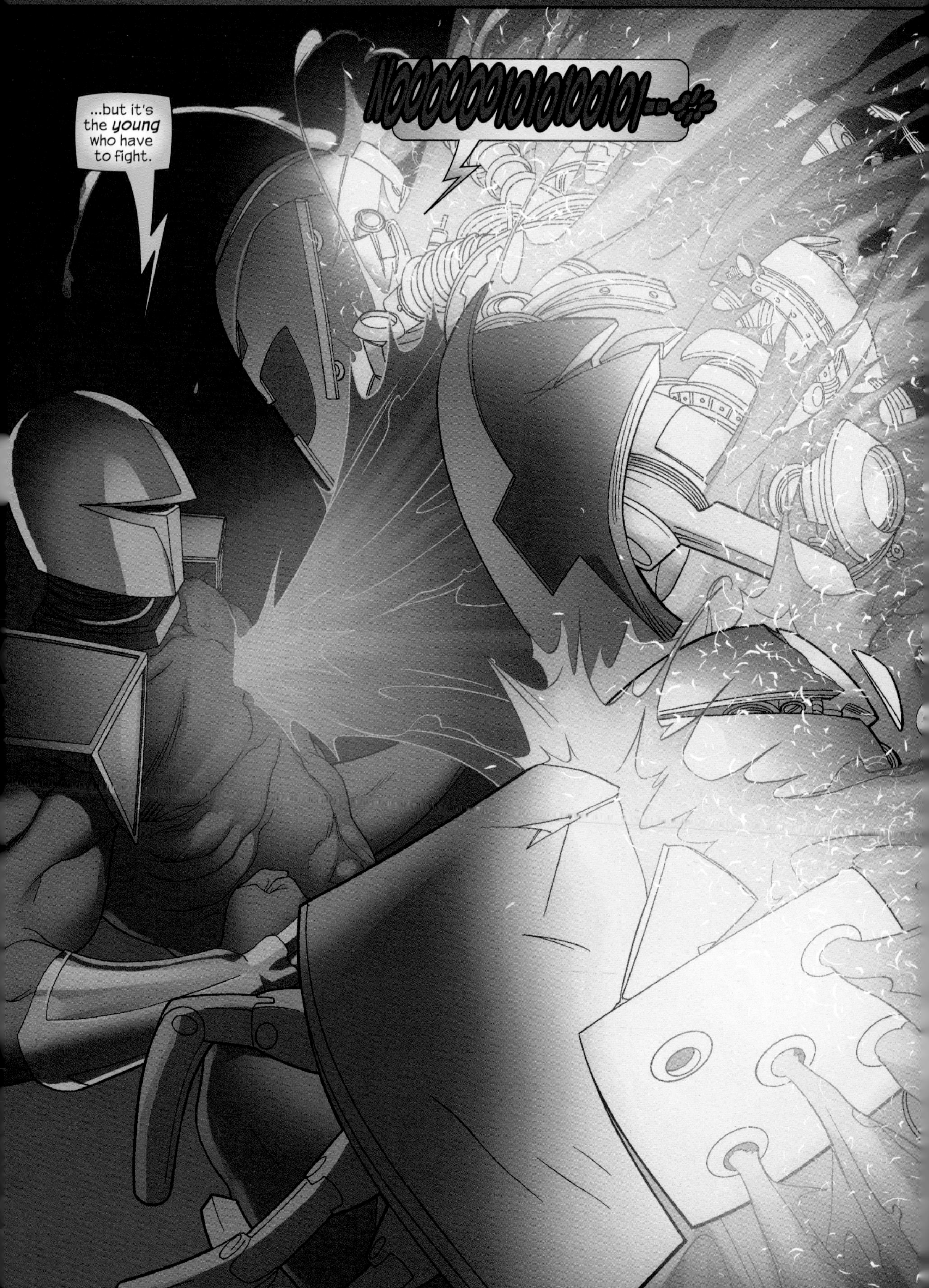

...but it's the *young* who have to fight.
NOOOOOOOIOIOIOOIOI--#

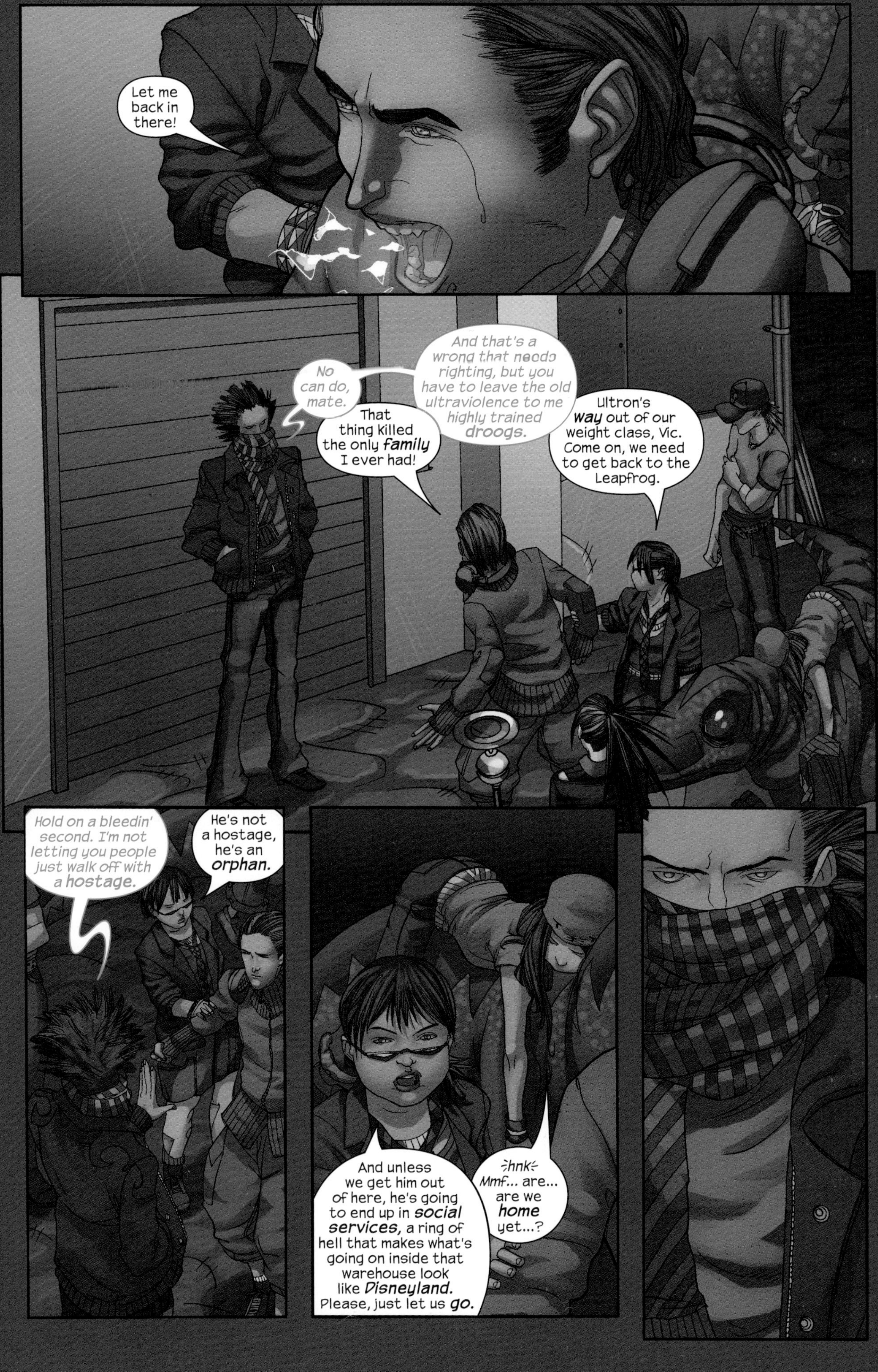
Let me back in there!
No can do, mate.
And that's a wrong that needs righting, but you have to leave the old ultraviolence to me highly trained droogs.
That thing killed the only family I ever had!
Ultron's way out of our weight class, Vic. Come on, we need to get back to the Leapfrog.
Hold on a bleedin' second. I'm not letting you people just walk off with a hostage.
He's not a hostage, he's an orphan.
And unless we get him out of here, he's going to end up in social services, a ring of hell that makes what's going on inside that warehouse look like Disneyland. Please, just let us go.
hnk Mmf... are... are we home yet...?

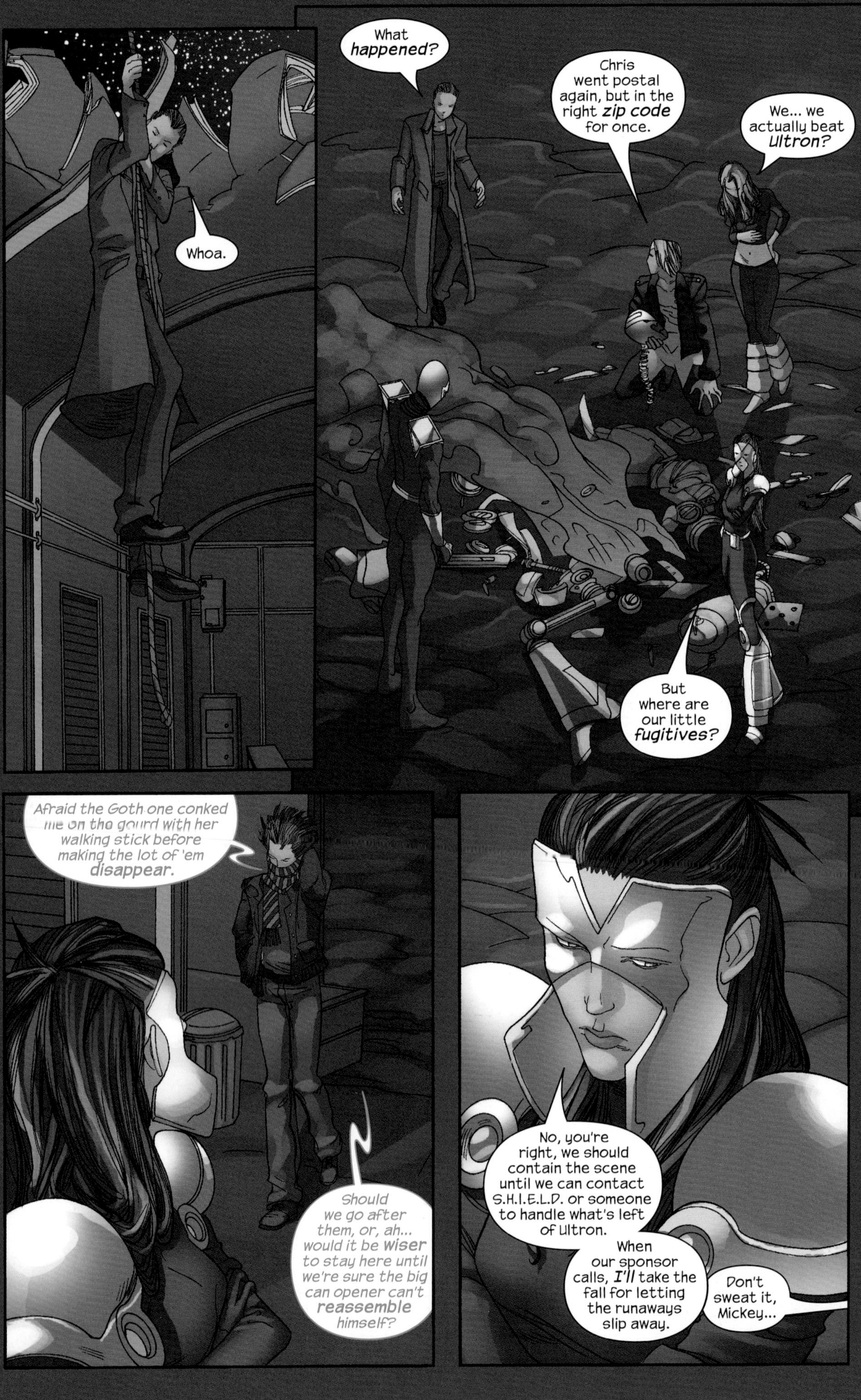
Whoa.
What happened?
Chris went postal again, but in the right zip code for once.
We... we actually beat Ultron?
But where are our little fugitives?
Afraid the Goth one conked me on the gourd with her walking stick before making the lot of 'em disappear.
Should we go after them, or, ah... would it be wiser to stay here until we're sure the big can opener can't reassemble himself?
No, you're right, we should contain the scene until we can contact S.H.I.E.L.D. or someone to handle what's left of Ultron.
When our sponsor calls, I'll take the fall for letting the runaways slip away.
Don't sweat it, Mickey...

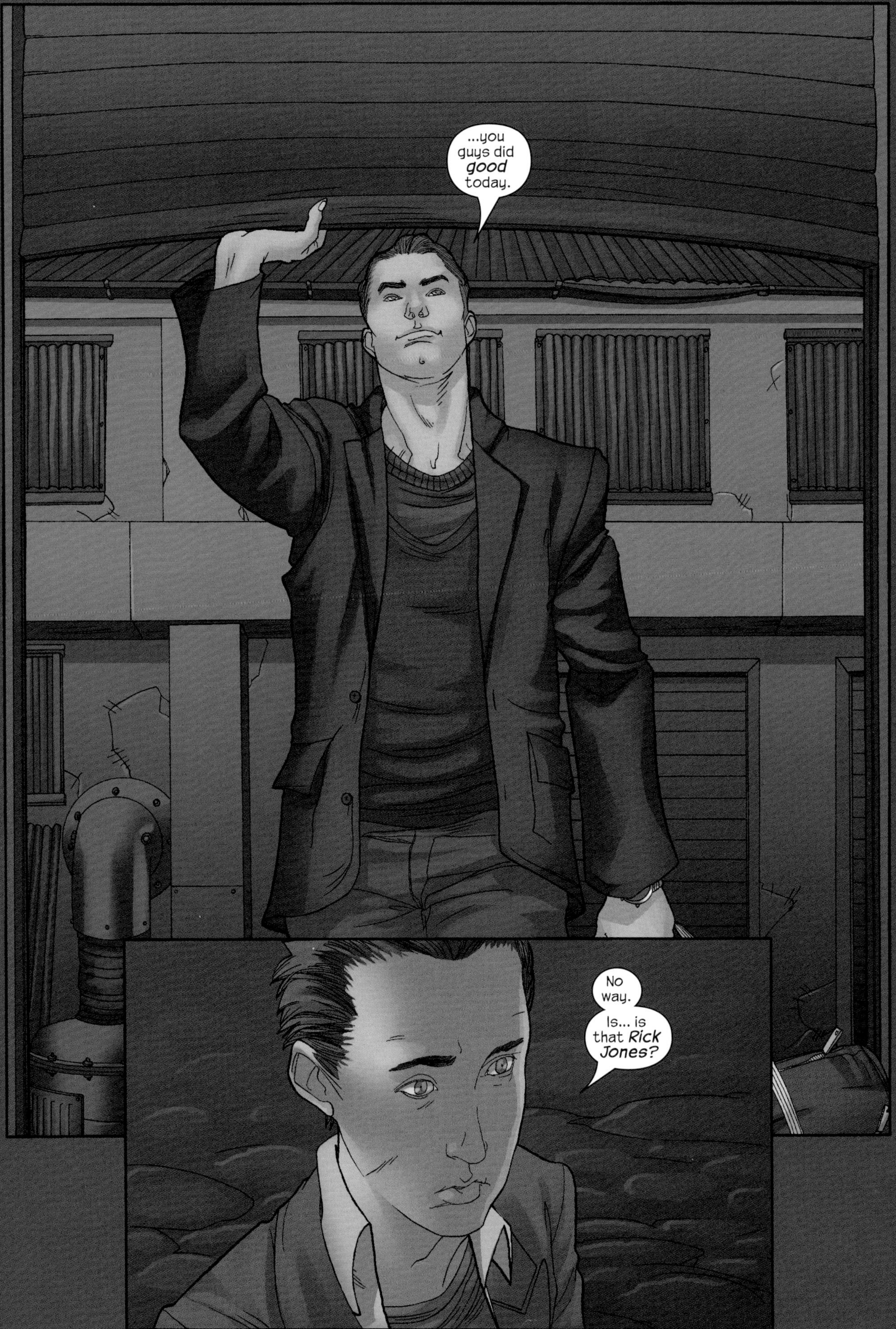
...you guys did *good* today.
No way.
Is... is that *Rick Jones?*

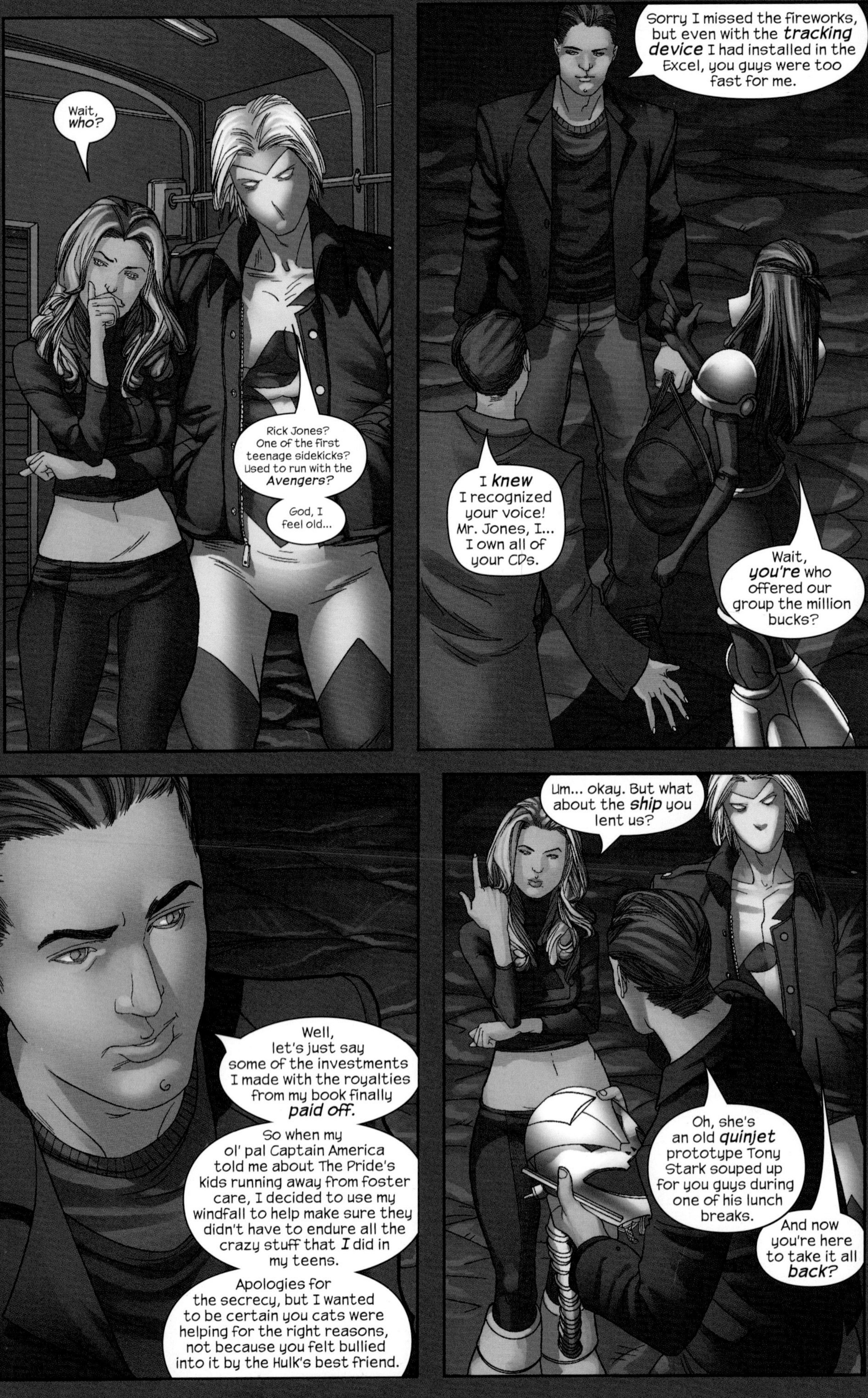

Wait, who?
Rick Jones? One of the first teenage sidekicks? Used to run with the Avengers?
God, I feel old...
Sorry I missed the fireworks, but even with the tracking device I had installed in the Excel, you guys were too fast for me.
I knew I recognized your voice! Mr. Jones, I... I own all of your CDs.
Wait, you're who offered our group the million bucks?
Well, let's just say some of the investments I made with the royalties from my book finally paid off.
So when my ol' pal Captain America told me about The Pride's kids running away from foster care, I decided to use my windfall to help make sure they didn't have to endure all the crazy stuff that I did in my teens.
Apologies for the secrecy, but I wanted to be certain you cats were helping for the right reasons, not because you felt bullied into it by the Hulk's best friend.
Um... okay. But what about the ship you lent us?
Oh, she's an old quinjet prototype Tony Stark souped up for you guys during one of his lunch breaks.
And now you're here to take it all back?

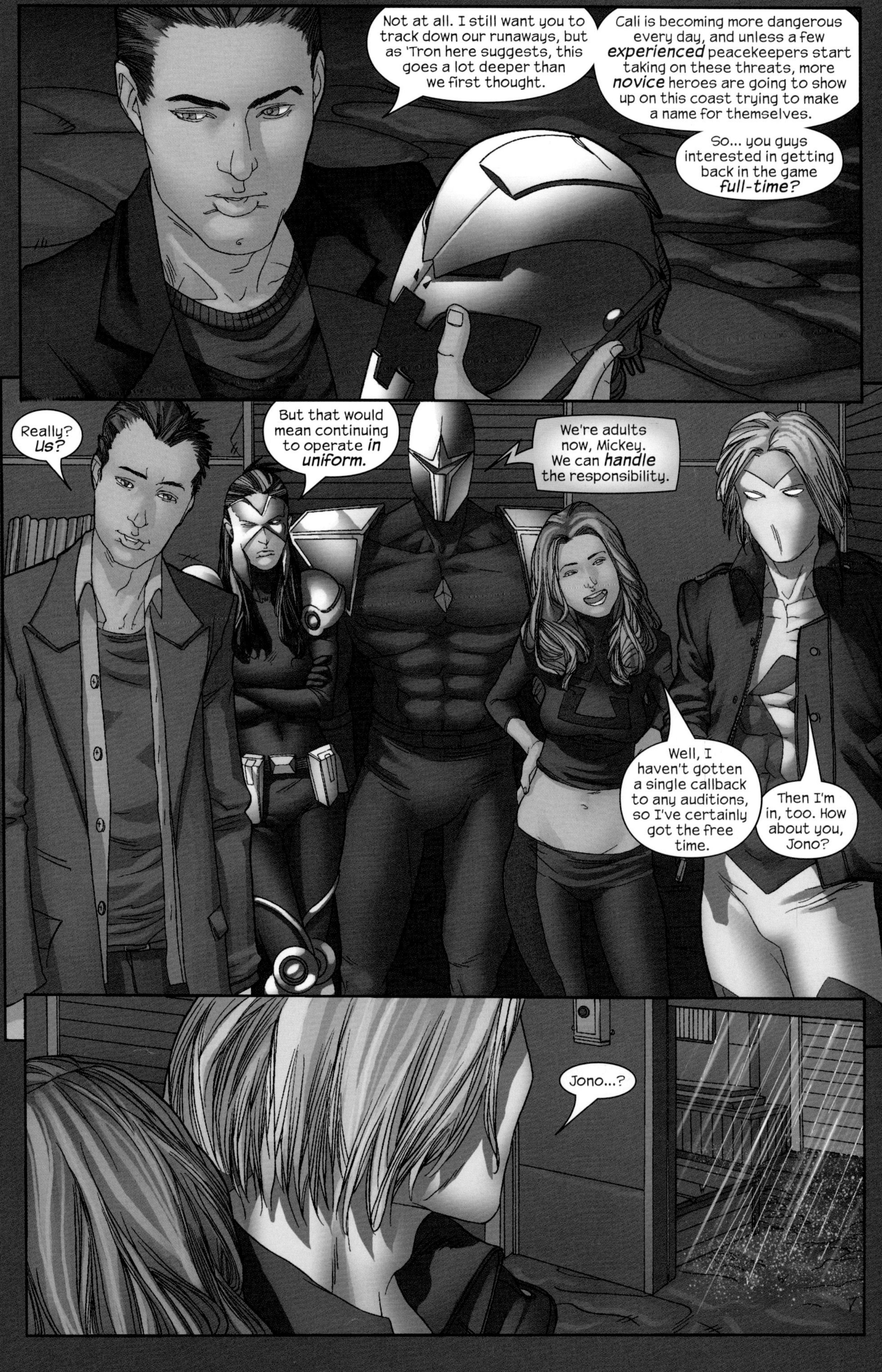
Not at all. I still want you to track down our runaways, but as 'Tron here suggests, this goes a lot deeper than we first thought.
Cali is becoming more dangerous every day, and unless a few *experienced* peacekeepers start taking on these threats, more *novice* heroes are going to show up on this coast trying to make a name for themselves.
So... you guys interested in getting back in the game *full-time?*
Really? *Us?*
But that would mean continuing to operate *in uniform.*
We're adults now, Mickey. We can *handle* the responsibility.
Well, I haven't gotten a single callback to any auditions, so I've certainly got the free time.
Then I'm in, too. How about you, Jono?
Jono...?

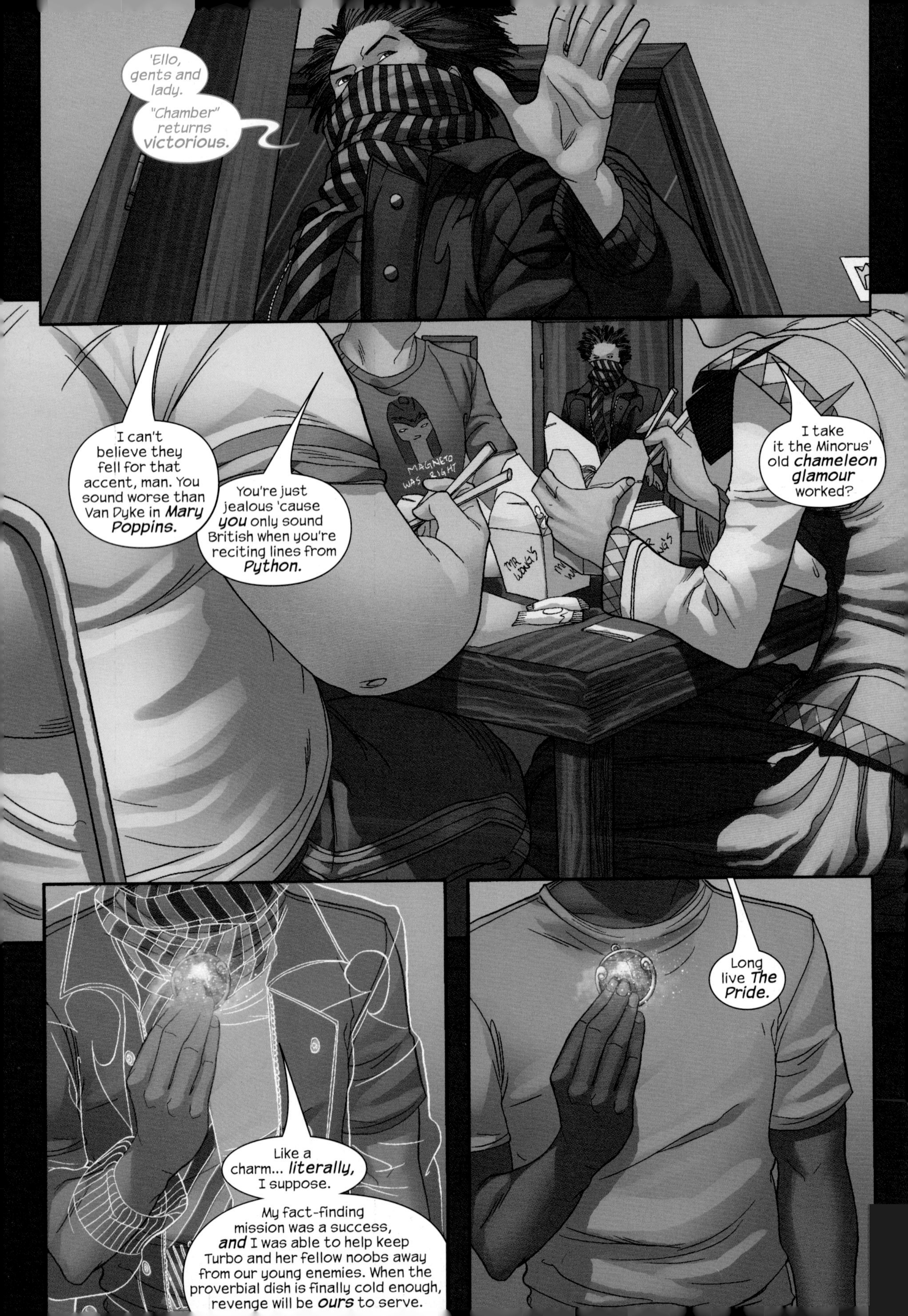

'Ello, gents and lady.
"Chamber" returns victorious.
I can't believe they fell for that accent, man. You sound worse than Van Dyke in Mary Poppins.
You're just jealous 'cause you only sound British when you're reciting lines from Python.
I take it the Minorus' old chameleon glamour worked?
MAGNETO WAS RIGHT
Like a charm... literally, I suppose.
My fact-finding mission was a success, and I was able to help keep Turbo and her fellow noobs away from our young enemies. When the proverbial dish is finally cold enough, revenge will be ours to serve.
Long live The Pride.

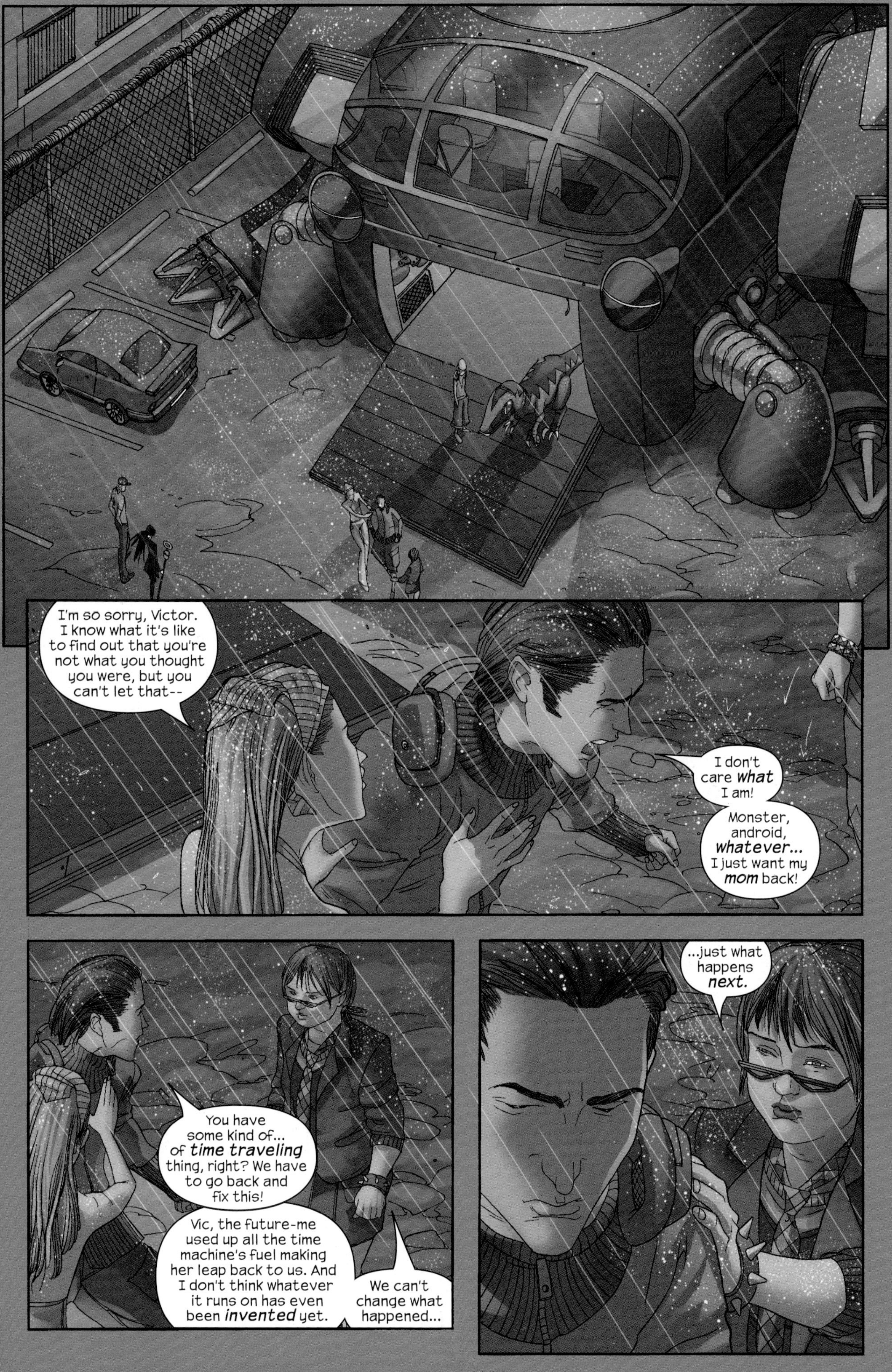

I'm so sorry, Victor. I know what it's like to find out that you're not what you thought you were, but you can't let that--
I don't care *what* I am!
Monster, android, *whatever...* I just want my *mom* back!
You have some kind of... of *time traveling* thing, right? We have to go back and fix this!
Vic, the future-me used up all the time machine's fuel making her leap back to us. And I don't think whatever it runs on has even been *invented* yet.
We can't change what happened...
...just what happens *next.*

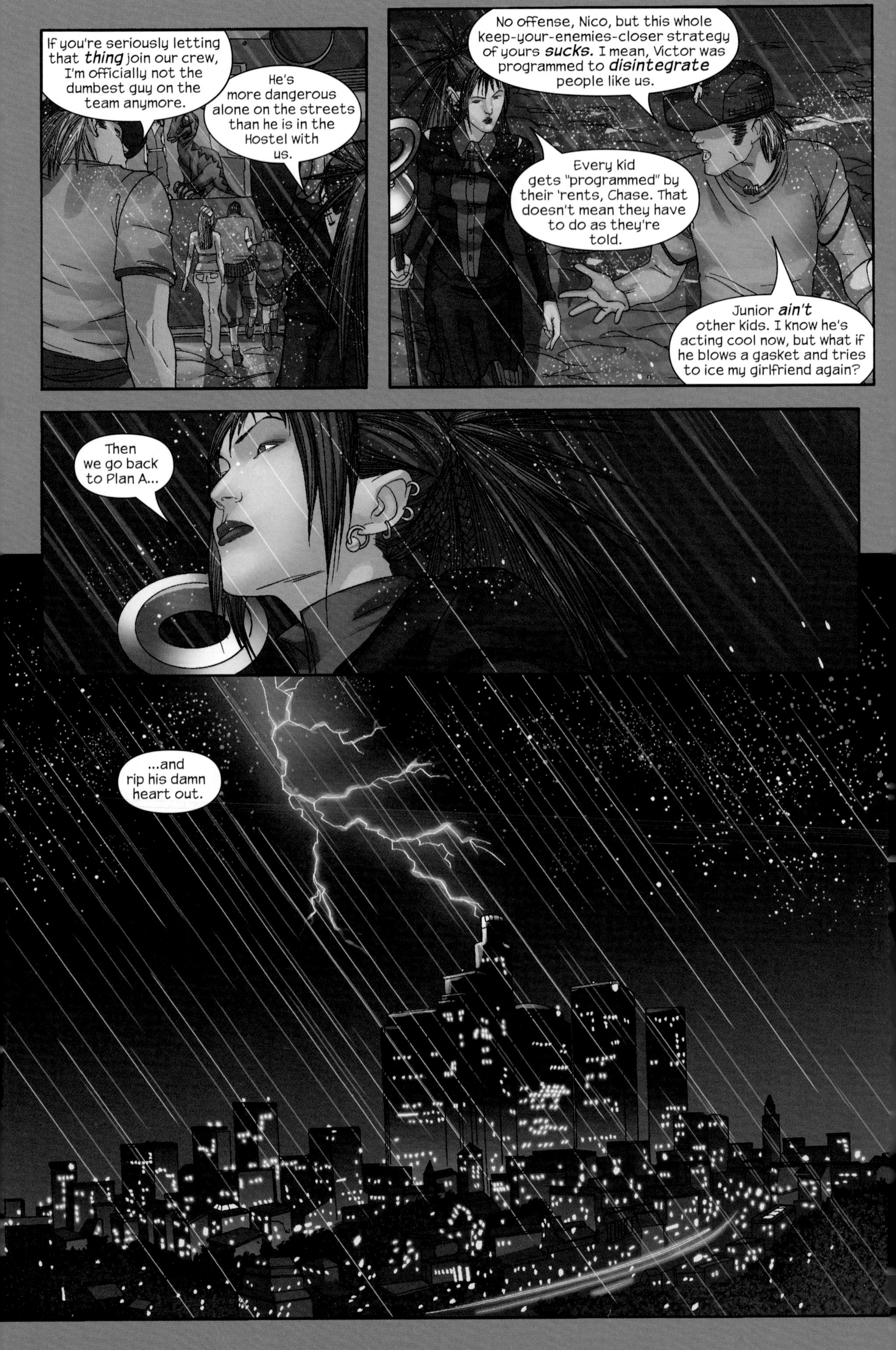
If you're seriously letting that *thing* join our crew, I'm officially not the dumbest guy on the team anymore.
He's more dangerous alone on the streets than he is in the Hostel with us.
No offense, Nico, but this whole keep-your-enemies-closer strategy of yours *sucks.* I mean, Victor was programmed to *disintegrate* people like us.
Every kid gets "programmed" by their 'rents, Chase. That doesn't mean they have to do as they're told.
Junior *ain't* other kids. I know he's acting cool now, but what if he blows a gasket and tries to ice my girlfriend again?
Then we go back to Plan A...
...and rip his damn heart out.

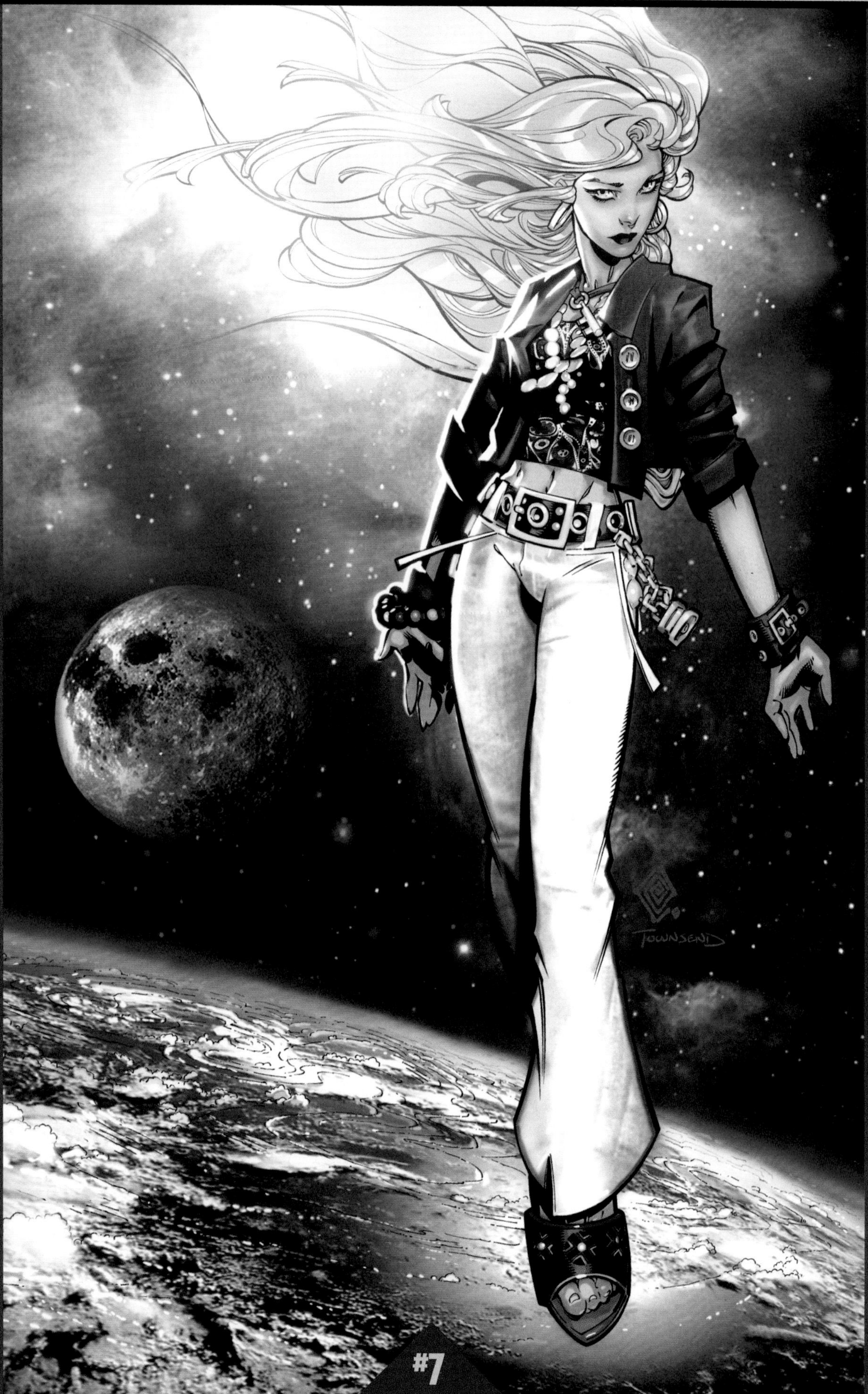
TOWNSEND
#7

STAR-CROSSED PART 1

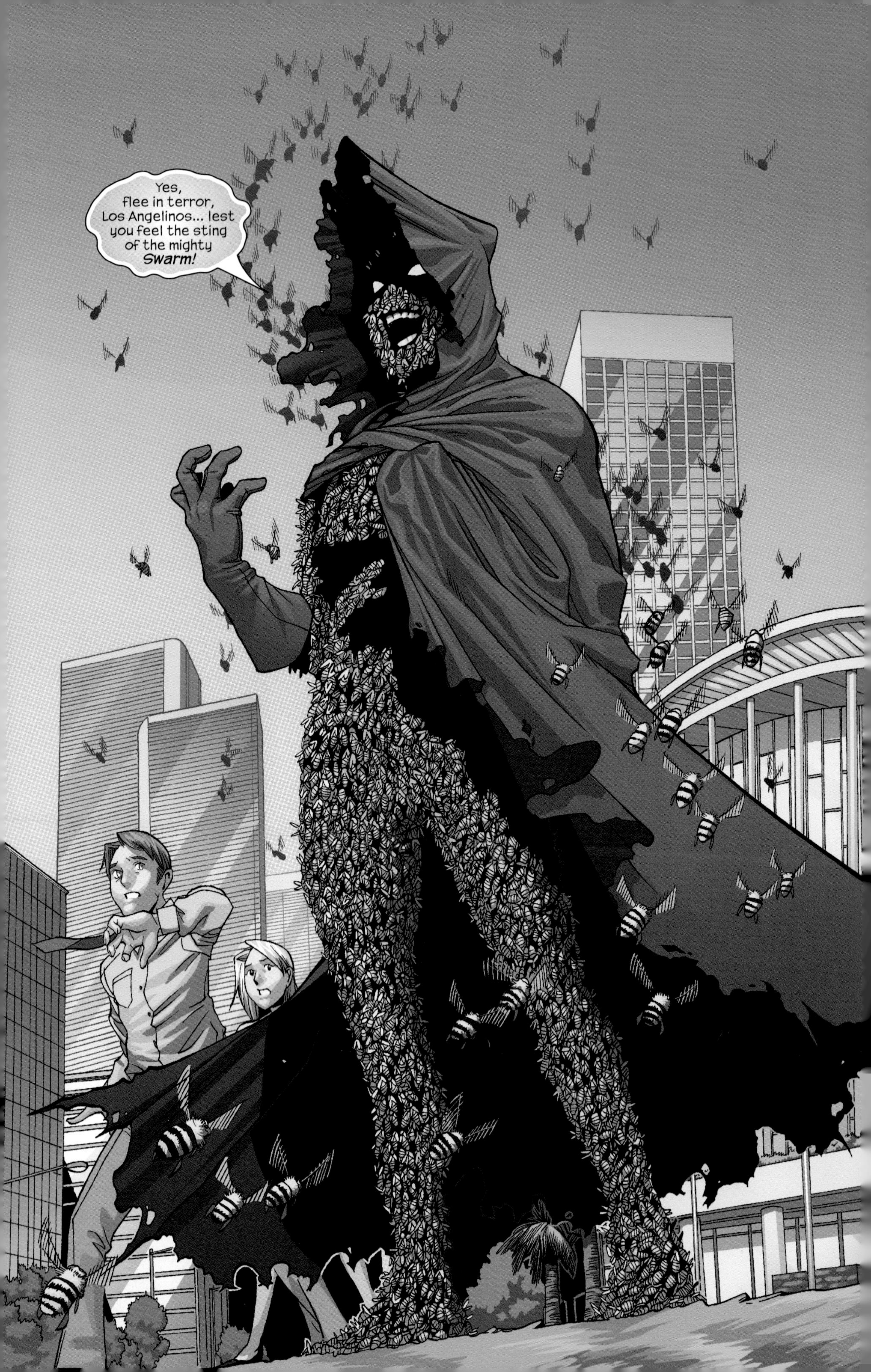
Yes, flee in terror, Los Angelinos... lest you feel the sting of the mighty *Swarm!*

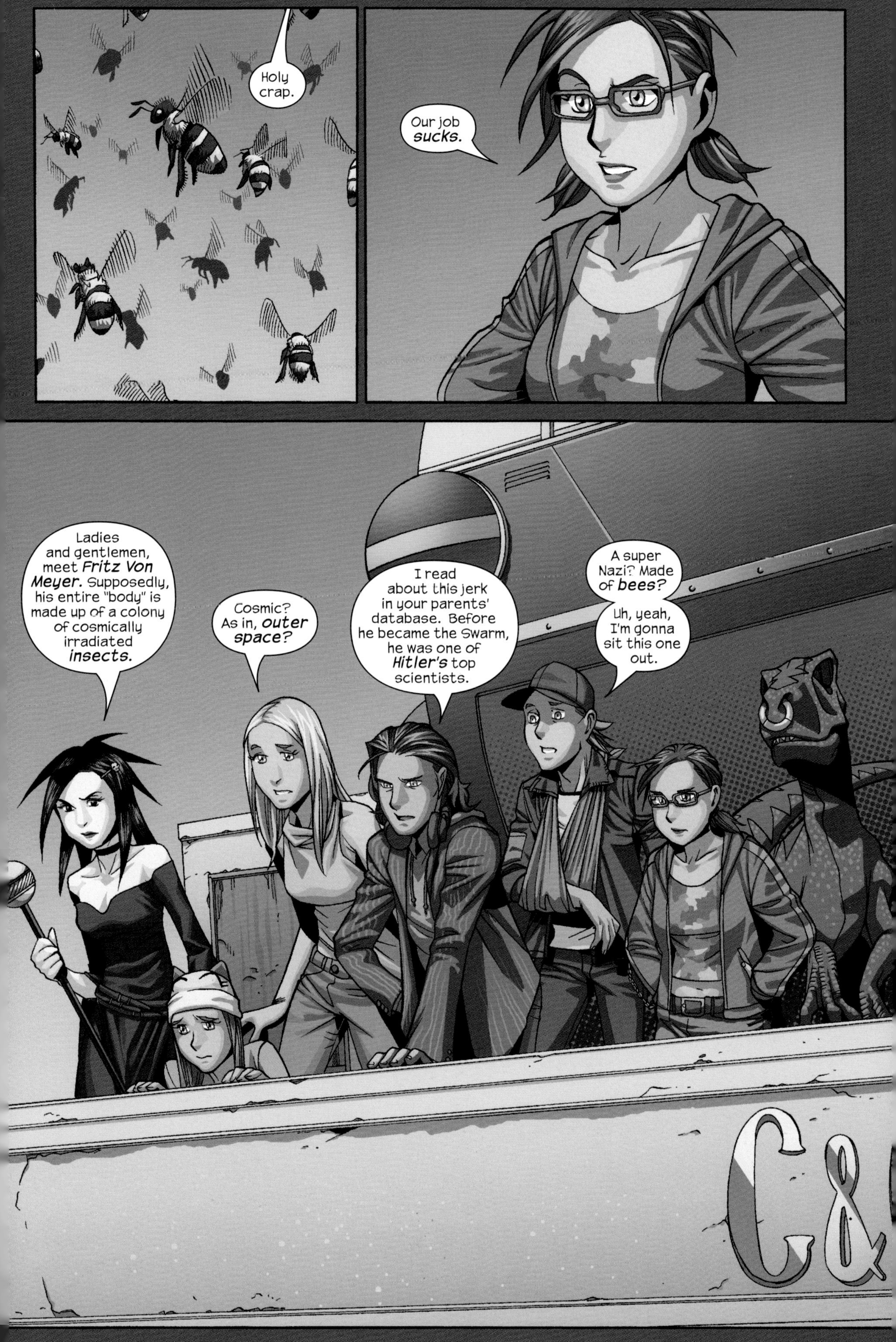

Holy crap.
Our job *sucks.*
Ladies and gentlemen, meet *Fritz Von Meyer.* Supposedly, his entire "body" is made up of a colony of cosmically irradiated *insects.*
Cosmic? As in, *outer space?*
I read about this jerk in your parents' database. Before he became the Swarm, he was one of *Hitler's* top scientists.
A super Nazi? Made of *bees?*
Uh, yeah, I'm gonna sit this one out.

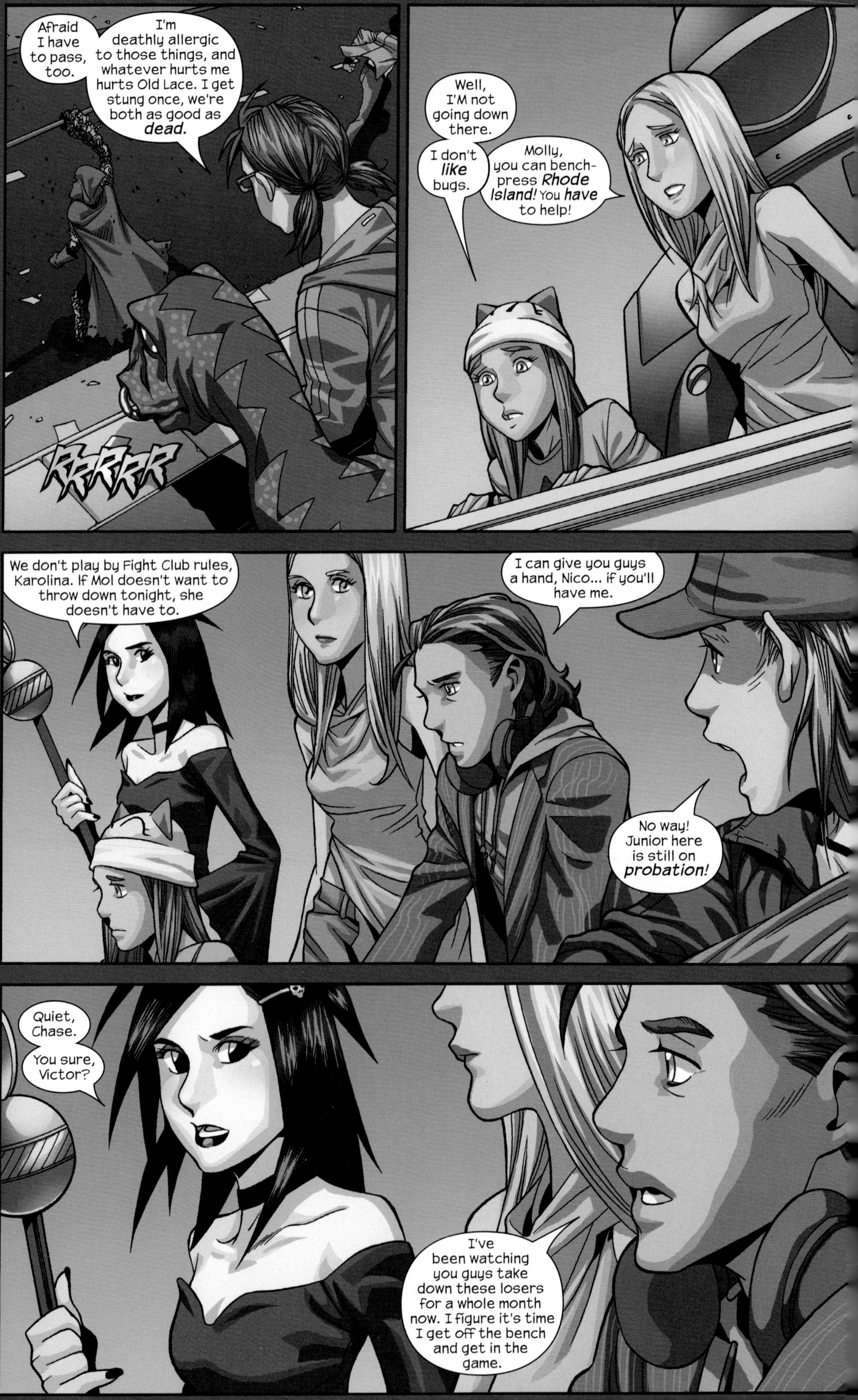
Afraid I have to pass, too.
I'm deathly allergic to those things, and whatever hurts me hurts Old Lace. I get stung once, we're both as good as dead.
RRRRR
Well, I'M not going down there.
Molly, you can bench-press Rhode Island! You have to help!
I don't like bugs.
We don't play by Fight Club rules, Karolina. If Mol doesn't want to throw down tonight, she doesn't have to.
I can give you guys a hand, Nico... if you'll have me.
No way! Junior here is still on probation!
Quiet, Chase.
You sure, Victor?
I've been watching you guys take down these losers for a whole month now. I figure it's time I get off the bench and get in the game.

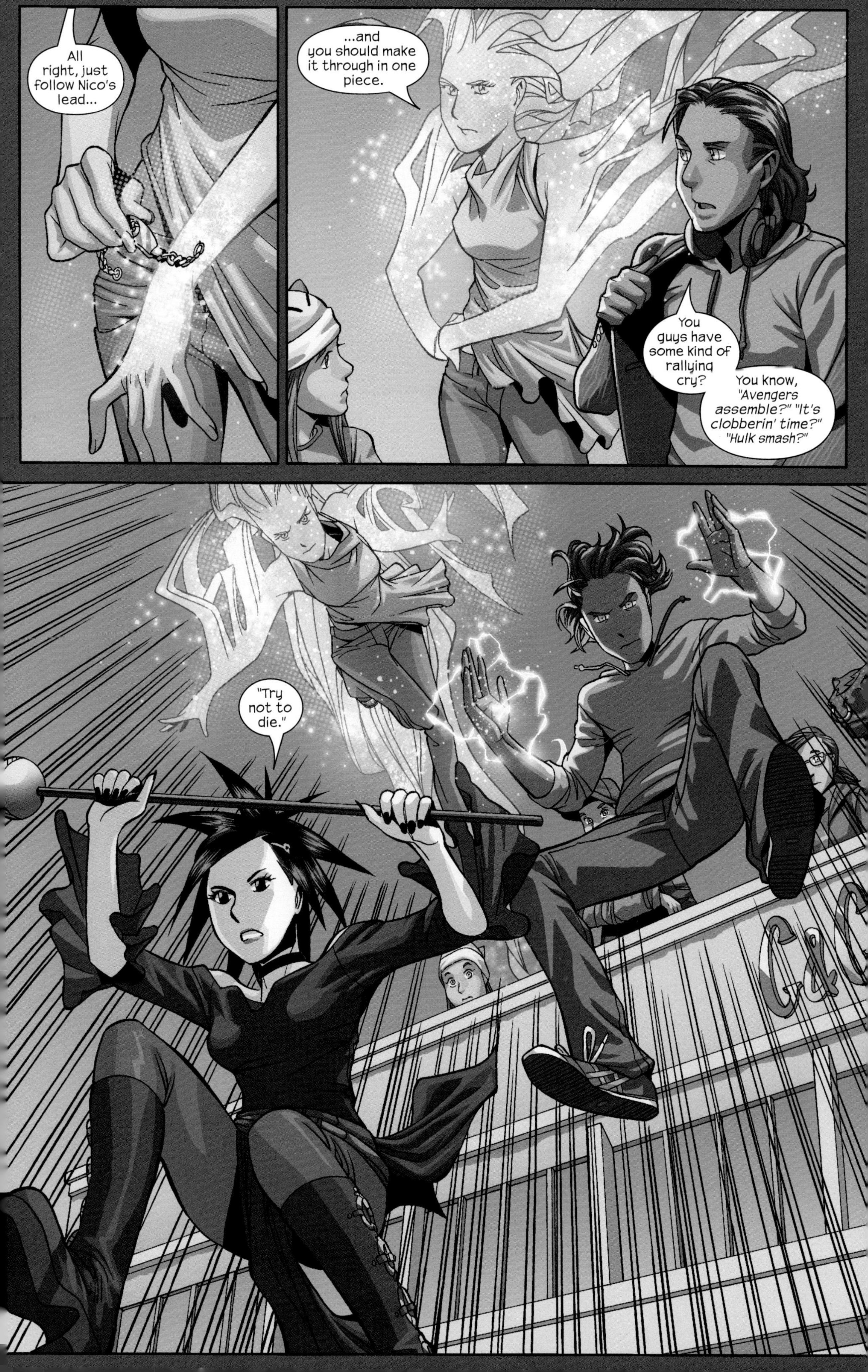
All right, just follow Nico's lead...
...and you should make it through in one piece.
You guys have some kind of rallying cry?
You know, "Avengers assemble?" "It's clobberin' time?" "Hulk smash?"
"Try not to die."

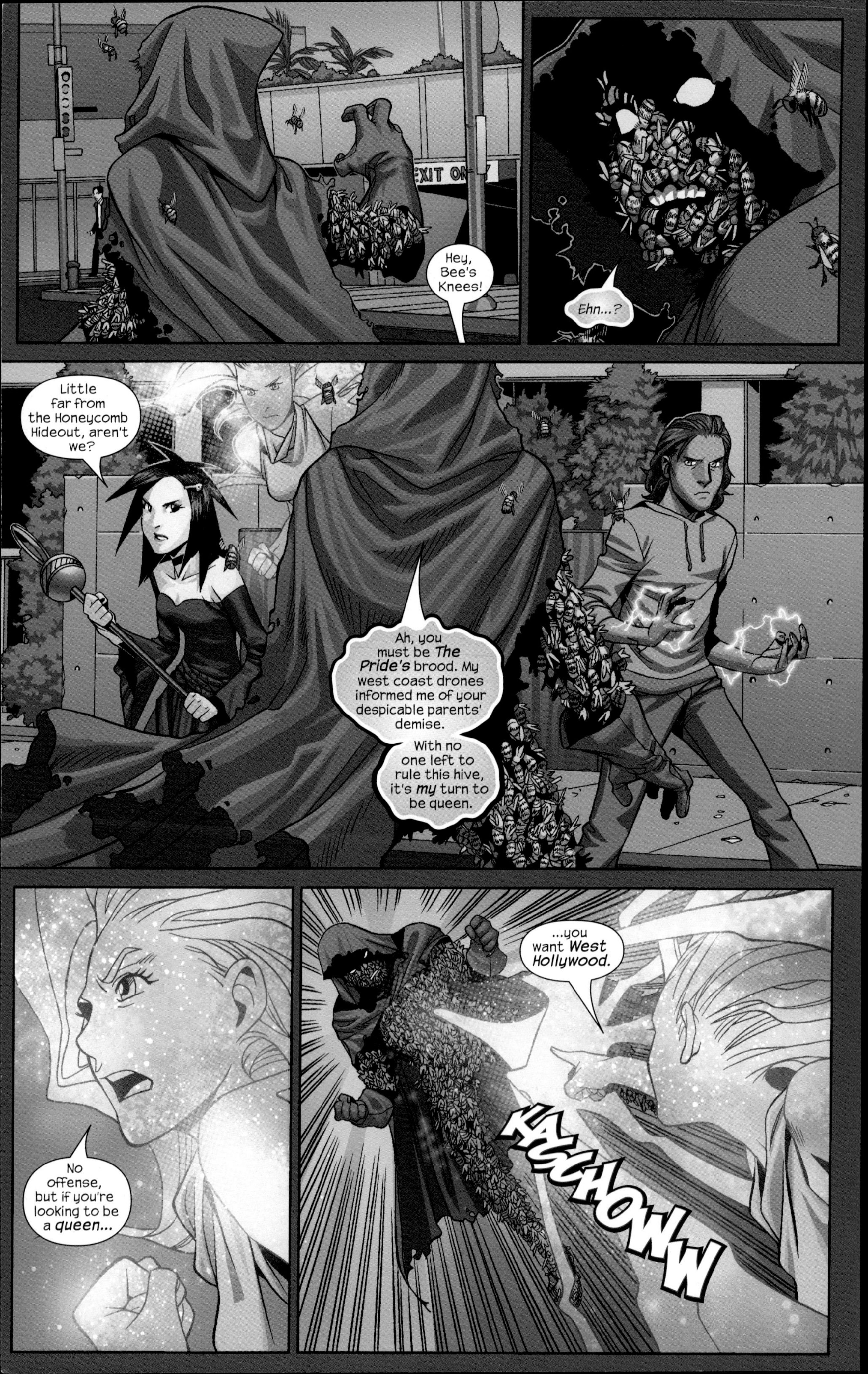
EXIT ONLY
Hey, Bee's Knees!
Ehn...?
Little far from the Honeycomb Hideout, aren't we?
Ah, you must be *The Pride's* brood. My west coast drones informed me of your despicable parents' demise.
With no one left to rule this hive, it's *my* turn to be queen.
No offense, but if you're looking to be a *queen*...
...you want *West Hollywood.*
KASCHOWW

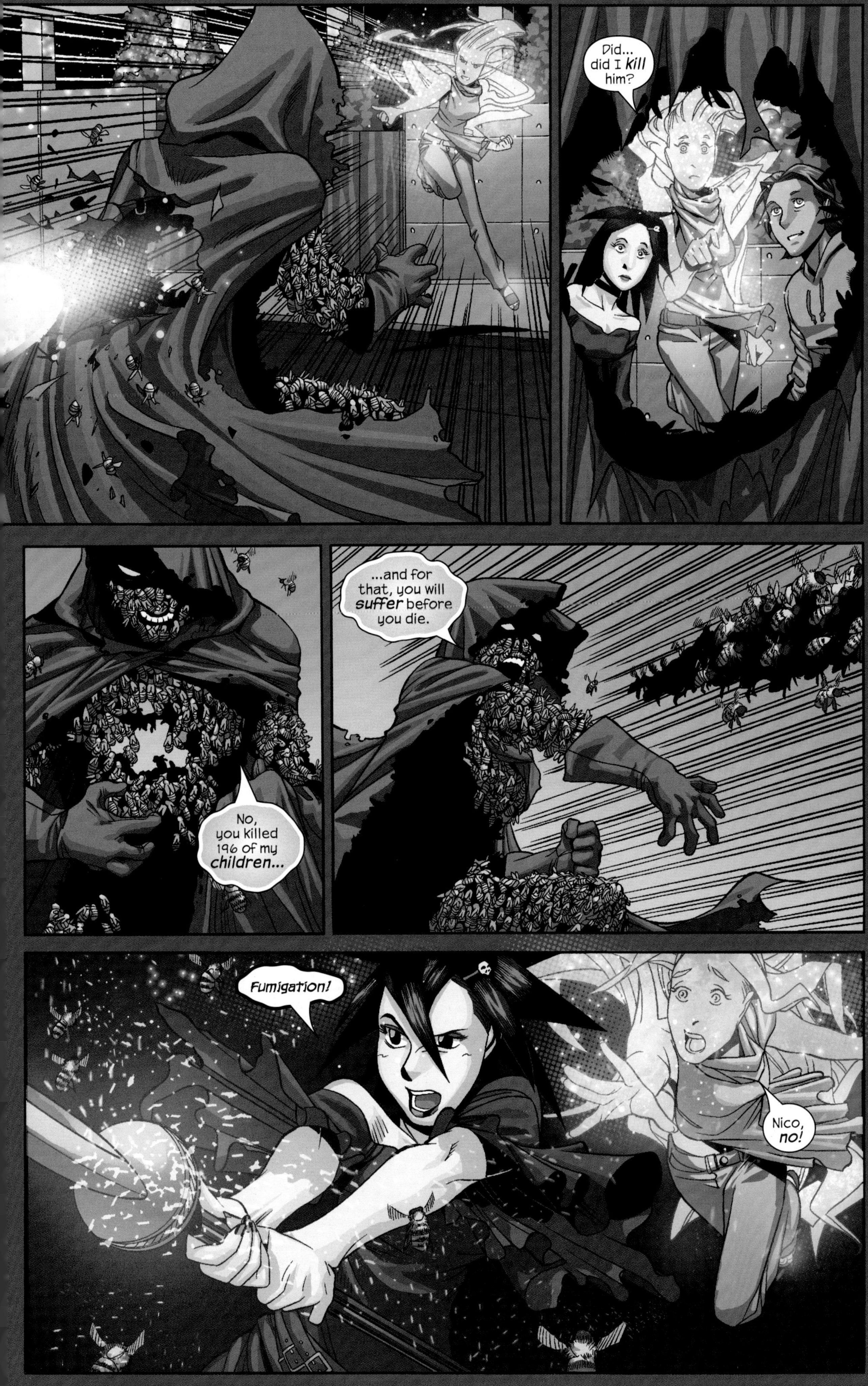
Did... did I *kill* him?
No, you killed 196 of my *children*...
...and for that, you will *suffer* before you die.
Fumigation!
Nico, *no!*

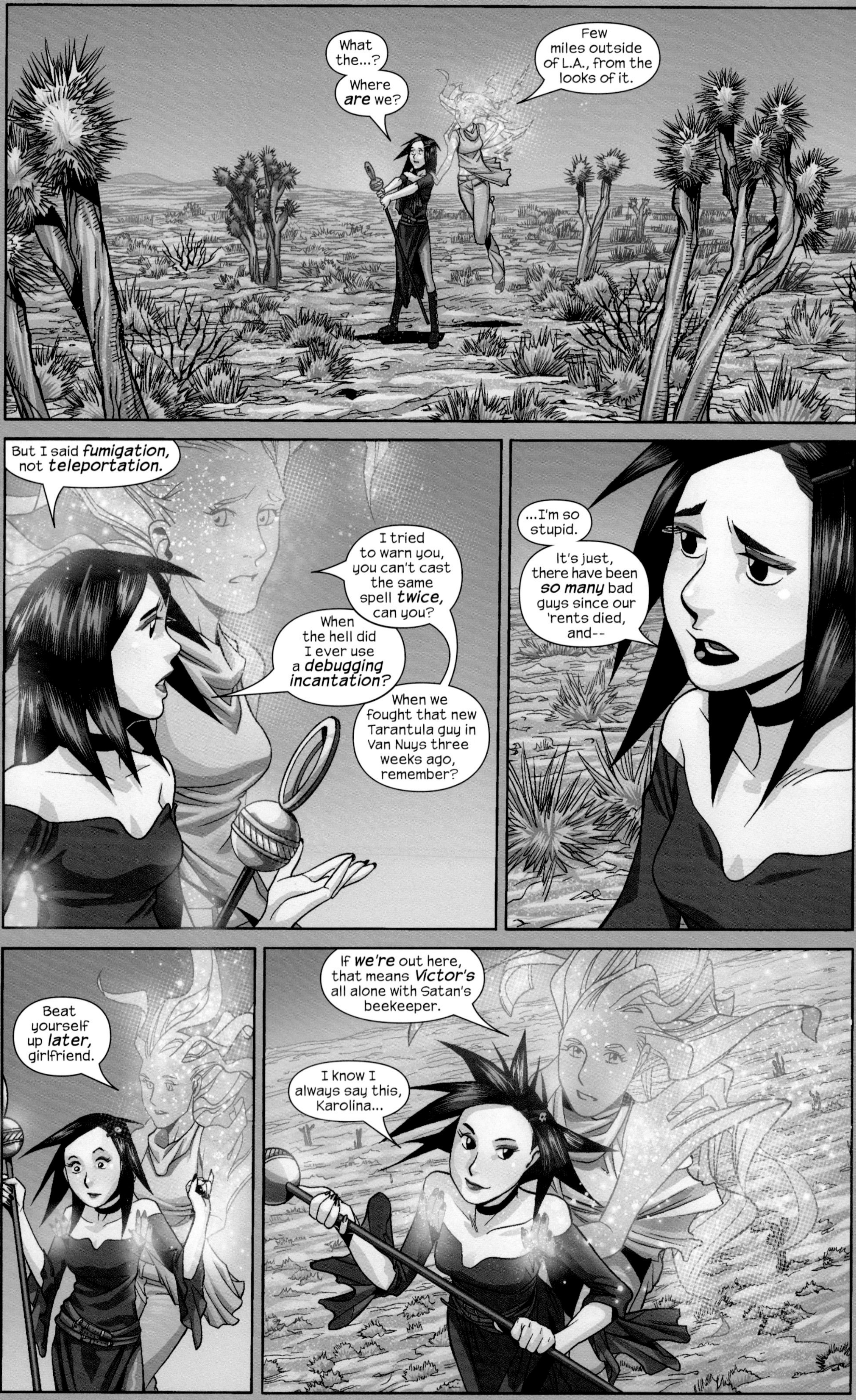
What the...?
Where *are* we?
Few miles outside of L.A., from the looks of it.
But I said *fumigation,* not *teleportation.*
I tried to warn you, you can't cast the same spell *twice,* can you?
When the hell did I ever use a *debugging incantation?*
When we fought that new Tarantula guy in Van Nuys three weeks ago, remember?
...I'm so stupid.
It's just, there have been *so many* bad guys since our 'rents died, and--
Beat yourself up *later,* girlfriend.
If *we're* out here, that means *Victor's* all alone with Satan's beekeeper.
I know I always say this, Karolina...

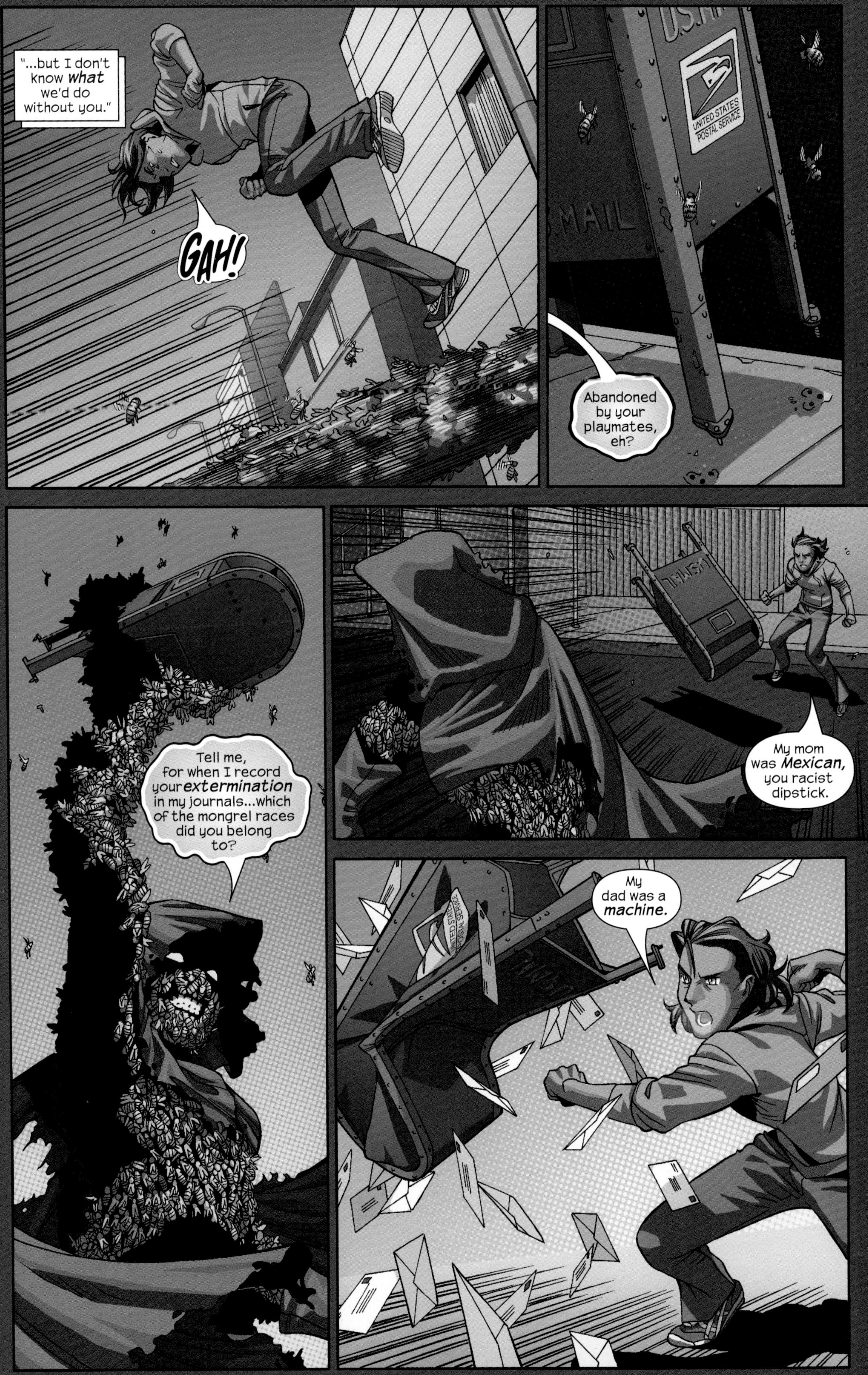

"...but I don't know *what* we'd do without you."
GAH!
U.S. MAIL
UNITED STATES POSTAL SERVICE
Abandoned by your playmates, eh?
Tell me, for when I record your *extermination* in my journals...which of the mongrel races did you belong to?
My mom was *Mexican,* you racist dipstick.
My dad was a *machine.*

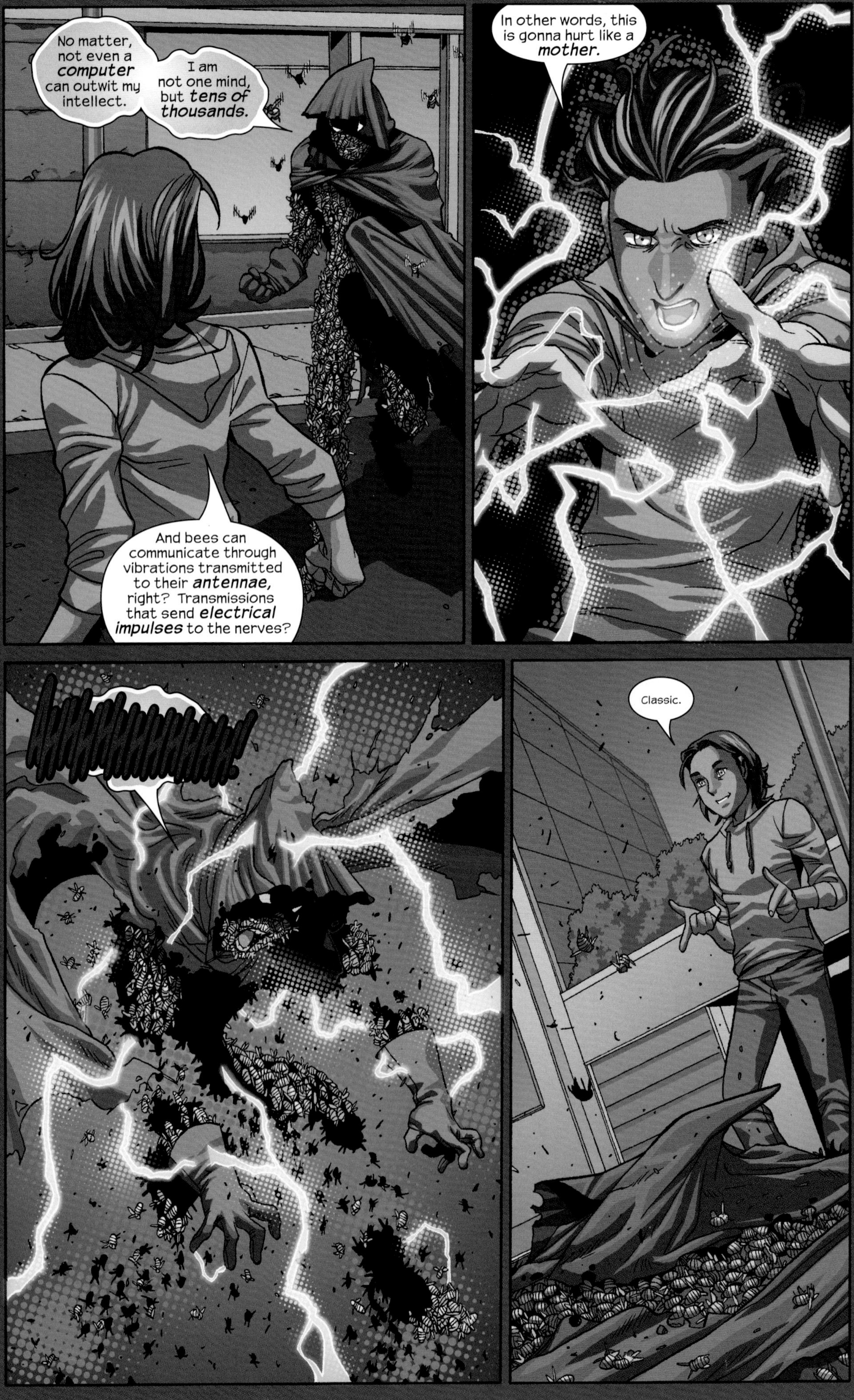
No matter, not even a computer can outwit my intellect.
I am not one mind, but tens of thousands.
And bees can communicate through vibrations transmitted to their antennae, right? Transmissions that send electrical impulses to the nerves?
In other words, this is gonna hurt like a mother.
Classic.

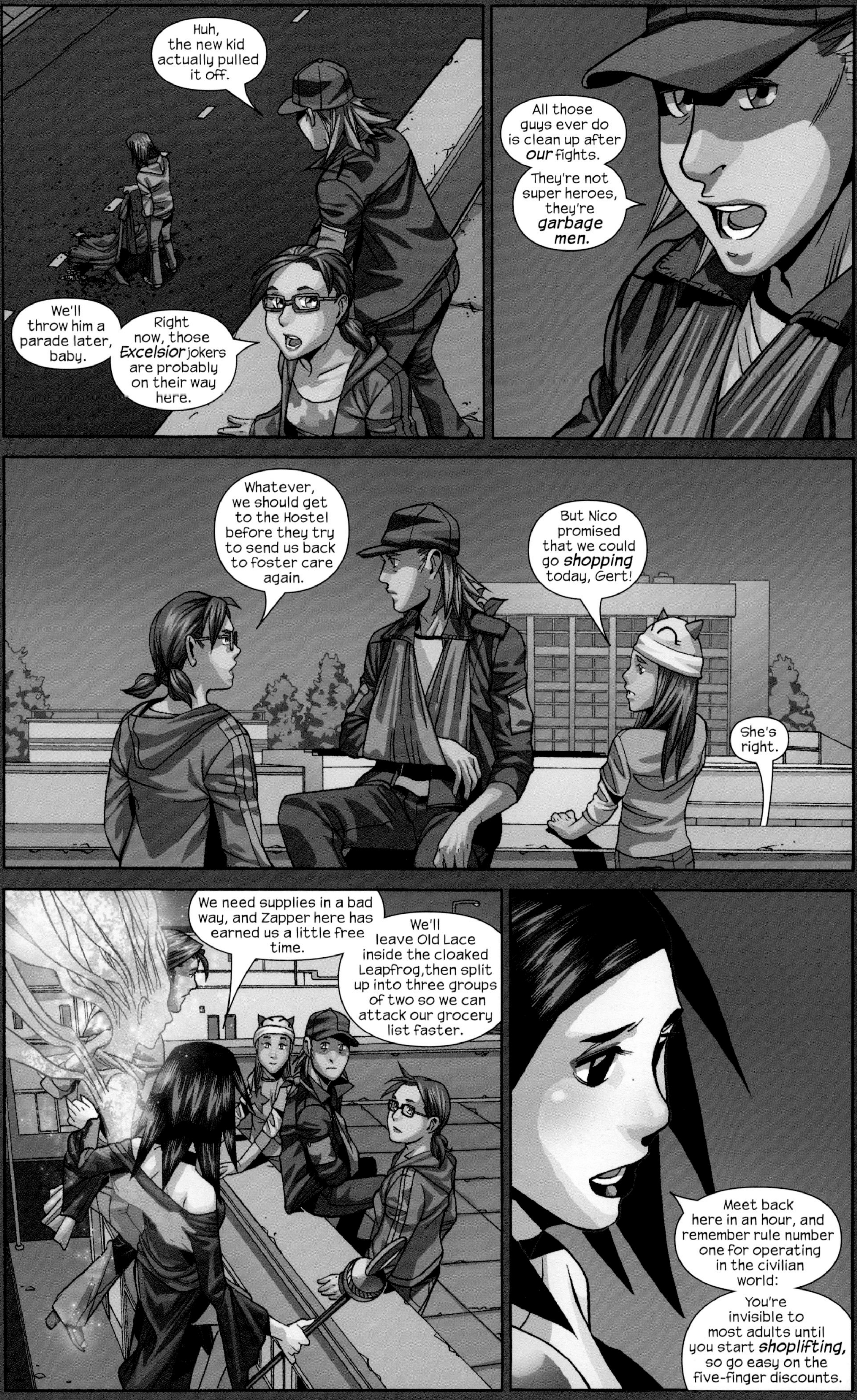

Huh, the new kid actually pulled it off.
We'll throw him a parade later, baby.
Right now, those Excelsior jokers are probably on their way here.
All those guys ever do is clean up after our fights.
They're not super heroes, they're garbage men.
Whatever, we should get to the Hostel before they try to send us back to foster care again.
But Nico promised that we could go shopping today, Gert!
She's right.
We need supplies in a bad way, and Zapper here has earned us a little free time.
We'll leave Old Lace inside the cloaked Leapfrog, then split up into three groups of two so we can attack our grocery list faster.
Meet back here in an hour, and remember rule number one for operating in the civilian world:
You're invisible to most adults until you start shoplifting, so go easy on the five-finger discounts.

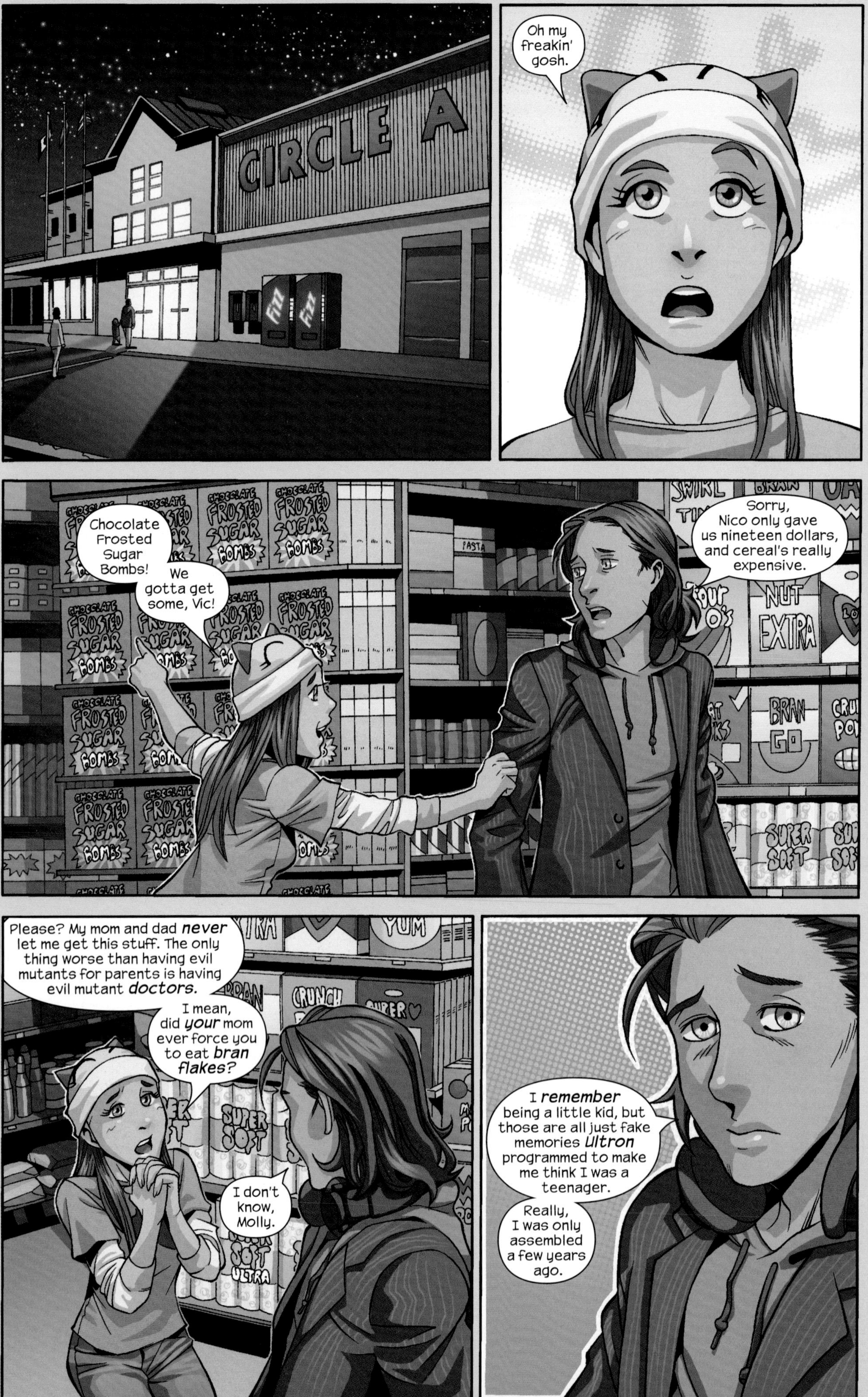
CIRCLE A
FIZZ
FIZZ
Oh my freakin' gosh.
CHOCOLATE FROSTED SUGAR BOMBS
Chocolate Frosted Sugar Bombs!
We gotta get some, Vic!
Sorry, Nico only gave us nineteen dollars, and cereal's really expensive.
PASTA
NUT EXTRA
BRAN GO
SUPER SOFT
Please? My mom and dad ***never*** let me get this stuff. The only thing worse than having evil mutants for parents is having evil mutant ***doctors***.
I mean, did ***your*** mom ever force you to eat ***bran flakes***?
I don't know, Molly.
CRUNCH
YUM
SUPER SOFT
I ***remember*** being a little kid, but those are all just fake memories ***Ultron*** programmed to make me think I was a teenager.
Really, I was only assembled a few years ago.

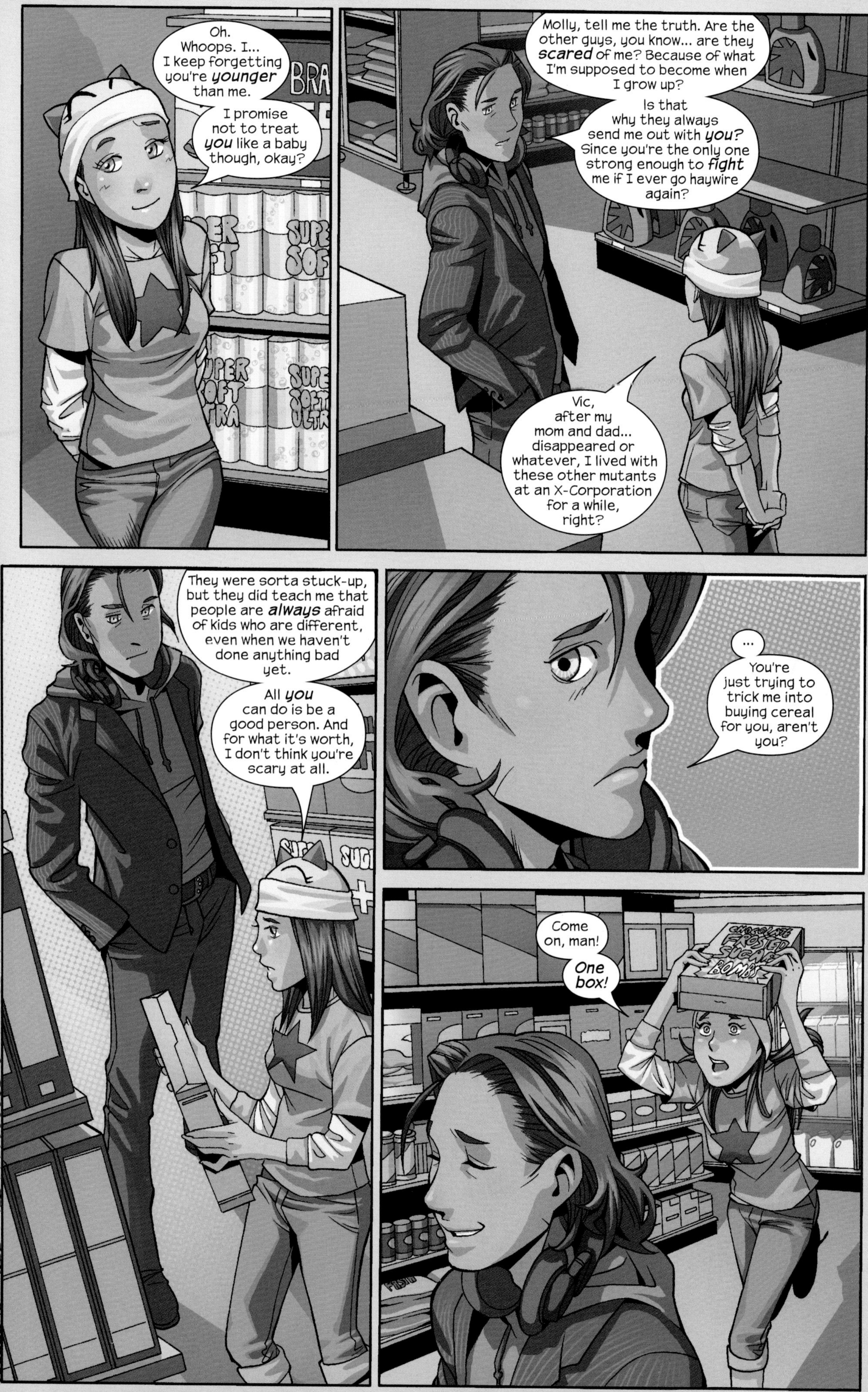
Oh. Whoops. I... I keep forgetting you're *younger* than me.
I promise not to treat *you* like a baby though, okay?
SUPER SOFT
Molly, tell me the truth. Are the other guys, you know... are they *scared* of me? Because of what I'm supposed to become when I grow up?
Is that why they always send me out with *you?* Since you're the only one strong enough to *fight* me if I ever go haywire again?
Vic, after my mom and dad... disappeared or whatever, I lived with these other mutants at an X-Corporation for a while, right?
They were sorta stuck-up, but they did teach me that people are *always* afraid of kids who are different, even when we haven't done anything bad yet.
All *you* can do is be a good person. And for what it's worth, I don't think you're scary at all.
...
You're just trying to trick me into buying cereal for you, aren't you?
Come on, man!
One box!
CHOCOLATE FROSTED SUGAR BOMBS

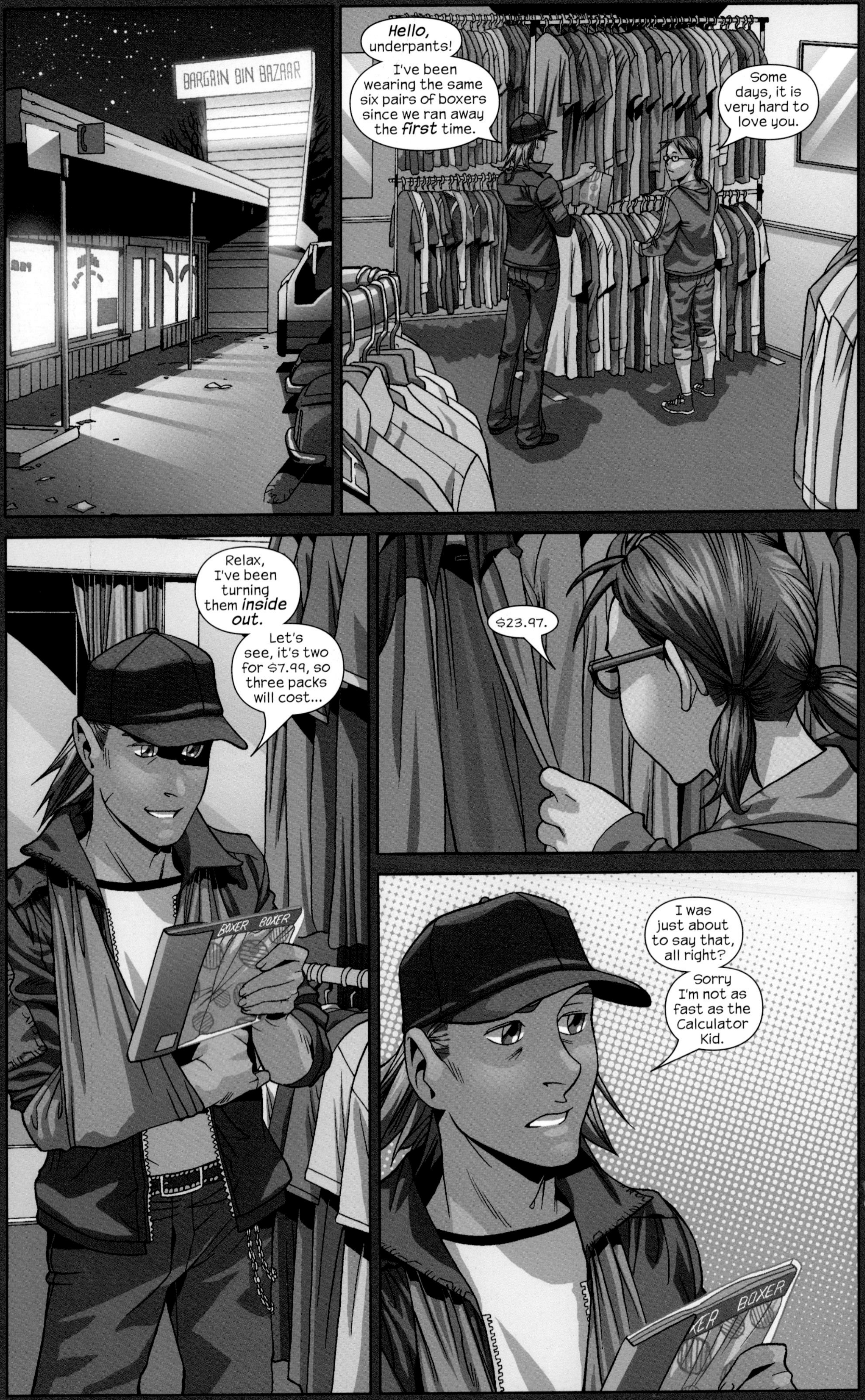
BARGAIN BIN BAZAAR
Hello, underpants!
I've been wearing the same six pairs of boxers since we ran away the first time.
Some days, it is very hard to love you.
Relax, I've been turning them inside out.
Let's see, it's two for $7.99, so three packs will cost...
$23.97.
I was just about to say that, all right?
Sorry I'm not as fast as the Calculator Kid.
BOXER BOXER

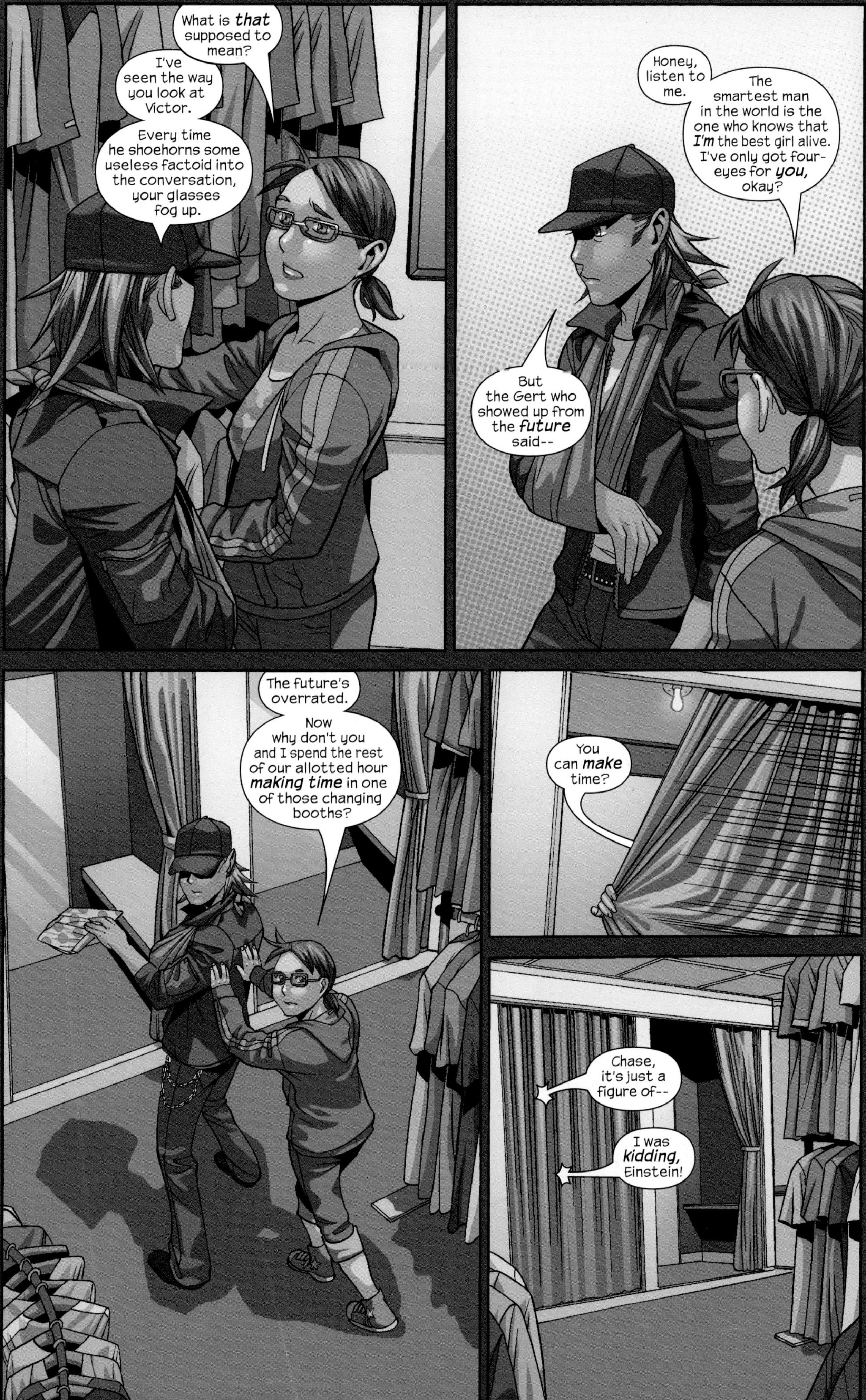
What is *that* supposed to mean?
I've seen the way you look at Victor.
Every time he shoehorns some useless factoid into the conversation, your glasses fog up.
Honey, listen to me.
The smartest man in the world is the one who knows that *I'm* the best girl alive. I've only got four-eyes for *you,* okay?
But the Gert who showed up from the *future* said--
The future's overrated.
Now why don't you and I spend the rest of our allotted hour *making time* in one of those changing booths?
You can *make* time?
Chase, it's just a figure of--
I was *kidding,* Einstein!

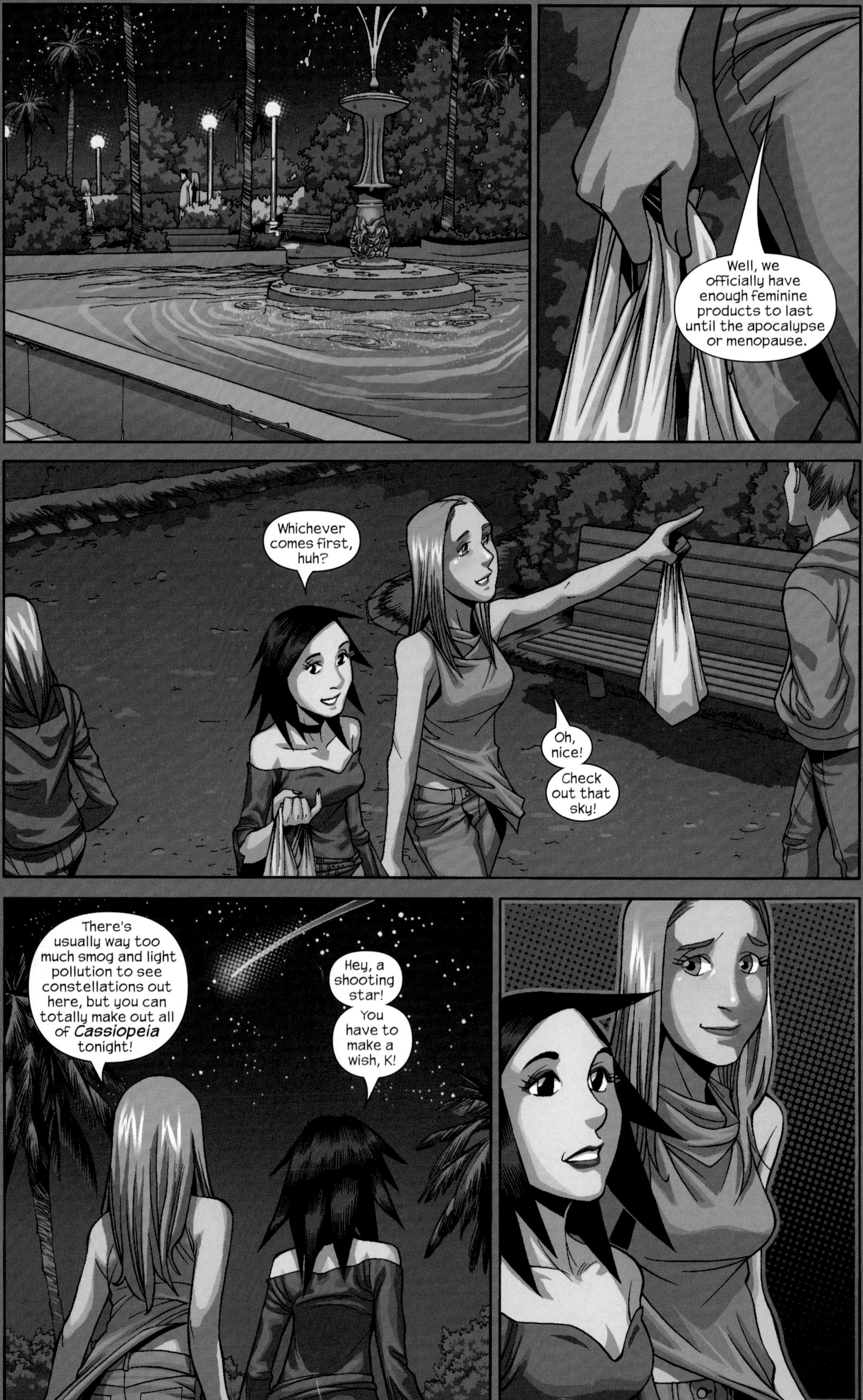
Well, we officially have enough feminine products to last until the apocalypse or menopause.
Whichever comes first, huh?
Oh, nice!
Check out that sky!
There's usually way too much smog and light pollution to see constellations out here, but you can totally make out all of *Cassiopeia* tonight!
Hey, a shooting star!
You have to make a wish, K!

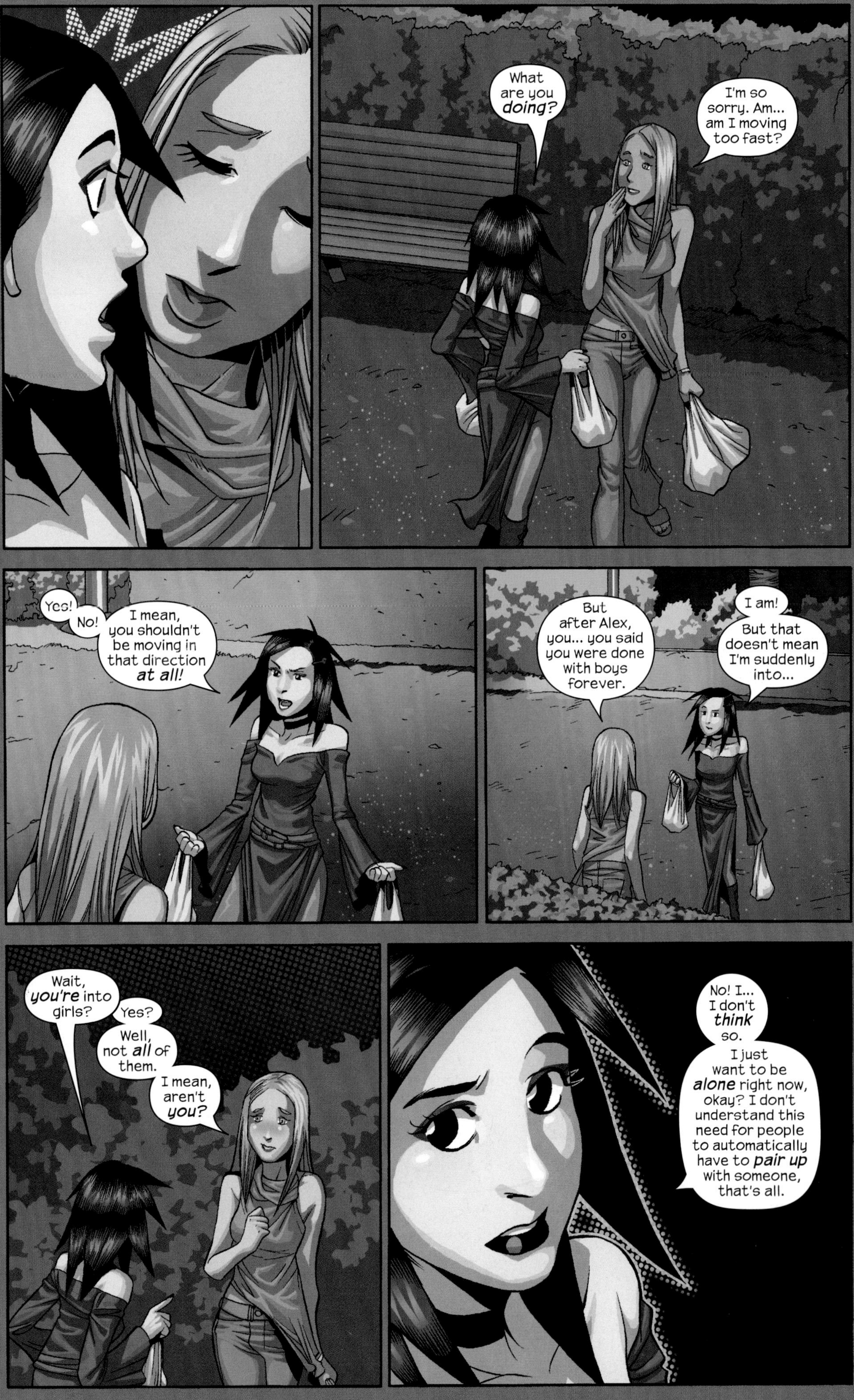

What are you *doing?*
I'm so sorry. Am... am I moving too fast?
Yes!
No!
I mean, you shouldn't be moving in that direction *at all!*
But after Alex, you... you said you were done with boys forever.
I am!
But that doesn't mean I'm suddenly into...
Wait, *you're* into girls?
Yes?
Well, not *all* of them.
I mean, aren't *you?*
No! I... I don't *think* so.
I just want to be *alone* right now, okay? I don't understand this need for people to automatically have to *pair up* with someone, that's all.

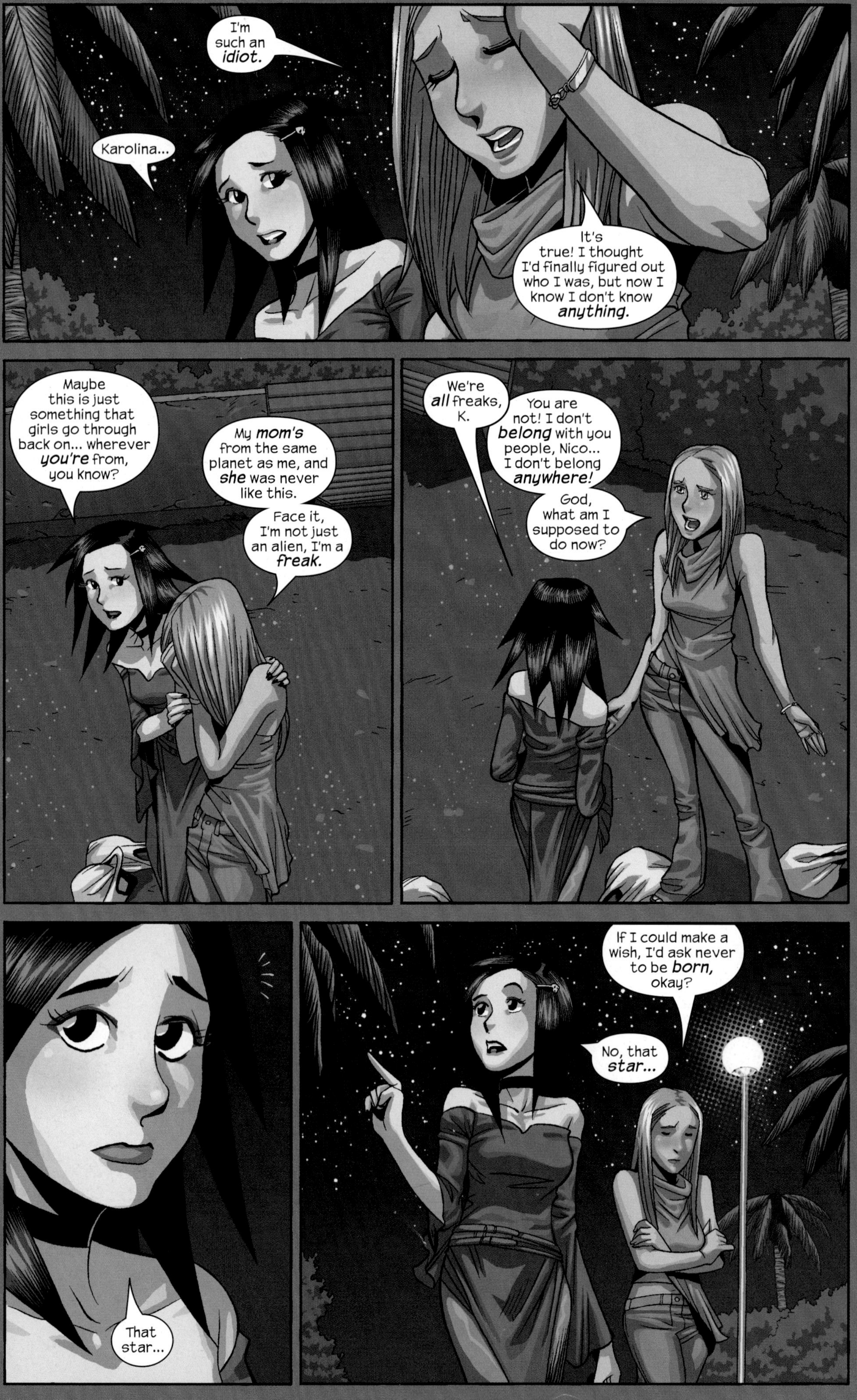
I'm such an idiot.
Karolina...
It's true! I thought I'd finally figured out who I was, but now I know I don't know anything.
Maybe this is just something that girls go through back on... wherever you're from, you know?
My mom's from the same planet as me, and she was never like this.
Face it, I'm not just an alien, I'm a freak.
We're all freaks, K.
You are not! I don't belong with you people, Nico... I don't belong anywhere!
God, what am I supposed to do now?
That star...
If I could make a wish, I'd ask never to be born, okay?
No, that star...

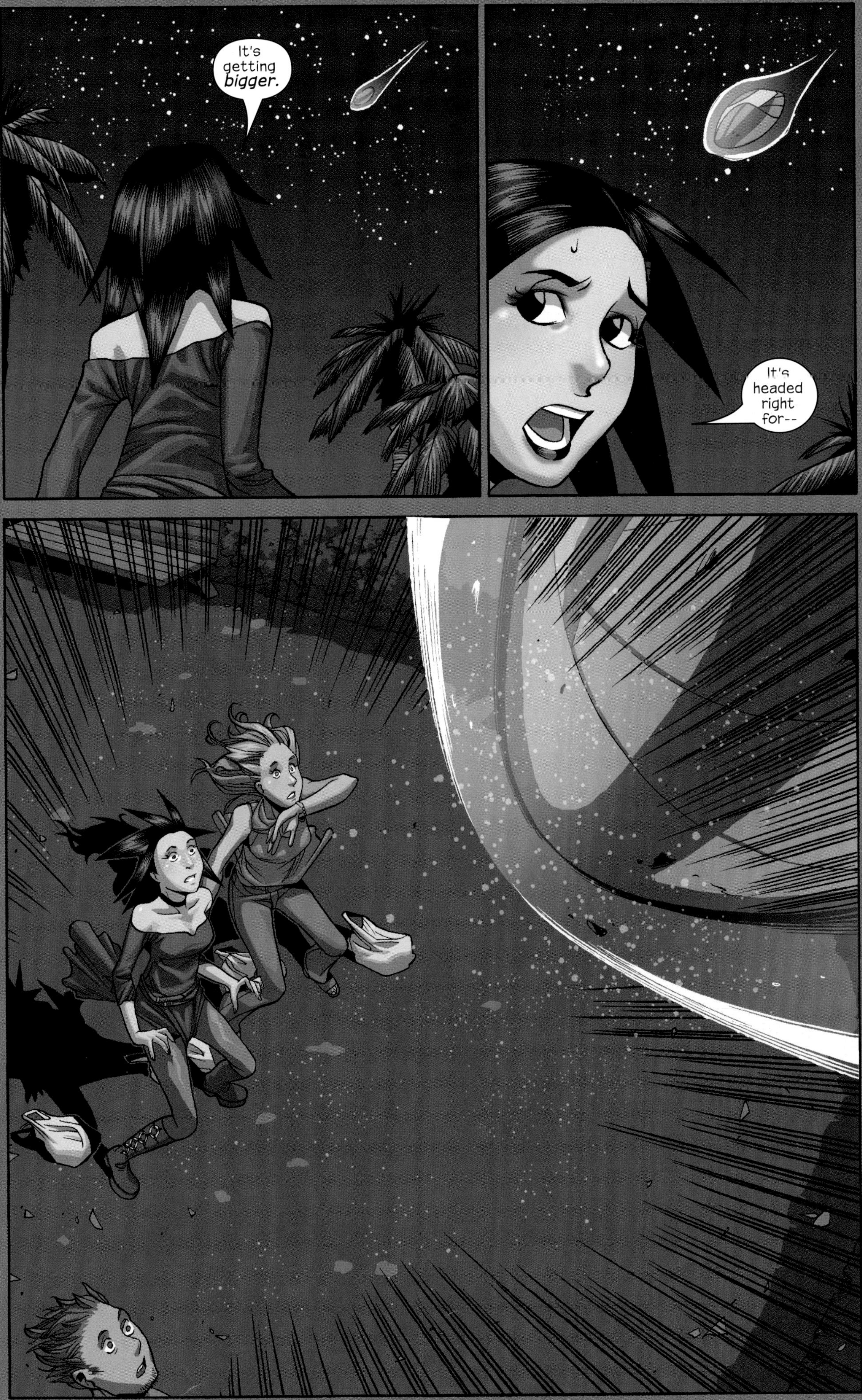
It's getting *bigger*.
It's headed right for--

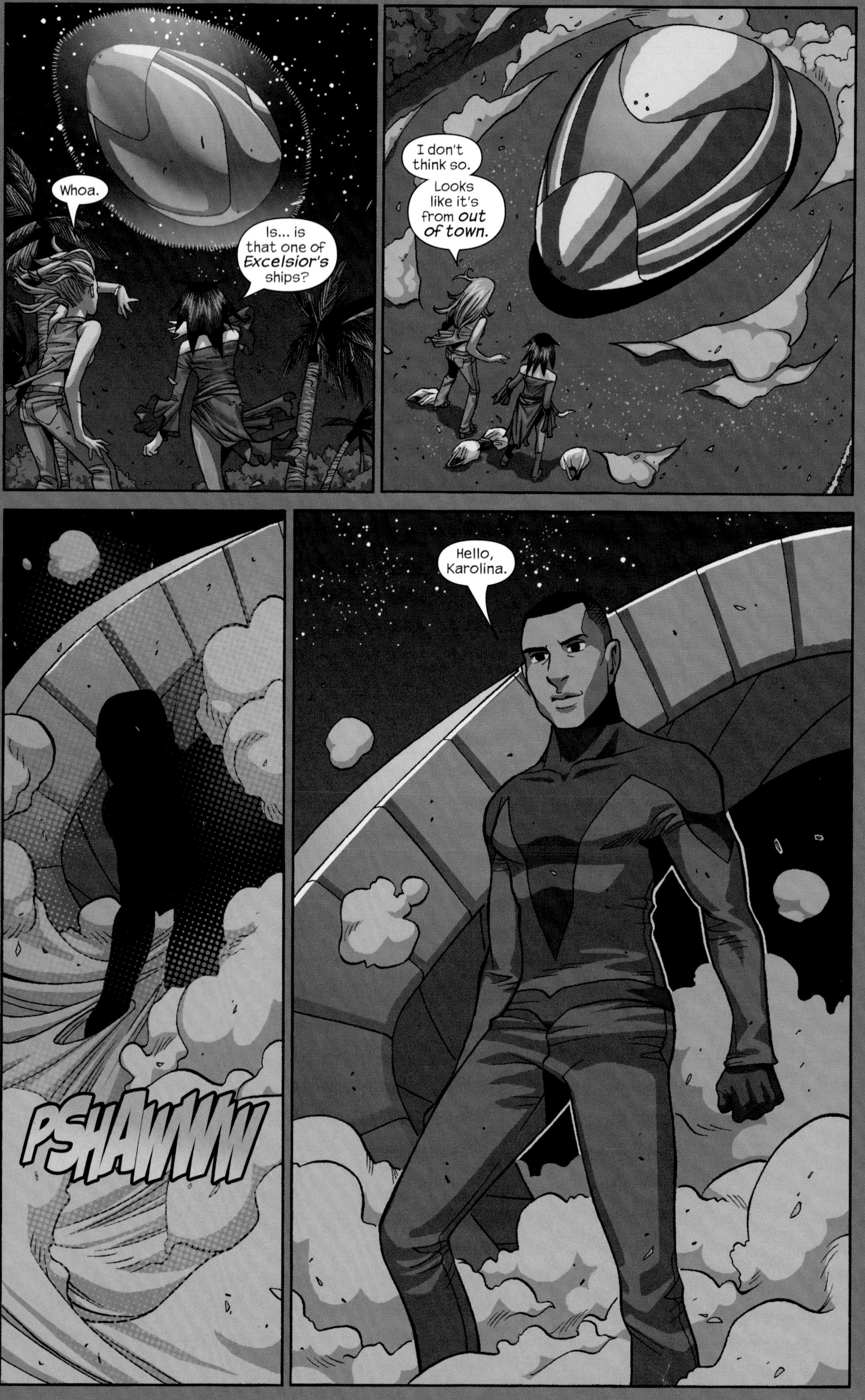

Whoa.
Is... is that one of Excelsior's ships?
I don't think so.
Looks like it's from out of town.
PSHAWWW
Hello, Karolina.

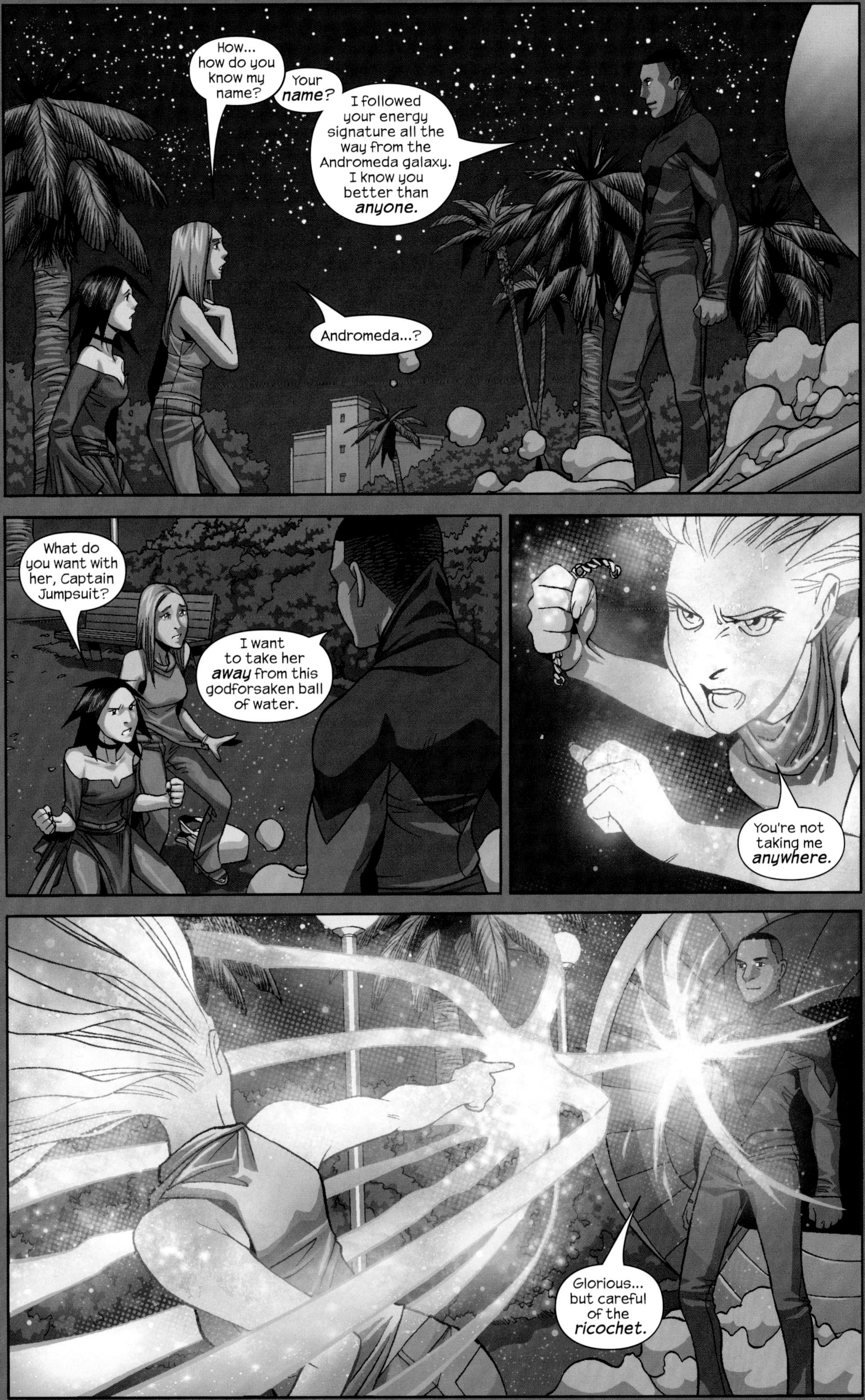
How... how do you know my name?
Your name?
I followed your energy signature all the way from the Andromeda galaxy. I know you better than anyone.
Andromeda...?
What do you want with her, Captain Jumpsuit?
I want to take her away from this godforsaken ball of water.
You're not taking me anywhere.
Glorious... but careful of the ricochet.

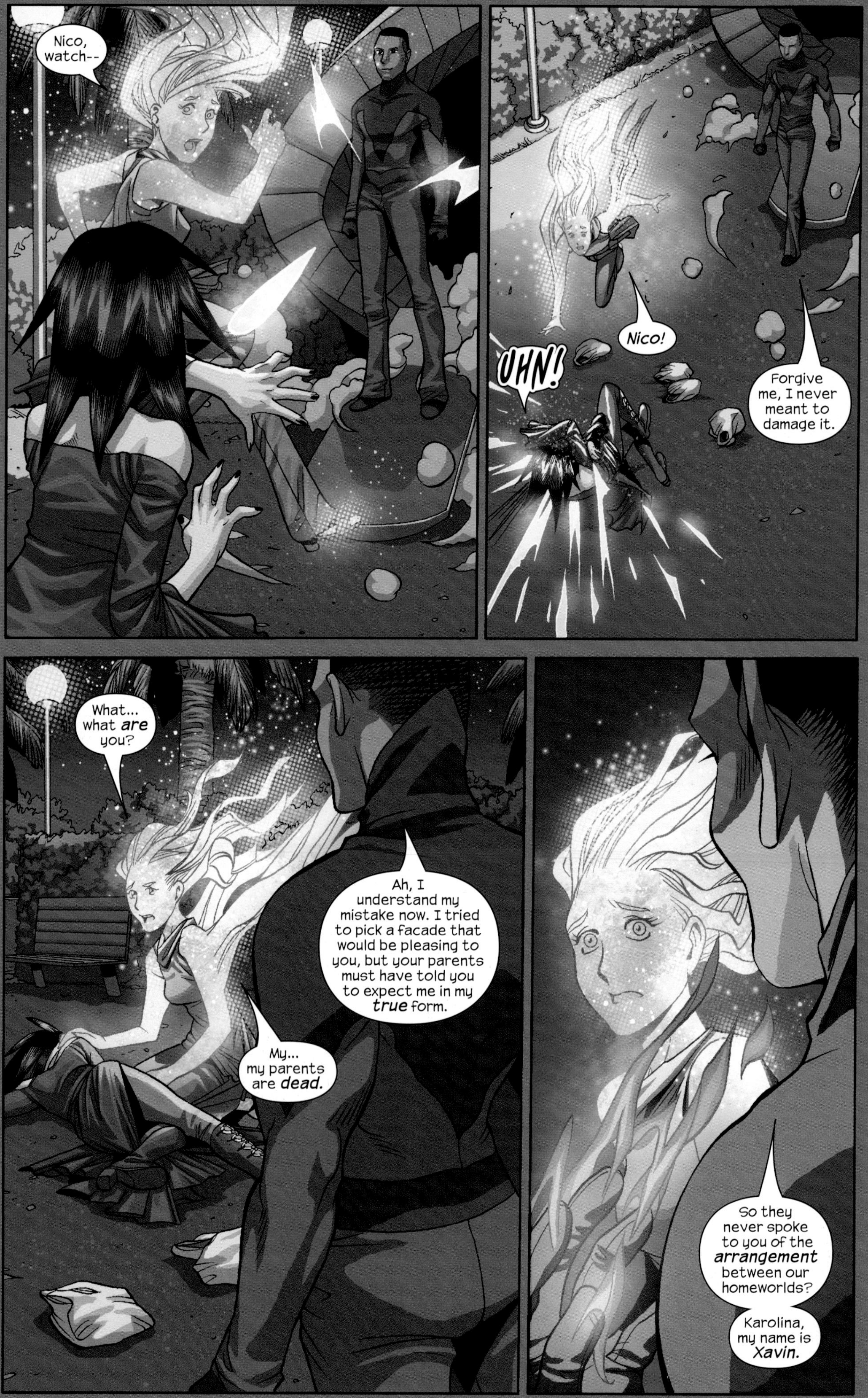
Nico, watch--
Nico!
UHN!
Forgive me, I never meant to damage it.
What... what *are* you?
Ah, I understand my mistake now. I tried to pick a facade that would be pleasing to you, but your parents must have told you to expect me in my *true* form.
My... my parents are *dead.*
So they never spoke to you of the *arrangement* between our homeworlds?
Karolina, my name is *Xavin.*

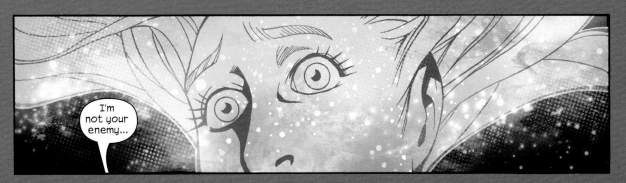

I'm not your enemy...

...I'm your fiancé.

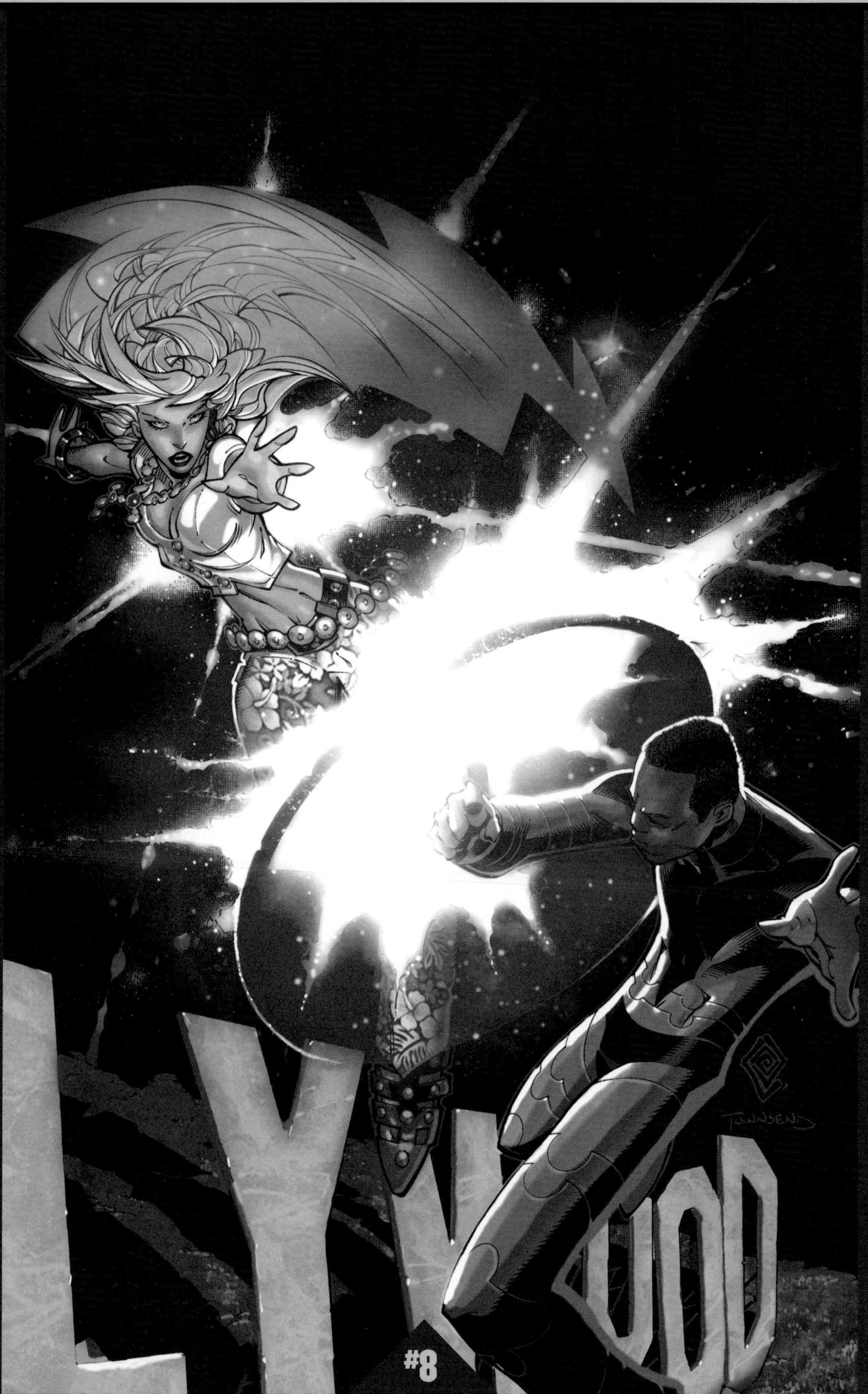
TOWNSEND

#8

STAR-CROSSED PART 2

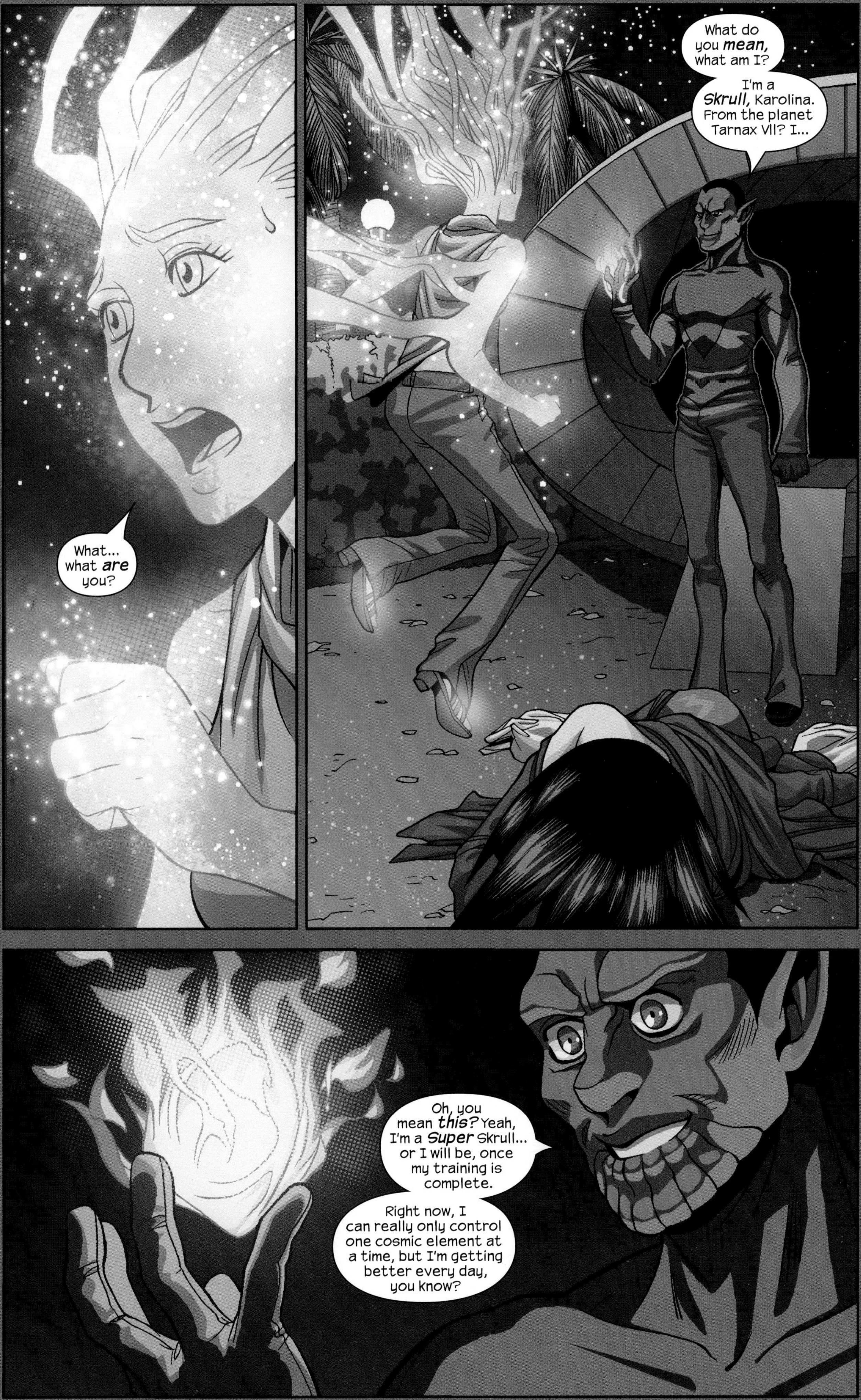
What... what are you?
What do you mean, what am I?
I'm a Skrull, Karolina. From the planet Tarnax VII? I...
Oh, you mean this? Yeah, I'm a Super Skrull... or I will be, once my training is complete.
Right now, I can really only control one cosmic element at a time, but I'm getting better every day, you know?

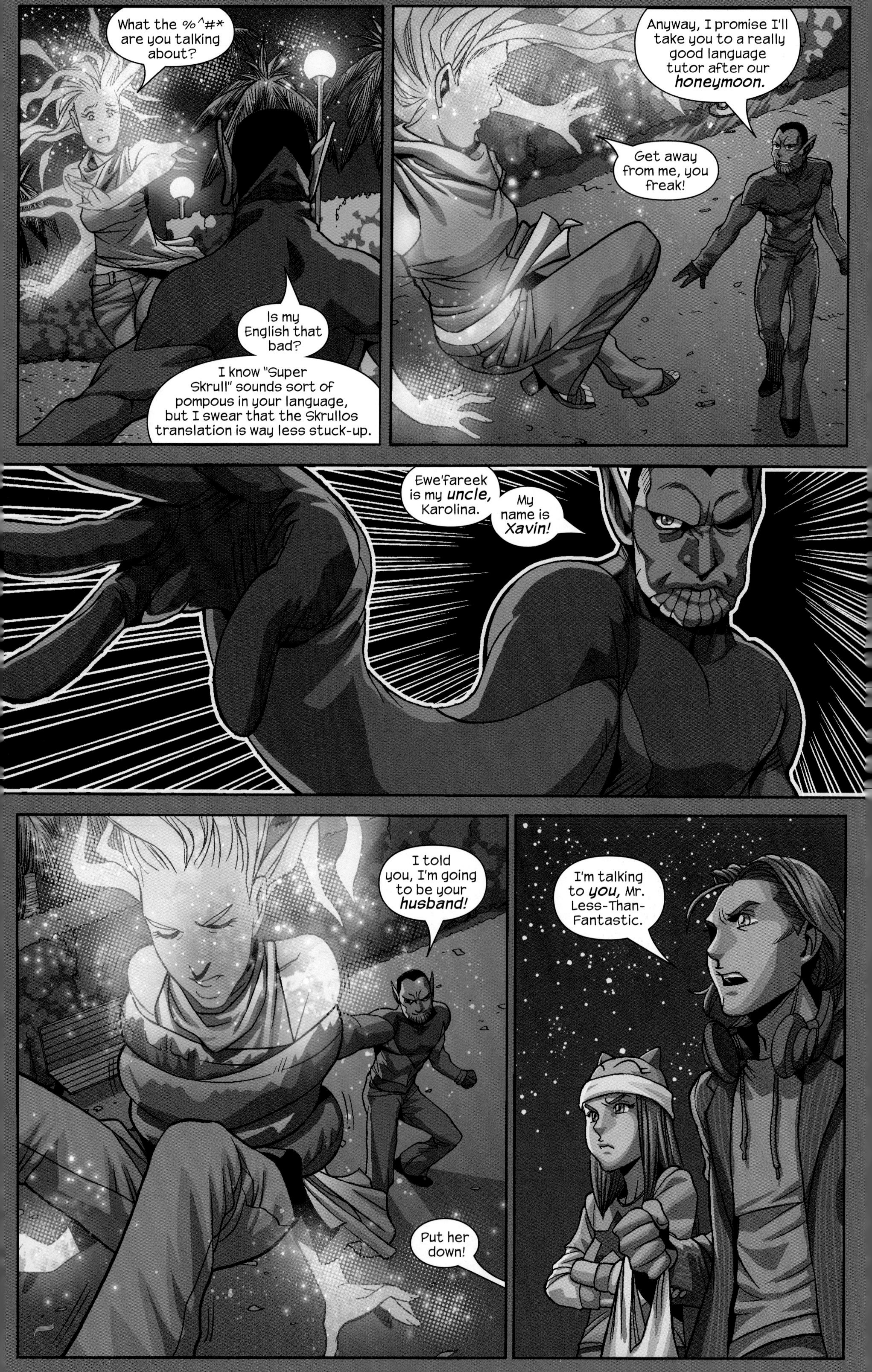

What the %^#* are you talking about?
Is my English that bad?
I know "Super Skrull" sounds sort of pompous in your language, but I swear that the Skrullos translation is way less stuck-up.
Anyway, I promise I'll take you to a really good language tutor after our honeymoon.
Get away from me, you freak!
Ewe'fareek is my uncle, Karolina.
My name is Xavin!
I told you, I'm going to be your husband!
Put her down!
I'm talking to you, Mr. Less-Than-Fantastic.

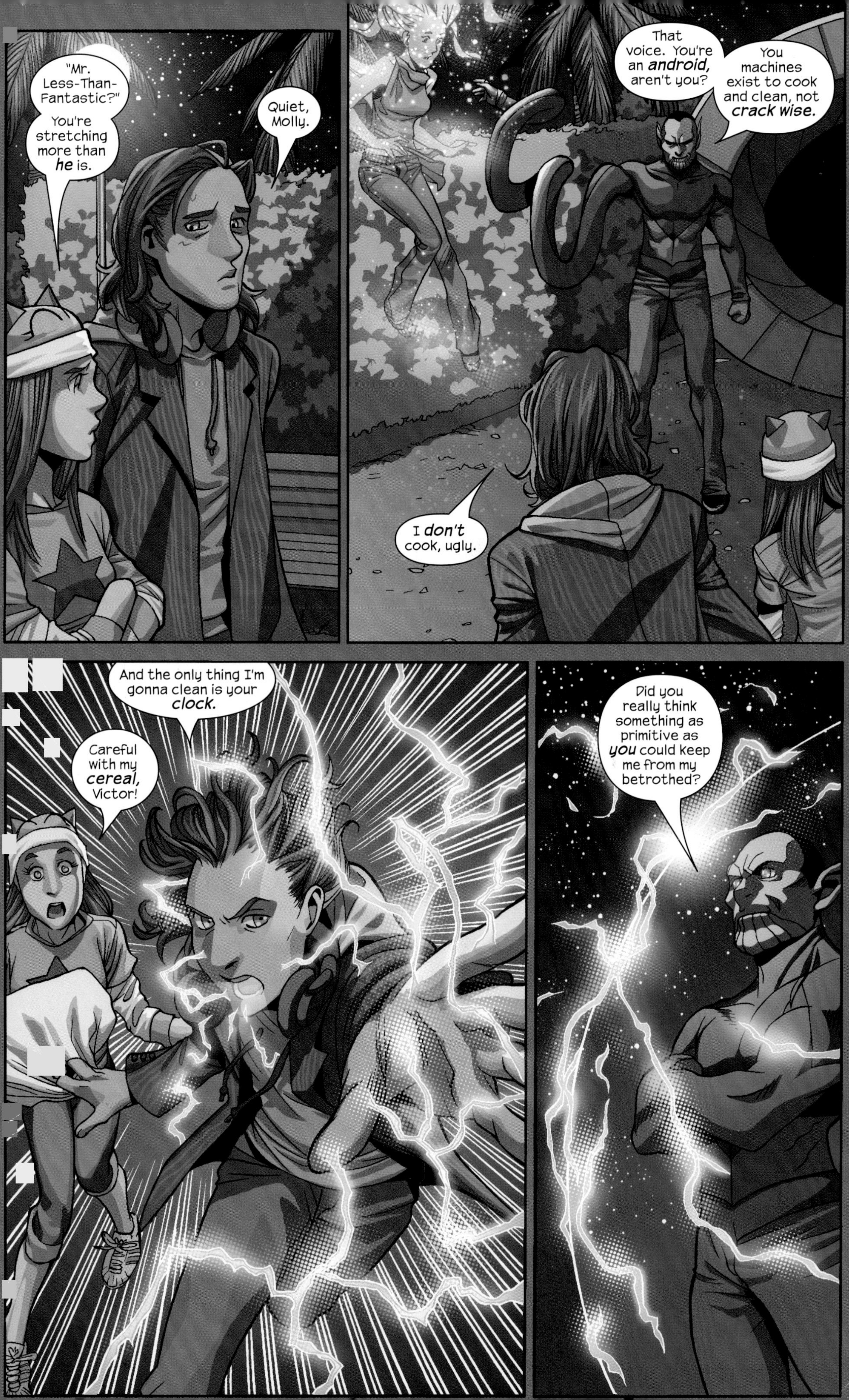
"Mr. Less-Than-Fantastic?"
You're stretching more than *he* is.
Quiet, Molly.
That voice. You're an *android,* aren't you?
You machines exist to cook and clean, not *crack wise.*
I *don't* cook, ugly.
And the only thing I'm gonna clean is your *clock.*
Careful with my *cereal,* Victor!
Did you really think something as primitive as *you* could keep me from my betrothed?

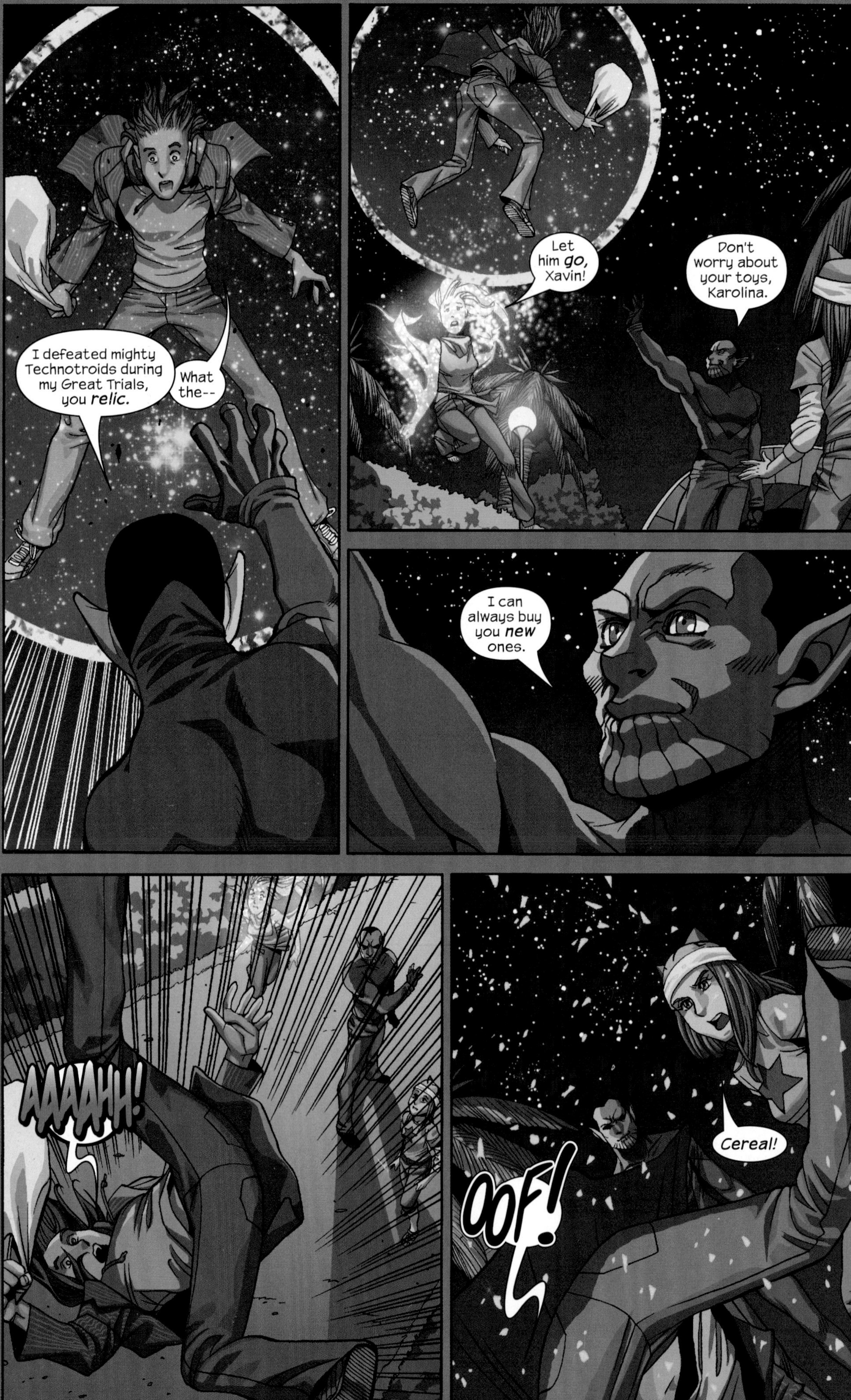

I defeated mighty Technotroids during my Great Trials, you relic.
What the--
Let him go, Xavin!
Don't worry about your toys, Karolina.
I can always buy you new ones.
AAAAHH!
Cereal!
OOF!

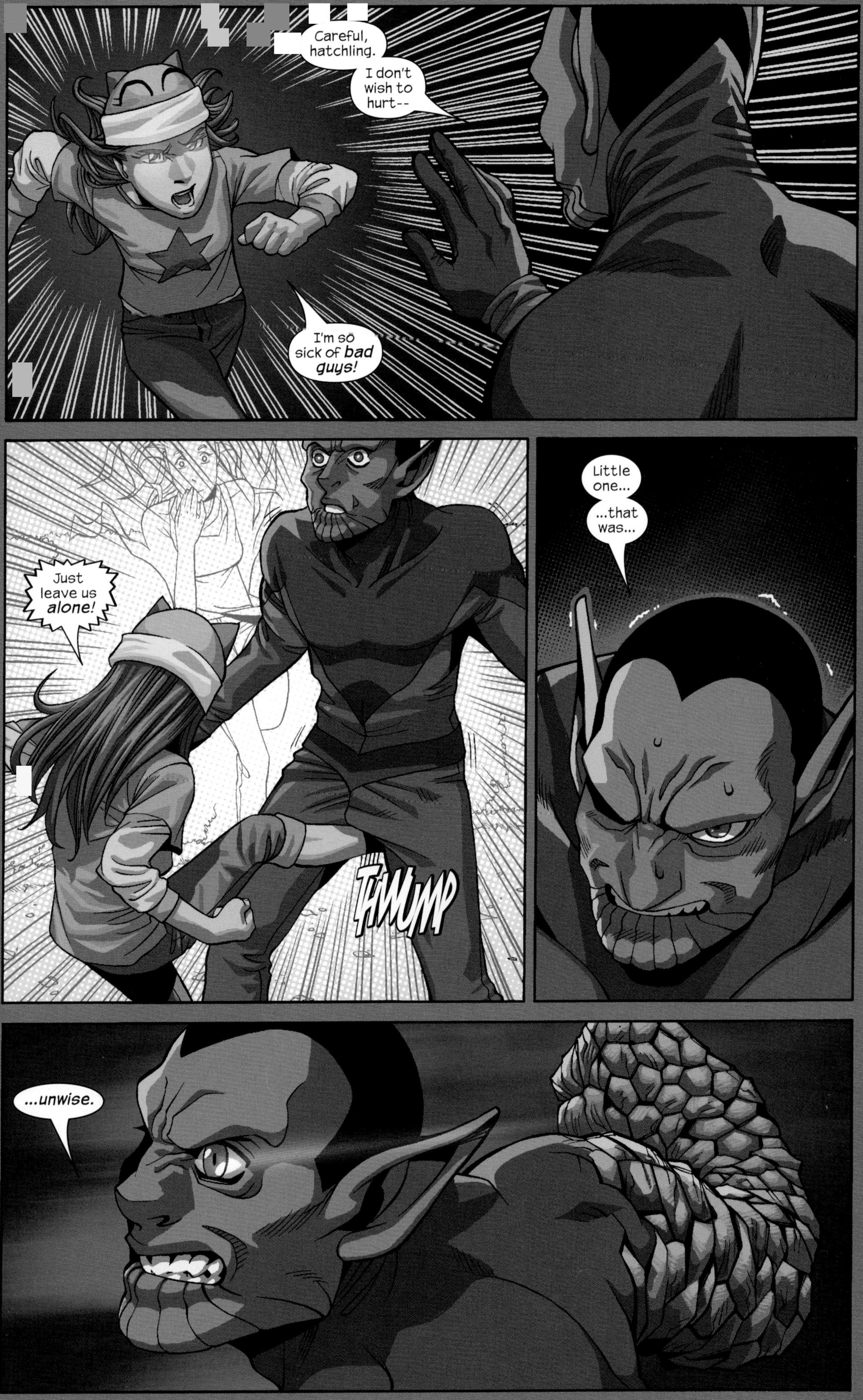
Careful, hatchling.
I don't wish to hurt--
I'm so sick of bad guys!
Just leave us alone!
THWUMP
Little one...
...that was...
...unwise.

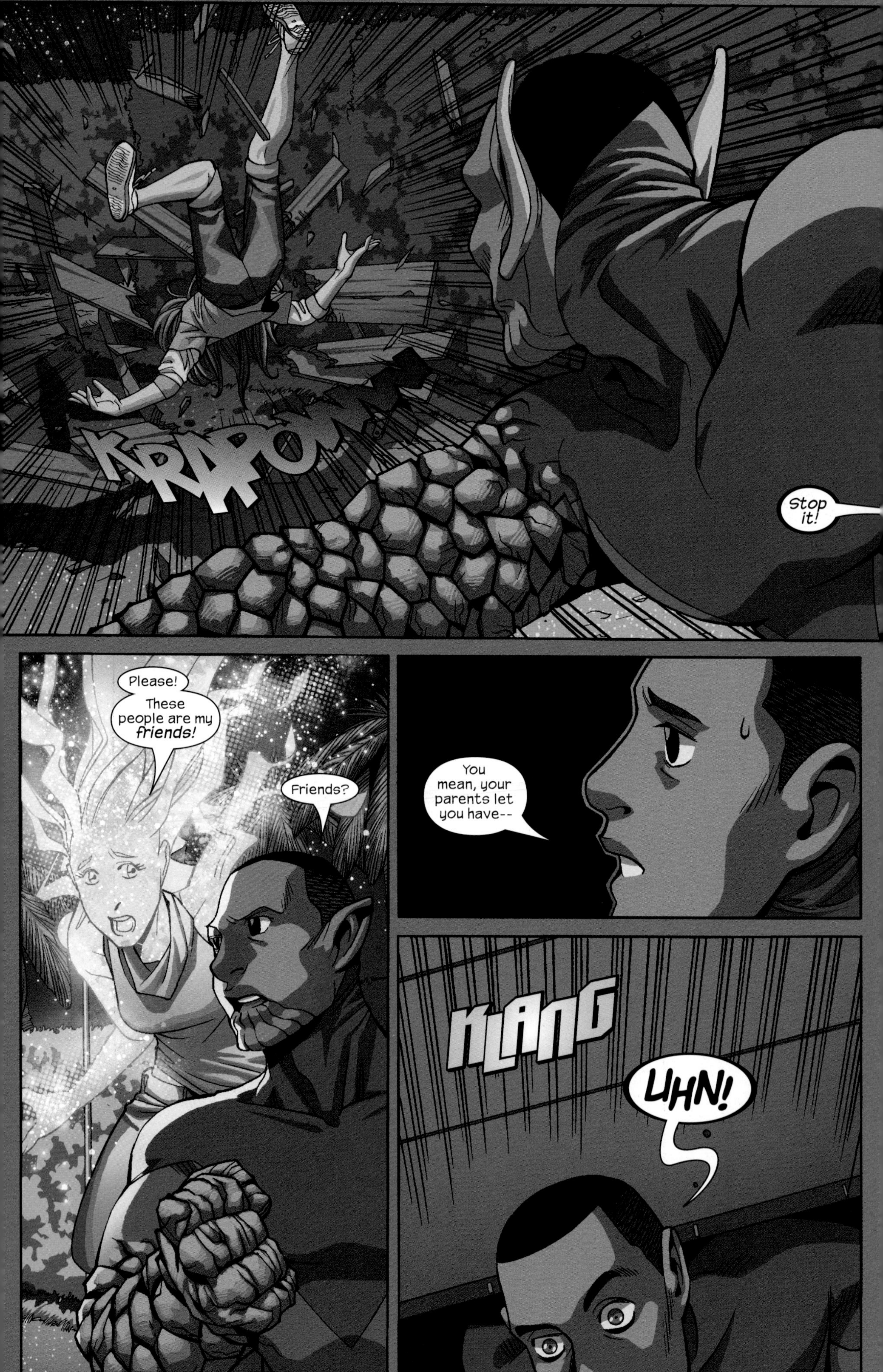
KRAPOW
Stop it!
Please! These people are my friends!
Friends?
You mean, your parents let you have--
KLANG
UHN!

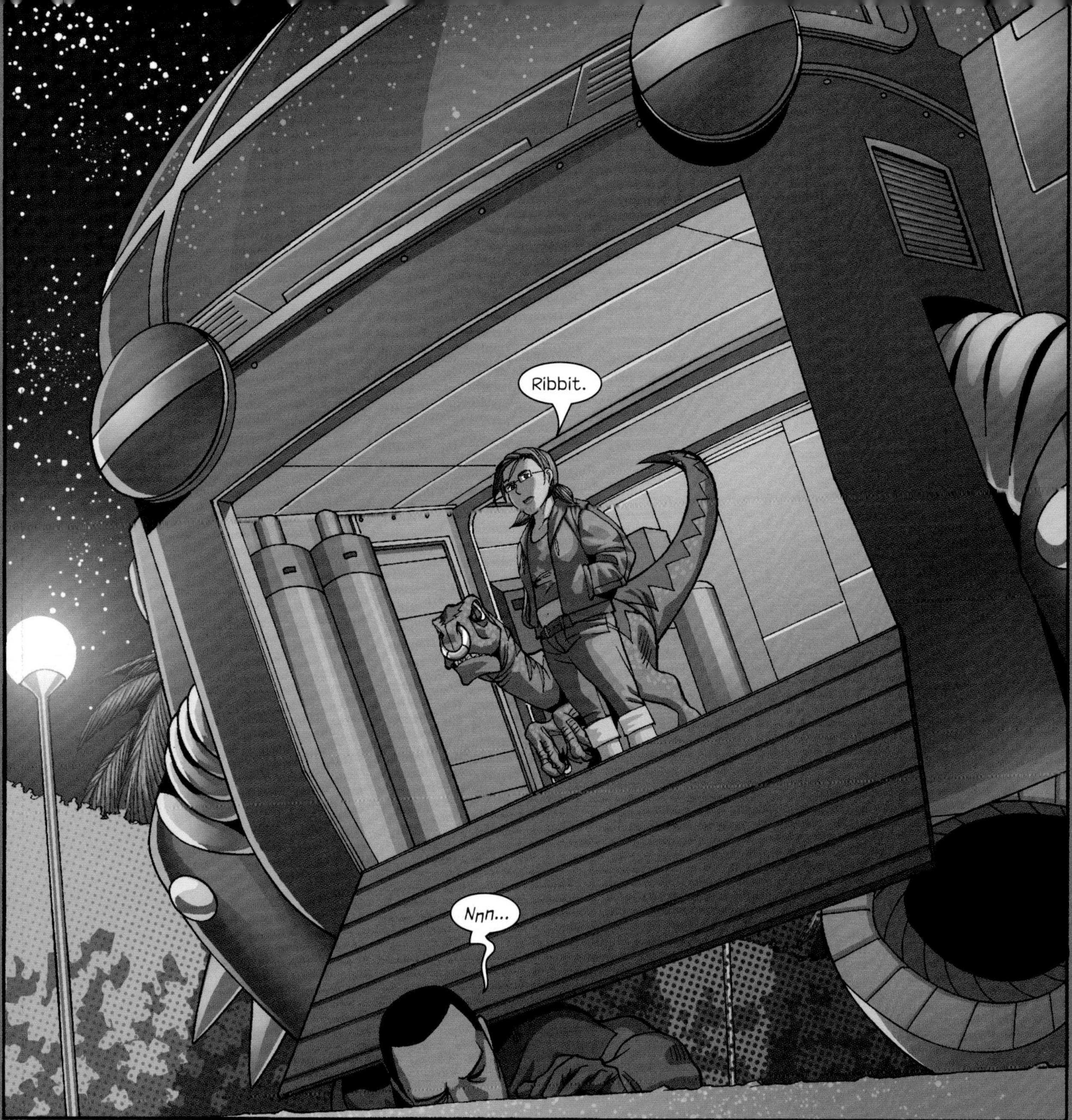
Ribbit.
Nnn...

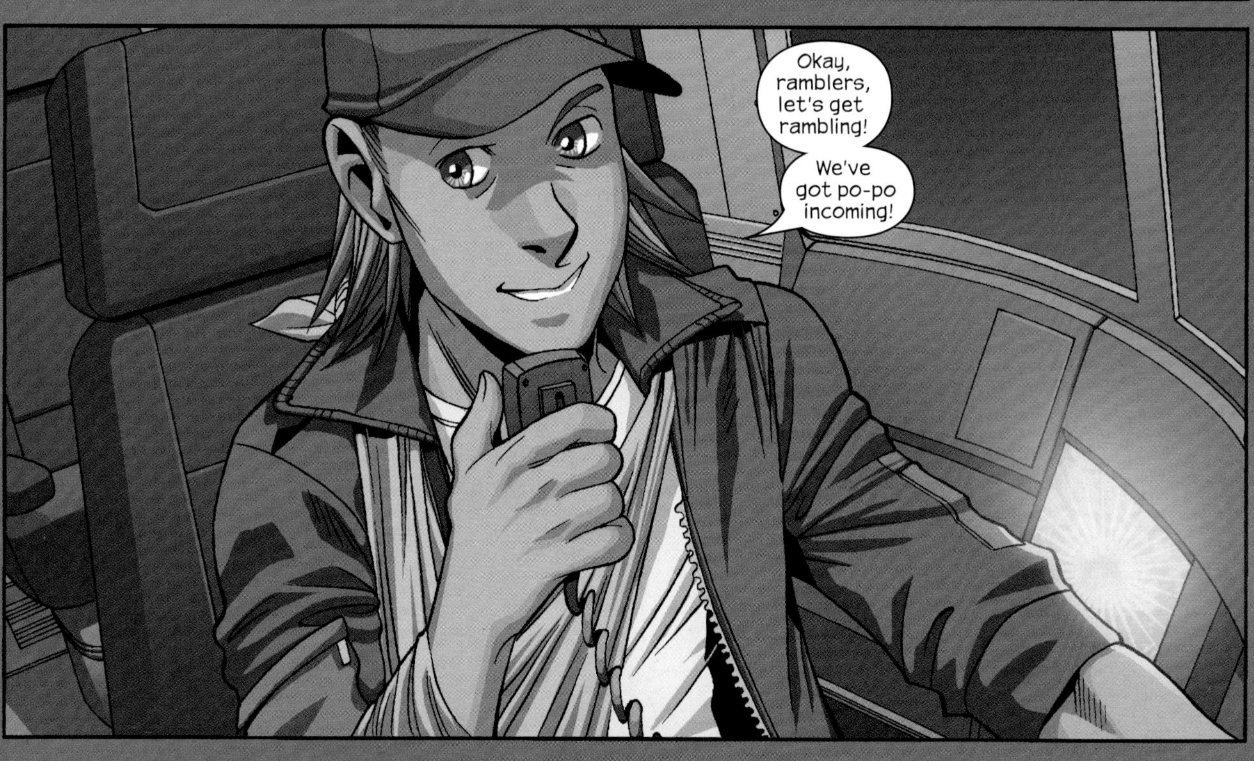
Okay, ramblers, let's get rambling!
We've got po-po incoming!

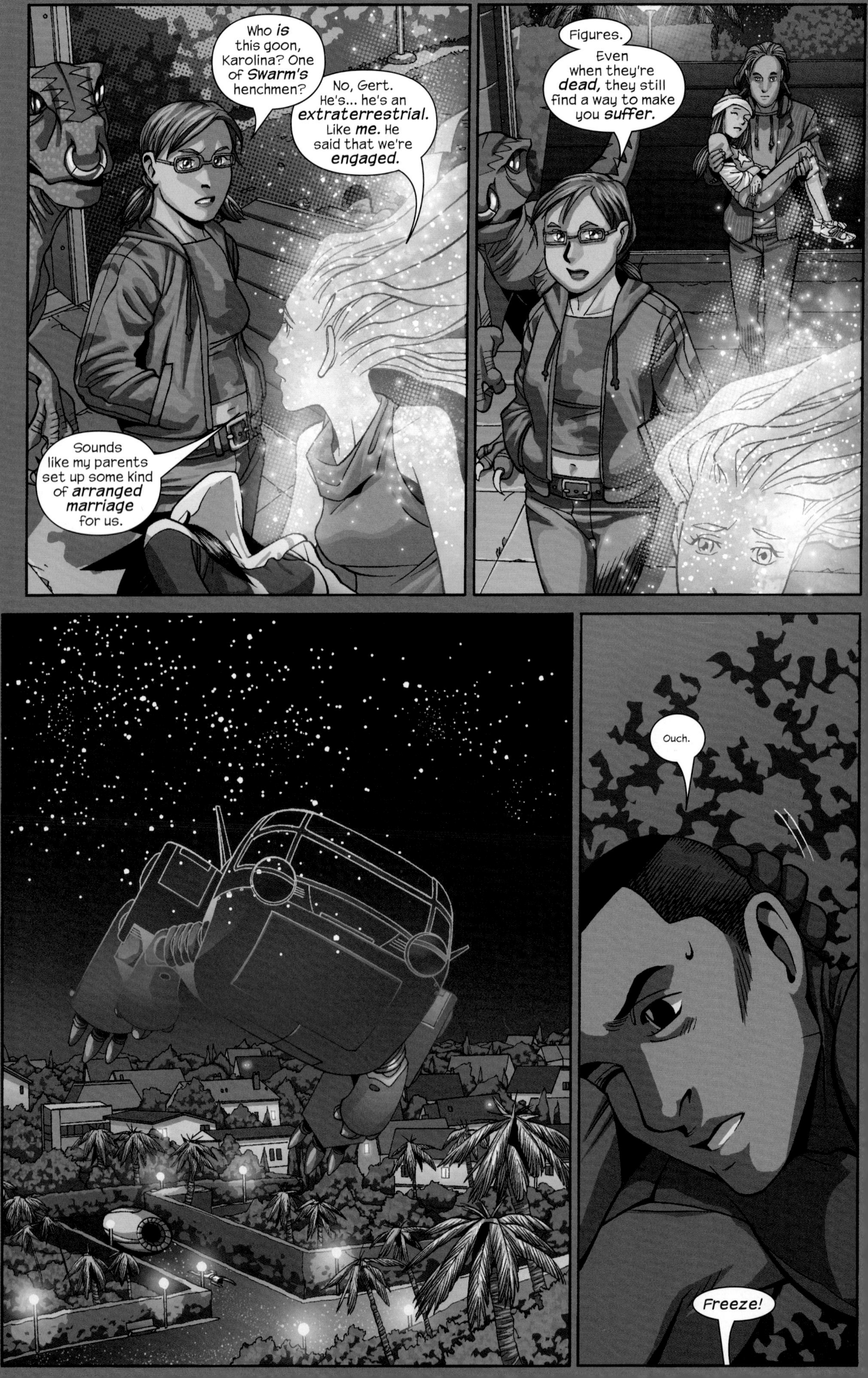
Who is this goon, Karolina? One of Swarm's henchmen?
No, Gert. He's... he's an extraterrestrial. Like me. He said that we're engaged.
Sounds like my parents set up some kind of arranged marriage for us.
Figures.
Even when they're dead, they still find a way to make you suffer.
Ouch.
Freeze!

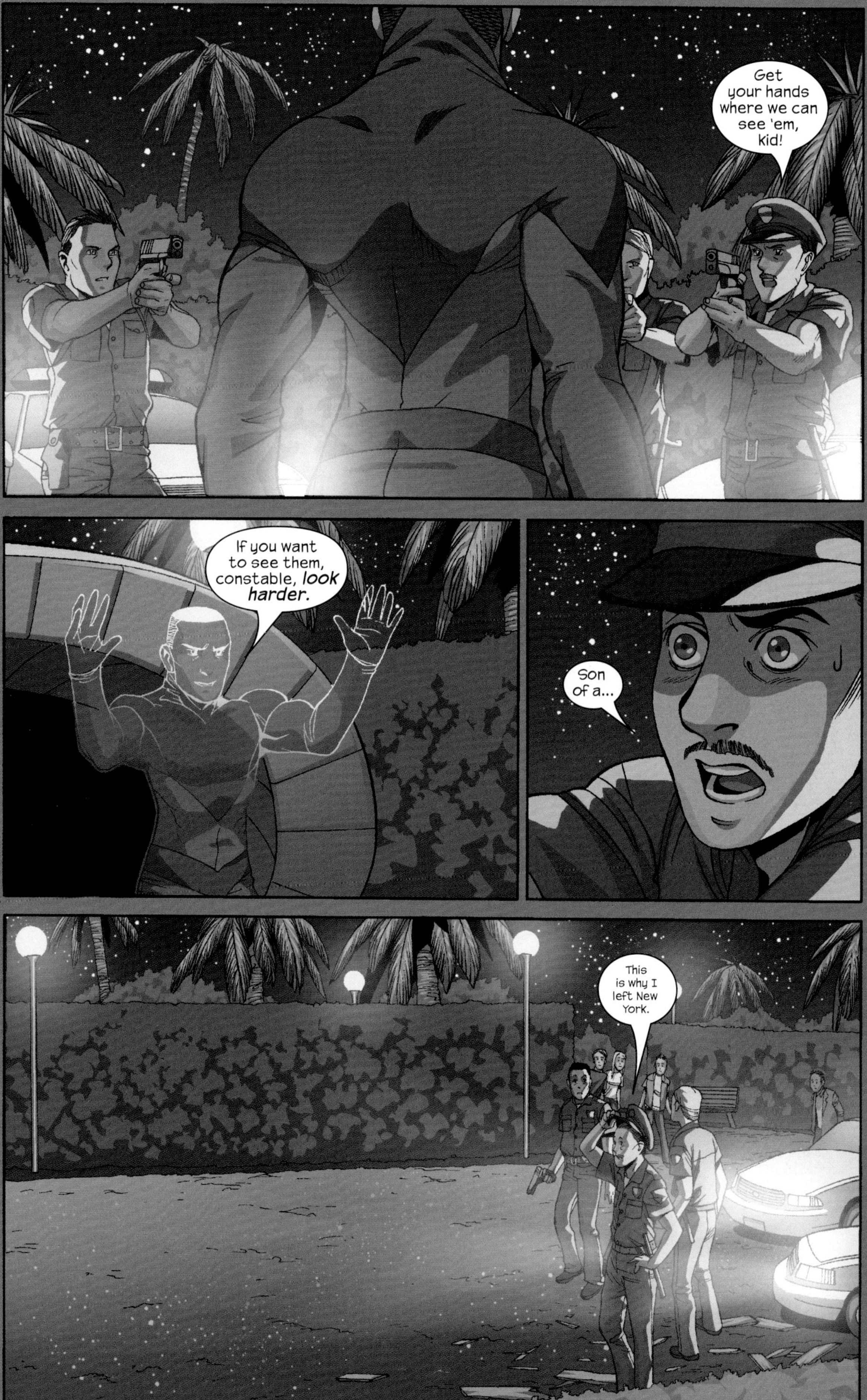

Get your hands where we can see 'em, kid!
If you want to see them, constable, *look harder.*
Son of a...
This is why I left New York.

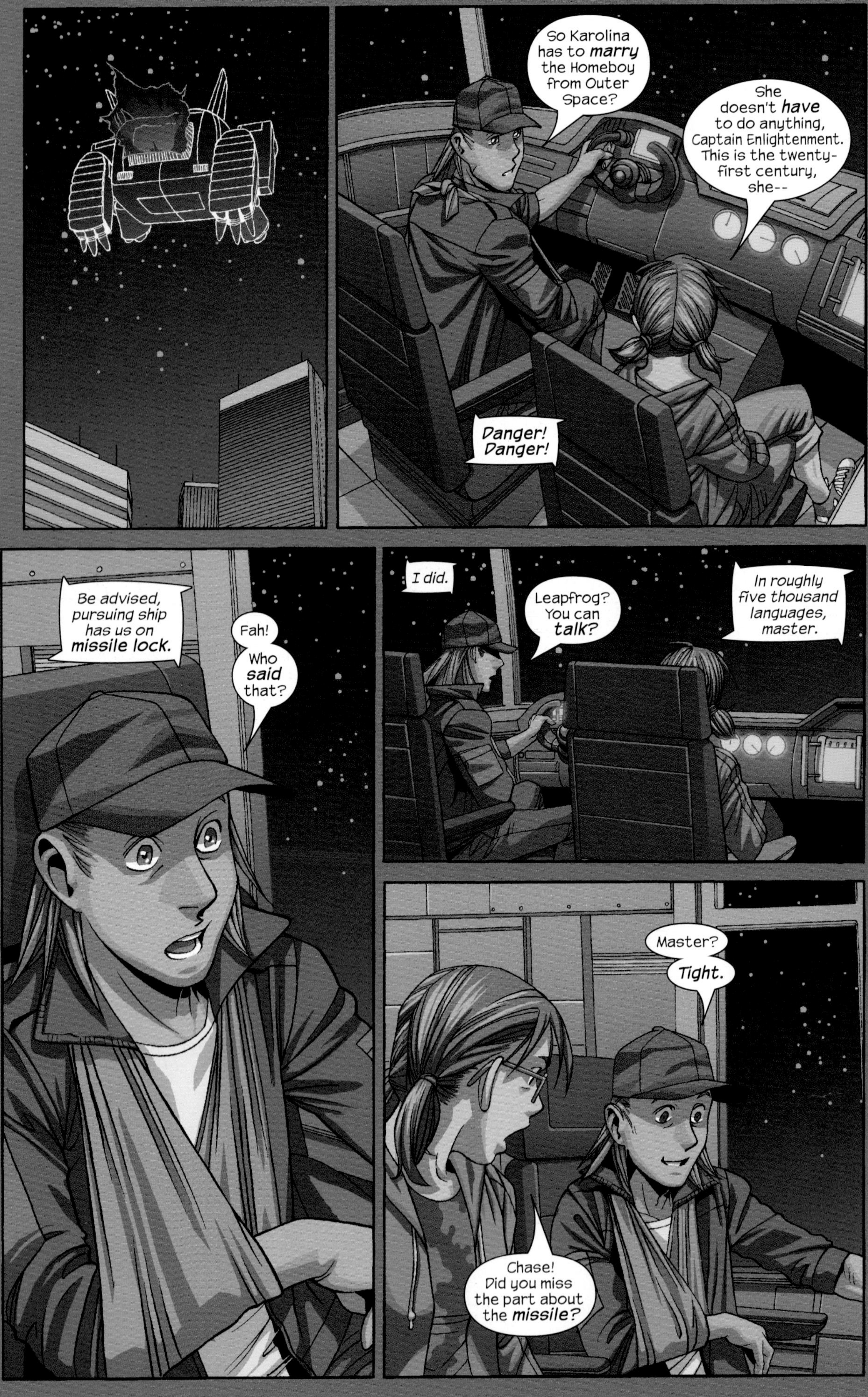

So Karolina has to *marry* the Homeboy from Outer Space?
She doesn't *have* to do anything, Captain Enlightenment. This is the twenty-first century, she--
Danger! Danger!
Be advised, pursuing ship has us on **missile lock.**
Fah!
Who *said* that?
I did.
Leapfrog? You can *talk?*
In roughly five thousand languages, master.
Master?
Tight.
Chase! Did you miss the part about the *missile?*

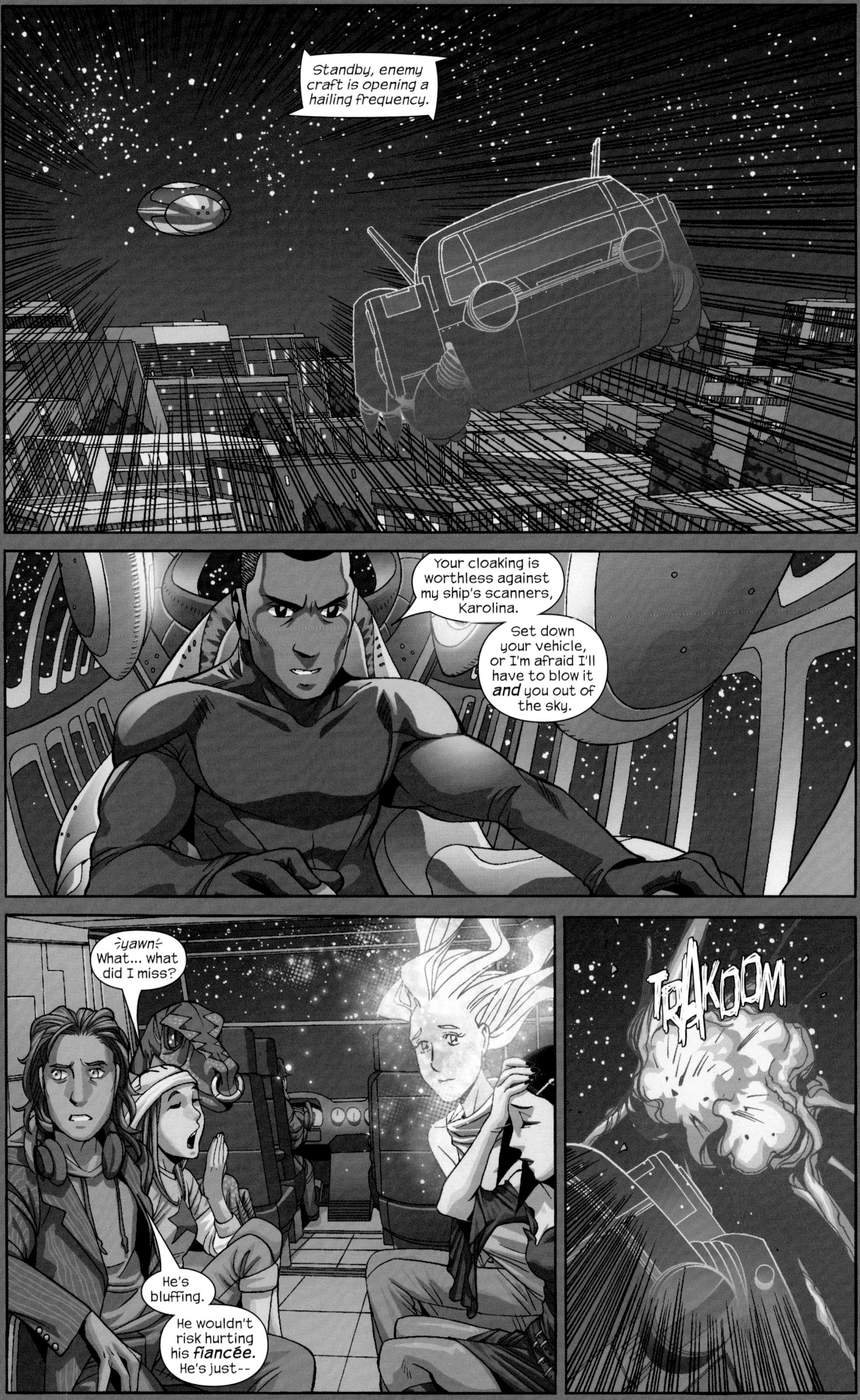
Standby, enemy craft is opening a hailing frequency.
Your cloaking is worthless against my ship's scanners, Karolina.
Set down your vehicle, or I'm afraid I'll have to blow it *and* you out of the sky.
yawn
What... what did I miss?
He's bluffing.
He wouldn't risk hurting his *fiancée.* He's just--
TRAKOOM

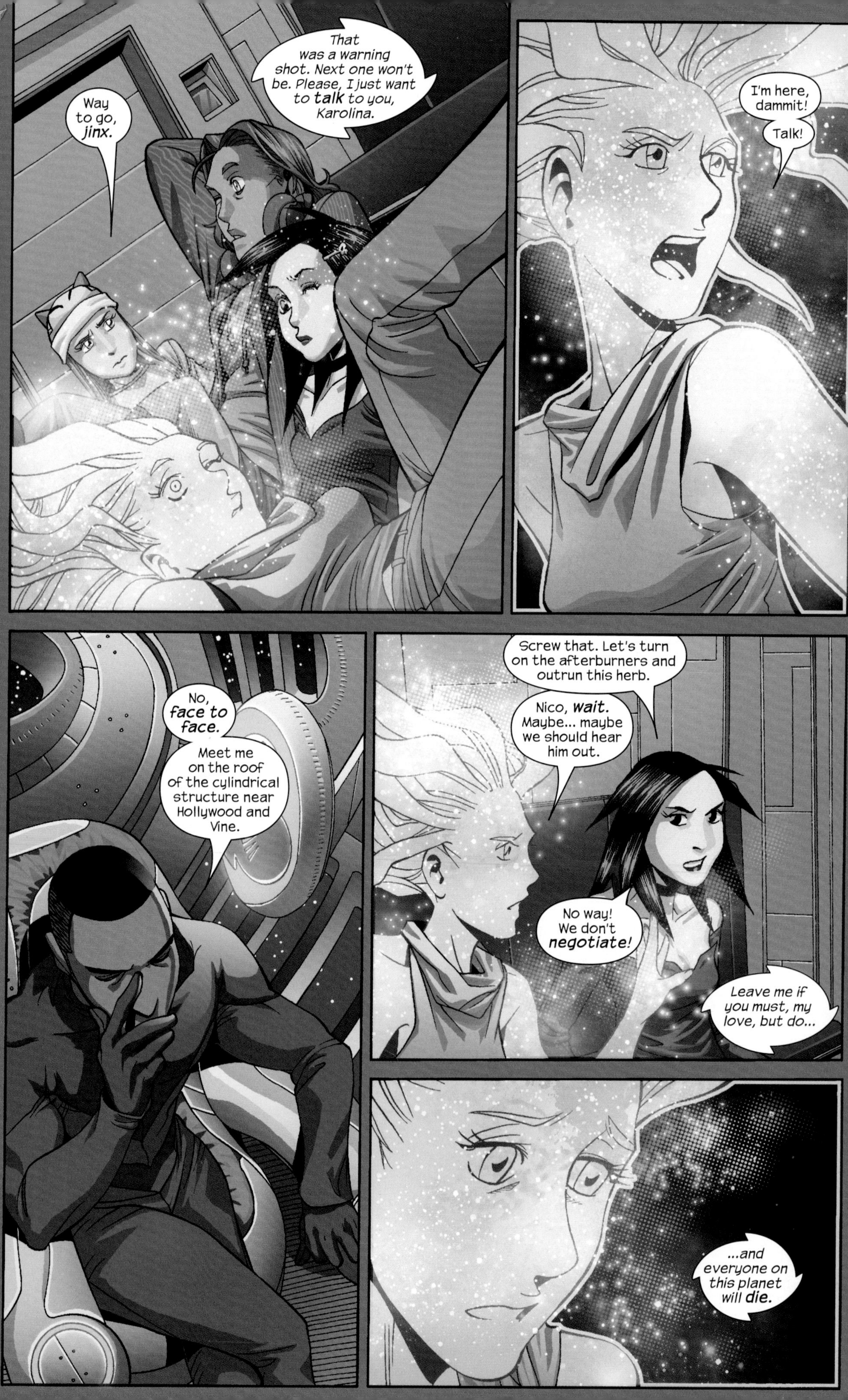
Way to go, *jinx.*
That was a warning shot. Next one won't be. Please, I just want to **talk** to you, Karolina.
I'm here, dammit!
Talk!
No, ***face to face.***
Meet me on the roof of the cylindrical structure near Hollywood and Vine.
Screw that. Let's turn on the afterburners and outrun this herb.
Nico, ***wait.*** Maybe... maybe we should hear him out.
No way! We don't ***negotiate!***
Leave me if you must, my love, but do...
...and everyone on this planet will **die.**

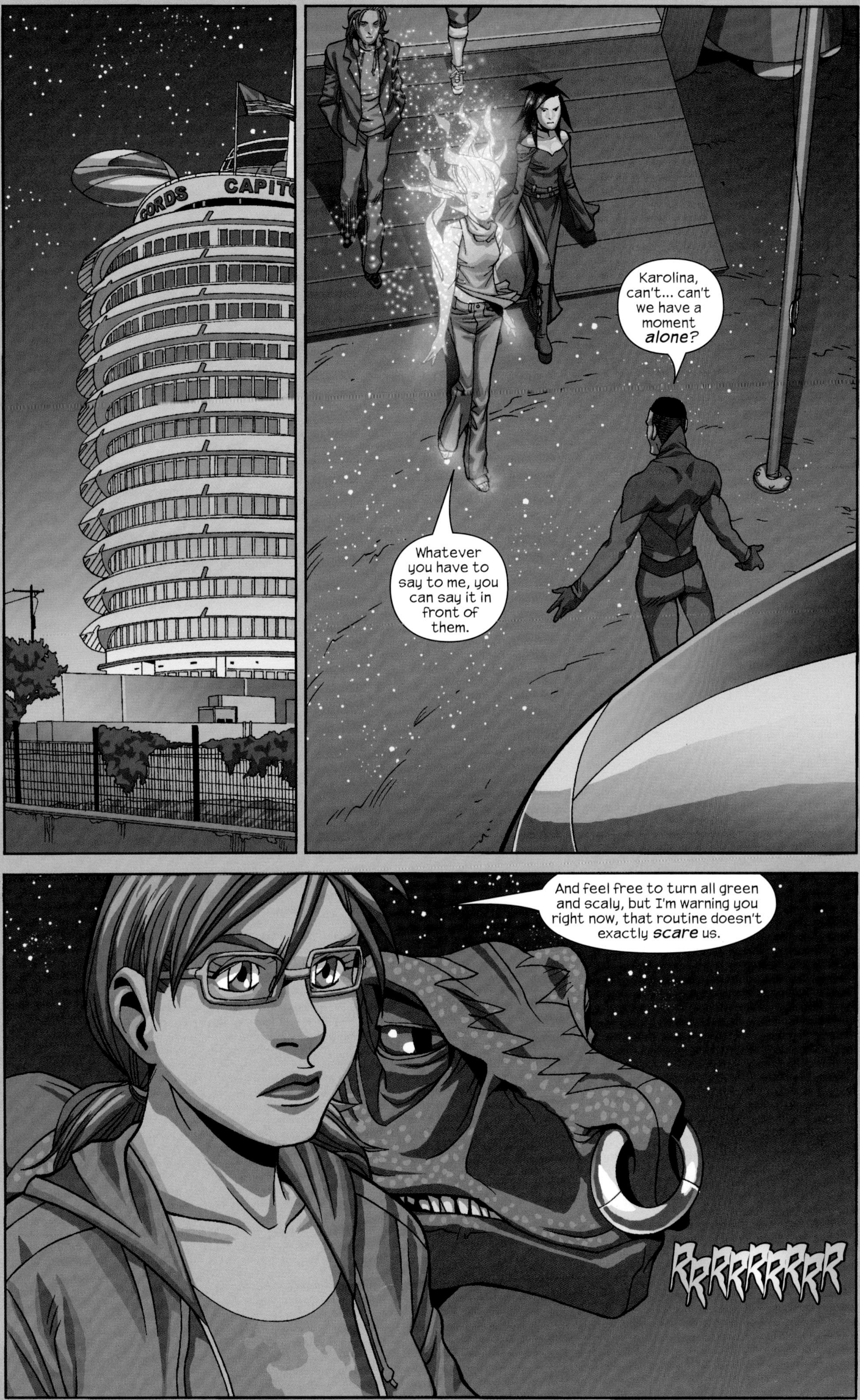
CAPITO
CORDS
Karolina, can't... can't we have a moment *alone*?
Whatever you have to say to me, you can say it in front of them.
And feel free to turn all green and scaly, but I'm warning you right now, that routine doesn't exactly *scare* us.
RRRRRRRRR

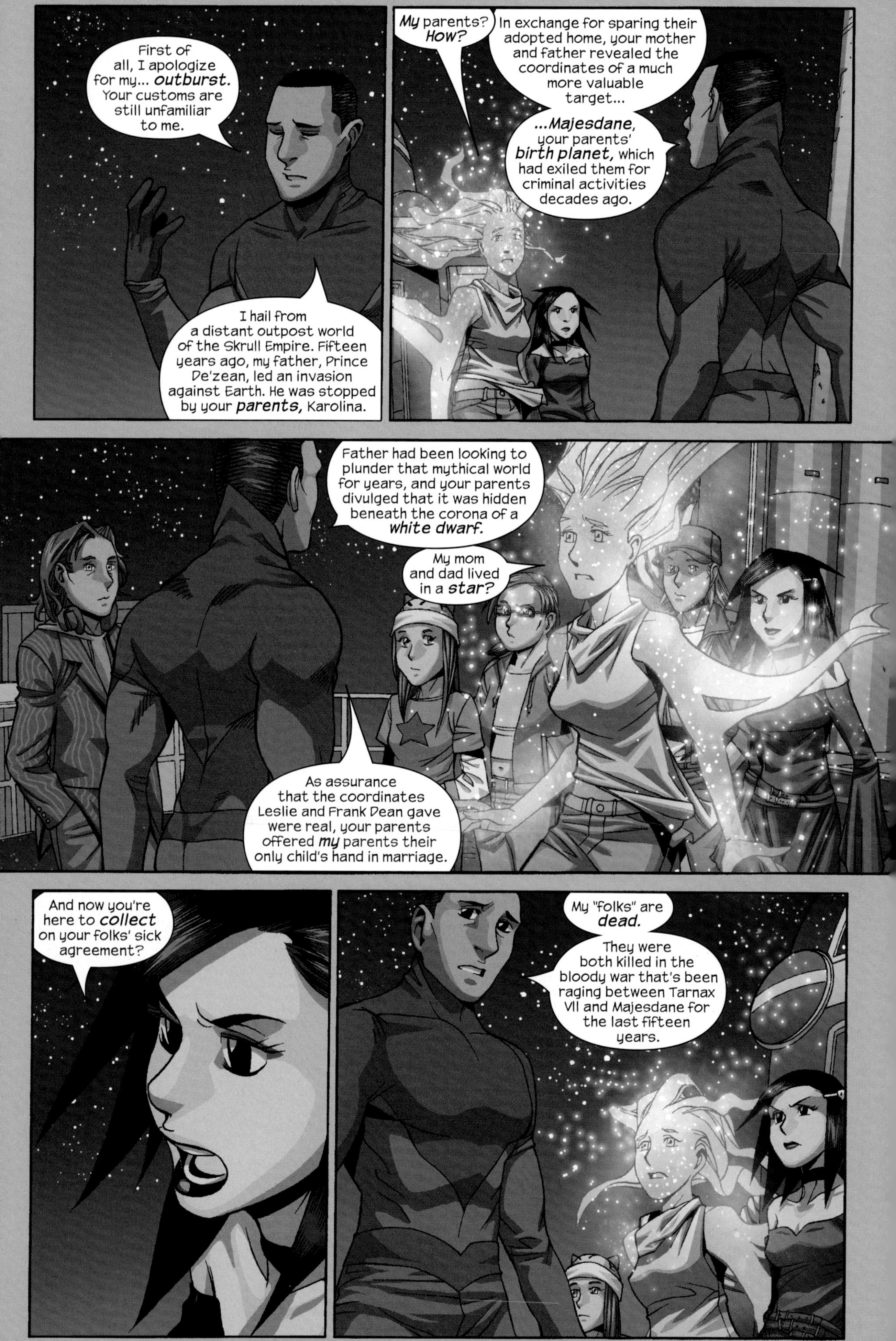

First of all, I apologize for my... outburst. Your customs are still unfamiliar to me.
I hail from a distant outpost world of the Skrull Empire. Fifteen years ago, my father, Prince De'zean, led an invasion against Earth. He was stopped by your parents, Karolina.
My parents? How?
In exchange for sparing their adopted home, your mother and father revealed the coordinates of a much more valuable target...
...Majesdane, your parents' birth planet, which had exiled them for criminal activities decades ago.
Father had been looking to plunder that mythical world for years, and your parents divulged that it was hidden beneath the corona of a white dwarf.
My mom and dad lived in a star?
As assurance that the coordinates Leslie and Frank Dean gave were real, your parents offered my parents their only child's hand in marriage.
And now you're here to collect on your folks' sick agreement?
My "folks" are dead.
They were both killed in the bloody war that's been raging between Tarnax VII and Majesdane for the last fifteen years.

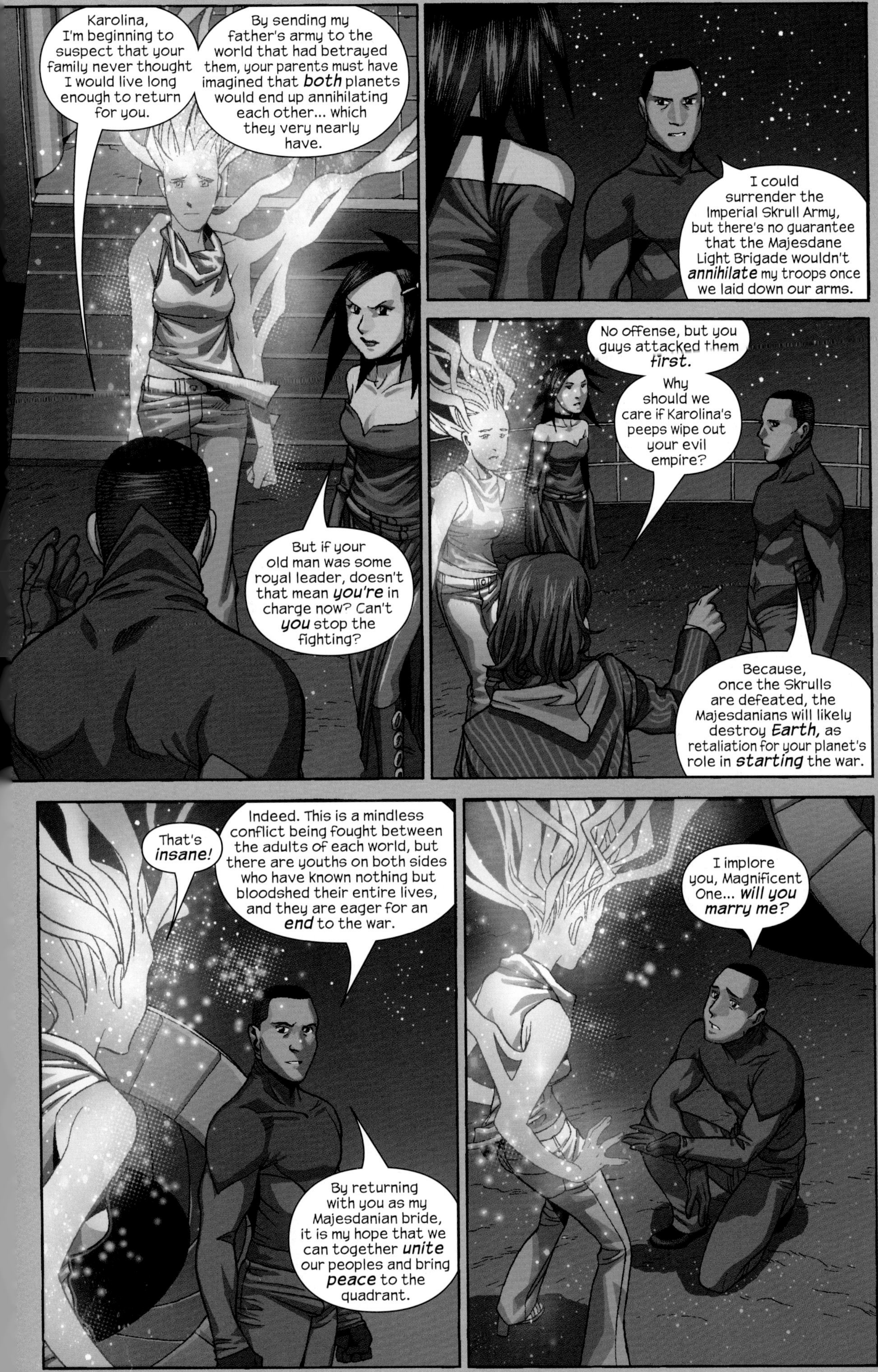
Karolina, I'm beginning to suspect that your family never thought I would live long enough to return for you.
By sending my father's army to the world that had betrayed them, your parents must have imagined that *both* planets would end up annihilating each other... which they very nearly have.
But if your old man was some royal leader, doesn't that mean *you're* in charge now? Can't *you* stop the fighting?
I could surrender the Imperial Skrull Army, but there's no guarantee that the Majesdane Light Brigade wouldn't *annihilate* my troops once we laid down our arms.
No offense, but you guys attacked them *first.*
Why should we care if Karolina's peeps wipe out your evil empire?
Because, once the Skrulls are defeated, the Majesdanians will likely destroy *Earth,* as retaliation for your planet's role in *starting* the war.
That's *insane!*
Indeed. This is a mindless conflict being fought between the adults of each world, but there are youths on both sides who have known nothing but bloodshed their entire lives, and they are eager for an *end* to the war.
By returning with you as my Majesdanian bride, it is my hope that we can together *unite* our peoples and bring *peace* to the quadrant.
I implore you, Magnificent One... *will you marry me?*

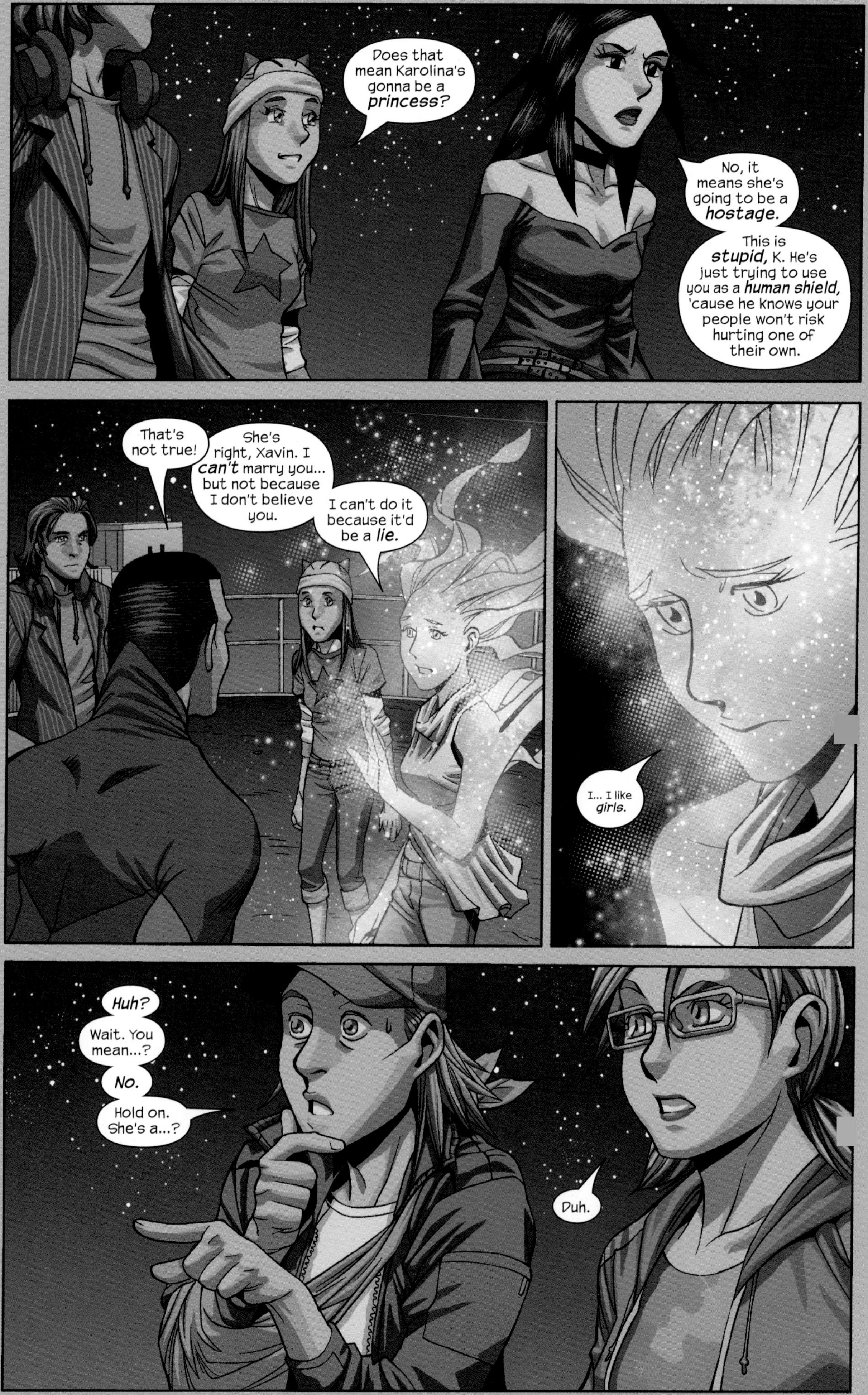
Does that mean Karolina's gonna be a *princess?*
No, it means she's going to be a ***hostage.***
This is ***stupid,*** K. He's just trying to use you as a ***human shield,*** 'cause he knows your people won't risk hurting one of their own.
That's not true!
She's right, Xavin. I ***can't*** marry you... but not because I don't believe you.
I can't do it because it'd be a ***lie.***
I... I like ***girls.***
Huh?
Wait. You mean...?
No.
Hold on. She's a...?
Duh.

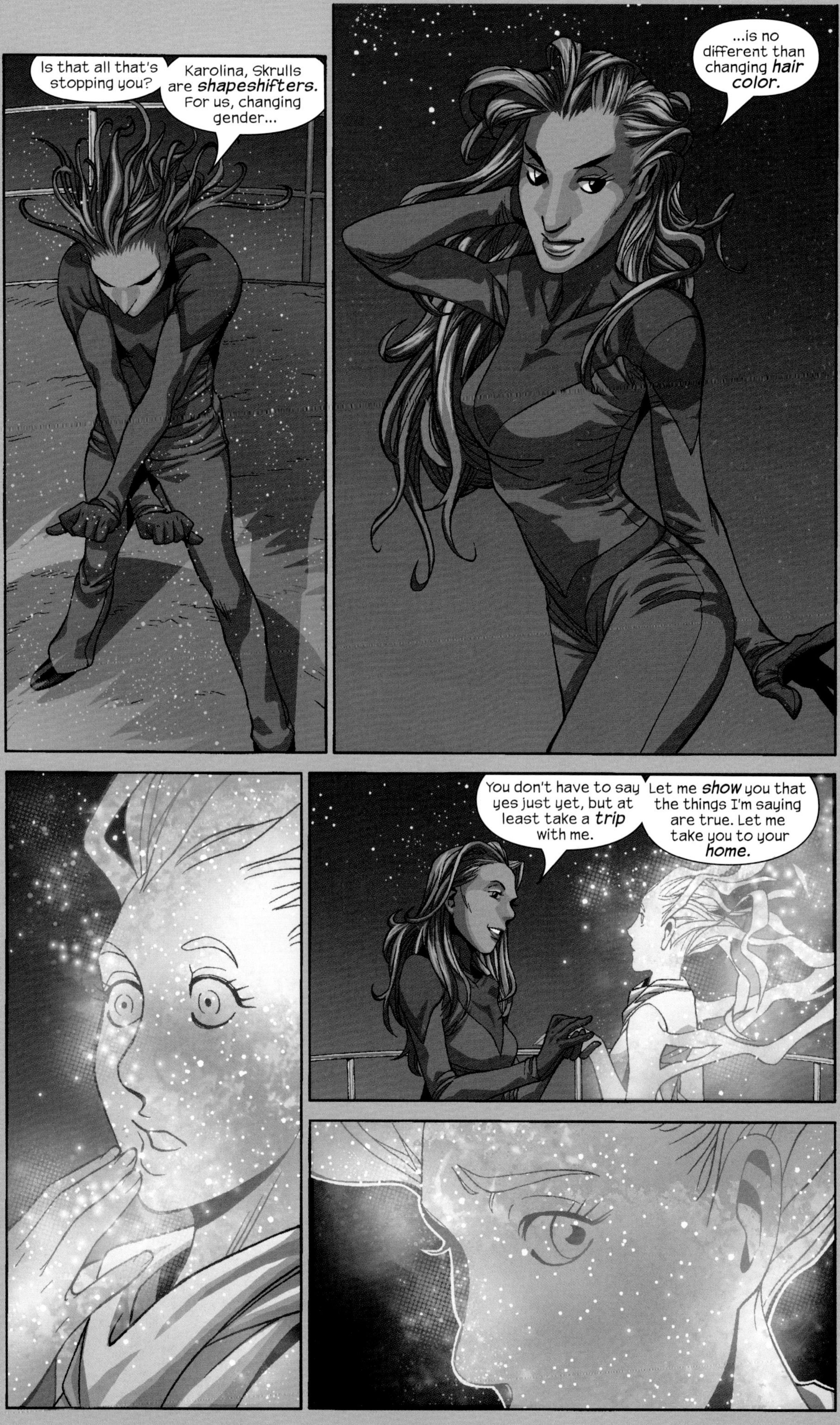
Is that all that's stopping you?
Karolina, Skrulls are shapeshifters. For us, changing gender...
...is no different than changing hair color.
You don't have to say yes just yet, but at least take a trip with me.
Let me show you that the things I'm saying are true. Let me take you to your home.

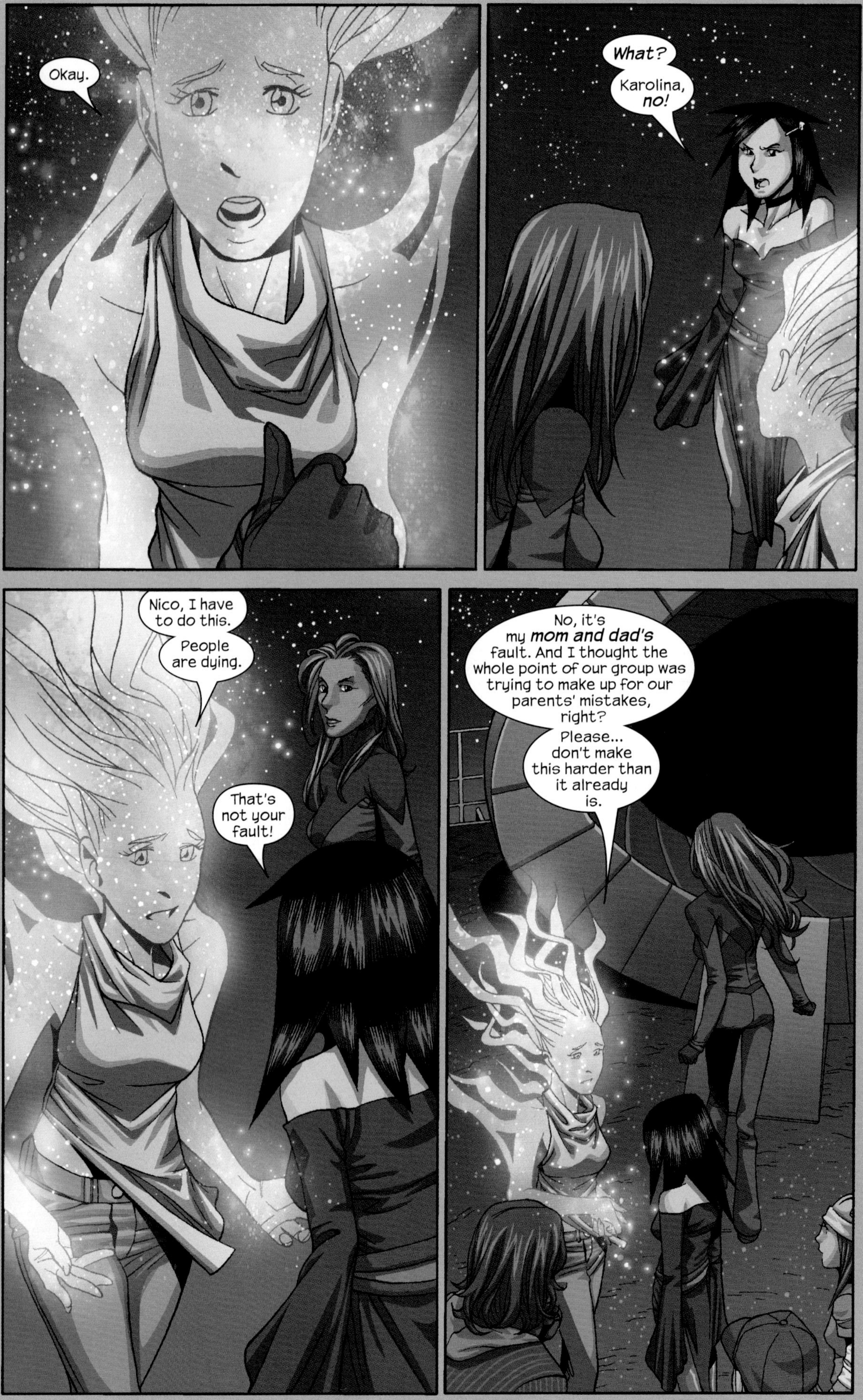
Okay.
What?
Karolina, no!
Nico, I have to do this.
People are dying.
That's not your fault!
No, it's my mom and dad's fault. And I thought the whole point of our group was trying to make up for our parents' mistakes, right?
Please... don't make this harder than it already is.

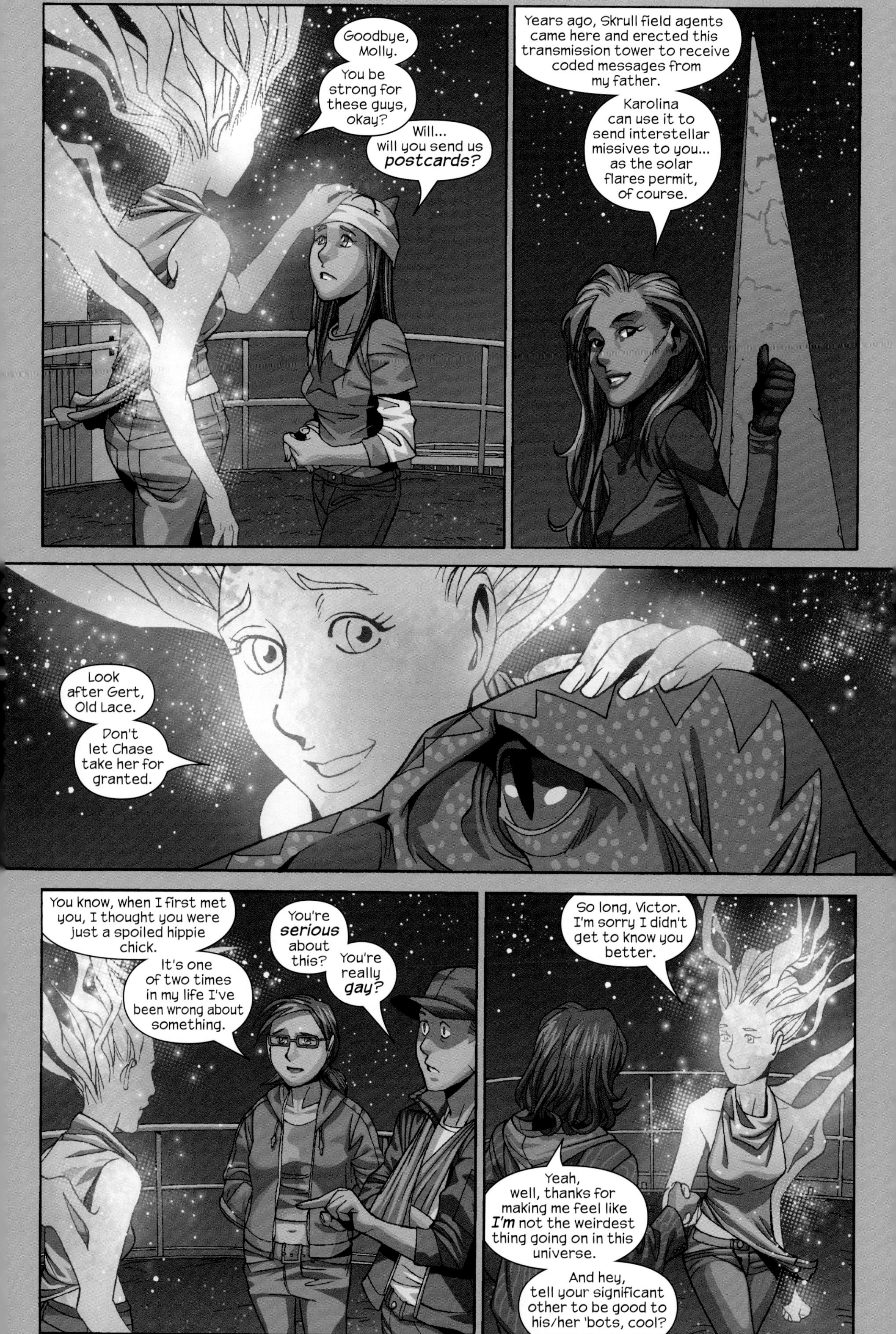
Goodbye, Molly.
You be strong for these guys, okay?
Will... will you send us *postcards?*
Years ago, Skrull field agents came here and erected this transmission tower to receive coded messages from my father.
Karolina can use it to send interstellar missives to you... as the solar flares permit, of course.
Look after Gert, Old Lace.
Don't let Chase take her for granted.
You know, when I first met you, I thought you were just a spoiled hippie chick.
It's one of two times in my life I've been wrong about something.
You're *serious* about this?
You're really *gay?*
So long, Victor. I'm sorry I didn't get to know you better.
Yeah, well, thanks for making me feel like *I'm* not the weirdest thing going on in this universe.
And hey, tell your significant other to be good to his/her 'bots, cool?

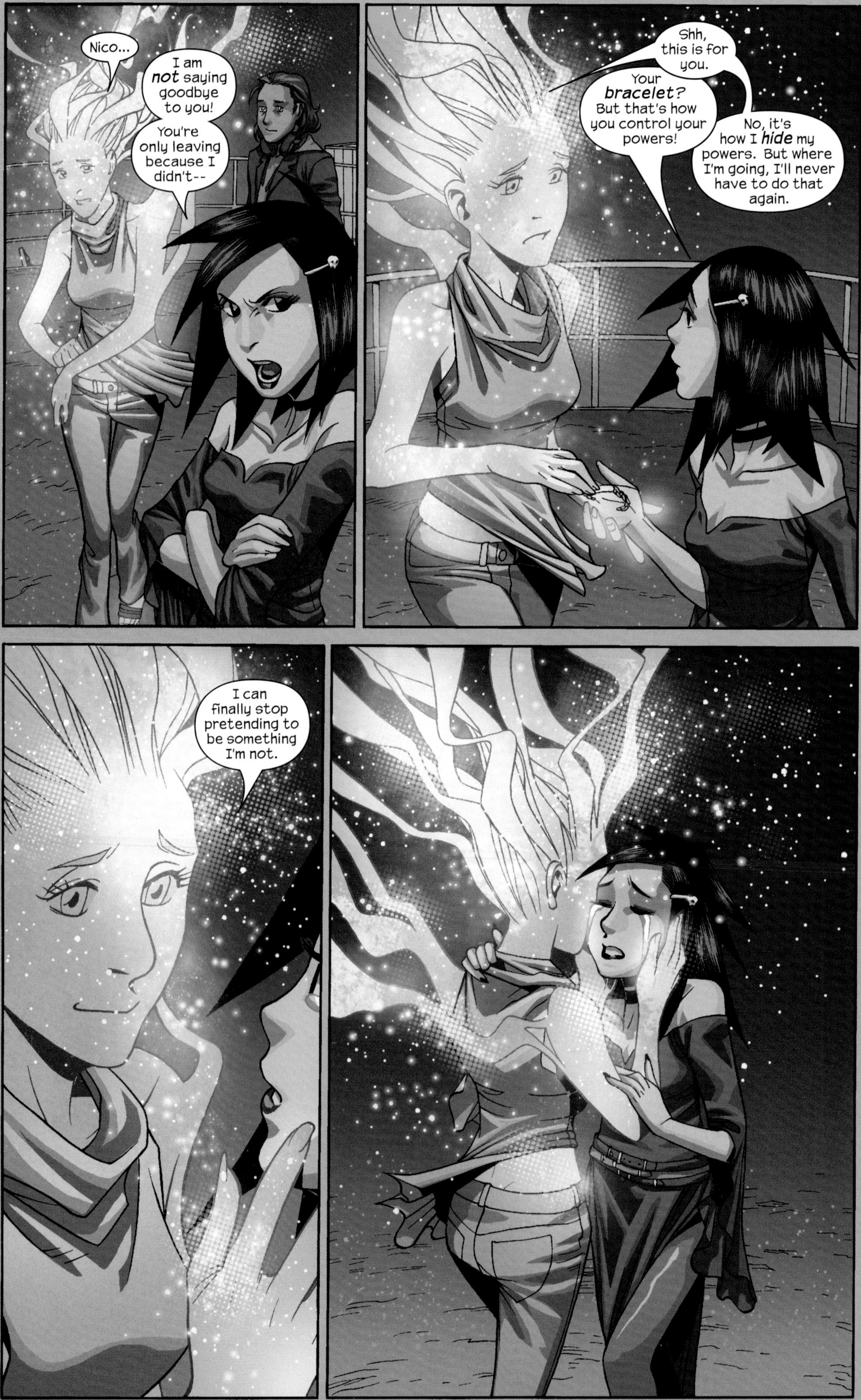
Nico...
I am **not** saying goodbye to you!
You're only leaving because I didn't--
Shh, this is for you.
Your **bracelet**? But that's how you control your powers!
No, it's how I **hide** my powers. But where I'm going, I'll never have to do that again.
I can finally stop pretending to be something I'm not.

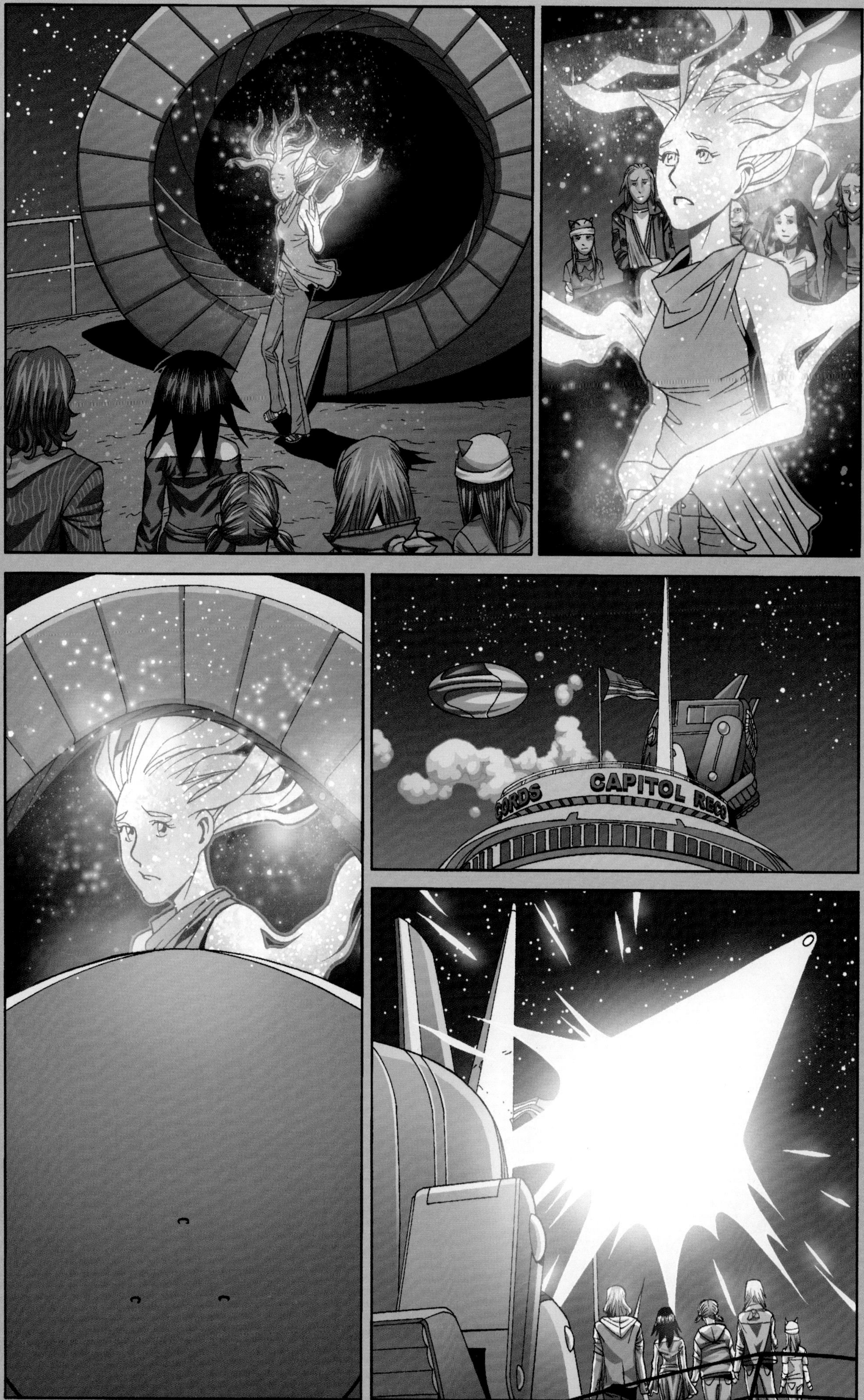
CORDS
CAPITOL RECO

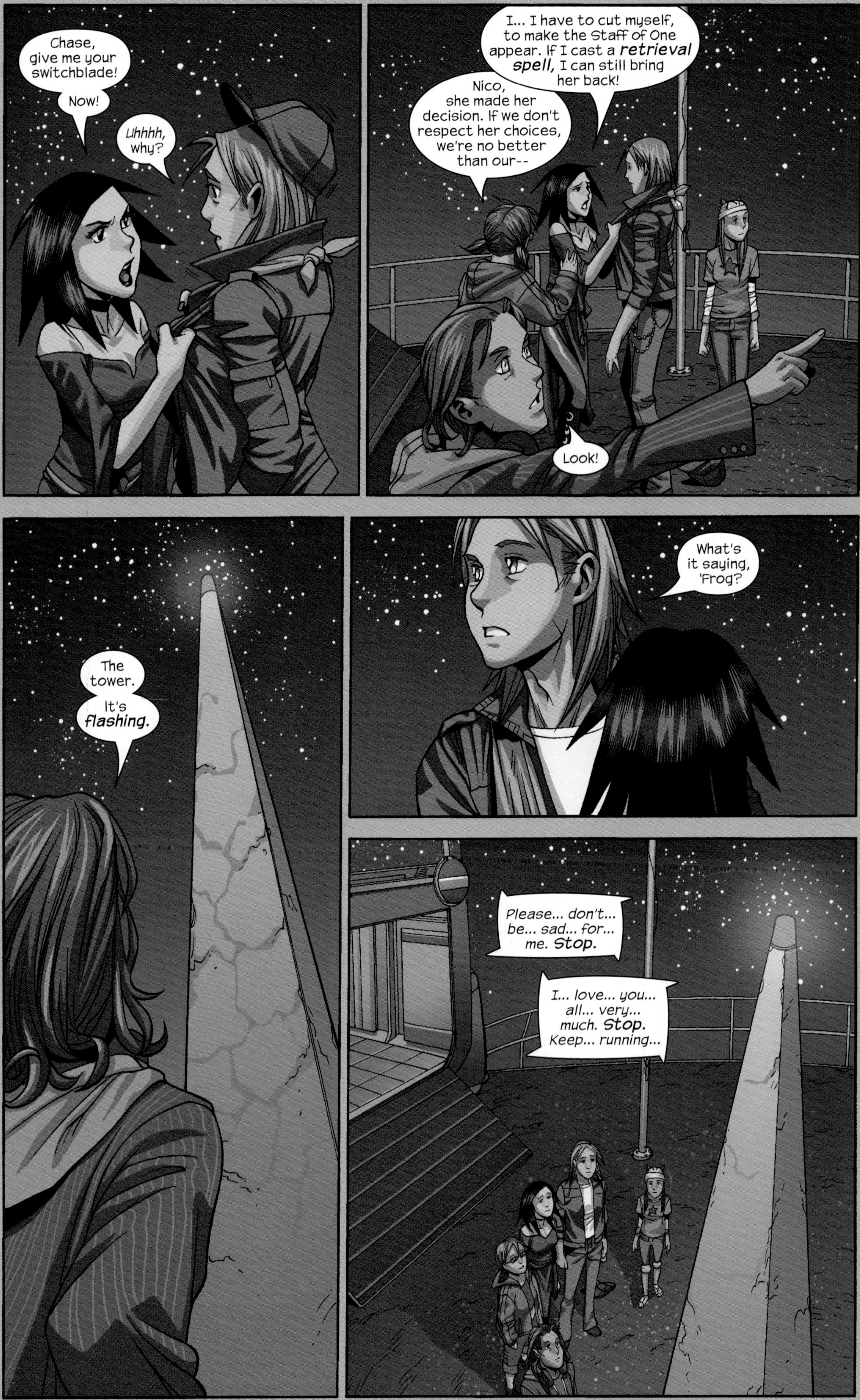
Chase, give me your switchblade!
Now!
Uhhhh, why?
I... I have to cut myself, to make the Staff of One appear. If I cast a *retrieval spell,* I can still bring her back!
Nico, she made her decision. If we don't respect her choices, we're no better than our--
Look!
The tower.
It's *flashing.*
What's it saying, 'Frog?
Please... don't... be... sad... for... me. **Stop.**
I... love... you... all... very... much. **Stop.** Keep... running...

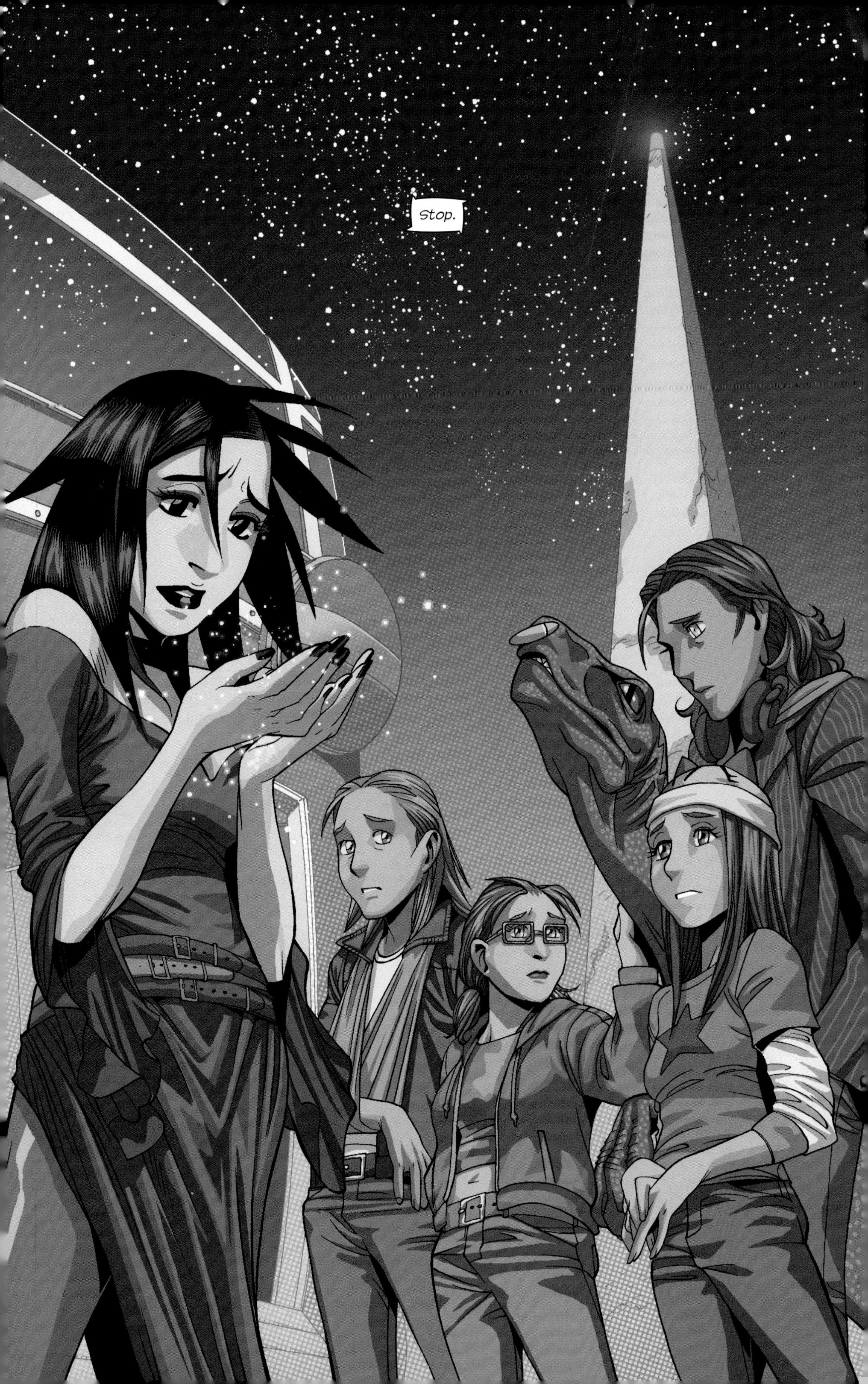
Stop.

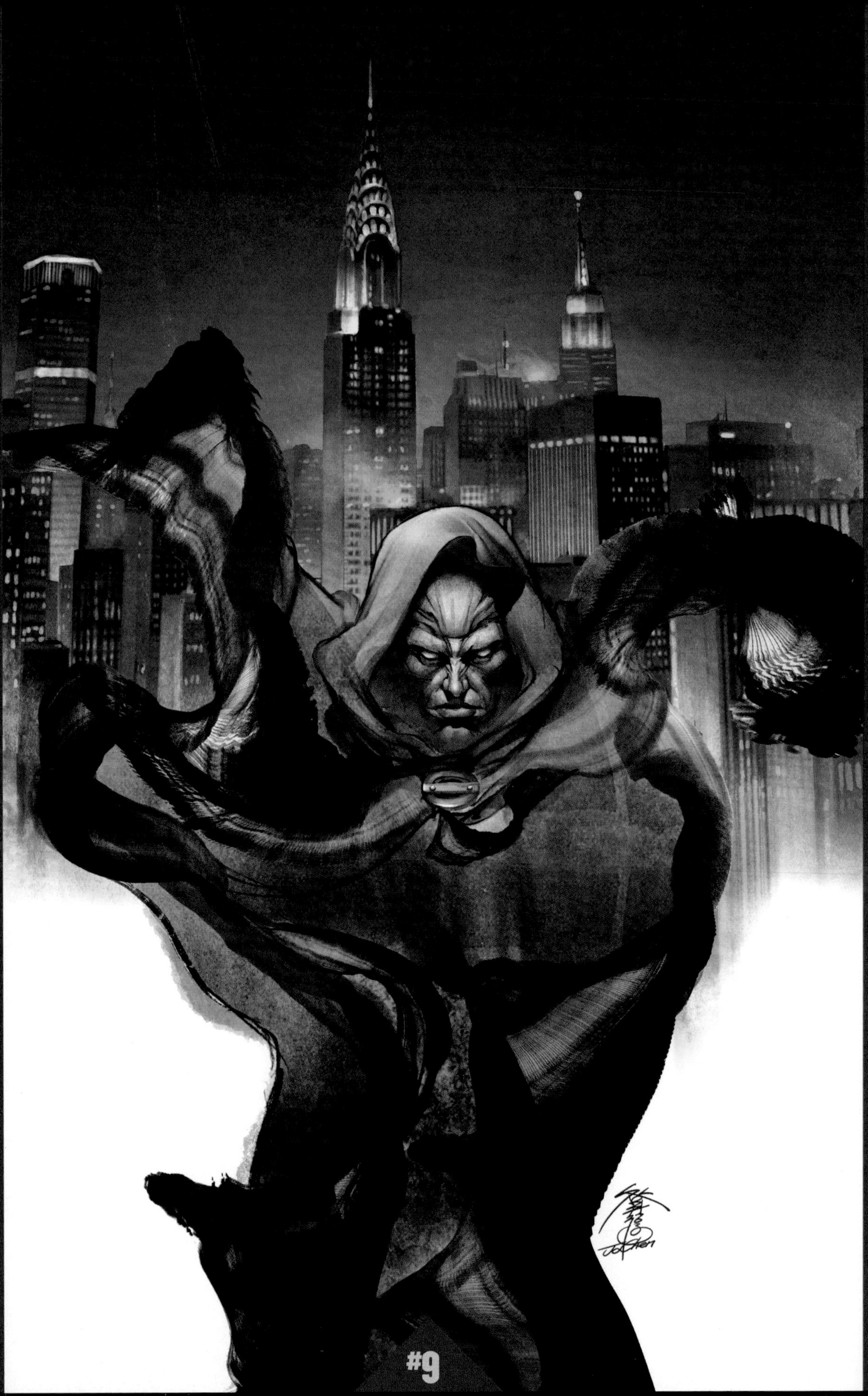
#9

EAST COAST/WEST COAST PART 1

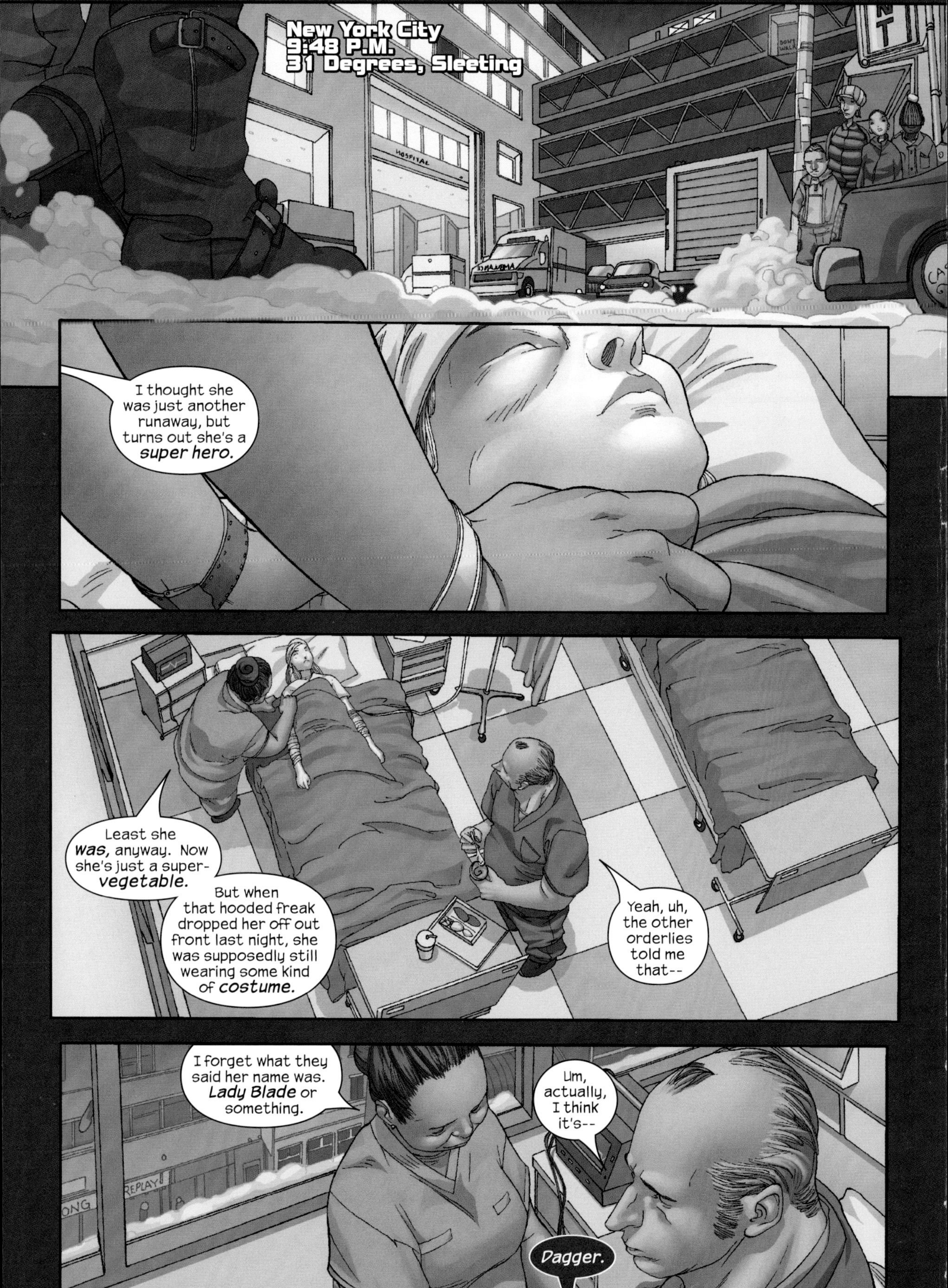
New York City
9:48 P.M.
31 Degrees, Sleeting
HOSPITAL
AMBULANCE
I thought she was just another runaway, but turns out she's a *super hero.*
Least she *was,* anyway. Now she's just a super-*vegetable.*
But when that hooded freak dropped her off out front last night, she was supposedly still wearing some kind of *costume.*
Yeah, uh, the other orderlies told me that--
I forget what they said her name was. *Lady Blade* or something.
Um, actually, I think it's--
Dagger.
REPLAY

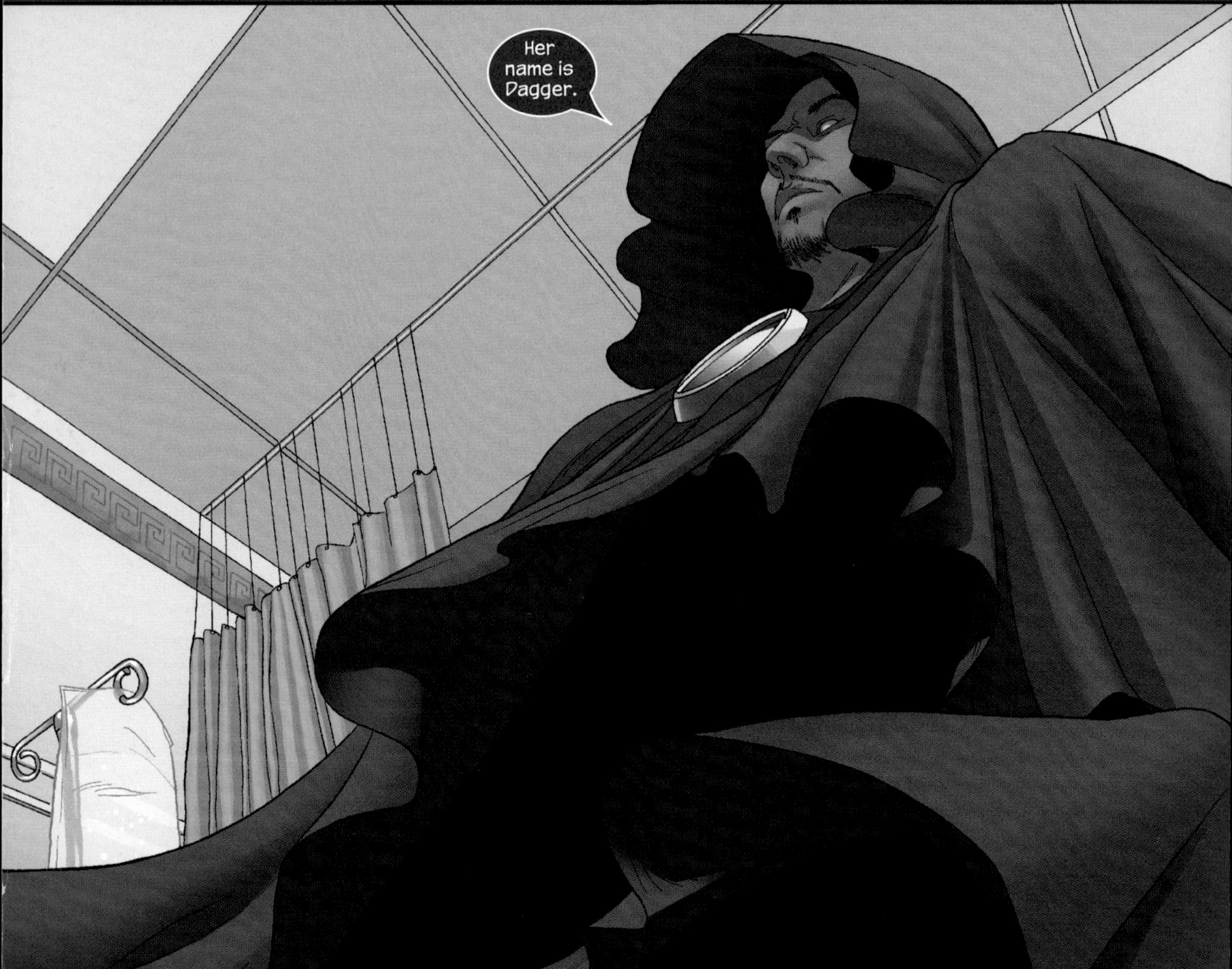
Her name is Dagger.

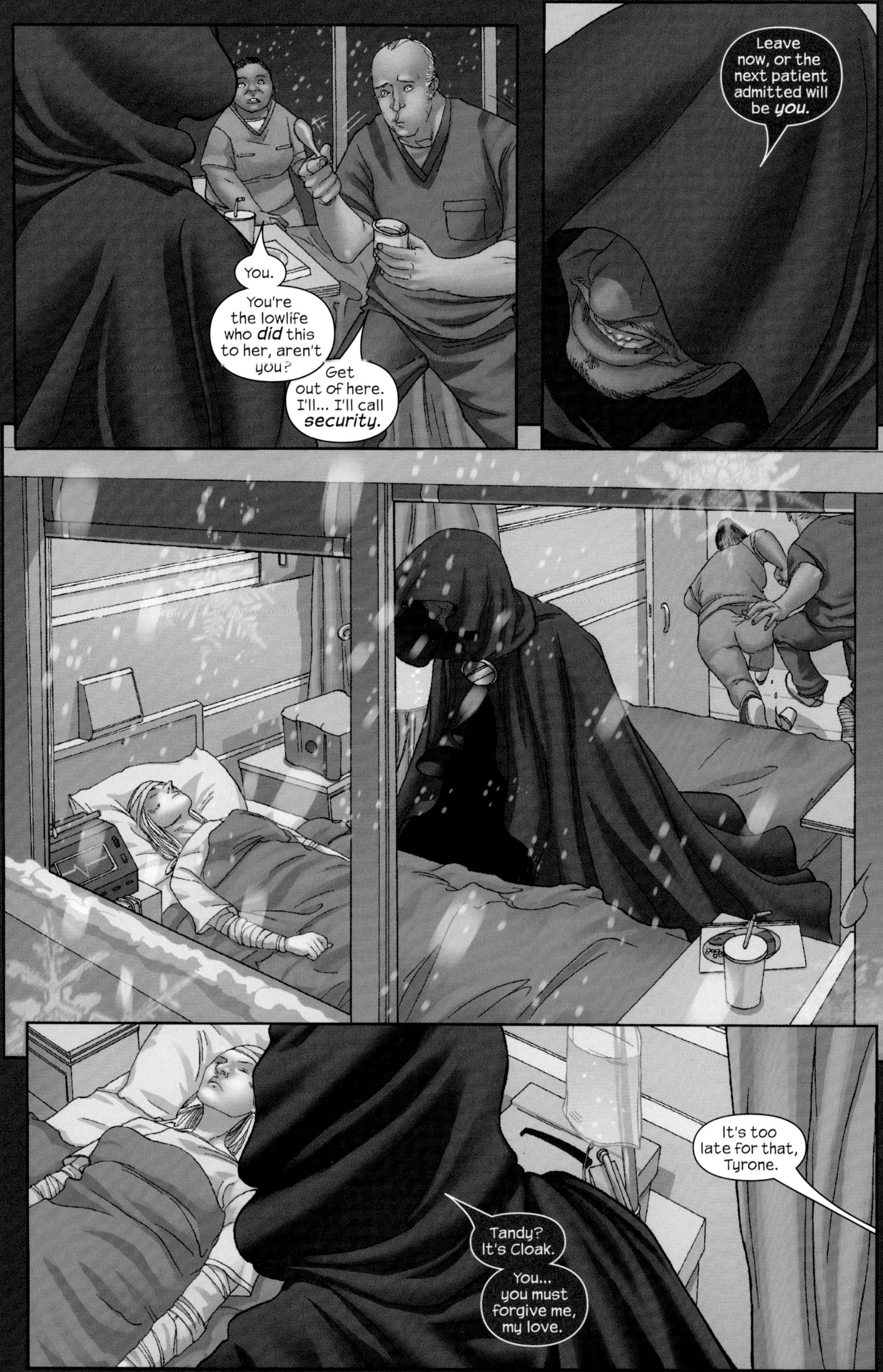
You.
You're the lowlife who *did* this to her, aren't you?
Get out of here. I'll... I'll call *security.*
Leave now, or the next patient admitted will be *you.*
Tandy? It's Cloak.
You... you must forgive me, my love.
It's too late for that, Tyrone.

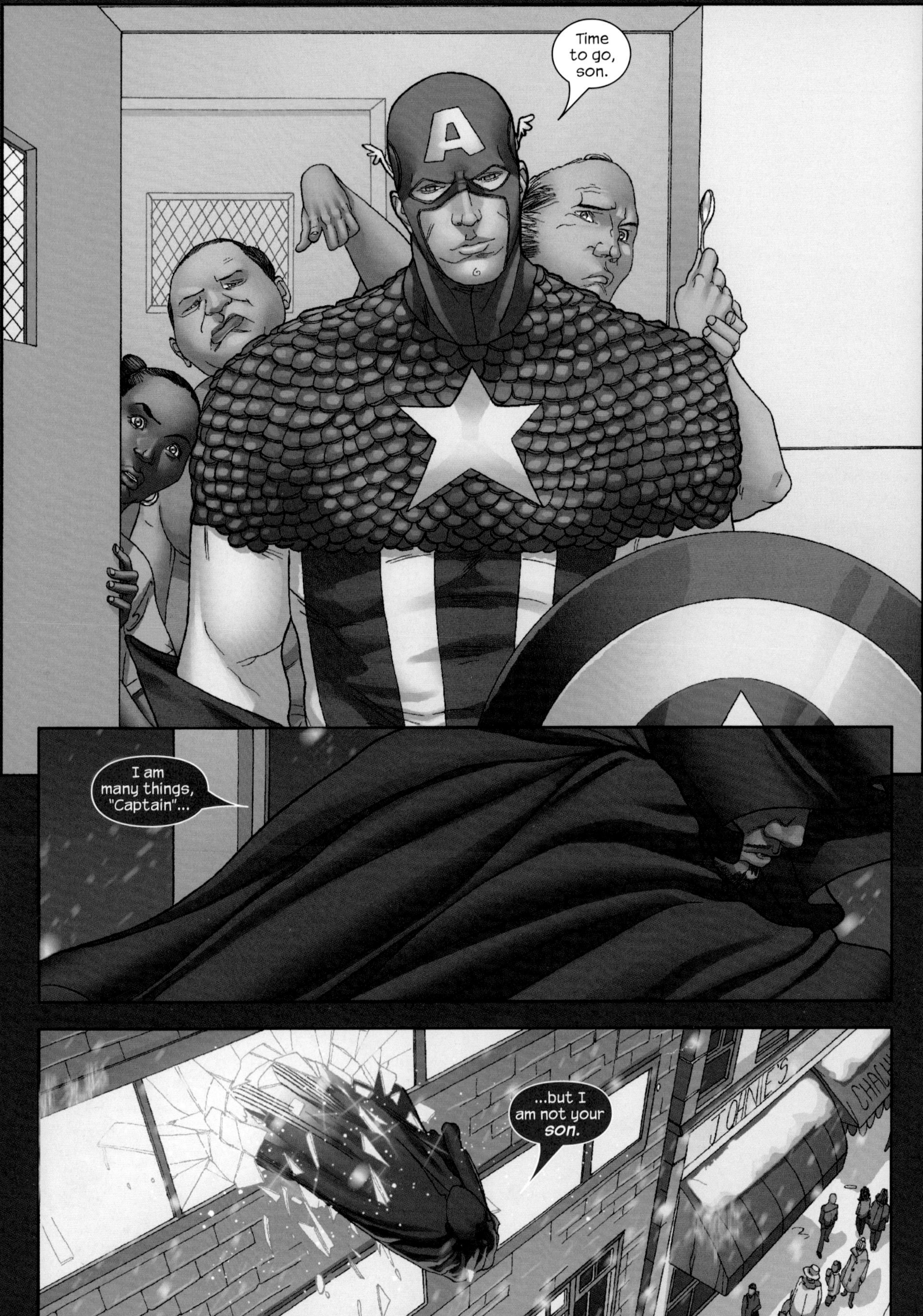
Time to go, son.
I am many things, "Captain"...
...but I am not your son.
JOHNIE'S

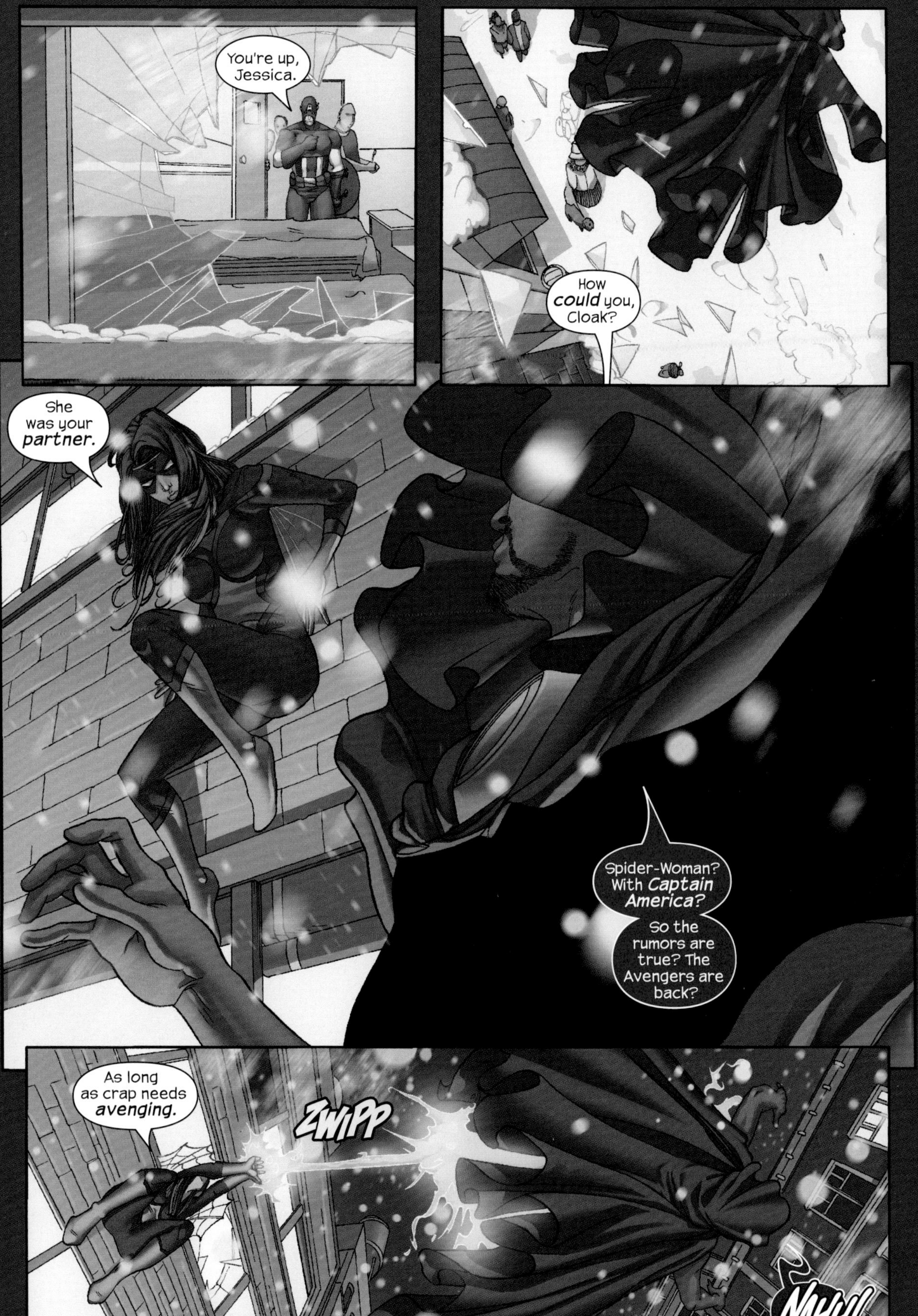
You're up, Jessica.
How could you, Cloak?
She was your partner.
Spider-Woman? With Captain America?
So the rumors are true? The Avengers are back?
As long as crap needs avenging.
ZWIPP
NAHH!

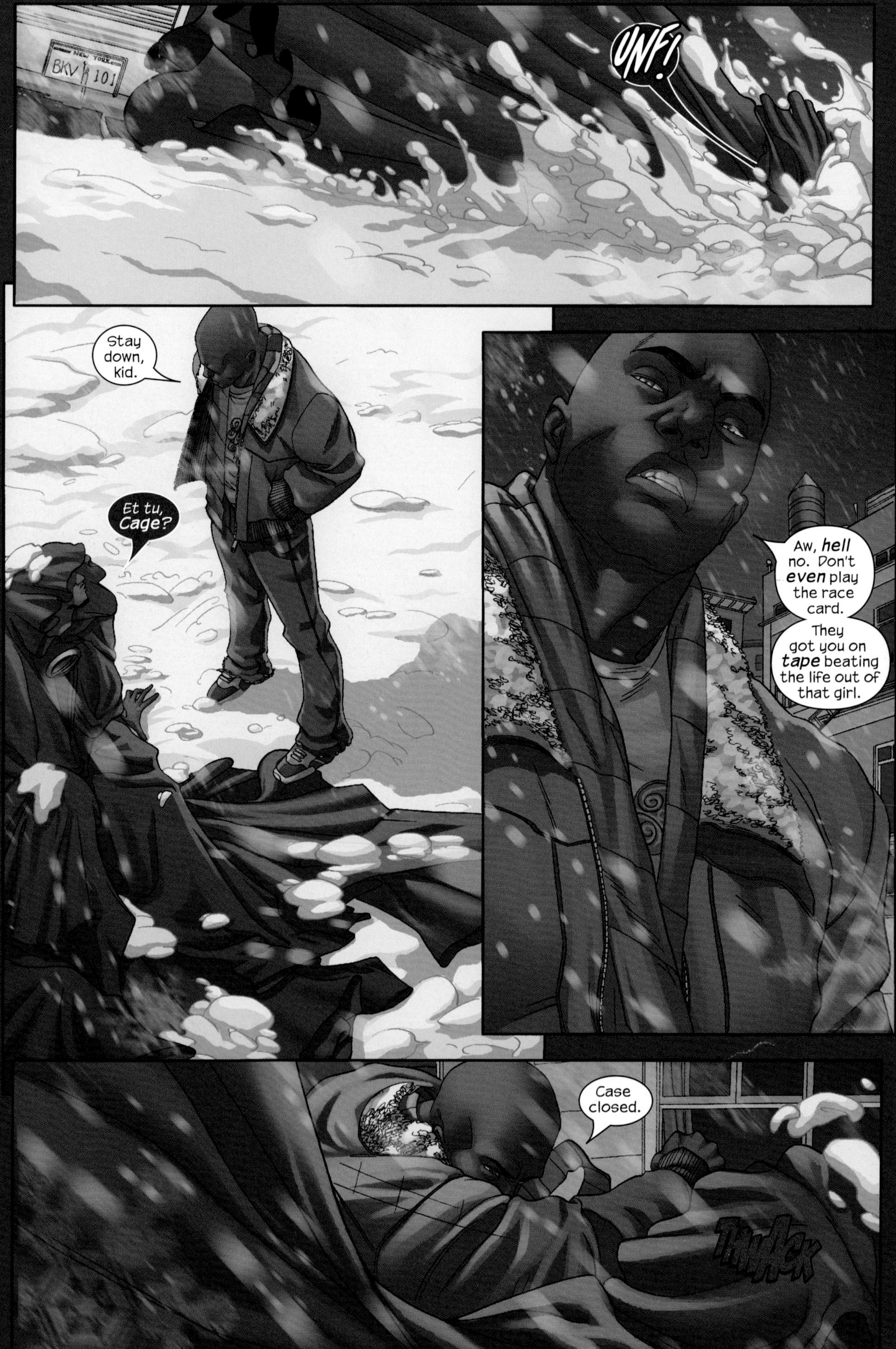

UNF!
Stay down, kid.
Et tu, Cage?
Aw, hell no. Don't even play the race card.
They got you on tape beating the life out of that girl.
Case closed.
THWACK

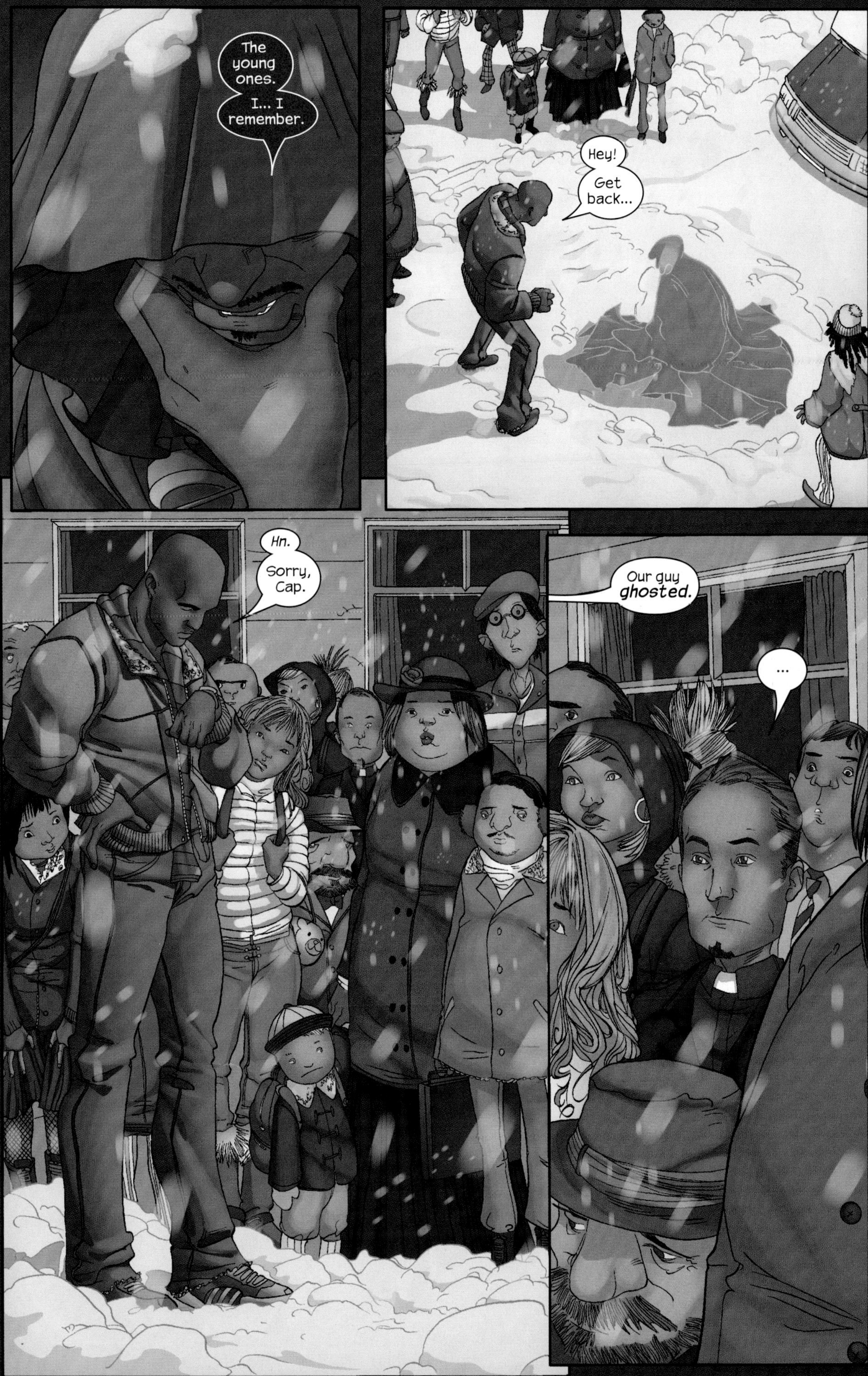
The young ones.
I... I remember.
Hey!
Get back...
Hn.
Sorry, Cap.
Our guy ghosted.
...

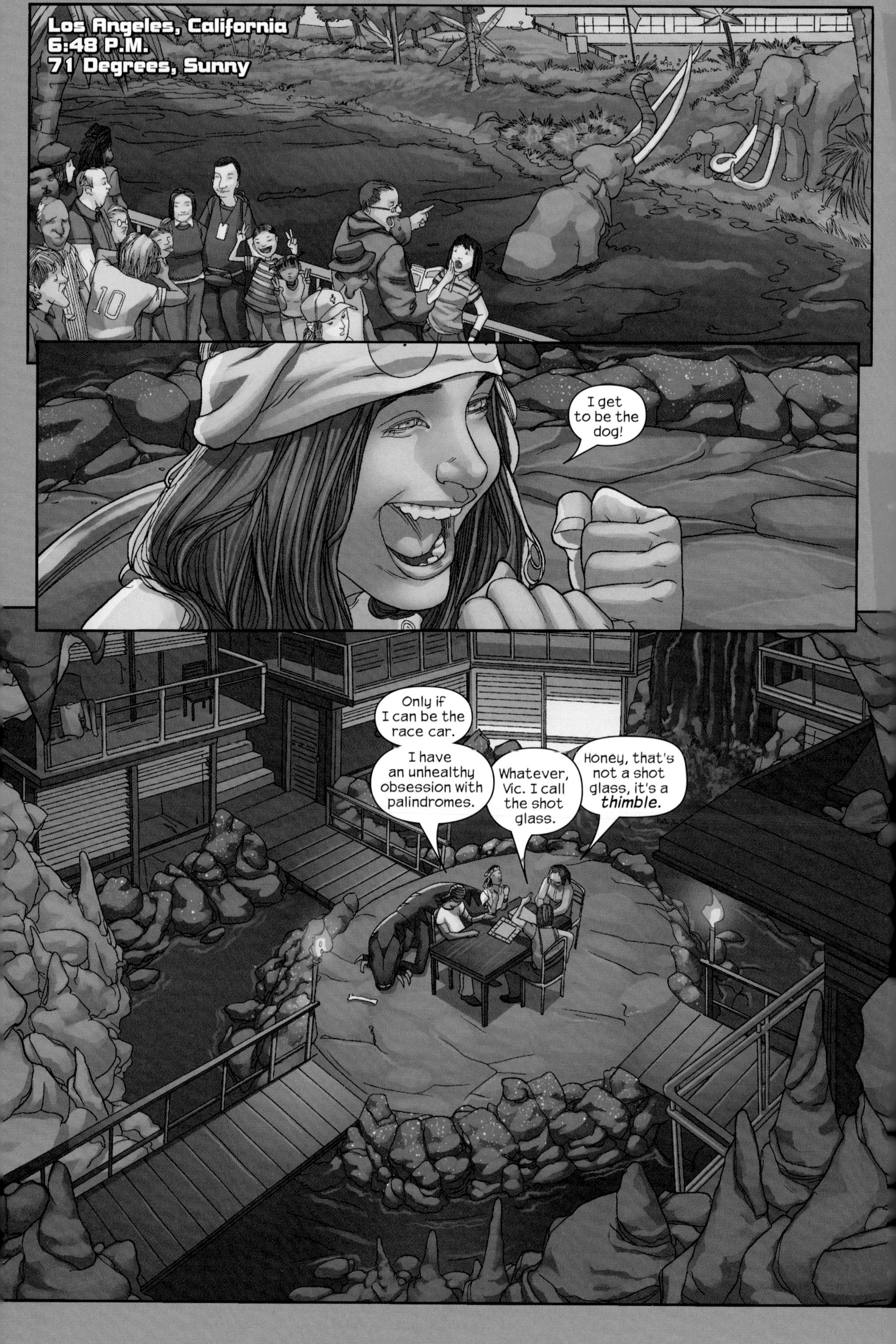
Los Angeles, California
6:48 P.M.
71 Degrees, Sunny
I get to be the dog!
Only if I can be the race car.
I have an unhealthy obsession with palindromes.
Whatever, Vic. I call the shot glass.
Honey, that's not a shot glass, it's a *thimble.*

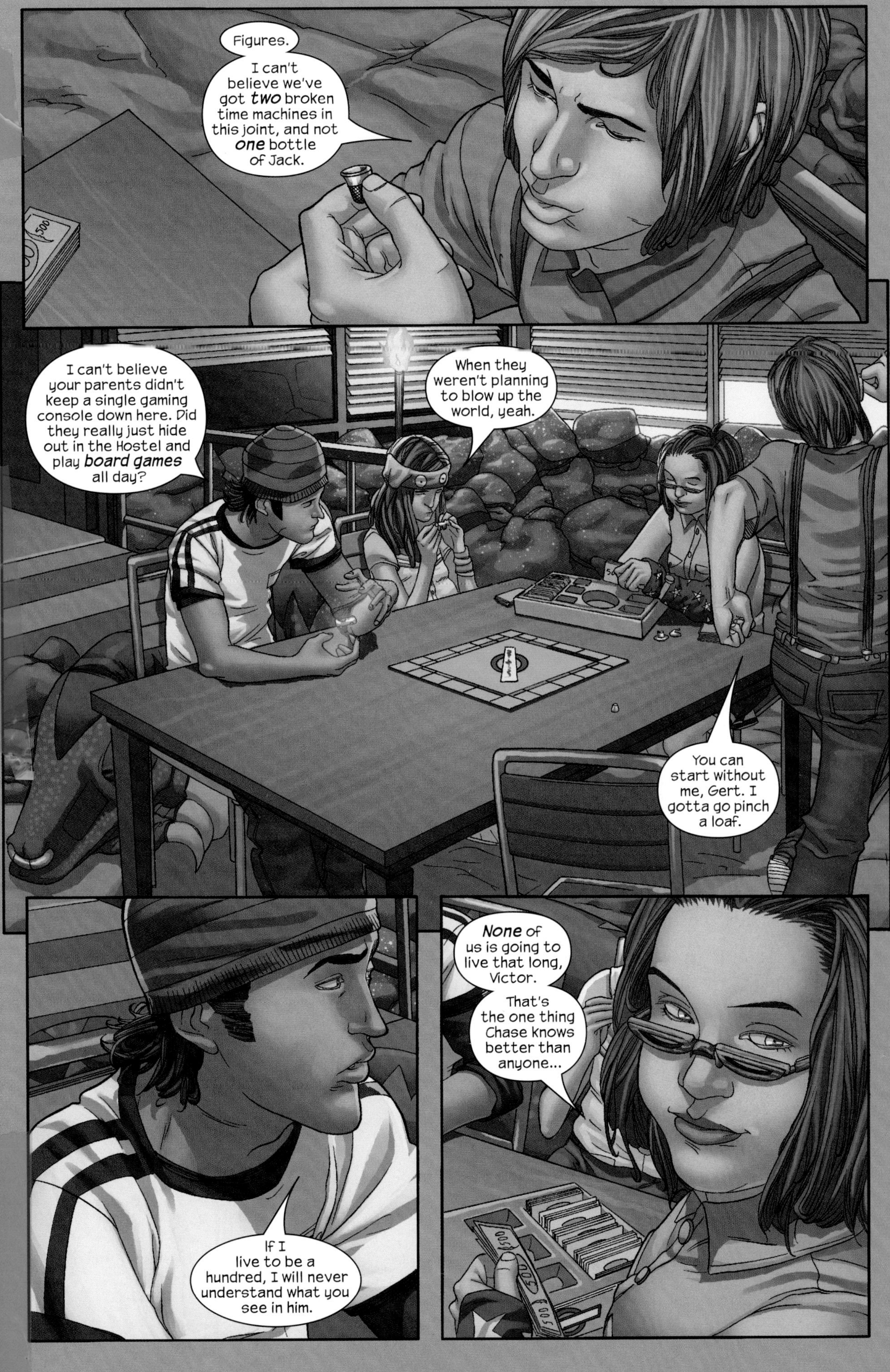
Figures.
I can't believe we've got *two* broken time machines in this joint, and not *one* bottle of Jack.
I can't believe your parents didn't keep a single gaming console down here. Did they really just hide out in the Hostel and play **board games** all day?
When they weren't planning to blow up the world, yeah.
You can start without me, Gert. I gotta go pinch a loaf.
If I live to be a hundred, I will never understand what you see in him.
None of us is going to live that long, Victor.
That's the one thing Chase knows better than anyone...

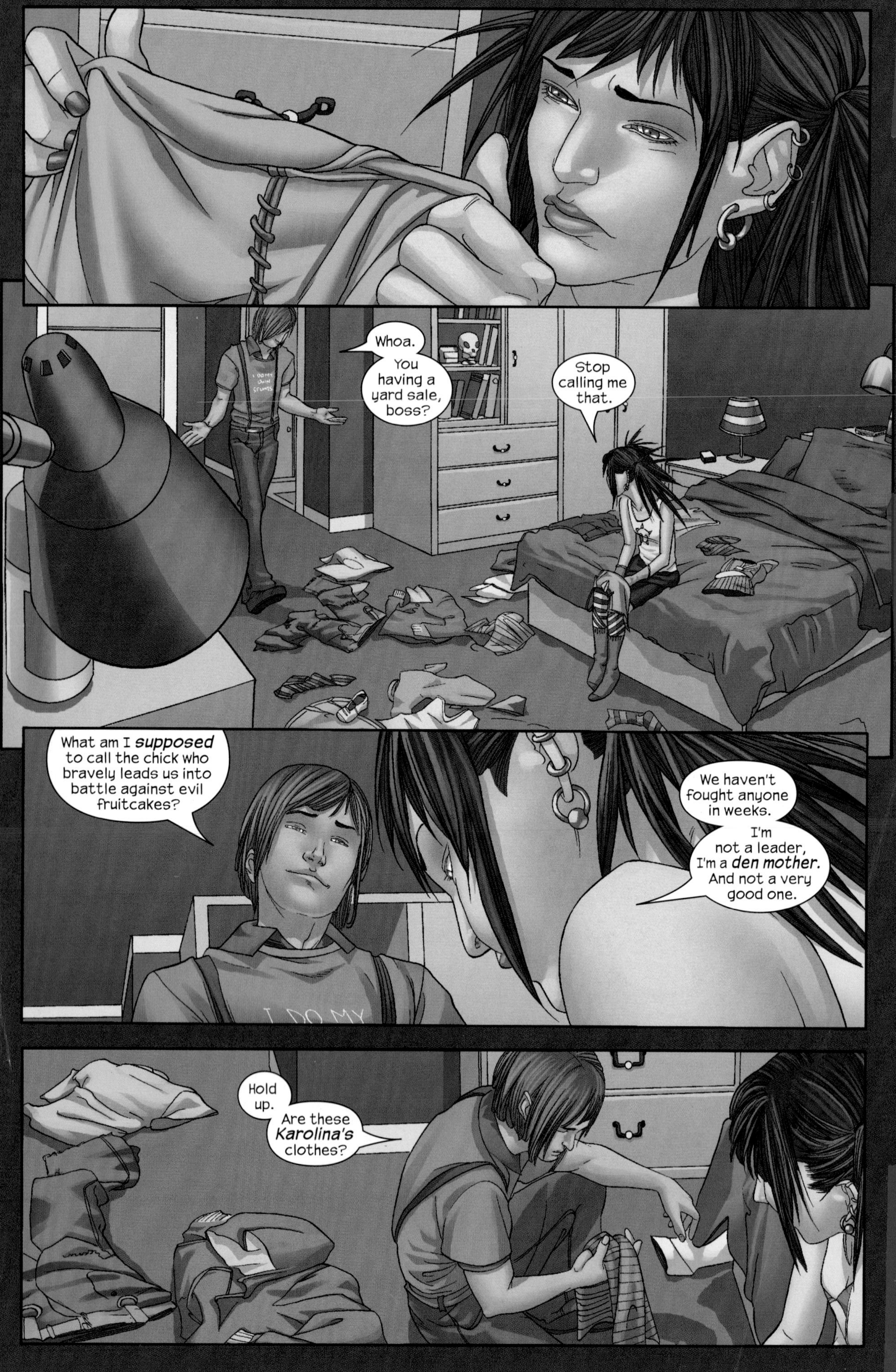
Whoa.
You having a yard sale, boss?
Stop calling me that.
What am I *supposed* to call the chick who bravely leads us into battle against evil fruitcakes?
We haven't fought anyone in weeks.
I'm not a leader, I'm a *den mother.* And not a very good one.
Hold up.
Are these *Karolina's* clothes?

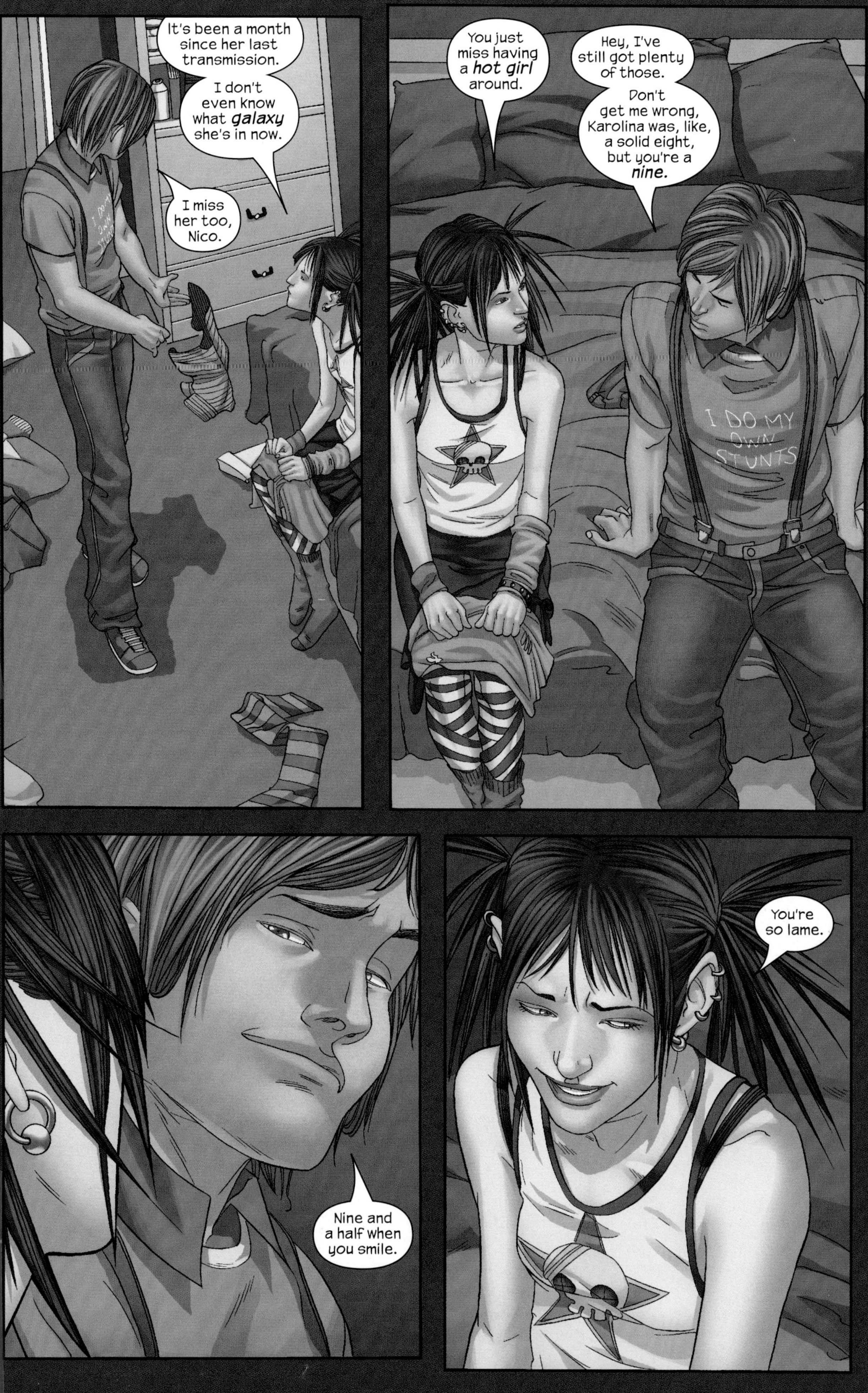
It's been a month since her last transmission.
I don't even know what *galaxy* she's in now.
I miss her too, Nico.
I DO MY OWN STUNTS
You just miss having a ***hot girl*** around.
Hey, I've still got plenty of those.
Don't get me wrong, Karolina was, like, a solid eight, but you're a ***nine.***
I DO MY OWN STUNTS
Nine and a half when you smile.
You're so lame.

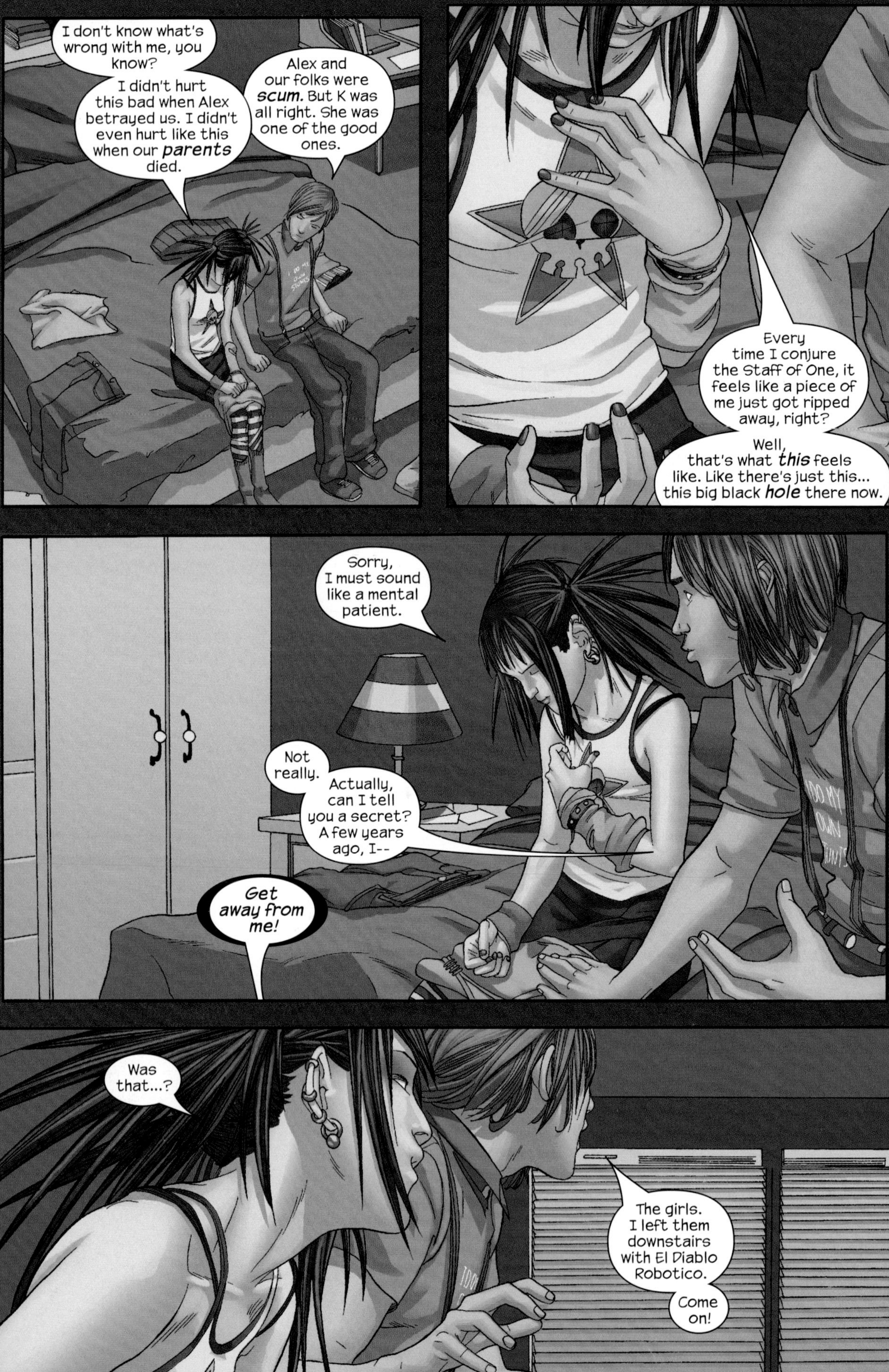
I don't know what's wrong with me, you know?
I didn't hurt this bad when Alex betrayed us. I didn't even hurt like this when our *parents* died.
Alex and our folks were ***scum.*** But K was all right. She was one of the good ones.
Every time I conjure the Staff of One, it feels like a piece of me just got ripped away, right?
Well, that's what ***this*** feels like. Like there's just this... this big black ***hole*** there now.
Sorry, I must sound like a mental patient.
Not really.
Actually, can I tell you a secret? A few years ago, I--
Get away from me!
Was that...?
The girls. I left them downstairs with El Diablo Robotico.
Come on!

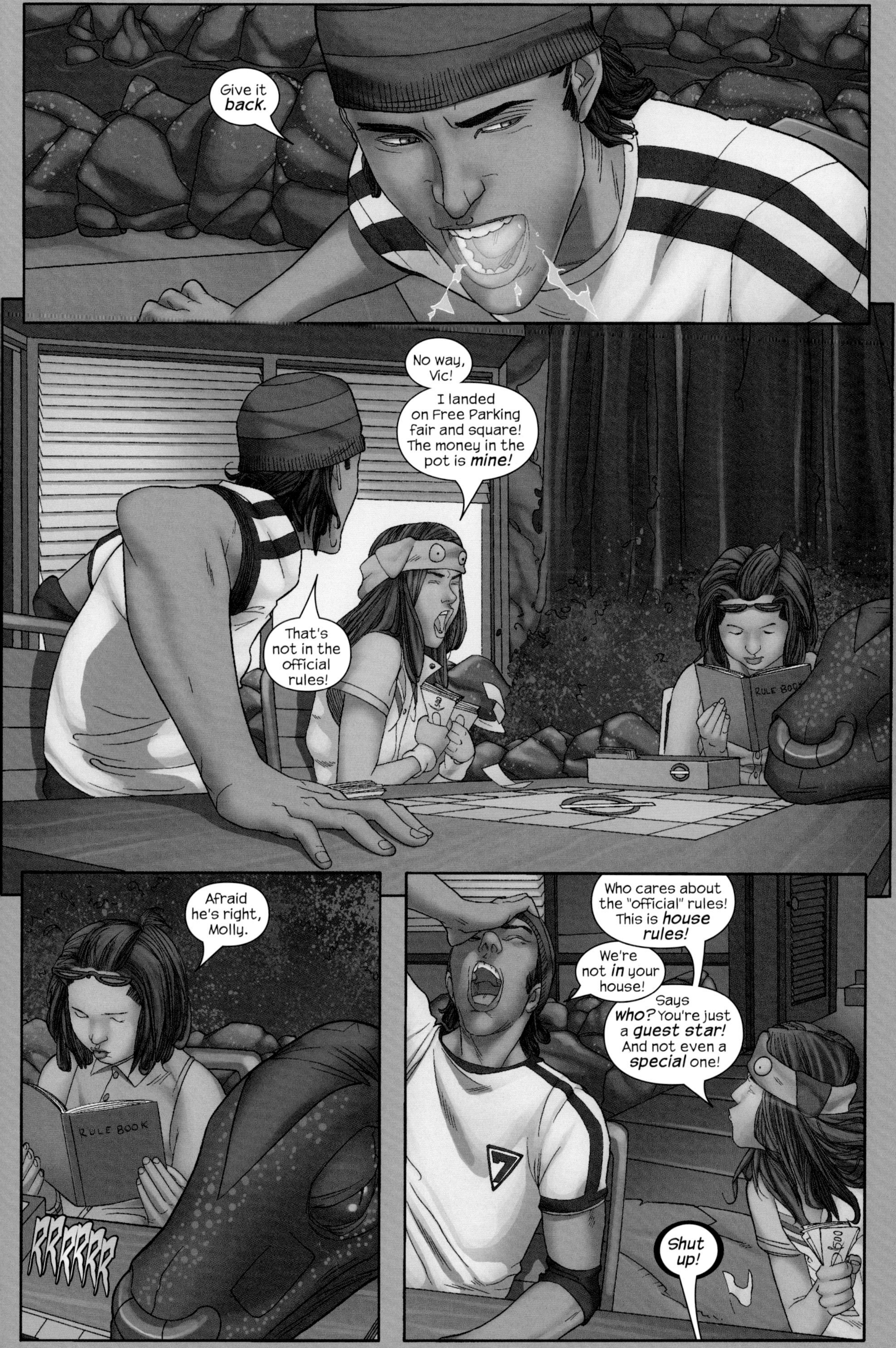

Give it back.
No way, Vic!
I landed on Free Parking fair and square! The money in the pot is mine!
That's not in the official rules!
RULE BOOK
Afraid he's right, Molly.
RULE BOOK
RRRRRR
Who cares about the "official" rules! This is house rules!
We're not in your house!
Says who? You're just a guest star! And not even a special one!
Shut up!

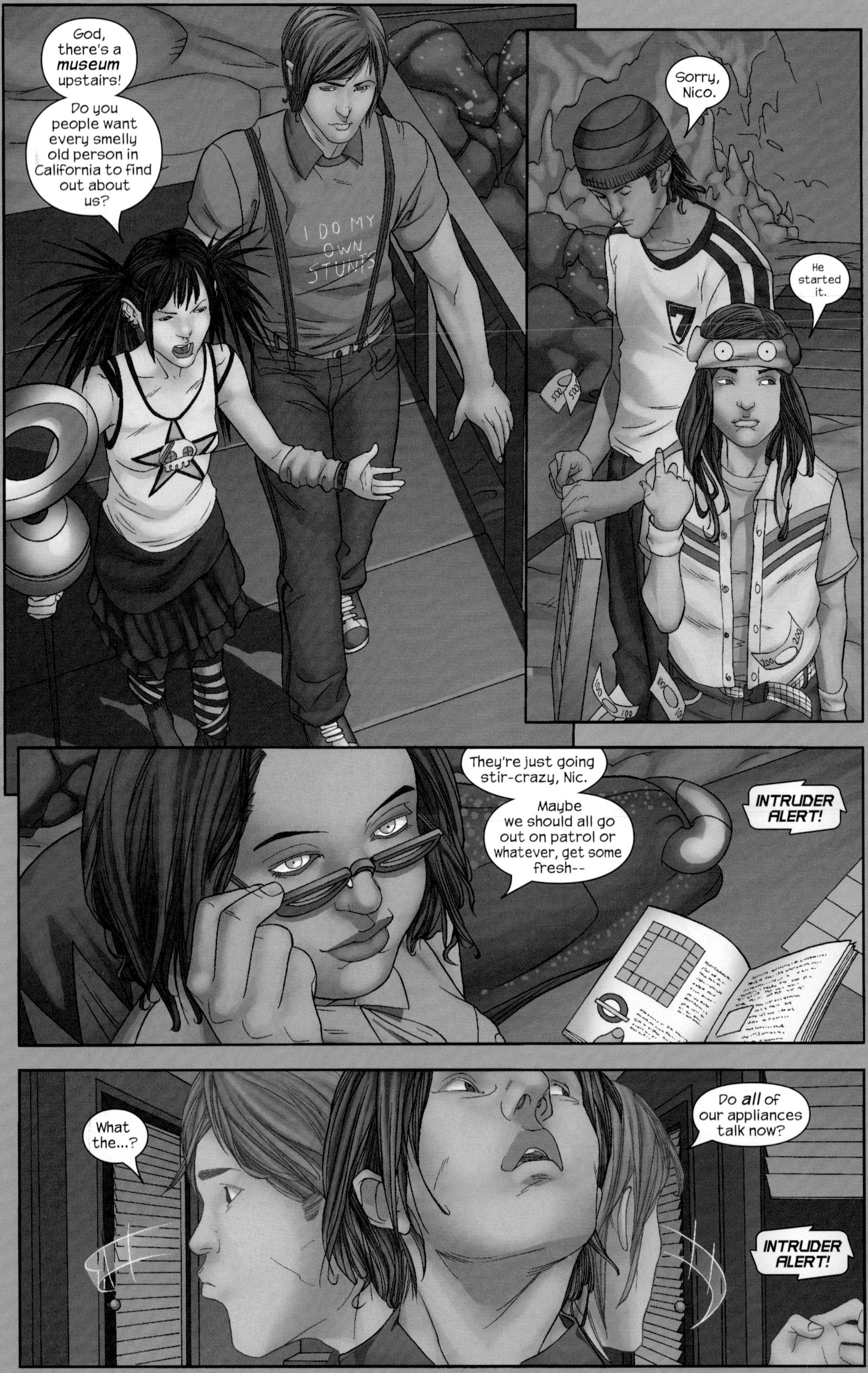
God, there's a museum upstairs!
Do you people want every smelly old person in California to find out about us?
I DO MY OWN STUNTS
Sorry, Nico.
He started it.
They're just going stir-crazy, Nic.
Maybe we should all go out on patrol or whatever, get some fresh--
INTRUDER ALERT!
What the...?
Do all of our appliances talk now?
INTRUDER ALERT!

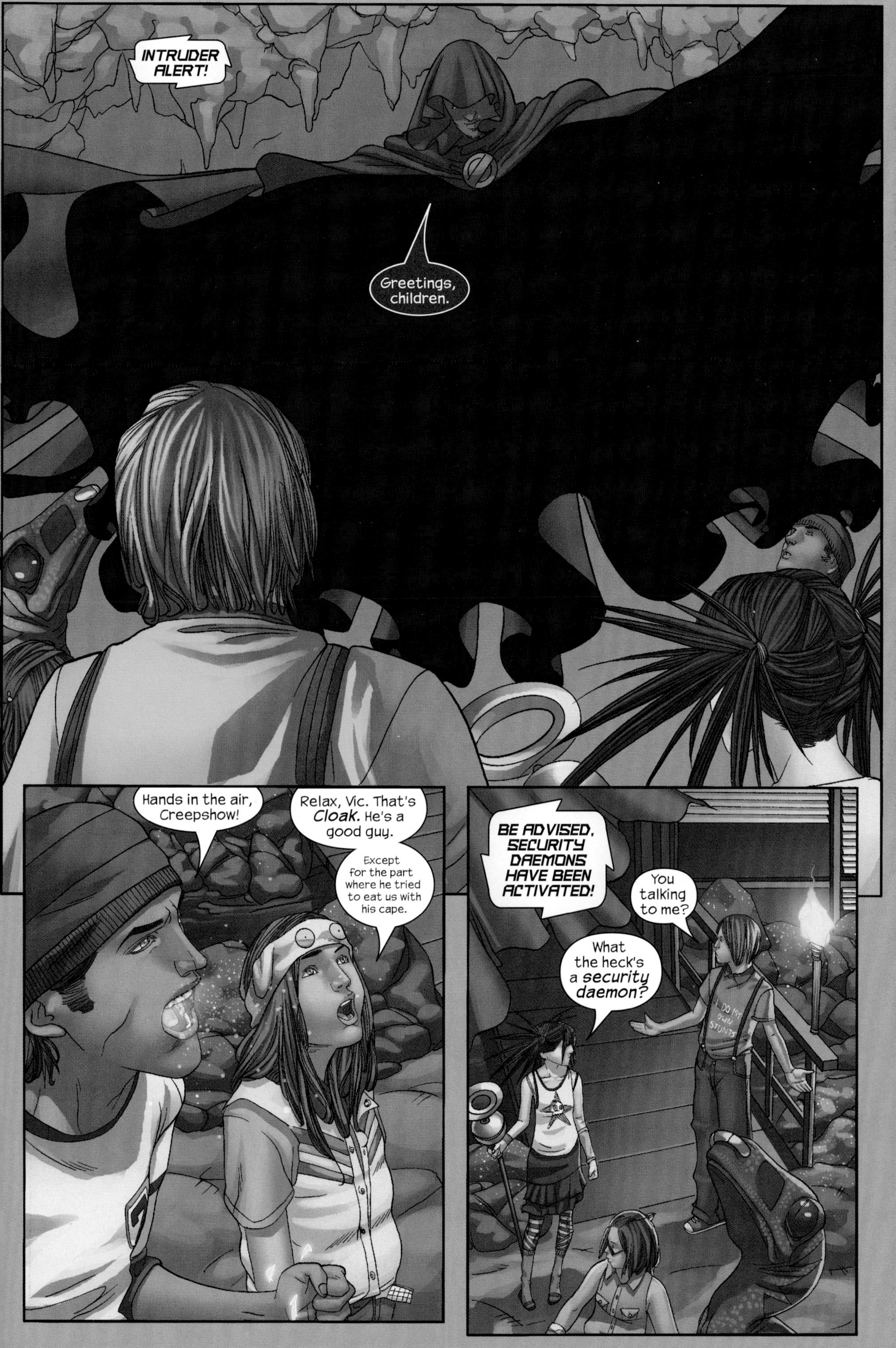
INTRUDER ALERT!
Greetings, children.
Hands in the air, Creepshow!
Relax, Vic. That's *Cloak.* He's a good guy.
Except for the part where he tried to eat us with his cape.
BE ADVISED, SECURITY DAEMONS HAVE BEEN ACTIVATED!
You talking to me?
What the heck's a *security daemon?*

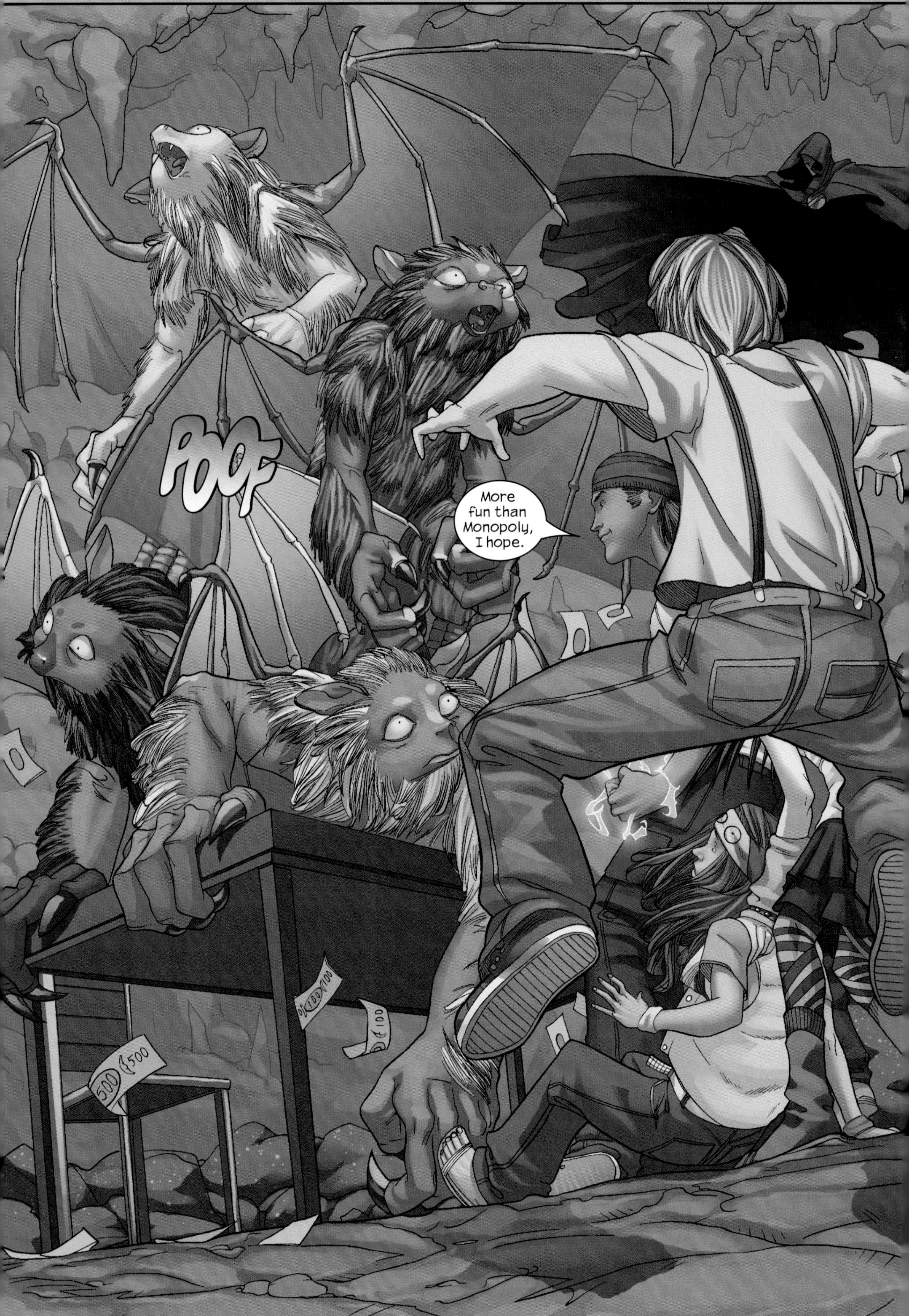
POOF
More fun than Monopoly, I hope.

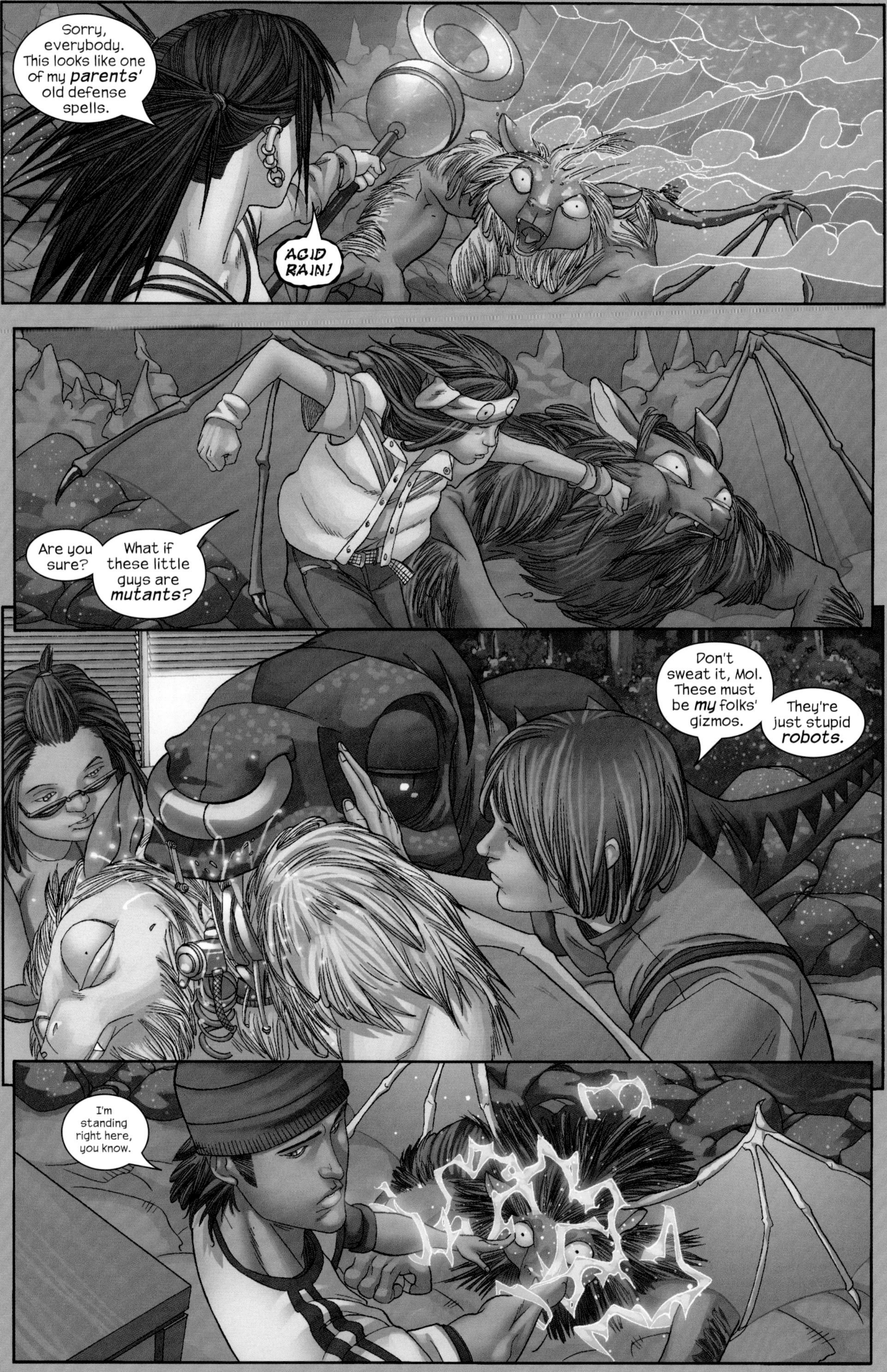
Sorry, everybody. This looks like one of my *parents'* old defense spells.
ACID RAIN!
Are you sure?
What if these little guys are *mutants?*
Don't sweat it, Mol. These must be *my* folks' gizmos.
They're just stupid **robots.**
I'm standing right here, you know.

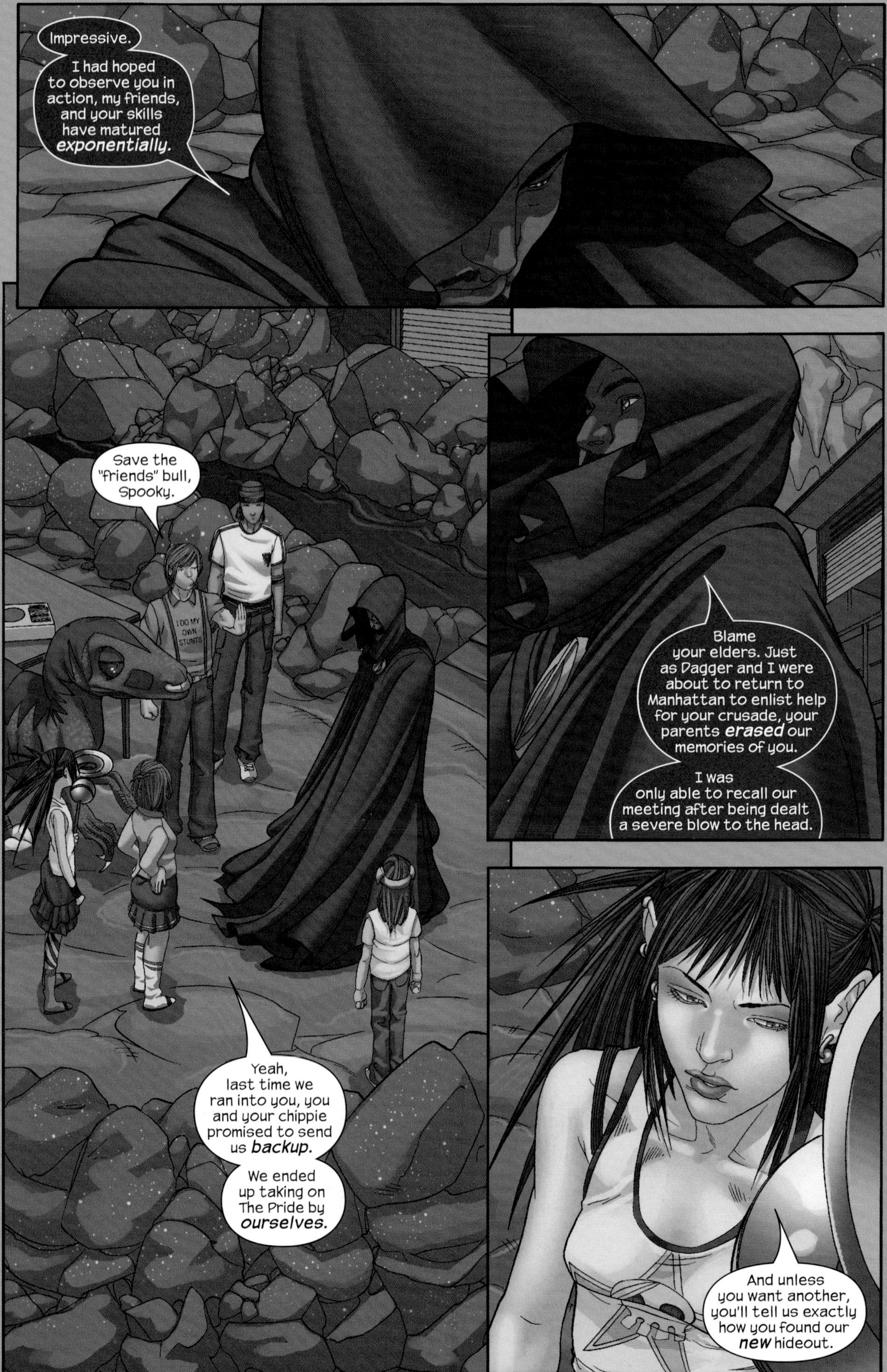

Impressive.
I had hoped to observe you in action, my friends, and your skills have matured *exponentially.*
Save the "friends" bull, Spooky.
I DO MY OWN STUNTS
Yeah, last time we ran into you, you and your chippie promised to send us *backup.*
We ended up taking on The Pride by *ourselves.*
Blame your elders. Just as Dagger and I were about to return to Manhattan to enlist help for your crusade, your parents *erased* our memories of you.
I was only able to recall our meeting after being dealt a severe blow to the head.
And unless you want another, you'll tell us exactly how you found our *new* hideout.

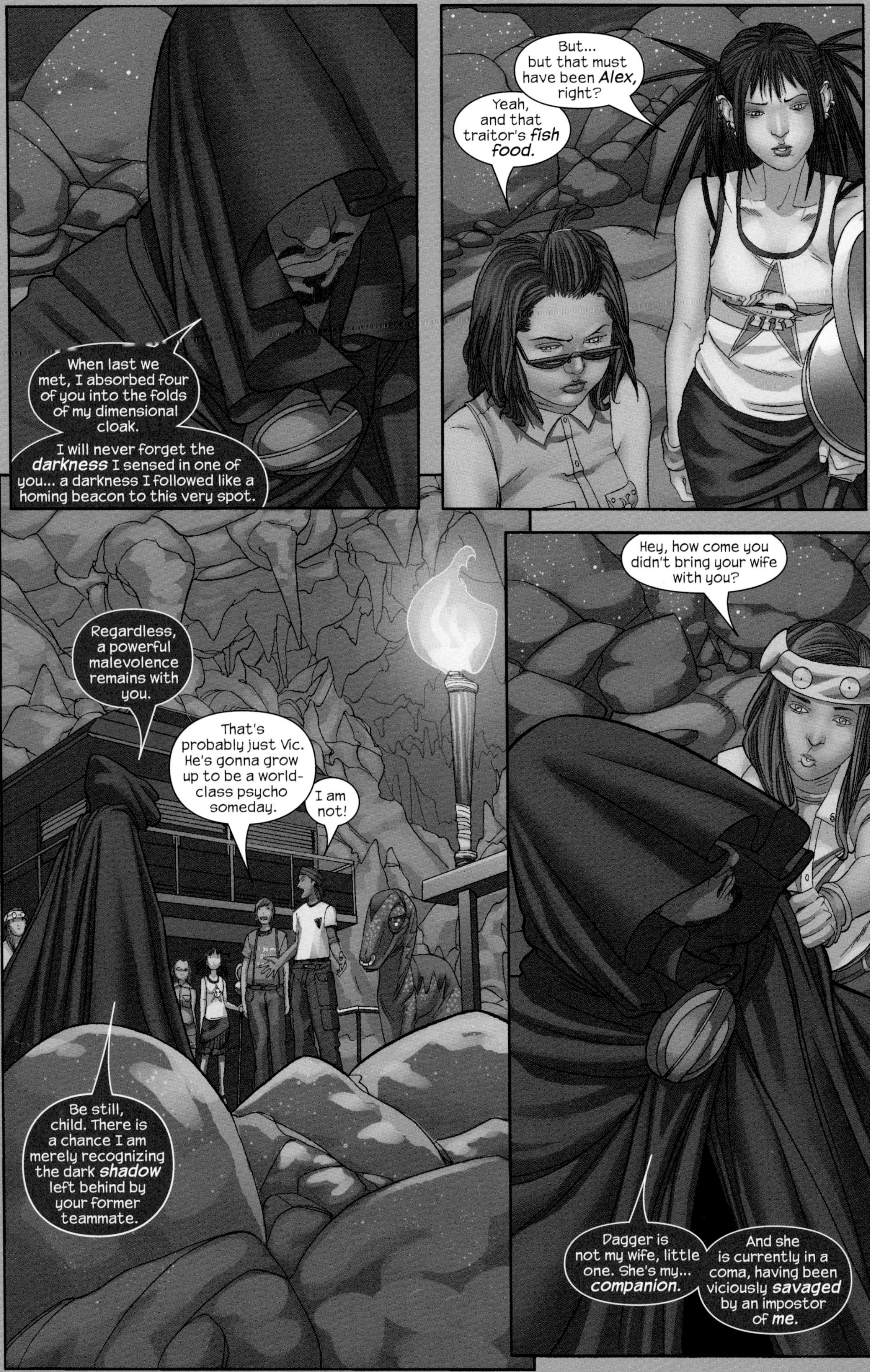
When last we met, I absorbed four of you into the folds of my dimensional cloak.
I will never forget the *darkness* I sensed in one of you... a darkness I followed like a homing beacon to this very spot.
But... but that must have been *Alex,* right?
Yeah, and that traitor's *fish food.*
Regardless, a powerful malevolence remains with you.
That's probably just Vic. He's gonna grow up to be a world-class psycho someday.
I am not!
Be still, child. There is a chance I am merely recognizing the dark *shadow* left behind by your former teammate.
Hey, how come you didn't bring your wife with you?
Dagger is not my wife, little one. She's my... *companion.*
And she is currently in a coma, having been viciously *savaged* by an impostor of *me.*

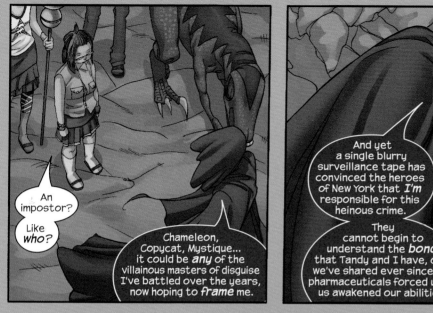

An impostor?

Like *who*?

Chameleon, Copycat, Mystique... it could be *any* of the villainous masters of disguise I've battled over the years, now hoping to *frame* me.

And yet a single blurry surveillance tape has convinced the heroes of New York that *I'm* responsible for this heinous crime.

They cannot begin to understand the *bond* that Tandy and I have, one we've shared ever since the pharmaceuticals forced upon us awakened our abilities.

Wait, back up. Your secret origin is *drugs*?

Doesn't that kinda set a bad example for little kids?

I AM NOT YOUR ROLE MODEL!

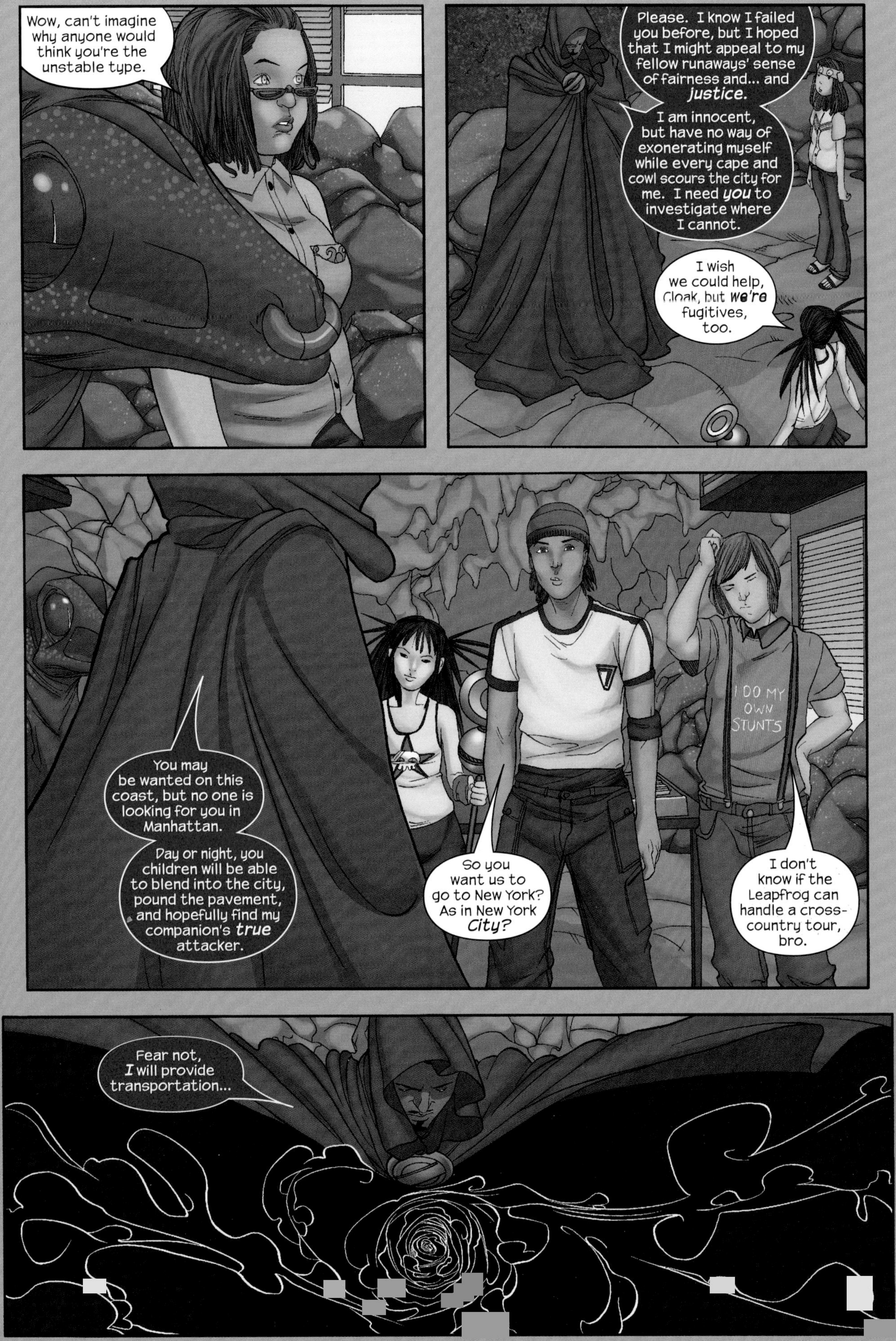
Wow, can't imagine why anyone would think you're the unstable type.
Please. I know I failed you before, but I hoped that I might appeal to my fellow runaways' sense of fairness and... and justice.
I am innocent, but have no way of exonerating myself while every cape and cowl scours the city for me. I need you to investigate where I cannot.
I wish we could help, Cloak, but we're fugitives, too.
I DO MY OWN STUNTS
You may be wanted on this coast, but no one is looking for you in Manhattan.
Day or night, you children will be able to blend into the city, pound the pavement, and hopefully find my companion's true attacker.
So you want us to go to New York? As in New York City?
I don't know if the Leapfrog can handle a cross-country tour, bro.
Fear not, I will provide transportation...

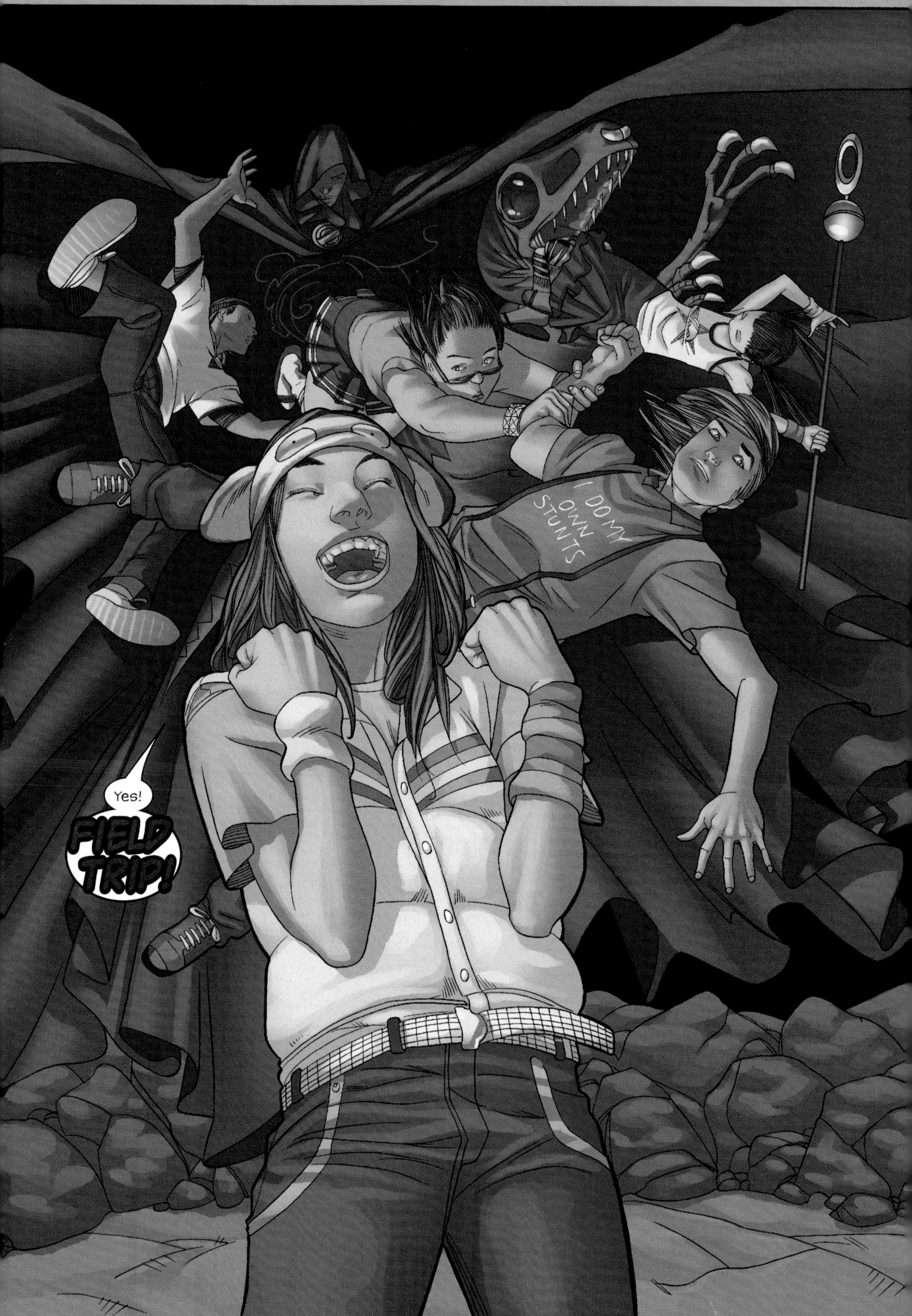
Yes! FIELD TRIP!
I DO MY OWN STUNTS

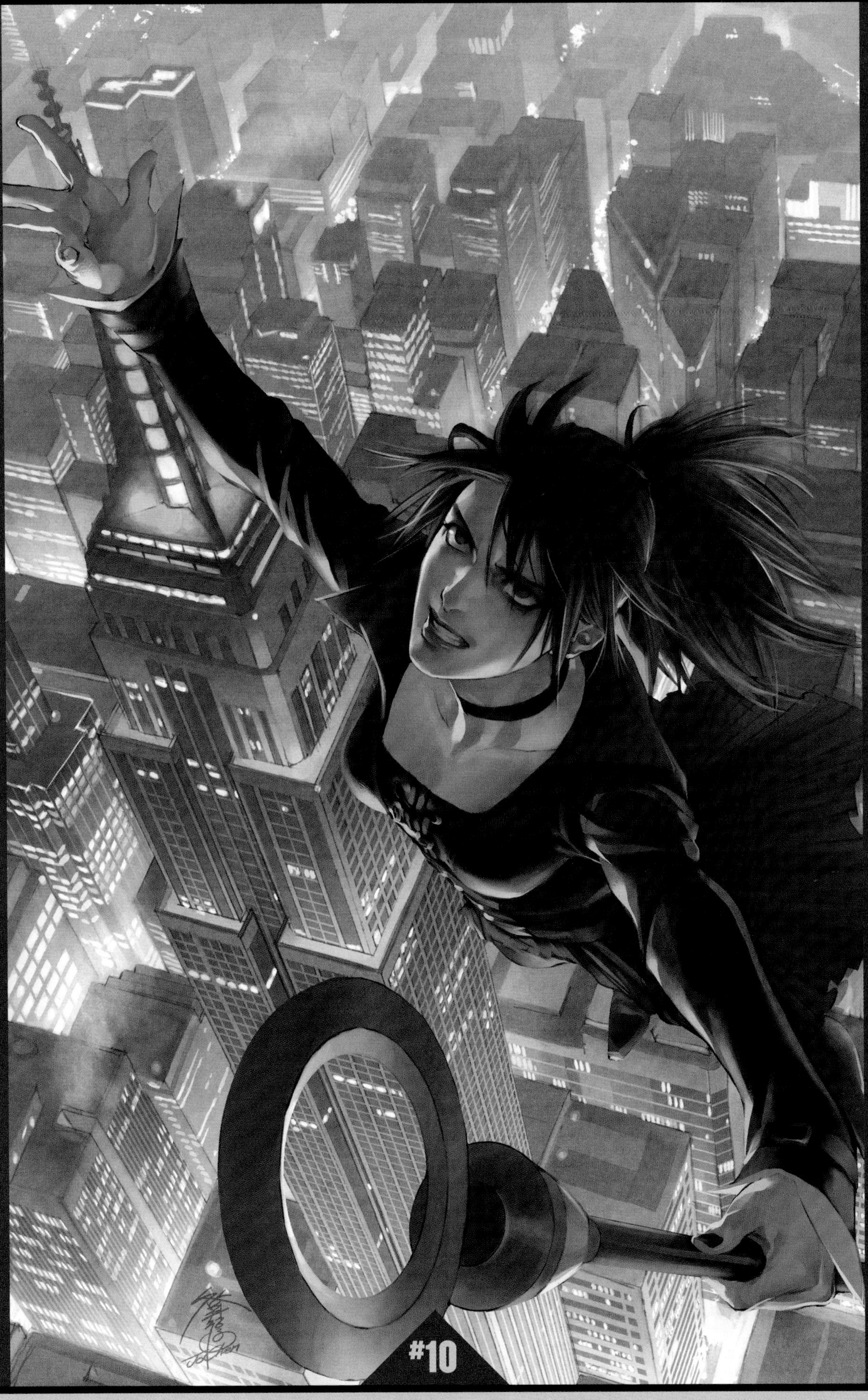
#10

EAST COAST/WEST COAST PART 2

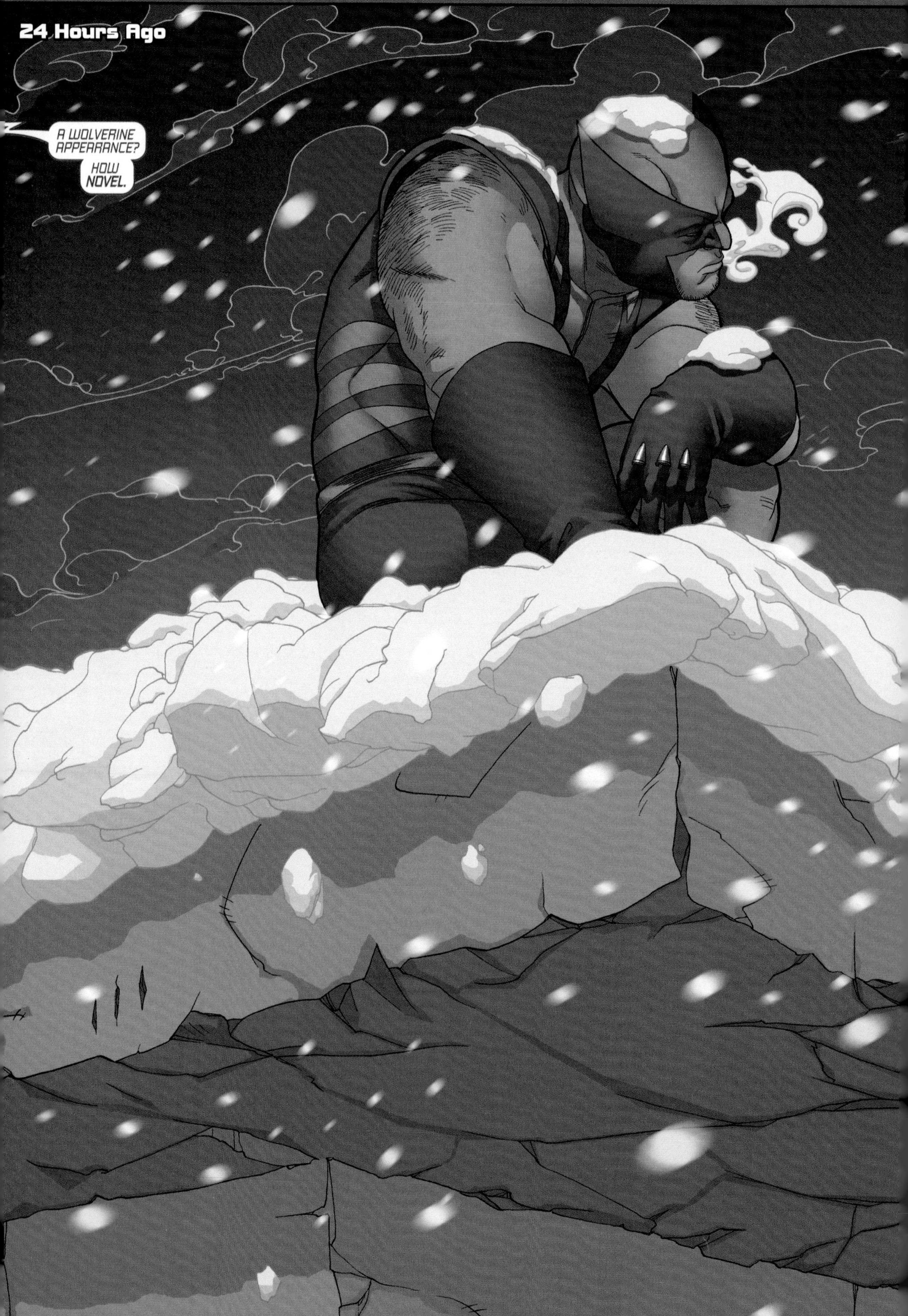
24 Hours Ago
A WOLVERINE APPEARANCE? HOW NOVEL.

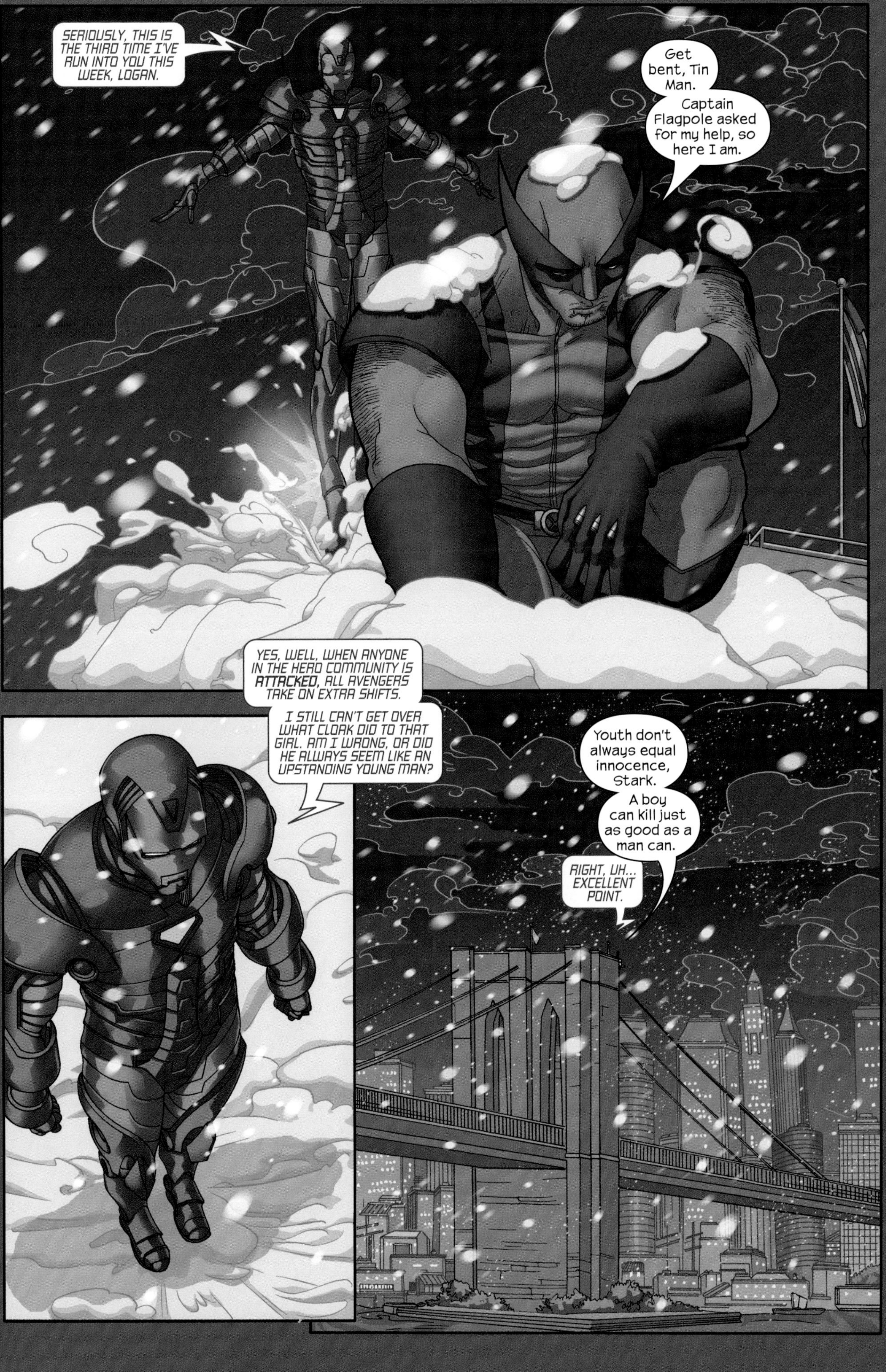
SERIOUSLY, THIS IS THE THIRD TIME I'VE RUN INTO YOU THIS WEEK, LOGAN.
Get bent, Tin Man.
Captain Flagpole asked for my help, so here I am.
YES, WELL, WHEN ANYONE IN THE HERO COMMUNITY IS ATTACKED, ALL AVENGERS TAKE ON EXTRA SHIFTS.
I STILL CAN'T GET OVER WHAT CLOAK DID TO THAT GIRL. AM I WRONG, OR DID HE ALWAYS SEEM LIKE AN UPSTANDING YOUNG MAN?
Youth don't always equal innocence, Stark.
A boy can kill just as good as a man can.
RIGHT, UH... EXCELLENT POINT.

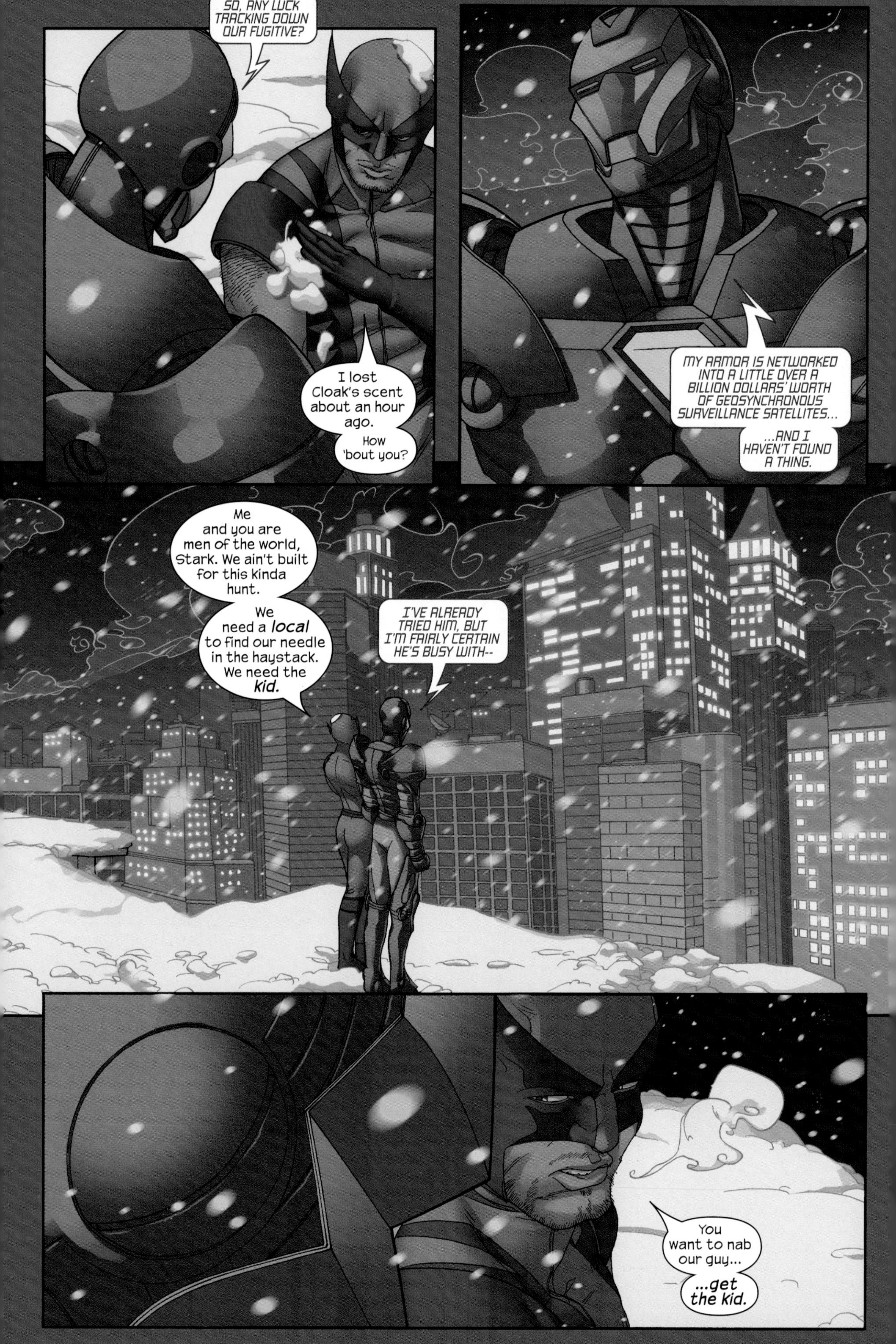
SO, ANY LUCK TRACKING DOWN OUR FUGITIVE?
I lost Cloak's scent about an hour ago.
How 'bout you?
MY ARMOR IS NETWORKED INTO A LITTLE OVER A BILLION DOLLARS' WORTH OF GEOSYNCHRONOUS SURVEILLANCE SATELLITES...
...AND I HAVEN'T FOUND A THING.
Me and you are men of the world, Stark. We ain't built for this kinda hunt.
We need a *local* to find our needle in the haystack. We need the ***kid.***
I'VE ALREADY TRIED HIM, BUT I'M FAIRLY CERTAIN HE'S BUSY WITH--
You want to nab our guy...
...get the kid.

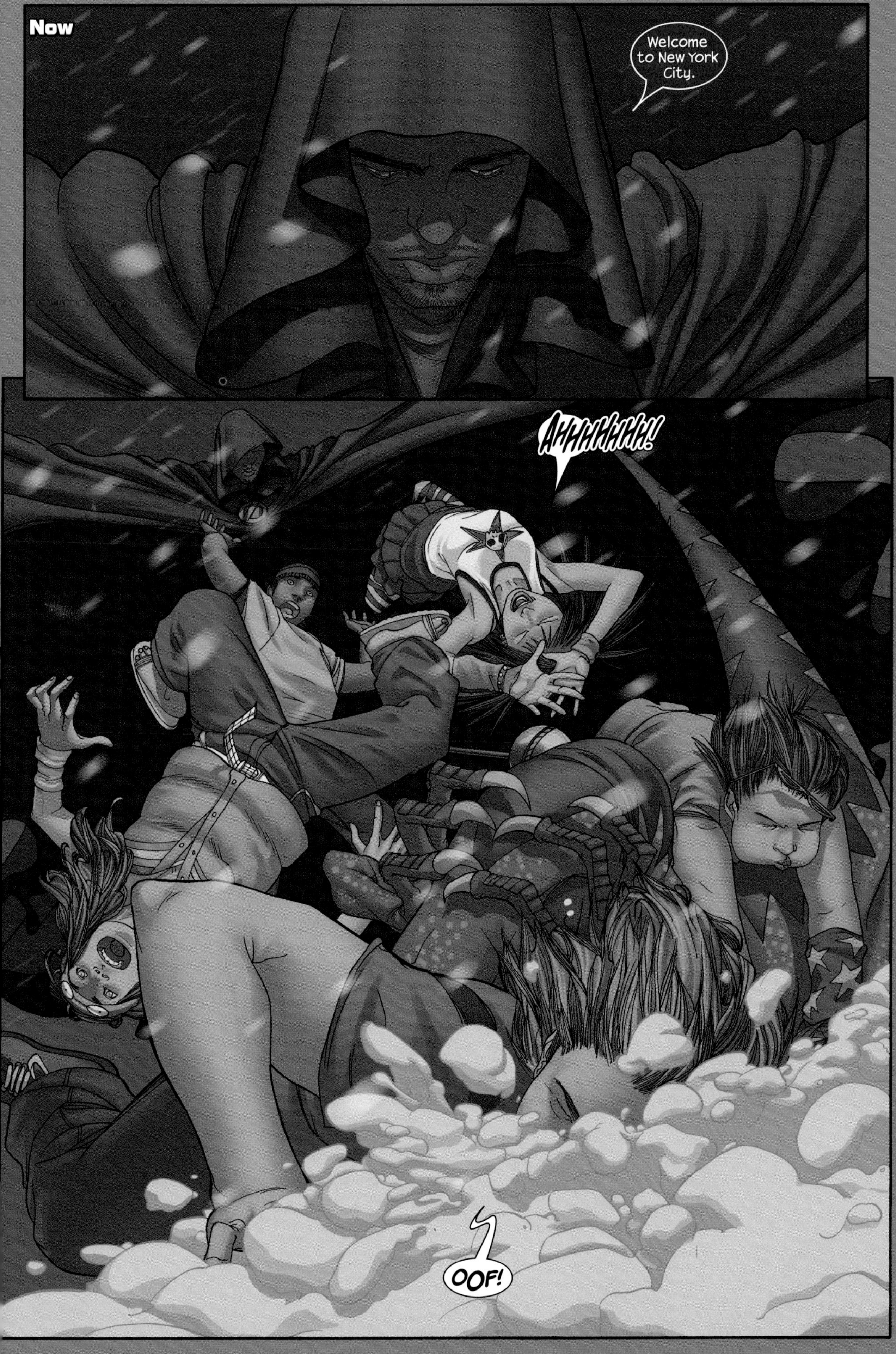
Now
Welcome to New York City.
AHHHHHHH!
OOF!

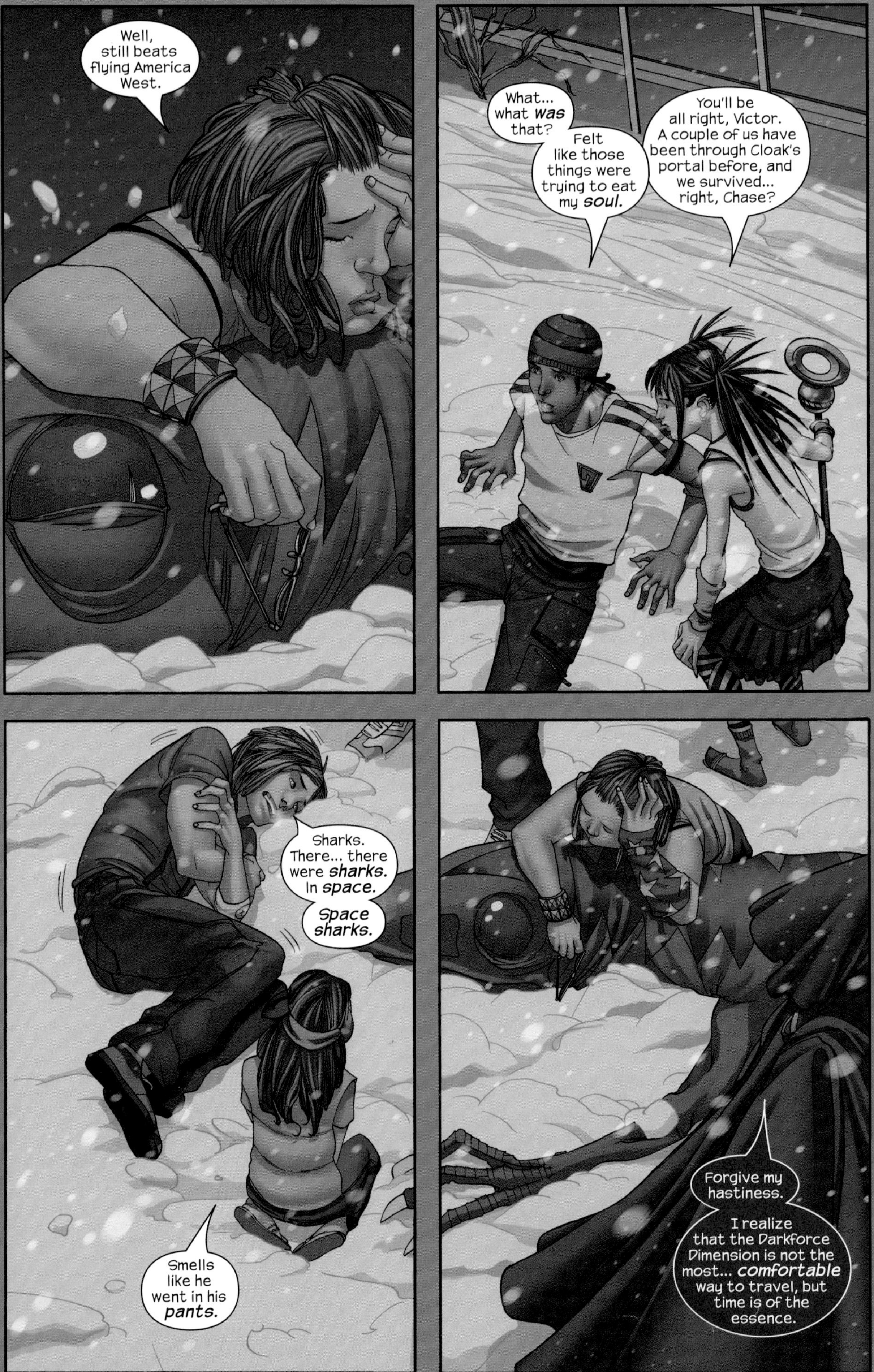
Well, still beats flying America West.
What... what *was* that?
Felt like those things were trying to eat my *soul.*
You'll be all right, Victor. A couple of us have been through Cloak's portal before, and we survived... right, Chase?
Sharks. There... there were *sharks.* In *space.*
Space sharks.
Smells like he went in his *pants.*
Forgive my hastiness.
I realize that the Darkforce Dimension is not the most... *comfortable* way to travel, but time is of the essence.

You could have at least given us a second to grab a coat or something!

Chase, we've lived our entire lives in Los Angeles.

Do you even *own* winter clothes?

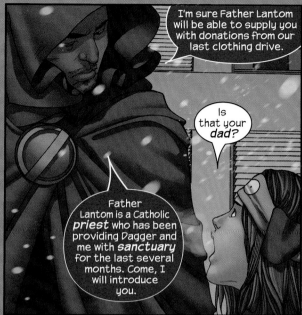

I'm sure Father Lantom will be able to supply you with donations from our last clothing drive.

Is that your *dad*?

Father Lantom is a Catholic *priest* who has been providing Dagger and me with *sanctuary* for the last several months. Come, I will introduce you.

Whoa, can we just take a moment to appreciate this?

I mean, we're in the *Big Apple*, home of Spider-Man, Daredevil... the Fantastic Freakin' Four live here!

This is hallowed ground, people.

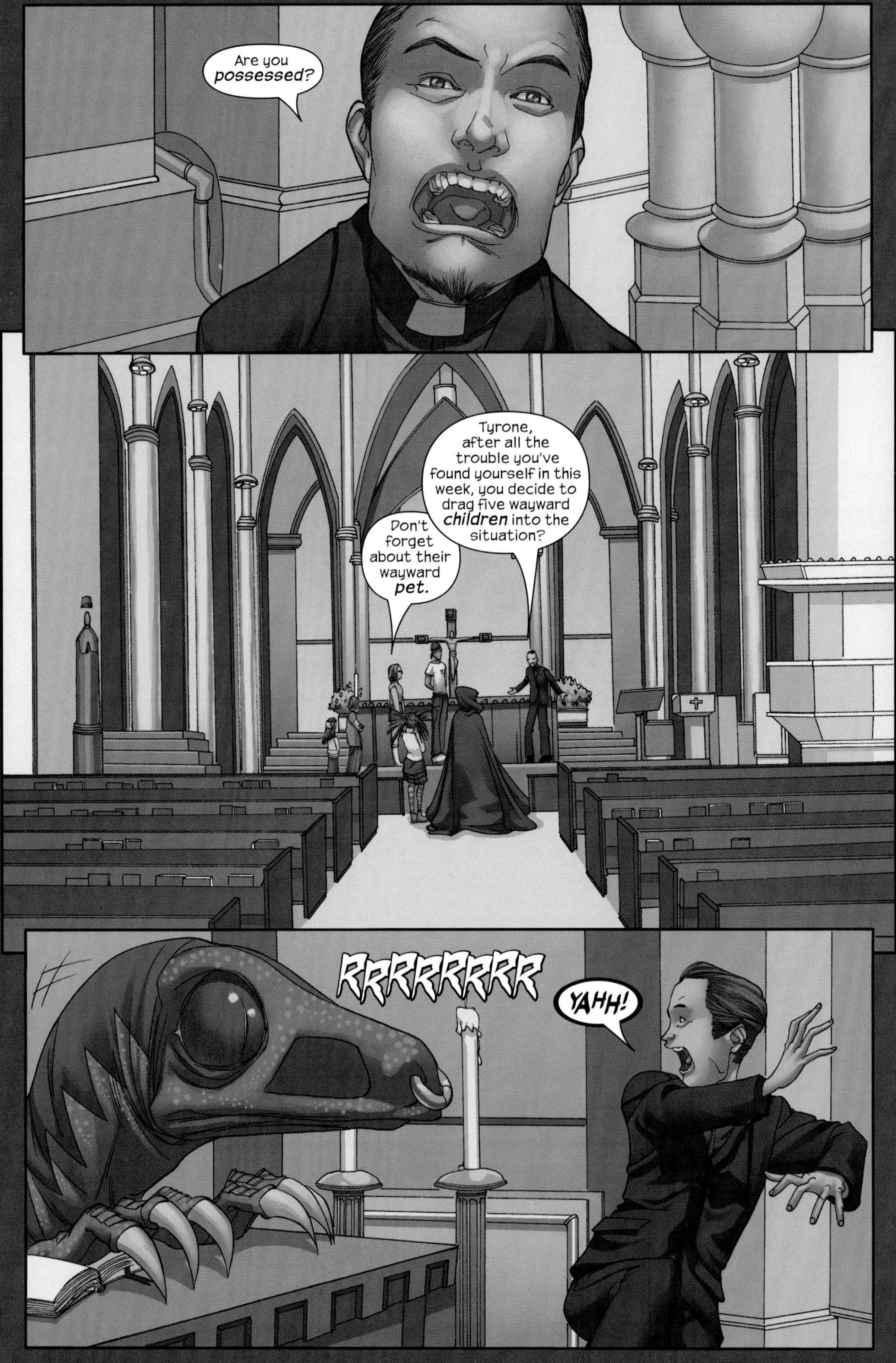
Are you possessed?
Tyrone, after all the trouble you've found yourself in this week, you decide to drag five wayward children into the situation?
Don't forget about their wayward pet.
RRRRRRRR
YAHH!

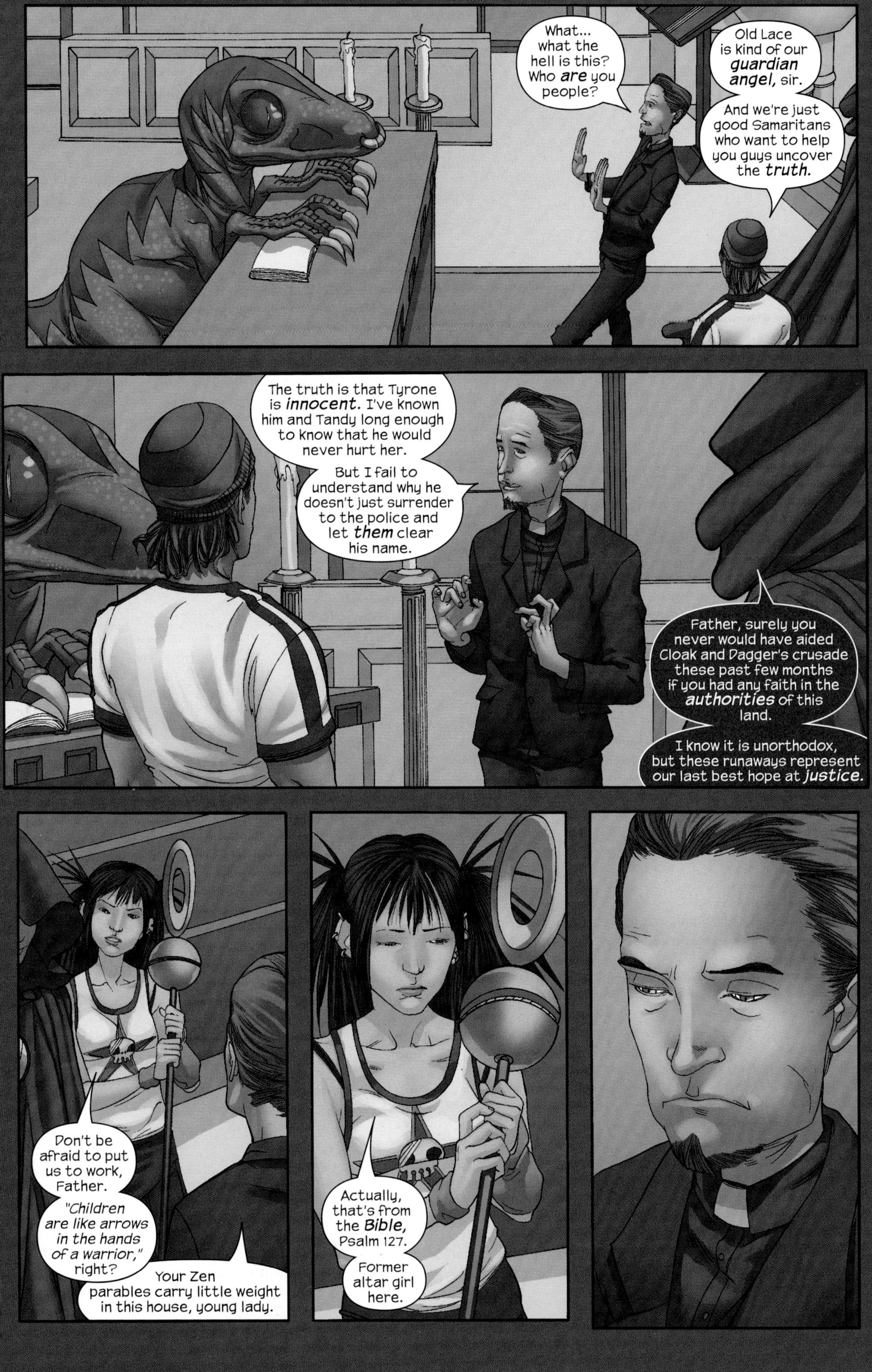
What... what the hell is this? Who *are* you people?
Old Lace is kind of our *guardian angel,* sir.
And we're just good Samaritans who want to help you guys uncover the *truth.*
The truth is that Tyrone is *innocent.* I've known him and Tandy long enough to know that he would never hurt her.
But I fail to understand why he doesn't just surrender to the police and let *them* clear his name.
Father, surely you never would have aided Cloak and Dagger's crusade these past few months if you had any faith in the *authorities* of this land.
I know it is unorthodox, but these runaways represent our last best hope at *justice.*
Don't be afraid to put us to work, Father.
"Children are like arrows in the hands of a warrior," right?
Your Zen parables carry little weight in this house, young lady.
Actually, that's from the *Bible,* Psalm 127.
Former altar girl here.

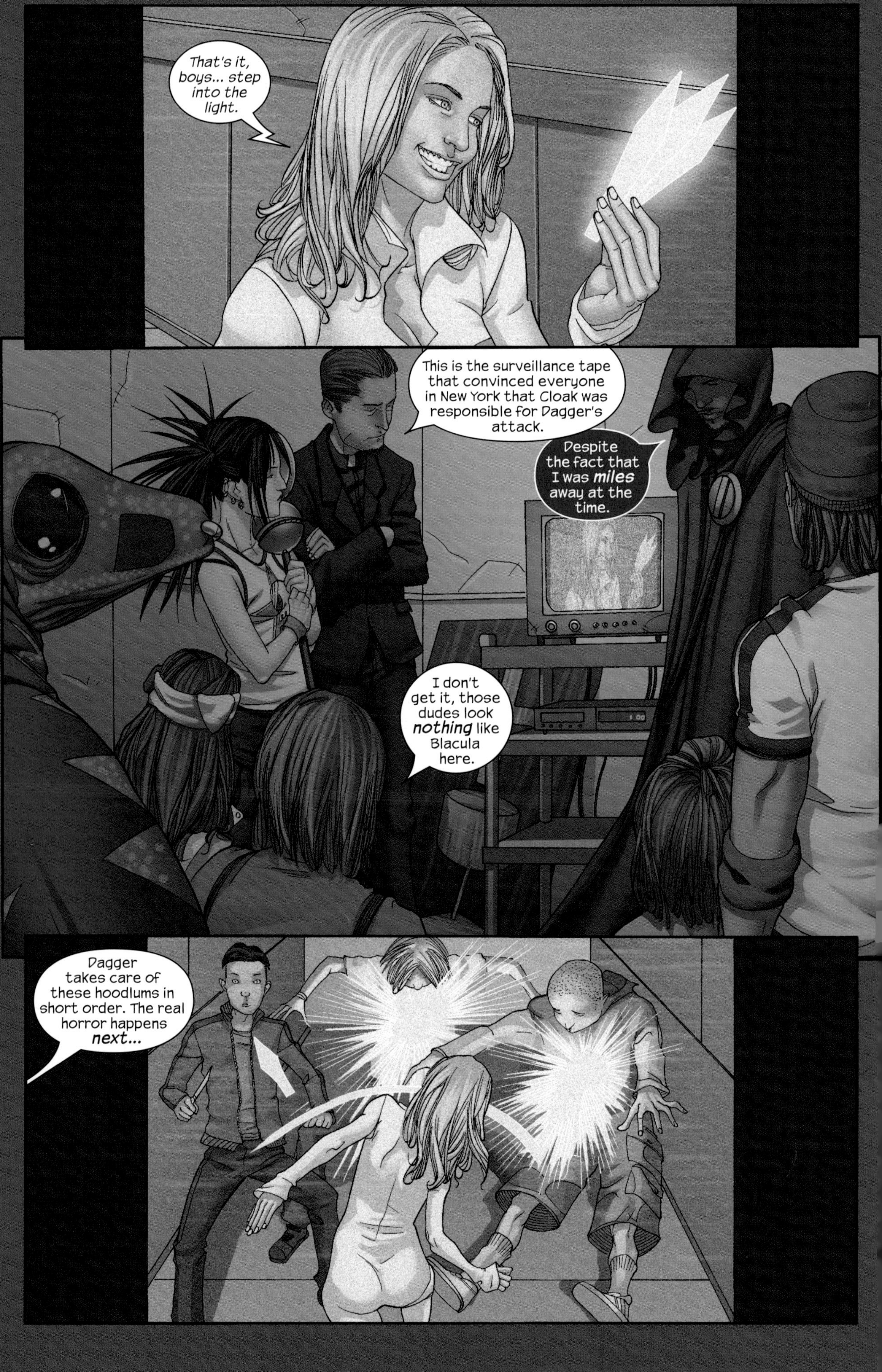
That's it, boys... step into the light.
This is the surveillance tape that convinced everyone in New York that Cloak was responsible for Dagger's attack.
Despite the fact that I was *miles* away at the time.
I don't get it, those dudes look *nothing* like Blacula here.
Dagger takes care of these hoodlums in short order. The real horror happens *next...*

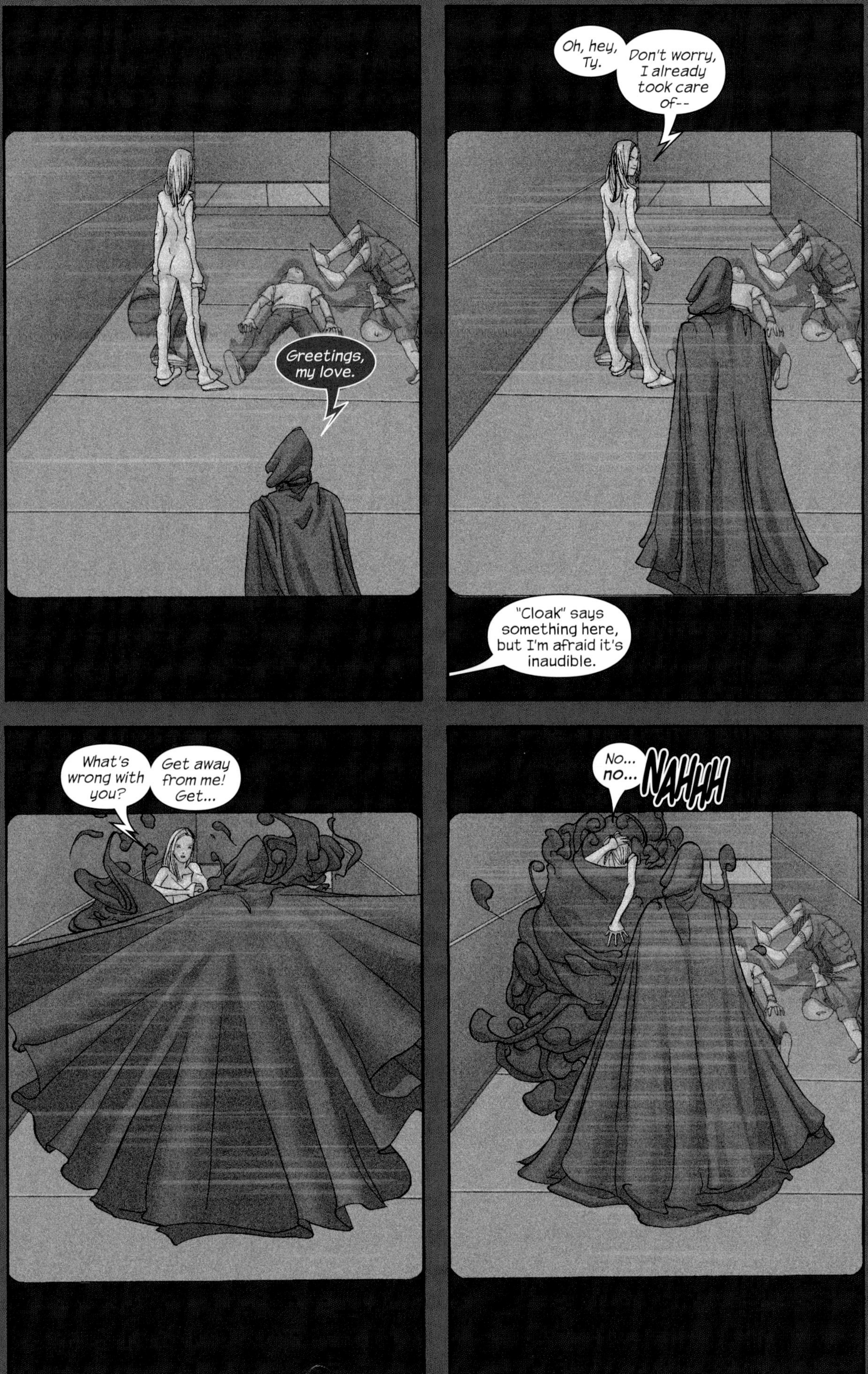
Greetings, my love.
Oh, hey, Ty.
Don't worry, I already took care of--
"Cloak" says something here, but I'm afraid it's inaudible.
What's wrong with you?
Get away from me! Get...
No... no...
NAHHH

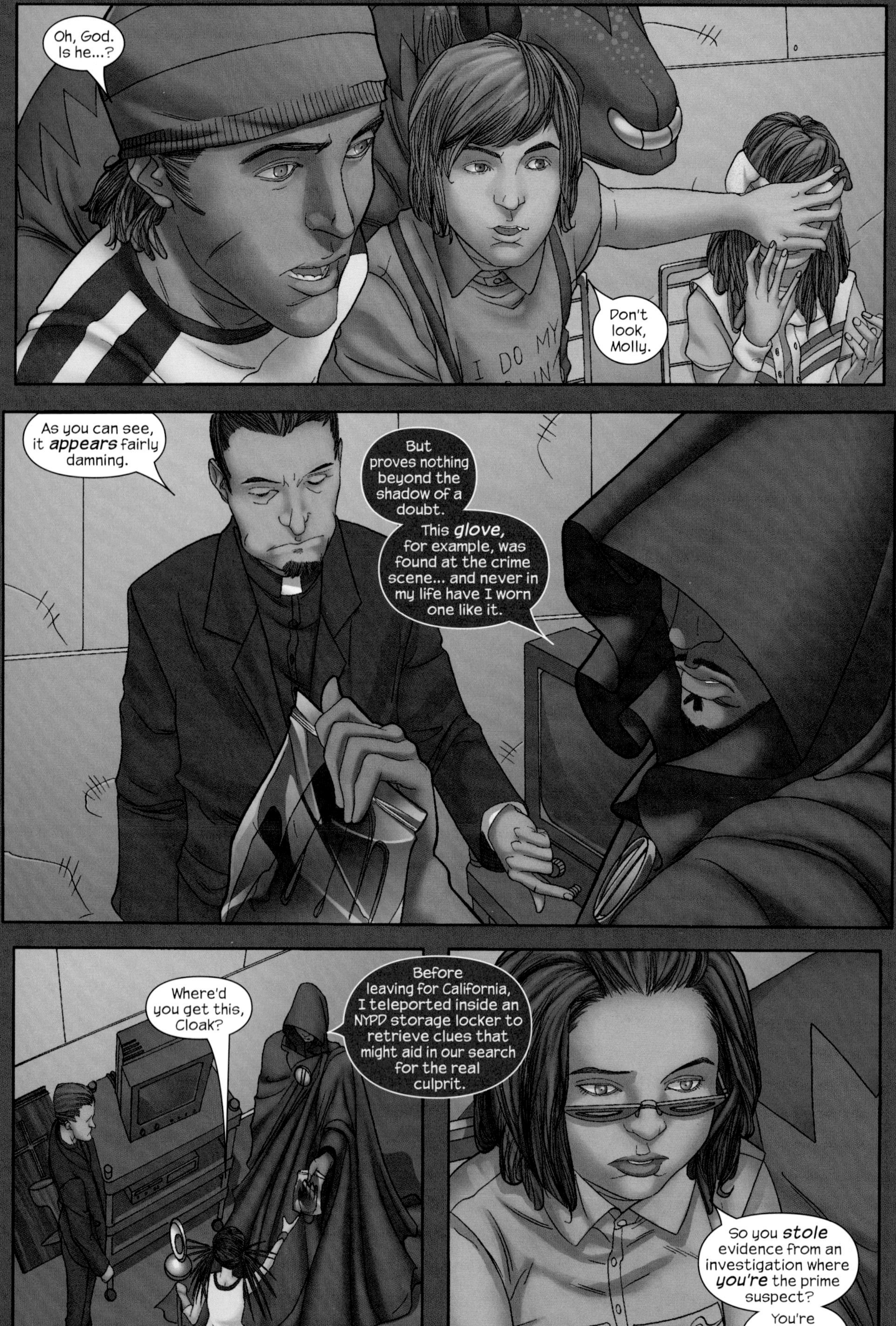

Oh, God. Is he...?
Don't look, Molly.
As you can see, it *appears* fairly damning.
But proves nothing beyond the shadow of a doubt.
This *glove,* for example, was found at the crime scene... and never in my life have I worn one like it.
Where'd you get this, Cloak?
Before leaving for California, I teleported inside an NYPD storage locker to retrieve clues that might aid in our search for the real culprit.
So you *stole* evidence from an investigation where *you're* the prime suspect?
You're not exactly helping your case, O.J.

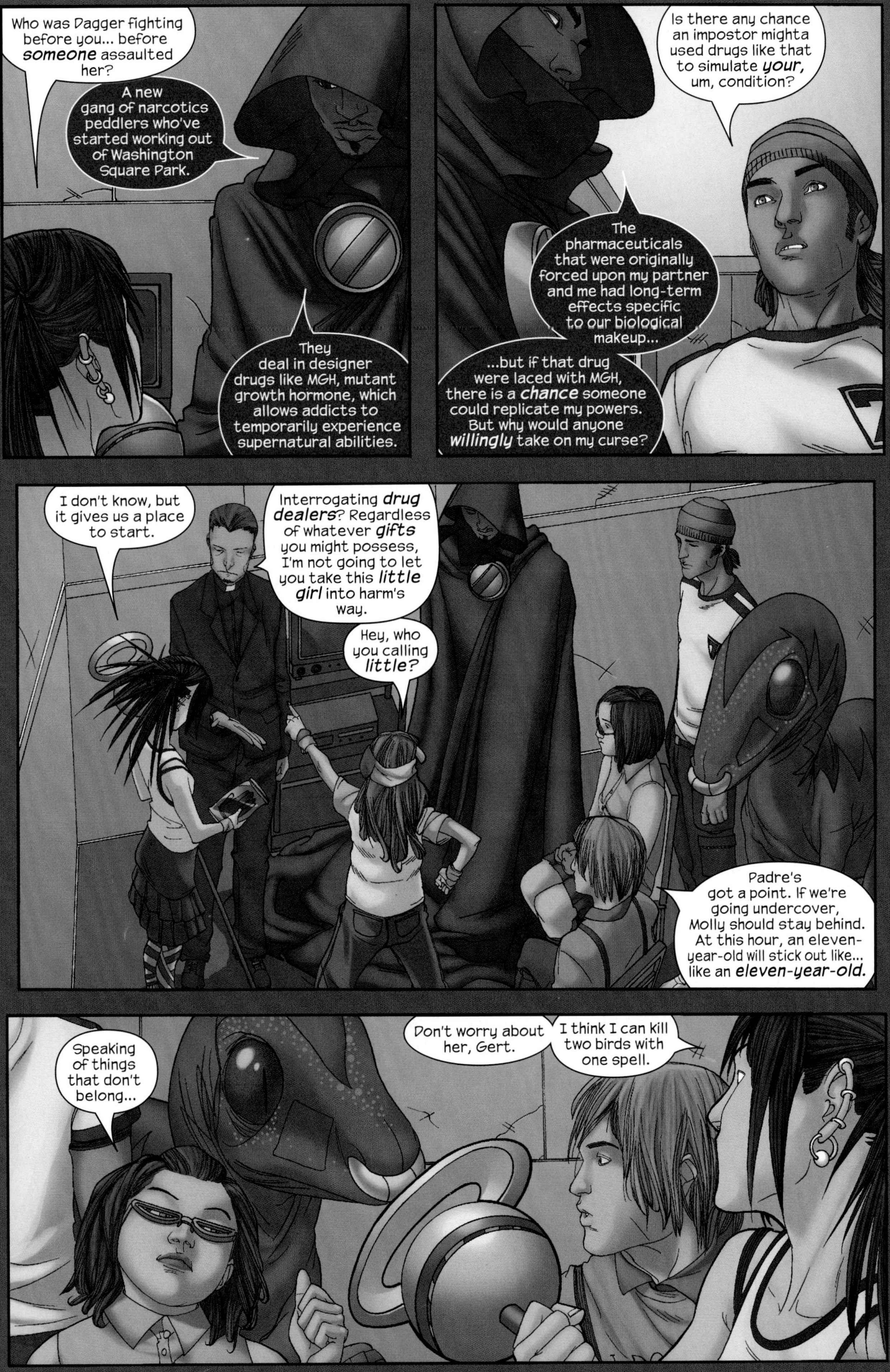

Who was Dagger fighting before you... before someone assaulted her?
A new gang of narcotics peddlers who've started working out of Washington Square Park.
They deal in designer drugs like MGH, mutant growth hormone, which allows addicts to temporarily experience supernatural abilities.
Is there any chance an impostor mighta used drugs like that to simulate your, um, condition?
The pharmaceuticals that were originally forced upon my partner and me had long-term effects specific to our biological makeup...
...but if that drug were laced with MGH, there is a chance someone could replicate my powers. But why would anyone willingly take on my curse?
I don't know, but it gives us a place to start.
Interrogating drug dealers? Regardless of whatever gifts you might possess, I'm not going to let you take this little girl into harm's way.
Hey, who you calling little?
Padre's got a point. If we're going undercover, Molly should stay behind. At this hour, an eleven-year-old will stick out like... like an eleven-year-old.
Speaking of things that don't belong...
Don't worry about her, Gert.
I think I can kill two birds with one spell.

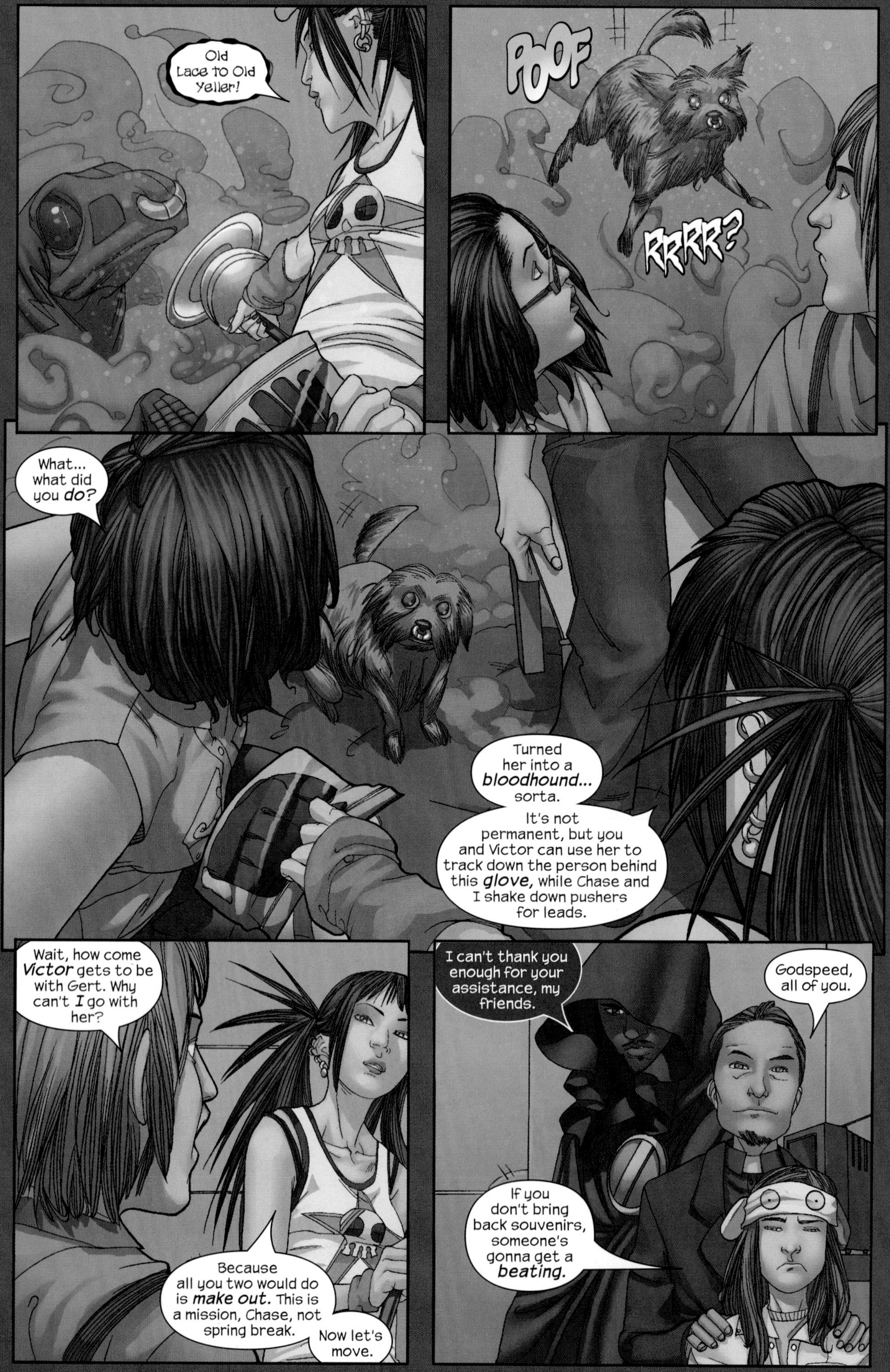
Old Lace to Old Yeller!
POOF
RRRR?
What... what did you *do*?
Turned her into a *bloodhound...* sorta.
It's not permanent, but you and Victor can use her to track down the person behind this *glove,* while Chase and I shake down pushers for leads.
Wait, how come *Victor* gets to be with Gert. Why can't *I* go with her?
Because all you two would do is *make out.* This is a mission, Chase, not spring break.
Now let's move.
I can't thank you enough for your assistance, my friends.
Godspeed, all of you.
If you don't bring back souvenirs, someone's gonna get a *beating.*

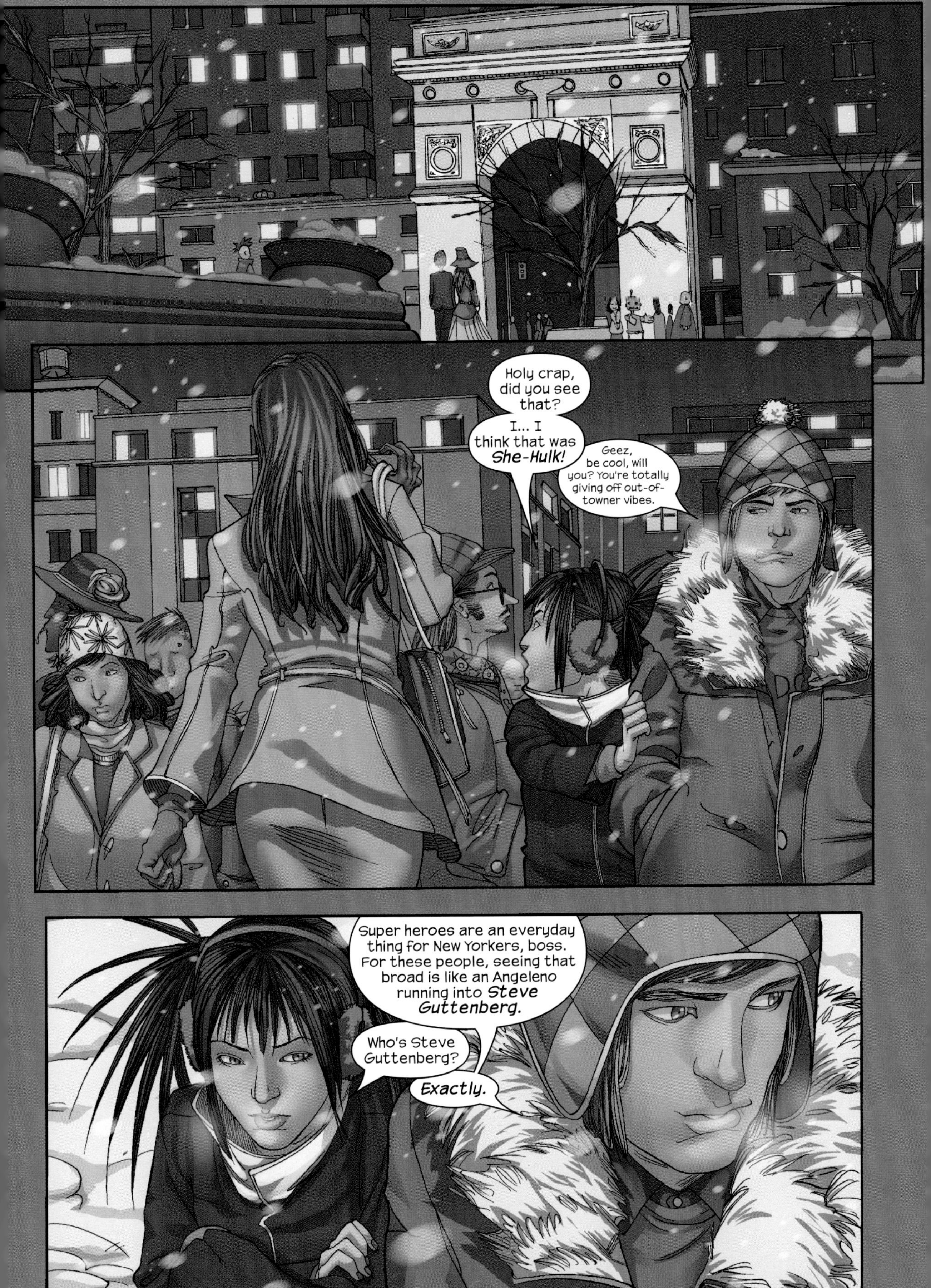
Holy crap, did you see that?
I... I think that was She-Hulk!
Geez, be cool, will you? You're totally giving off out-of-towner vibes.
Super heroes are an everyday thing for New Yorkers, boss. For these people, seeing that broad is like an Angeleno running into Steve Guttenberg.
Who's Steve Guttenberg?
Exactly.

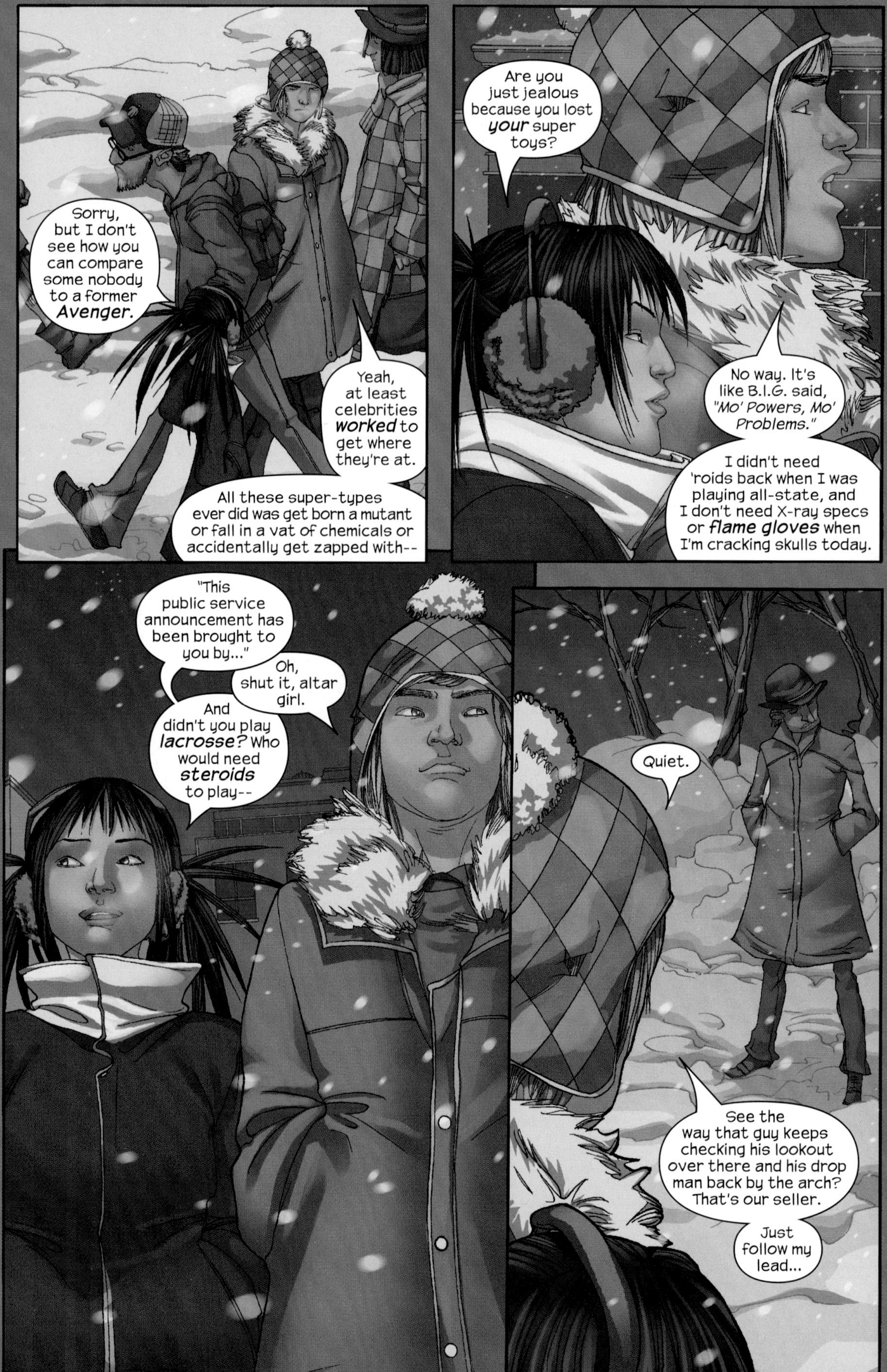
Sorry, but I don't see how you can compare some nobody to a former *Avenger.*
Yeah, at least celebrities ***worked*** to get where they're at.
All these super-types ever did was get born a mutant or fall in a vat of chemicals or accidentally get zapped with--
Are you just jealous because you lost ***your*** super toys?
No way. It's like B.I.G. said, *"Mo' Powers, Mo' Problems."*
I didn't need 'roids back when I was playing all-state, and I don't need X-ray specs or ***flame gloves*** when I'm cracking skulls today.
"This public service announcement has been brought to you by..."
Oh, shut it, altar girl.
And didn't you play ***lacrosse?*** Who would need ***steroids*** to play--
Quiet.
See the way that guy keeps checking his lookout over there and his drop man back by the arch? That's our seller.
Just follow my lead...

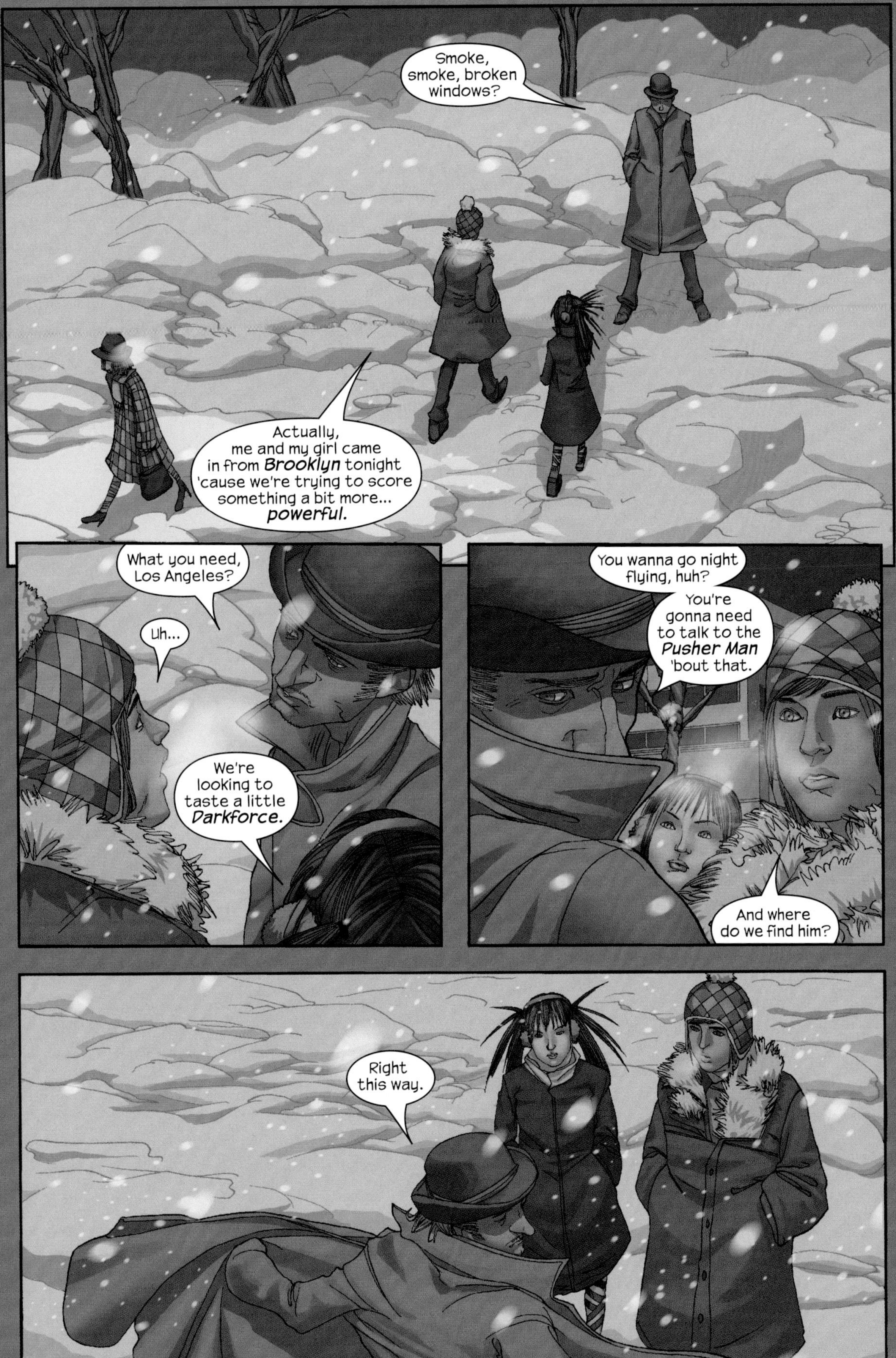
Smoke, smoke, broken windows?
Actually, me and my girl came in from Brooklyn tonight 'cause we're trying to score something a bit more... powerful.
What you need, Los Angeles?
Uh...
We're looking to taste a little Darkforce.
You wanna go night flying, huh?
You're gonna need to talk to the Pusher Man 'bout that.
And where do we find him?
Right this way.

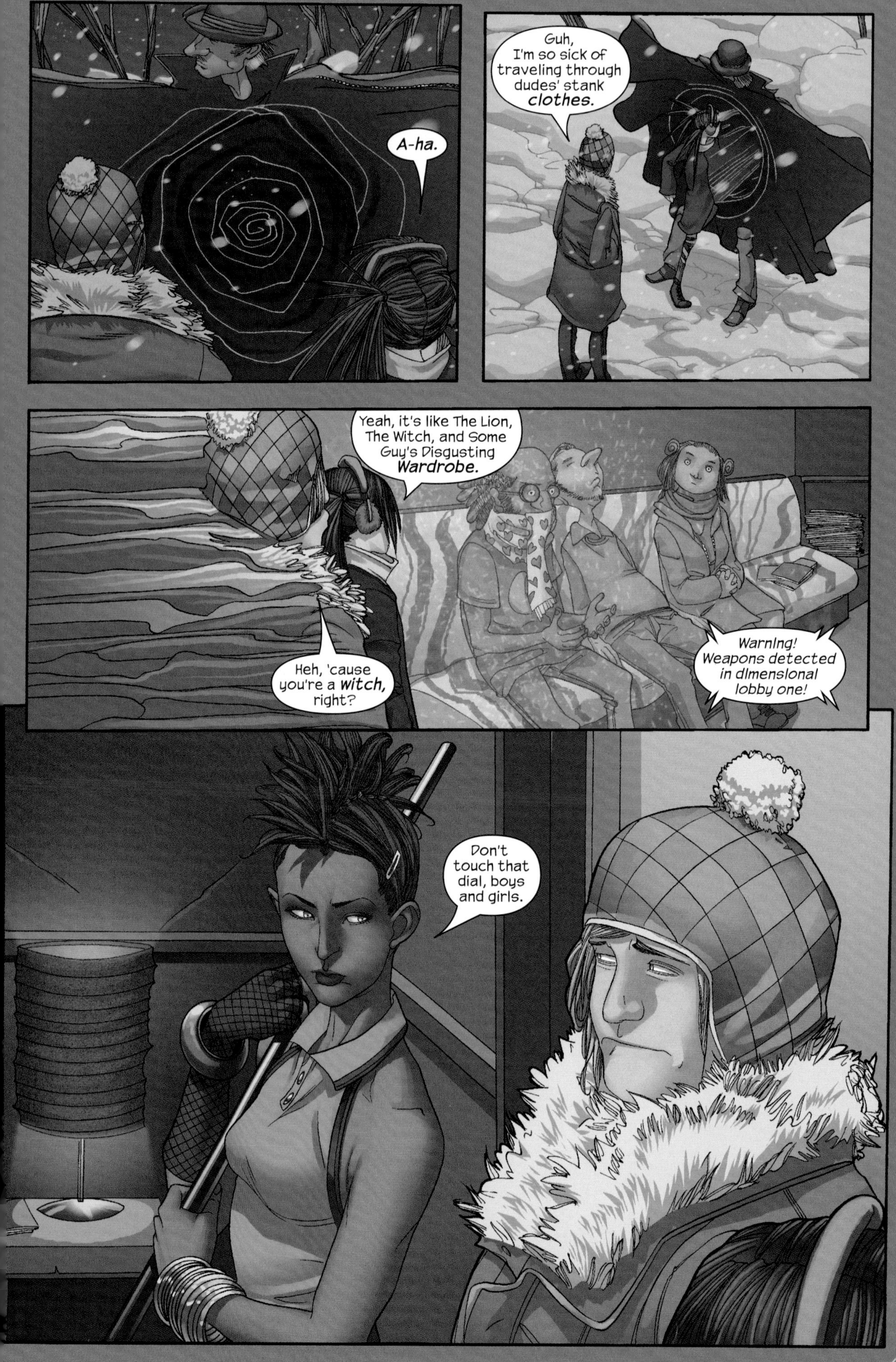
A-ha.
Guh, I'm so sick of traveling through dudes' stank *clothes*.
Yeah, it's like The Lion, The Witch, and Some Guy's Disgusting *Wardrobe*.
Heh, 'cause you're a *witch*, right?
Warning! Weapons detected in dimensional lobby one!
Don't touch that dial, boys and girls.

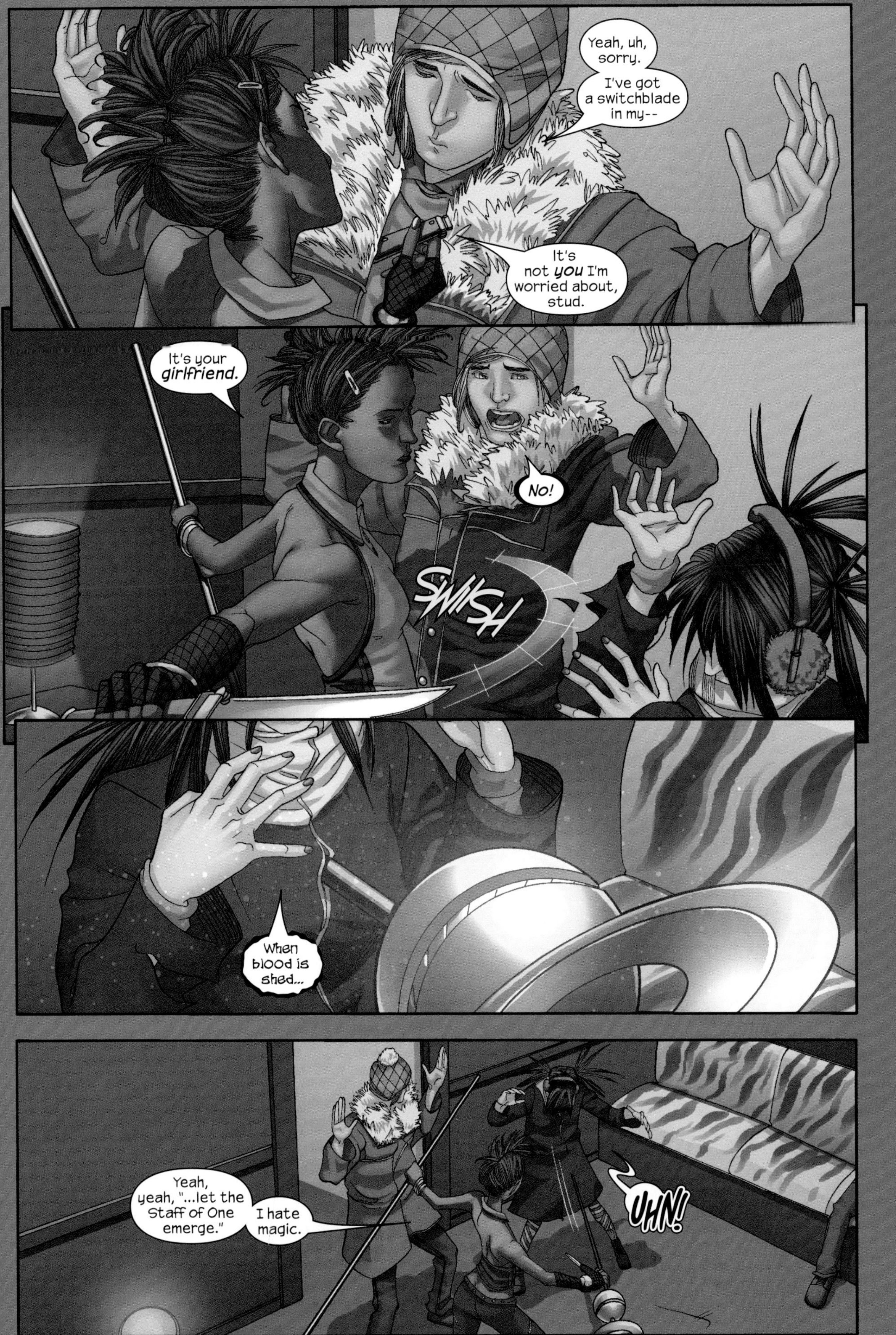
Yeah, uh, sorry.
I've got a switchblade in my--
It's not *you* I'm worried about, stud.
It's your *girlfriend.*
No!
SWISH
When blood is shed...
Yeah, yeah, "...let the Staff of One emerge."
I hate magic.
UHN!

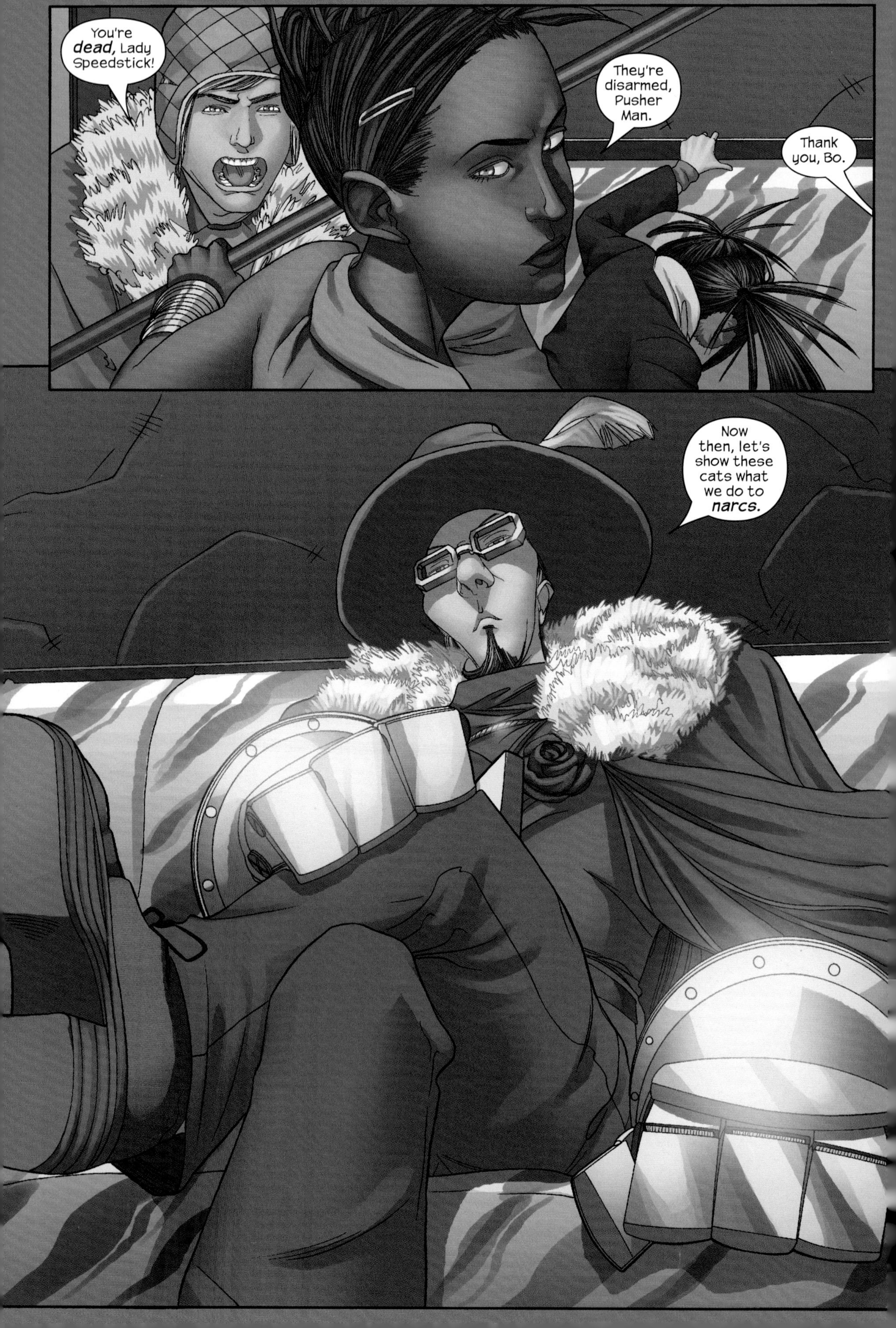
You're ***dead,*** Lady Speedstick!
They're disarmed, Pusher Man.
Thank you, Bo.
Now then, let's show these cats what we do to ***narcs.***

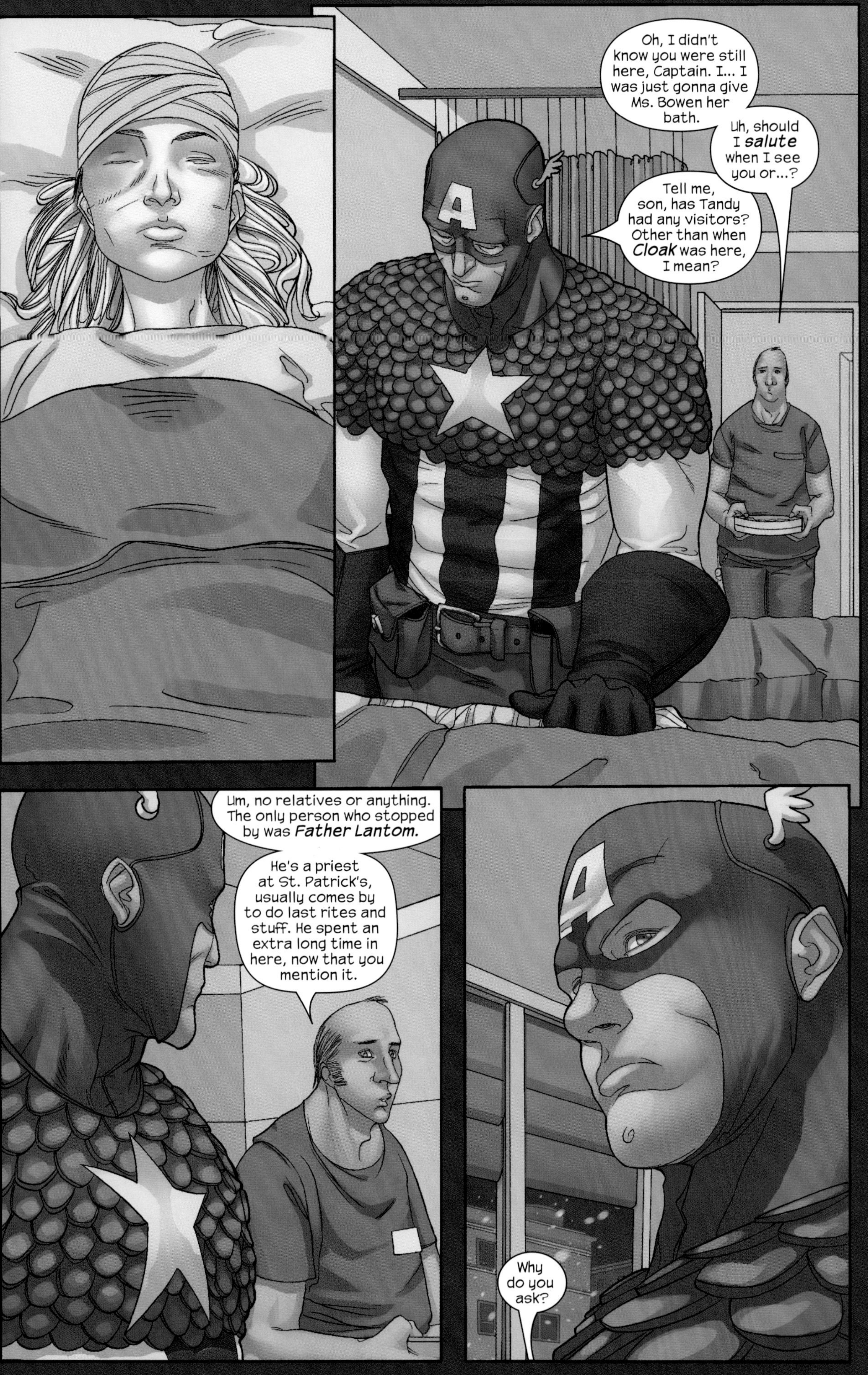
Oh, I didn't know you were still here, Captain. I... I was just gonna give Ms. Bowen her bath.
Uh, should I *salute* when I see you or...?
Tell me, son, has Tandy had any visitors? Other than when *Cloak* was here, I mean?
Um, no relatives or anything. The only person who stopped by was *Father Lantom.*
He's a priest at St. Patrick's, usually comes by to do last rites and stuff. He spent an extra long time in here, now that you mention it.
Why do you ask?

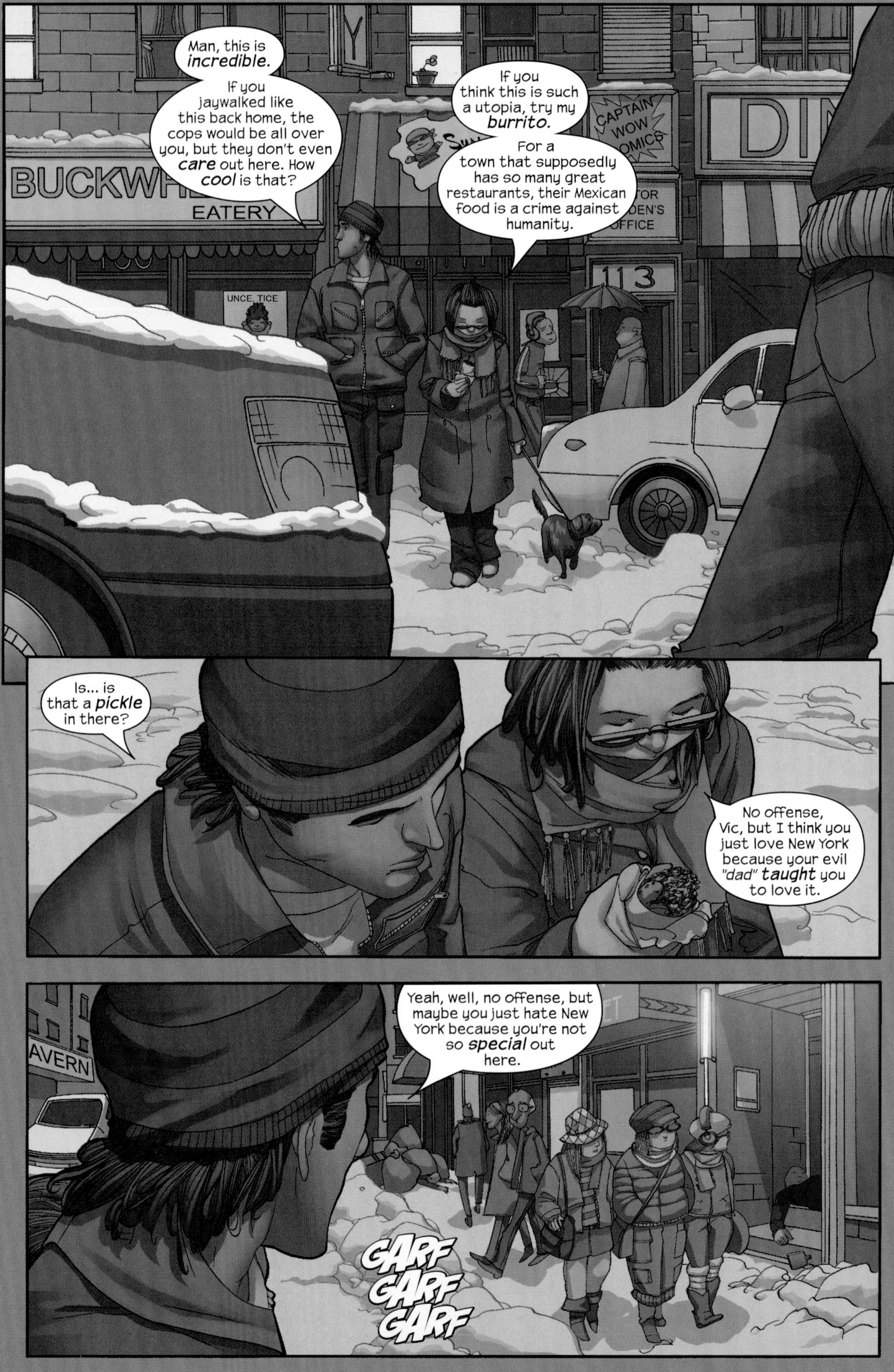
Man, this is *incredible.*
If you jaywalked like this back home, the cops would be all over you, but they don't even *care* out here. How *cool* is that?
If you think this is such a utopia, try my *burrito.*
For a town that supposedly has so many great restaurants, their Mexican food is a crime against humanity.
BUCKWHE
EATERY
CAPTAIN WOW COMICS
DIN
113
Is... is that a *pickle* in there?
No offense, Vic, but I think you just love New York because your evil *"dad" taught* you to love it.
Yeah, well, no offense, but maybe you just hate New York because you're not so *special* out here.
AVERN
GARF GARF GARF

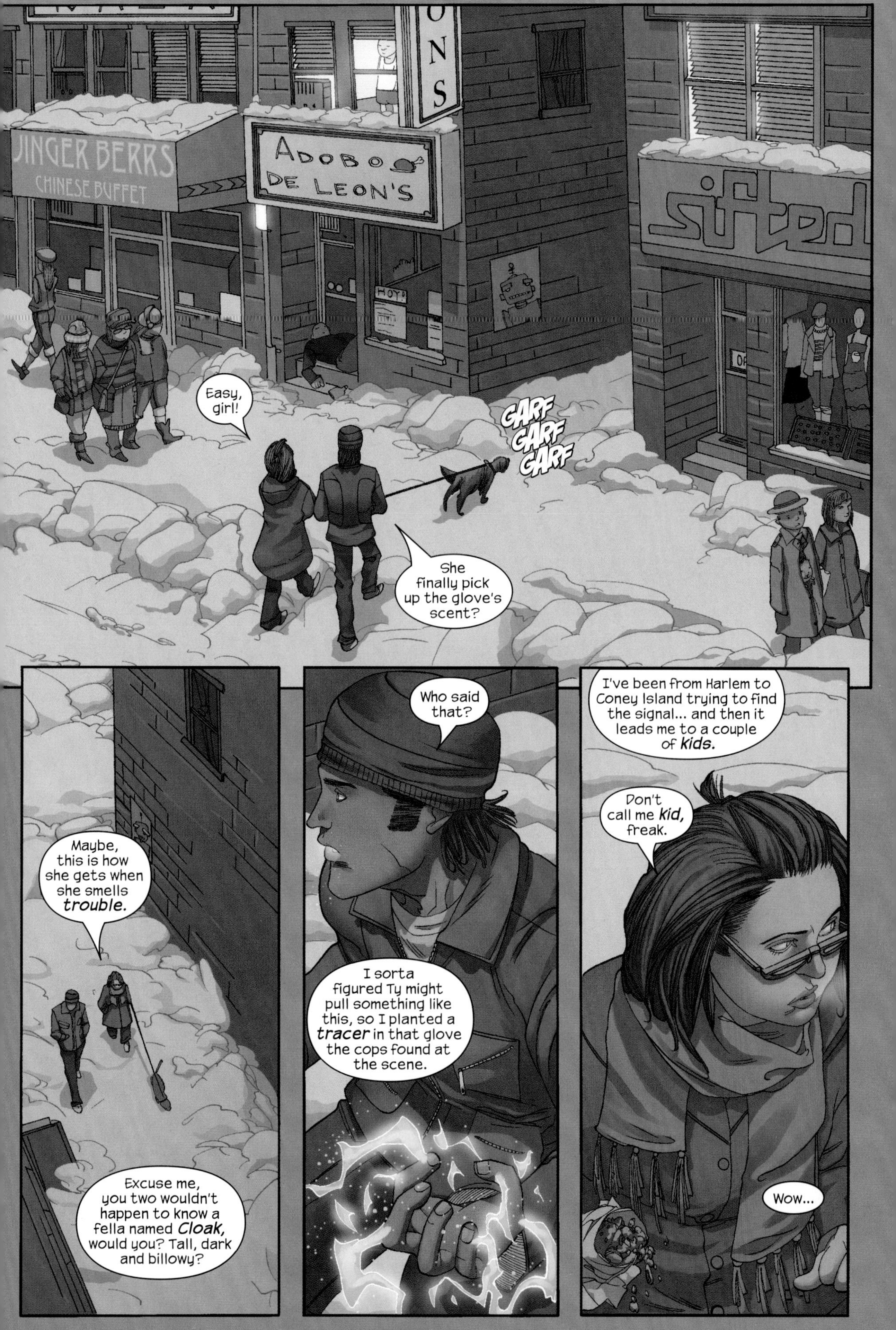
JINGER BERRS
CHINESE BUFFET
ADOBO
DE LEON'S
sifted
HOY!
Easy, girl!
GARF GARF GARF
She finally pick up the glove's scent?
Maybe, this is how she gets when she smells *trouble.*
Excuse me, you two wouldn't happen to know a fella named *Cloak,* would you? Tall, dark and billowy?
Who said that?
I sorta figured Ty might pull something like this, so I planted a *tracer* in that glove the cops found at the scene.
I've been from Harlem to Coney Island trying to find the signal... and then it leads me to a couple of *kids.*
Don't call me *kid,* freak.
Wow...

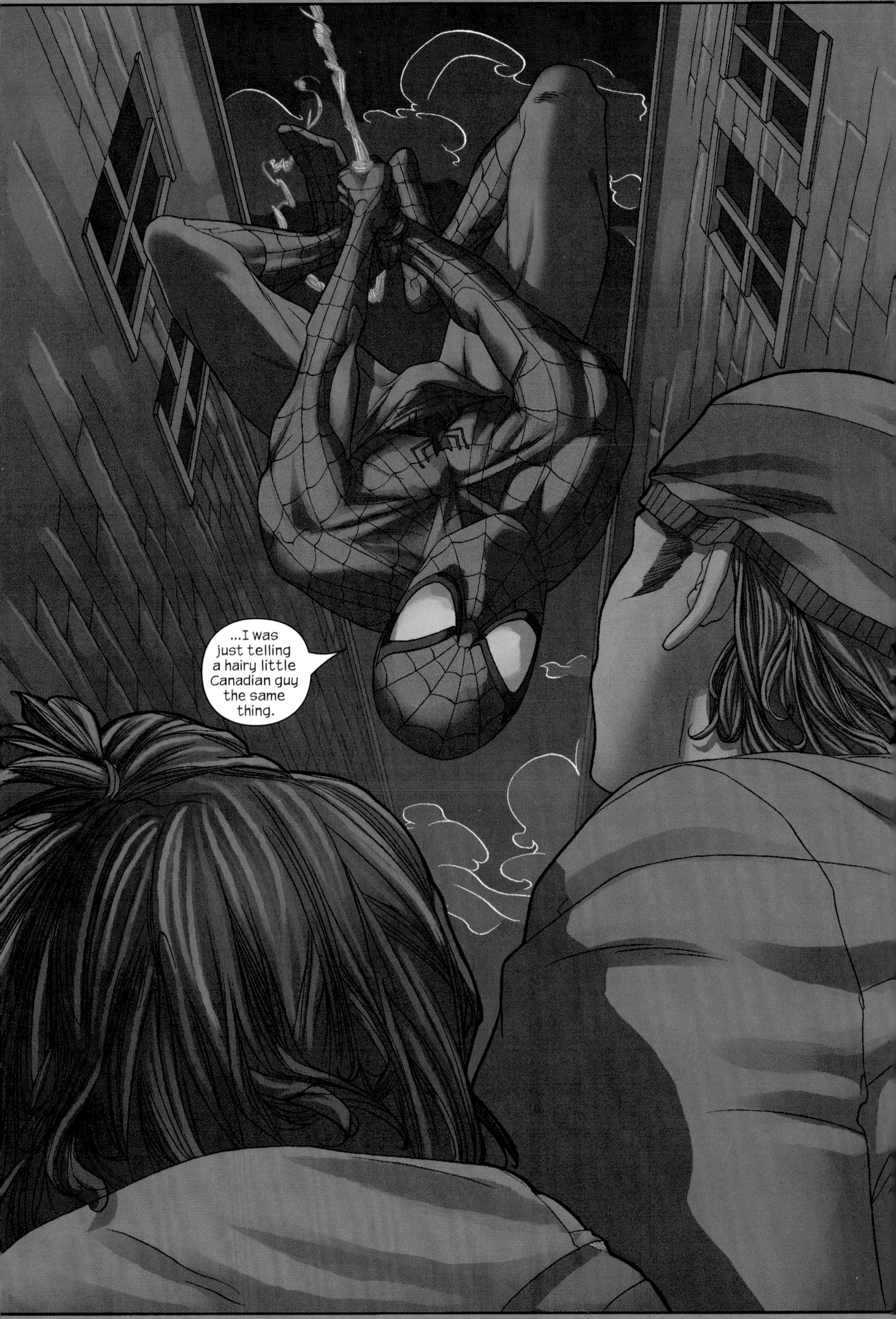
...I was just telling a hairy little Canadian guy the same thing.

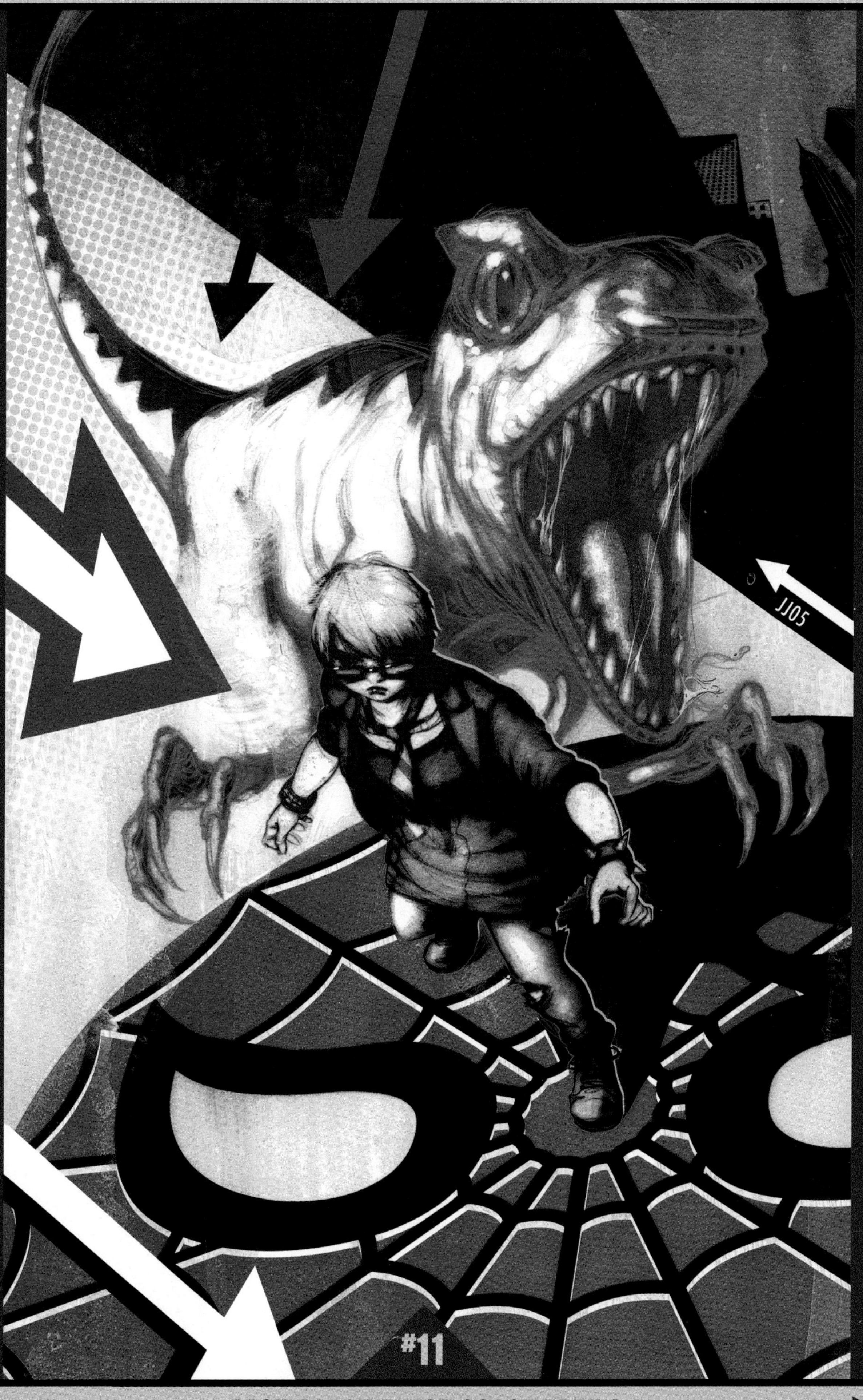
JJ05
#11

EAST COAST/WEST COAST PART 3

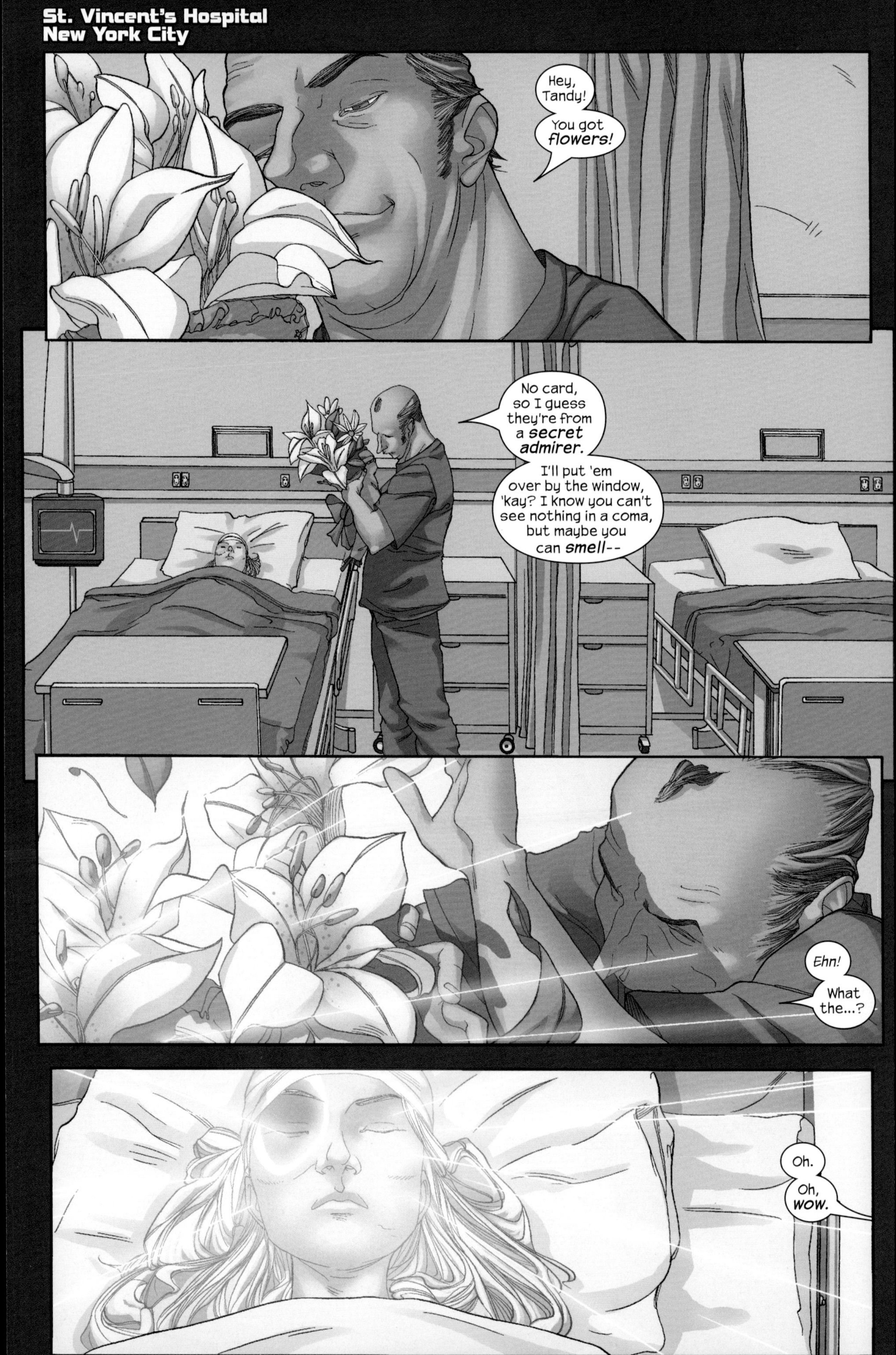

St. Vincent's Hospital
New York City
Hey, Tandy!
You got flowers!
No card, so I guess they're from a secret admirer.
I'll put 'em over by the window, 'kay? I know you can't see nothing in a coma, but maybe you can smell--
Ehn!
What the...?
Oh.
Oh, wow.

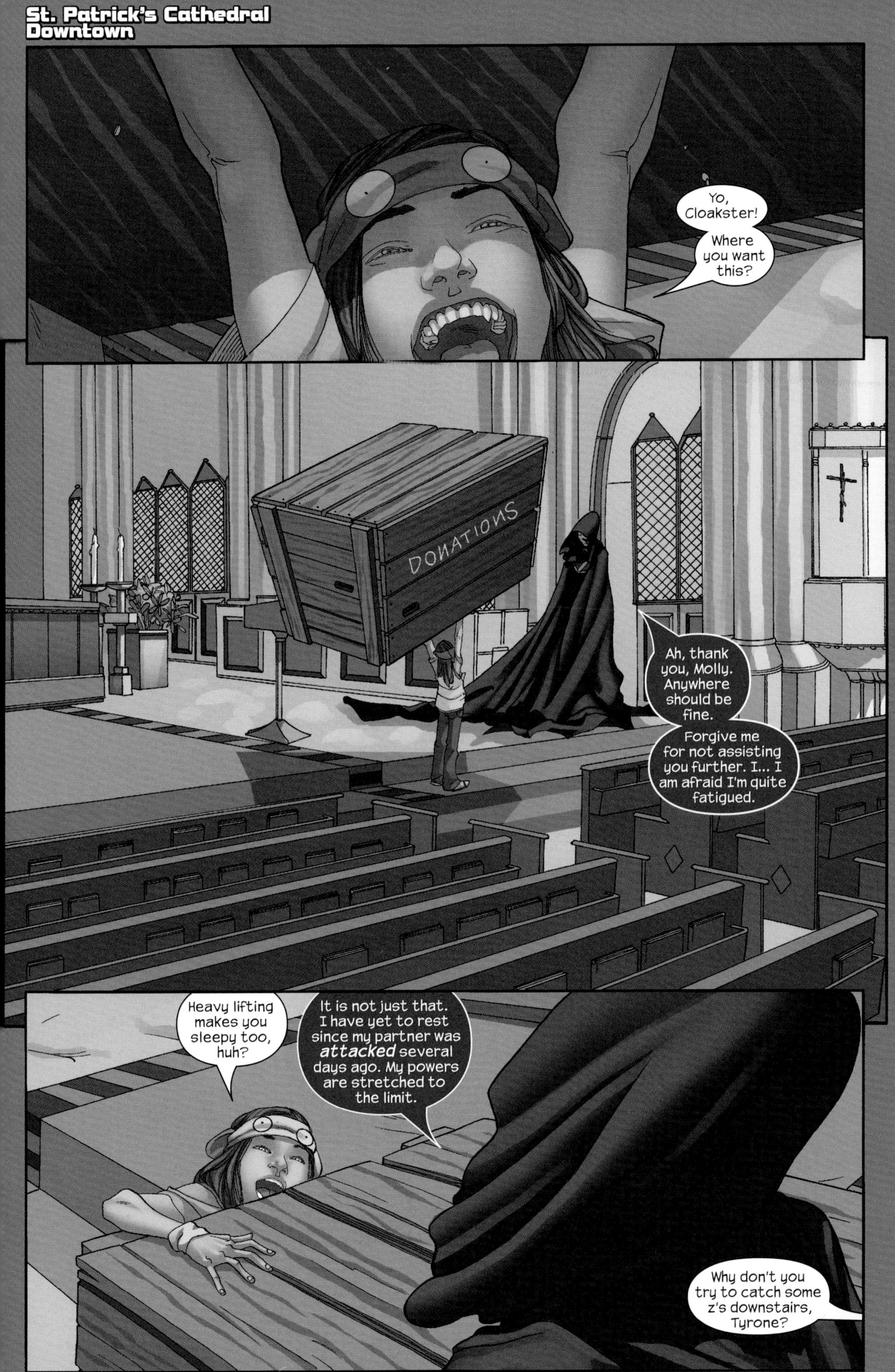
St. Patrick's Cathedral
Downtown
Yo, Cloakster!
Where you want this?
DONATIONS
Ah, thank you, Molly. Anywhere should be fine.
Forgive me for not assisting you further. I... I am afraid I'm quite fatigued.
Heavy lifting makes you sleepy too, huh?
It is not just that. I have yet to rest since my partner was *attacked* several days ago. My powers are stretched to the limit.
Why don't you try to catch some z's downstairs, Tyrone?

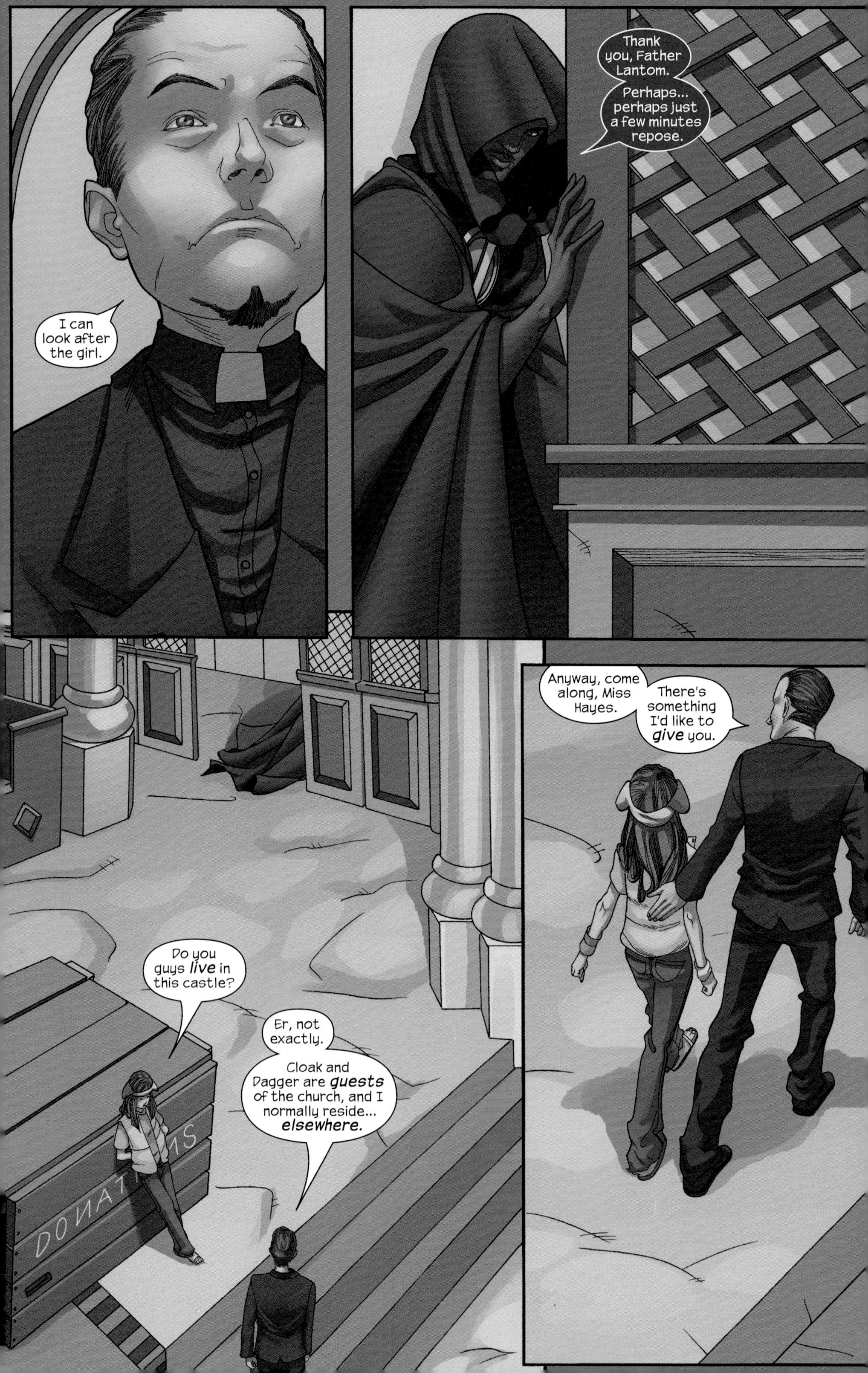
I can look after the girl.
Thank you, Father Lantom.
Perhaps... perhaps just a few minutes repose.
Do you guys *live* in this castle?
Er, not exactly.
Cloak and Dagger are *guests* of the church, and I normally reside... ***elsewhere.***
DONATIONS
Anyway, come along, Miss Hayes.
There's something I'd like to ***give*** you.

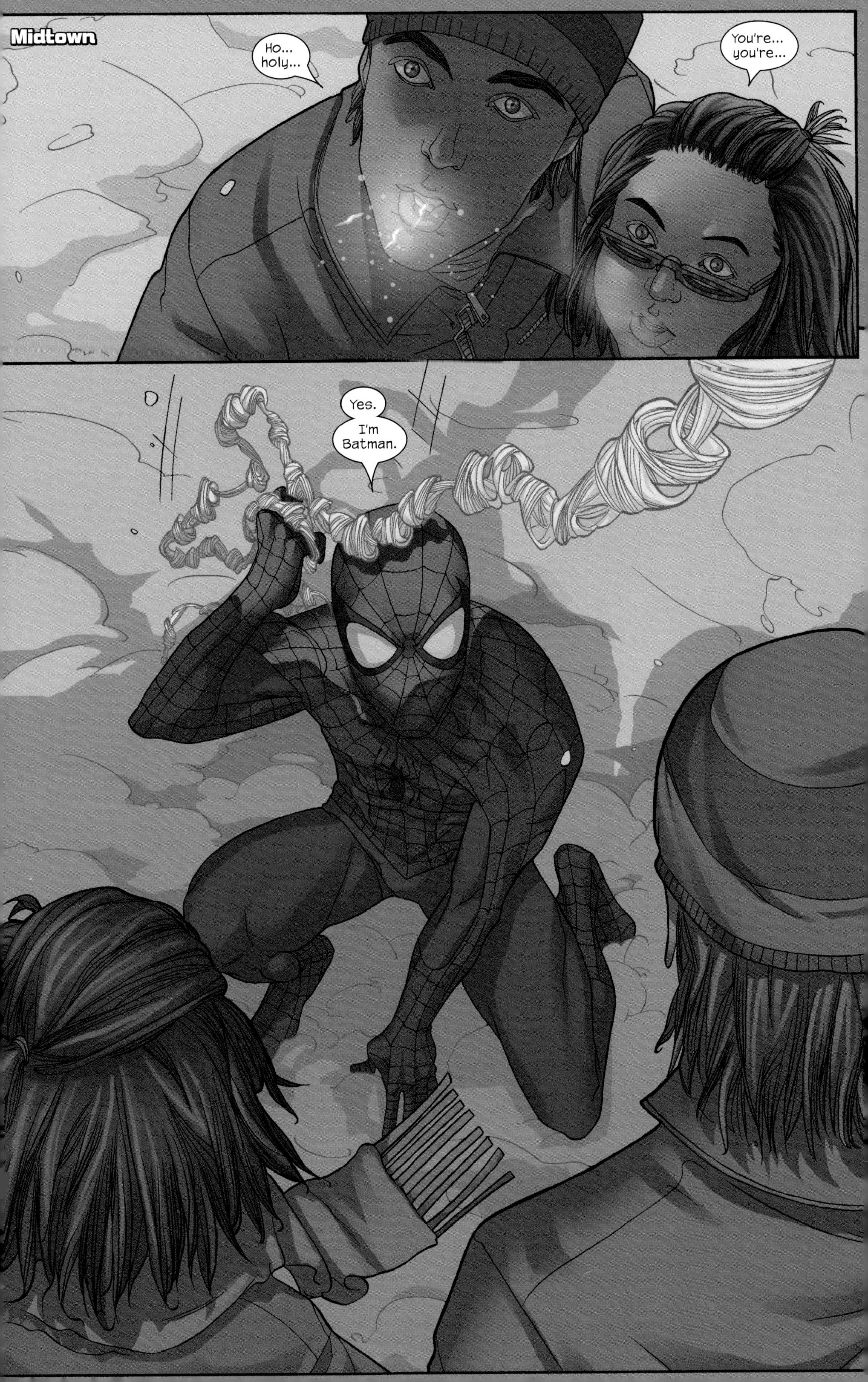
Midtown
Ho... holy...
You're... you're...
Yes.
I'm Batman.

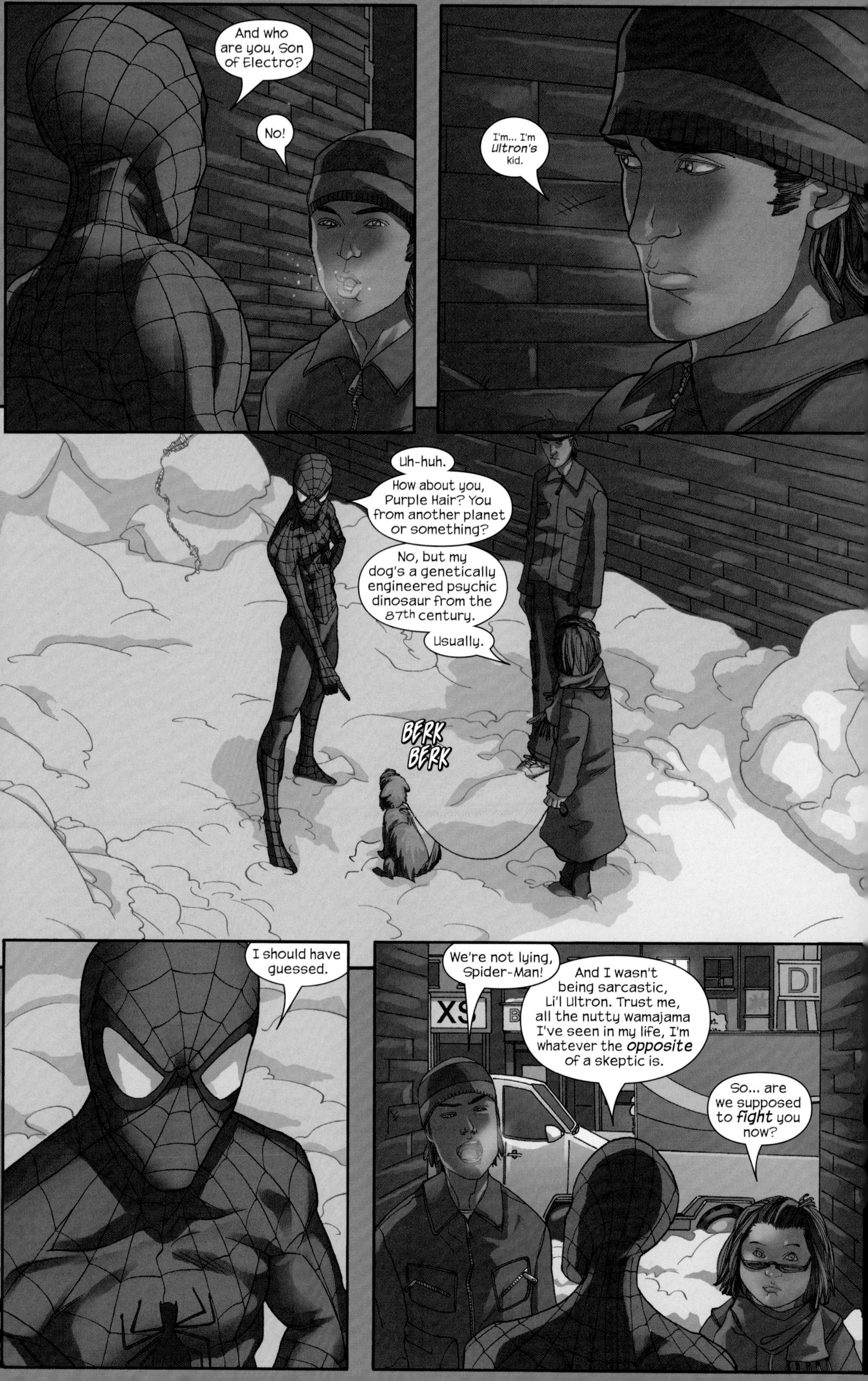

And who are you, Son of Electro?
No!
I'm... I'm *Ultron's* kid.
Uh-huh.
How about you, Purple Hair? You from another planet or something?
No, but my dog's a genetically engineered psychic dinosaur from the 87th century.
Usually.
BERK BERK
I should have guessed.
We're not lying, Spider-Man!
And I wasn't being sarcastic, Li'l Ultron. Trust me, all the nutty wamajama I've seen in my life, I'm whatever the *opposite* of a skeptic is.
So... are we supposed to *fight* you now?

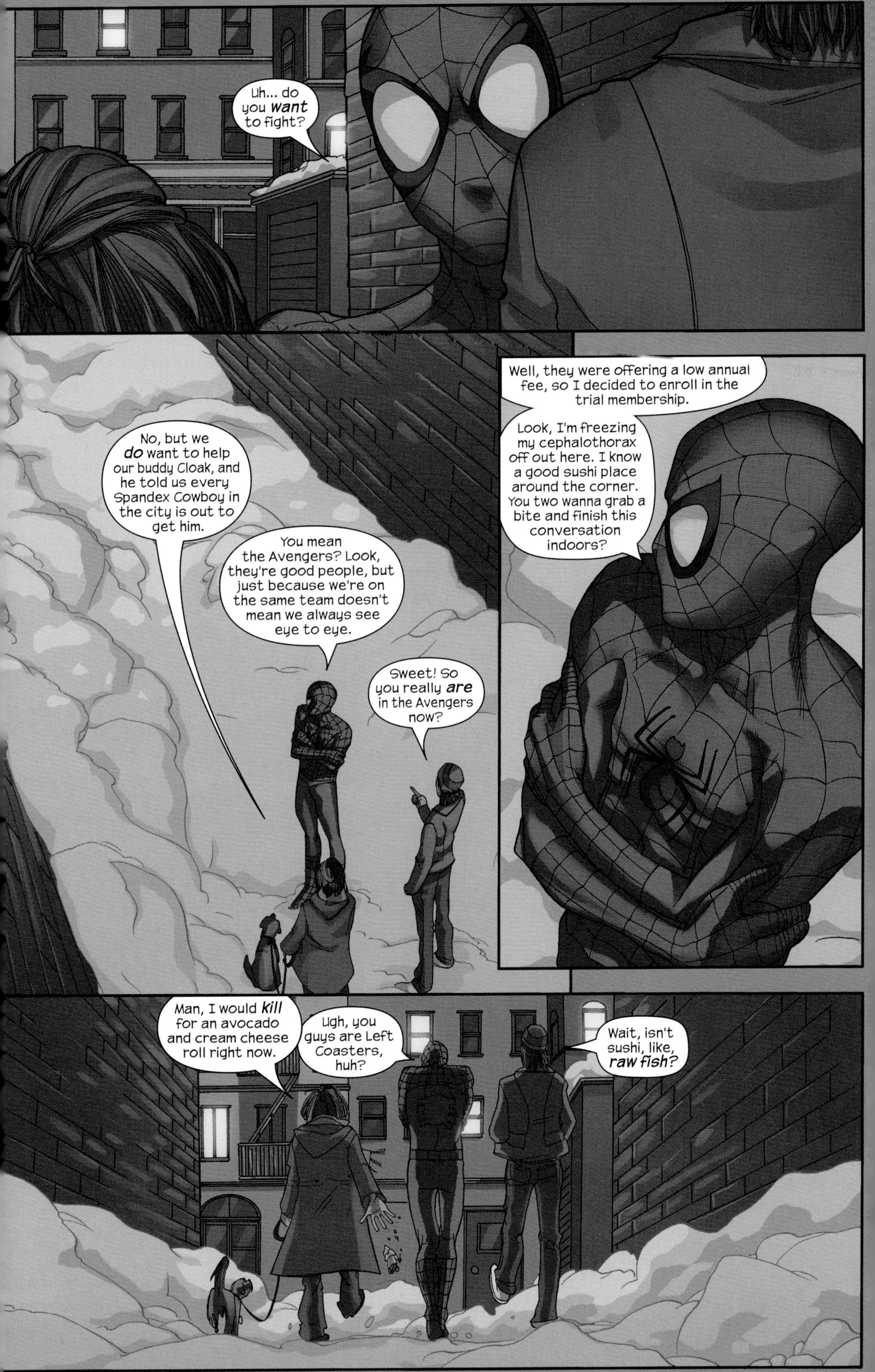

Uh... do you *want* to fight?
No, but we *do* want to help our buddy Cloak, and he told us every Spandex Cowboy in the city is out to get him.
You mean the Avengers? Look, they're good people, but just because we're on the same team doesn't mean we always see eye to eye.
Sweet! So you really *are* in the Avengers now?
Well, they were offering a low annual fee, so I decided to enroll in the trial membership.
Look, I'm freezing my cephalothorax off out here. I know a good sushi place around the corner. You two wanna grab a bite and finish this conversation indoors?
Man, I would *kill* for an avocado and cream cheese roll right now.
Ugh, you guys are Left Coasters, huh?
Wait, isn't sushi, like, *raw fish*?

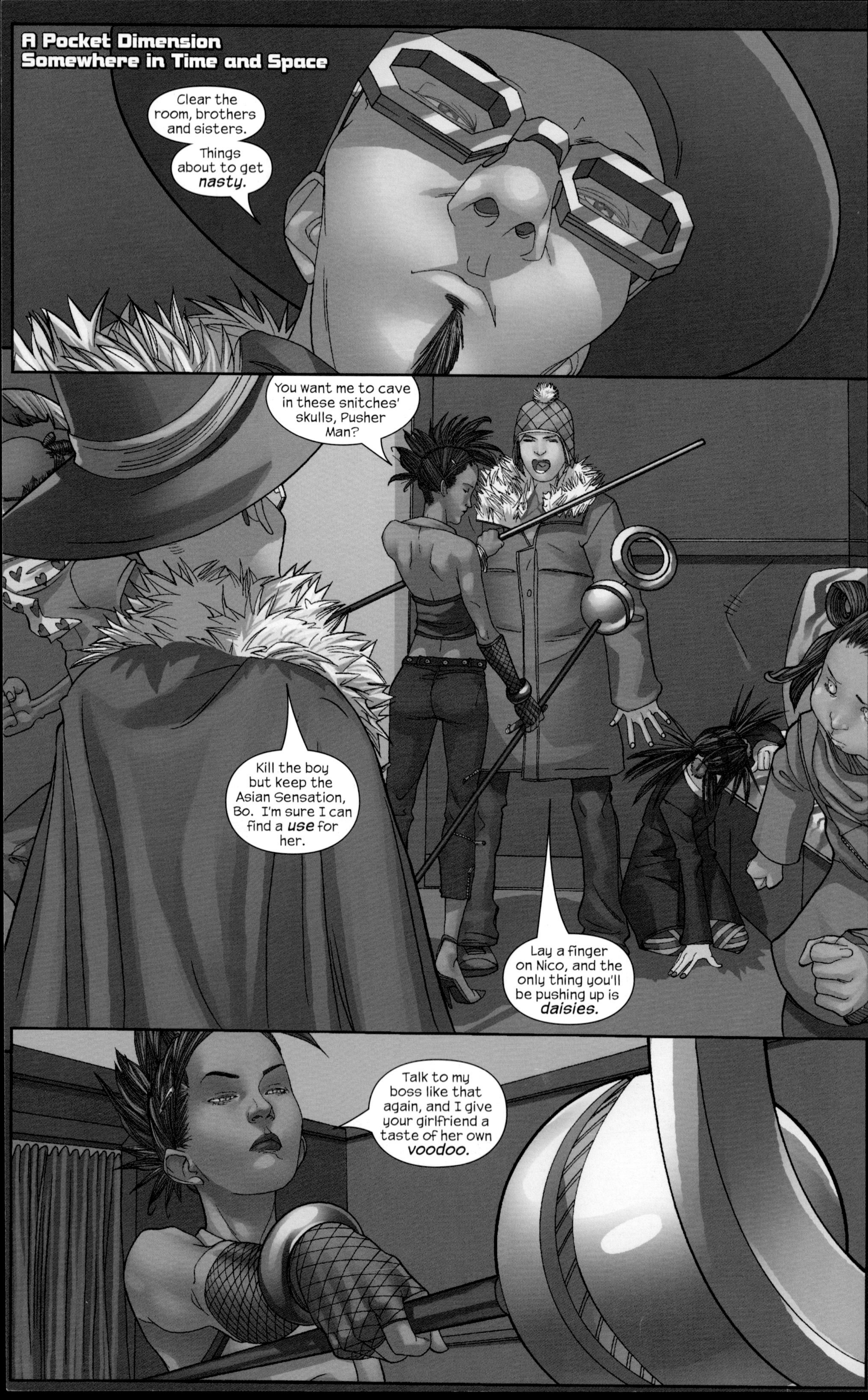
A Pocket Dimension
Somewhere in Time and Space
Clear the room, brothers and sisters.
Things about to get nasty.
You want me to cave in these snitches' skulls, Pusher Man?
Kill the boy but keep the Asian Sensation, Bo. I'm sure I can find a use for her.
Lay a finger on Nico, and the only thing you'll be pushing up is daisies.
Talk to my boss like that again, and I give your girlfriend a taste of her own voodoo.

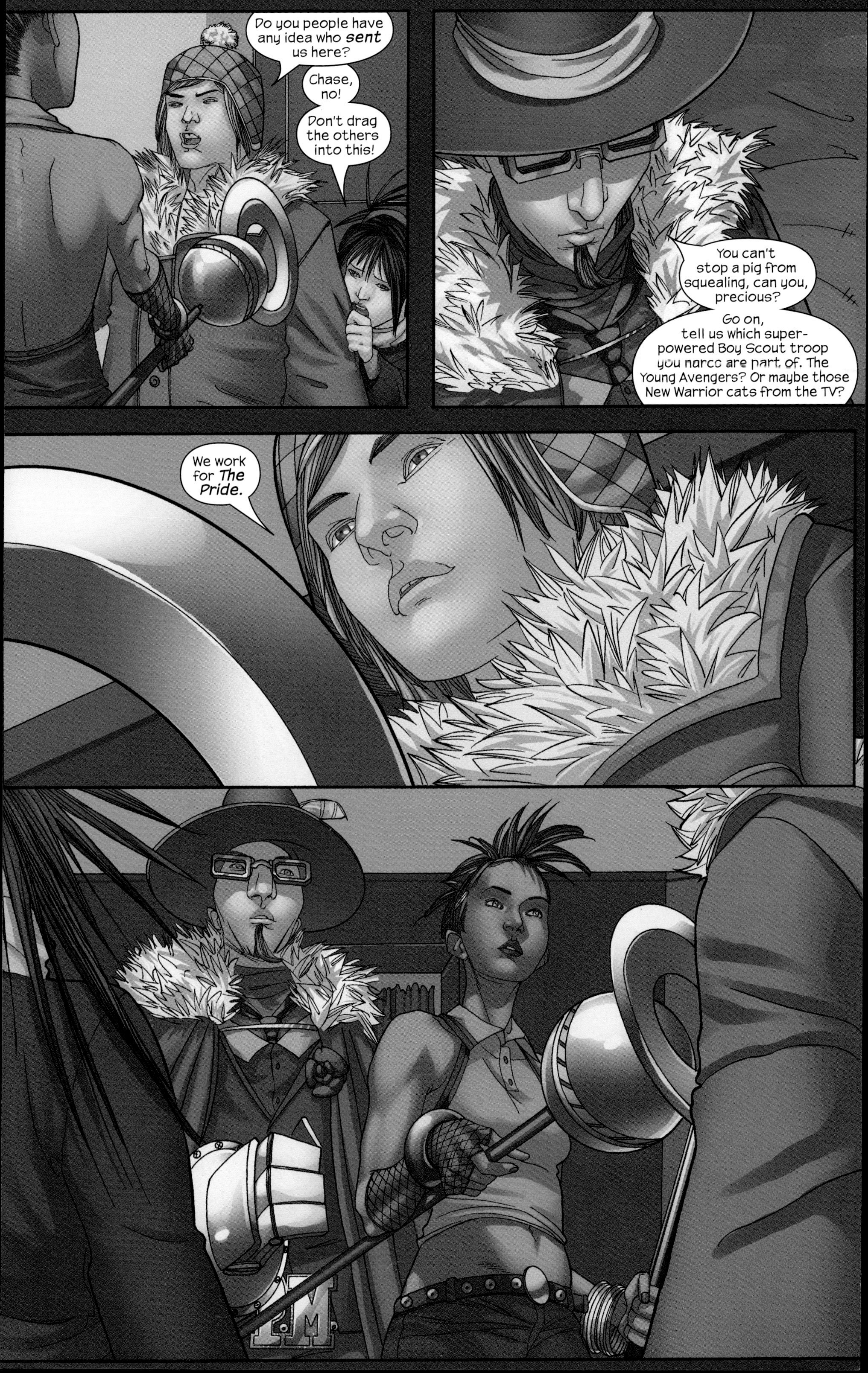
Do you people have any idea who *sent* us here?
Chase, no!
Don't drag the others into this!
You can't stop a pig from squealing, can you, precious?
Go on, tell us which super-powered Boy Scout troop you narcs are part of. The Young Avengers? Or maybe those New Warrior cats from the TV?
We work for *The Pride.*

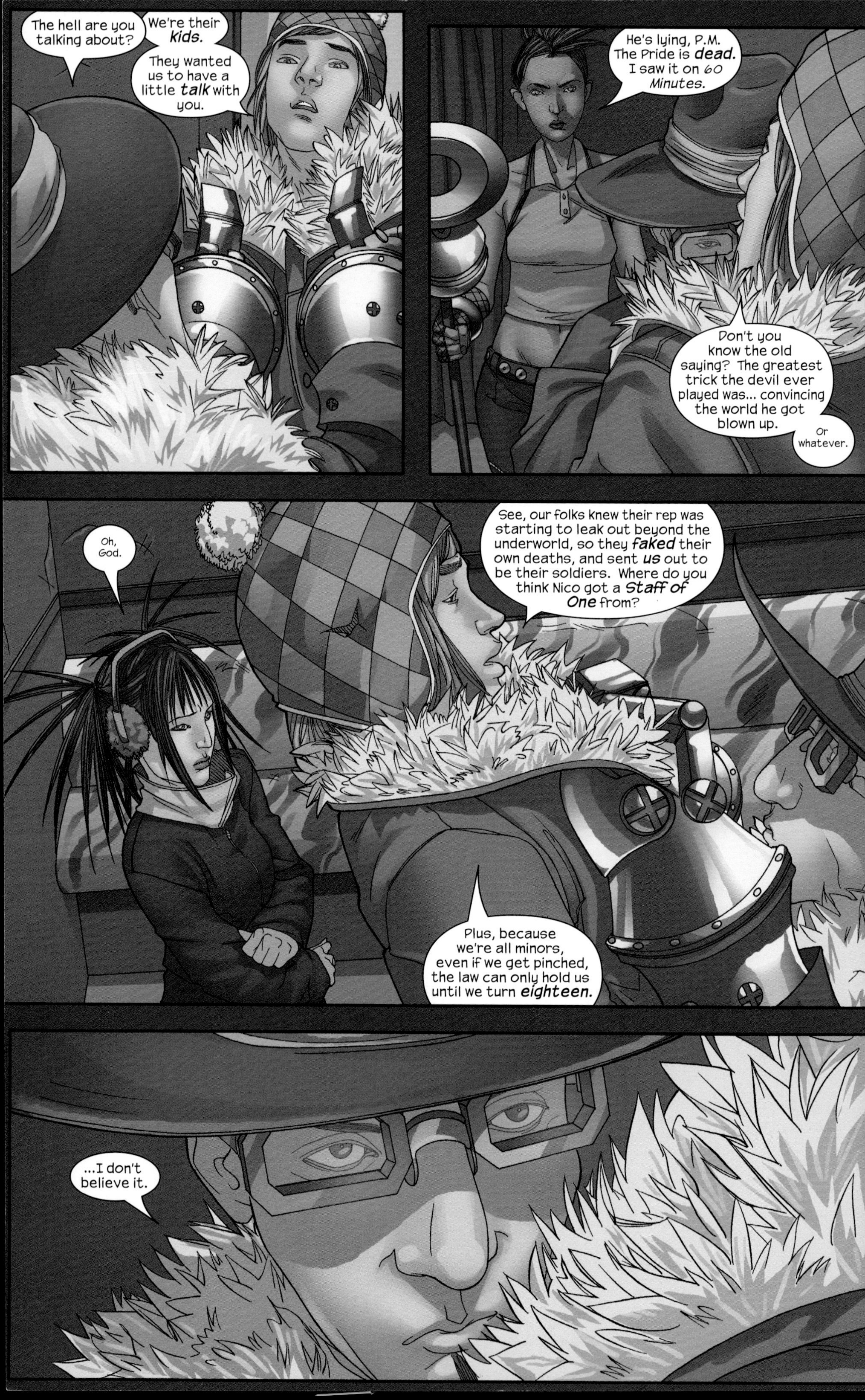
The hell are you talking about?
We're their *kids.*
They wanted us to have a little *talk* with you.
He's lying, P.M. The Pride is *dead.* I saw it on *60 Minutes.*
Don't you know the old saying? The greatest trick the devil ever played was... convincing the world he got blown up.
Or whatever.
Oh, God.
See, our folks knew their rep was starting to leak out beyond the underworld, so they *faked* their own deaths, and sent *us* out to be their soldiers. Where do you think Nico got a *Staff of One* from?
Plus, because we're all minors, even if we get pinched, the law can only hold us until we turn *eighteen.*
...I don't believe it.

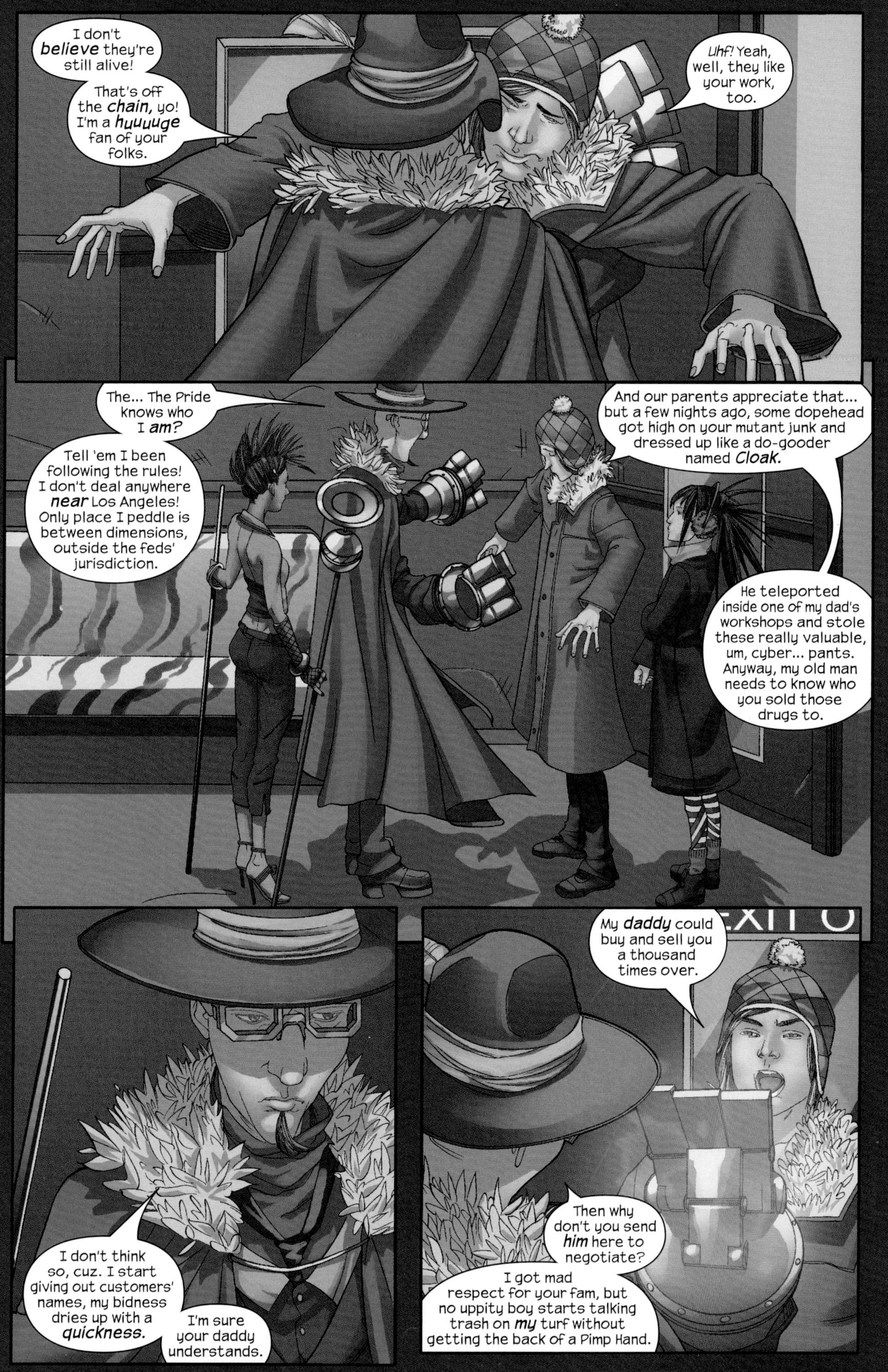

I don't *believe* they're still alive!
That's off the *chain,* yo! I'm a *huuuuge* fan of your folks.
Uhf! Yeah, well, they like your work, too.
The... The Pride knows who I *am?*
Tell 'em I been following the rules! I don't deal anywhere *near* Los Angeles! Only place I peddle is between dimensions, outside the feds' jurisdiction.
And our parents appreciate that... but a few nights ago, some dopehead got high on your mutant junk and dressed up like a do-gooder named *Cloak.*
He teleported inside one of my dad's workshops and stole these really valuable, um, cyber... pants. Anyway, my old man needs to know who you sold those drugs to.
I don't think so, cuz. I start giving out customers' names, my bidness dries up with a *quickness.*
I'm sure your daddy understands.
EXIT
My *daddy* could buy and sell you a thousand times over.
Then why don't you send *him* here to negotiate?
I got mad respect for your fam, but no uppity boy starts talking trash on *my* turf without getting the back of a Pimp Hand.

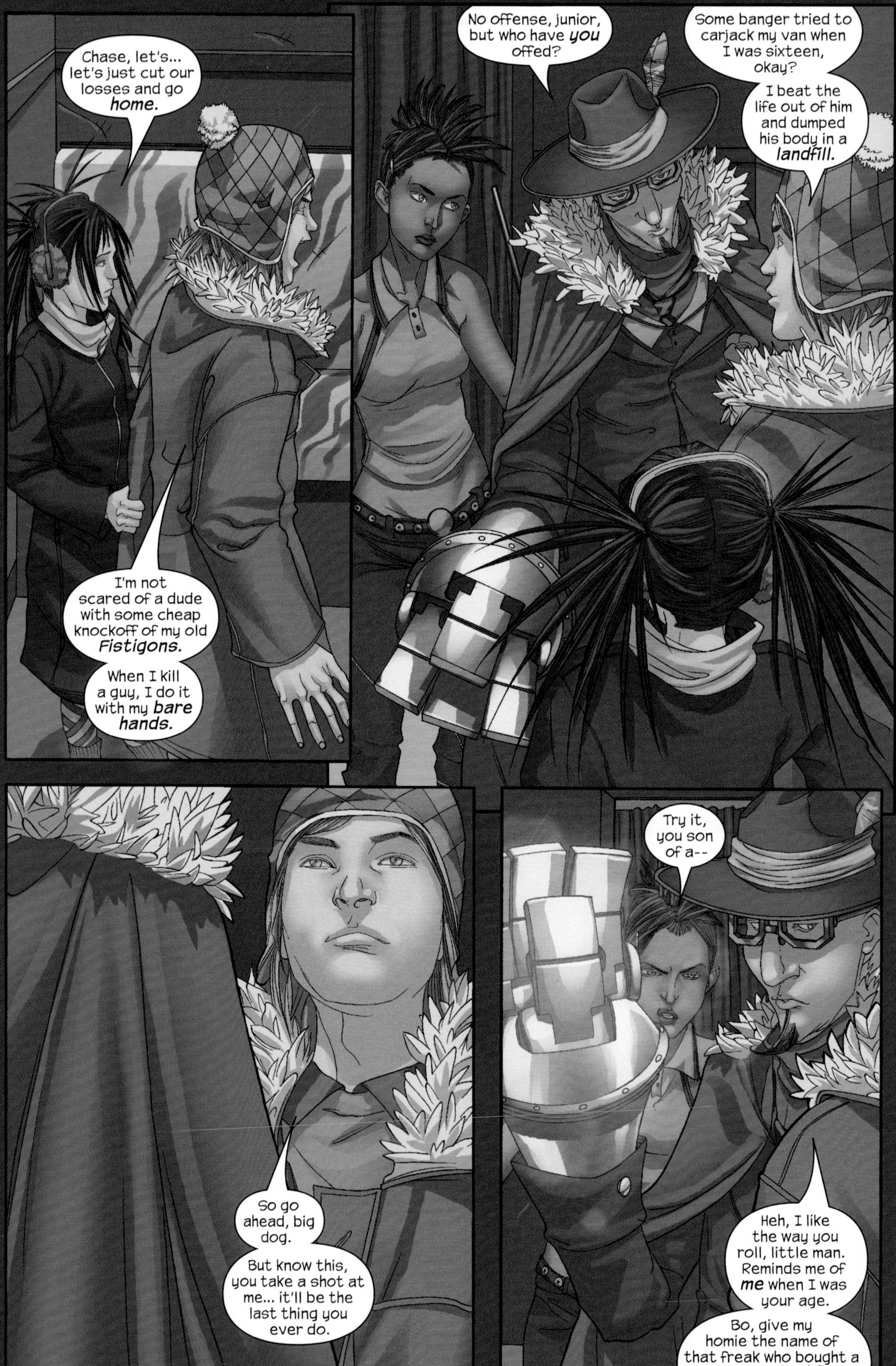
Chase, let's... let's just cut our losses and go *home.*
No offense, junior, but who have *you* offed?
Some banger tried to carjack my van when I was sixteen, okay?
I beat the life out of him and dumped his body in a *landfill.*
I'm not scared of a dude with some cheap knockoff of my old *Fistigons.*
When I kill a guy, I do it with my *bare hands.*
So go ahead, big dog.
But know this, you take a shot at me... it'll be the last thing you ever do.
Try it, you son of a--
Heh, I like the way you roll, little man. Reminds me of *me* when I was your age.
Bo, give my homie the name of that freak who bought a dime bag of *Darkforce* from us last week.

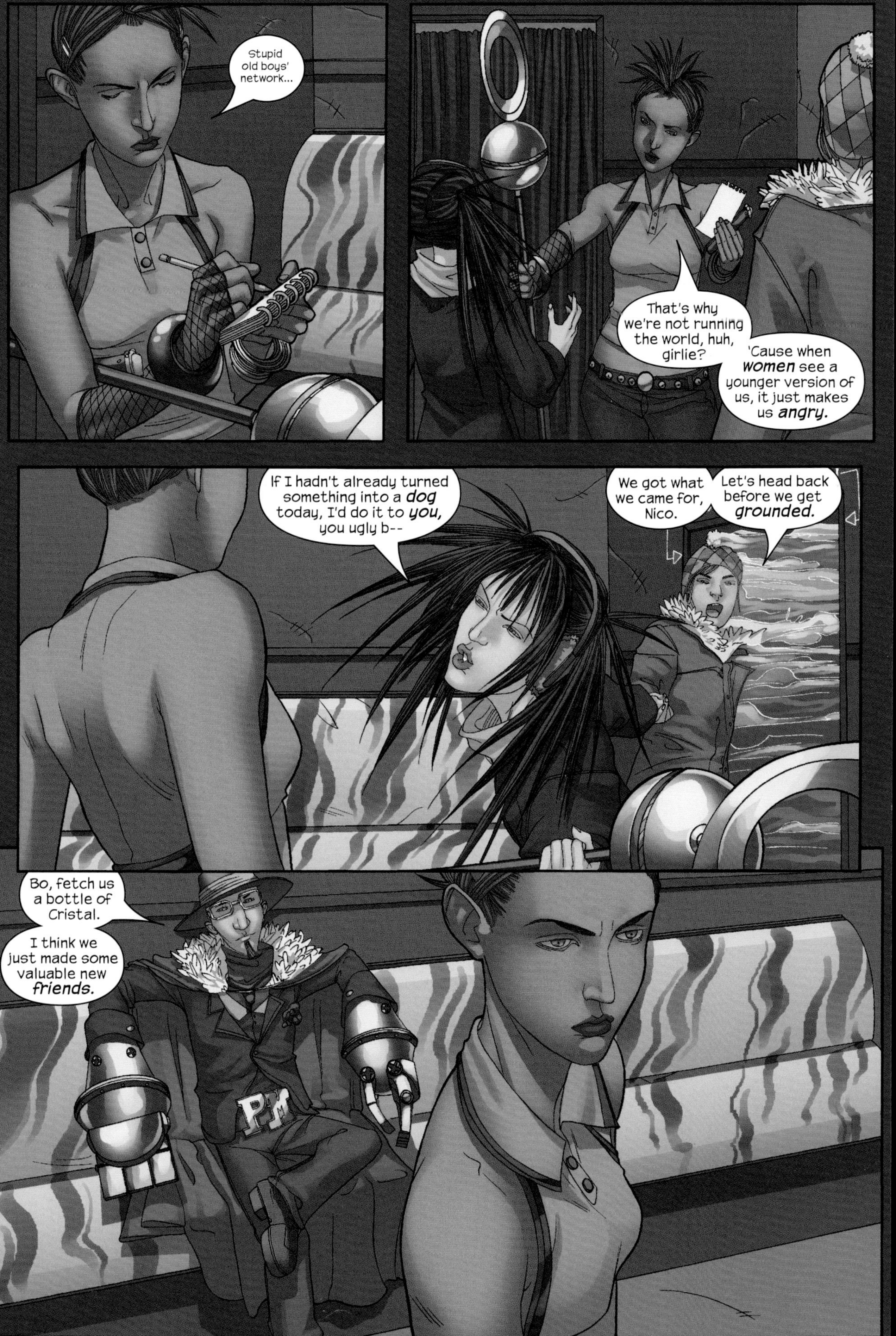

Stupid old boys' network...
That's why we're not running the world, huh, girlie?
'Cause when *women* see a younger version of us, it just makes us *angry.*
If I hadn't already turned something into a *dog* today, I'd do it to *you,* you ugly b--
We got what we came for, Nico.
Let's head back before we get *grounded.*
Bo, fetch us a bottle of Cristal.
I think we just made some valuable new *friends.*
PM

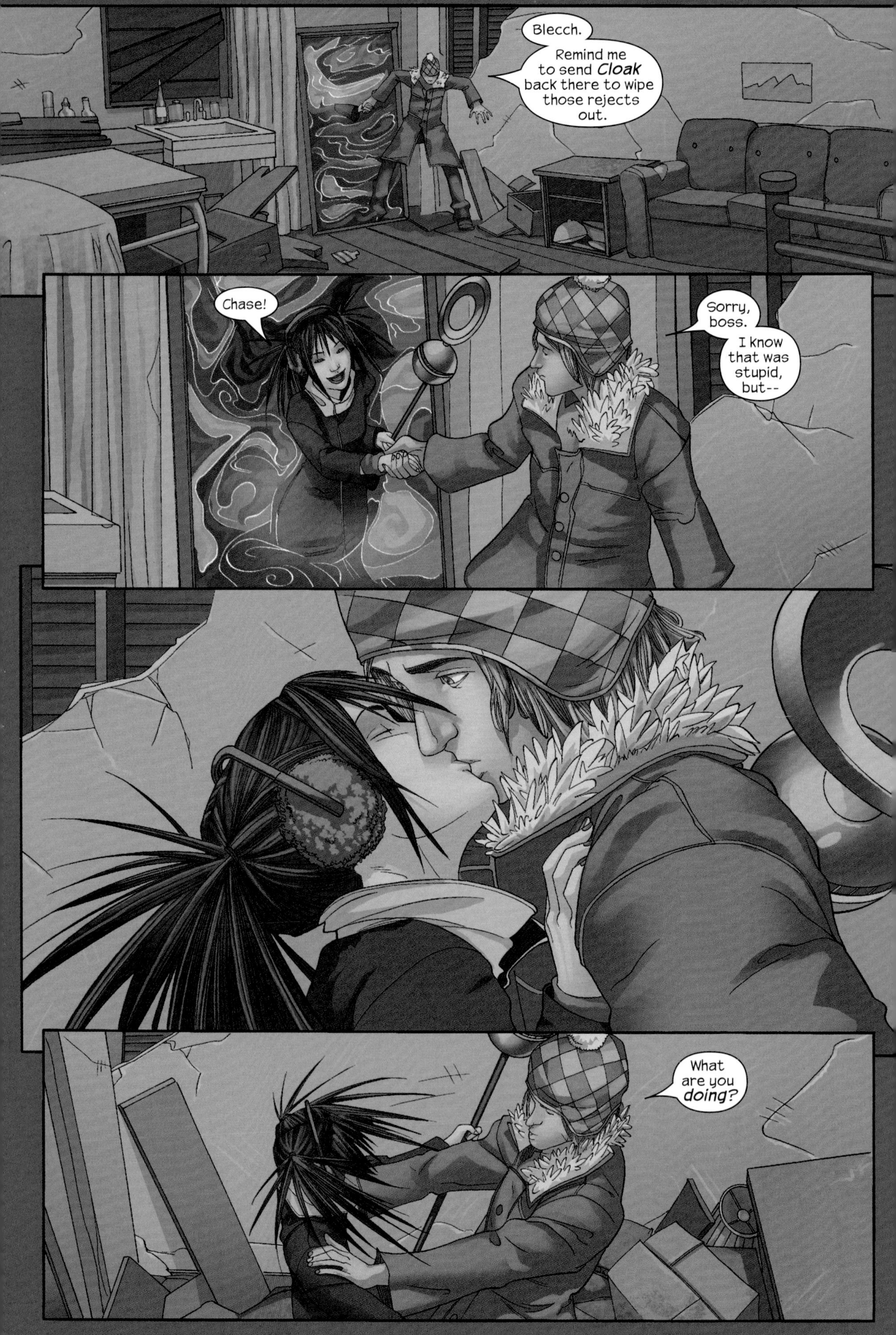
Blecch.
Remind me to send Cloak back there to wipe those rejects out.
Chase!
Sorry, boss.
I know that was stupid, but--
What are you doing?

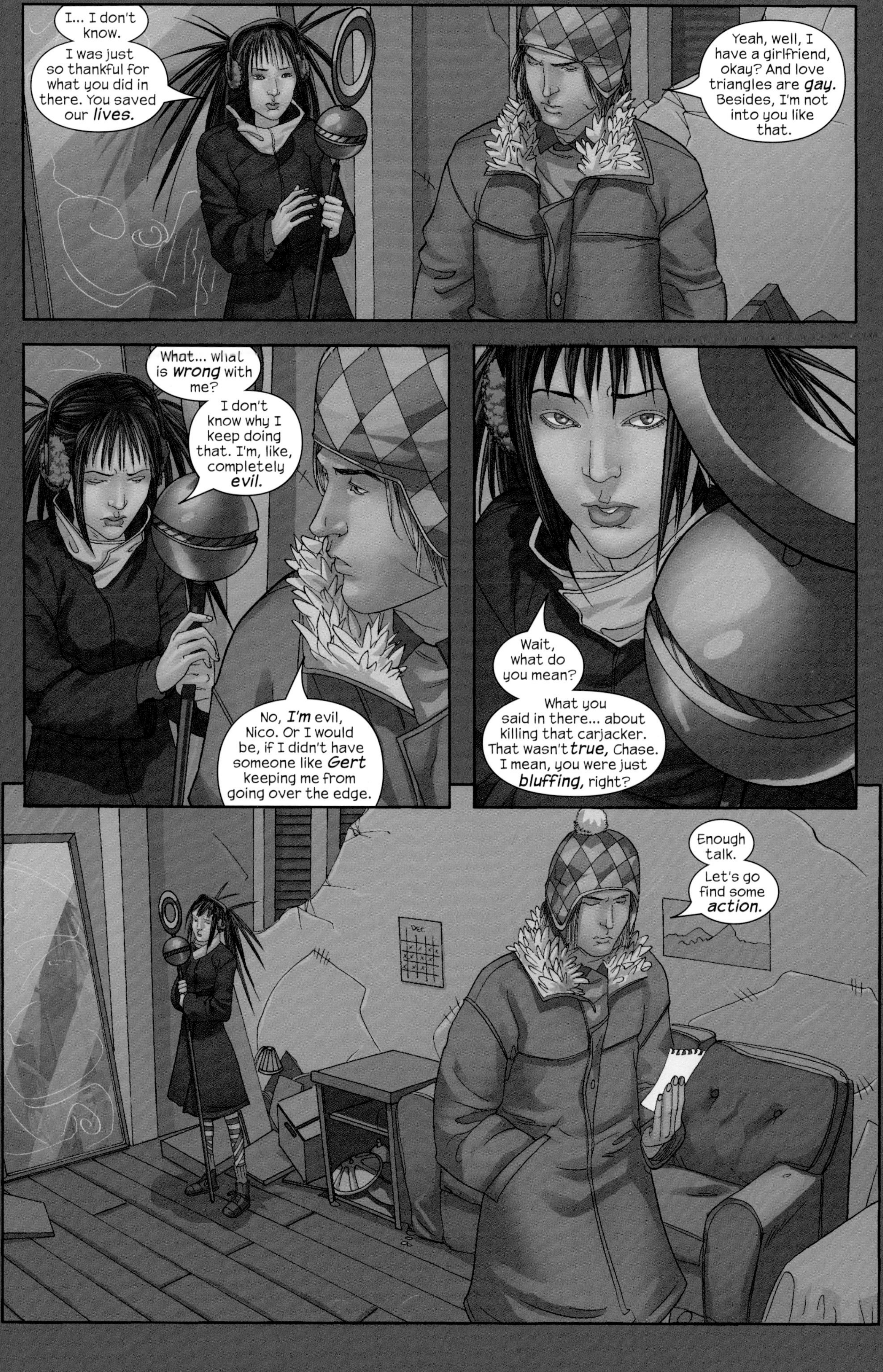
I... I don't know.
I was just so thankful for what you did in there. You saved our lives.
Yeah, well, I have a girlfriend, okay? And love triangles are gay. Besides, I'm not into you like that.
What... what is wrong with me?
I don't know why I keep doing that. I'm, like, completely evil.
No, I'm evil, Nico. Or I would be, if I didn't have someone like Gert keeping me from going over the edge.
Wait, what do you mean?
What you said in there... about killing that carjacker. That wasn't true, Chase. I mean, you were just bluffing, right?
Enough talk.
Let's go find some action.

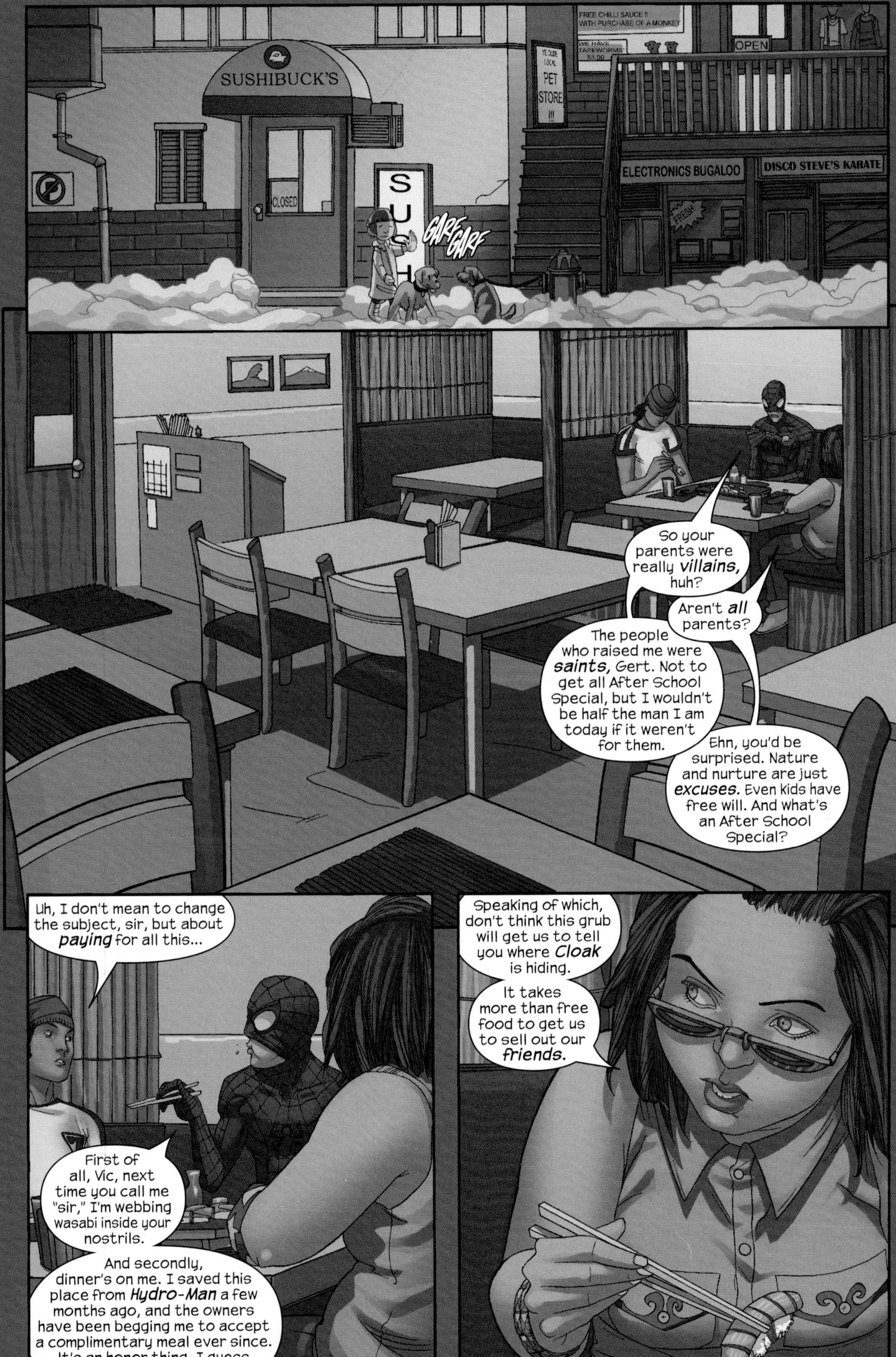

SUSHIBUCK'S
CLOSED
SUSH
YE OLDE LOCAL PET STORE !!!
FREE CHILLI SAUCE !! WITH PURCHASE OF A MONKEY
WE HAVE TAPEWORMS $3.00
OPEN
ELECTRONICS BUGALOO
DISCO STEVE'S KARATE
FRESH
GARF GARF
So your parents were really villains, huh?
Aren't all parents?
The people who raised me were saints, Gert. Not to get all After School Special, but I wouldn't be half the man I am today if it weren't for them.
Ehn, you'd be surprised. Nature and nurture are just excuses. Even kids have free will. And what's an After School Special?
Uh, I don't mean to change the subject, sir, but about paying for all this...
First of all, Vic, next time you call me "sir," I'm webbing wasabi inside your nostrils.
And secondly, dinner's on me. I saved this place from Hydro-Man a few months ago, and the owners have been begging me to accept a complimentary meal ever since. It's an honor thing, I guess.
Speaking of which, don't think this grub will get us to tell you where Cloak is hiding.
It takes more than free food to get us to sell out our friends.

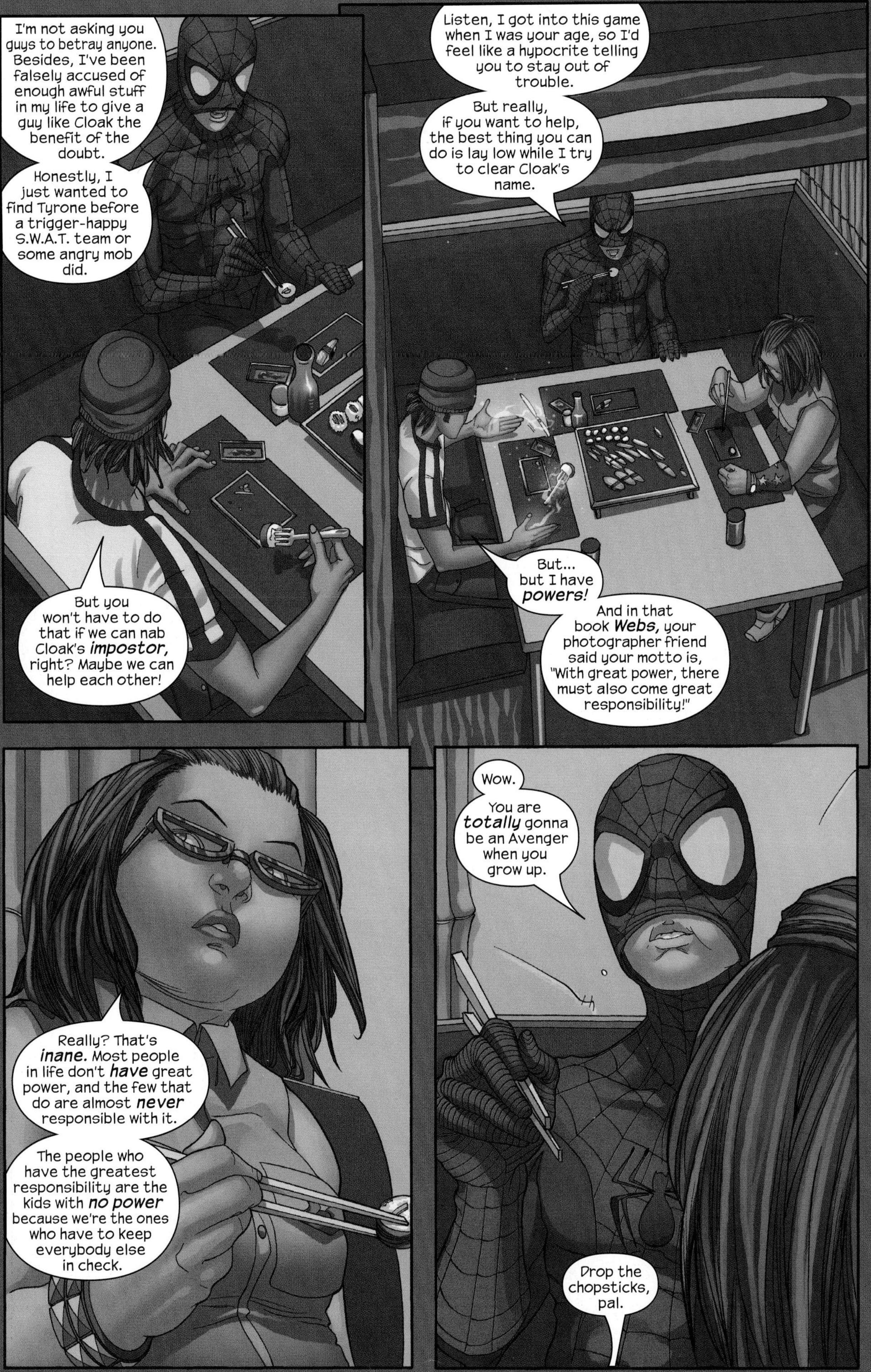
I'm not asking you guys to betray anyone. Besides, I've been falsely accused of enough awful stuff in my life to give a guy like Cloak the benefit of the doubt.
Honestly, I just wanted to find Tyrone before a trigger-happy S.W.A.T. team or some angry mob did.
But you won't have to do that if we can nab Cloak's *impostor,* right? Maybe we can help each other!
Listen, I got into this game when I was your age, so I'd feel like a hypocrite telling you to stay out of trouble.
But really, if you want to help, the best thing you can do is lay low while I try to clear Cloak's name.
But... but I have *powers!*
And in that book *Webs,* your photographer friend said your motto is, "With great power, there must also come great responsibility!"
Really? That's *inane.* Most people in life don't *have* great power, and the few that do are almost *never* responsible with it.
The people who have the greatest responsibility are the kids with *no power* because we're the ones who have to keep everybody else in check.
Wow.
You are *totally* gonna be an Avenger when you grow up.
Drop the chopsticks, pal.

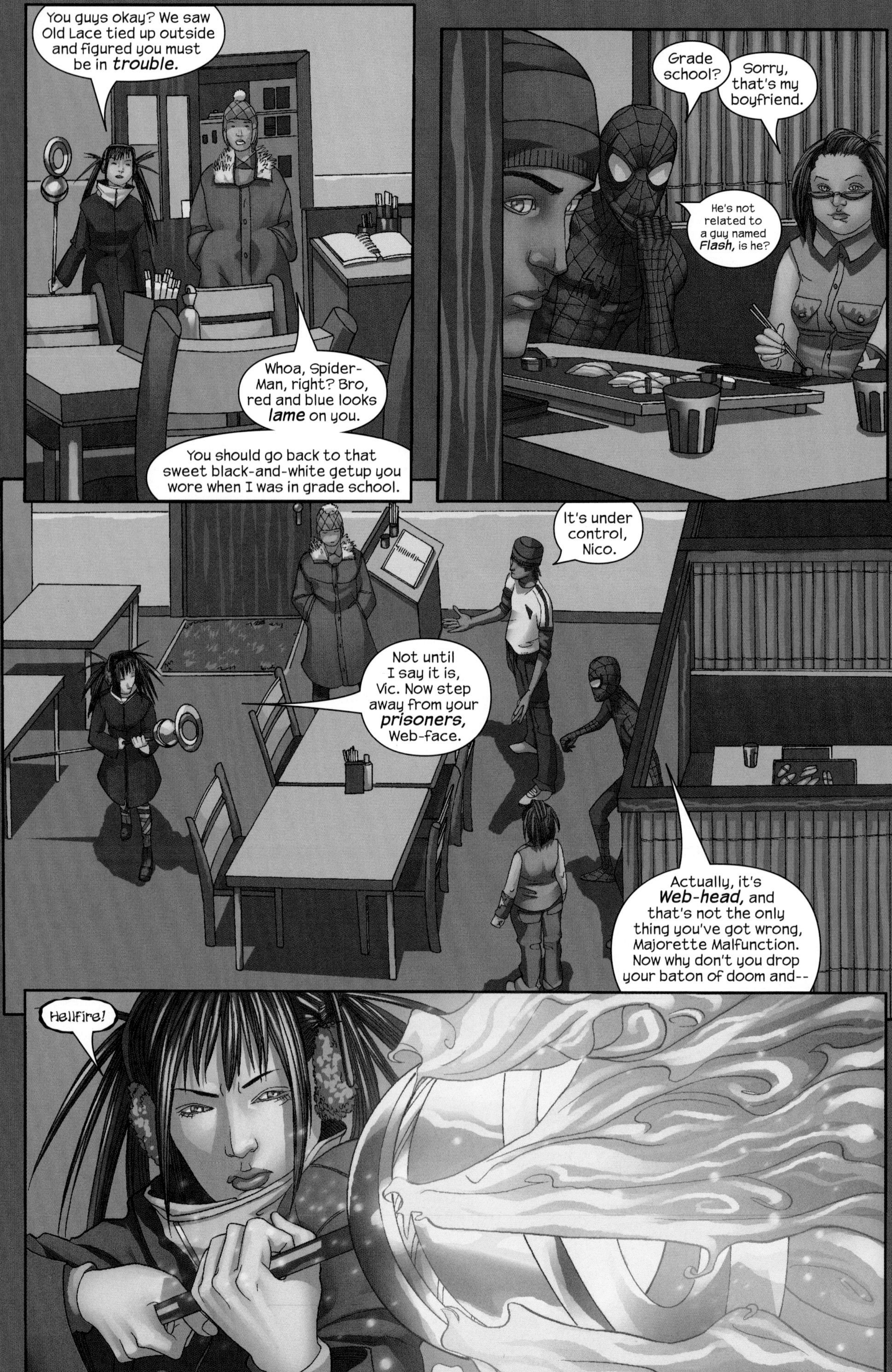
You guys okay? We saw Old Lace tied up outside and figured you must be in *trouble.*
Whoa, Spider-Man, right? Bro, red and blue looks *lame* on you.
You should go back to that sweet black-and-white getup you wore when I was in grade school.
Grade school?
Sorry, that's my boyfriend.
He's not related to a guy named *Flash,* is he?
It's under control, Nico.
Not until I say it is, Vic. Now step away from your *prisoners,* Web-face.
Actually, it's *Web-head,* and that's not the only thing you've got wrong, Majorette Malfunction. Now why don't you drop your baton of doom and--
Hellfire!

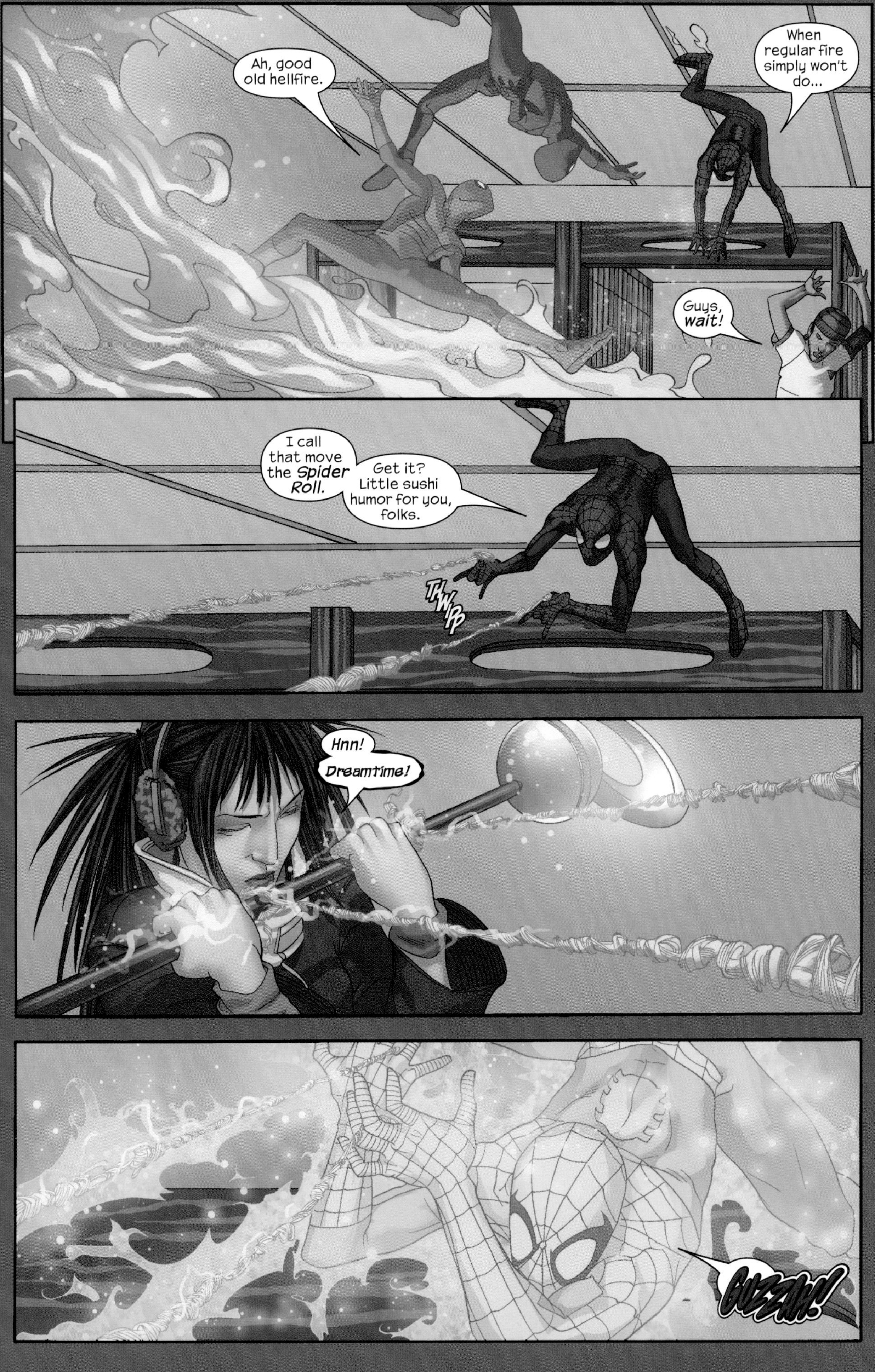

Ah, good old hellfire.
When regular fire simply won't do...
Guys, *wait!*
I call that move the *Spider Roll.*
Get it? Little sushi humor for you, folks.
THWIP
Hnn!
Dreamtime!

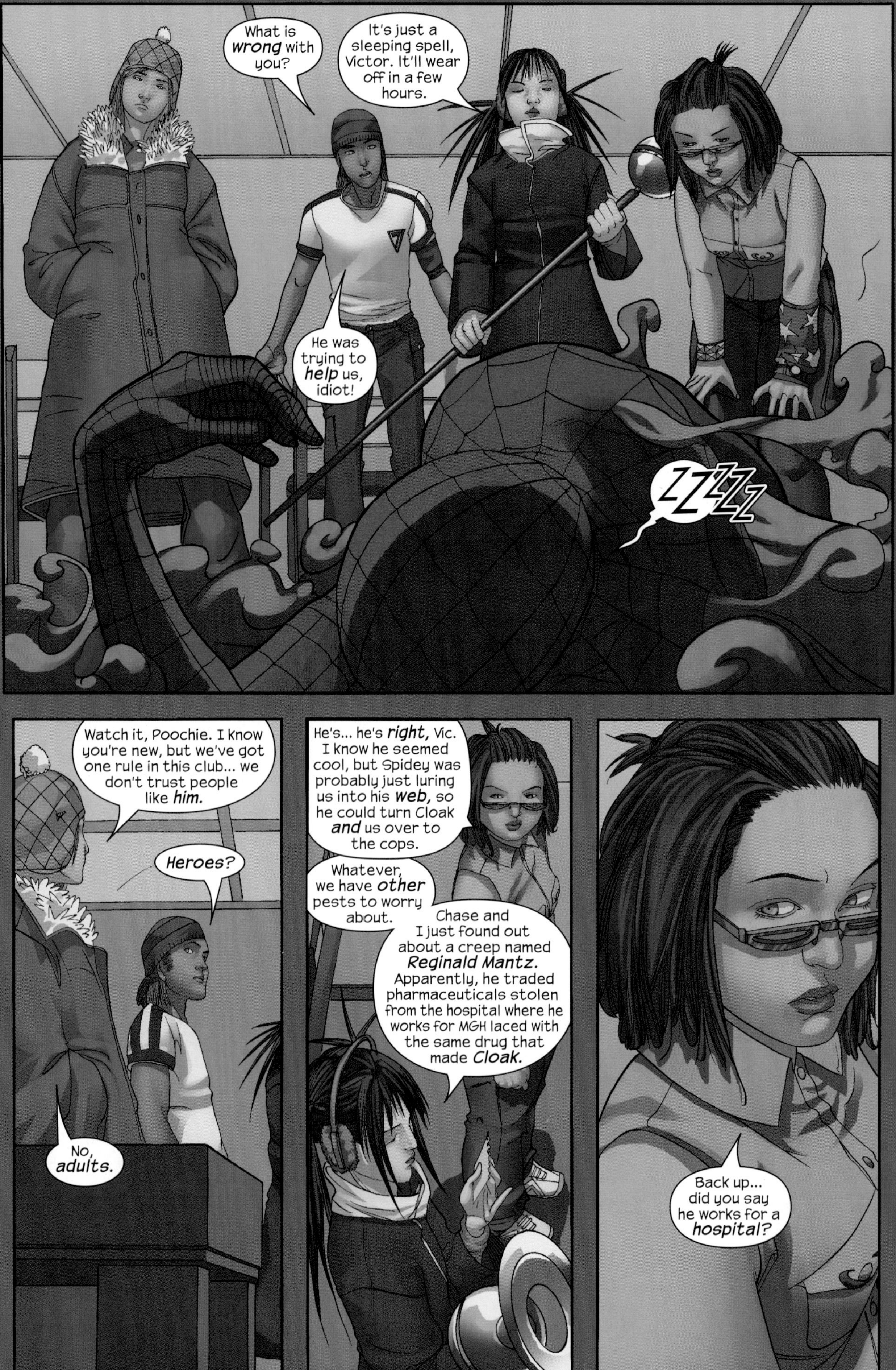
What is wrong with you?
It's just a sleeping spell, Victor. It'll wear off in a few hours.
He was trying to help us, idiot!
ZZZZZ
Watch it, Poochie. I know you're new, but we've got one rule in this club... we don't trust people like him.
Heroes?
No, adults.
He's... he's right, Vic. I know he seemed cool, but Spidey was probably just luring us into his web, so he could turn Cloak and us over to the cops.
Whatever, we have other pests to worry about.
Chase and I just found out about a creep named Reginald Mantz. Apparently, he traded pharmaceuticals stolen from the hospital where he works for MGH laced with the same drug that made Cloak.
Back up... did you say he works for a hospital?

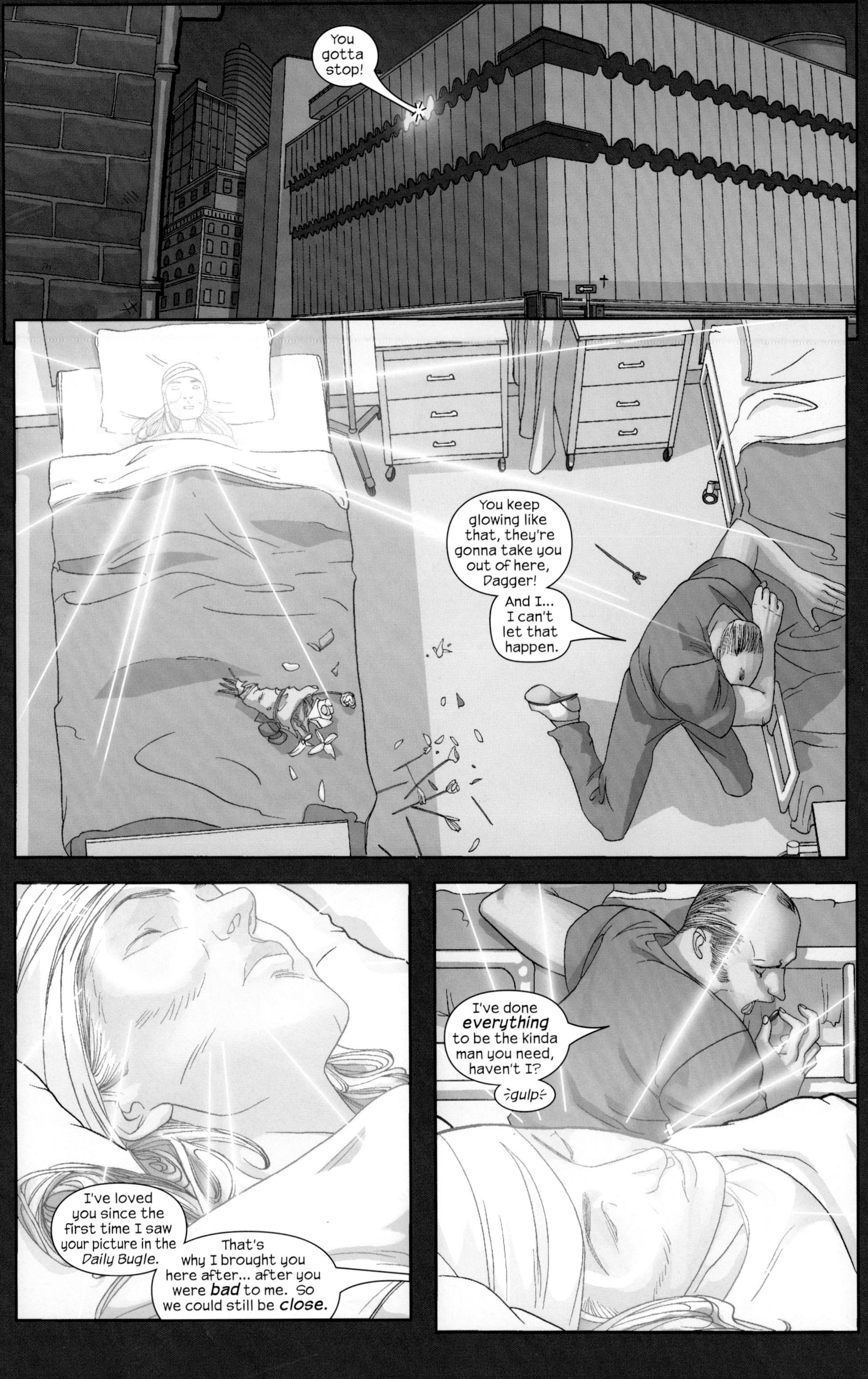
You gotta stop!
You keep glowing like that, they're gonna take you out of here, Dagger!
And I... I can't let that happen.
I've loved you since the first time I saw your picture in the *Daily Bugle.*
That's why I brought you here after... after you were ***bad*** to me. So we could still be ***close.***
I've done ***everything*** to be the kinda man you need, haven't I?
gulp

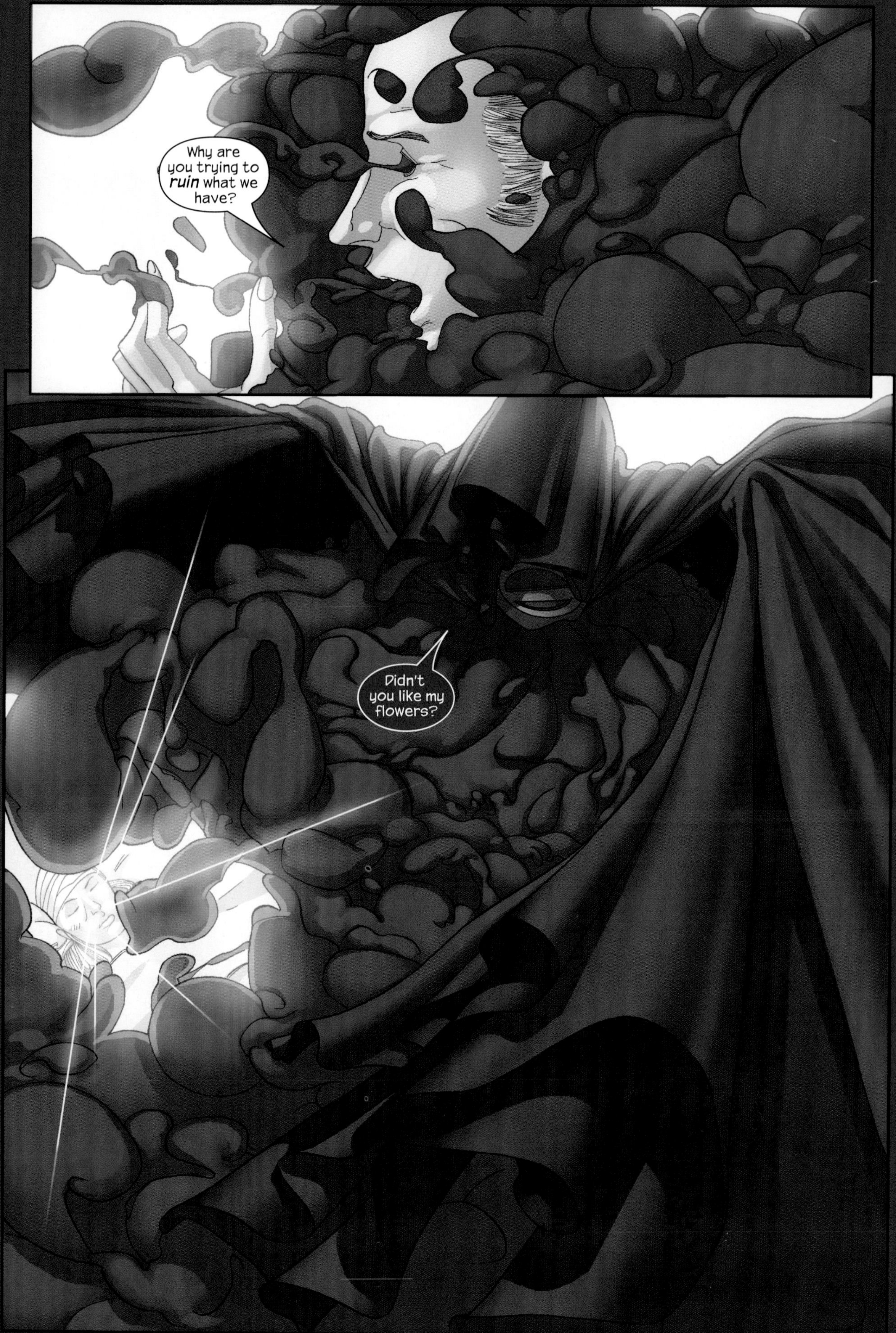

Why are you trying to *ruin* what we have?
Didn't you like my flowers?

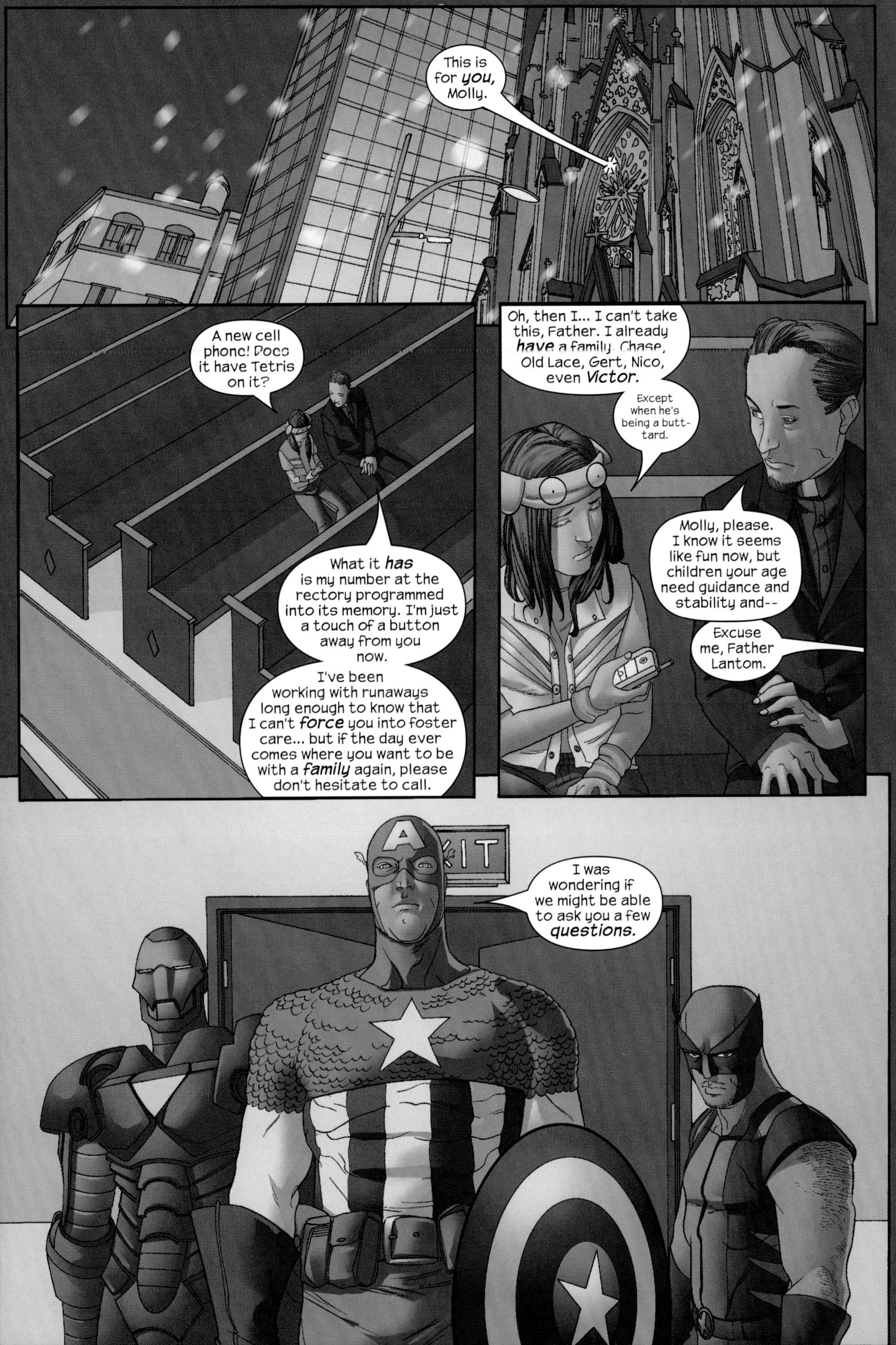
This is for you, Molly.
A new cell phone! Does it have Tetris on it?
What it has is my number at the rectory programmed into its memory. I'm just a touch of a button away from you now.
I've been working with runaways long enough to know that I can't force you into foster care... but if the day ever comes where you want to be with a family again, please don't hesitate to call.
Oh, then I... I can't take this, Father. I already have a family. Chase, Old Lace, Gert, Nico, even Victor.
Except when he's being a butt-tard.
Molly, please. I know it seems like fun now, but children your age need guidance and stability and--
Excuse me, Father Lantom.
I was wondering if we might be able to ask you a few questions.

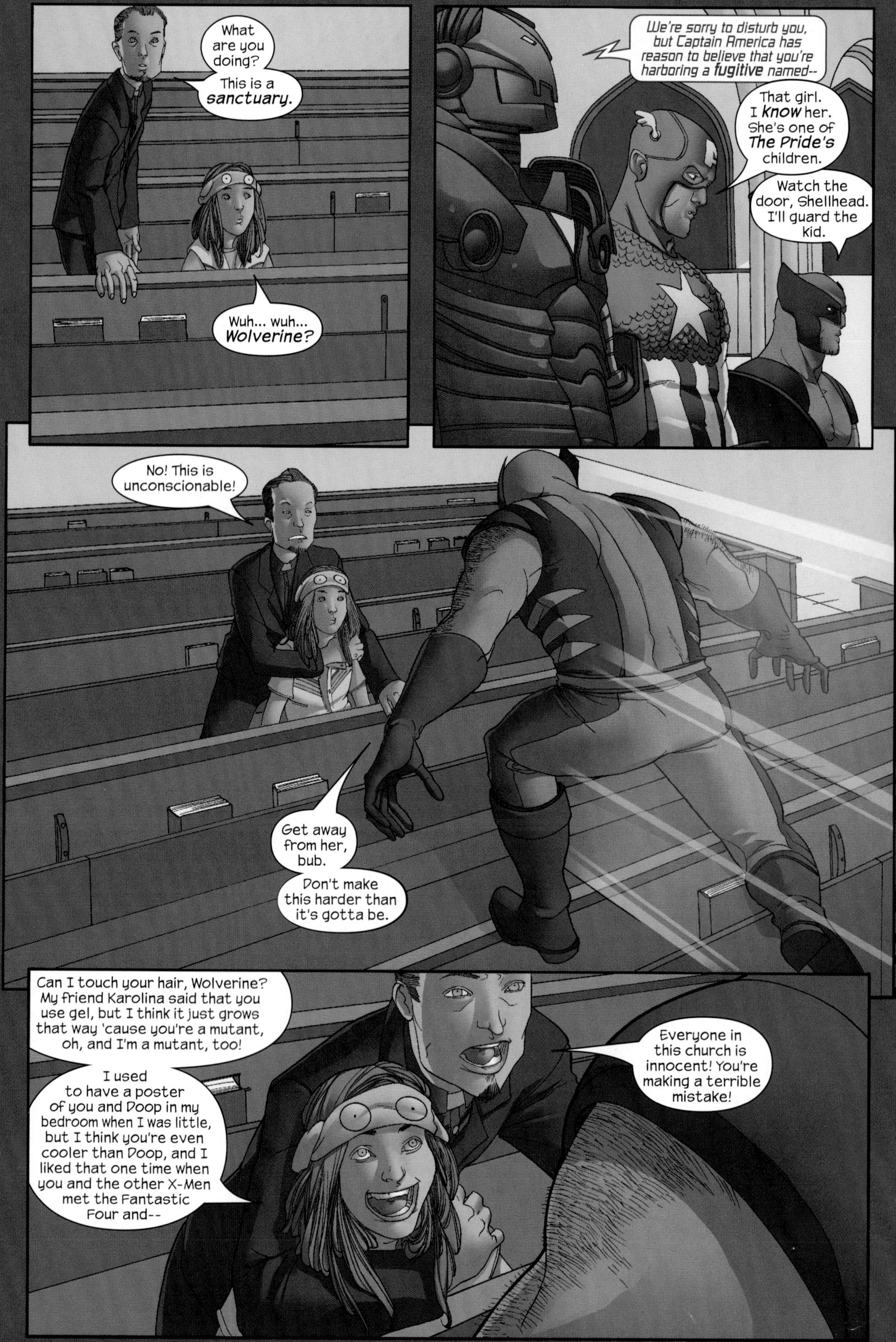
What are you doing? This is a sanctuary.
Wuh... wuh... Wolverine?
We're sorry to disturb you, but Captain America has reason to believe that you're harboring a fugitive named--
That girl. I know her. She's one of The Pride's children.
Watch the door, Shellhead. I'll guard the kid.
No! This is unconscionable!
Get away from her, bub.
Don't make this harder than it's gotta be.
Can I touch your hair, Wolverine? My friend Karolina said that you use gel, but I think it just grows that way 'cause you're a mutant, oh, and I'm a mutant, too!
I used to have a poster of you and Doop in my bedroom when I was little, but I think you're even cooler than Doop, and I liked that one time when you and the other X-Men met the Fantastic Four and--
Everyone in this church is innocent! You're making a terrible mistake!

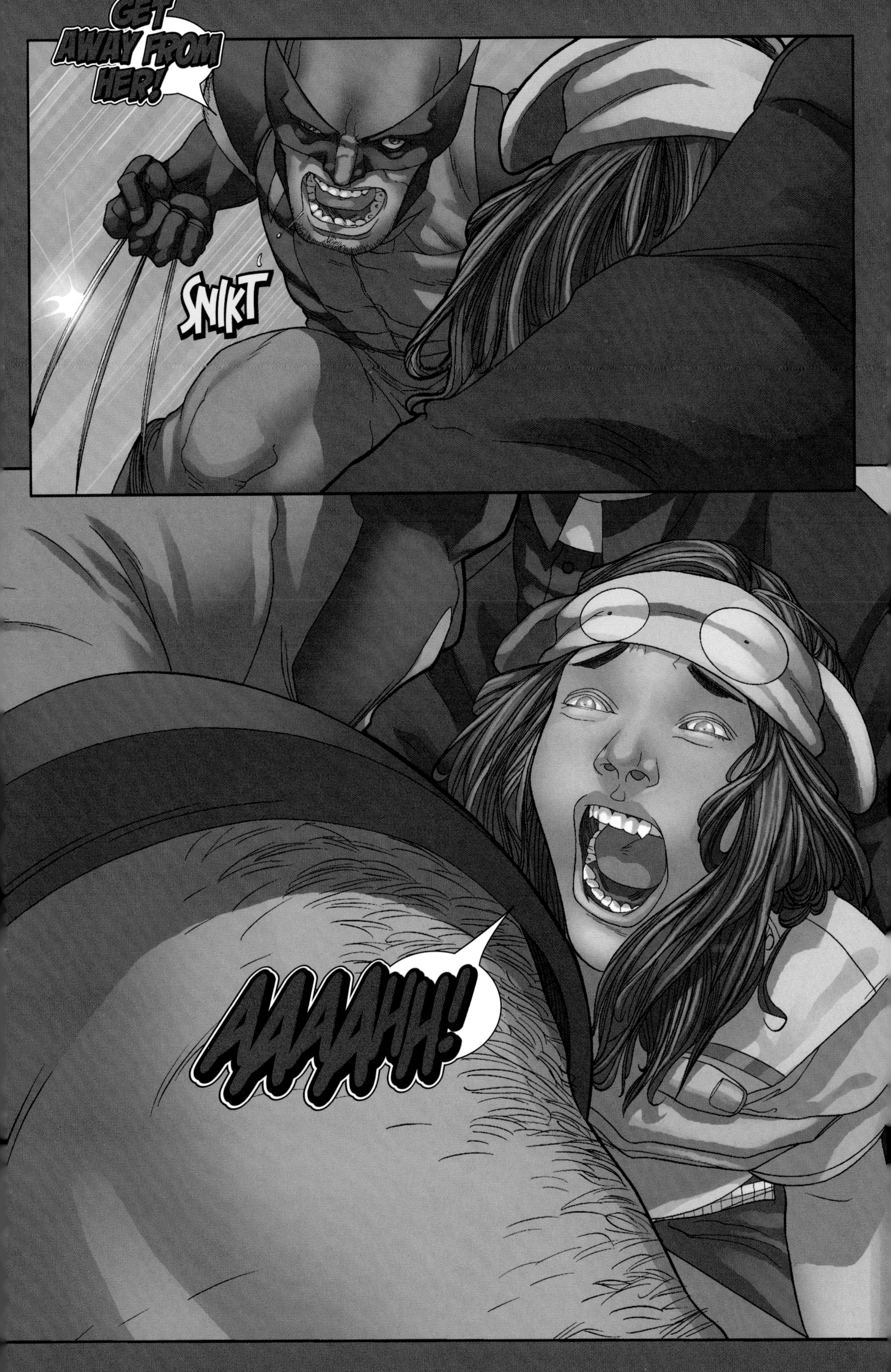
GET AWAY FROM HER!
SNIKT
AAAAHH!

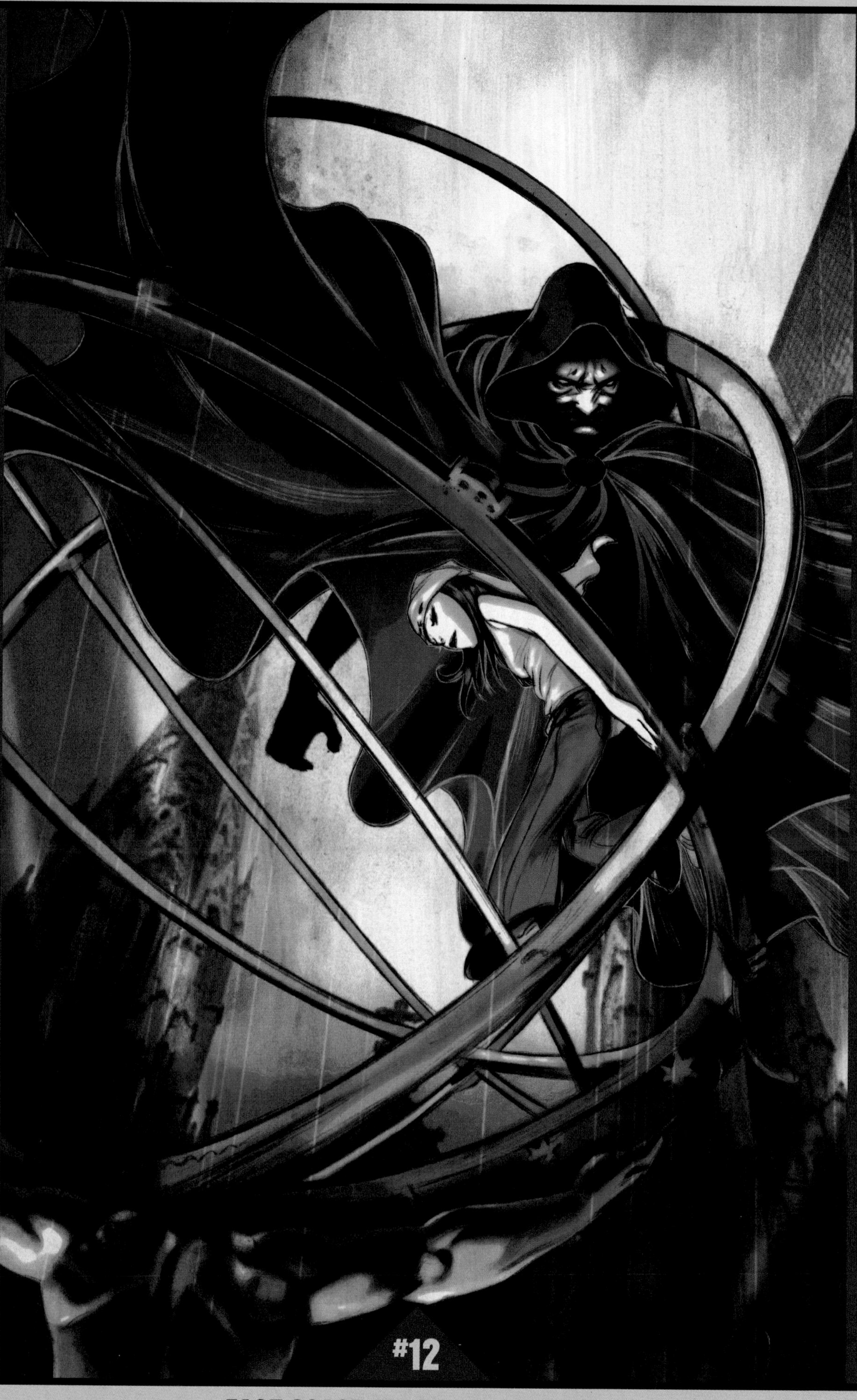
#12

EAST COAST/WEST COAST PART 4

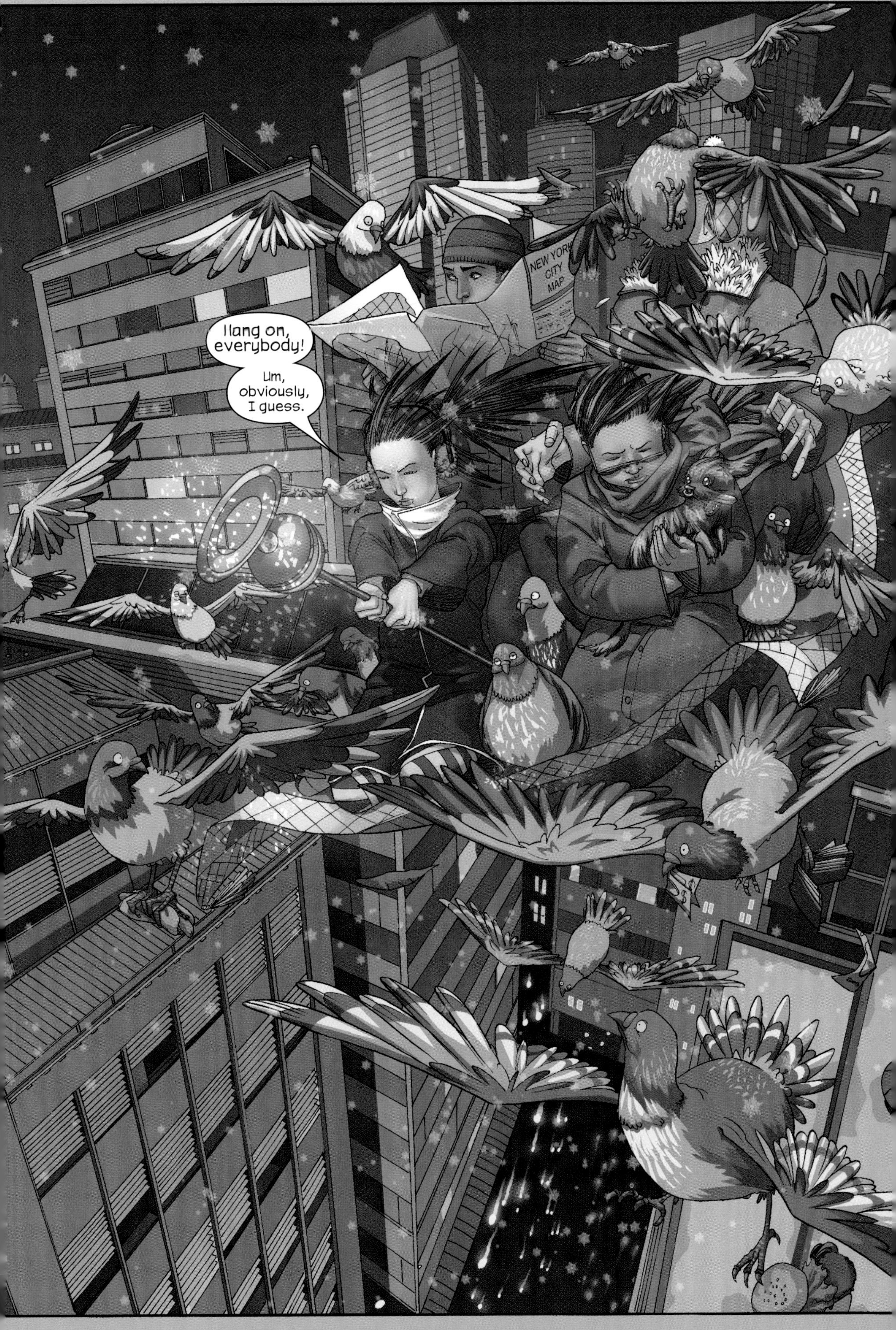
NEW YORK CITY MAP
Hang on, everybody!
Um, obviously, I guess.

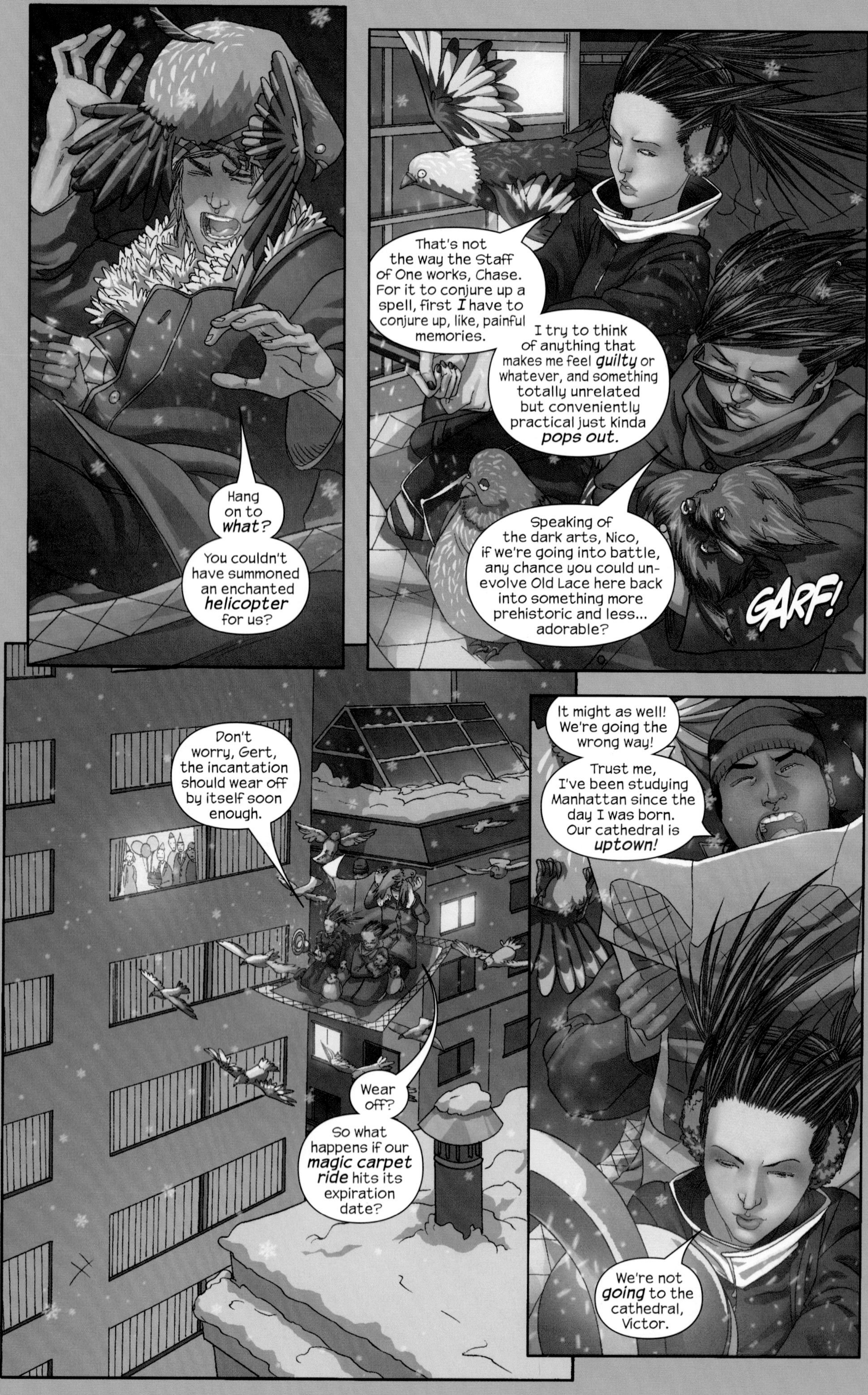

That's not the way the Staff of One works, Chase. For it to conjure up a spell, first I have to conjure up, like, painful memories.
I try to think of anything that makes me feel guilty or whatever, and something totally unrelated but conveniently practical just kinda pops out.
Hang on to what?
You couldn't have summoned an enchanted helicopter for us?
Speaking of the dark arts, Nico, if we're going into battle, any chance you could un-evolve Old Lace here back into something more prehistoric and less... adorable?
GARF!
Don't worry, Gert, the incantation should wear off by itself soon enough.
Wear off?
So what happens if our magic carpet ride hits its expiration date?
It might as well! We're going the wrong way!
Trust me, I've been studying Manhattan since the day I was born. Our cathedral is uptown!
We're not going to the cathedral, Victor.

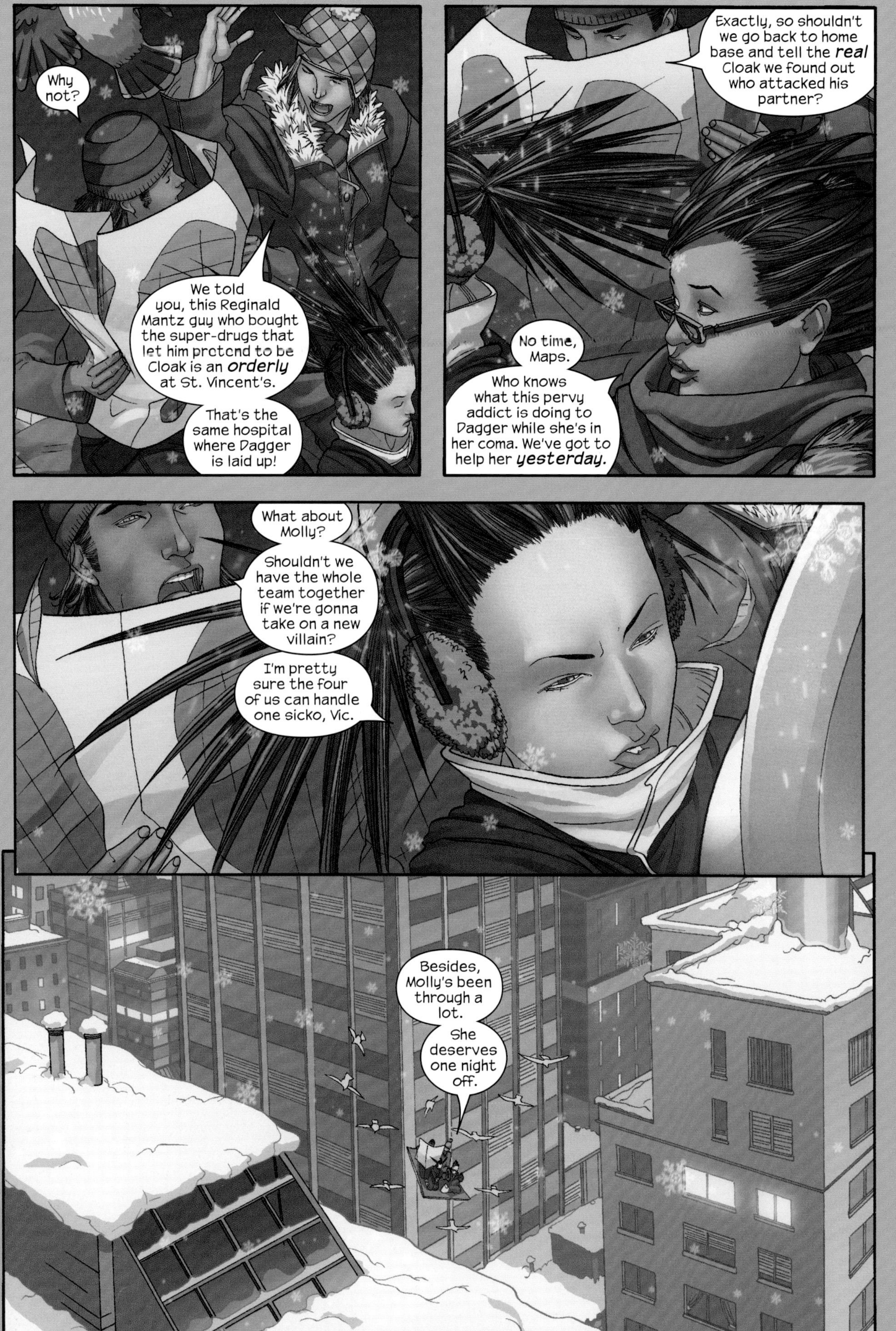
Why not?
We told you, this Reginald Mantz guy who bought the super-drugs that let him pretend to be Cloak is an *orderly* at St. Vincent's.
That's the same hospital where Dagger is laid up!
Exactly, so shouldn't we go back to home base and tell the *real* Cloak we found out who attacked his partner?
No time, Maps.
Who knows what this pervy addict is doing to Dagger while she's in her coma. We've got to help her *yesterday.*
What about Molly?
Shouldn't we have the whole team together if we're gonna take on a new villain?
I'm pretty sure the four of us can handle one sicko, Vic.
Besides, Molly's been through a lot.
She deserves one night off.

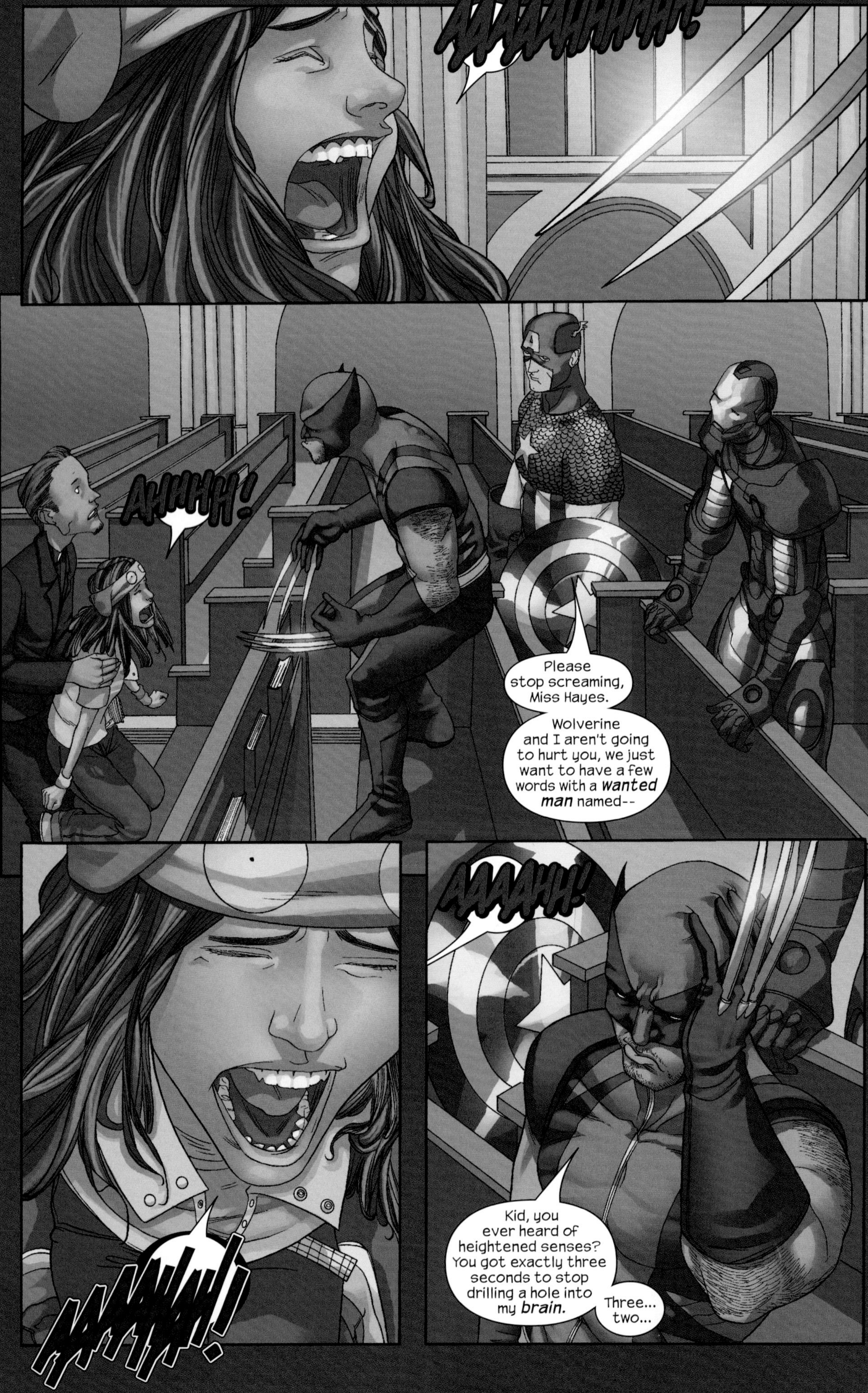
AAAAAAHHHHHH!
AHHHHH!
Please stop screaming, Miss Hayes.
Wolverine and I aren't going to hurt you, we just want to have a few words with a ***wanted man*** named--
AAAAAHH!
AAAAAAAAAAH!
Kid, you ever heard of heightened senses? You got exactly three seconds to stop drilling a hole into my ***brain.***
Three... two...

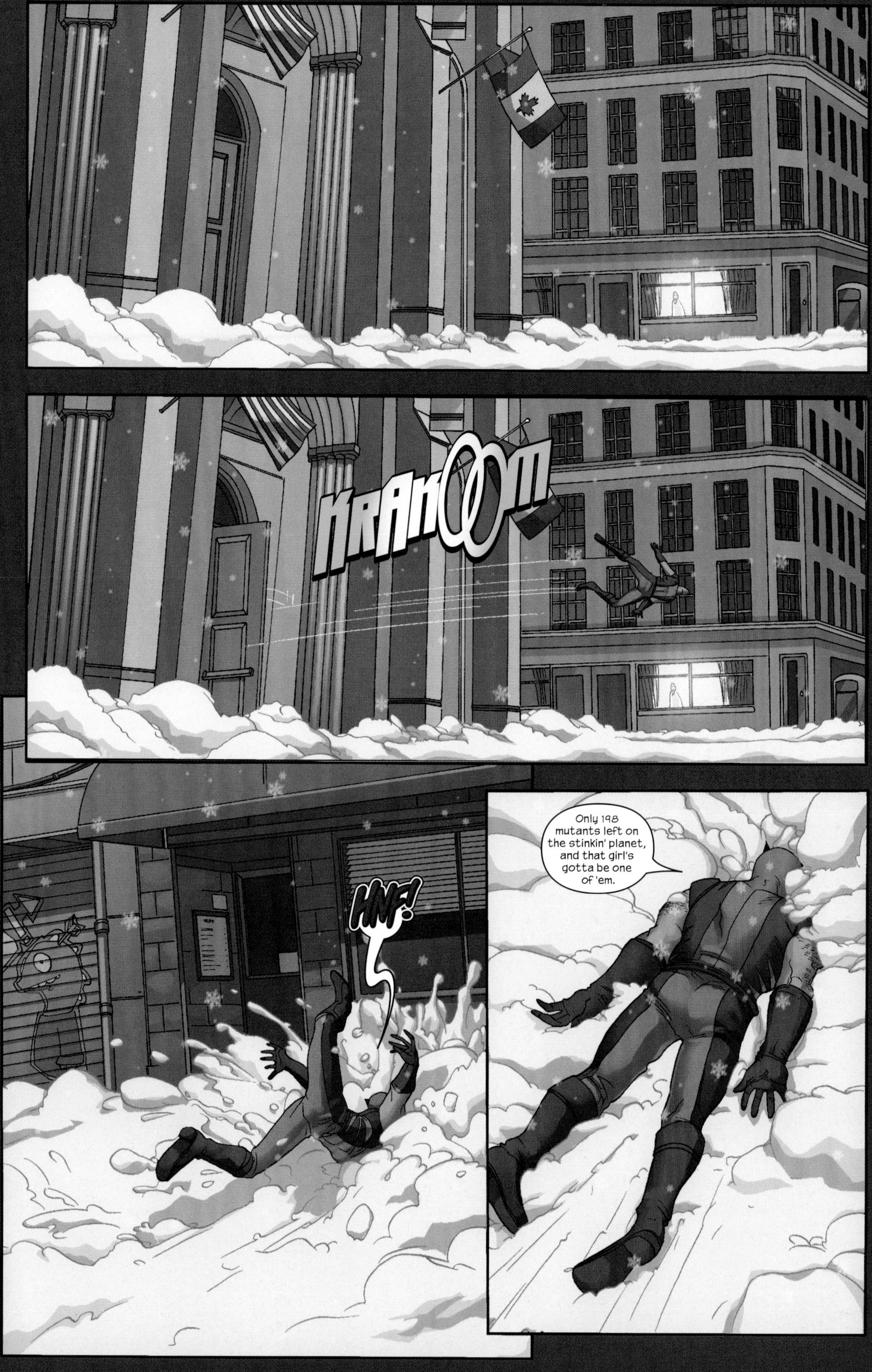

KRAKOOM
HNF!
Only 198 mutants left on the stinkin' planet, and that girl's gotta be one of 'em.

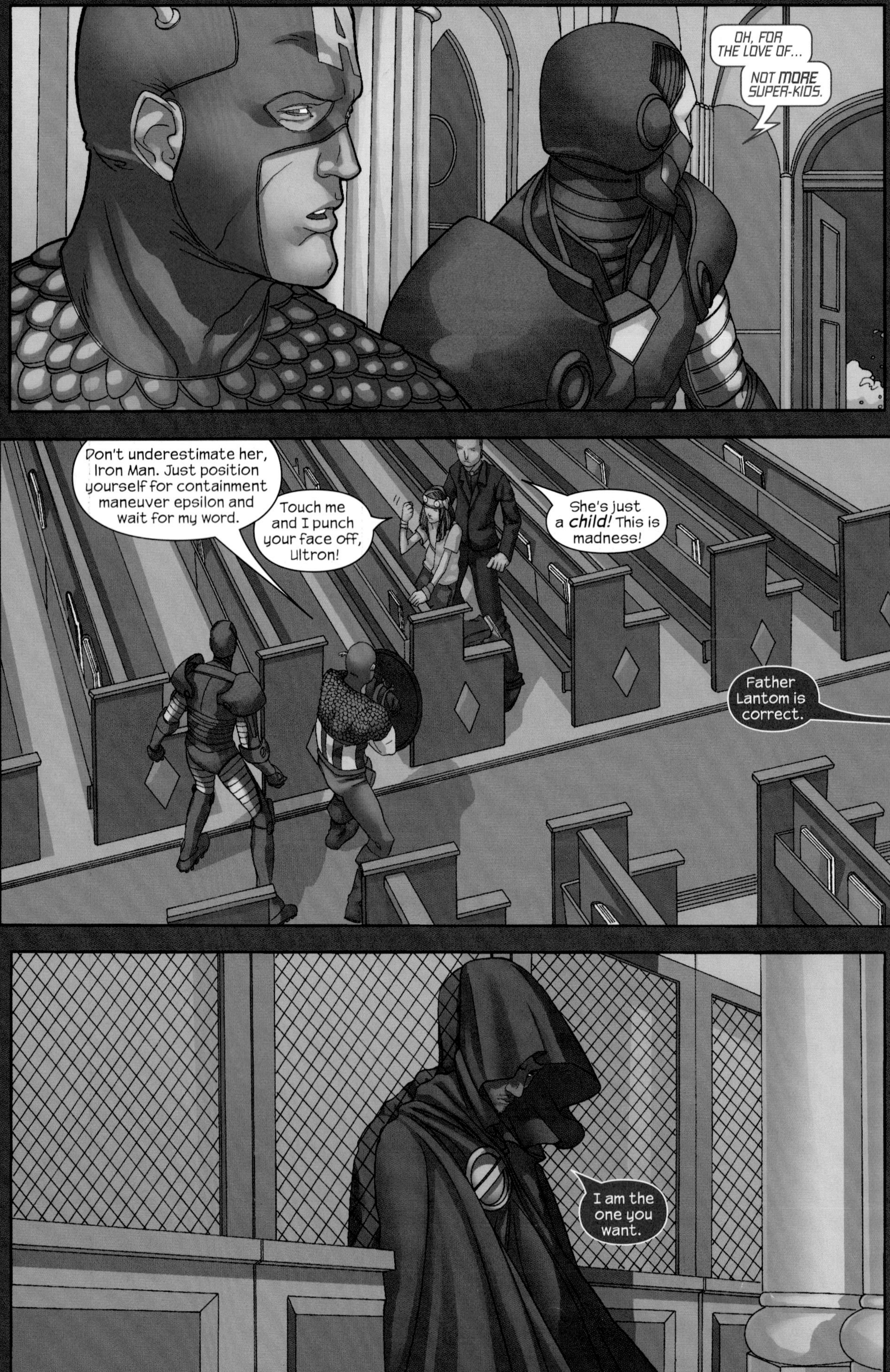
OH, FOR THE LOVE OF...
NOT MORE SUPER-KIDS.
Don't underestimate her, Iron Man. Just position yourself for containment maneuver epsilon and wait for my word.
Touch me and I punch your face off, Ultron!
She's just a child! This is madness!
Father Lantom is correct.
I am the one you want.

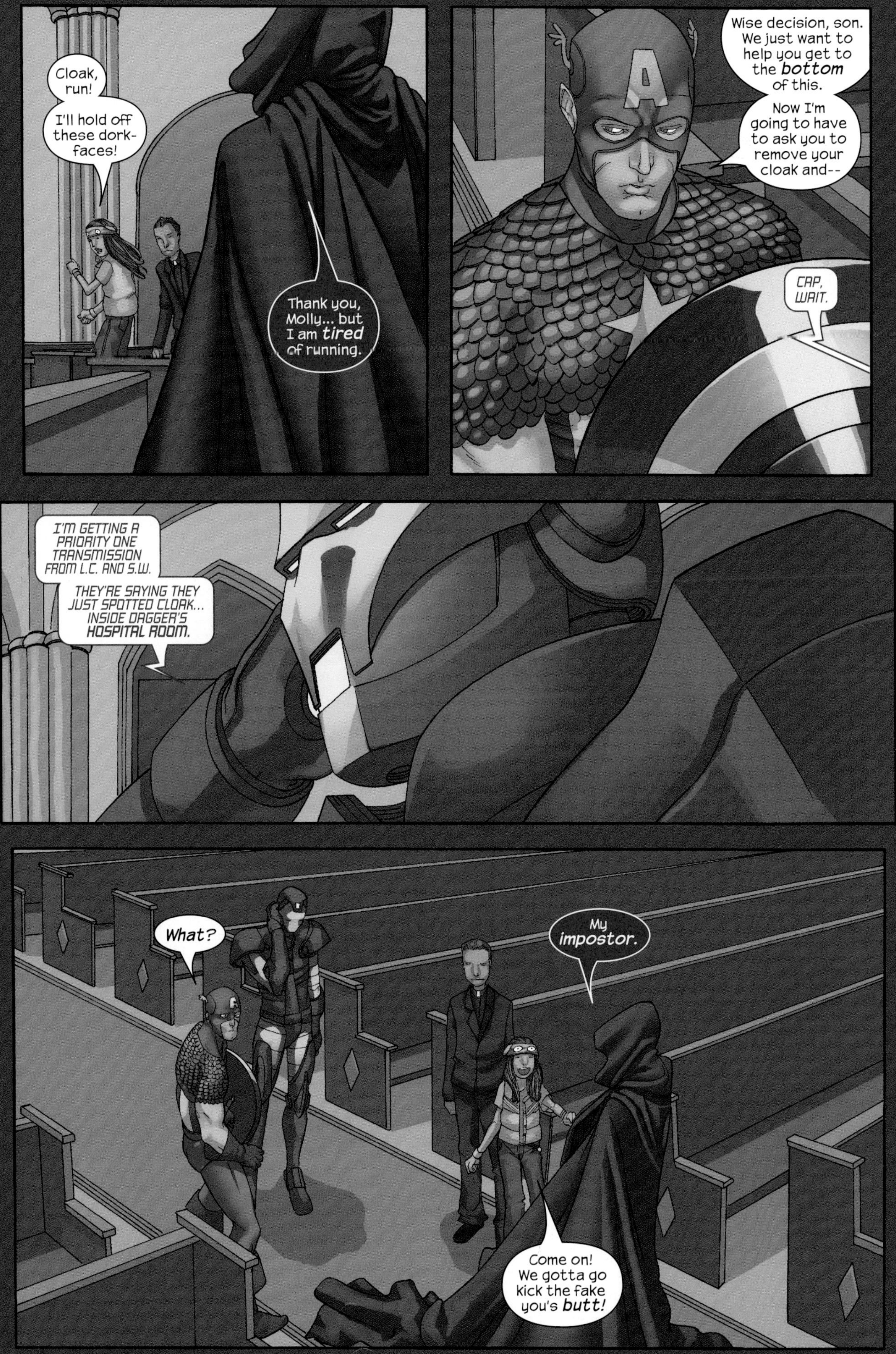
Cloak, run!
I'll hold off these dork-faces!
Thank you, Molly... but I am tired of running.
Wise decision, son. We just want to help you get to the bottom of this.
Now I'm going to have to ask you to remove your cloak and--
CAP, WAIT.
I'M GETTING A PRIORITY ONE TRANSMISSION FROM L.C. AND S.W.
THEY'RE SAYING THEY JUST SPOTTED CLOAK... INSIDE DAGGER'S HOSPITAL ROOM.
What?
My impostor.
Come on! We gotta go kick the fake you's butt!

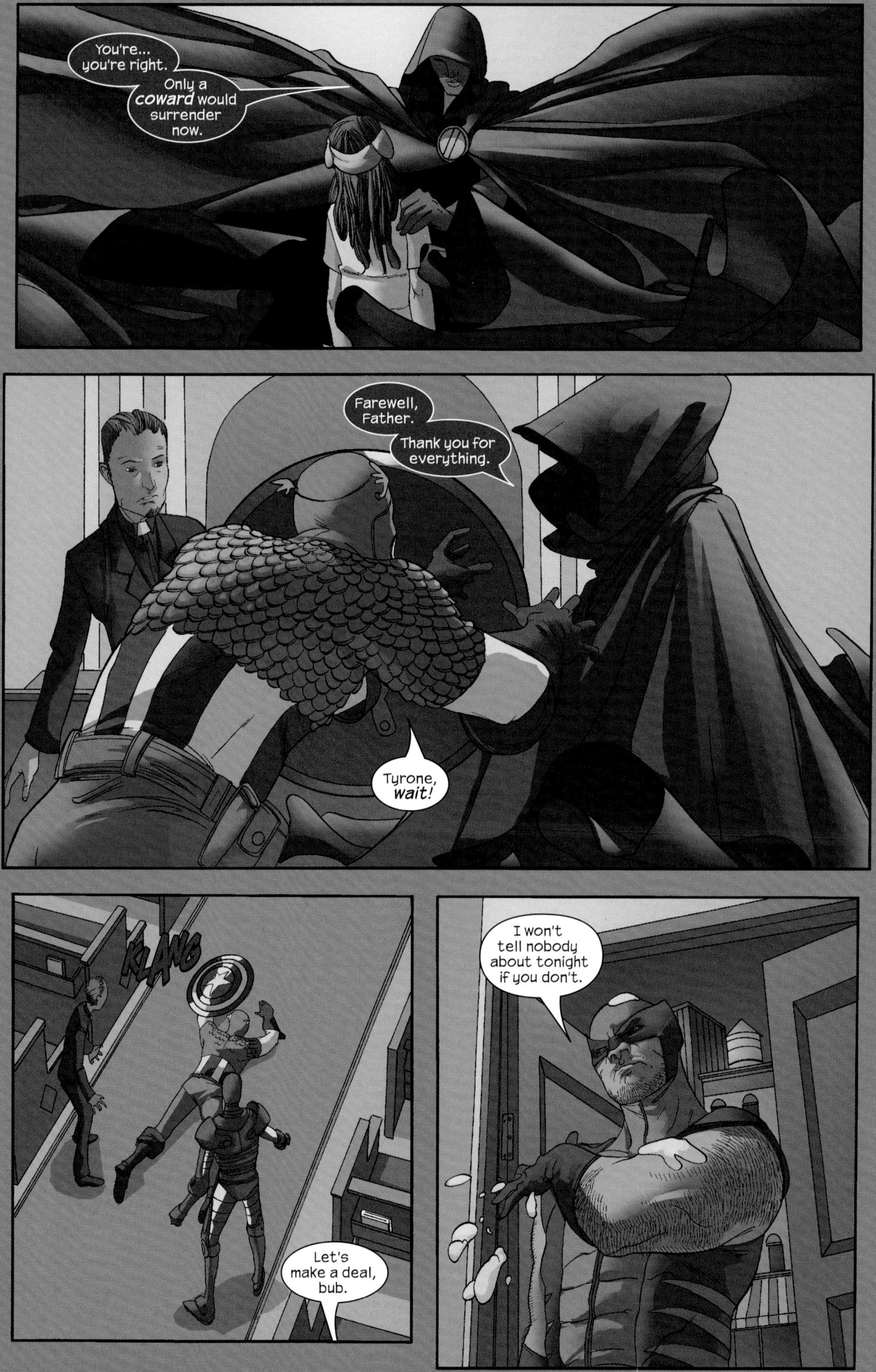
You're... you're right.
Only a coward would surrender now.
Farewell, Father.
Thank you for everything.
Tyrone, wait!
KLANG
Let's make a deal, bub.
I won't tell nobody about tonight if you don't.

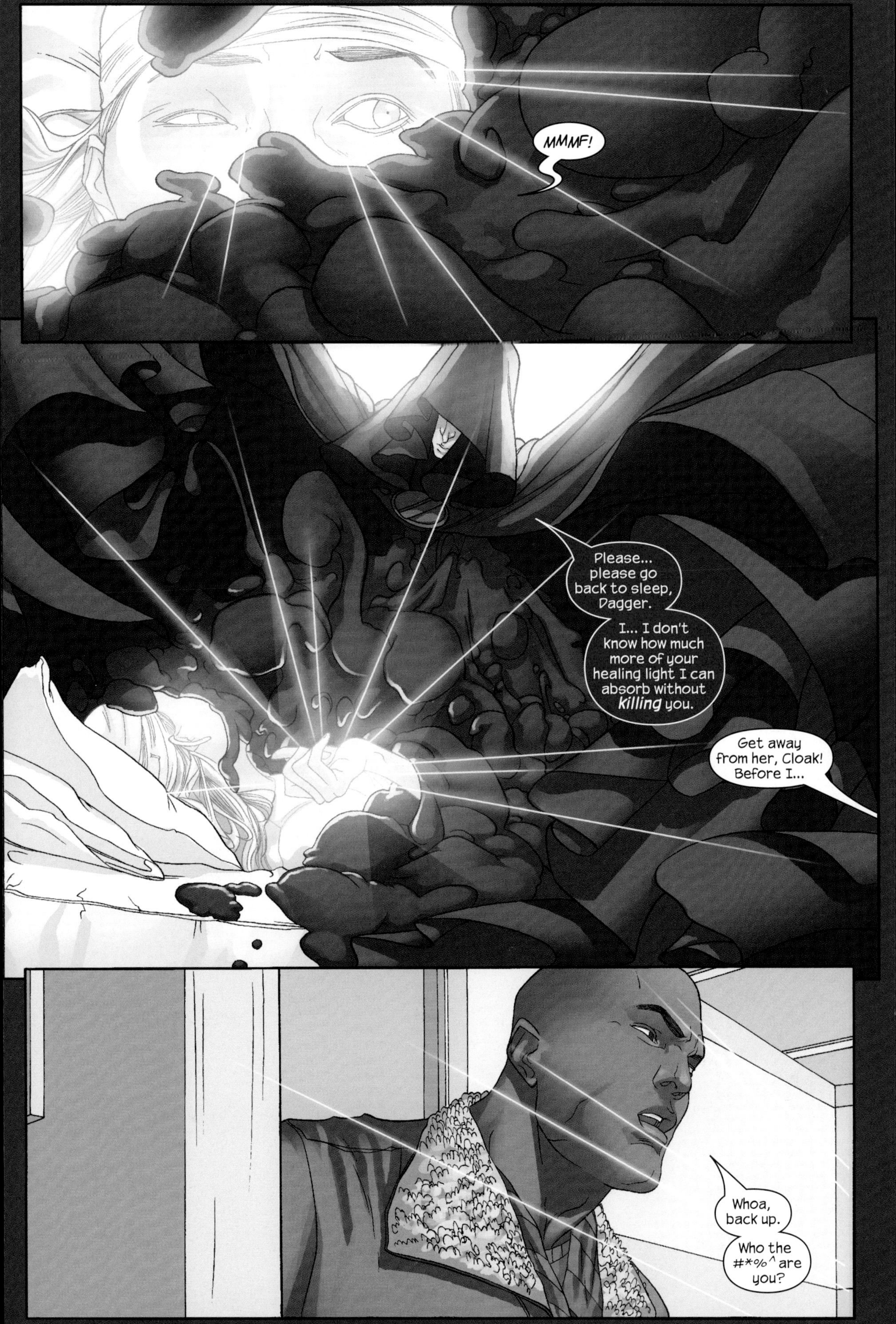
MMMF!
Please... please go back to sleep, Dagger.
I... I don't know how much more of your healing light I can absorb without *killing* you.
Get away from her, Cloak! Before I...
Whoa, back up.
Who the #*%^ are you?

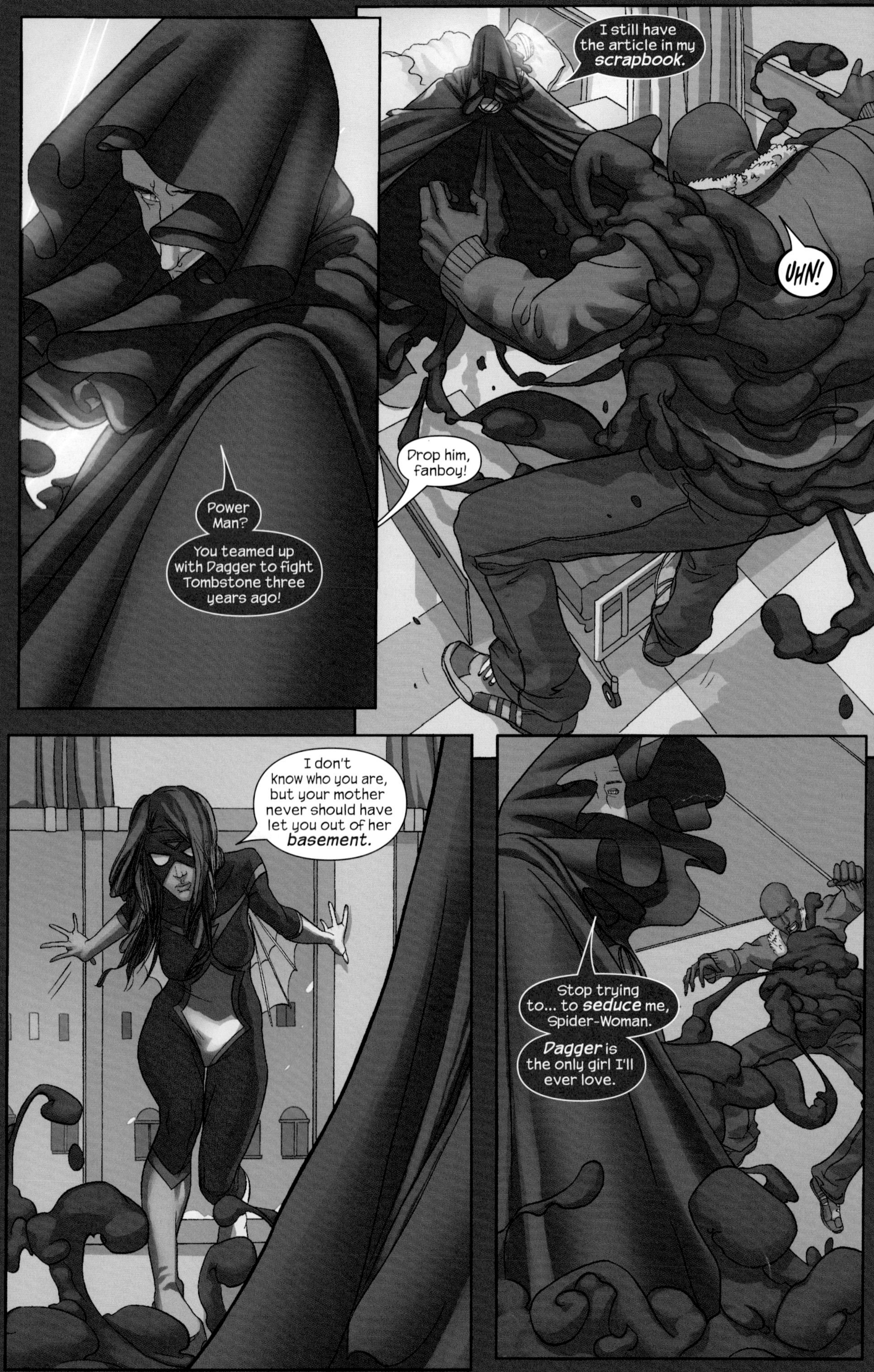
Power Man?
You teamed up with Dagger to fight Tombstone three years ago!
I still have the article in my scrapbook.
UHN!
Drop him, fanboy!
I don't know who you are, but your mother never should have let you out of her basement.
Stop trying to... to seduce me, Spider-Woman.
Dagger is the only girl I'll ever love.

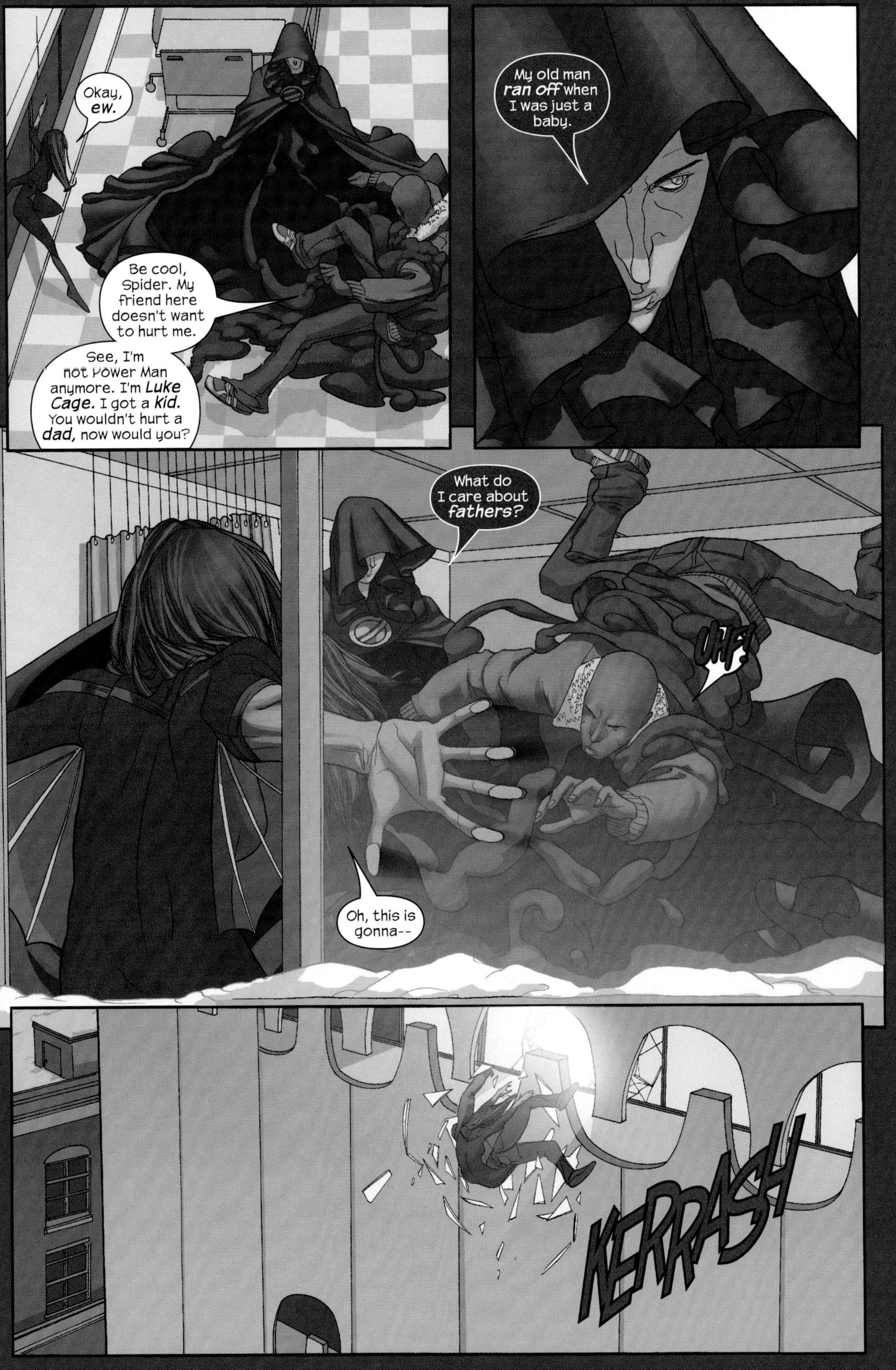

Okay, *ew.*
Be cool, Spider. My friend here doesn't want to hurt me.
See, I'm not Power Man anymore. I'm *Luke Cage.* I got a *kid.* You wouldn't hurt a *dad,* now would you?
My old man *ran off* when I was just a baby.
What do I care about *fathers?*
UHF!
Oh, this is gonna--
KERRASH

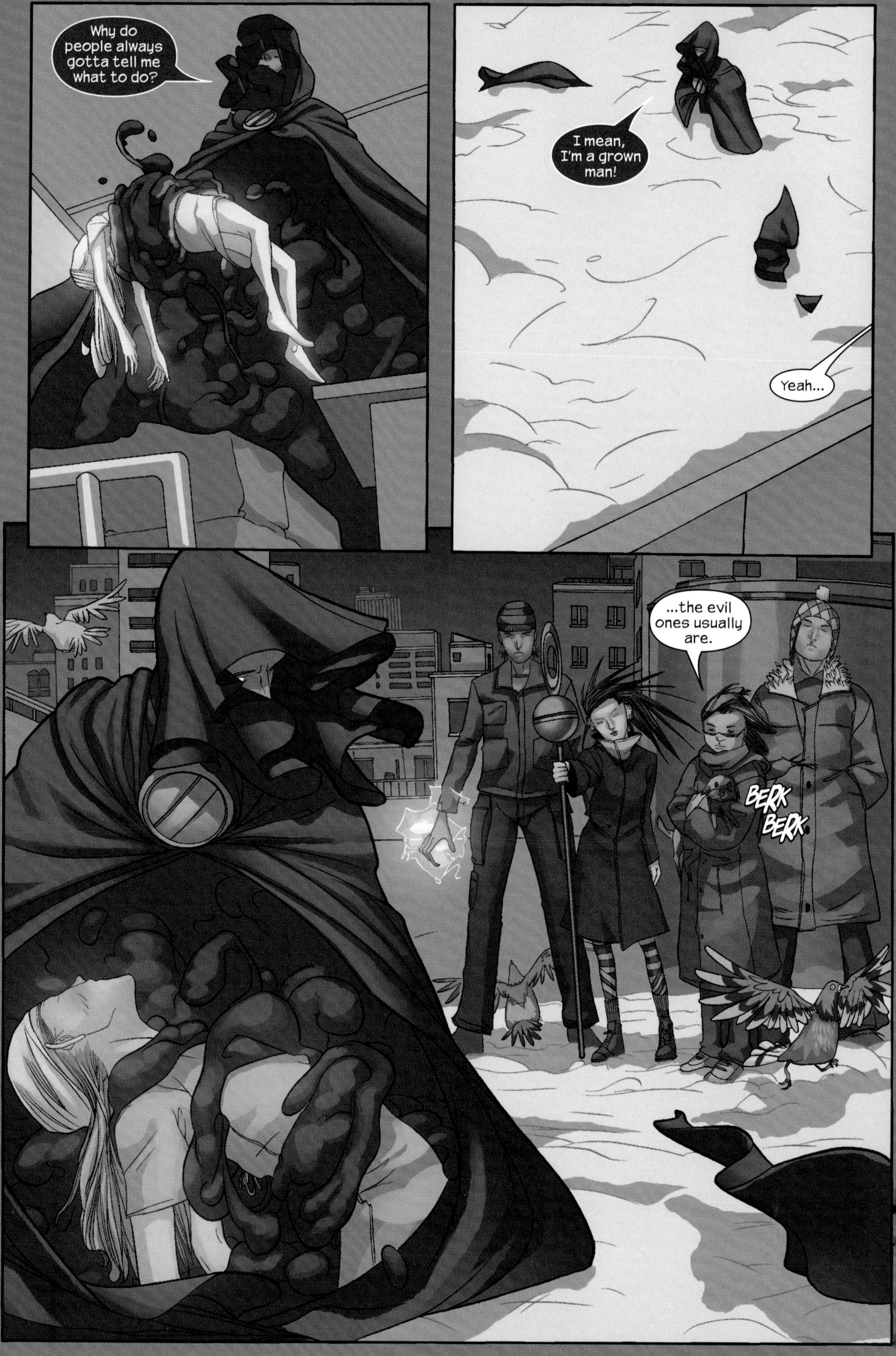

Why do people always gotta tell me what to do?
I mean, I'm a grown man!
Yeah...
...the evil ones usually are.
BERK BERK

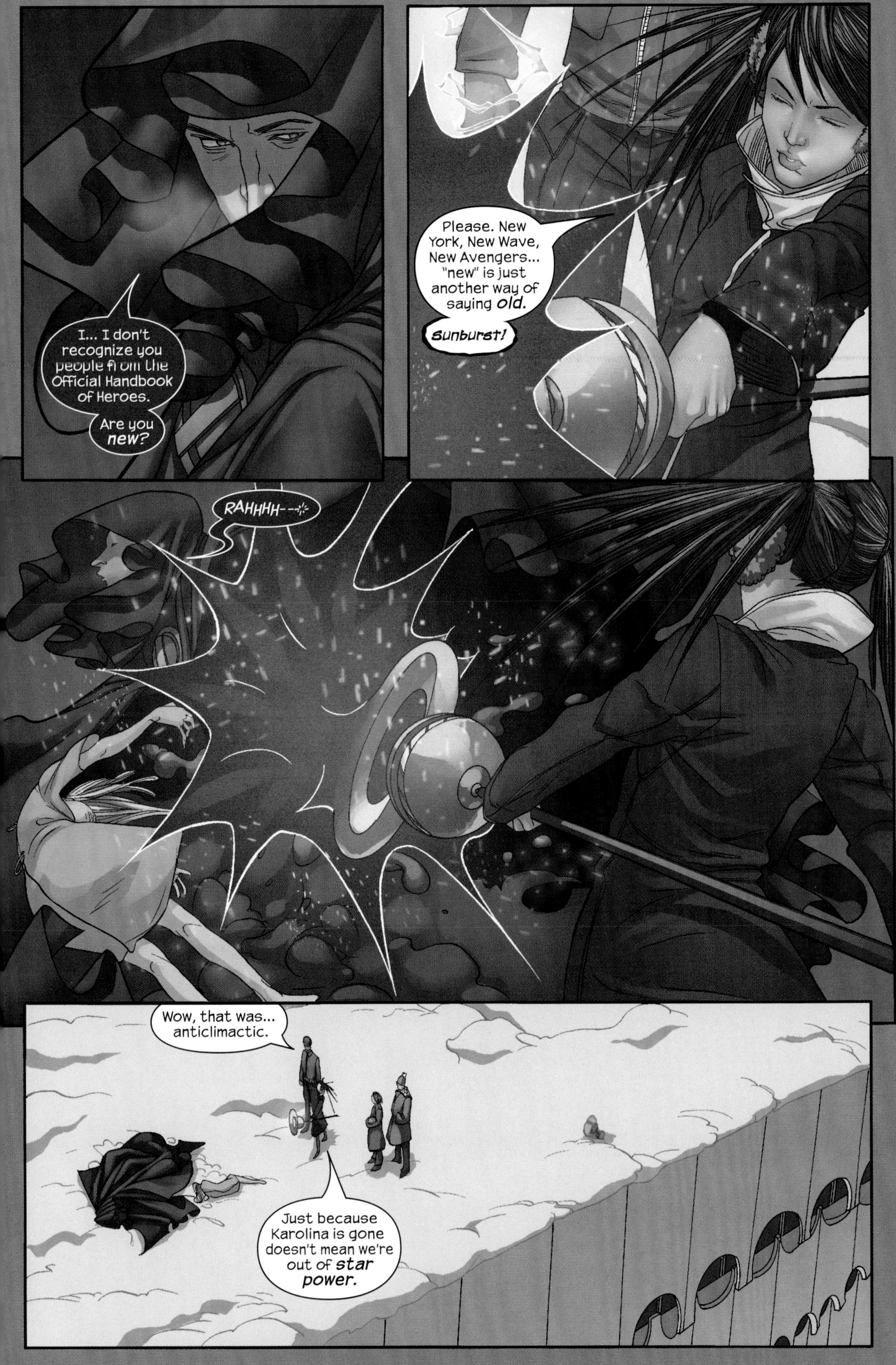
I... I don't recognize you people from the Official Handbook of Heroes.
Are you new?
Please. New York, New Wave, New Avengers... "new" is just another way of saying old.
Sunburst!
RAHHHH--
Wow, that was... anticlimactic.
Just because Karolina is gone doesn't mean we're out of star power.

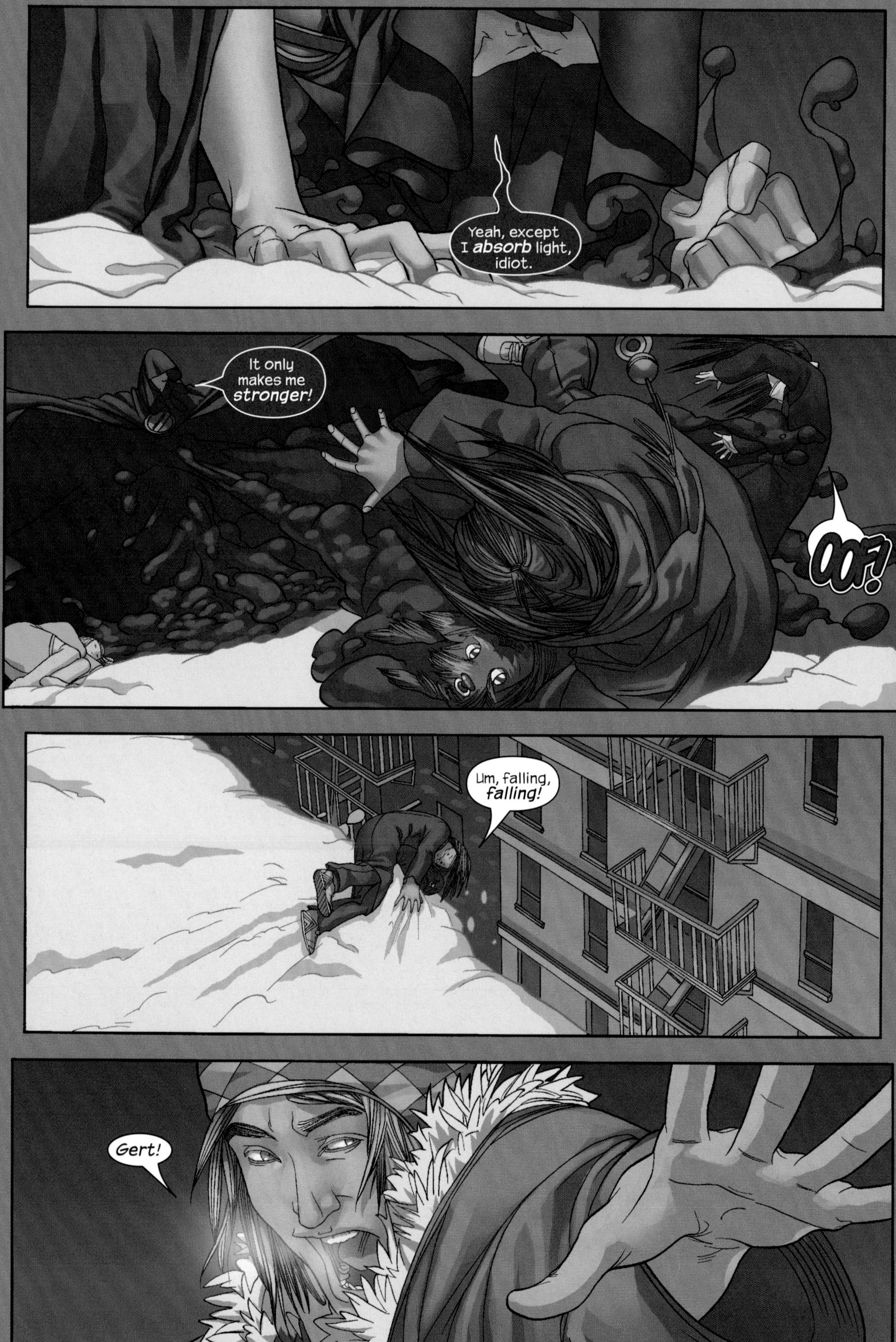
Yeah, except I *absorb* light, idiot.
It only makes me *stronger!*
OOF!
Um, falling, *falling!*
Gert!

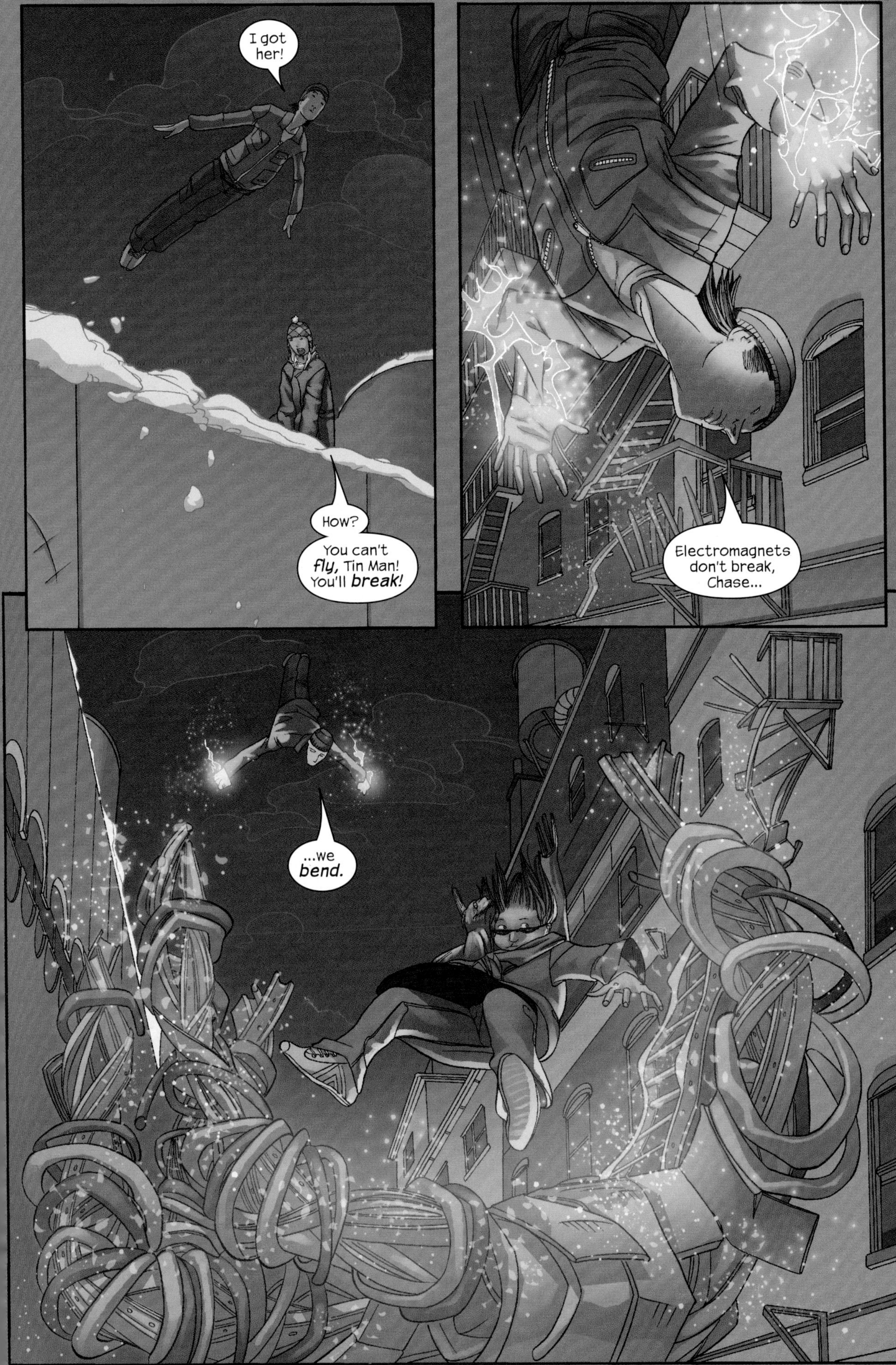
I got her!
How?
You can't *fly,* Tin Man! You'll *break!*
Electromagnets don't break, Chase...
...we *bend.*

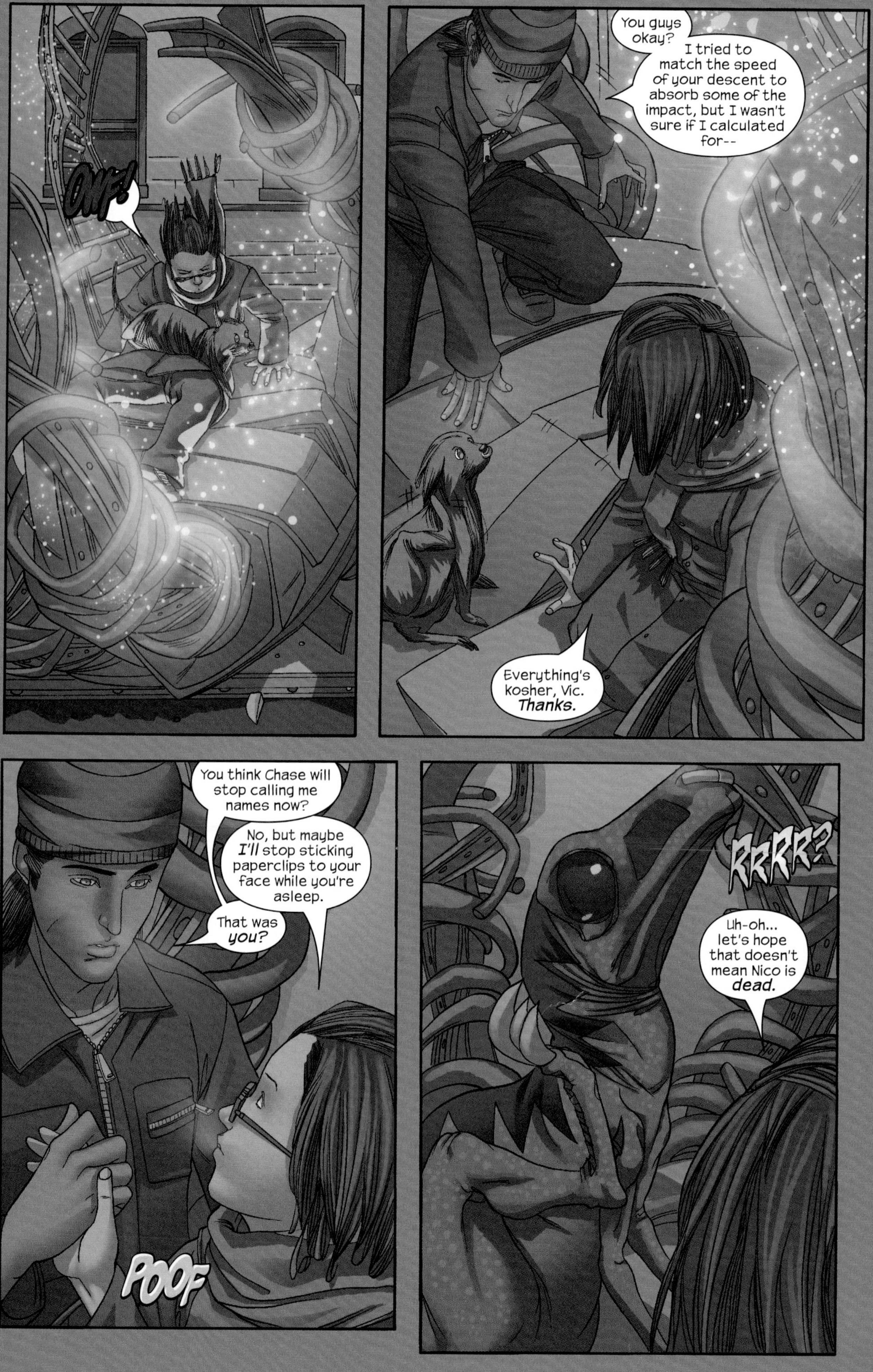
OMF!
You guys okay?
I tried to match the speed of your descent to absorb some of the impact, but I wasn't sure if I calculated for--
Everything's kosher, Vic. Thanks.
You think Chase will stop calling me names now?
No, but maybe I'll stop sticking paperclips to your face while you're asleep.
That was you?
POOF
RRRR?
Uh-oh... let's hope that doesn't mean Nico is dead.

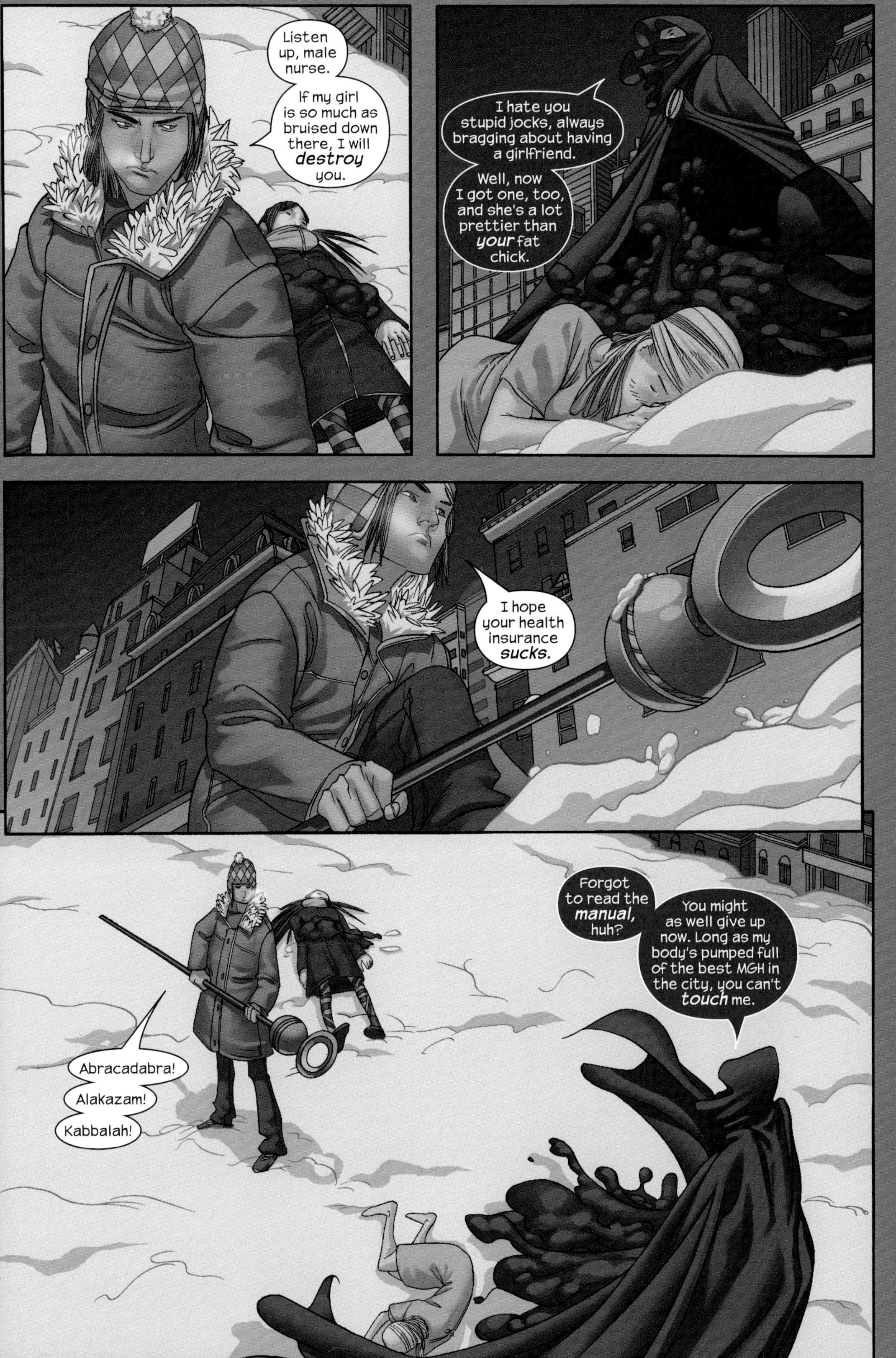

Listen up, male nurse.
If my girl is so much as bruised down there, I will *destroy* you.
I hate you stupid jocks, always bragging about having a girlfriend.
Well, now I got one, too, and she's a lot prettier than *your* fat chick.
I hope your health insurance *sucks.*
Abracadabra!
Alakazam!
Kabbalah!
Forgot to read the *manual,* huh?
You might as well give up now. Long as my body's pumped full of the best MGH in the city, you can't *touch* me.

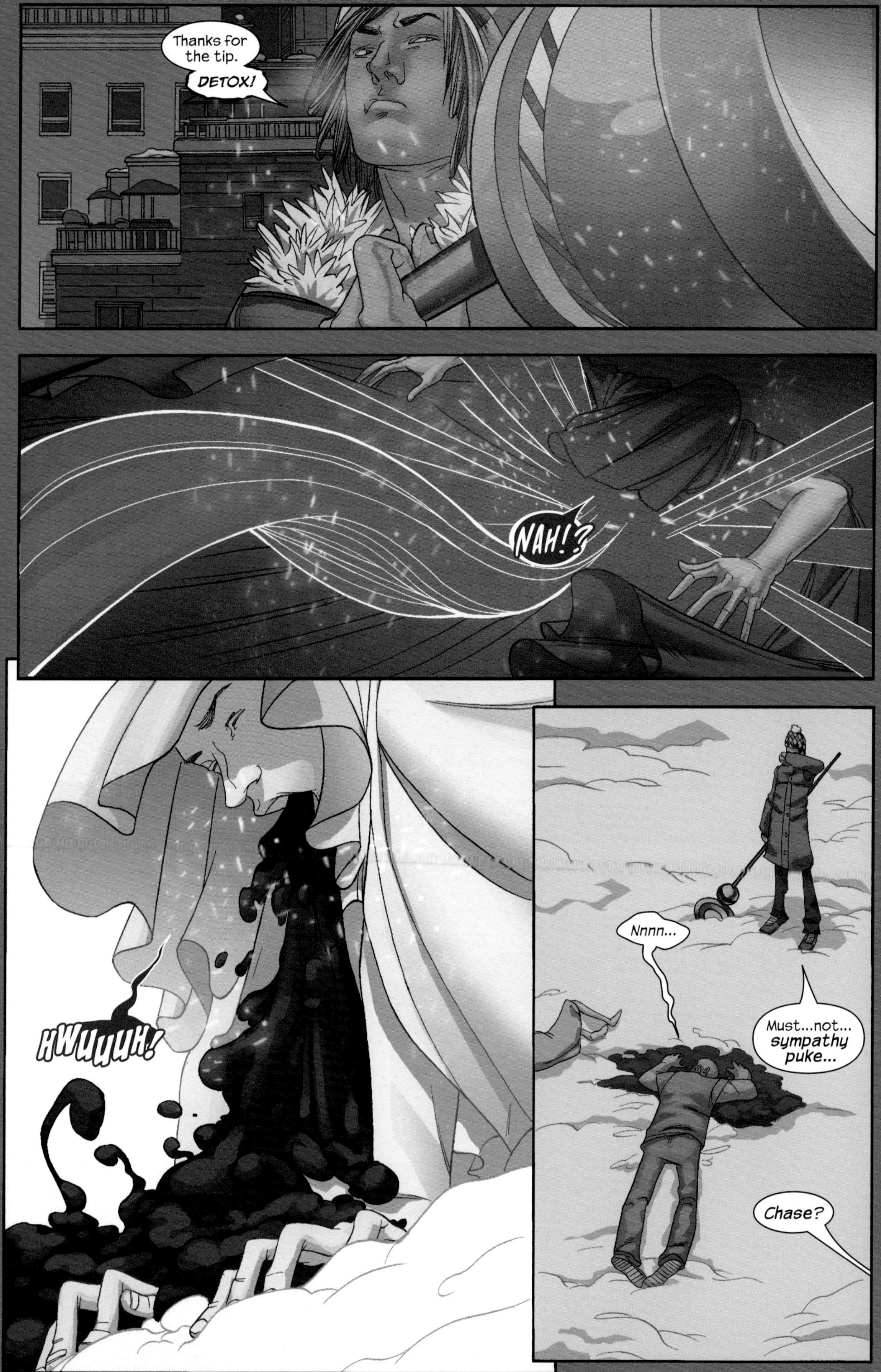

Thanks for the tip.
DETOX!
NAH!?
HWUUUUH!
Nnnn...
Must...not... sympathy puke...
Chase?

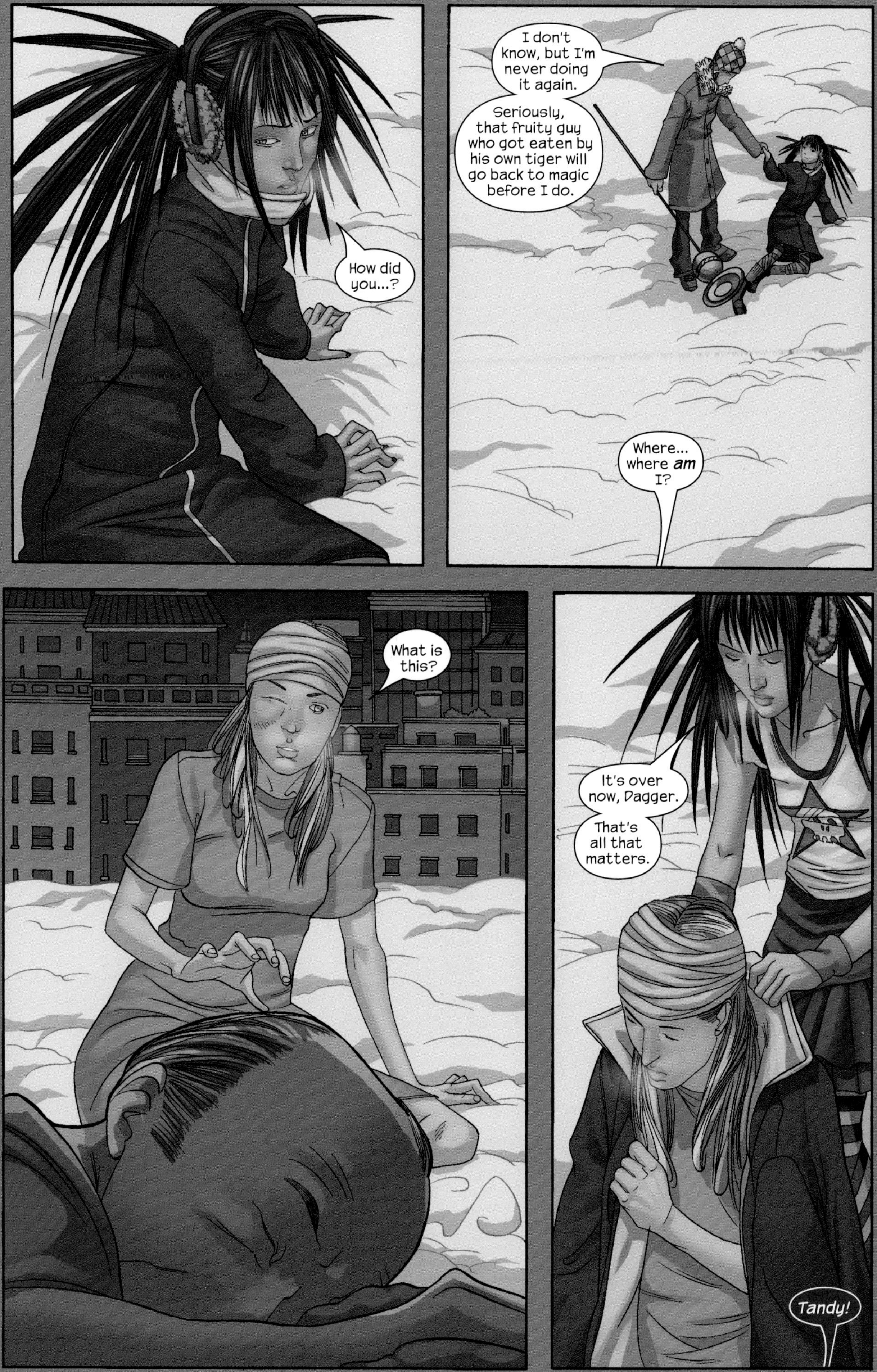
How did you...?
I don't know, but I'm never doing it again.
Seriously, that fruity guy who got eaten by his own tiger will go back to magic before I do.
Where... where *am* I?
What is this?
It's over now, Dagger.
That's all that matters.
Tandy!

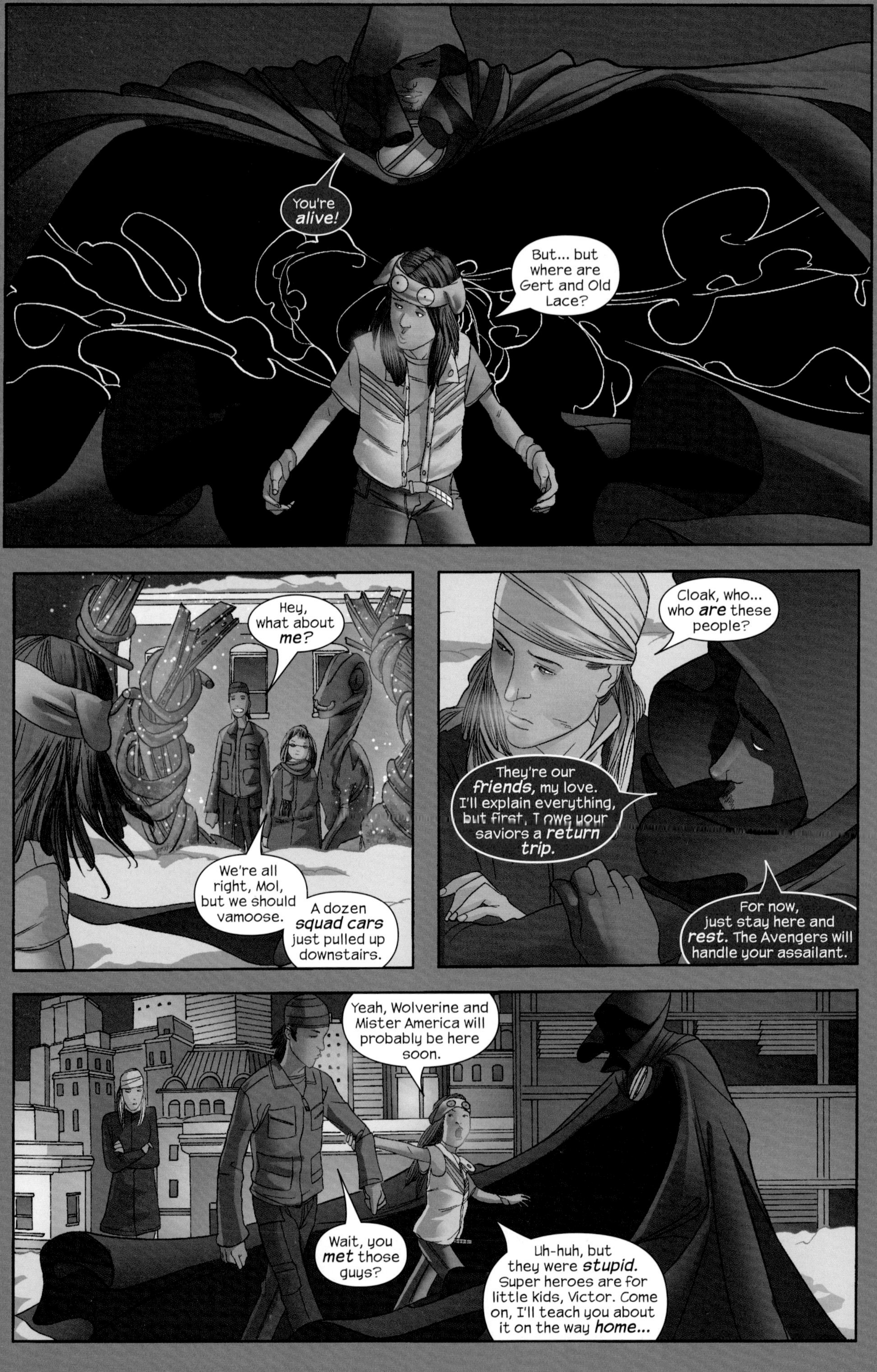
You're alive!
But... but where are Gert and Old Lace?
Hey, what about me?
We're all right, Mol, but we should vamoose.
A dozen squad cars just pulled up downstairs.
Cloak, who... who are these people?
They're our friends, my love. I'll explain everything, but first, I owe your saviors a return trip.
For now, just stay here and rest. The Avengers will handle your assailant.
Yeah, Wolverine and Mister America will probably be here soon.
Wait, you met those guys?
Uh-huh, but they were stupid. Super heroes are for little kids, Victor. Come on, I'll teach you about it on the way home...

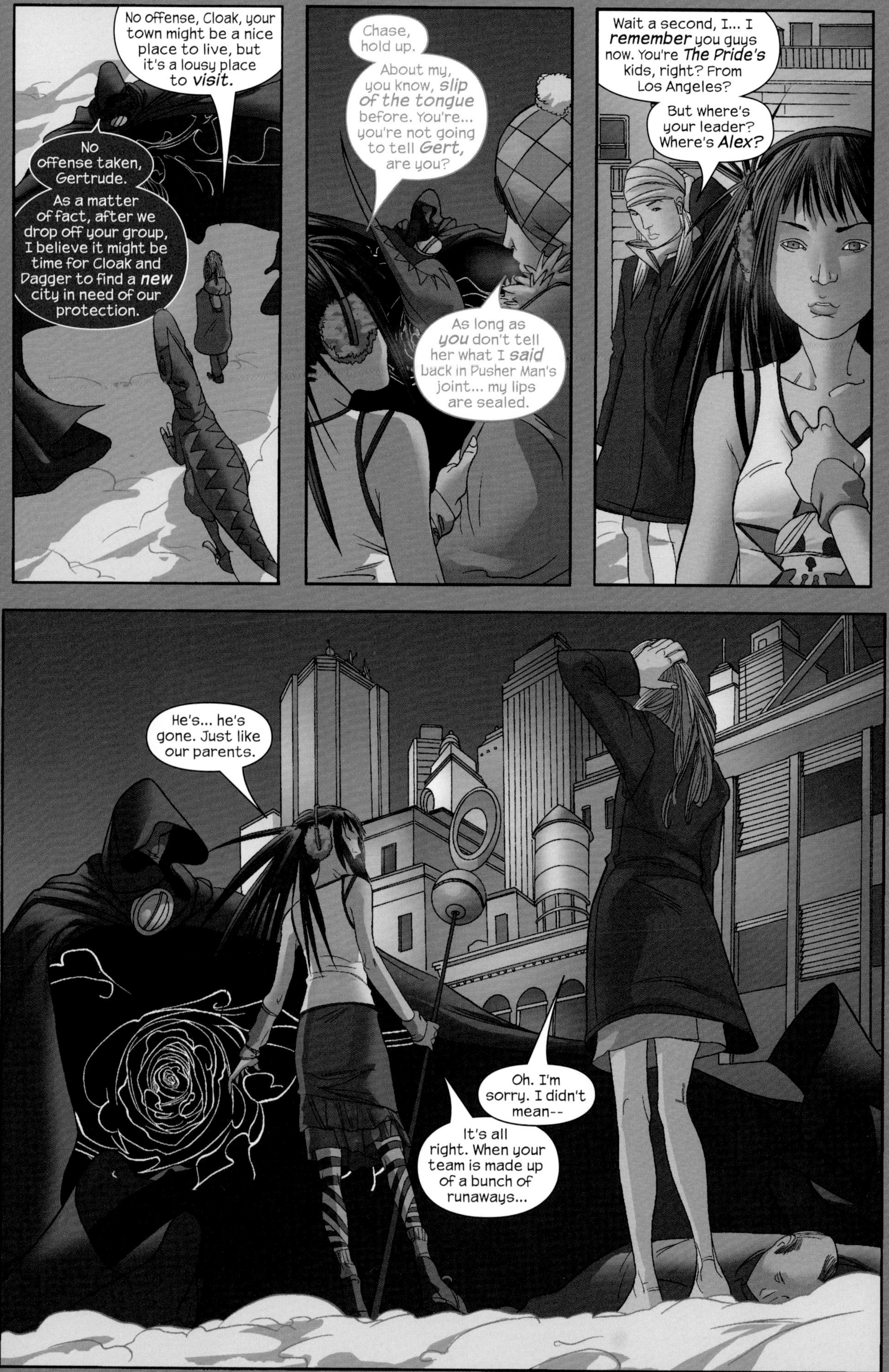
No offense, Cloak, your town might be a nice place to live, but it's a lousy place to *visit.*
No offense taken, Gertrude.
As a matter of fact, after we drop off your group, I believe it might be time for Cloak and Dagger to find a *new* city in need of our protection.
Chase, hold up.
About my, you know, *slip of the tongue* before. You're... you're not going to tell *Gert,* are you?
As long as *you* don't tell her what I *said* back in Pusher Man's joint... my lips are sealed.
Wait a second, I... I *remember* you guys now. You're *The Pride's* kids, right? From Los Angeles?
But where's your leader? Where's *Alex?*
He's... he's gone. Just like our parents.
Oh. I'm sorry. I didn't mean--
It's all right. When your team is made up of a bunch of runaways...

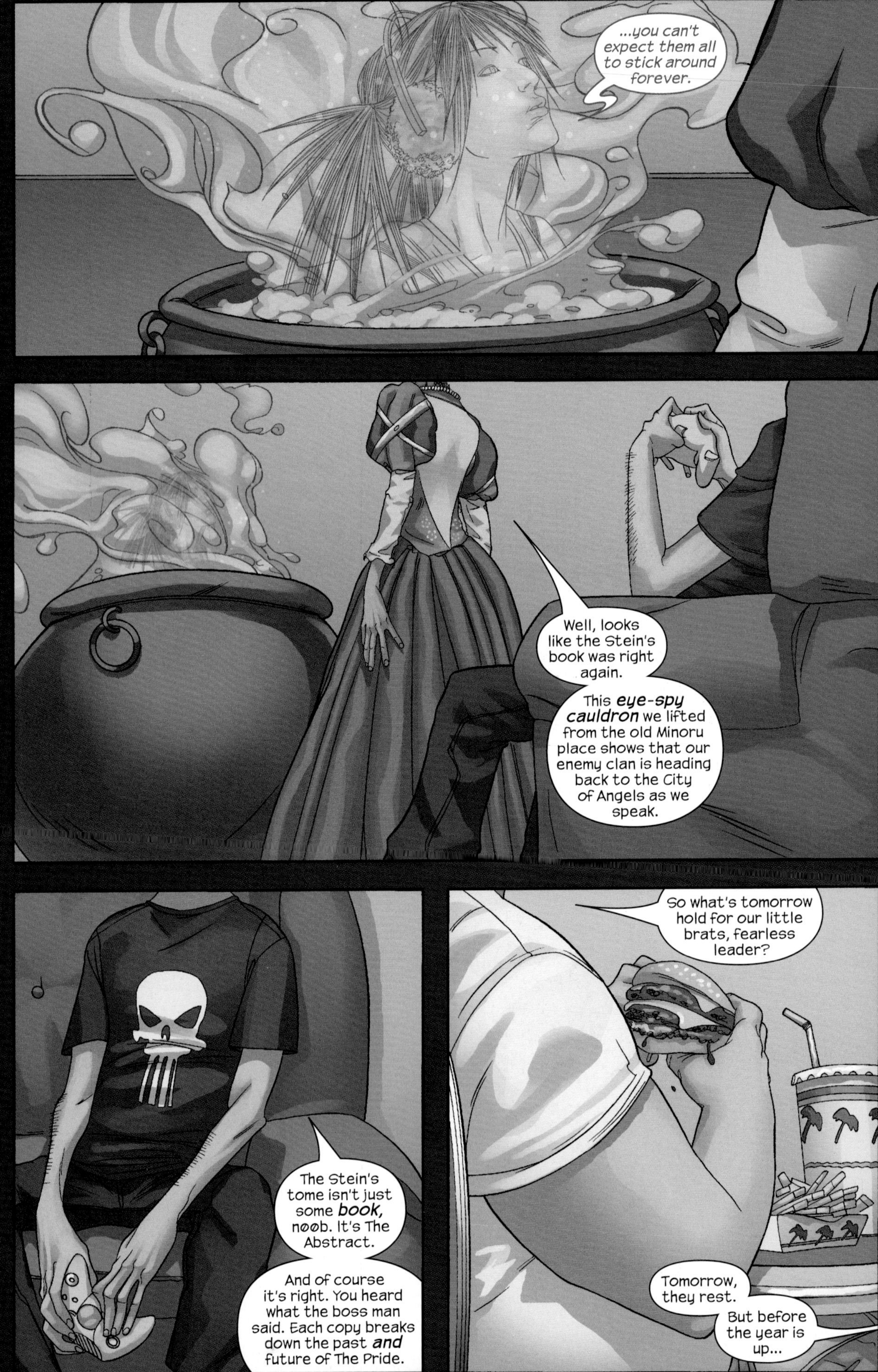
...you can't expect them all to stick around forever.
Well, looks like the Stein's book was right again.
This **eye-spy cauldron** we lifted from the old Minoru place shows that our enemy clan is heading back to the City of Angels as we speak.
The Stein's tome isn't just some **book,** n00b. It's The Abstract.
And of course it's right. You heard what the boss man said. Each copy breaks down the past **and** future of The Pride.
So what's tomorrow hold for our little brats, fearless leader?
Tomorrow, they rest.
But before the year is up...

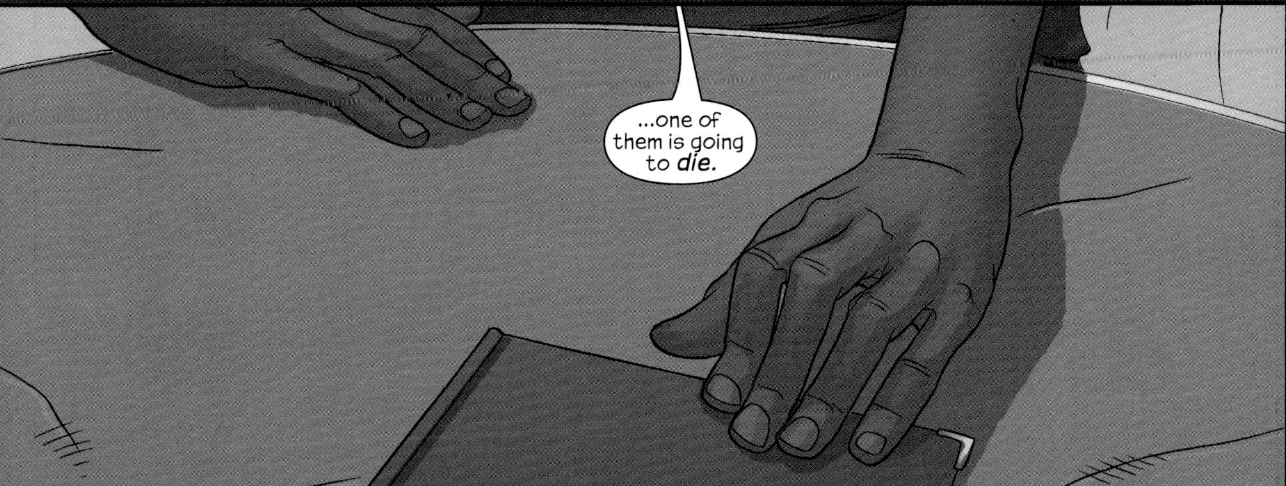
...one of them is going to *die.*

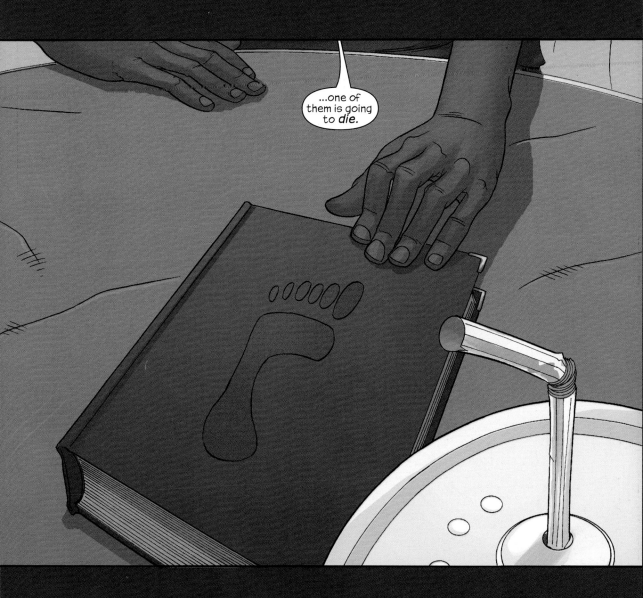

To Be Continued...

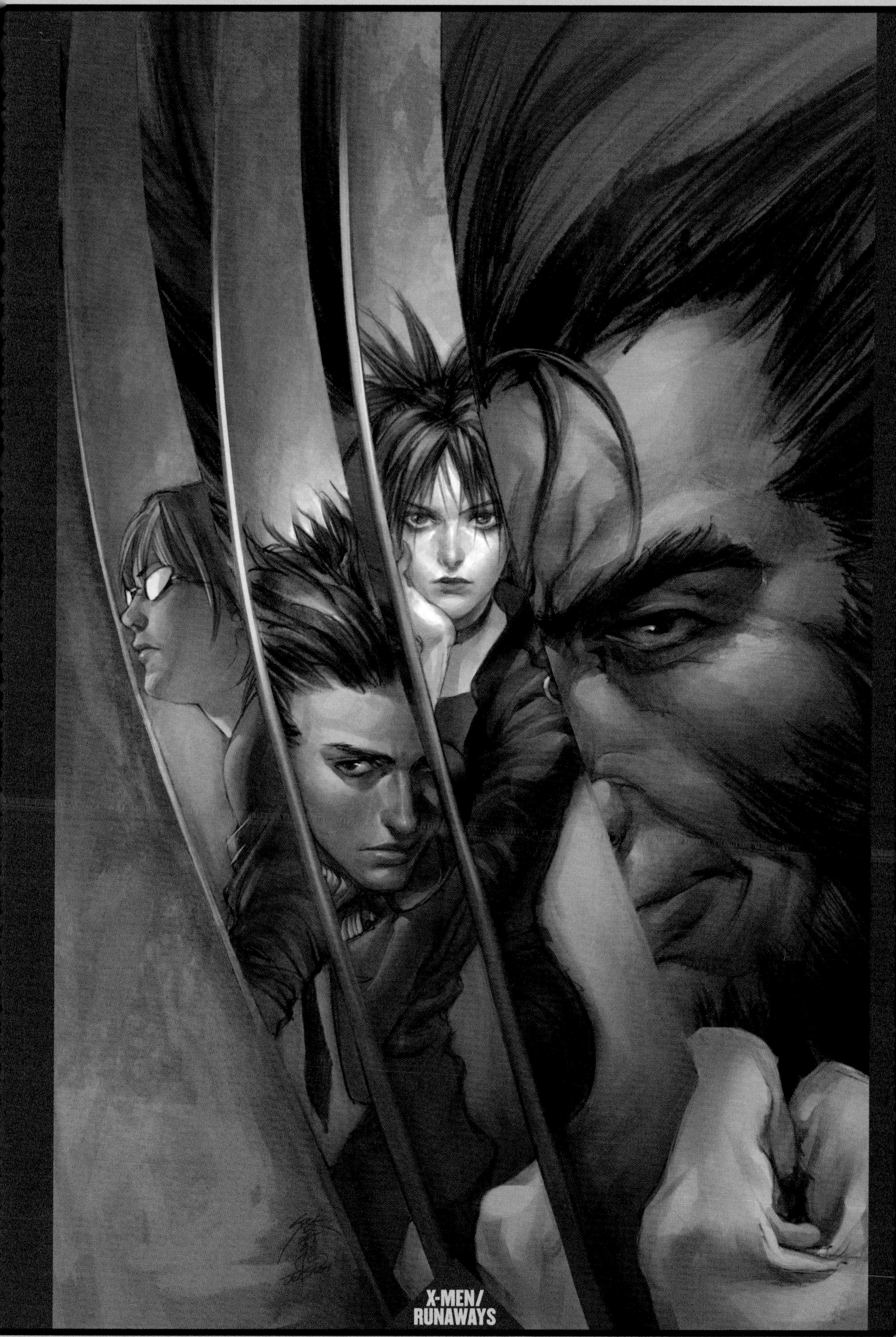
X-MEN/
RUNAWAYS

FREE

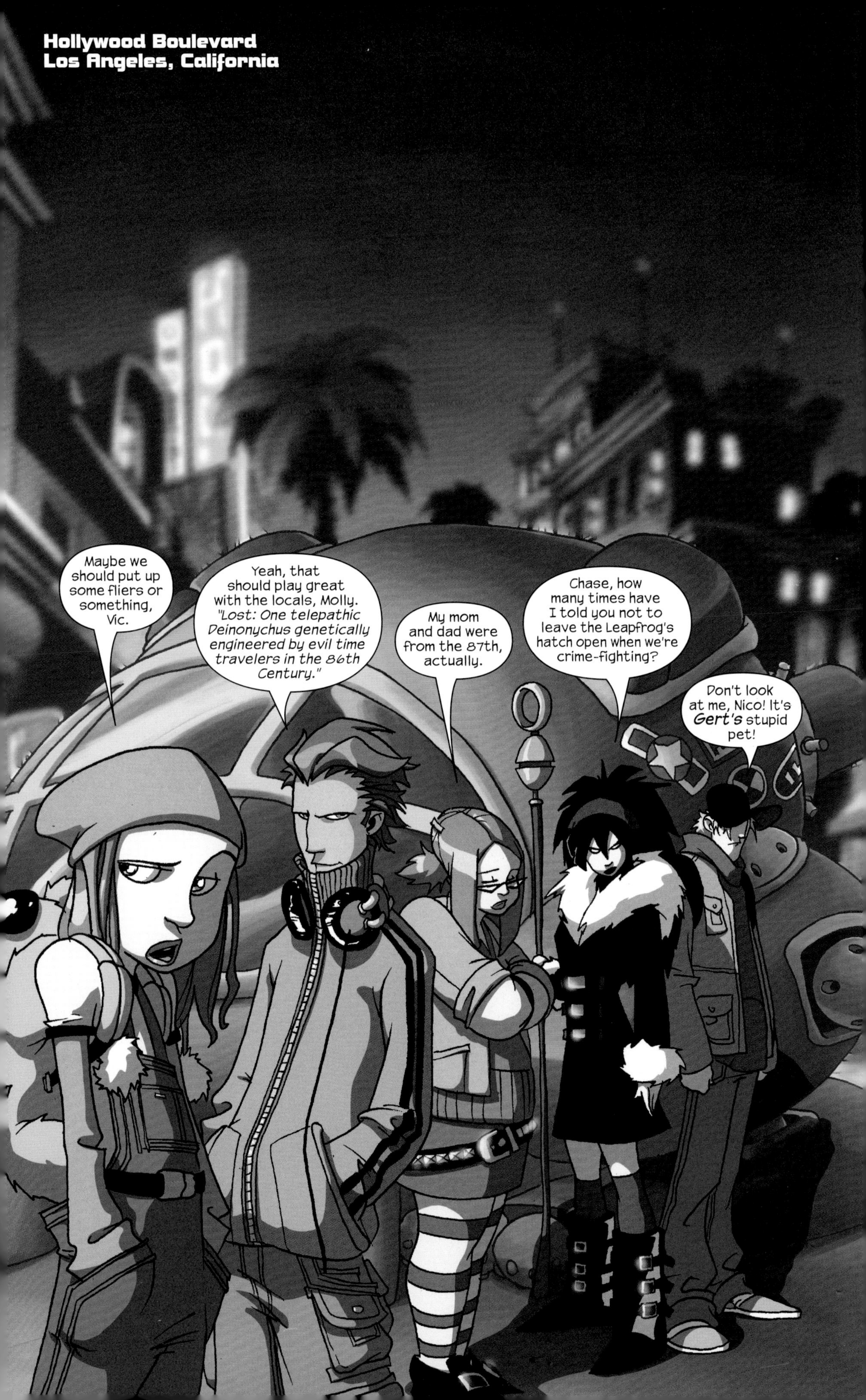
Hollywood Boulevard
Los Angeles, California
Maybe we should put up some fliers or something, Vic.
Yeah, that should play great with the locals, Molly. *"Lost: One telepathic Deinonychus genetically engineered by evil time travelers in the 86th Century."*
My mom and dad were from the 87th, actually.
Chase, how many times have I told you not to leave the Leapfrog's hatch open when we're crime-fighting?
Don't look at me, Nico! It's ***Gert's*** stupid pet!

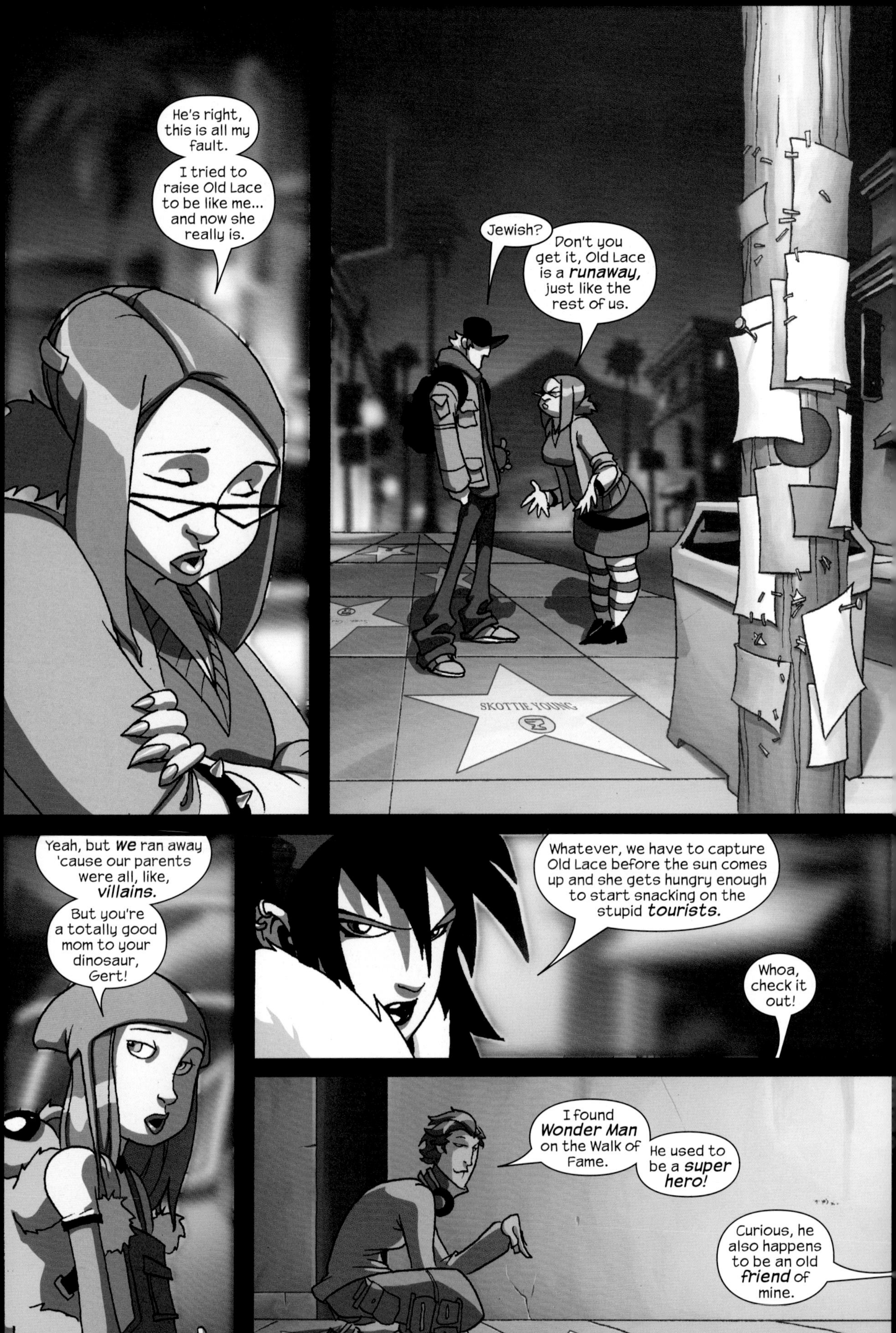
He's right, this is all my fault.
I tried to raise Old Lace to be like me... and now she really is.
Jewish?
Don't you get it, Old Lace is a runaway, just like the rest of us.
SKOTTIE YOUNG
Yeah, but we ran away 'cause our parents were all, like, villains.
But you're a totally good mom to your dinosaur, Gert!
Whatever, we have to capture Old Lace before the sun comes up and she gets hungry enough to start snacking on the stupid tourists.
Whoa, check it out!
I found Wonder Man on the Walk of Fame.
He used to be a super hero!
Curious, he also happens to be an old friend of mine.

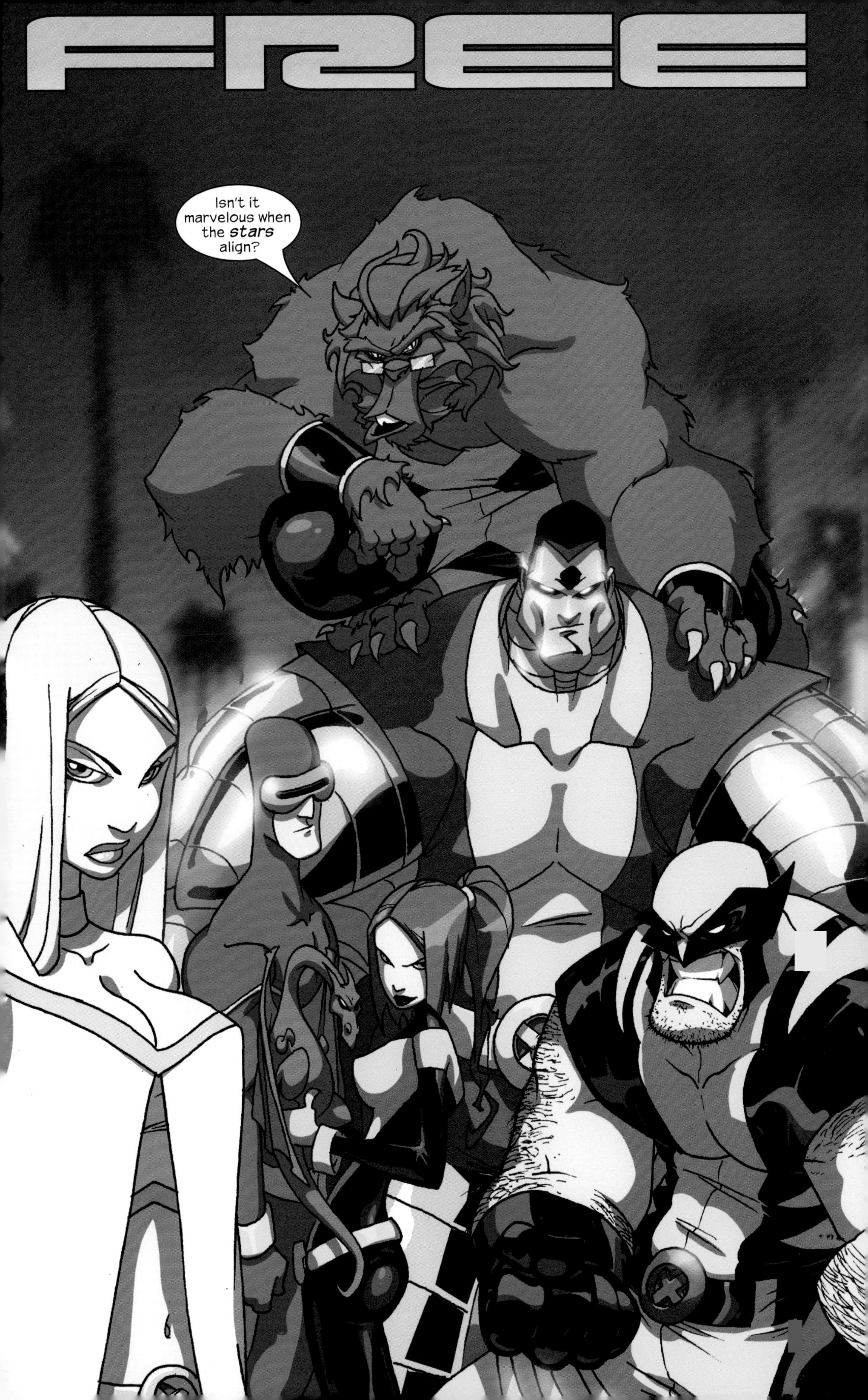
FREE
Isn't it marvelous when the *stars* align?

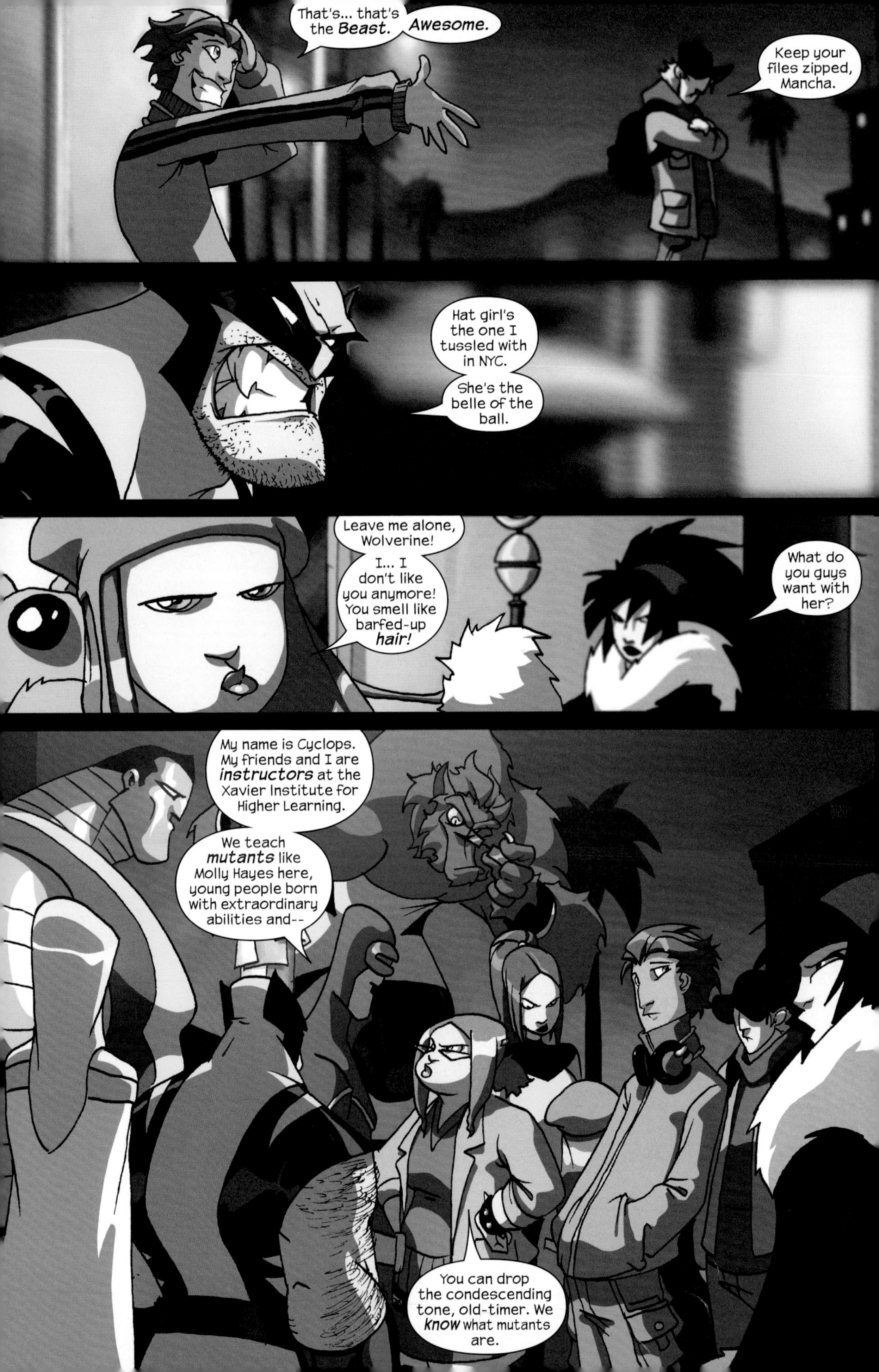
That's... that's the *Beast.*
Awesome.
Keep your files zipped, Mancha.
Hat girl's the one I tussled with in NYC.
She's the belle of the ball.
Leave me alone, Wolverine!
I... I don't like you anymore! You smell like barfed-up *hair!*
What do you guys want with her?
My name is Cyclops. My friends and I are *instructors* at the Xavier Institute for Higher Learning.
We teach *mutants* like Molly Hayes here, young people born with extraordinary abilities and--
You can drop the condescending tone, old-timer. We *know* what mutants are.

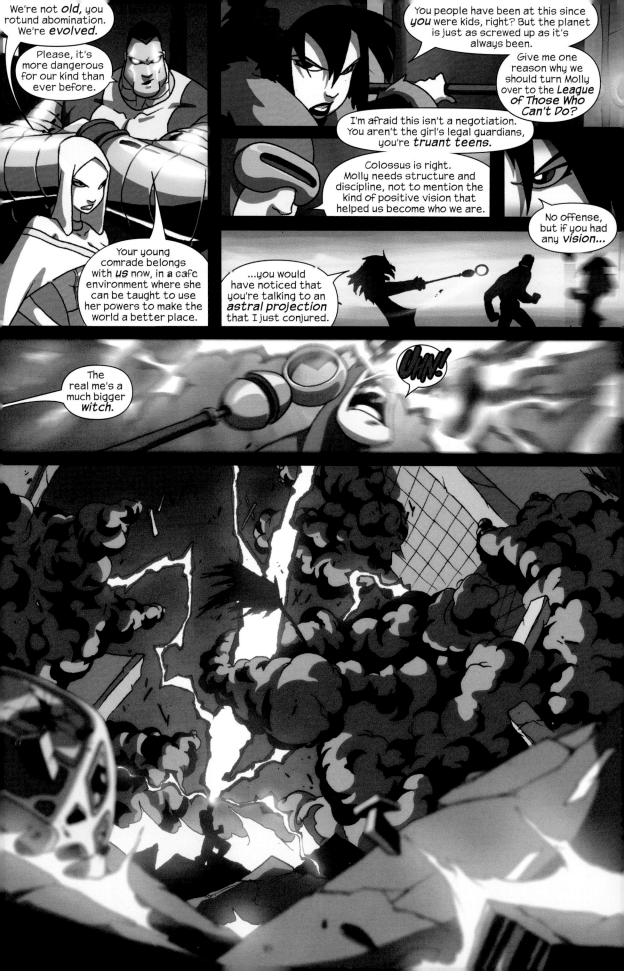

We're not **old**, you rotund abomination. We're **evolved**.

Please, it's more dangerous for our kind than ever before.

You people have been at this since **you** were kids, right? But the planet is just as screwed up as it's always been.

Give me one reason why we should turn Molly over to the **League of Those Who Can't Do?**

I'm afraid this isn't a negotiation. You aren't the girl's legal guardians, you're **truant teens.**

Colossus is right. Molly needs structure and discipline, not to mention the kind of positive vision that helped us become who we are.

No offense, but if you had any **vision**...

Your young comrade belongs with **us** now, in a safe environment where she can be taught to use her powers to make the world a better place.

...you would have noticed that you're talking to an **astral projection** that I just conjured.

UHN!

The real me's a much bigger **witch.**

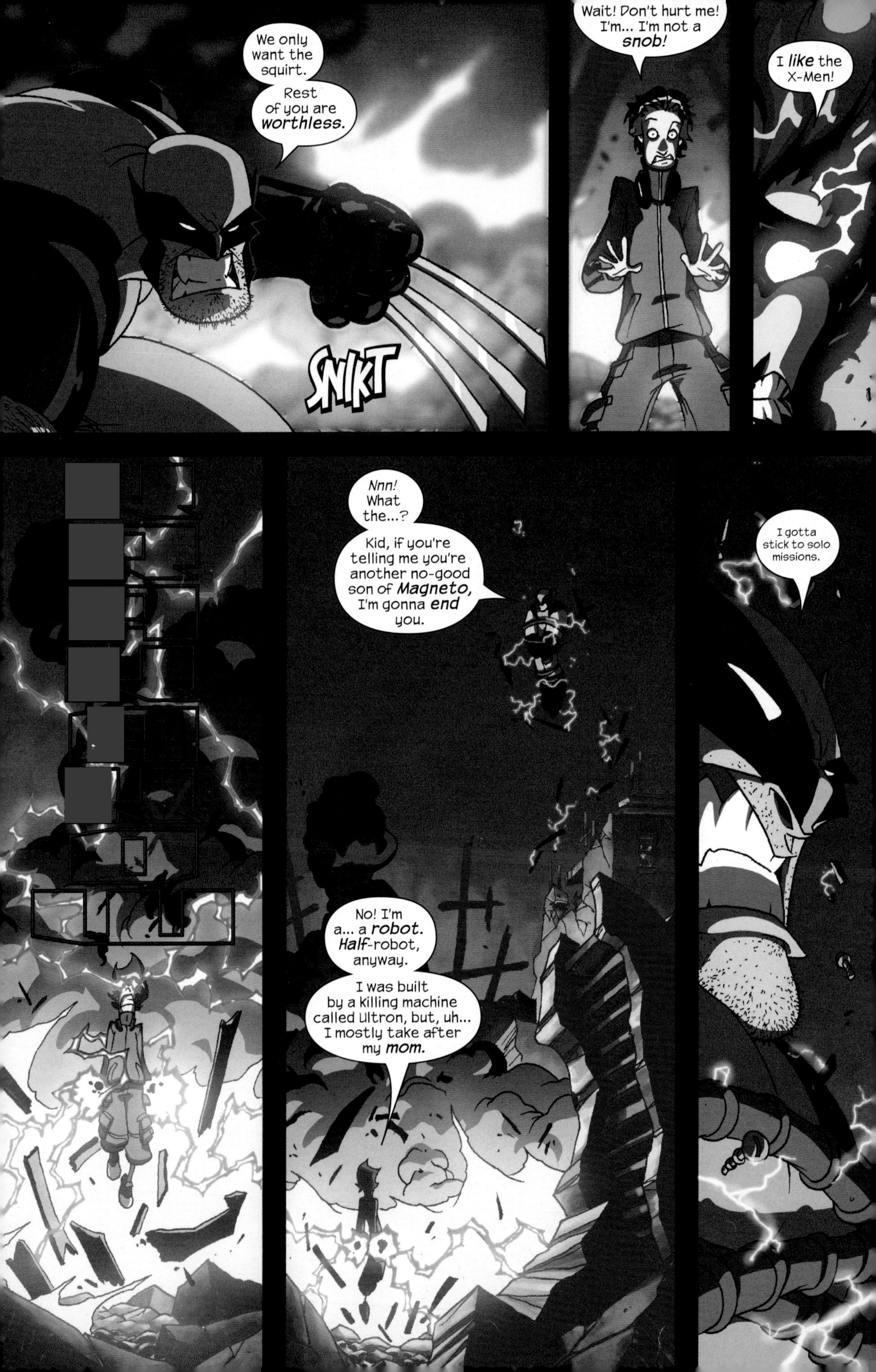
We only want the squirt.
Rest of you are worthless.
SNIKT
Wait! Don't hurt me! I'm... I'm not a snob!
I like the X-Men!
Nnn! What the...?
Kid, if you're telling me you're another no-good son of Magneto, I'm gonna end you.
No! I'm a... a robot. Half-robot, anyway.
I was built by a killing machine called Ultron, but, uh... I mostly take after my mom.
I gotta stick to solo missions.

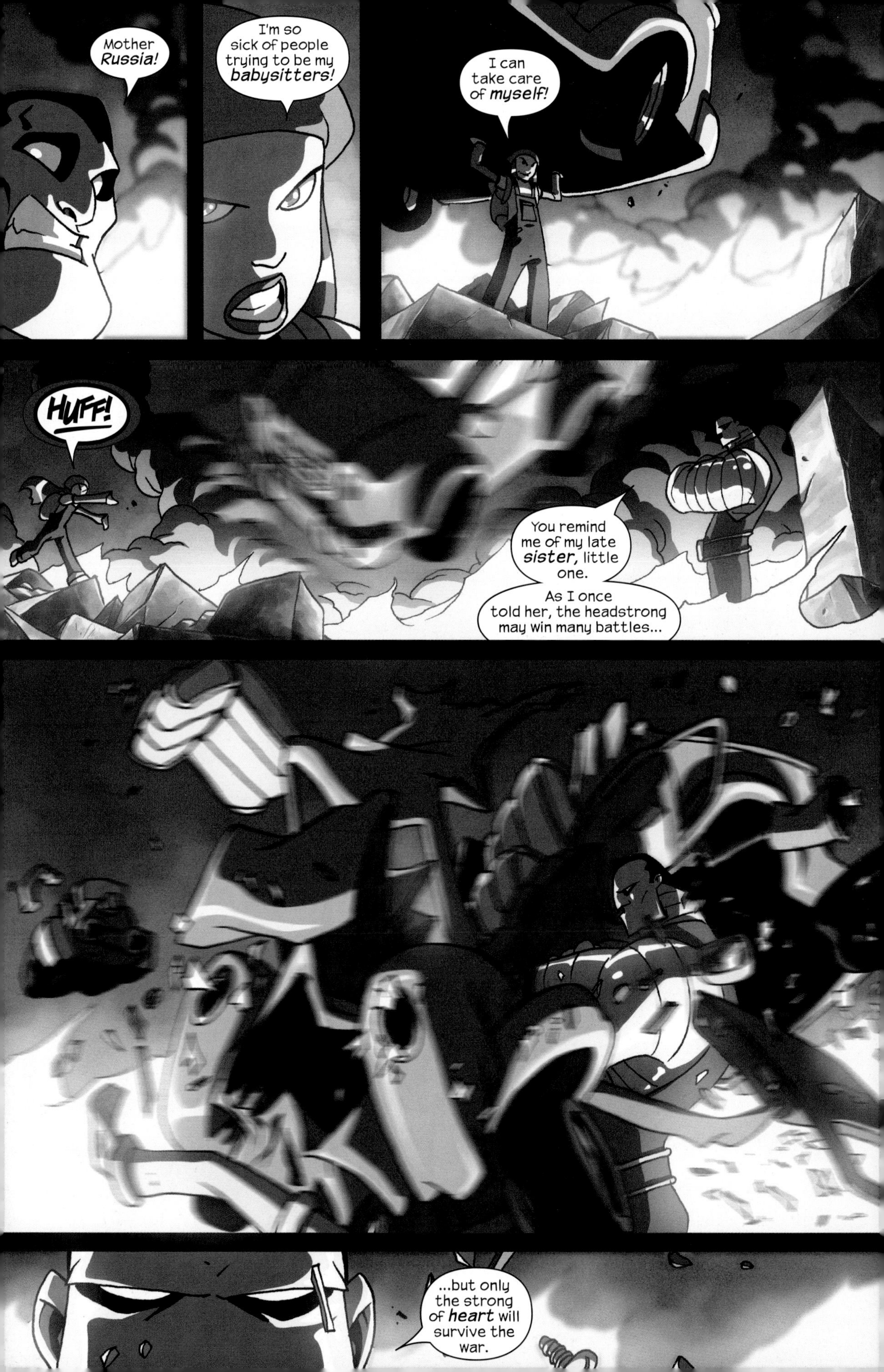
Mother Russia!
I'm so sick of people trying to be my babysitters!
I can take care of myself!
HUFF!
You remind me of my late sister, little one.
As I once told her, the headstrong may win many battles...
...but only the strong of heart will survive the war.

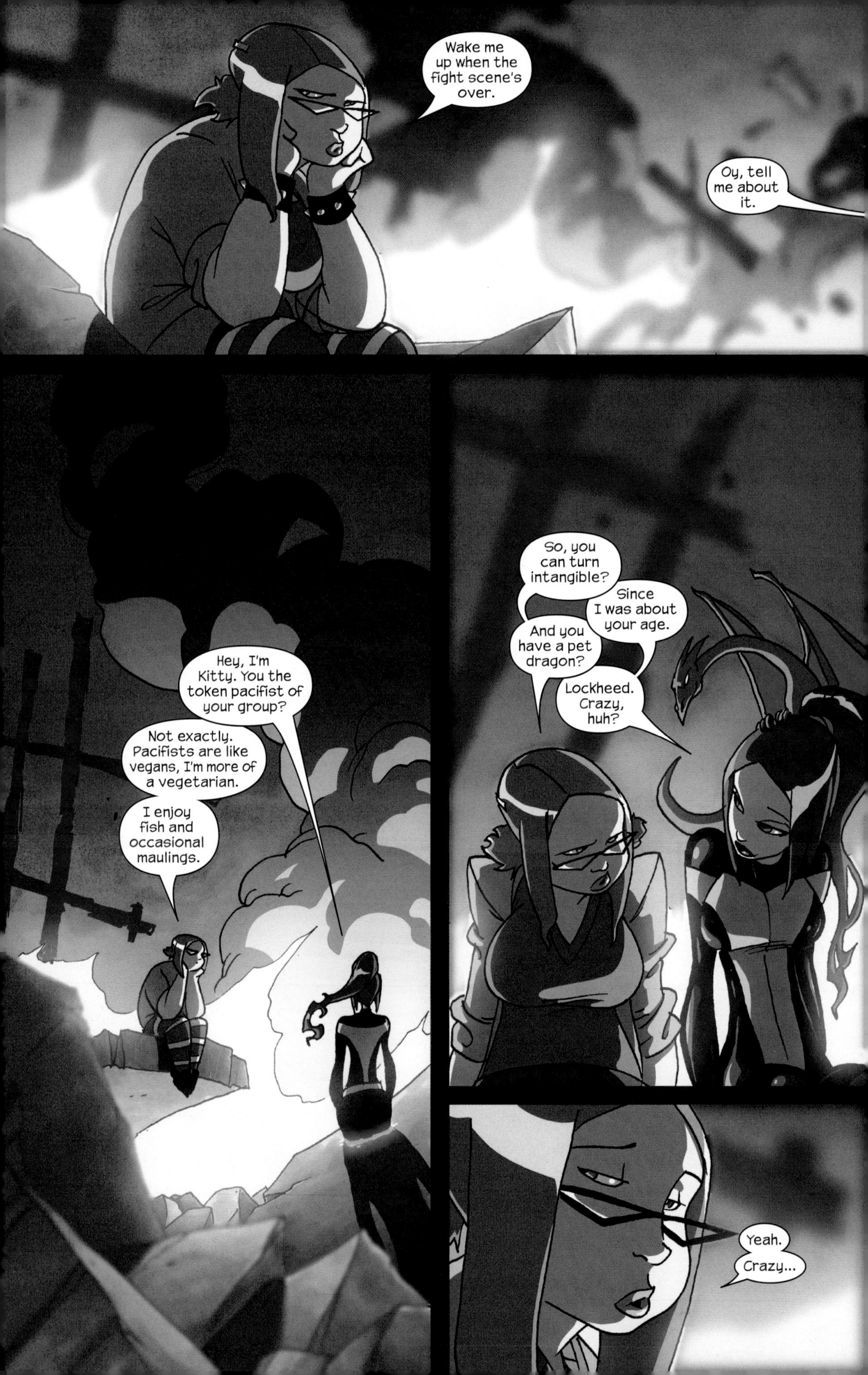

Wake me up when the fight scene's over.
Oy, tell me about it.
Hey, I'm Kitty. You the token pacifist of your group?
Not exactly. Pacifists are like vegans, I'm more of a vegetarian.
I enjoy fish and occasional maulings.
So, you can turn intangible?
Since I was about your age.
And you have a pet dragon?
Lockheed. Crazy, huh?
Yeah.
Crazy...

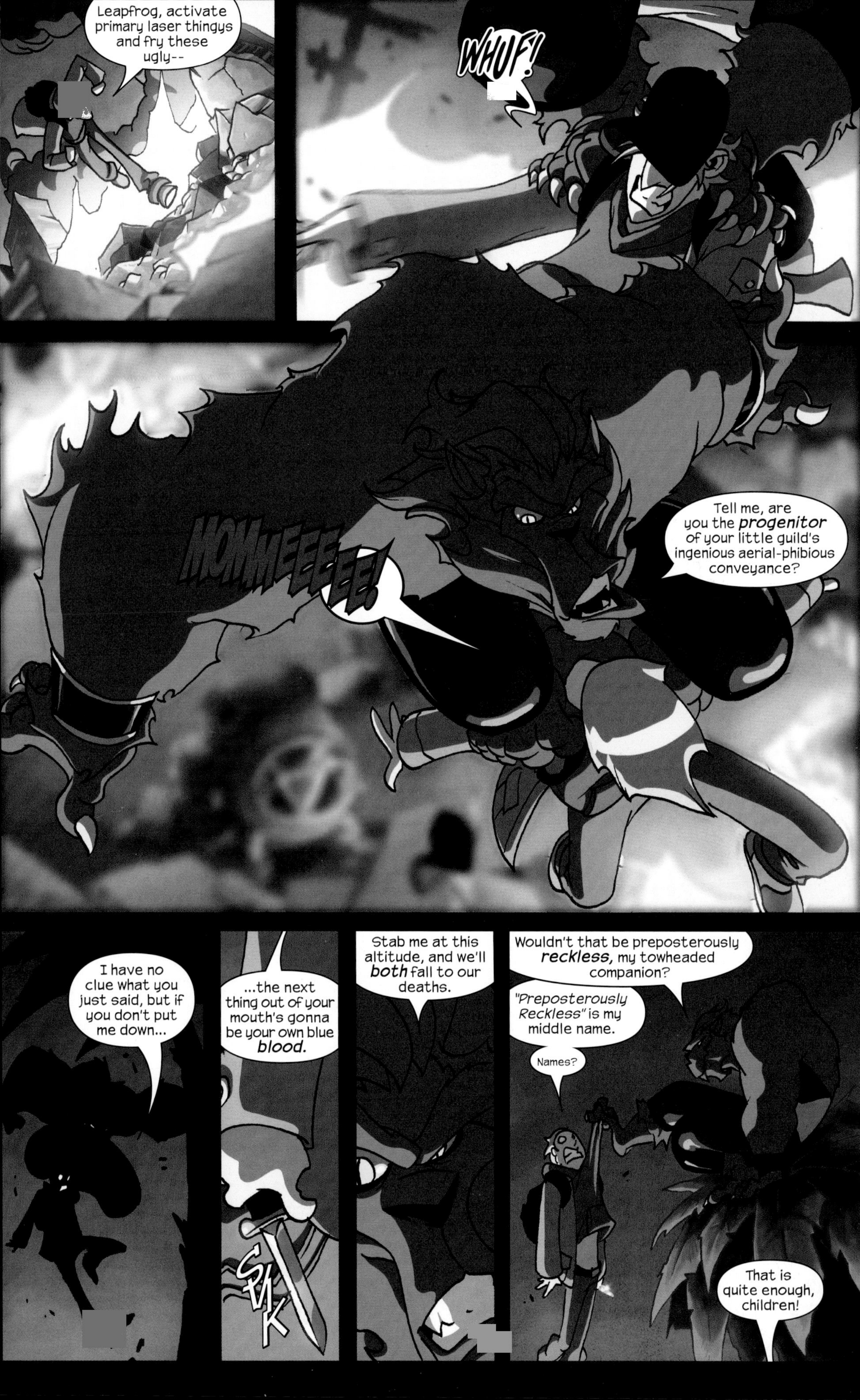

Leapfrog, activate primary laser thingys and fry these ugly--
WHUF!
MOMMEEEEE!
Tell me, are you the progenitor of your little guild's ingenious aerial-phibious conveyance?
I have no clue what you just said, but if you don't put me down...
...the next thing out of your mouth's gonna be your own blue blood.
SNIK
Stab me at this altitude, and we'll both fall to our deaths.
Wouldn't that be preposterously reckless, my towheaded companion?
"Preposterously Reckless" is my middle name.
Names?
That is quite enough, children!

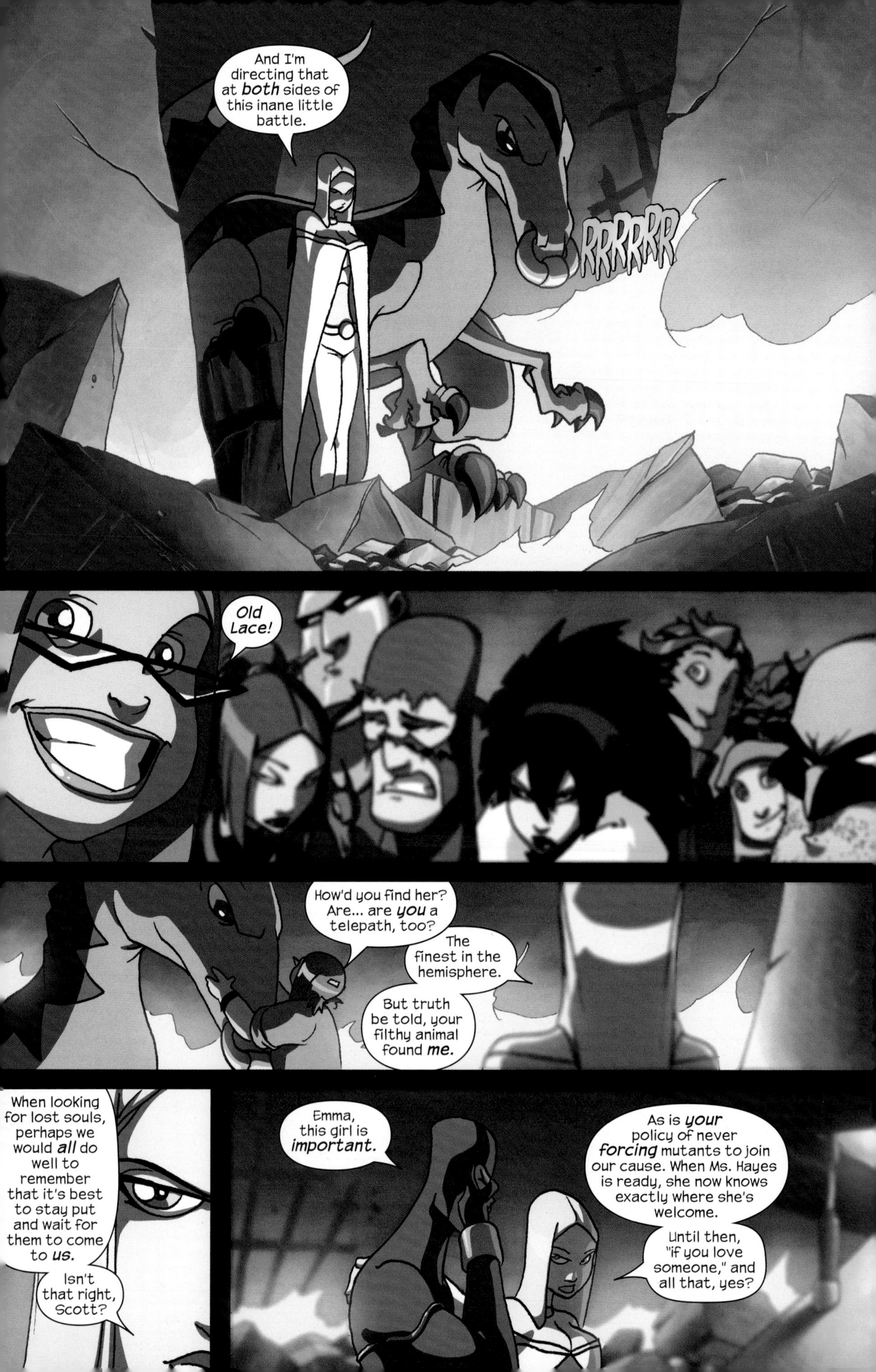

And I'm directing that at *both* sides of this inane little battle.
RRRRRR
Old Lace!
How'd you find her? Are... are *you* a telepath, too?
The finest in the hemisphere.
But truth be told, your filthy animal found *me.*
When looking for lost souls, perhaps we would *all* do well to remember that it's best to stay put and wait for them to come to *us.*
Isn't that right, Scott?
Emma, this girl is *important.*
As is *your* policy of never *forcing* mutants to join our cause. When Ms. Hayes is ready, she now knows exactly where she's welcome.
Until then, "if you love someone," and all that, yes?

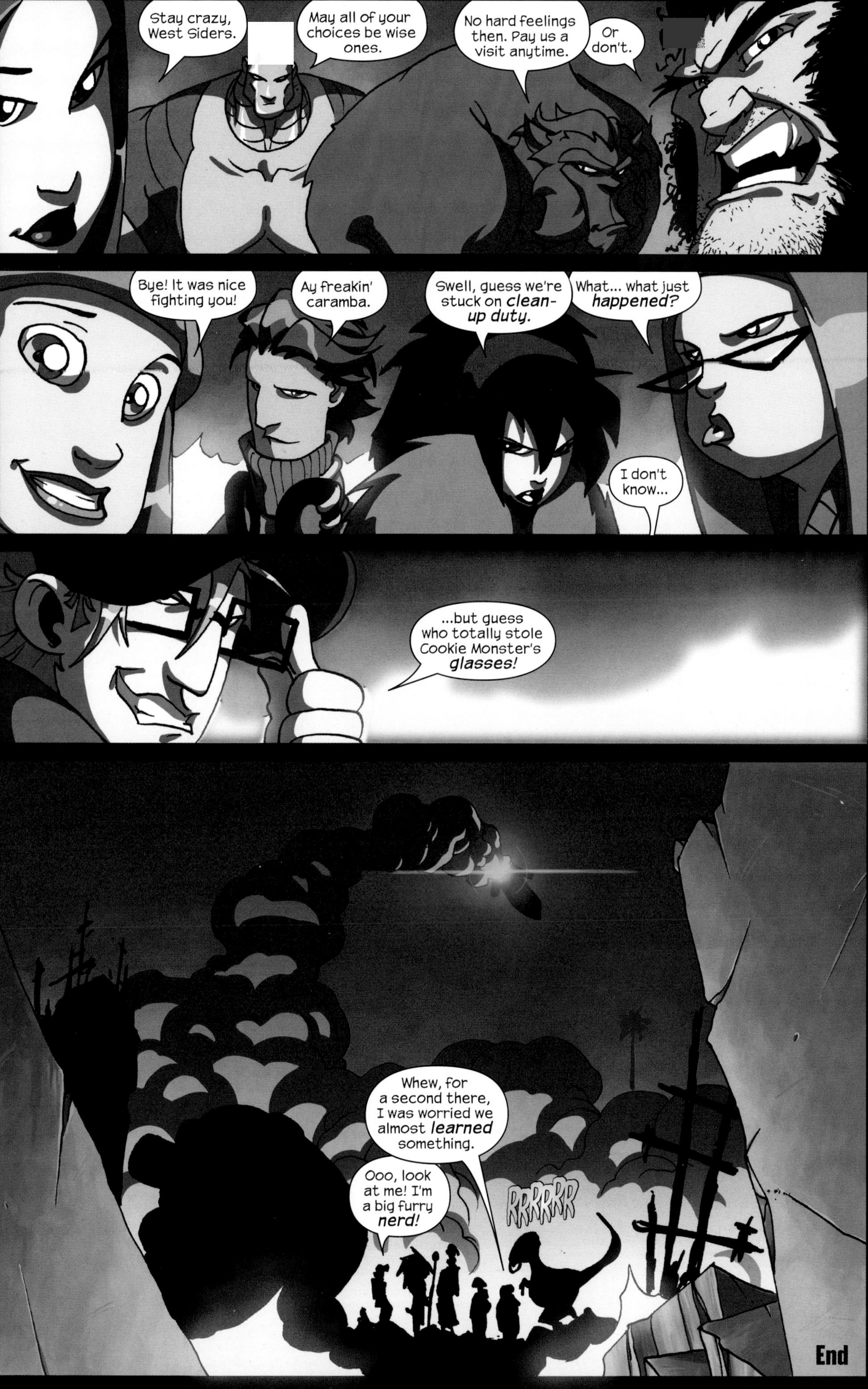
Stay crazy, West Siders.
May all of your choices be wise ones.
No hard feelings then. Pay us a visit anytime.
Or don't.
[redacted]
Bye! It was nice fighting you!
Ay freakin' caramba.
Swell, guess we're stuck on *clean-up duty.*
What... what just *happened?*
I don't know...
...but guess who totally stole Cookie Monster's *glasses!*
Whew, for a second there, I was worried we almost *learned* something.
Ooo, look at me! I'm a big furry *nerd!*
RRRRRR
End

"True Believers, Chapter One"
The Full Script for
(NEW) RUNAWAYS #1
Prepared for Marvel Comics
September 21, 2004

[Welcome back, everybody! Adrian, this first script is a big one, but it's got a lot of fun ▮▮▮ in it, and mostly pages made up of four panels or less, so hopefully, you can burn right through it. We've got a lot of new characters to introduce, but that's what you're best at, so I know you'll knock this one out of the park. Have fun!]

Page One

Page One, Panel One

Okay, we open with this page-wide, letterbox, establishing shot of Downtown Los Angeles, maybe a smaller version of your lovely final splash from our last ish.

1) Overlay in Upper Left-hand Corner (not a caption box, please!):

Los Angeles, California
9:17 pm

2) Tailless: Okay, if you could be any hero working today... who'd it be?

Page One, Panel Two

Cut inside of a teenager's bedroom for this largest panel of the page, at least a half-SPLASH. We're looking at two Hispanic teenagers, a well-dressed, athletic 16-year-old kid named VICTOR MANCHA (who will become a new member of our cast, so design him with care!), and his overweight, more "thuggish" 16-year-old buddy, JORGE.

This is Victor's room, which is cluttered with whatever cool, contemporary stuff you think kids would have, Adrian. However, it's important that we see some Marvel Heroes stuff in here, like a big poster of Captain America on the wall that says, *"DRUGS HURT AMERICA!"* Please leave some room for this exchange:

3) Victor: Easy. Spider-Man. No question.

4) Jorge: *Spider-Man?* You're off your meds, son. The correct answer is *Mr. Fantastic*...stretch yourself out to eight feet, get a fat NBA contract.

5) Jorge: Besides, Spidey ain't even a hero. He's just another banger.

6) Victor: Oh, he is *not*. The only people who think he's a criminal are Fox News and The Daily Bugle.

And the Bugle is, like, the least respected paper in New York City.

Page One, Panel Three

Push in on chubby Jorge for this shot. Over his shoulder in the background, we can see a CRUDE HOMEMADE ELECTRONIC DEVICE, a blinking/flashing radio that Victor built out of spare video game console parts, old speakers, etc.

7) Jorge: What do *you* know about New York, Victor? You've barely been outside *Pasadena* before.

8) Jorge: Your mom won't even let you go to *band camp* without--

9) Electronic (from device): *-kzzk- All units, be advised... possible 10-39 in progress at East First and South San Pedro. -kzzk-*

Page Two

Page Two, Panel One

Pull out to a shot of both kids for this largest panel of the page. Jorge turns around to touch Victor's homemade radio, but Victor LEAPS UP to pull his pal away.

1) Jorge: Yo, E.T., your home planet's on the line.

2) Victor: It's not a phone, dummy, that's the *police scanner* I built. Did they just say *10-39?*

3) Jorge: I guess. Why, what's that, spaz? Naked chicks on parade?

Page Two, Panel Two

This is just a dramatic shot of Victor, as he calmly says:

4) Victor: No, it's a masked felony.

5) Victor: That's cop talk for *super-villains.*

Page Two, Panel Three

Pull out to another shot of both teens. Jorge looks excited as hell, but Victor seems sad.

6) Jorge: Real bad guys? *Here?* We gotta check 'em out!

7) Victor: I...I can't. My curfew's 8:30 on school nights.

8) Jorge: This is a once-in-a-lifetime opportunity, Vic! We *never* get costumes out here!

9) Jorge (small, an aside): Except maybe Wonder Man, and he don't count.

Page Two, Panel Four

Push in closer on the two. Jorge looks disappointed in his crestfallen friend.

10) Victor: Sorry, Jorge. It's my mom's house, her rules.

11) <u>Victor</u>: What am I supposed to do? *Run away?*

12) <u>Jorge</u>: Fft, you're gonna look back on this and *hate* yourself someday, bro. It's like the song goes, when you're an old man, you don't regret the stuff you did...

Page Two, Panel Five
          This is just a small, silent shot of Victor, longingly staring out his bedroom window.

13) <u>Jorge (from off)</u>: ...you regret the stuff you *didn't*.

Page Three

Page Three, Panel One
          Cut to elsewhere in Los Angeles for this page-wide establishing shot of a classy bank on an empty, palm-lined street (maybe something like this: http://www.movieplaces.tv/Heat-136.html, but feel free to use your imagination). There should clearly be a huge HOLE in the wall of this bank, with smoke coming out of it.

1) <u>Overlay in Upper Left-hand Corner</u>:

Third Bank of California
9:19 pm

Page Three, Panel Two
          Cut inside the bank for this close-up of a new villain named EXCAVATOR, the 17-year-old son of Piledriver. His costume can look a bit like his father's (though maybe a different color), and we should be able to see his blonde hair sticking straight out of the top of his mask. Excavator (who has a silver SHOVEL resting on his shoulder here) is smiling at a big wad of CASH that he's holding up in front of his eyes.

2) <u>Excavator</u>: Scrilla fo' rilla!

3) <u>Excavator</u>: This haul gonna be *taut.*

Page Three, Panel Three
          Pull out to the largest panel of the page (at least a half-SPLASH), as we reveal that we're just outside of a smashed-into BANK VAULT (something like this: http://images.encarta.msn.com/xrefmedia/sharemed/targets/images/pho/000a5/000a5038.jpg). Walking out of this vault are all four members of THE WRECKING CREW (C.B. and Mac can get you better reference, but here's something to get you started: http://www.classicmarvel.com/cast/wreckingcrew.htm). THUNDERBALL, PILE-DRIVER, BULLDOZER, and WRECKER (lined up in that order) are all carrying bags of cash here. We can see Excavator in the background, taking up the rear.

4) <u>Thunderball</u>: Piledriver, if "Excavator" here continues affecting that manner of speech, I'm going to smash him in the face with his own enchanted *shovel.*

5) <u>Piledriver</u>: Settle down, Thunderball. That's just the way teenagers talk these days.

6) <u>Bulldozer</u>: I dunno, P.D. I still think dragging your *kid* along for this score was a dumb play. This ain't the

Wrecking Crew and *Son.*

7) <u>Wrecker</u>: Yeah, bad enough I hadda split my power with *you* ungrateful lunks, now I gotta share it with one of your long-lost *brats?*

Page Four

Page Four, Panel One
          Push in for this shot of just Wrecker, as he defends his bastard son.

1) <u>Piledriver</u>: Wrecker, you're the one who's always saying we gotta start thinking about the *future,* right? Well, I'm just training a new generation who can *kick up* to us when we retire.

2) <u>Piledriver</u>: Besides, this ain't *NYC.* It's not like there's gonna be any annoying "heroes" around to interfere with the kid's first heist.

3) <u>Piledriver (small, an aside)</u>: Except maybe Wonder Man, and he don't count.

Page Four, Panel Two
          Change angles for this largest panel of the page, a shot of Bulldozer and the curious young Excavator (and anyone else you have room to draw), as they step out of the hole in the bank wall and onto the streets of Los Angeles.

4) <u>Excavator</u>: Hey, 'Dozer, if this town's so ripe for the picking, how come you guys didn't jump coasts sooner?

5) <u>Bulldozer</u>: 'Cause L.A. used to be run by a dozen stone-cold psychos called *The Pride.*

6) <u>Bulldozer</u>: This was *their* turf. Any mask who tried to make a play for a slice would get sent back to the Big Apple...piece by piece.

Page Four, Panel Three
          Change angles again, as Excavator turns to talk with the grumpy, crowbar-wielding Wrecker.

7) <u>Excavator</u>: They in stir now, Mr. Wrecker?

8) <u>Wrecker</u>: No, they're not "in stir," you annoying piece of...

9) <u>Wrecker</u>: The Pride is *dead,* okay? They were betrayed by their spoiled children, in what should have been a valuable *lesson* to every hood who's got an "accident" or two out there.

Page Four, Panel Four
          Change angles one last time, as Piledriver lovingly puts his arm around his son.

10) <u>Piledriver</u>: You got nothing to worry about with *my* boy, Wrecks. He's a chip off the old--

11) <u>Someone's Voice (from off)</u>: Hey, Village People!

Page Five

Page Five, Panel One
      Cut over to the street in front of the off-panel Wrecking Crew for this largest panel of the page, at least a half-SPLASH. It's a heroic shot of four of our Runaways: GERT, NICO, KAROLINA and MOLLY (lined up in that order, please). I'm sure we'll talk about our characters' new looks before we begin, but these girls should look confident and tough as hell here, Adrian! They don't have costumes, weapons, or even their dinosaur, but they still look ready to kick ▬.

1) <u>Gert</u>: Step away from the minor.

2) <u>Molly</u>: Or else you're in for some *major...*

3) <u>Molly (small, an aside)</u>: ...you know, bad stuff.

Page Five, Panel Two
      Cut back to the Wrecking Crew, who are all staring at the off-panel Runaways. They look super-confused, except for the hard-headed Bulldozer, who's just smiling here.

4) <u>Thunderball</u>: The hell is this?

5) <u>Bulldozer</u>: I don't know, but I'll take a box of *Thin Mints.*

Page Five, Panel Three
      Cut over to Nico and Karolina.

6) <u>Nico</u>: Listen, we don't care about whatever money you stole. We know the bank is insured.

7) <u>Nico</u>: Just give us the *kid,* and you can be on your way.

8) <u>Karolina</u>: Haven't you seen the news, Ricky? Your grandparents are worried *sick* about you.

Page Six

Page Six, Panel One
      Cut over to Piledriver and his son. Excavator is defiant, but his old man is looking back at his off-panel crewmates like a proud papa.

1) <u>Excavator</u>: My *grandparents?* Those stank old fogies can choke on their *dentures* for all I care. I'm running with my *dad* now.

2) <u>Piledriver</u>: Check it out, four ladies fighting over him already.

3) <u>Piledriver</u>: Told you he takes after his pops.

Page Six, Panel Two
      Cut back to a pissed-off Nico and Karolina, as Karolina RIPS off her own bracelet. She begins to GLOW with her alien power.

4) <u>Nico</u>: And that concludes the *negotiation* segment of our program.

5) <u>Nico</u>: Karolina?

6) <u>Karolina</u>: Plan B it is, boss.

Page Six, Panel Three
      Pull out to the largest panel of the page for a big group shot of all of our players, as a now-floating Karolina BLASTS Piledriver, knocking him backwards!

7) <u>SFX</u>: *KASCHOWW*

8) <u>Excavator</u>: DAD!

Page Six, Panel Four
      This is just a shot of the crowbar-wielding Wrecker, as he yells out an order.

9) <u>Wrecker</u>: They're *muties!*

10) <u>Wrecker</u>: Light 'em up!

Page Seven

Page Seven, Panel One
      Cut over to Karolina (still floating and firing at the off-panel Wrecking Crew) and Molly, who's beneath her, angrily punching one of her own hands in preparation for battle.

1) <u>Karolina</u>: Excuse me.

2) <u>Karolina</u>: I'm an *extraterrestrial...*and proud *of* it, thank you very much.

3) <u>Molly</u>: Besides, the word "mutie" is really offensive to people like me, you freakin' *racists.*

Page Seven, Panel Two
      Cut over to Excavator, who's running right at us. He has his enchanted shovel raised over his head.

4) <u>Excavator</u>: I'll *kill* you!

5) <u>Excavator</u>: I'll kill--

Page Seven, Panel Three
      Pull out to the largest panel of the page, as Excavator SWINGS the shovel into Molly's head. Molly doesn't even flinch at the magic tool SNAPS IN HALF across her little skull.

6) <u>SFX</u>: *KRACK*

Page Seven, Panel Four
      This is just a small close-up of the frowning Molly, her eyes GLOWING brightly here.

7) <u>Molly</u>: Too bad.

8) <u>Molly</u>: Our club coulda used another boy.

Page Seven, Panel Five
      Pull out to a bigger shot, as Molly PUNCHES Excavator in the gut, sending him FLYING down the street!

      No Copy *((KAAPOW!!))*

Page Eight

Page Eight, Panel One

We're with Nico in the foreground of this shot, as she yells at the off-panel Molly. Behind him, Wrecker is approaching, with his crowbar at the ready.

1) Nico: Molly, go sit on him or something!

2) Nico: We'll finish off the grown-ups!

3) Wrecker: Sister, you just earned yourself a taste of the *big stick*.

Page Eight, Panel Two

This is just a shot of Nico, as she turns to shoot us a scary look. Her hair is beginning to blow with mystical force.

4) Nico: Bet mine's bigger than yours.

Page Eight, Panel Three

Pull out for another shot of Wrecker and Nico. A stunned Wrecker DROPS his crowbar as the GLOWING STAFF OF ONE begins *growing* out of a pained Nico's chest!

5) Wrecker: Ah, crap.

6) Wrecker: Not *witches*. I *hate*--

Page Eight, Panel Four

Pull out to the largest panel of the page, as Nico aims her fully formed, glowing staff at Wrecker, who instantaneously BREAKS into a hundred different pieces! Adrian, this shouldn't be the least bit gory, it's more like a *picture* of Wrecker being torn into many little pieces. No blood or guts!

7) Nico (creepy font): DECONSTRUCT.

8) Wrecker: *NOOOOO!*

Page Nine

Page Nine, Panel One

Change angles, as a flying Karolina SWOOPS down next to the staff-wielding Nico, who's standing next to all of the pieces of Wrecker. Karolina looks concerned.

1) Karolina: Nico!

2) Nico: It's all right, Karolina. He'll come together in an hour or two...probably.

3) Karolina: But I thought you could only use the Staff of One after your *blood* was shed? And you never...

Page Nine, Panel Two

This is just a small silent shot of Nico, as she looks over at the off-panel Karolina, and shoots her a knowing look.

No Copy

Page Nine, Panel Three

And this is just a small shot of the glowing Karolina, as she finally understands what's going on.

4) Karolina (small, under her breath): Oh. Right.

5) Karolina (small, under her breath): That time of the month...

6) Another Voice (from off): ENOUGH!

Page Nine, Panel Four

Cut over to Thunderball and Gert for this largest panel of the page. Thunderball is menacingly SWINGING his wrecking ball in a circle over his head, as he approaches a confident Gert, who's backing towards a nearby tree.

7) Thunderball: You girls stand down *posthaste*...or I smash your friend here into oblivion.

Page Ten

Page Ten, Panel One

Push in closer on Gert and Thunderball. Thunderball suddenly looks a little concerned.

1) Gert: Bad idea, Mean Green.

2) Gert: I've got the power to make grown men lose control of their *bowels*.

3) Thunderball: Really...?

Page Ten, Panel Two

Cut back to Gert for this largest panel of the page, as OLD LACE suddenly comes LEAPING out from behind the nearby tree. The velociraptor's mouth is wide open here, so she can show off her fangs.

4) Gert: More or less.

5) SFX by Old Lace (not in a balloon, please!): *RAAAARRR*

Page Ten, Panel Three

Change angles on the three. As Old Lace POUNCES on top of a fallen Thunderball, Gert just shakes her head.

6) Thunderball: AHHHHHH!

7) Gert: Why couldn't my 'rents have given you to me for my *bat mitzvah*, Old Lace? A telepathic velociraptor from the 87th Century would have made middle school a lot more tolerab--

Page Ten, Panel Four

Push in close on Gert, as a FIST (belonging to Bulldozer) suddenly enters the frame and PUNCHES Gert in the face, knocking her glasses off!

8) SFX: *THWACK*

Page Eleven

Page Eleven, Panel One
        Change angles to reveal that BULLDOZER is now standing over Gert, who's fallen on her ▬. She's reaching for her glasses here. Bulldozer is standing in the middle of the street, and we can't see anyone except for him and Gert in this shot.

1) Bulldozer: I got you all figured out, fatty.

2) Bulldozer: Wizards, gene freaks, *time travelers*...you're *The Pride's* kids, ain't you?

3) Gert: Wow, maybe your head isn't as dense as it *looks*... which is too bad, considering what's about to land on *top* of it.

Page Eleven, Panel Two
        Push in for this tight shot of Bulldozer, who nervously looks up, as a DARK SHADOW suddenly falls over him.

4) Bulldozer: Huh?

Page Eleven, Panel Three
        Pull out to the largest panel of the page, a three-quarter SPLASH, as the Runaways' LEAPFROG suddenly comes SMASHING down in the middle of the street, presumably squashing Bulldozer flat! The ship narrowly misses Gert, who protects her face with her arm as the ship loudly LANDS inches away from her.

5) SFX:
                K
                R
                O
                O
                O
                M

Page Twelve

Page Twelve, Panel One
        Cut into the control panels of the Leapfrog, as CHASE looks out at us! He's wearing racing gloves, and maybe some kind of new goggles resting on his forehead. We can talk about his new look, Adrian, whatever you like...

1) Chase: Sorry I'm late, baby!

2) Chase: I totally forgot to gas up the Leapfrog last night. Had to "borrow" ninety gallons of unleaded from the Circle A...

Page Twelve, Panel Two
        Cut back down to the street for this shot of an excited Molly, who's now standing next to Gert (who's putting her glasses back on).

3) Gert (small, an aside): We are the worst good guys of all time.

4) Molly: Chase!

5) Molly: Did you see who we got to beat up tonight? Their costumes were really pretty!

Page Twelve, Panel Three
        Pull out to the largest panel of the page for this group shot. Chase is now walking down out of the opening mouth/ramp of the Leapfrog, as he approaches the assembled girls. A still-glowing Karolina looks pissed, but Gert (standing next to Old Lace) tries to calm her down. Nico is looking off in the direction of the off-panel Excavator. We can see POLICE CARS approaching in the distant background.

6) Chase: What did we talk about, Mol? Costumes are *gay*.

7) Karolina: Hey! I warned you, misuse that word one more time and--

8) Gert: Save it, Karolina. If we're not legs up in the next thirty seconds, the pigs are gonna send us back to *foster care*.

9) Nico: What about the boy, Gert? Are we really just going to let him get hauled off to *juvie*? I mean, he's in the same boat as us.

Page Twelve, Panel Four
        This is just a small shot of Gert.

10) Gert: No, I'd say he went overboard the second he saw his father as someone to *look up* to.

11) Gert: Let him go, Nico. No offense to your drearily departed boyfriend, but the last thing we need is another *Alex* to stab us in the back.

Page Twelve, Panel Five
        And this is just a silent shot of a somber Nico, still looking in the direction of the off-panel Excavator.

12) Gert (from off): Face it, some kids are a *lost cause*...

Page Thirteen

Page Thirteen, Panel One
        Cut to later that night for this establishing shot of a little church in Los Angeles (http://www.fresno.edu/preserve/lrhr/110.htm). In the foreground of this shot, we should *clearly* see one of those CHURCH SIGNS with movable letters (http://www.churchsigngenerator.com/index1.php) that reads:

1) Sign in Foreground:
                Excelsior Meeting - 9:30
                Church Basement

Page Thirteen, Panel Two
        Cut into a dimly lit church basement for this largest panel of the page, a nice semi-SPLASH. We're behind a row of four people sitting in folding chairs, but we can't see their faces yet. We *can* see the two young people standing in front of them: MICKEY MUSASHI (the New Warrior's Turbo) and PHIL URICH (the former heroic

Green Goblin). Mickey and Phil are both wearing cool, contemporary clothing. They're both about 22-years-old, so they should look older than our Runaways, but younger than regular Marvel heroes like Captain America. Phil is giving a little wave to everybody, as Mickey introduces herself. Please leave some room for their brief opening remarks:

2) Mickey: Right, so...as some of you already know, my name is Michiko Musashi, but pretty much everybody calls me *Mickey*.

3) Mickey: I moved here three months ago after I got a job with the Los Angeles Times, thanks to a recommendation from my good pal, Phil Urich.

4) Phil: Howdy. Mickey and I have been talking about starting a group like this for a while now, so we really appreciate you guys coming out to our first meeting.

5) Phil: We don't exactly have a budget or anything, so we're starting off small, but we hope to expand Excelsior into a *nationwide* outreach program someday soon.

Page Thirteen, Panel Three
　　　This is just a close-up of Mickey, as she makes this dramatic revelation:

6) Mickey: Like everyone here tonight, Phil and I are former teenage superheroes.

Page Fourteen

Page Fourteen, Panel One
　　　Change angles on Mickey, as she reveals her secret origin. Remember, this whole scene should be dark and shadowy, Adrian, eerily lit from above!

1) Mickey: From the time I was a sophomore in college up until a few months ago, I'd been living a double life as the New Warrior's *Turbo*.

2) Mickey: But late last year, I was fighting some Z-lister, and I had this...this *epiphany*. I realized that I could do more good with my *education* than I ever could with some hi-tech *costume.*That's when I decided to get back into investigative journalism.

Page Fourteen, Panel Two
　　　Change angles for this largest panel of the page, a shot of Mickey, as she turns her attention to one of the people seated in the first row (we can't see the others yet). This is CHRIS POWELL, the 19-year-old alter ego of Darkhawk (again, our esteemed editors will get you reference, Adrian!).

3) Mickey: Anyway, I'm obviously not the only one here with a story like that. Chris, why don't you keep it going?

4) Chris: Oh, uh, sure. My name's Chris Powell, and I'm...well, I *used* to be Darkhawk.

5) Chris: I found this *amulet* back when I was in high school, and it changed me into this...this *thing*. You know the drill.

Page Fourteen, Panel Three
　　　This is just a shot of Chris, as he hangs his head and nervously recounts how he got here.

6) Chris: I used the powers it gave me as a *vigilante* for a couple of years, which was cool and all, but I...

7) Chris: I started having these *nightmares*. Really intense ones. I mean, I was in New York when some pretty bad stuff went down, and I...I just had to get away.

Page Fourteen, Panel Four
　　　Change angles, as Phil Urich walks over and puts a hand on Chris' shoulder. Phil looks over at another one of the off-panel guests at this meeting.

8) Chris: I'm not cut out for seeing all the stuff I've seen, you know? I don't think *anyone* my age is. I'm sure I sound like a *coward*, but--

9) Phil: You're a brave guy, Chris. You always have been.

10) Phil: Julie, why don't you take the floor?

Page Fifteen

Page Fifteen, Panel One
　　　Cut over to another guest for this largest panel of the page, as a smiling JULIE POWER stands, like a teacher's pet addressing her speech class. Julie is the grown-up version of Lightspeed from Power Pack. She's about 18 years old here, so she should look older than the Runaways' girls, but younger than Mickey. She's wearing something sexy, but not too slutty. She looks like she could be a movie star.

1) Julie: *Ahem.* Thank you, Mr. Urich. Hi, everybody. I'm Julie Power. And yes, before you ask, that *is* my real name.

2) Julie: Actually, I've had *lots* of names over the years: Lightspeed, Starstreak, Molecula, Mistress of Density...

Page Fifteen, Panel Two
　　　Push in closer on Julie, as she suddenly gets more serious.

3) Julie: See, when I was just ten years old, my brothers and sister and I met someone from...well, from far away. Long story short, we became *Power Pack*.

4) Julie: When my siblings and I were fighting crime, I thought it was all just fun and games. I had no idea I was actually being robbed of a *normal childhood*.

Page Fifteen, Panel Three
　　　Pull out for this shot of Julie and Mickey, as Mickey politely interrupts her.

5) Julie: With the help of a lot of therapy, I'm trying to get some of that innocence *back*.

6) Julie: I've always loved fantasy and drama, so I'm living

in Hollywood now, just taking auditions and looking for an agent. So, ah, if anyone wants to *network* after this...

7) <u>Mickey</u>: Thanks, Julie. You want to share, Johnny?

Page Fifteen, Panel Four

Cut over to JOHNNY GALLO, the 19-year-old kid who used to be the Slingers' Ricochet. He looks like ▬▬ here, disheveled and depressed.

8) <u>Johnny</u>: I don't know, man. I...I feel totally outclassed here. I mean, you guys have probably never even *heard* of me.

9) <u>Johnny</u>: My team...my team didn't even have a *name*. We were just a bunch of Spider-Man wannabes. I used to be this guy called *Ricochet*.

Page Fifteen, Panel Five

Change angles on poor ol' Johnny, as he continues talking:

10) <u>Johnny</u>: When my powers first materialized, I thought fulltime hero-ing was gonna be my *life*. And for a while, I guess it was. It was *awesome*.

11) <u>Johnny</u>: But before I knew it, it was *over*. I'd even *look* for crimes and stuff, but by the time I'd get to one, somebody like *Iron Fist* or *Moon Knight* was already taking care of it.

12) <u>Johnny</u>: I wasn't a superhero...I was *superfluous*.

Page Sixteen

Page Sixteen, Panel One

Pull out to a larger panel, as Mickey and Phil try to console Johnny.

1) <u>Johnny</u>: And I really loved the spotlight, man. What kid wouldn't? But when you get so much, so young, so *fast*...nobody tells you how to deal when that spotlight inevitably shuts off, you know?

2) <u>Mickey</u>: Well, we founded Excelsior to help with *every* stage of your transition into adulthood and a healthy civilian life. Right, Phil?

3) <u>Phil</u>: Absolutely. I'd be lying if I said I didn't enjoy *my* time as the Green Goblin, but now I know what a dangerous message people like us were sending to impressionable young--

Page Sixteen, Panel Two

Cut over to CHAMBER, our last member of Excelsior, as he suddenly JUMPS to his feet and OPENS his bandages, exposing the GLOWING BIOKINETIC FIRE in his chest.

4) <u>Chamber (unique font)</u>: Hold the bleedin' phone!

5) <u>Chamber (unique font)</u>: This kid's the *Green Goblin?*

Page Sixteen, Panel Three

Pull out to the largest panel of the page for a big group shot, as Phil nervously backs away from the glowing Chamber. All of the other kids look scared, as Mickey tries to calm down Chamber.

6) <u>Phil</u>: Oh, I...I wasn't the *evil* Green Goblin. I just found one of his suits, and used the equipment to protect--

7) <u>Chamber (unique font)</u>: There was a *good* Green Goblin? That is the absolute *stupidest* thing I've ever heard!

8) <u>Mickey</u>: Jonothan, why don't you put your *blast furnace* away and introduce yourself to the nice--

Page Sixteen, Panel Four

This is just a shot of Chamber, as he begins resealing himself with the black wraps that hide the big glowing hole in his face and chest.

9) <u>Chamber (unique font)</u>: The name's *Jono*, luv. Or Chamber. Whichever strikes.

10) <u>Chamber (unique font)</u>: Right then, Reader's Digest: I'm a mutant, did some time as a soldier with the X-Men after I blew half me own face off. A group of sods called Weapon X patched me up, but I went and ripped a *new* hole in myself when some drunk in Fresno made me mad.

11) <u>Chamber (unique font)</u>: Anyway, just enduring this sob-fest for the free pizza I read about in the email.

Page Seventeen

Page Seventeen, Panel One

Change angles for this shot of Julie, Johnny and Mickey. Julie and Johnny are staring at the off-panel Chamber, while Mickey pulls out her little CELL PHONE.

1) <u>Julie</u>: Pizza? I hope this isn't insensitive, Jono, but if you don't have a *mouth...?*

2) <u>Johnny</u>: Wait, you were part of the *X-Men?* As in, Professor *Xavier's* X-Men? They wouldn't even return my--

3) <u>SFX (from off)</u>: *DEET DEET DOO*

4) <u>Mickey</u>: If you guys could excuse me for a second, that's probably my *editor*.

Page Seventeen, Panel Two

Pull out to the largest panel of the page, as Mickey walks towards us, away from the talkative group in the background of this shot, and into the shadowy back of the church basement. She's talking on her phone now.

5) <u>Mickey</u>: Musashi here.

6) <u>Tailless (electronic)</u>: Way to go, girl. Your little group's a cool idea, very well executed.

Page Seventeen, Panel Three
        Push in close on Mickey, who suddenly looks angry and a little sacred.

7) Mickey: Who *is* this? How'd you get this number?

8) Tailless (electronic): Yeah, that's not really important right now, Mick.

9) Tailless (electronic): What is important is that there are other people out there who need Excelsior's help. Not *former* heroes, but underage kids who are putting their necks on the line even as we--

Page Seventeen, Panel Four
        Cut to an unknown location for this shot of A SHADOWY FIGURE. This is a male, but we can't tell who it is, or where he's at, Adrian!

10) Tailless (electronic): I didn't start wearing a mask *yesterday*, pal. If you think I'm gonna start running *errands* for some mystery benefactor, you can kiss my--

11) From Figure: All I'm asking your team to do is help me find five runaways...

12) From Figure: ...and in exchange, I'll give your organization *one million dollars,* enough to reach out to every cape and cowl who's ever lived the life.

Page Seventeen, Panel Five
        Finally, cut back to a quietly intrigued Mickey for this closing extreme close-up.

13) Mickey: Keep talking.

Page Eighteen

Page Eighteen, Panel One
        Cut to later that night for this establishing shot of THE LA BREA TAR PITS (something like this: http://www.davidphenry.com/States/LaBreaTarPitMuseum.jpg, and if you draw those elephants in the tar, they should clearly be FAKE).

1) Overlay in Upper Left-hand Corner:

The La Brea Tar Pits
10:01 pm *((Don't put time here))*

Page Eighteen, Panel Two
        Cut into the massive caves underneath the tar pits for a three-quarter SPLASH, our first look at THE HOSTEL II! The Leapfrog is parked here, and the kids are walking away from it, in this order from left to right: Molly, Karolina (no longer glowing), Gert (with Old Lace), Chase, Karolina, and Nico (no longer holding her staff). The kids can just be smallish figures in this torch-lit shot. They're walking underneath a GIANT FRAMED PORTRAIT of the twelve members of THE PRIDE, all in their villain costumes. Feel free to fill the lair with whatever other cool super-villain crap you wanna draw, Adrian!

2) Molly: I wish we had put our hideout under an *In & Out Burger.* I'm so sick of eating whatever junk my mom *pickled* down here before she...you know.

3) Karolina: Just be glad we have *someplace* for our new Hostel, Molly.

4) Gert: Yeah, if we hadn't found our parents' old *lair,* the five of us would still be cloaked on Venice Beach, sleeping in the same smelly ship.

5) Chase: With all these evil fruit loops to beat down, we're practically living inside the 'Frog, *anyway.* That Space Ghost-looking *Flag-Smasher* guy last week, *Typeface* the week before that...

6) Nico: Well, this is *our* fault, you know. We're the ones who created the power vacuum.

Page Nineteen

Page Nineteen, Panel One
        Push in on Chase and Gert. As Chase makes a joke, Gert blushes and elbows him in the side playfully. In the background, we can see a disgusted Molly rolling her eyes.

1) Chase: Heh, "power vacuum." That should be Gert's new codename.

2) Gert: You're disgusting.

3) Molly: Can you two go back to hating each other, please? It made me barf in my mouth less.

Page Nineteen, Panel Two
        Cut over to Nico, looking deadly severe.

4) Nico: I'm *serious.* Us taking down The Pride was like the U.S. taking down *Saddam.* We got rid of a monster, but we didn't plan for what would happen *next.*

5) Nico: Our parents may have been awful people, but at least they maintained some kind of...of *order.*

Page Nineteen, Panel Three
        Change angles for this shot of Chase, Karolina and Nico. Chase is pointing at Gert's parents' TIME MACHINE, the gazebo-looking thing you drew during our first season, which is sitting dusty and broken in a corner of this crowded old lair. Karolina and Nico are berating Chase.

6) Chase: Hey, if you want your mommy and daddy back so bad, why don't you hop in the Yorkes' old *time machine* and rescue 'em from the past?

7) Karolina: Because she *doesn't* want them back, Chase. She's just saying we have a responsibility to clean up their *mess,* right, Nico?

8) Nico: And for the son of two mad *scientists,* you sure do have trouble comprehending the fact that Gert's parents' 4D-thing has been *busted* for--

Page Nineteen, Panel Four
        Pull out to the largest panel of the page for a big group shot. The kids all cover their eyes, as ANOTHER version of the Yorkes' time machine appears in the lair in a blinding flash of light! We can see a figure silhouetted inside this time machine, but we can't see who it is yet.

9) SFX: *FWASH*

Page Twenty

Page Twenty, Panel One
        Cut over to this newly arrived time machine for a three-quarter SPLASH. Standing in the middle of this steamy contraption is a SUPER-HEROINE. She's about 35 years old, five-foot-six, raven-haired, busty, thin, and very, very attractive. She's wearing a long cape, skirt, boots, and a tight corset-type top (her costume is torn and dirty in places, like she's just survived a terrible fight). As she steps into the low-hanging fog surrounding the bottom of this machine, she's clutching her stomach, which appears to be bleeding (though we need to be very subtle with this...maybe it blends in with her dark-colored outfit?).

1) Heroine: Please...please tell me what year this is...

Page Twenty, Panel Two
        We're looking over the Heroine's shoulder in the foreground of this shot, over at an angry Gert and a confused Old Lace in the background.

2) Heroine: Oh...Karolina's still here...

3) Heroine: Must be *2005*...

4) Gert: Lady, you take another step, and my dinosaur will *end* you.

Page Twenty, Panel Three
        This is just an extreme close-up of the Heroine, as she drops this bombshell:

5) Heroine: I seriously doubt that, Gertrude.

6) Heroine: Seeing how I'm *you*...

Page Twenty-one

Page Twenty-one, Panel One
        Pull out to the largest panel of the page for a big group shot, as the Heroine (still clutching her stomach) limps towards the stunned kids. The Heroine kindly strokes a friendly Old Lace's head, as the dino brushes up against her.

1) Nico: *What?*

2) Gert: She's *lying*. I wouldn't be caught *dead* in that get-up.

3) Heroine: Funny choice of words, kid...and you'll realize how much things can *change*...in about twenty years... when you start leading the *Avengers*...

Page Twenty-one, Panel Two
        Change angles for this shot of Heroine and a wide-eyed Molly.

4) Molly: Gert's gonna be a *superhero?*

5) Heroine: It's not as fun as it sounds, Mol...

6) Heroine: She's going to be betrayed...by someone she's *stupid* enough to put on her team...

Page Twenty-one, Panel Three
        Change angles for this shot of Heroine and Chase, as Chase rushes over to help hold up the injured woman.

7) Heroine: I barely escaped...with my life. He just *slaughtered* my Avengers...used my *files* to kill the others...

8) Heroine: Hisako and her X-Men, Daredevil, the Fantastic Fourteen...he murdered *all* of them...every hero on the planet...

9) Chase: *Who* did?

Page Twenty-one, Panel Four
        This is just a close-up of Heroine, as she looks at the off-panel Chase and says:

10) Heroine: A supposed "champion" named *Victorious*. He's the most powerful man...on the *planet*...

11) Heroine: Please...you're the future's only *hope*...Iron Woman sacrificed her *life* to help power my one last trip... because I need you children...to *stop* him...

Page Twenty-two

Page Twenty-two, Panel One
        Change angles for this shot of Karolina and the Heroine, who's still being held up by Chase. Heroine is reaching for something in her belt here.

1) Karolina: Us?

2) Karolina: Ma'am, how are we supposed to stop something if the *grown-up* us's can't?

3) Heroine: You have to find Victorious when he was just a boy...before he becomes too strong...

Page Twenty-two, Panel Two
        Push in on Heroine, as she holds up a torn-at-the-edges, slightly faded photo of VICTOR MANCHA, who looks exactly like he did at the beginning of this issue!

4) Heroine: His real name is *Victor Mancha*.

5) Heroine: He grew up...in Pasadena...

Page Twenty-two, Panel Three
        Pull out to a shot of Chase and the Heroine, as she begins to slump to the floor. Chase kneels with her, gently easing her to the ground in his arms.

6) Heroine: Don't trust him. He's not who he says he is... I knew only you guys would understand...

7) Heroine: His father...is a villain from your time..the greatest evil...in the *universe*...

8) Chase: What's that mean? Who's this guy the son of?

Page Twenty-two, Panel Four

Push in closer on the two. Chase is cradling Older Gert much like Younger Gert cradled him when he "died" back in Issue #15. The Heroine lovingly looks up at Chase through half-shut eyes and breathes her last breath here.

9) Heroine (small, groggy): Sweet Chase...

10) Heroine (small, trailing off): In all those years… I never told you...how much I loved...*

Page Twenty-three

Page Twenty-three, Panel One

Pull out to a larger shot of Chase and the now-lifeless Heroine. He's still looking down at her.

No Copy

Page Twenty-three, Panel Two

Cut over to the other Runaways (and Old Lace). Karolina covers her mouth in horror. The others don't know what to say.

1) Chase (from off): She's dead.

Page Twenty-three, Panel Three

Pull out to the largest panel of the page, as the girls begin to argue.

2) Molly: I'm...I'm really sorry, Gert.

3) Gert: That was *not* me! This is probably just another... another *lie* from our parents, one last *mind-freak* from the grave!

4) Karolina: But Old Lace seemed pretty sure--

Page Twenty-three, Panel Four

Cut over to Nico, as she tries to take control of the situation.

5) Nico: *Quiet.* Let's think about this for a second.

6) Nico: What if this woman *was* telling the truth? Even if there really *is* someone out there who's gonna kill every hero on earth someday, what do we do about it *now?*

Page Twenty-four

Page Twenty-four, SPLASH

Finally, we close on this dramatic SPLASH (with room at the *bottom* of this page for title and closing credits, please!). This is a somewhat high-angle downshot on Chase, still cradling the Heroine's lifeless body (she still has Victor's photo in her hands). We can now see that Chase has TEARS streaming down his face, as he looks up at us, and through angrily gritted teeth, says:

1) Chase: We find him...and we rip his damn heart out.

2) Title: **TRUE BELIEVERS**
chapter one

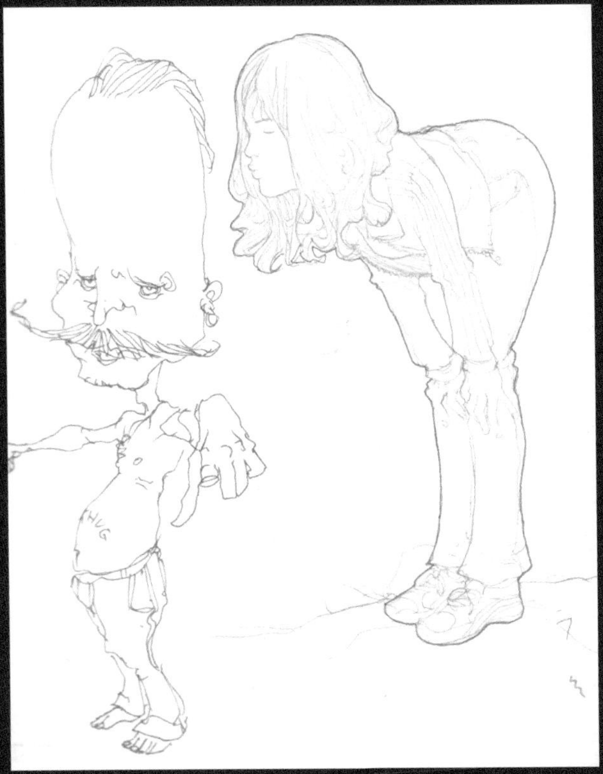

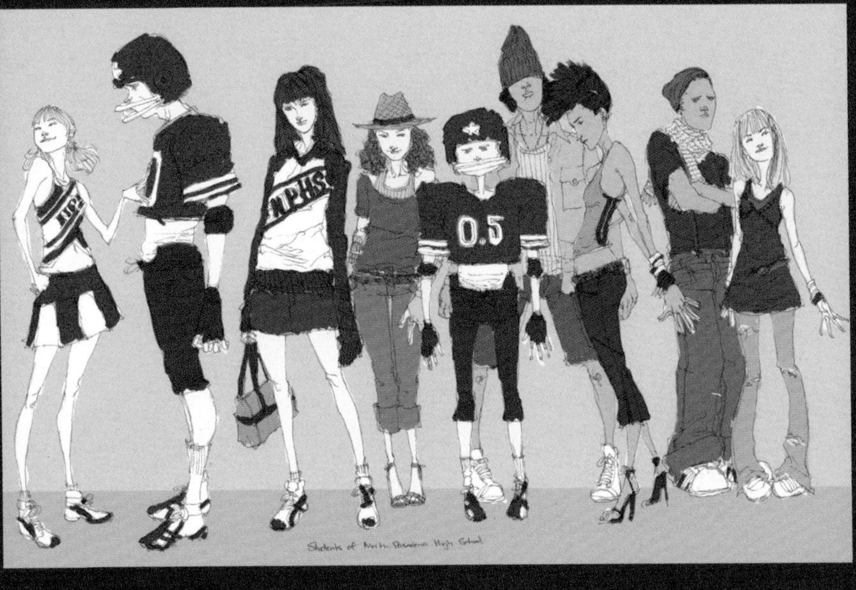
NPHS
0.5

ADRIAN ALPHONA SKETCHBOOK

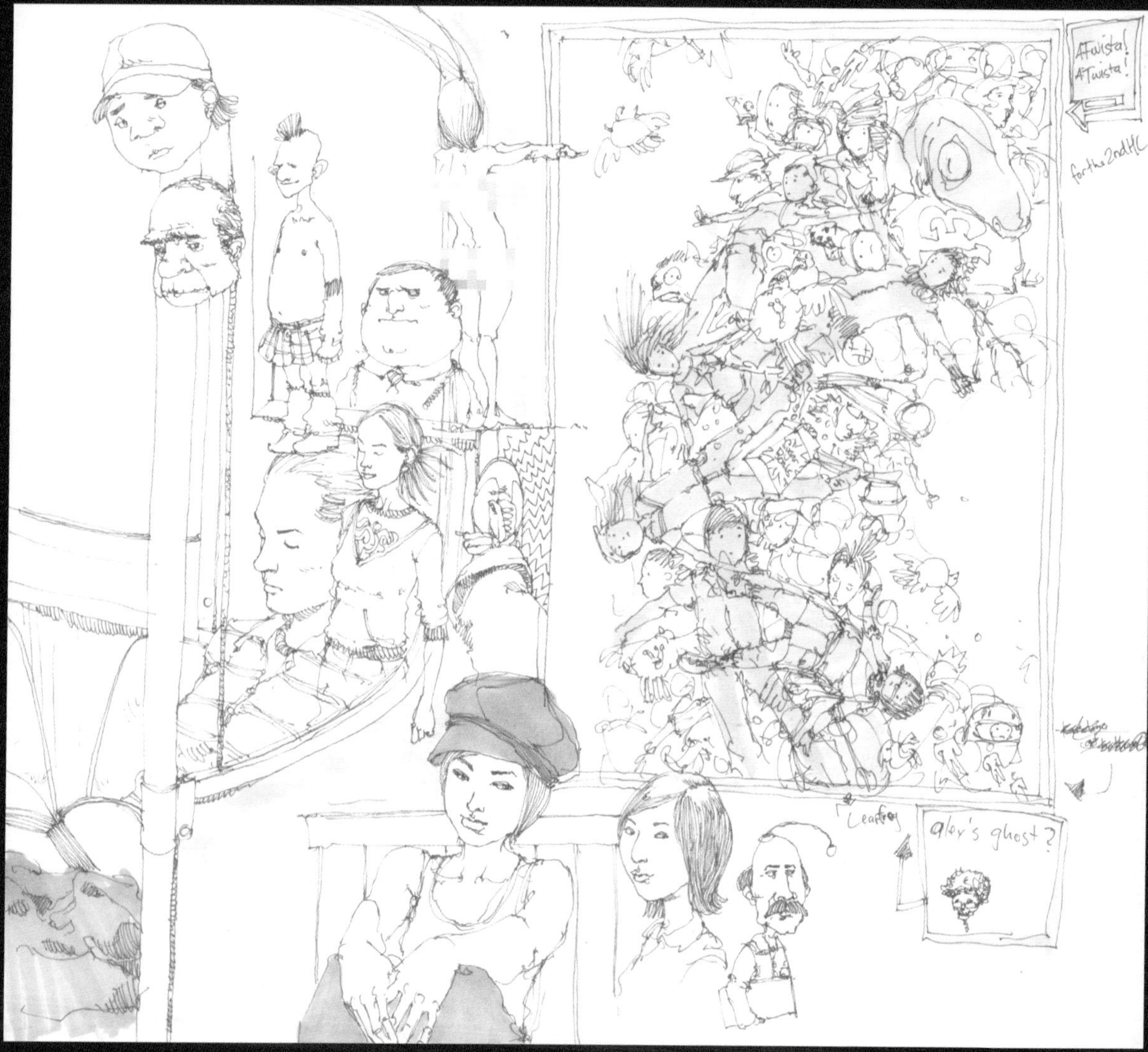

A Twista!
A Twista!
for the 2nd HC
Leapfrog
alex's ghost?

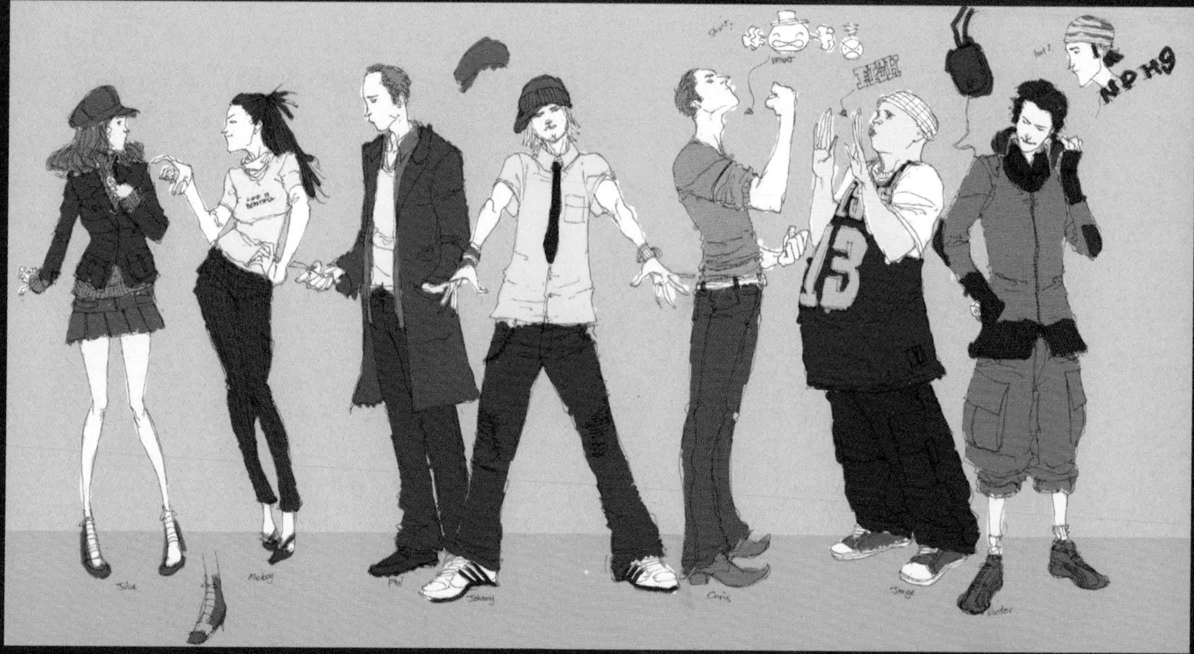

NPH9
Julie
Mickey
Phil
Johnny
Chris
Jorge
Victor

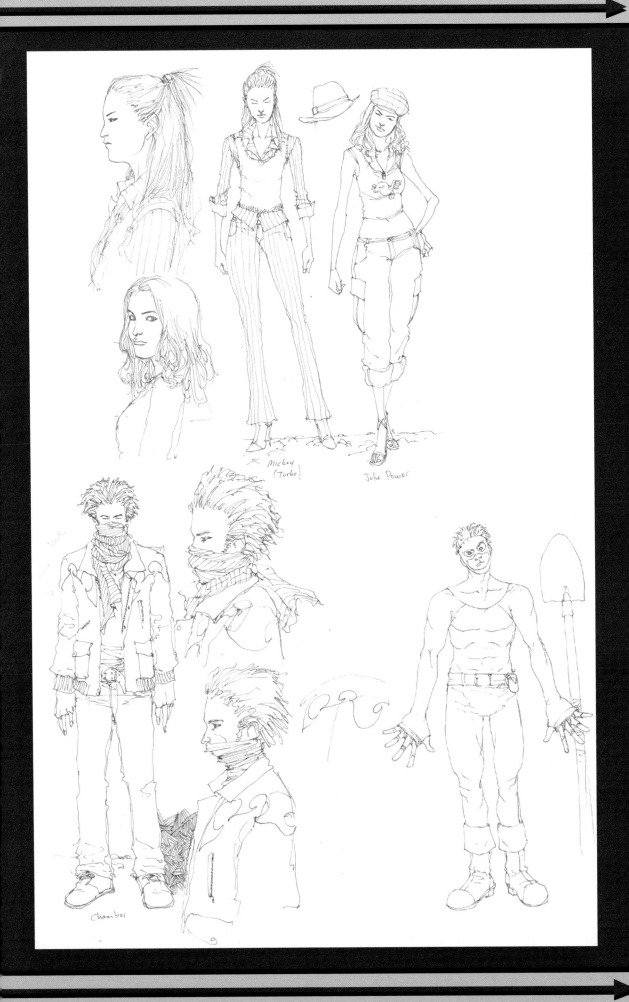

Mickey
(Turbo)

Jolie Power

Chamber

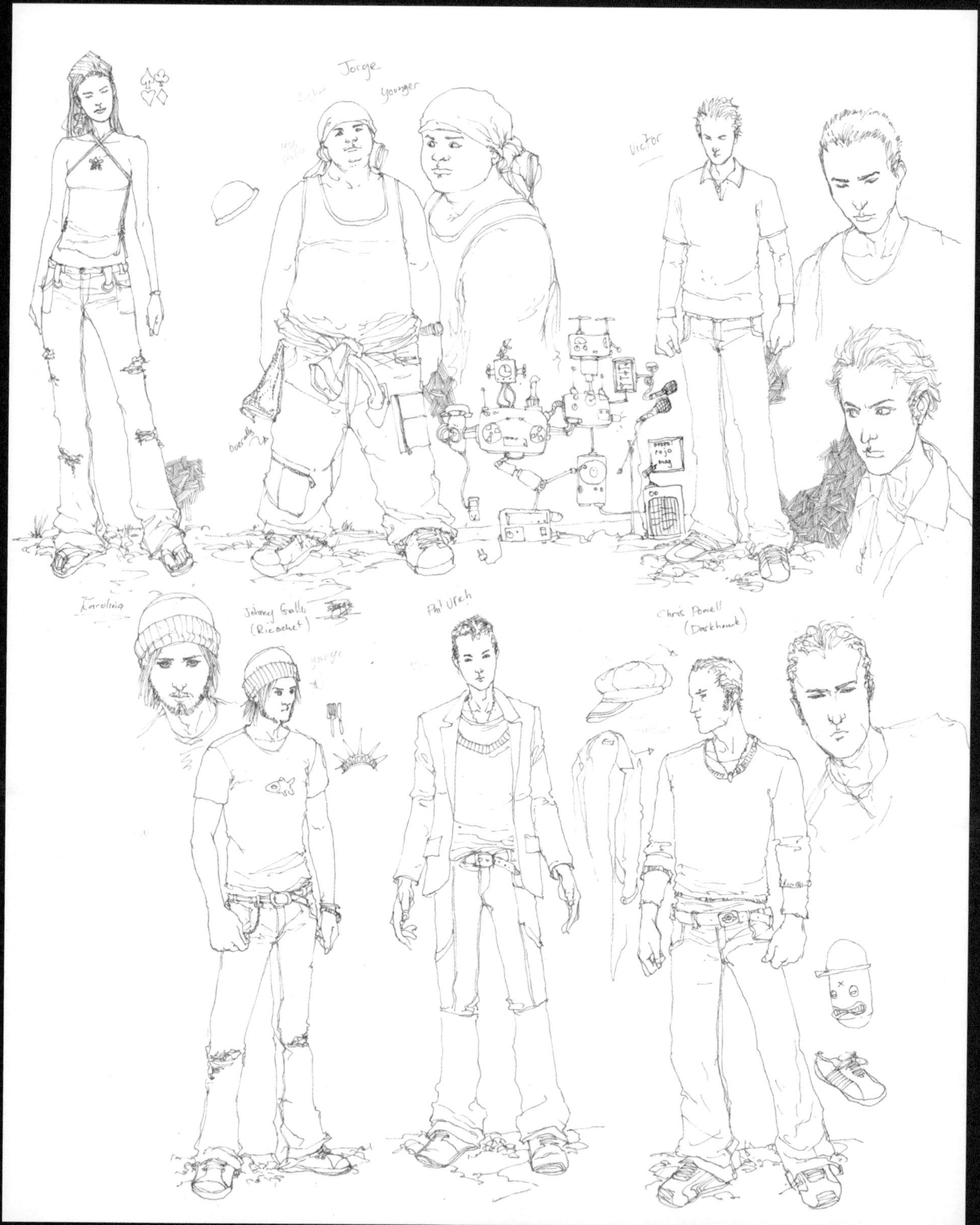
Jorge
younger
Victor
Karolina
Johnny Gallo
(Ricochet)
Phil Urich
Chris Powell
(Darkhawk)

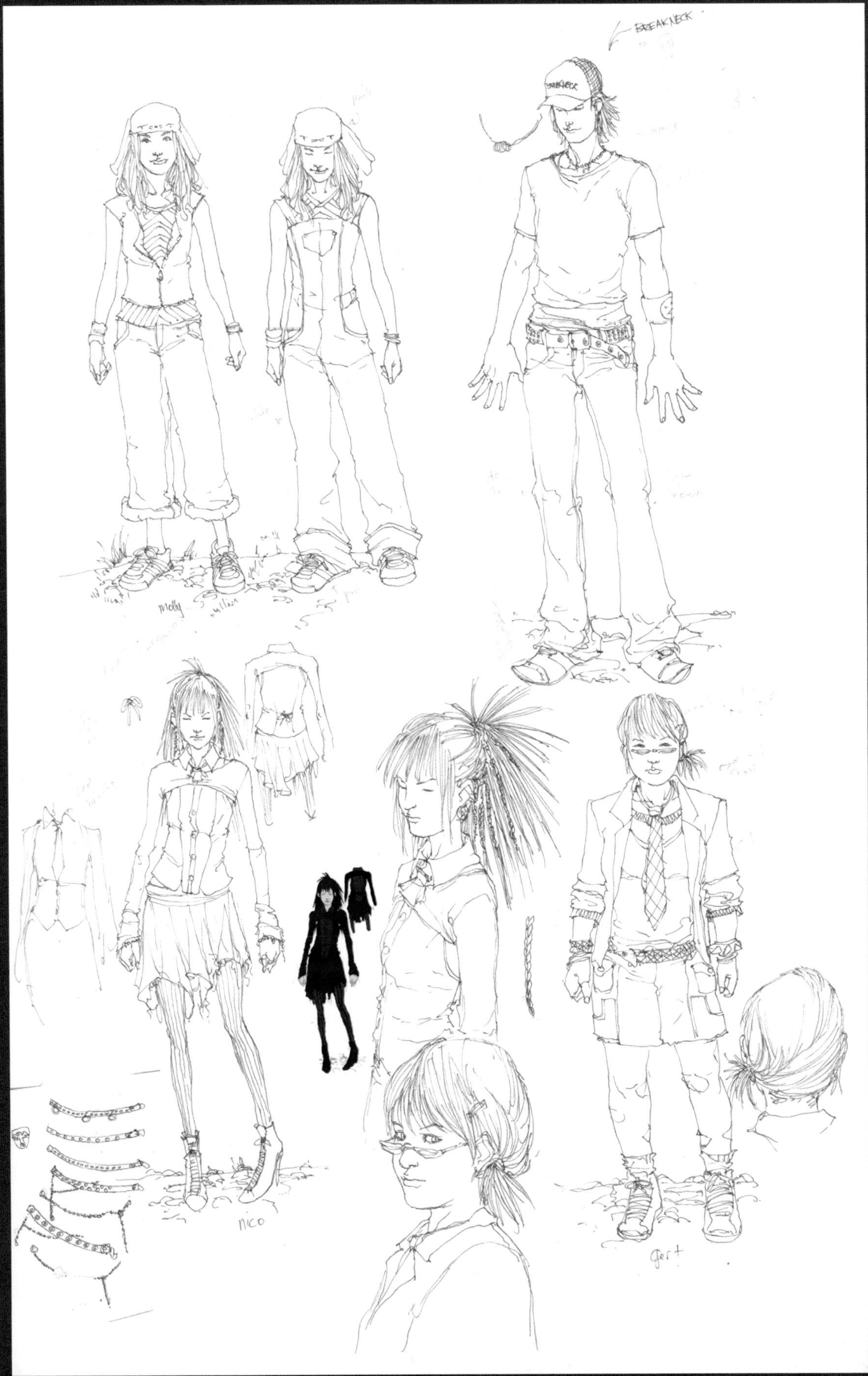
BREAKNECK
BREAKNECK
molly
nico
Gert

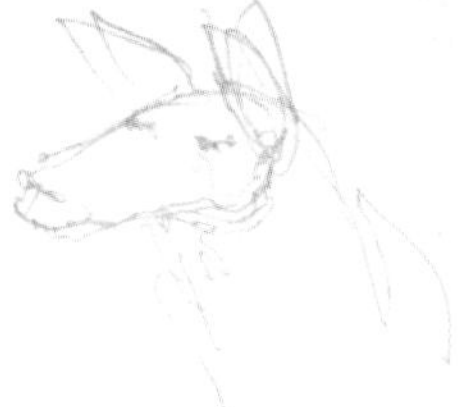

Page Sixteen

Page Sixteen, SPLASH

Pull out to this SPLASH for a big group shot of Cloak and all of our Runaways, as FOUR LITTLE WINGED GOBLINS suddenly appear in midair bursts of smoke! Everyone looks freaked out, except for Victor, who smiles as he continues to charge up his glowing hands with electricity. Cloak takes a step back here, Adrian, deciding to *observe* the Runaways rather than fight.

Security Daemon

1) Victor: More fun than Monopoly, I hope.

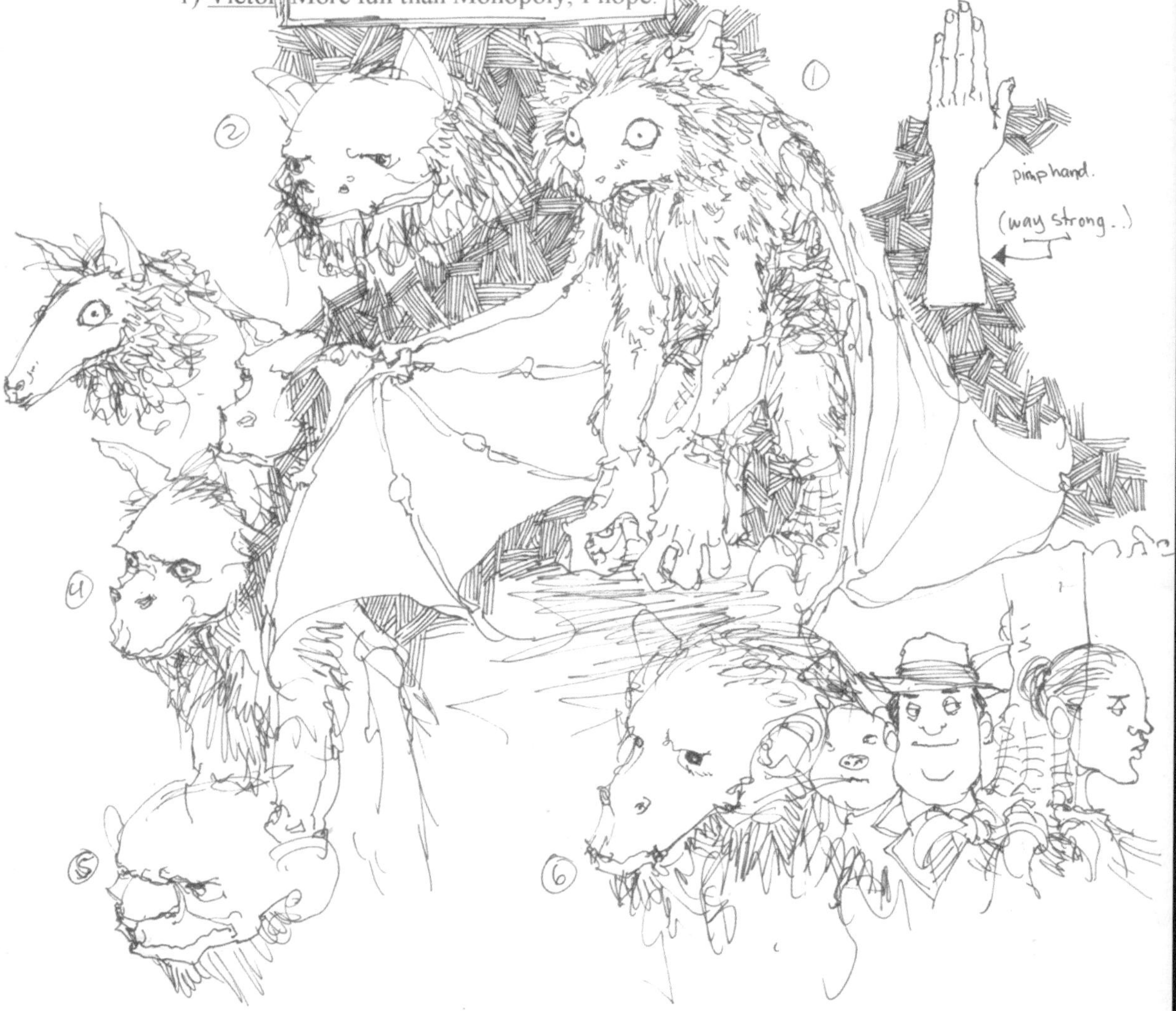

pimp hand.
(way strong..)

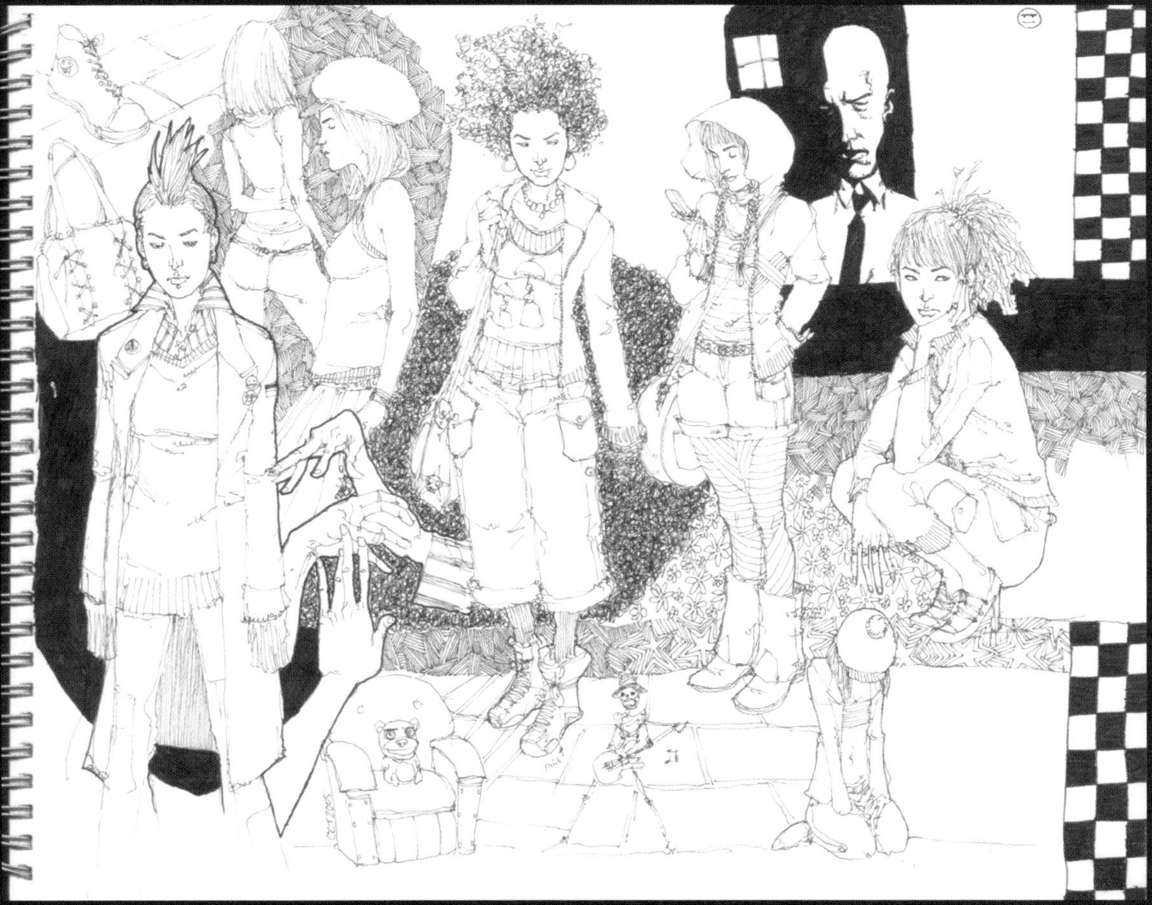

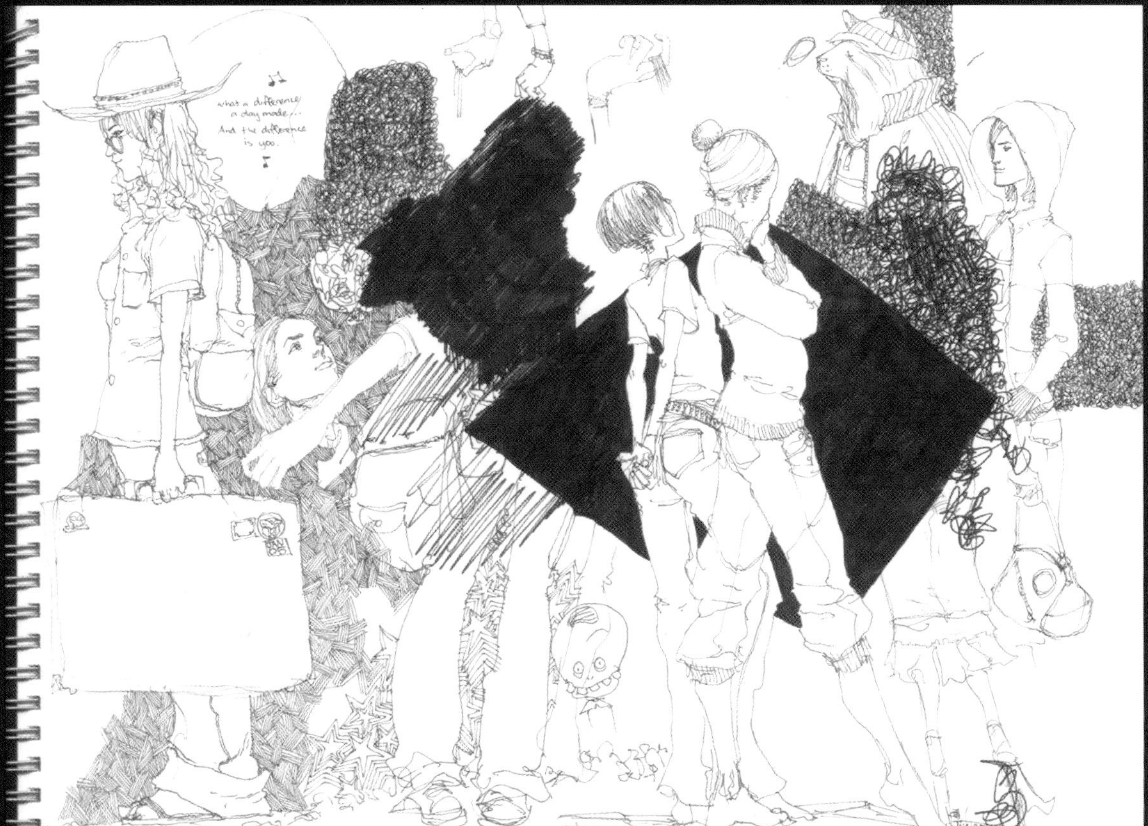
what a difference a day made... And the difference is you.

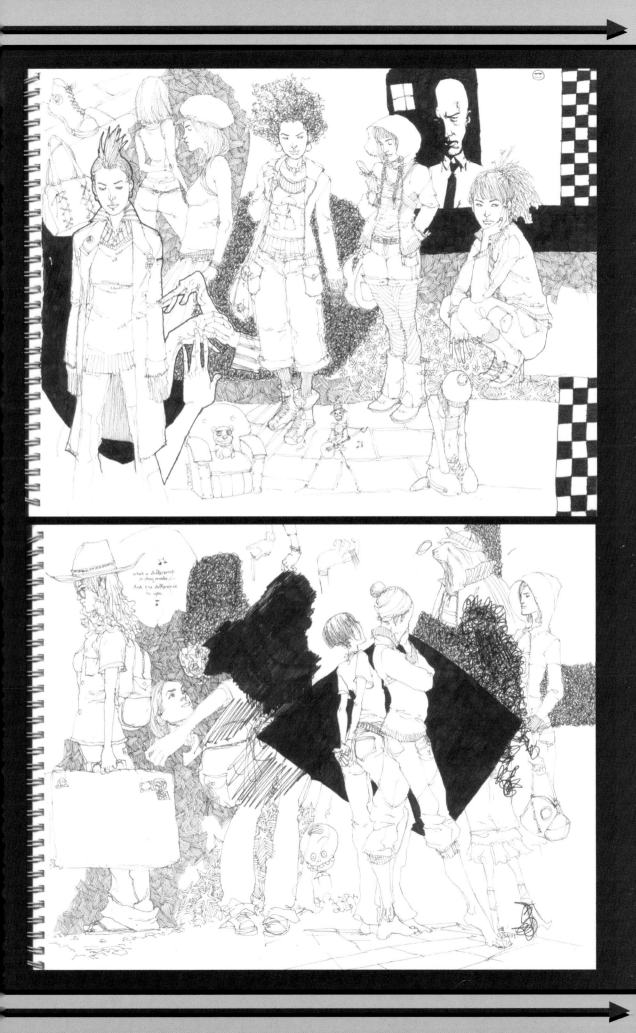

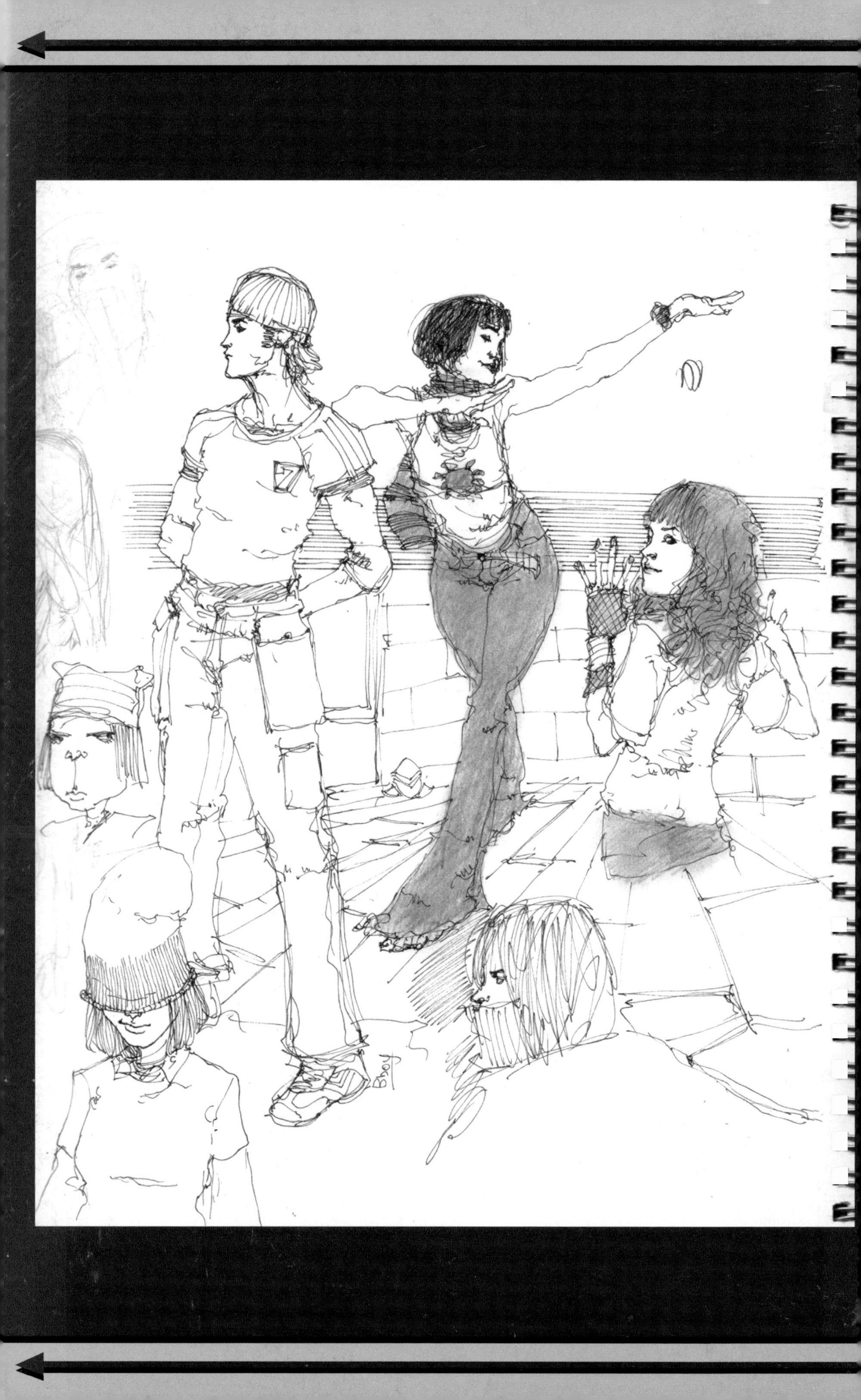
Bboy